S0-AAH-552

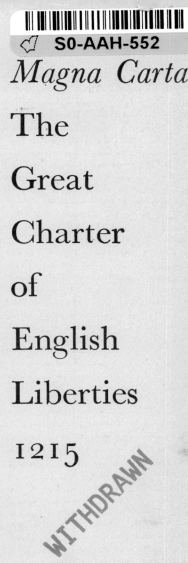

Magna Carta

The
Great
Charter
of
English
Liberties
1215

WITHDRAWN

$1.50

Voices of Liberty

THE MACMILLAN COMPANY
NEW YORK · BOSTON · CHICAGO
DALLAS · ATLANTA · SAN FRANCISCO

MACMILLAN AND CO., LIMITED
LONDON · BOMBAY · CALCUTTA
MADRAS · MELBOURNE

**THE MACMILLAN COMPANY
OF CANADA, LIMITED**
TORONTO

VOICES OF LIBERTY

EDITED BY

Finley M. K. Foster
WESTERN RESERVE UNIVERSITY

Homer A. Watt
NEW YORK UNIVERSITY

Short Story Index

NEW YORK · *The Macmillan Company* · 1941

Copyright, 1941, by

THE MACMILLAN COMPANY

All Rights Reserved

Published April, 1941

PRINTED IN THE UNITED STATES OF AMERICA

820.8
F84v

42768

PN
6071
L5
F6

PREFACE

A COURSE in college composition would be incomplete without student analysis of specimens of good writing. The "readers" which provide this material have varied greatly. Often they are essentially magazines of good literature designed to illustrate the various forms of discourse. More often the specimens assembled all deal with some central theme or subject, such as college life, the world at work, or shifting social or economic patterns, and so give to the book in which they appear a unity and articulation that keeps it from being a mere miscellany. Such an anthology is justified only if the specimens selected represent sound interests and are so well written that they guide the young writer in his own attempts at effective expression. These two principles have determined the making of the present collection: first, subject-matter that is of the utmost present interest and importance, and second, high literary quality. A few words about each of these principles will make the purpose and the plan of this book clearer.

There can be no disagreement with the statement that the paramount issue in the world today is the struggle between the democratic way of life and the totalitarian way that has sprung up to challenge it. And there will be little disagreement with the added statement that although the Americans are a people of mixed bloods and antecedents, their political and social ideologies have an essential kinship with those of Great Britain, the other English-speaking democracy, rather than with those of the totalitarian states. Social injustices have existed and will continue to exist under the democratic form of government, for it is man-made and to err is human; but the British and Americans who have been committed to this form of government are also committed to the belief that liberty, freedom, and social justice have a better chance of survival under a rule of the people than under a dictatorship or an oligarchy. Whether as individuals we Americans like the idea or not, it is certain that for an indefinite period our patterns of living are to be determined largely by our democratic creeds and by our political kinship with Great Britain. It would seem to be highly important, therefore, that we have a clear conception of the ancestry, the development, and the characteristics of our own ideas and ideals of liberty. To give such a conception as soundly and as simply as possible is the purpose of this book. From it speak those voices of liberty in England and America which have expressed from time to time, from Magna Carta to the present, the democratic ideas that are determining our way of life today.

To reveal the history and development of democratic ideas the selections have been grouped into four divisions. Of these, the first shows how, in the "fortress isle" of England, "freedom slowly broadens down from precedent to precedent," and how a succession of tyrannies have been checked by those who were oppressed. In this section, too, speak the wise British statesmen who saw in the American struggles to establish and to preserve freedom in a new democracy the counterpart of English struggles for liberty. The second part presents the development of the democratic ideas in America from the beginnings of the republic to the present moment. The third part moves out of the realm of ideas into that of personalities in a series of biographical essays intended to delineate notable Americans, foreign-born or native. Part four, finally, is a group of stories of American life from the colonial days to the New Deal, in which the operations of the democratic way of life are revealed in fiction more vivid than truth. In all four parts the order is chronological, and in each part an attempt has been made to co-ordinate selections with those in other parts of the book. The purpose of the whole, as has been said, is to make clear the origins, development, and essential characteristics of the democratic idea.

In choosing materials which are centered in the spacious theme of liberty and democracy, the editors have not forgotten at the same time the necessity of providing for student writers a group of selections that are excellently written and that present collectively a variety of literary types. Narrative writing is here in abundance in the forms of history, biography, and story; and expository and argumentative composition is represented in the speeches and essays of prose-masters of many generations. Excepting, finally, for one or two legalistic items in the first part of the book, the compositions are all excellent as examples of effective writing. Possibly the clarity of style and the vigor of expression reflect the earnestness of those who spoke for liberty and truth. However this may be, the student writer will find here much help in disciplining his own expression, for the authors here represented, old and new, are artisans in words as well as philosophers in ideas.

With the thought, therefore, of furnishing material that will stimulate to good writing as well as clarify thinking, the editors have assembled this book. It is their hope that it may create a clearer understanding of democratic principles, both in their English origins and in their American developments, and that it may confirm once more the validity of our democracy as an expression of civil liberty.

F. M. K. F.

H. A. W.

February 12, 1941.

TABLE OF CONTENTS

Part One
The Spirit of Liberty
In England

This royal throne of kings, this sceptered isle,
This earth of majesty, this seat of Mars,
This other Eden, demi-paradise,
This fortress built by Nature for herself
Against infection and the hand of war,

    . . . . . .
This blessed plot, this earth, this realm, this England.

SHAKESPEARE: Richard II, *II,* 1.

This England never did, nor never shall,
Lie at the proud foot of a conqueror,
But when it first did help to wound itself,
Now these her princes are come home again,
Come the three corners of the world in arms
And we shall shock them, nought shall make us rue
If England to itself do rest but true.

SHAKESPEARE: King John, *V,* 7.

And yet, with all thy theoretic platitudes, what a depth of practical
sense in thee, great England! A depth of sense, of justice, and courage;
in which under all emergencies and world-bewilderments, and under
this most complex of emergencies we now live in, there is still hope,
there is still assurance! CARLYLE: Past and Present (*III,* 5).

Thomas Babington Macaulay
(1800-1859)

THOMAS BABINGTON MACAULAY came naturally by his love of liberty and justice, for his father was Zachary Macaulay, anti-slavery philanthropist and reformer. Macaulay's literary career began with his famous essay on Milton, which appeared in the *Edinburgh Review* when the author was only twenty-five; and his political career began with his election to Parliament in 1830. Four years later saw him in India as legal adviser to the Supreme Council. He returned to England in 1838 and was sent to Parliament to represent Edinburgh. A lull in his political activities gave him time to devote to his literary work. *The Lays of Ancient Rome,* a series of stirring poems on Roman history, appeared in 1842, and he continued to write for the *Edinburgh Review.* But what he chose to regard as his life work, his *History of England from the Accession of James II,* occupied his time until his death in 1859. Of this popular history the first two volumes appeared in 1848, volumes three and four in 1855, and the fifth and last shortly before his death. He died in 1859 and was buried in the Poets' Corner of Westminster Abbey.

Macaulay's *History of England* owes its popularity both to his theory of history and his skill in writing. To him the story of the past should be recreated in vivid and detailed pageantry. The historian, he believed, should be somewhat of a dramatist; so he brought his figures into active, breathing life. It was Sir Walter Scott whom he admired as a historian—not Dr. Dryasdust. The following selection is taken from Volume I, Chapter I. Here his ardent love for popular government—he was a Whig in politics— appears. The titles which the editors have given this section is meant to summarize Macaulay's expressed belief that resistance against tyranny was in the blood of the English from their beginnings as a people.

3

The Natural Liberalism
of the English

The old English government was one of a class of limited monarchies which sprang up in Western Europe during the middle
ages, and which, notwithstanding many diversities, bore to one
another a strong family likeness. That there should have been
such a likeness is not strange. The countries in which those monarchies arose had been provinces of the same great civilized empire, and had been overrun and conquered, about the same time,
by tribes of the same rude and warlike nation. They were members of the same great coalition against Islam. They were in communion with the same superb and ambitious Church. Their
polity naturally took the same form. They had institutions derived partly from imperial Rome, partly from papal Rome, partly
from the old Germany. All had Kings; and in all the kingly office
became by degrees strictly hereditary. All had nobles bearing
titles which had originally indicated military rank. The dignity
of knighthood, the rules of heraldry, were common to all. All had
richly endowed ecclesiastical establishments, municipal corporations enjoying large franchises, and senates whose consent was
necessary to the validity of some public acts.

Of these kindred constitutions the English was, from an early
period, justly reputed the best. The prerogatives of the sovereign
were undoubtedly extensive. The spirit of religion, and the spirit
of chivalry, concurred to exalt his dignity. The sacred oil had
been poured on his head. It was no disparagement to the bravest
and noblest knights to kneel at his feet. His person was invio-
lable. He alone was entitled to convoke the Estates of the realm:
he could at his pleasure dismiss them; and his assent was necessary to all their legislative acts. He was the chief of the executive
administration, the sole organ of communication with foreign
powers, the captain of the military and naval forces of the state,

4

the fountain of justice, of mercy, and of honor. He had large powers for the regulation of trade. It was by him that money was coined, that weights and measures were fixed, that marts and havens were appointed. His ecclesiastical patronage was immense. His hereditary revenues, economically administered, sufficed to meet the ordinary charges of government. His own domains were of vast extent. He was also feudal lord paramount of the whole soil of his kingdom, and, in that capacity, possessed many lucrative and many formidable rights, which enabled him to annoy and depress those who thwarted him, and to enrich and aggrandize, without any cost to himself, those who enjoyed his favor.

But his power, though ample, was limited by three great constitutional principles, so ancient that none can say when they began to exist, so potent that their natural development, continued through many generations, has produced the order of things under which we now live.

First, the King could not legislate without the consent of his Parliament. Secondly, he could impose no taxes without the consent of his Parliament. Thirdly, he was bound to conduct the executive administration according to the laws of the land, and, if he broke those laws, his advisers and his agents were responsible.

No candid Tory will deny that these principles had, five hundred years ago, acquired the authority of fundamental rules. On the other hand, no candid Whig will affirm that they were, till a later period, cleared from all ambiguity, or followed out to all their consequences. A constitution of the middle ages was not, like a constitution of the eighteenth or nineteenth century, created entire by a single act, and fully set forth in a single document. It is only in a refined and speculative age that a polity is constructed on system. In rude societies the progress of government resembles the progress of language and of versification. Rude societies have language, and often copious and energetic language: but they have no scientific grammar, no definitions of nouns and verbs, no names for declensions, moods, tenses, and voices. Rude societies have versification, and often versification of great power and sweetness: but they have no metrical canons; and the minstrel whose numbers, regulated solely by his ear, are the delight of his audience, would himself be unable to say of

how many dactyls and trochees each of his lines consists. As eloquence exists before syntax, and song before prosody, so government may exist in a high degree of excellence long before the
limits of legislative, executive, and judicial power have been
traced with precision.

It was thus in our country. The line which bounded the royal
prerogative, though in general sufficiently clear, had not everywhere been drawn with accuracy and distinctness. There was,
therefore, near the border some debatable ground on which in-
cursions and reprisals continued to take place, till, after ages of
strife, plain and durable landmarks were at length set up. It may
be instructive to note in what way, and to what extent, our
ancient sovereigns were in the habit of violating the three great
principles by which the liberties of the nation were protected.

No English King has ever laid claim to the general legislative
power. The most violent and imperious Plantagenet never fancied
himself competent to enact, without the consent of his great
council, that a jury should consist of ten persons instead of twelve,
that a widow's dower should be a fourth part instead of a third,
that perjury should be a felony, or that the custom of gavelkind
should be introduced into Yorkshire. But the King had the power
of pardoning offenders; and there is one point at which the power
of pardoning and the power of legislating seem to fade into each
other, and may easily, at least in a simple age, be confounded. A
penal statute is virtually annulled if the penalties which it imposes are regularly remitted as often as they are incurred. The
sovereign was undoubtedly competent to remit penalties without
limit. He was therefore competent to annul virtually a penal
statute. It might seem that there could be no serious objection to
his doing formally what he might do virtually. Thus, with the
help of subtle and courtly lawyers, grew up, on the doubtful
frontier which separates executive from legislative functions, that
great anomaly known as the dispensing power.

That the King could not impose taxes without the consent of
Parliament is admitted to have been, from time immemorial, a
fundamental law of England. It was among the articles which
John was compelled by the Barons to sign. Edward the First ventured to break through the rule: but, able, powerful, and popular
as he was, he encountered an opposition to which he found it

expedient to yield. He covenanted accordingly in express terms, for himself and his heirs, that they would never again levy any aid without the assent and good-will of the Estates of the realm. His powerful and victorious grandson attempted to violate this solemn compact: but the attempt was strenuously withstood. At length the Plantagenets gave up the point in despair; but though they ceased to infringe the law openly, they occasionally contrived, by evading it, to procure an extraordinary supply for a temporary purpose. They were interdicted from taxing; but they claimed the right of begging and borrowing. They therefore sometimes begged in a tone not to be distinguished from that of command, and sometimes borrowed with small thought of repaying. But the fact that it was thought necessary to disguise these exactions under the names of benevolences and loans sufficiently proves that the authority of the great constitutional rule was universally recognized.

The principle that the King of England was bound to conduct the administration according to law, and that, if he did anything against law, his advisers and agents were answerable, was established at a very early period, as the severe judgments pronounced and executed on many royal favorites sufficiently prove. It is, however, certain that the rights of individuals were often violated by the Plantagenets, and that the injured parties were often unable to obtain redress. According to law no Englishman could be arrested or detained in confinement merely by the mandate of the sovereign. In fact, persons obnoxious to the government were frequently imprisoned without any other authority than a royal order. According to law, torture, the disgrace of the Roman jurisprudence, could not, in any circumstances, be inflicted on an English subject. Nevertheless, during the troubles of the fifteenth century, a rack was introduced into the Tower, and was occasionally used under the plea of political necessity. But it would be a great error to infer from such irregularities that the English monarchs were, either in theory or in practice, absolute. We live in a highly civilized society, in which intelligence is so rapidly diffused by means of the press and of the post office, that any gross act of oppression committed in any part of our island is, in a few hours, discussed by millions. If the sovereign were now to immure a subject in defiance of the writ of Habeas Corpus, or to put a conspirator to the torture, the whole nation would be instantly electrified by the news. In the middle ages the state of society was widely different. Rarely and with great difficulty did the wrongs of individuals come to the knowledge of the public. A man might be illegally confined during many months in the castle of Carlisle or Norwich; and no whisper of the transaction might reach London. It is highly probable that the rack had been many years in use before the great majority of the nation had the least suspicion that it was ever employed. Nor were our ancestors by any means so much alive as we are to the importance of maintaining great general rules. We have been taught by long experience that we cannot without danger suffer any breach of the constitution to pass unnoticed. It is therefore now universally held that a government which unnecessarily exceeds its powers ought to be visited with severe parliamentary censure, and that a government which, under the pressure of a great exigency, and with pure intentions, has exceeded its powers, ought without delay to apply to Parliament for an act of indemnity. But such were not the feelings of the Englishmen of the fourteenth and fifteenth centuries. They were little disposed to contend for a principle merely as a principle, or to cry out against an irregularity which was not also felt to be a grievance. As long as the general spirit of the administration was mild and popular, they were willing to allow some latitude to their sovereign. If, for ends generally acknowledged to be good, he exerted a vigor beyond the law, they not only forgave, but applauded him, and, while they enjoyed security and prosperity under his rule, were but too ready to believe that whoever had incurred his displeasure had deserved it. But to this indulgence there was a limit: nor was that King wise who presumed far on the forbearance of the English people. They might sometimes allow him to overstep the constitutional line; but they also claimed the privilege of overstepping that line themselves, whenever his encroachments were so serious as to excite alarm. If, not content with occasionally oppressing individuals, he dared to oppress great masses, his subjects promptly appealed to the laws, and, that appeal failing, appealed as promptly to the God of battles.

They might indeed safely tolerate a king in a few excesses; for they had in reserve a check which soon brought the fiercest and proudest king to reason, the check of physical force. It is difficult for an Englishman of the nineteenth century to image to himself the facility and rapidity with which, four hundred years ago, this check was applied. The people have long unlearned the use of arms. The art of war has been carried to a perfection unknown to our forefathers, and the knowledge of that art is confined to a particular class. A hundred thousand troops, well disciplined and commanded, will keep down millions of plowmen and artisans. A few regiments of household troops are sufficient to overawe all the discontented spirits of a large capital. In the meantime the effect of the constant progress of wealth has been to make insurrection far more terrible to thinking men than maladministration. Immense sums have been expended on works which, if a rebellion broke out, might perish in a few hours. The mass of movable wealth collected in the shops and warehouses of London alone exceeds five-hundredfold that which the whole island contained in the days of the Plantagenets; and, if the government were subverted by physical force, all this movable wealth would be exposed to imminent risk of spoliation and destruction. Still greater would be the risk to public credit, on which thousands of families directly depend for subsistence, and with which the credit of the whole commercial world is inseparably connected. It is no exaggeration to say that a civil war of a week on English ground would now produce disasters which would be felt from the Hoangho to the Missouri, and of which the traces would be discernible at the distance of a century. In such a state of society resistance must be regarded as a cure more desperate than almost any malady which can afflict the state. In the middle ages, on the contrary, resistance was an ordinary remedy for political distempers, a remedy which was always at hand, and which, though doubtless sharp at the moment, produced no deep or lasting ill effects. If a popular chief raised his standard in a popular cause, an irregular army could be assembled in a day. Regular army there was none. Every man had a slight tincture of soldiership, and scarcely any man more than a slight tincture. The national wealth consisted chiefly in flocks and herds, in the harvest of the year, and in the simple buildings inhabited by the people. All the furniture, the stock of shops, the machinery which could be found in the realm was of less value than the property which some single parishes now contain. Manufactures were rude; credit was almost unknown. Society, therefore, recovered from the shock as soon as the actual conflict was over. The calamities of civil war were confined to the slaughter on the field of battle, and to a few subsequent executions and confiscations. In a week the peasant was driving his team and the esquire flying his hawks over the field of Towton, or of Bosworth, as if no extraordinary event had interrupted the regular course of human life.

A hundred and sixty years have now elapsed since the English people have by force subverted a government. During the hundred and sixty years which preceded the union of the Roses, nine Kings reigned in England. Six of these nine Kings were deposed. Five lost their lives as well as their crowns. It is evident, therefore, that any comparison between our ancient and our modern polity must lead to most erroneous conclusions, unless large allowance be made for the effect of that restraint which resistance and the fear of resistance constantly imposed on the Plantagenets. As our ancestors had against tyranny a most important security which we want, they might safely dispense with some securities to which we justly attach the highest importance. As we cannot, without the risk of evils from which the imagination recoils, employ physical force as a check on misgovernment, it is evidently our wisdom to keep all the constitutional checks on misgovernment in the highest state of efficiency, to watch with jealousy the first beginnings of encroachment, and never to suffer irregularities, even when harmless in themselves, to pass unchallenged, lest they acquire the force of precedents. Four hundred years ago such minute vigilance might seem unnecessary. A nation of hardy archers and spearmen might, with small risk to its liberties, connive at some illegal acts on the part of a prince whose general administration was good, and whose throne was not defended by a single company of regular soldiers.

Under this system, rude as it may appear when compared with those elaborate constitutions of which the last seventy years have been fruitful, the English long enjoyed a large measure of freedom and happiness. Though during the feeble reign of Henry the Sixth the state was torn first by factions, and at length by civil war, though Edward the Fourth was a prince of dissolute and imperious character, though Richard the Third has generally been represented as a monster of depravity, though the exactions of Henry the Seventh caused great repining, it is certain that our ancestors, under those Kings, were far better governed than the Belgians under Philip, surnamed the Good, or the French under that Louis who was styled the Father of his people. Even while the wars of the Roses were actually raging, our country appears to have been in a happier condition than the neighboring realms during years of profound peace. Comines was one of the most enlightened statesmen of his time. He had seen all the richest and most highly civilized parts of the Continent. He had lived in the opulent towns of Flanders, the Manchesters and Liverpools of the fifteenth century. He had visited Florence, recently adorned by the magnificence of Lorenzo, and Venice, not yet humbled by the confederates of Cambray. This eminent man deliberately pronounced England to be the best governed country of which he had any knowledge. Her constitution he emphatically designated as a just and holy thing, which, while it protected the people, really strengthened the hands of a prince who respected it. In no other country, he said, were men so effectually secured from wrong. The calamities produced by our intestine wars seemed to him to be confined to the nobles and the fighting men, and to leave no traces such as he had been accustomed to see elsewhere, no ruined dwellings, no depopulated cities.

John Richard Green
(1837-1883)

FOLLOWING in general Macaulay's theory of history, John Richard Green avoided the technicalities of constitutional law, parliamentary bills, and foreign treaties, and wrote the "simple annals" of the common man of England. His *Short History of the English People* (1874) is, therefore, a distinctly democratic work, simple in style, clear and easy in narrative. After a training in Jesus College, Oxford, Green took orders as an Anglican clergyman in 1860 but resigned his charge later as the result of a growing skepticism, and devoted himself to historical writing. In addition to his masterpiece, he wrote *The Making of England* (1882) and *The Conquest of England* (1883). If the reader of Green's histories were not aware of the fact, he would never suspect that the easy and sparkling prose was written by a sick man who fought down disease and raced with death to complete his history.

Green's story of the signing of Magna Carta is taken from Volume I, Chapter III, Sections II and III of the *Short History*. The Great Charter of English liberties is to the British what the Declaration of Independence is to the Americans. It was signed by King John and twenty-five of his barons who wrested their ancient liberties from him. Of it Dr. William Stubbs wrote: "The whole of the Constitutional History of England is a commentary on this charter." Of this famous document, written in Latin, there are extant four copies of the original with King John's signature—not one only, as Green has said. Of these, two are in the British Museum, one in the archives of Salisbury Cathedral, and one in the archives of Lincoln Cathedral. This fourth copy was brought to America in 1939 for exhibition in the British Pavilion at the New York World's Fair. Upon the closing of the Fair, it was deposited for safe keeping in the Library of Congress in Washington.

The Great Charter (1215)

It is to the victory of Bouvines that England owes her Great Charter. From the hour of his submission to the Papacy, John's vengeance on the barons had only been delayed till he should return a conqueror from the fields of France. A sense of their danger nerved the baronage to resistance; they refused to follow the king on his foreign campaign till the excommunication were removed, and when it was removed they still refused, on the plea that they were not bound to serve in wars without the realm. Furious as he was at this new attitude of resistance, the time had not yet come for vengeance, and John sailed for Poitou with the dream of a great victory which should lay Philip and the barons alike at his feet. He returned from his defeat to find the nobles no longer banded together in secret conspiracies, but openly united in a definite claim of liberty and law. The leader in this great change was the new Archbishop whom Innocent had set on the throne of Canterbury. From the moment of his landing in England, Stephen Langton had assumed the constitutional position of the Primate as champion of the old English customs and law against the personal despotism of the kings. As Anselm had withstood William the Red, as Theobald had rescued England from the lawlessness of Stephen, so Langton prepared to withstand and rescue his country from the tyranny of John. He had already forced him to swear to observe the laws of the Confessor, a phrase in which the whole of the national liberties were summed up. When the baronage refused to sail to Poitou, he compelled the king to deal with them not by arms but by process of law. Far however from being satisfied with resistance such as this to isolated acts of tyranny, it was the Archbishop's aim to restore on a formal basis the older freedom of the realm. The pledges of Henry the First had long been forgotten when the

Justiciar, Geoffrey Fitz-Peter, brought them to light at a Council held at St. Albans. There in the king's name the Justiciar promised good government for the time to come, and forbade all royal officers to practice extortion as they prized life and limb. The king's peace was pledged to those who had opposed him in the past; and observance of the laws of Henry the First was enjoined upon all within the realm. Langton saw the vast importance of such a precedent. In a fresh meeting of the barons at St. Paul's he produced the Charter of Henry the First, and it was at once welcomed as a base for the needed reforms. All hope however hung on the fortunes of the French campaign; the victory at Bouvines gave strength to John's opponents, and after the king's landing the barons secretly met at St. Edmundsbury, and swore to demand from him, if needful by force of arms, the restoration of their liberties by Charter under the king's seal. Early in January in the year 1215 they presented themselves in arms before the king, and preferred their claim. The few months that followed showed John the uselessness of resistance; nobles and Churchmen were alike arrayed against him, and the commissioners whom he sent to plead his cause at shire-courts brought back the news that no man would help him against the Charter. At Easter the barons again gathered in arms at Brackley, and renewed their claim. "Why do they not ask for my kingdom?" cried John in a burst of passion; but the whole country rose as one man at his refusal. London threw open her gates to the forces of the barons, now organized under Robert Fitz-Walter as "Marshal of the Army of God and Holy Church." The example of the capital was followed by Exeter and Lincoln; promises of aid came from Scotland and Wales; the northern barons marched hastily to join their comrades in London. There was a moment when John found himself with seven knights at his back, and before him a nation in arms. He had summoned mercenaries and appealed to his liege lord, the Pope; but summons and appeal were alike too late. Nursing wrath in his heart the tyrant bowed to necessity, and called the barons to a conference at Runnymede.

An island in the Thames between Staines and Windsor had been chosen as the place of conference: the king encamped on one bank, while the barons covered the marshy flat, still known by the name of Runnymede, on the other. Their delegates met in the island between them, but the negotiations were a mere cloak to cover John's purpose of unconditional submission. The Great Charter was discussed, agreed to, and signed in a single day.

One copy of it still remains in the British Museum, injured by age and fire, but with the royal seal still hanging from the brown, shriveled parchment. It is impossible to gaze without reverence on the earliest monument of English freedom which we can see with our own eyes and touch with our own hands, the Great Charter to which from age to age patriots have looked back as the basis of English liberty. But in itself the Charter was no novelty, nor did it claim to establish any new constitutional principles. The Charter of Henry the First formed the basis of the whole, and the additions to it are for the most part formal recognitions of the judicial and administrative changes introduced by Henry the Second. But the vague expressions of the older charter were now exchanged for precise and elaborate provisions. The bonds of unwritten custom which the older grant did little more than recognize had proved too weak to hold the Angevins; and the baronage now threw them aside for the restraints of written law. It is in this way that the Great Charter marks the transition from the age of traditional rights, preserved in the nation's memory and officially declared by the Primate, to the age of written legislation, of Parliaments and Statutes, which was soon to come. The Church had shown its power of self-defense in the struggle over the interdict, and the clause which recognized its rights alone retained the older and general form. But all vagueness ceases when the Charter passes on to deal with the rights of Englishmen at large, their right to justice, to security of person and property, to good government. "No freeman," ran the memorable article that lies at the base of our whole judicial system, "shall be seized or imprisoned, or dispossessed, or outlawed, or in any way brought to ruin: we will not go against any man nor send against him, save by legal judgment of his peers or by the law of the land." "To no man will we sell," runs another, "or deny, or delay, right or justice." The great reforms of the past reigns were now formally recognized; judges of assize were to hold their circuits four times in the year, and the King's Court was no longer to follow the king in his wanderings over the realm, but to sit in a fixed place. But the denial of justice under John was a small danger compared with the lawless exactions both of himself and his predecessor. Richard had increased the amount of the scutage which Henry the Second had introduced, and applied it to raise funds for his ransom. He had restored the Danegeld, or land-tax, so often abolished, under the new name of "carucage," had seized the wool of the Cistercians and the plate of the churches, and rated movables as well as land. John had again raised the rate of scutage, and imposed aids, fines, and ransoms at his pleasure without counsel of the baronage. The Great Charter met this abuse by the provision on which our constitutional system rests. With the exception of the three customary feudal aids which still remained to the crown, "no scutage or aid shall be imposed in our realm save by the common council of the realm"; and to this Great Council it was provided that prelates and the greater barons should be summoned by special writ, and all tenants in chief through the sheriffs and bailiffs, at least forty days before. The provision defined what had probably been the common usage of the realm; but the definition turned it into a national right, a right so momentous that on it rests our whole Parliamentary life.

The rights which the barons claimed for themselves they claimed for the nation at large. The boon of free and unbought justice was a boon for all, but a special provision protected the poor. The forfeiture of the freeman on conviction of felony was never to include his tenement, or that of the merchant his wares, or that of the countryman his wain. The means of actual livelihood were to be left even to the worst. The under-tenants or farmers were protected against all lawless exactions of their lords in precisely the same terms as these were protected against the lawless exactions of the crown. The towns were secured in the enjoyment of their municipal privileges, their freedom from arbitrary taxation, their rights of justice, of common deliberation, of regulation of trade. "Let the city of London have all its old liberties and its free customs, as well by land as by water. Besides this, we will and grant that all other cities, and boroughs, and towns, and ports, have all their liberties and free customs." The influence of the trading class is seen in two other enactments, by which freedom of journeying and trade was secured to foreign merchants, and an uniformity of weights and measures was ordered to be enforced throughout the realm. There remained only one question, and that the most difficult of all; the question how to secure this order which the Charter had established in the actual government of the realm. The immediate abuses were easily swept away, the hostages restored to their homes, the foreigners banished from the country. But it was less easy to provide means for the control of a king whom no man could trust, and a council of twenty-five barons was chosen from the general body of their order to enforce on John the observance of the Charter, with the right of declaring war on the king should its provisions be infringed. Finally, the Charter was published throughout the whole country and sworn to at every hundred-mote and town-mote by order from the king.

"They have given me five-and-twenty over-kings," cried John in a burst of fury, flinging himself on the floor and gnawing sticks and straw in his impotent rage. But the rage soon passed into the subtle policy of which he was a master. Some days after, he left Windsor, and lingered for months along the southern shore, waiting for news of the aid he had solicited from Rome and from the Continent. It was not without definite purpose that he had become the vassal of Rome. While Innocent was dreaming of a vast Christian Empire with the Pope at its head to enforce justice and religion on his under-kings, John believed that the Papal protection would enable him to rule as tyrannically as he would. The thunders of the Papacy were to be ever at hand for his protection, as the armies of England are at hand to protect the vileness and oppression of a Turkish Sultan or a Nizam of Hyderabad. His envoys were already at Rome, and Innocent, indignant that a matter which might have been brought before his court of appeal as overlord should have been dealt with by armed revolt, annulled the Great Charter and suspended Stephen Langton from the exercise of his office as Primate. Autumn brought a host of foreign soldiers from oversea to the king's standard, and advancing against the disorganized forces of the barons, John starved Rochester into submission and marched ravaging through the midland counties to the north, while his mercenaries spread like locusts over the whole face of the land. From Berwick the king turned back triumphant to coop up his enemies in London, while fresh Papal excommunications fell on the barons and the city. But the burghers set Innocent at defiance. "The ordering of secular matters appertaineth not to the Pope," they said, in words that seem like mutterings of the coming Lollardry; and at the advice of Simon Langton, the Archbishop's brother, bells swung out and mass was celebrated as before. With the undisciplined militia of the country and the towns, however, success was impossible against the trained forces of the king, and despair drove the barons to seek aid from France. Philip had long been waiting the opportunity for his revenge upon John, and his son Louis at once accepted the crown in spite of Innocent's excommunications, and landed in Kent with a considerable force. As the barons had foreseen, the French mercenaries who constituted John's host refused to fight against the French sovereign. The whole aspect of affairs was suddenly reversed. Deserted by the bulk of his troops, the king was forced to fall rapidly back on the Welsh Marches, while his rival entered London and received the submission of the larger part of England. Only Dover held out obstinately against Louis. By a series of rapid marches John succeeded in distracting the plans of the barons and in relieving Lincoln; then after a short stay at Lynn he crossed the Wash in a fresh movement to the north. In crossing, however, his army was surprised by the tide, and his baggage with the royal treasures washed away.

The fever which seized the baffled tyrant in the abbey of Swineshead was inflamed by a gluttonous debauch, and John entered Newark only to die. His death changed the whole face of affairs, for his son Henry was but a child of nine years old, and the royal authority passed into the hands of one who stands high among English patriots, William Marshal. The boy-king was hardly crowned when the earl and the Papal Legate issued in his name the very Charter against which his father had died fighting; only the clauses which regulated taxation and the summoning of Parliament were as yet declared to be suspended. The nobles soon streamed away from the French camp; for national jealousy and suspicions of treason told heavily against Louis, while the pity which was excited by the youth and helplessness of Henry was aided by a sense of injustice in burthening the child with the iniquity of his father. One bold stroke of William Marshal decided the struggle. A joint army of French and English barons under the Count of Perche and Robert Fitz-Walter was besieging Lincoln, when the earl, rapidly gathering forces from the royal castles, marched to its relief. Cooped up in the steep narrow streets, and attacked at once by the earl and the garrison, the barons fled in hopeless rout; the Count of Perche fell on the field; Robert Fitz-Walter was taken prisoner. Louis, who was investing Dover, retreated to London, and called for aid from France. But a more terrible defeat crushed his remaining hopes. A small English fleet, which had set sail from Dover under Hubert de Burgh, fell boldly on the reinforcements which were crossing under the escort of Eustace the Monk, a well-known freebooter of the Channel. The fight admirably illustrates the naval warfare of the time. From the decks of the English vessels bowmen poured their arrows into the crowded transports, others hurled quicklime into their enemies' faces, while the more active vessels crashed with their armed prows into the sides of the French ships. The skill of the mariners of the Cinque Ports decided the day against the larger forces of their opponents, and the fleet of Eustace was utterly destroyed. The royal army at once closed in upon London, but resistance was really at an end. By the treaty of Lambeth Louis promised to withdraw from England on payment of a sum which he claimed as debt; his adherents were restored to their possessions, the liberties of London and other towns confirmed, and the prisoners on either side set at liberty. The expulsion of the stranger left English statesmen free to take up again the work of reform; and a fresh issue of the Charter, though in its modified form, proclaimed clearly the temper and policy of the Earl Marshal.

James Anthony Froude
(1818-1894)

AMONG the most popular of modern British historians is James Anthony Froude. Educated at Oxford, he came under the influence of that powerful religious reform known as the Oxford Movement, but became ultimately a skeptic and wrote *The Nemesis of Faith* which cost him his Oxford fellowship. In 1849 he became acquainted with Thomas Carlyle, who influenced him greatly. Froude lectured in Great Britain and the United States and wrote with tireless energy. His longest work is *The History of England from the Fall of Wolsey to the Defeat of the Spanish Armada* (12 vols., 1856–1870). In 1892 he was appointed regius professor of modern history at Oxford, and his lectures were published in several volumes. *The Defeat of the Armada,* reprinted here, is Lecture IX of a series entitled *English Seamen in the Sixteenth Century*. These lectures were delivered at Oxford during the Easter Terms of 1893–4 and were published in 1895. In lecturing and writing Froude's style was fluent and graceful. He has been accused, however, of prolixity in expression and, what is more serious, of inaccuracy in historical facts. But the selection here is historically correct.

In 1066 William the Conqueror, Duke of Normandy, invaded England, defeated Harold, the last of the Saxon kings, at Hastings, and occupied the country. Since then there have been no successful attempts to conquer the "island fortress," although the Spaniards attempted it in 1588, and Napoleon's plan to seize England had to be dashed by Lord Nelson's brilliant defeat of the French navy at the Battle of Trafalgar in 1805. Froude's story of the earlier of these attacks is vivid and moving, and he makes clear the part played in the defeat of the Armada not only by the courage of the English sea-dogs but by the hand of God in sending a storm to scatter the invading fleet.

Defeat of the Armada (1588)

In the gallery at Madrid there is a picture, painted by Titian, representing the Genius of Spain coming to the delivery of the afflicted Bride of Christ. Titian was dead, but the temper of the age survived, and in the study of that great picture you will see the spirit in which the Spanish nation had set out for the conquest of England. The scene is the seashore. The Church a naked Andromeda, with disheveled hair, fastened to the trunk of an ancient disbranched tree. The cross lies at her feet, the cup overturned, the serpents of heresy biting at her from behind with uplifted crests. Coming on before a leading breeze is the sea monster, the Moslem fleet, eager for their prey; while in front is Perseus, the Genius of Spain, banner in hand, with the legions of the faithful laying not raiment before him, but shield and helmet, the apparel of war for the Lady of Nations to clothe herself with strength and smite her foes.

In the Armada the crusading enthusiasm had reached its point and focus. England was the stake to which the Virgin, the daughter of Sion, was bound in captivity. Perseus had come at last in the person of the Duke of Medina Sidonia, and with him all that was best and brightest in the countrymen of Cervantes, to break her bonds and replace her on her throne. They had sailed into the channel in pious hope, with the blessed banner waving over their heads.

To be the executor of the decrees of Providence is a lofty ambition, but men in a state of high emotion overlook the precautions which are not to be dispensed with even on the sublimest of errands. Don Quixote, when he set out to redress the wrongs of humanity, forgot that a change of linen might be necessary, and

From *English Seamen in the Sixteenth Century* (1895); reprinted by permission of Longmans, Green & Co.

that he must take money with him to pay his hotel bills. Philip II, in sending the Armada to England, and confident in supernatural protection, imagined an unresisted triumphal procession. He forgot that contractors might be rascals, that water four months in the casks in a hot climate turned putrid, and that putrid water would poison his ships' companies, though his crews were companies of angels. He forgot that the servants of the evil one might fight for their mistress after all, and that he must send adequate supplies of powder, and, worst forgetfulness of all, that a great naval expedition required a leader who understood his business. Perseus, in the shape of the Duke of Medina Sidonia, after a week of disastrous battles, found himself at the end of it in an exposed roadstead, where he ought never to have been, nine-tenths of his provisions thrown overboard as unfit for food, his ammunition exhausted by the unforeseen demands upon it, the seamen and soldiers harassed and dispirited, officers the whole week without sleep, and the enemy, who had hunted him from Plymouth to Calais, anchored within half a league of him.

Still, after all his misadventures, he had brought the fleet, if not to the North Foreland, yet within a few miles of it, and to outward appearance not materially injured. Two of the galleons had been taken; a third, the *Santa Aña*, had strayed; and his galleys had left him, being found too weak for the channel sea; but the great armament had reached its destination substantially uninjured so far as English eyes could see. Hundreds of men had been killed and hundreds more wounded, and the spirit of the rest had been shaken. But the loss of life could only be conjectured on board the English fleet. The English admiral could only see that the Duke was now in touch with Parma. Parma, they knew, had an army at Dunkirk with him, which was to cross to England. He had been collecting men, barges, and transports all the winter and spring, and the backward state of Parma's preparations could not be anticipated, still less relied upon. The Calais anchorage was unsafe; but at that season of the year, especially after a wet summer, the weather usually settled; and to attack the Spaniards in a French port might be dangerous for many reasons. It was uncertain after the day of the Barricades whether the Duke of Guise or Henry of Valois was master of France, and a violation of the neutrality laws might easily at that moment bring Guise and France into the field on the Spaniards' side. It was, no doubt, with some such expectation that the Duke and his advisers had chosen Calais as the point at which to bring up. It was now Saturday, the 7th of August. The governor of the town came off in the evening to the *San Martin*. He expressed surprise to see the Spanish fleet in so exposed a position, but he was profuse in his offers of service. Anything which the Duke required should be provided, especially every facility for communicating with Dunkirk and Parma. The Duke thanked him, said that he supposed Parma to be already embarked with his troops, ready for the passage, and that his own stay in the roads would be but brief. On Monday morning at latest he expected that the attempt to cross would be made. The governor took his leave, and the Duke, relieved from his anxieties, was left to a peaceful night. He was disturbed on the Sunday morning by an express from Parma informing him that, so far from being embarked, the army could not be ready for a fortnight. The barges were not in condition for sea. The troops were in camp. The arms and stores were on the quays at Dunkirk. As for the fly-boats and ammunition which the Duke had asked for, he had none to spare. He had himself looked to be supplied from the Armada. He promised to use his best expedition, but the Duke, meanwhile, must see to the safety of the fleet.

Unwelcome news to a harassed landsman thrust into the position of an admiral and eager to be rid of his responsibilities. If by evil fortune the northwester should come down upon him, with the shoals and sandbanks close under his lee, he would be in a bad way. Nor was the view behind him calculated for comfort. There lay the enemy almost within gunshot, who, though scarcely more than half his numbers, had hunted him like a pack of bloodhounds, and, worse than all, in double strength; for the Thames squadron—three Queen's ships and thirty London adventurers—under Lord H. Seymour and Sir John Hawkins, had crossed in the night. There they were between him and Cape Grisnez, and the reinforcements meant plainly enough that mischief was in the wind.

After a week so trying the Spanish crews would have been glad of a Sunday's rest if they could have had it; but the rough handling which they had gone through had thrown everything into disorder. The sick and wounded had to be cared for, torn rigging looked to, splintered timbers mended, decks scoured, and guns and arms cleaned up and put to rights. And so it was that no rest could be allowed; so much had to be done, and so busy was every one, that the usual rations were not served out and the Sunday was kept as a fast. In the afternoon the stewards went ashore for fresh meat and vegetables. They came back with their boats loaded, and the prospect seemed a little less gloomy. Suddenly, as the Duke and a group of officers were watching the English fleet from the *San Martin's* poop deck, a small smart pinnace, carrying a gun in her bow, shot out from Howard's lines, bore down on the *San Martin,* sailed round her, sending in a shot or two as she passed, and went off unhurt. The Spanish officers could not help admiring such airy impertinence. Hugo de Monçada sent a ball after the pinnace, which went through her mainsail, but did no damage, and the pinnace again disappeared behind the English ships.

So a Spanish officer describes the scene. The English story says nothing of the pinnace; but she doubtless came and went as the Spaniard says, and for sufficient purpose. The English, too, were in straits, though the Duke did not dream of it. You will remember that the last supplies which the Queen had allowed to the fleet had been issued in the middle of June. They were to serve for a month, and the contractors were forbidden to prepare more. The Queen had clung to her hope that her differences with Philip were to be settled by the Commission at Ostend; and she feared that if Drake and Howard were too well furnished they would venture some fresh rash stroke on the coast of Spain, which might mar the negotiations. Their month's provisions had been stretched to serve for six weeks, and when the Armada appeared but two full days' rations remained. On these they had fought their way up Channel. Something had been brought out by private exertion on the Dorsetshire coast, and Seymour had, perhaps, brought a little more. But they were still in extremity. The contractors had warned the Government that they could provide nothing without notice, and notice had not been given. The adventurers were in better state, having been equipped by private owners. But the Queen's ships in a day or two more must either go home or their crews would be starving. They had been on reduced rations for near two months. Worse than that, they were still poisoned by the sour beer. The Queen had changed her mind so often, now ordering the fleet to prepare for sea, then recalling her instructions and paying off the men, that those whom Howard had with him had been enlisted in haste, had come on board as they were, and their clothes were hanging in rags on them. The fighting and the sight of the flying Spaniards were meat and drink, and clothing too, and had made them careless of all else. There was no fear of mutiny; but there was a limit to the toughest endurance. If the Armada was left undisturbed a long struggle might be still before them. The enemy would recover from its flurry, and Parma would come out from Dunkirk. To attack them directly in French waters might lead to perilous complications, while delay meant famine. The Spanish fleet had to be started from the roads in some way. Done it must be, and done immediately.

Then, on that same Sunday afternoon a memorable council of war was held in the *Ark's* main cabin. Howard, Drake, Seymour, Hawkins, Martin Frobisher, and two or three others met to consult, knowing that on them at that moment the liberties of England were depending. Their resolution was taken promptly. There was no time for talk. After nightfall a strong flood tide would be setting up along shore to the Spanish anchorage. They would try what could be done with fire ships, and the excursion of the pinnace, which was taken for bravado, was probably for a survey of the Armada's exact position. Meantime eight useless vessels were coated with pitch—hulls, spars, and rigging. Pitch was poured on the decks and over the sides, and parties were told off to steer them to their destination and then fire and leave them.

The hours stole on, and twilight passed into dark. The night was without a moon. The Duke paced his deck late with uneasy sense of danger. He observed lights moving up and down the English lines, and imagining that the *endemoniada gente*—the infernal devils—might be up to mischief, ordered a sharp lookout. A faint westerly air was curling the water, and towards midnight the watchers on board the galleons made out dimly several ships which seemed to be drifting down upon them. Their experience since the action off Plymouth had been so strange and unlooked for that anything unintelligible which the English did was alarming.

The phantom forms drew nearer, and were almost among them

when they broke into a blaze from water-line to truck, and the
two fleets were seen by the lurid light of the conflagration; the
anchorage, the walls and windows of Calais, and the sea shining
red as far as eye could reach, as if the ocean itself was burning.
Among the dangers which they might have to encounter, English
fireworks had been especially dreaded by the Spaniards. Fire
ships—a fit device of heretics—had worked havoc among the
Spanish troops, when the bridge was blown up, at Antwerp. They
imagined that similar infernal machines were approaching the
Armada. A capable commander would have sent a few launches to
grapple the burning hulks, which of course were now deserted,
and tow them out of harm's way. Spanish sailors were not cowards,
and would not have flinched from duty because it might be dangerous; but the Duke and Diego Florez lost their heads again. A
signal gun from the *San Martin* ordered the whole fleet to slip
their cables and stand out to sea.

Orders given in panic are doubly unwise, for they spread the
terror in which they originate. The danger from the fire ships was
chiefly from the effect on the imagination, for they appear to
have drifted by and done no real injury. And it speaks well for
the seamanship and courage of the Spaniards that they were able,
crowded together as they were, at midnight and in sudden alarm
to set their canvas and clear out without running into one another. They buoyed their cables, expecting to return for them at
daylight, and with only a single accident, to be mentioned directly, they executed successfully a really difficult maneuver.

The Duke was delighted with himself. The fire ships burned
harmlessly out. He had baffled the inventions of the *endemoniada
gente*. He brought up a league outside the harbor, and supposed
that the whole Armada had done the same. Unluckily for himself, he found it at daylight divided into two bodies. The *San
Martin* with forty of the best appointed of the galleons were riding together at their anchors. The rest, two thirds of the whole,
having no second anchors ready, and inexperienced in Channel
tides and currents, had been lying to. The west wind was blowing up. Without seeing where they were going they had drifted to
leeward, and were two leagues off, towards Gravelines, dangerously near the shore. The Duke was too ignorant to realize the
full peril of his situation. He signaled to them to return and

rejoin him. As the wind and tide stood it was impossible. He proposed to follow them. The pilots told him that if he did the whole fleet might be lost on the banks. Towards the land the look of things was not more encouraging.

One accident only had happened the night before. The *Capitana* galleass, with Don Hugo de Monçada and eight hundred men on board, had fouled her helm in a cable in getting under way and had become unmanageable. The galley slaves disobeyed orders, or else Don Hugo was as incompetent as his commander-in-chief. The galleass had gone on the sands, and as the tide ebbed, had fallen over on her side. Howard, seeing her condition, had followed her in the *Ark* with four or five other of the Queen's ships, and was furiously attacking her with his boats, careless of neutrality laws. Howard's theory was, as he said, to pluck the feathers one by one from the Spaniard's wing, and here was a feather worth picking up. The galleass was the most splendid vessel of her kind afloat, Don Hugo one of the greatest of Spanish grandees.

Howard was making a double mistake. He took the galleass at last after three hours' fighting. Don Hugo was killed by a musket ball. The vessel was plundered, and Howard's men took possession, meaning to carry her away when the tide rose. The French authorities ordered him off, threatening to fire upon him; and after wasting the forenoon, he was obliged at last to leave her where she lay. Worse than this, he had lost three precious hours, and had lost along with them, in the opinion of the Prince of Parma, the honors of the great day.

Drake and Hawkins knew better than to waste time plucking single feathers. The fire ships had been more effective than they could have dared to hope. The enemy was broken up. The Duke was shorn of half his strength, and the Lord had delivered him into their hand. He had got under way, still signaling wildly, and uncertain in which direction to turn. His uncertainties were ended for him by seeing Drake bear down upon him with the whole English fleet, save those which were loitering about the galleass. The English had now the advantage of numbers. The superiority of their guns he knew already, and their greater speed allowed him no hope to escape a battle. Forty ships alone were left to him to defend the banner of the crusade and the honor of

Castile; but those forty were the largest and most powerfully armed and manned that he had, and on board them were Oquendo, De Leyva, Recalde, Bretandona, the best officers in the Spanish navy next to the lost Don Pedro.

It was now or never for England. The scene of the action which was to decide the future of Europe was between Calais and Dunkirk, a few miles off shore, and within sight of Parma's camp. There was no more maneuvering for the weather-gauge, no more fighting at long range. Drake dashed straight upon his prey as the falcon swoops upon its quarry. A chance had fallen to him which might never return; not for the vain distinction of carrying prizes into English ports, not for the ray of honor which would fall on him if he could carry off the sacred banner itself and hang it in the Abbey at Westminster, but a chance so to handle the Armada that it should never be seen again in English waters, and deal such a blow on Philip that the Spanish Empire should reel with it. The English ships had the same superiority over the galleons which steamers have now over sailing vessels. They had twice the speed; they could lie two points nearer to the wind. Sweeping round them at cable's length, crowding them in one upon the other, yet never once giving them a chance to grapple, they hurled in their cataracts of round shot. Short as was the powder supply, there was no sparing it that morning. The hours went on, and still the battle raged, if battle it could be called where the blows were all dealt on one side and the suffering was all on the other. Never on sea or land did the Spaniards show themselves worthier of their great name than on that day. But from the first they could do nothing. It was said afterwards in Spain that the Duke showed the white feather, that he charged his pilot to keep him out of harm's way, that he shut himself up in his cabin, buried in woolpacks, and so on. The Duke had faults enough, but poltroonery was not one of them. He, who till he entered the English Channel had never been in action on sea or land, found himself, as he said, in the midst of the most furious engagement recorded in the history of the world. As to being out of harm's way, the standard at his masthead drew the hottest of the fire upon him. The *San Martin's* timbers were of oak and a foot thick, but the shot, he said, went through them enough to shatter a rock. Her deck was a slaughterhouse; half his company were killed or wounded, and no more would have been heard or seen of the *San Martin* or her commander had not Oquendo and De Leyva pushed in to the rescue and enabled him to creep away under their cover. He himself saw nothing more of the action after this. The smoke, he said, was so thick that he could make out nothing, even from his masthead. But all round it was but a repetition of the same scene. The Spanish shot flew high, as before, above the low English hulls, and they were themselves helpless butts to the English guns. And it is noticeable and supremely creditable to them that not a single galleon struck her colors. One of them, after a long duel with an Englishman, was on the point of sinking. An English officer, admiring the courage which the Spaniards had shown, ran out upon his bowsprit, told them that they had done all which became men, and urged them to surrender and save their lives. For answer they cursed the English as cowards and chickens because they refused to close. The officer was shot. His fall brought a last broadside on them, which finished the work. They went down, and the water closed over them. Rather death to the soldiers of the Cross than surrender to a heretic.

The deadly hail rained on. In some ships blood was seen streaming out of the scupper-holes. Yet there was no yielding; all ranks showed equal heroism. The priests went up and down in the midst of the carnage, holding the crucifix before the eyes of the dying. At midday Howard came up to claim a second share in a victory which was no longer doubtful. Towards the afternoon the Spanish fire slackened. Their powder was gone, and they could make no return to the cannonade which was still overwhelming them. They admitted freely afterwards that if the attack had been continued but two hours more they must all have struck or gone ashore. But the English magazines were empty also; the last cartridge was shot away, and the battle ended from mere inability to keep it up. It had been fought on both sides with peculiar determination. In the English there was the accumulated resentment of thirty years of menace to their country and their creed, with the enemy in tangible shape at last to be caught and grappled with; in the Spanish, the sense that if their cause had not brought them the help they looked for from above, the honor and faith of Castile should not suffer in their hands.

It was over. The English drew off, regretting that their thrifty mistress had limited their means of fighting for her, and so obliged them to leave their work half done. When the cannon ceased the wind rose, the smoke rolled away, and in the level light of the sunset they could see the results of the action.

A galleon in Recalde's squadron was sinking with all hands. The *San Philip* and the *San Matteo* were drifting dismasted towards the Dutch coast, where they were afterwards wrecked. Those which were left with canvas still showing were crawling slowly after their comrades who had not been engaged, the spars and rigging so cut up that they could scarce bear their sails. The loss of life could only be conjectured, but it had been obviously terrible. The nor'-wester was blowing up and was pressing the wounded ships upon the shoals, from which, if it held, it seemed impossible in their crippled state they would be able to work off.

In this condition Drake left them for the night, not to rest, but from any quarter to collect, if he could, more food and powder. The snake had been scotched, but not killed. More than half the great fleet were far away, untouched by shot, perhaps able to fight a second battle if they recovered heart. To follow, to drive them on the banks if the wind held, or into the North Sea, anywhere so that he left them no chance of joining hands with Parma again, and to use the time before they had rallied from his blows, that was the present necessity. His own poor fellows were famished and in rags; but neither he nor they had leisure to think of themselves. There was but one thought in the whole of them, to be again in chase of the flying foe. Howard was resolute as Drake. All that was possible was swiftly done. Seymour and the Thames squadron were to stay in the straits and watch Parma. From every obtainable source food and powder were collected for the rest—far short in both ways of what ought to have been, but, as Drake said, "we were resolved to put on a brag and go on as if we needed nothing." Before dawn the admiral and he were again off on the chase.

The brag was unneeded. What man could do had been done, and the rest was left to the elements. Never again could Spanish seamen be brought to face the English guns with Medina Sidonia to lead them. They had a fool at their head. The Invisible Powers in whom they had been taught to trust had deserted them. Their confidence was gone and their spirit broken. Drearily the morning broke on the Duke and his consorts the day after the battle. The Armada had collected in the night. The nor'-wester had freshened to a gale, and they were laboring heavily along, making fatal leeway towards the shoals.

It was St. Lawrence's Day, Philip's patron saint, whose shoulder-bone he had lately added to the treasures of the Escurial; but St. Lawrence was as heedless as St. Dominic. The *San Martin* had but six fathoms under her. Those nearer to the land signaled five, and right before them they could see the brown foam of the breakers curling over the sands, while on their weather-beam, a mile distant and clinging to them like the shadow of death, were the English ships which had pursued them from Plymouth like the dogs of the Furies. The Spanish sailors and soldiers had been without food since the evening when they anchored at Calais. All Sunday they had been at work, no rest allowed them to eat. On the Sunday night they had been stirred out of their sleep by the fire ships. Monday they had been fighting, and Monday night committing their dead to the sea. Now they seemed advancing directly upon inevitable destruction. As the wind stood there was still room for them to wear and thus escape the banks, but they would then have to face the enemy, who seemed only refraining from attacking them because while they continued on their present course the winds and waves would finish the work without help from man. Recalde, De Leyva, Oquendo, and other officers were sent for to the *San Martin* to consult. Oquendo came last. "Ah, Señor Oquendo," said the Duke as the heroic Biscayan stepped on board, "que haremos?" (what shall we do?) "Let your Excellency bid load the guns again," was Oquendo's gallant answer. It could not be. De Leyva himself said that the men would not fight the English again. Florez advised surrender. The Duke wavered. It was said that a boat was actually lowered to go off to Howard and make terms, and that Oquendo swore that if the boat left the *San Martin* on such an errand he would fling Florez into the sea. Oquendo's advice would have, perhaps, been the safest if the Duke could have taken it. There were still seventy ships in the Armada little hurt. The English were "bragging," as Drake said, and in no condition themselves for another serious engagement. But the temper of the entire fleet made a coura-

geous course impossible. There was but one Oquendo. Discipline
was gone. The soldiers in their desperation had taken the command out of the hands of the seamen. Officers and men alike
abandoned hope, and, with no human prospect of salvation left
to them, they flung themselves on their knees upon the decks and
prayed the Almighty to have pity on them. But two weeks were
gone since they had knelt on those same decks on the first sight
of the English shore to thank Him for having brought them so
far on an enterprise so glorious. Two weeks; and what weeks!
Wrecked, torn by cannon shot, ten thousand of them dead or
dying—for this was the estimated loss by battle—the survivors
could now but pray to be delivered from a miserable death by
the elements. In cyclones the wind often changes suddenly back
from north-west to west, from west to south. At that moment, as
if in answer to their petition, one of these sudden shifts of wind
saved them from the immediate peril. The gale backed round to
S.S.W., and ceased to press them on the shoals. They could ease
their sheets, draw off into open water, and steer a course up the
middle of the North Sea.

So only that they went north, Drake was content to leave them
unmolested. Once away into the high latitudes they might go
where they would. Neither Howard nor he, in the low state of
their own magazines, desired any unnecessary fighting. If the
Armada turned back they must close with it. If it held its present
course they must follow it till they could be assured it would
communicate no more for that summer with the Prince of Parma.
Drake thought they would perhaps make for the Baltic or some
port in Norway. They would meet no hospitable reception from
either Swedes or Danes, but they would probably try. One only
imminent danger remained to be provided against. If they turned
into the Forth, it was still possible for the Spaniards to redeem
their defeat, and even yet shake Elizabeth's throne. Among the
many plans which had been formed for the invasion of England,
a landing in Scotland had long been the favorite. Guise had
always preferred Scotland when it was intended that Guise should
be the leader. Santa Cruz had been in close correspondence with
Guise on this very subject, and many officers in the Armada must
have been acquainted with Santa Cruz's views. The Scotch Catholic nobles were still savage at Mary Stuart's execution, and had

the Armada anchored in Leith Roads with twenty thousand men, half a million ducats, and a Santa Cruz at its head, it might have kindled a blaze at that moment from John o'Groat's Land to the Border.

But no such purpose occurred to the Duke of Medina Sidonia. He probably knew nothing at all of Scotland or its parties. Among the many deficiencies which he had pleaded to Philip as unfitting him for the command, he had said that Santa Cruz had acquaintances among the English and Scotch peers. He had himself none. The small information which he had of anything did not go beyond his orange gardens and his tunny fishing. His chief merit was that he was conscious of his incapacity; and, detesting a service into which he had been fooled by a hysterical nun, his only anxiety was to carry home the still considerable fleet which had been trusted to him without further loss. Beyond Scotland and the Scotch isles there was the open ocean, and in the open ocean there were no sandbanks and no English guns. Thus, with all sail set he went on before the wind. Drake and Howard attended him till they had seen him past the Forth, and knew then that there was no more to fear. It was time to see to the wants of their own poor fellows, who had endured so patiently and fought so magnificently. On the 13th of August they saw the last of the Armada, turned back, and made their way to the Thames.

But the story has yet to be told of the final fate of the great "enterprise of England" (the "empresa de Inglaterra"), the object of so many prayers, on which the hopes of the Catholic world had been so long and passionately fixed. It had been ostentatiously a religious crusade. The preparations had been attended with peculiar solemnities. In the eyes of the faithful it was to be the execution of Divine justice on a wicked princess and a wicked people. In the eyes of millions whose convictions were less decided it was an appeal to God's judgment to decide between the Reformation and the Pope. There was an appropriateness, therefore, if due to accident, that other causes besides the action of man should have combined in its overthrow.

The Spaniards were experienced sailors; a voyage round the Orkneys and round Ireland to Spain might be tedious, but at that season of the year need not have seemed either dangerous or difficult. On inquiry, however, it was found that the condition of the fleet was seriously alarming. The provisions placed on board at Lisbon had been found unfit for food, and almost all had been thrown into the sea. The fresh stores taken in at Corunna had been consumed, and it was found that at the present rate there would be nothing left in a fortnight. Worse than all, the water-casks refilled there had been carelessly stowed. They had been shot through in the fighting and were empty; while of clothing or other comforts for the cold regions which they were entering no thought had been taken. The mules and horses were flung overboard, and Scotch smacks, which had followed the retreating fleet, reported that they had sailed for miles through floating carcasses.

The rations were reduced for each man to a daily half-pound of biscuit, a pint of water, and a pint of wine. Thus, sick and hungry, the wounded left to the care of a medical officer, who went from ship to ship, the subjects of so many prayers were left to encounter the climate of the North Atlantic. The Duke blamed all but himself; he hanged one poor captain for neglect of orders, and would have hanged another had he dared; but his authority was gone. They passed the Orkneys in a single body. They then parted, it was said in a fog; but each commander had to look out for himself and his men. In many ships water must be had somewhere, or they would die. The *San Martin,* with sixty consorts, went north to the sixtieth parallel. From that height the pilots promised to take them down clear of the coast. The wind still clung to the west, each day blowing harder than the last. When they braced round to it their wounded spars gave way. Their rigging parted. With the greatest difficulty they made at last sufficient offing, and rolled down somehow out of sight of land, dipping their yards in the enormous seas. Of the rest, one or two went down among the Western Isles and became wrecks there, their crews, or part of them, making their way through Scotland to Flanders. Others went north to Shetland or the Faroe Islands. Between thirty or forty were tempted in upon the Irish coasts. There were Irishmen in the fleet, who must have told them that they would find the water there for which they were perishing, safe harbors, and a friendly Catholic people; and they found either harbors which they could not reach or sea-washed sands and reefs. They were all wrecked at various places between Donegal and the Blaskets. Something like eight thousand half-drowned wretches struggled on shore alive. Many were gentlemen, richly dressed, with velvet coats, gold chains, and rings. The common sailors and soldiers had been paid their wages before they started, and each had a bag of ducats lashed to his waist when he landed through the surf. The wild Irish of the coast, tempted by the booty, knocked unknown numbers of them on the head with their battle-axes, or stripped them naked and left them to die of the cold. On one long sand strip in Sligo an English officer counted eleven hundred bodies, and he heard that there were as many more a few miles distant.

The better educated of the Ulster chiefs, the O'Rourke and O'Donnell, hurried down to stop the butchery and spare Ireland the shame of murdering helpless Catholic friends. Many—how many cannot be said—found protection in their castles. But even so it seemed as if some inexorable fate pursued all who had sailed in that doomed expedition. Alonzo de Leyva, with half a hundred young Spanish nobles of high rank who were under his special charge, made his way in a galleass into Killibeg. He was himself disabled in landing. O'Donnell received and took care of him and his companions. After remaining in O'Donnell's castle for a month he recovered. The weather appeared to mend. The galleass was patched up, and De Leyva ventured an attempt to make his way in her to Scotland. He had passed the worst danger, and Scotland was almost in sight; but fate would have its victims. The galleass struck a rock off Dunluce and went to pieces, and Don Alonzo and the princely youths who had sailed with him were washed ashore all dead, to find an unmarked grave in Antrim.

Most pitiful of all was the fate of those who fell into the hands of the English garrisons in Galway and Mayo. Galleons had found their way into Galway Bay—one of them had reached Galway itself—the crews half dead with famine and offering a cask of wine for a cask of water. The Galway townsmen were human, and tried to feed and care for them. Most were too far gone to be revived, and died of exhaustion. Some might have recovered, but recovered they would be a danger to the State. The English in the West of Ireland were but a handful in the midst of a sullen, half conquered population. The ashes of the Desmond rebellion were still smoking, and Dr. Sanders and his Legatine Commission were fresh in immediate memory. The defeat of the Armada in the Channel could only have been vaguely heard of. All that English officers could have accurately known must have been that an enormous expedition had been sent to England by Philip to restore the Pope; and Spaniards, they found, were landing in thousands in the midst of them with arms and money; distressed for the moment, but sure, if allowed time to get their strength again, to set Connaught in a blaze. They had no fortresses to hold so many prisoners, no means of feeding them, no men to spare to escort them to Dublin. They were responsible to the Queen's Government for the safety of the country. The Spaniards had not come on any errand of mercy to her or hers. The stern order went out to kill them all wherever they might be found, and two thousand or more were shot, hanged, or put to the sword. Dreadful! Yes, but war itself is dreadful and has its own necessities.

The sixty ships which had followed the *San Martin* succeeded at last in getting round Cape Clear, but in a condition scarcely less miserable than that of their companions who had perished in Ireland. Half their companions died—died of untended wounds, hunger, thirst, and famine fever. The survivors were moving skeletons, more shadows and ghosts than living men, with scarce strength left them to draw a rope or handle a tiller. In some ships there was no water for fourteen days. The weather in the lower latitudes lost part of its violence, or not one of them would have seen Spain again. As it was they drifted on outside Scilly and into the Bay of Biscay, and in the second week of September they dropped in one by one. Recalde, with better success than the rest, made Corunna. The Duke, not knowing where he was, found himself in sight of Corunna also. The crew of the *San Martin* were prostrate, and could not work her in. They signaled for help, but none came, and they dropped away to leeward to Bilboa. Oquendo had fallen off still farther to Santander, and the rest of the sixty arrived in the following days at one or other of the Biscay ports. On board them, of the thirty thousand who had left those shores but two months before in high hope and passionate enthusiasm, nine thousand only came back alive—if alive they could be called. It is touching to read in a letter from Bilboa of their joy at warm Spanish sun, the sight of the grapes on the white walls, and the taste of fresh home bread and water again. But it came too late to save them, and those whose bodies might have rallied died of broken hearts and disappointed dreams. Santa Cruz's old companions could not survive the ruin of the Spanish navy. Recalde died two days after he landed at Bilboa. Santander was Oquendo's home. He had a wife and children there, but he refused to see them, turned his face to the wall, and died too. The common seamen and soldiers were too weak to help themselves. They had to be left on board the poisoned ships till hospitals could be prepared to take them in. The authorities of Church and State did all that men could do; but the case was past help, and before September was out all but a few hundred needed no further care.

Philip, it must be said for him, spared nothing to relieve the misery. The widows and orphans were pensioned by the State. The stroke which had fallen was received with a dignified submission to the inscrutable purposes of Heaven. Diego Florez escaped with a brief imprisonment at Burgos. None else were punished for faults which lay chiefly in the King's own presumption in imagining himself the instrument of Providence.

The Duke thought himself more sinned against than sinning. He did not die, like Recalde or Oquendo, seeing no occasion for it. He flung down his command and retired to his palace at St. Lucan; and so far was Philip from resenting the loss of the Armada or its commander, that he continued him in his governorship of Cadiz, where Essex found him seven years later, and where he ran from Essex as he had run from Drake.

The Spaniards made no attempt to conceal the greatness of their defeat. Unwilling to allow that the Upper Powers had been against them, they set it frankly down to the superior fighting powers of the English.

The English themselves, the Prince of Parma said, were modest in their victory. They thought little of their own gallantry. To them the defeat and destruction of the Spanish fleet was a declaration of the Almighty in the cause of their country and the Protestant faith. Both sides had appealed to Heaven, and Heaven had spoken.

It was the turn of the tide. The wave of the reconquest of the

Netherlands ebbed from that moment. Parma took no more towns from the Hollanders. The Catholic peers and gentlemen of England, who had held aloof from the Established Church, waiting *ad illud tempus* for a religious revolution, accepted the verdict of Providence. They discovered that in Anglicanism they could keep the faith of their fathers, yet remain in communion with their Protestant fellow-countrymen, use the same liturgy, and pray in the same temples. For the first time since Elizabeth's father broke the bonds of Rome the English became a united nation, joined in loyal enthusiasm for the Queen, and were satisfied that thenceforward no Italian priest should tithe or toll in her dominions.

But all that, and all that went with it, the passing from Spain to England of the scepter of the seas, must be left to other lectures, or other lecturers who have more years before them than I. My own theme has been the poor Protestant adventurers who fought through that perilous week in the English Channel and saved their country and their country's liberty.

Sir Walter Raleigh
(1552?-1618)

EVERY schoolboy knows Sir Walter Raleigh as the courtier who, the story goes, spread his cloak over a patch of mud so that the great Queen Elizabeth might not soil her shoes. But he was more than a courtier; he was also a brave soldier, an intrepid sailor, an explorer, and—strange but true—a poet and prose-writer. He was born in Devonshire of distinguished parentage and educated at Oxford and by association with such famous Elizabethans as his friend Spenser. He saw military and diplomatic service in Ireland and France, and accompanied his half-brother, Sir Humphrey Gilbert, on a voyage of discovery to North America. Later, in command of his own expeditions, he founded the ill-fated Roanoke colony and explored Guiana. Although Raleigh did not always have the favor of Queen Elizabeth, his fortunes under her successor James I were even less happy. After a fourteen year imprisonment in the Tower of London on the charge of conspiracy, he was released to undertake an unfortunate expedition to South America in the course of which he attacked a Spanish colony, was arrested on his return, and executed in 1618. Thus perished one of the last of the vivid and bold adventurers of the "spacious days" of Queen Elizabeth.

Raleigh's account of Sir Richard Grenville's magnificent single-ship fight against fifteen Spanish vessels off Flores was published in the *Principal Navigations, Voyages, and Discoveries of the English Nation* of Richard Hakluyt (1552?–1616). To one who knows the tales of the Elizabethan sea-dogs, it must seem that the spirits of Drake and Howard, commanders of the fleet against the "Invincible Armada," and of the great-souled Sir Richard must be reincarnated today in the captains of the *Ajax,* of the *Jervis Bay,* and of other British ships that have been sailed and fought with more valor than discretion.

The Last Fight
of the Revenge *(1591)*

Because the rumors are diversely spread, as well in England as in the low countries and elsewhere, of this late encounter between her Majesty's ships and the Armada of Spain; and that the Spaniards, according to their usual manner, fill the world with their vainglorious vaunts, making great appearance of victories, when on the contrary themselves are most commonly and shamefully beaten and dishonored, thereby hoping to possess the ignorant multitude by anticipating and forerunning false reports: it is agreeable with all good reason (for manifestation of the truth, to overcome falsehood and untruth) that the beginning, continuance, and success of this late honorable encounter of Sir Richard Grenville, and other her Majesty's captains, with the Armada of Spain, should be truly set down and published without partiality or false imaginations. And it is no marvel that the Spaniards should seek by false and slanderous pamphlets, advisos, and letters to cover their own loss, and to derogate from others their due honors (especially in this fight, being performed far off), seeing they were not ashamed in the year 1588, when they purposed the invasion of this land, to publish in sundry languages, in print, great victories (in words) which they pleaded to have obtained against this realm, and spread the same in a most false sort over all parts of France, Italy, and elsewhere. . . .

The Lord Thomas Howard, with six of her Majesty's ships, six victuallers of London, the bark *Raleigh,* and two or three pinnaces riding at anchor near unto Flores, one of the westerly islands of the Azores, the last of August in the afternoon, had intelligence by one Captain Middleton of the approach of the Spanish Armada. Which Middleton, being in a very good sailer, had kept them company three days before, of good purpose both to discover their forces the more, as also to give advice to my Lord Thomas of their approach.

He had no sooner delivered the news but the fleet was in sight. Many of our ships' companies were on shore in the island, some providing ballast for their ships, others filling of water and refreshing themselves from the land with such things as they could either for money or by force recover. By reason whereof our ships being all pestered, and rummaging, every thing out of order, very light for want of ballast. And that which was most to our disadvantage, the one half part of the men of every ship sick and utterly unserviceable. For in the *Revenge* there were ninety diseased; in the *Bonaventure,* not so many in health as could handle her mainsail. For had not twenty men been taken out of a bark of Sir George Cary's, his being commanded to be sunk, and those appointed to her, she had hardly ever recovered England. The rest, for the most part, were in little better state.

The names of her Majesty's ships were these, as followeth: the *Defiance,* which was Admiral; the *Revenge,* Vice Admiral; the *Bonaventure,* commanded by Captain Crosse; the *Lion,* by George Fenner; the *Foresight,* by Thomas Vavisour; and the *Crane,* by Duffield. The *Foresight* and the *Crane* being but small ships only; the other were of middle size. The rest, besides the bark *Raleigh,* commanded by Captain Thin, were victuallers, and of small force or none.

The Spanish fleet, having shrouded their approach by reason of the island, were now so soon at hand as our ships had scarce time to weigh their anchors, but some of them were driven to let slip their cables and set sail. Sir Richard Grenville was the last weighed, to recover the men that were upon the island, which otherwise had been lost. The Lord Thomas with the rest very hardly recovered the wind, which Sir Richard Grenville not being able to do, was persuaded by the master and others to cut his mainsail and cast about, and to trust to the sailing of his ship: for the squadron of Seville were on his weather bow. But Sir Richard utterly refused to turn from the enemy, alleging that he would rather choose to die, than to dishonor himself, his country, and her Majesty's ship; persuading his company that he would pass through the two squadrons in despite of them, and enforce those of Seville to give him way. Which he performed upon divers of the foremost, who, as the mariners term it, sprang their luff, and fell under the lee of the *Revenge.* But the other course had

been the better, and might right well have been answered in so
great an impossibility of prevailing. Notwithstanding out of the
greatness of his mind he could not be persuaded.

In the meanwhile, as he attended those which were nearest
him, the great *San Philip,* being in the wind of him, and coming
towards him, becalmed his sails in such sort as the ship could
neither way nor feel the helm: so huge and high carged was the
Spanish ship, being of a thousand and five hundred tons; who after
laid the *Revenge* aboard. When he was thus bereft of his sails,
the ships that were under his lee, luffing up, also laid him aboard;
of which the next was the admiral of the Biscayans, a very mighty
and puissant ship commanded by Britan Dona. The said *Philip*
carried three tier of ordnance on a side, and eleven pieces in
every tier. She shot eight forthright out of her chase, besides those
of her stern ports.

After the *Revenge* was entangled with this *Philip,* four others
boarded her, two on her larboard, and two on her starboard. The
fight, thus beginning at three of the clock in the afternoon, continued very terrible all that evening. But the great *San Philip,*
having received the lower tier of the *Revenge,* discharged with
crossbar shot, shifted herself with all diligence from her sides,
utterly misliking her first entertainment. Some say that the ship
foundered, but we cannot report it for truth, unless we were assured. The Spanish ships were filled with companies of soldiers,—
in some two hundred besides the mariners, in some five, in others
eight hundred. In ours there were none at all beside the mariners
but the servants of the commanders and some few voluntary gentlemen only. After many interchanged volleys of great ordnance
and small shot, the Spaniards deliberated to enter the *Revenge,*
and made divers attempts, hoping to force her by the multitudes
of their armed soldiers and musketeers, but were still repulsed
again and again, and at all times beaten back into their own
ships, or into the seas. In the beginning of the fight, the *George
Noble* of London, having received some shot through her by the
armadas, fell under the lee of the *Revenge,* and asked Sir Richard what he would command him, being but one of the victuallers and of small force. Sir Richard bade him save himself, and
leave him to his fortune. After the fight had thus, without inter-
mission, continued while the day lasted and some hours of the

night, many of our men were slain and hurt, and one of the great galleons of the armada, and the admiral of the hulks both sunk, and in many other of the Spanish ships great slaughter was made. Some write that Sir Richard was very dangerously hurt almost in the beginning of the fight, and lay speechless for a time ere he recovered. But two of the *Revenge's* own company brought home in a ship of Lima from the islands, examined by some of the lords and others affirmed that he was never so wounded as that he forsook the upper deck, till an hour before midnight: and then being shot into the body with a musket as he was a-dressing, was again shot into the head, and withal his surgeon wounded to death. This agreeth also with an examination taken by Sir Francis Godolphin, of four other mariners of the same ship being returned, which examination, the said Sir Francis sent unto Master William Killigrew, of her Majesty's privy chamber.

But to return to the fight, the Spanish ships which attempted to board the *Revenge,* as they were wounded and beaten off, so always others came in their places, she having never less than two mighty galleons by her sides, and aboard her: so that ere the morning, from three of the clock the day before, there had fifteen several armadas assailed her; and all so ill approved their entertainment, as they were by the break of day, far more willing to hearken to a composition than hastily to make any more assaults or entries. But as the day increased, so our men decreased: and as the light grew more and more, by so much more grew our discomforts. For none appeared in sight but enemies, saving one small ship called the *Pilgrim,* commanded by Jacob Whiddon, who hovered all night to see the success: but in the morning bearing with the *Revenge* was hunted like a hare amongst many ravenous hounds, but escaped.

All the powder of the *Revenge* to the last barrel was now spent, all her pikes broken, forty of her best men slain, and the most part of the rest hurt. In the beginning of the fight she had but one hundred free from sickness, and fourscore and ten sick, laid in hold upon the ballast. A small troop to man such a ship, and a weak garrison to resist so mighty an army. By those hundred all was sustained, the volleys, boardings, and enterings of fifteen ships of war, besides those which beat her at large. On the contrary, the Spanish were always supplied with soldiers brought from every squadron: all manner of arms and powder at will. Unto ours there remained no comfort at all, no hope, no supply either of ships, men, or weapons; the masts all beaten overboard, all her tackle cut asunder, her upper work altogether razed, and in effect evened she was with the water, but the very foundation or bottom of a ship, nothing being left overhead either for flight or defense. Sir Richard finding himself in this distress, and unable any longer to make resistance, having endured in this fifteen hours' fight, the assault of fifteen several armadas, all by turns aboard him, and by estimation eight hundred shot of great artillery, besides many assaults and entries; and that himself and the ship must needs be possessed by the enemy, who were now all cast in a ring around about him, the *Revenge* not able to move one way or other but as she was moved by the waves and billows of the sea,—commanded the master gunner, whom he knew to be a most resolute man, to split and sink the ship, that thereby nothing might remain of glory or victory to the Spaniards, seeing in so many hours' fight, and with so great a navy, they were not able to take her, having had fifteen hours' time, fifteen thousand men, and fifty and three sail of men-of-war to perform it withal; and persuaded the company, or as many as he could induce, to yield themselves unto God, and to the mercy of none else, but, as they had, like valiant resolute men, repulsed so many enemies, they should not now shorten the honor of their nation by prolonging their own lives for a few hours or a few days.

The master gunner readily condescended, and divers others. But the Captain and the Master were of another opinion and besought Sir Richard to have care of them, alleging that the Spaniard would be as ready to entertain a composition as they were willing to offer the same, and that there being divers sufficient and valiant men yet living, and whose wounds were not mortal, they might do their country and prince acceptable service hereafter. And, that where Sir Richard had alleged that the Spaniards should never glory to have taken one ship of her Majesty's, seeing that they had so long and so notably defended themselves, they answered that the ship had six foot of water in hold, three shot under water which were so weakly stopped as, with the first working of the sea, she must needs sink, and was besides so crushed and bruised as she could never be removed out of the place.

And as the matter was thus in dispute, and Sir Richard refusing to hearken to any of those reasons, the Master of the *Revenge* (while the Captain won unto him the greater party) was convoyed aboard the General Don Alfonso Bassan, who finding none over hasty to enter the *Revenge* again, doubting lest Sir Richard would have blown them up and himself, and perceiving by the report of the Master of the *Revenge* his dangerous disposition, yielded that all their lives should be saved, the company sent for England, and the better sort to pay such reasonable ransom as their estate would bear, and in the mean season to be free from galley or imprisonment. To this he so much the rather condescended, as well, as I have said, for fear of further loss and mischief to themselves, as also for the desire he had to recover Sir Richard Grenville, whom for his notable valor he seemed greatly to honor and admire.

When this answer was returned, and that safety of life was promised, the common sort being now at the end of their peril, the most drew back from Sir Richard and the master gunner, being no hard matter to dissuade men from death to life. The master gunner finding himself and Sir Richard thus prevented and mastered by the greater number would have slain himself with a sword had he not been by force withheld and locked into his cabin. Then the General sent many boats aboard the *Revenge,* and divers of our men, fearing Sir Richard's disposition, stole away aboard the General and other ships. Sir Richard, thus overmatched, was sent unto by Alfonso Bassan to remove out of the *Revenge,* the ship being marvelous unsavory, filled with blood and bodies of dead and wounded men like a slaughterhouse. Sir Richard answered that he might do with his body what he list, for he esteemed it not; and as he was carried out of the ship he swooned, and reviving again, desired the company to pray for him. The General used Sir Richard with all humanity and left nothing unattempted that tended to his recovery, highly commending his valor and worthiness, and greatly bewailed the danger wherein he was, being unto them a rare spectacle, and a resolution seldom approved, to see one ship turn toward so many enemies, to endure the charge and boarding of so many huge armadas, and to resist and repel the assaults and entries of so many soldiers. All which, and more, is confirmed by a Spanish captain of the same Armada, and a present actor in the fight, who, being severed from the rest in a storm, was by the *Lion,* of London, a small ship, taken, and is now prisoner in London.

The General Commander of the Armada was Don Alfonso Bassan, brother to the Marquis of Santa Cruce. The Admiral of the Biscayan squadron was Britan Dona; of the squadron of Seville, Marquis of Arumburch. The Hulks and Fly-boats were commanded by Luis Cutino. There were slain and drowned in this fight well near two thousand of the enemies, and two especial commanders, Don Luis Saint John and Don George de Prunaria de Malaga, as the Spanish captain confesseth, besides divers others of special account, whereof as yet report is not made. . . .

John Richard Green
(1837-1883)

A BRIEF note on Green's life and work appears on p. 12. This second selection from his *A Short History of the English People* is taken from Volume II, Chapter VIII, Section III. It deals with the rebellion of Parliament against the tyranny of Charles I, a rebellion that ended with the trial and execution of the king in 1649 and the establishment in England of a Puritan Commonwealth instead of a monarchy. In 1628, however, the date of the parliamentary petition of right, neither Charles nor Parliament could have foreseen the tragic conclusion of his stiff-necked absolutism. If he had had a sense of justice and righteousness, he would have ruled as the magistrate of his people, not as their tyrant, and so would have saved his minister Buckingham and, ultimately, his own crown and life. The Petition of Right is a Stuart Magna Carta (see pp. 12 ff), a protest against tyranny, and a declaration of the rights of the English people to those ancient privileges that date back to King John and, indeed, to even earlier times.

The Petition of Right (1628)

The first result of Buckingham's folly was to force on Charles, overwhelmed as he was with debt and shame, the summoning of a new Parliament; a Parliament which met in a mood even more resolute than the last. The Court candidates were everywhere rejected. The patriot leaders were triumphantly returned. To have suffered in the recent resistance to arbitrary taxation was the sure road to a seat. In spite of Eliot's counsel, even the question of Buckingham's removal gave place to the craving for redress of wrongs done to personal liberty. "We must vindicate our ancient liberties," said Sir Thomas Wentworth, in words soon to be remembered against himself: "we must reinforce the laws made by our ancestors. We must set such a stamp upon them, as no licentious spirit shall dare hereafter to invade them." Heedless of sharp and menacing messages from the king, of demands that they should take his "royal word" for their liberties, the House bent itself to one great work, the drawing up a Petition of Right. The statutes that protected the subject against arbitrary taxation, against loans and benevolences, against punishment, outlawry, or deprivation of goods, otherwise than by lawful judgment of his peers, against arbitrary imprisonment without stated charge, against billeting of soldiery on the people or enactment of martial law in time of peace, were formally recited. The breaches of them under the last two sovereigns, and above all since the dissolution of the last Parliament, were recited as formally. At the close of this significant list, the Commons prayed "that no man hereafter be compelled to make or yield any gift, loan, benevolence, tax, or such like charge, without common consent by Act of Parliament. And that none be called to make answer, or to take such oaths, or to be confined or otherwise molested or disputed concerning the same, or for refusal thereof. And that no freeman may in such manner as is before mentioned be imprisoned or detained. And that your Majesty would be pleased to remove the said soldiers and mariners, and that your people may not be so burdened in time to come. And that the commissions for proceeding by martial law may be revoked and annulled, and that hereafter no commissions of like nature may issue forth to any person or persons whatsoever to be executed as aforesaid, lest by color of them any of your Majesty's subjects be destroyed and put to death, contrary to the laws and franchises of the land. All which they humbly pray of your most excellent Majesty, as their rights and liberties, according to the laws and statutes of the realm. And that your Majesty would also vouchsafe to declare that the awards, doings, and proceedings to the prejudice of your people in any of the premises shall not be drawn hereafter into consequence or example. And that your Majesty would be pleased graciously for the further comfort and safety of your people to declare your royal will and pleasure, that in the things aforesaid all your officers and ministers shall serve you according to the laws and statutes of this realm, as they tender the honor of your Majesty and the prosperity of the kingdom." It was in vain that the Lords desired to conciliate Charles by a reservation of his "sovereign power." "Our petition," Pym quietly replied, "is for the laws of England, and this power seems to be another power distinct from the power of the law." The Lords yielded, but Charles gave an evasive reply; and the failure of the more moderate counsels for which his own had been set aside, called Eliot again to the front. In a speech of unprecedented boldness he moved the presentation to the king of a Remonstrance on the state of the realm. But at the moment when he again touched on Buckingham's removal as the preliminary of any real improvement the Speaker of the House interposed. "There was a command laid on him," he said, "to interrupt any that should go about to lay an aspersion on the king's ministers." The breach of their privilege of free speech produced a scene in the Commons such as St. Stephen's had never witnessed before. Eliot sate abruptly down amidst the solemn silence of the House. "Then appeared such a spectacle of passions," says a letter of the time, "as the like had seldom been seen in such an assembly; some weeping, some expostulating, some prophesying of the fatal ruin

of our kingdom, some playing the divines in confessing their sins
and country's sins which drew these judgments upon us, some
finding, as it were, fault with those that wept. There were above
an hundred weeping eyes, many who offered to speak being interrupted and silenced by their own passions." Pym himself rose
only to sit down choked with tears. At last Sir Edward Coke
found words to blame himself for the timid counsels which had
checked Eliot at the beginning of the Session, and to protest "that
the author and source of all those miseries was the Duke of Buckingham."

Shouts of assent greeted the resolution to insert the Duke's
name in their Remonstrance. But at this moment Charles gave
way. To win supplies for a new expedition to Rochelle, Buckingham bent the king to consent to the Petition of Right. As Charles
understood it, indeed, the consent meant little. The point for
which he really cared was the power of keeping men in prison
without bringing them to trial or assigning causes for their imprisonment. On this he had consulted his judges; and they had
answered that his consent to the Petition left his rights untouched; like other laws, they said, the Petition would have to
be interpreted when it came before them, and the prerogative
remained unaffected. As to the rest, while waiving all claim to
levy taxes not granted by Parliament, Charles still reserved his
right to levy impositions paid customarily to the crown, and
amongst these he counted tonnage and poundage. Of these reserves however the Commons knew nothing. The king's consent
won a grant of subsidy from the Parliament, and such a ringing
of bells and lighting of bonfires from the people "as were never
seen but upon his majesty's return from Spain." But, like all
Charles's concessions, it came too late to effect the end at which
he aimed. The Commons persisted in presenting their Remonstrance. Charles received it coldly and ungraciously; while Buckingham, who had stood defiantly at his master's side as he was
denounced, fell on his knees to speak. "No, George!" said the
king as he raised him; and his demeanor gave emphatic proof
that the Duke's favor remained undiminished. "We will perish
together, George," he added at a later time, "if thou dost." No
shadow of his doom, in fact, had fallen over the brilliant favorite,
when, after the prorogation of the Parliament, he set out to take

command of a new expedition for the relief of Rochelle. But a lieutenant in the army, John Felton, soured by neglect and wrongs, had found in the Remonstrance some fancied sanction for the revenge he plotted; and, mixing with the throng which crowded the hall at Portsmouth, he stabbed Buckingham to the heart. Charles flung himself on his bed in a passion of tears when the news reached him; but outside the Court it was welcomed with a burst of joy. Young Oxford bachelors, grave London aldermen, vied with each other in drinking healths to Felton. "God bless thee, little David," cried an old woman, as the murderer passed manacled by; "the Lord comfort thee," shouted the crowd, as the Tower gates closed on him. The very crews of the Duke's armament at Portsmouth shouted to the king, as he witnessed their departure, a prayer that he would "spare John Felton, their sometime fellow soldier." But whatever national hopes the fall of Buckingham had aroused were quickly dispelled. Weston, a creature of the Duke, became Lord Treasurer, and his system remained unchanged. "Though our Achan is cut off," said Eliot, "the accursed thing remains."

John Milton
(1608-1674)

JOHN MILTON is usually thought of as the creator of *Paradise Lost* and of numerous short lyrics. But his love of liberty and his sense of justice also took the form of prose tracts and speeches of which the *Areopagitica* is one of the best examples. He was born in London in 1608 and educated at St. Paul's School and Christ College, Cambridge. After leaving college in 1632 he retired to his father's country estate at Horton, where for five years he studied the classics and composed several of his most famous poems, including *L'Allegro, Il Penseroso, Comus,* and *Lycidas.* The next two years he spent in travel, especially in Italy. On his return to England he married Mary Powell, tutored private pupils, and wrote numerous pamphlets on controversial themes. Upon the execution of King Charles I in 1649 he was appointed Latin secretary to the Council of State and began a vigorous defense of the people against the royalists. Shortly after the Restoration of 1660 he retired with his third wife to a house in London, where he spent his remaining years in writing *Paradise Lost, Paradise Regained, Samson Agonistes,* and several histories and tracts. These final works he had to dictate since he had become blind years before in the service of the Commonwealth.

The title of *The Areopagitica* came from Aeropagus, the hill of Mars at Athens on which the Upper Council of the city met for deliberations. In his speech Milton attacked the order of Parliament of June 14, 1643, that no book should henceforth be printed or sold "unless the same be first approved and licensed by such person or persons as both or either of the said House shall appoint. . . ." Milton's cry, "Give me the liberty to know, to utter, and to argue freely according to my conscience, above all liberties" has echoed wherever tyranny or folly would check the liberty of the platform or the freedom of the press.

The Areopagitica (1644)

A SPEECH FOR THE LIBERTY OF UNLICENSED
PRINTING, TO THE PARLIAMENT OF ENGLAND

They, who to states and governors of the Commonwealth direct
their speech, High Court of Parliament, or, wanting such access
in a private condition, write that which they foresee may advance
the public good; I suppose them, as at the beginning of no mean
endeavor, not a little altered and moved inwardly in their
minds: some with doubt of what will be the success, others with
fear of what will be the censure; some with hope, others with confidence of what they have to speak. And me perhaps each of these
dispositions, as the subject was whereon I entered, may have at
other times variously affected; and likely might in these foremost
expressions now also disclose which of them swayed most, but
that the very attempt of this address thus made, and the thought
of whom it hath recourse to, hath got the power within me to a
passion, far more welcome than incidental to a preface.

Which though I stay not to confess ere any ask, I shall be
blameless, if it be no other than the joy and gratulation which
it brings to all who wish and promote their country's liberty;
whereof this whole discourse proposed will be a certain testimony, if not a trophy. For this is not the liberty which we can
hope, that no grievance ever should arise in the Commonwealth
—that let no man in this world expect; but when complaints are
freely heard, deeply considered and speedily reformed, then is the
utmost bound of civil liberty attained that wise men look for. To
which if I now manifest by the very sound of this which I shall
utter, that we are already in good part arrived, and yet from such a
steep disadvantage of tyranny and superstition grounded into our
principles as was beyond the manhood of a Roman recovery, it
will be attributed first, as is most due, to the strong assistance of
God our deliverer, next to your faithful guidance and undaunted
wisdom, Lords and Commons of England. Neither is it in God's

esteem the diminution of His glory, when honorable things are spoken of good men and worthy magistrates; which if I now first should begin to do, after so fair a progress of your laudable deeds, and such a long obligement upon the whole realm to your indefatigable virtues, I might be justly reckoned among the tardiest, and the unwillingest of them that praise ye.

Nevertheless there being three principal things, without which all praising is but courtship and flattery: First, when that only is praised which is solidly worth praise: next, when greatest likelihoods are brought that such things are truly and really in those persons to whom they are ascribed: the other, when he who praises, by showing that such his actual persuasion is of whom he writes, can demonstrate that he flatters not; the former two of these I have heretofore endeavored, rescuing the employment from him who went about to impair your merits with a trivial and malignant encomium; the latter as belonging chiefly to mine own acquittal, that whom I so extolled I did not flatter, hath been reserved opportunely to this occasion.

For he who freely magnifies what hath been nobly done, and fears not to declare as freely what might be done better, gives ye the best covenant of his fidelity; and that his loyalest affection and his hope waits on your proceedings. His highest praising is not flattery, and his plainest advice is a kind of praising. For though I should affirm and hold by argument, that it would fare better with truth, with learning and the Commonwealth, if one of your published Orders, which I should name, were called in; yet at the same time it could not but much redound to the luster of your mild and equal government, whenas private persons are hereby animated to think ye better pleased with public advice, than other statists have been delighted heretofore with public flattery. And men will then see what difference there is between the magnanimity of a triennial Parliament, and that jealous haughtiness of prelates and Cabin Counselors that usurped of late, whenas they shall observe ye in the midst of your victories and successes more gently brooking written exceptions against a voted Order than other Courts, which had produced nothing worth memory but the weak ostentation of wealth, would have endured the least signified dislike at any sudden Proclamation.

If I should thus far presume upon the meek demeanor of

your civil and gentle greatness, Lords and Commons, as what your published Order hath directly said, that to gainsay, I might defend myself with ease, if any should accuse me of being new or insolent, did they but know how much better I find ye esteem it to imitate the old and elegant humanity of Greece, than the barbaric pride of a Hunnish and Norwegian stateliness. And out of those ages, to whose polite wisdom and letters we owe that we are not yet Goths and Jutlanders, I could name him who from his private house wrote that discourse to the Parliament of Athens, that persuades them to change the form of democracy which was then established. Such honor was done in those days to men who professed the study of wisdom and eloquence, not only in their own country, but in other lands, that cities and signiories heard them gladly, and with great respect, if they had aught in public to admonish the state. Thus did Dion Prusæus, a stranger and a private orator, counsel the Rhodians against a former edict; and I abound with other like examples, which to set here would be superfluous.

But if from the industry of a life wholly dedicated to studious labors, and those natural endowments haply not the worse for two and fifty degrees of northern latitude, so much must be derogated, as to count me not equal to any of those who had this privilege, I would obtain to be thought not so inferior, as yourselves are superior to the most of them who received their counsel: and how far you excel them, be assured, Lords and Commons, there can no greater testimony appear, than when your prudent spirit acknowledges and obeys the voice of reason from what quarter soever it be heard speaking; and renders ye as willing to repeal any Act of your own setting forth, as any set forth by your predecessors.

If ye be thus resolved, as it were injury to think ye were not, I know not what should withhold me from presenting ye with a fit instance wherein to show both that love of truth which ye eminently profess, and that uprightness of your judgment which is not wont to be partial to yourselves; by judging over again that Order which ye have ordained to regulate Printing:—that no book, pamphlet, or paper shall be henceforth printed, unless the same be first approved and licensed by such, or at least one of such, as shall be thereto appointed. For that part which preserves

justly every man's copy to himself, or provides for the poor, I
touch not, only wish they be not made pretenses to abuse and
persecute honest and painful men, who offend not in either of
these particulars. But that other clause of Licensing Books, which
we thought had died with his brother quadragesimal and matri-
monial when the prelates expired, I shall now attend with such a
homily, as shall lay before ye, first the inventors of it to be those
whom ye will be loth to own; next what is to be thought in general of reading, whatever sort the books be; and that this Order
avails nothing to the suppressing of scandalous, seditious, and
libelous books, which were mainly intended to be suppressed.
Last, that it will be primely to the discouragement of all learning, and the stop of Truth, not only by disexercising and blunt-
ing our abilities in what we know already, but by hindering and
cropping the discovery that might be yet further made both in
religious and civil Wisdom.

I deny not, but that it is of greatest concernment in the Church
and Commonwealth, to have a vigilant eye how books demean
themselves as well as men; and thereafter to confine, imprison,
and do sharpest justice on them as malefactors. For books are not
absolutely dead things, but do contain a potency of life in them
to be as active as that soul was whose progeny they are; nay, they
do preserve as in a vial the purest efficacy and extraction of that
living intellect that bred them. I know they are as lively, and
as vigorously productive, as those fabulous dragon's teeth; and
being sown up and down, may chance to spring up armed men.
And yet, on the other hand, unless wariness be used, as good almost kill a man as kill a good book. Who kills a man kills a reasonable creature, God's image; but he who destroys a good book,
kills reason itself, kills the image of God, as it were in the eye.
Many a man lives a burden to the earth; but a good book is the
precious life-blood of a master spirit, embalmed and treasured up
on purpose to a life beyond life. 'Tis true, no age can restore a
life, whereof perhaps there is no great loss; and revolutions of
ages do not oft recover the loss of a rejected truth, for the want
of which whole nations fare the worse.

We should be wary therefore what persecution we raise against
the living labors of public men, how we spill that seasoned life
of man, preserved and stored up in books; since we see a kind of

homicide may be thus committed, sometimes a martyrdom, and if it extend to the whole impression, a kind of massacre; whereof the execution ends not in the slaying of an elemental life, but strikes at that ethereal and fifth essence, the breath of reason itself, slays an immortality rather than a life. . . .

What advantage is it to be a man over it is to be a boy at school, if we have only escaped the ferula to come under the fescue of an Imprimatur, if serious and elaborate writings, as if they were no more than the theme of a grammar-lad under his pedagogue, must not be uttered without the cursory eyes of a temporizing and extemporizing licenser? He who is not trusted with his own actions, his drift not being known to be evil, and standing to the hazard of law and penalty, has no great argument to think himself reputed in the Commonwealth, wherein he was born, for other than a fool or a foreigner. When a man writes to the world, he summons up all his reason and deliberation to assist him; he searches, meditates, is industrious, and likely consults and confers with his judicious friends; after all which done he takes himself to be informed in what he writes, as well as any that writ before him. If, in this the most consummate act of his fidelity and ripeness, no years, no industry, no former proof of his abilities can bring him to that state of maturity, as not to be still mistrusted and suspected, unless he carry all his considerate diligence, all his midnight watchings and expense of Palladian oil, to the hasty view of an unleisured licenser, perhaps much his younger, perhaps far his inferior in judgment, perhaps one who never knew the labor of book-writing, and if he be not repulsed or slighted, must appear in print like a puny with his guardian, and his censor's hand on the back of his title to be his bail and surety that he is no idiot or seducer, it cannot be but a dishonor and derogation to the author, to the book, to the privilege and dignity of Learning.

And what if the author shall be one so copious of fancy, as to have many things well worth the adding come into his mind after licensing, while the book is yet under the press, which not seldom happens to the best and diligentest writers; and that perhaps a dozen times in one book? The printer dares not go beyond his licensed copy; so often then must the author trudge to his leave-giver, that those his new insertions may be viewed; and many a jaunt will be made, ere that licenser, for it must be the same man, can either be found, or found at leisure; meanwhile either the press must stand still, which is no small damage, or the author lose his accuratest thoughts, and send the book forth worse than he had made it, which to a diligent writer is the greatest melancholy and vexation that can befall.

And how can a man teach with authority, which is the life of teaching, how can he be a doctor in his book as he ought to be, or else had better be silent, whenas all he teaches, all he delivers, is but under the tuition, under the correction of his patriarchal licenser to blot or alter what precisely accords not with the hidebound humor which he calls his judgment? When every acute reader, upon the first sight of a pedantic license, will be ready with these like words to ding the book a quoit's distance from him: I hate a pupil teacher, I endure not an instructor that comes to me under the wardship of an over-seeing fist. I know nothing of the licenser, but that I have his own hand here for his arrogance; who shall warrant me his judgment? The State, sir, replies the stationer, but has a quick return: The State shall be my governors, but not my critics; they may be mistaken in the choice of a licenser, as easily as this licenser may be mistaken in an author; this is some common stuff; and he might add from Sir Francis Bacon, That such authorized books are but the language of the times. For though a licenser should happen to be judicious more than ordinary, which will be a great jeopardy of the next succession, yet his very office and his commission enjoins him to let pass nothing but what is vulgarly received already. . . .

And as for regulating the Press, let no man think to have the honor of advising ye better than yourselves have done in that Order published next before this, "that no book be Printed, unless the Printer's and the Author's name, or at least the Printer's, be registered." Those which otherwise come forth, if they be found mischievous and libelous, the fire and the executioner will be the timeliest and the most effectual remedy that man's prevention can use. For this authentic Spanish policy of licensing books, if I have said aught, will prove the most unlicensed book itself within a short while; and was the immediate image of a Star Chamber decree to that purpose made in those very times when that Court did the rest of those her pious works, for which she is now fallen from the stars with Lucifer. Whereby ye may guess what kind of state prudence, what love of the people, what care of Religion or good manners there was at the contriving, although with singular hypocrisy it pretended to bind books to their good behavior. And how it got the upper hand of your precedent Order so well constituted before, if we may believe those men whose profession gives them cause to enquire most, it may be doubted there was in it the fraud of some old patentees and monopolizers in the trade of bookselling; who under pretense of the poor in their Company not to be defrauded, and the just retaining of each man his several copy, which God forbid should be gainsaid, brought divers glosing colors to the House, which were indeed but colors, and serving to no end except it be to exercise a superiority over their neighbors; men who do not therefore labor in an honest profession to which learning is indebted, that they should be made other men's vassals. Another end is thought was aimed at by some of them in procuring by petition this Order, that, having power in their hands, malignant books might the easier scape abroad, as the event shows.

But of these sophisms and elenchs of merchandise I skill not. This I know, that errors in a good government and in a bad are equally almost incident; for what Magistrate may not be misinformed, and much the sooner, if Liberty of Printing be reduced into the power of a few? But to redress willingly and speedily what hath been erred, and in highest authority to esteem a plain advertisement more than others have done a sumptuous bribe, is a virtue (honored Lords and Commons) answerable to your highest actions, and whereof none can participate but greatest and wisest men.

Thomas Babington Macaulay
(1800-1859)

THE CONTRIBUTIONS of Lord Macaulay to English thought and literature have been outlined on p. 3. The following selection from *The History of England* is taken from Volume II, Chapter IX. It has to do with the revolt of the people against what has been sometimes called "the second Stuart tyranny," the absolutism of King James II, a stubborn monarch who failed to profit by the fate of his father Charles I. The declaration of William of Orange, son-in-law of the English ruler, followed the petition of a group of English leaders that he come to England and in the name of his wife Mary take over the government. This he did in 1688 in the "Bloodless Revolution" which put William and Mary on the throne as joint rulers. William's declaration was his initial pledge to his people. With the accession of William and Mary, the Stuart theory of "the divine right of kings" came to an end forever, and Great Britain was thenceforth to be a limited monarchy, essentially, with its Tories and its Whigs, its Conservatives and its Liberals, a democratic form of government.

The Declaration
of William of Orange (1688)

The difference between the expedition of 1685 and the expedition of 1688 was sufficiently marked by the difference between the manifestoes which the leaders of those expeditions published. For Monmouth Ferguson had scribbled an absurd and brutal libel about the burning of London, the strangling of Godfrey, the butchering of Essex, and the poisoning of Charles. The Declaration of William was drawn up by the Grand Pensionary Fagel, who was highly renowned as a publicist. Though weighty and learned, it was, in its original form, much too prolix: but it was abridged and translated into English by Burnet, who well understood the art of popular composition. It began by a solemn preamble, setting forth that, in every community, the strict observance of law was necessary alike to the happiness of nations and to the security of governments. The Prince of Orange had therefore seen with deep concern that the fundamental laws of a kingdom, with which he was by blood and by marriage closely connected, had, by the advice of evil counselors, been grossly and systematically violated. The power of dispensing with Acts of Parliament had been strained to such a point that the whole legislative authority had been transferred to the crown. Decisions at variance with the spirit of the constitution had been obtained from the tribunals by turning out Judge after Judge, till the bench had been filled with men ready to obey implicitly the directions of the government. Notwithstanding the King's repeated assurances that he would maintain the established religion, persons notoriously hostile to that religion had been promoted, not only to civil offices, but also to ecclesiastical benefices. The government of the Church had, in defiance of express statutes, been entrusted to a new court of High Commission; and in that court one avowed Papist had a seat. Good subjects, for refusing to violate their duty and their oaths, had been ejected from their property, in contempt of the

Great Charter of the liberties of England. Meanwhile persons who could not legally set foot on the island had been placed at the head of seminaries for the corruption of youth. Lieutenants, Deputy Lieutenants, Justices of the Peace had been dismissed in multitudes for refusing to support a pernicious and unconstitutional policy. The franchises of almost every borough in the realm had been invaded. The courts of justice were in such a state that their decisions, even in civil matters, had ceased to inspire confidence, and that their servility in criminal cases had brought on the kingdom the stain of innocent blood. All these abuses, loathed by the English nation, were to be defended, it seemed, by an army of Irish Papists. Nor was this all. The most arbitrary princes had never accounted it an offense in a subject modestly and peaceably to represent his grievances and to ask for relief. But supplication was now treated as a high misdemeanor in England. For no crime but that of offering to the Sovereign a petition drawn up in the most respectful terms, the fathers of the Church had been imprisoned and prosecuted; and every Judge who gave his voice in their favor had instantly been turned out. The calling of a free and lawful Parliament might indeed be an effectual remedy for all these evils: but such a Parliament, unless the whole spirit of the administration were changed, the nation could not hope to see. It was evidently the intention of the court to bring together, by means of regulated corporations and of Popish returning officers, a body which would be a House of Commons in name alone. Lastly, there were circumstances which raised a grave suspicion that the child who was called Prince of Wales was not really born of the Queen. For these reasons the Prince, mindful of his near relation to the royal house, and grateful for the affection which the English people had ever shown to his beloved wife and to himself, had resolved, in compliance with the request of many Lords Spiritual and Temporal, and of many other persons of all ranks, to go over at the head of a force sufficient to repel violence. He abjured all thought of conquest. He protested that, while his troops remained in the island, they should be kept under the strictest restraints of discipline, and that, as soon as the nation had been delivered from tyranny, they should be sent back. His single object was to have a free and legal Parliament assembled: and to the decision of such a Parliament he solemnly pledged himself to leave all questions both public and private.

Statutes of the Realm
(1689)

THE DECLARATION of William of Orange of 1688 was carried over into the fuller and more formal Bill of Rights of 1689. This Bill was, in effect, a renewed covenant or contract made between the rulers and the ruled by which justice and right were assured to all. Under its liberal provisions no absolutism was possible. Under the Stuarts the rulers came to believe, with Shakespeare's tyrant Claudius, that there is a divinity that "doth hedge a king." With the Bill of Rights, however, the king's authority was secured not by divine right but by the authority of the governed, and the king was not the absolute ruler but the magistrate and servant of his people. The following parts of the Bill of Rights are taken from the *Statutes of the Realm,* Volume VI, pp. 142, ff.

The Bill of Rights (1689)

Whereas the said late King James II having abdicated the government, and the throne being thereby vacant, his Highness the prince of Orange (whom it hath pleased Almighty God to make the glorious instrument of delivering this kingdom from popery and arbitrary power) did (by the advice of the lords spiritual and temporal, and diverse principal persons of the Commons) cause letters to be written to the lords spiritual and temporal, being Protestants, and other letters to the several counties, cities, universities, boroughs, and Cinque Ports, for the choosing of such persons to represent them, as were of right to be sent to parliament, to meet and sit at Westminster upon the two-and-twentieth day of January, in this year 1689, in order to such an establishment as that their religion, laws, and liberties might not again be in danger of being subverted; upon which letters elections have been accordingly made.

And thereupon the said lords spiritual and temporal and Commons, pursuant to their respective letters and elections, being now assembled in a full and free representation of this nation, taking into their most serious consideration the best means for attaining the ends aforesaid, do in the first place (as their ancestors in like case have usually done), for the vindicating and asserting their ancient rights and liberties, declare:

1. That the pretended power of suspending laws, or the execution of laws, by regal authority, without consent of parliament, is illegal.

2. That the pretended power of dispensing with laws, or the execution of laws, by regal authority, as it hath been assumed and exercised of late, is illegal.

3. That the commission for erecting the late court of commissioners for ecclesiastical causes, and all other commissions and courts of like nature, are illegal and pernicious.

4. That levying money for or to the use of the crown by pretense of prerogative, without grant of parliament, for longer time or in other manner than the same is or shall be granted, is illegal.

5. That it is the right of the subjects to petition the king, and all commitments and prosecutions for such petitioning are illegal.

6. That the raising or keeping a standing army within the kingdom in time of peace, unless it be with consent of parliament, is against law.

7. That the subjects which are Protestants may have arms for their defense suitable to their conditions, and as allowed by law.

8. That election of members of parliament ought to be free.

9. That the freedom of speech, and debates or proceedings in parliament, ought not to be impeached or questioned in any court or place out of parliament.

10. That excessive bail ought not to be required, nor excessive fines imposed, nor cruel and unusual punishments inflicted.

11. That jurors ought to be duly impaneled and returned, and jurors which pass upon men in trials for high treason ought to be freeholders.

12. That all grants and promises of fines and forfeitures of particular persons before conviction are illegal and void.

13. And that for redress of all grievances, and for the amending, strengthening, and preserving of the laws, parliament ought to be held frequently.

And they do claim, demand, and insist upon all and singular the premises, as their undoubted rights and liberties; and that no declarations, judgments, doings, or proceedings, to the prejudice of the people in any of the said premises, ought in any wise to be drawn hereafter into consequence or example.

To which demand of their rights they are particularly encouraged by the declaration of his Highness the prince of Orange, as being the only means for obtaining a full redress and remedy therein.

Having therefore an entire confidence that his said Highness the prince of Orange will perfect the deliverance so far advanced by him, and will still preserve them from the violation of their rights, which they have here asserted, and from all other attempts upon their religion, rights, and liberties:

The said lords spiritual and temporal, and commons, assem-

bled at Westminster, do resolve that William and Mary, prince
and princess of Orange, be, and be declared king and queen of
England, France, and Ireland, and the dominions thereunto belonging, to hold the crown and royal dignity of the said kingdoms
and dominions to them the said prince and princess during their
lives, and the life of the survivor of them; and that the sole and
full exercise of the regal power be only in, and executed by, the
said prince of Orange, in the names of the said prince and princess, during their joint lives; and after their deceases, the said
crown and royal dignity of the said kingdoms and dominions to
be to the heirs of the body of the said princess; and for default of
such issue to the princess Anne of Denmark, and the heirs of her
body; and for default of such issue to the heirs of the body of
the said prince of Orange. And the lords spiritual and temporal,
and commons, do pray the said prince and princess to accept the
same accordingly. . . .

Upon which their said Majesties did accept the crown and royal
dignity of the kingdoms of England, France, and Ireland, and the
dominions thereunto belonging, according to the resolution and
desire of the said lords and commons contained in the said declaration.

John Locke
(1632-1704)

JOHN LOCKE was the most influential English philosopher of the seventeenth century. After an education at Christ Church, Oxford, he took up the study of medicine but seems to have acted as a physician only to his patron, Anthony Ashley Cooper, first Earl of Shaftesbury, of whose household he was for some time a member. On the political fall of Shaftesbury, Locke was exiled to the Netherlands, but he returned to England after the Revolution of 1688. Under William and Mary he held many minor diplomatic posts. Locke's most important work is his *Essay Concerning Human Understanding* (1690), an analysis of the nature of knowledge and of the methods of thought. His political and religious essays reveal his persistent love of liberty and of religious toleration. Locke attacked the doctrine of the divine right of kings and represented government as essentially a contract between ruler and ruled. Thus his political theories were definitely opposed to those of the Stuart kings but were in harmony with those of their successors to the English throne.

Locke's *Of Conquest* is Chapter XVI of Book II of his *Two Treatises of Civil Government* (1690). In this clearly written essay he expresses his ideas of the unrighteous and unsound status of the conquering invader, who cannot by any reasoning be regarded as holding any right to control those people whose lands he has seized.

Of Conquest (1690)

Though governments can originally have no other rise than that before mentioned, nor polities be founded on anything but the consent of the people, yet such have been the disorders ambition has filled the world with, that in the noise of war, which makes so great a part of the history of mankind, this consent is little taken notice of; and, therefore, many have mistaken the force of arms for the consent of the people, and reckon conquest as one of the originals of government. But conquest is as far from setting up any government as demolishing a house is from building a new one in the place. Indeed, it often makes way for a new frame of a commonwealth by destroying the former; but, without the consent of the people, can never erect a new one.

That the aggressor, who puts himself into the state of war with another, and unjustly invades another man's right, can, by such an unjust war, never come to have a right over the conquered, will be easily agreed by all men, who will not think that robbers and pirates have a right of empire over whomsoever they have force enough to master, or that men are bound by promises which unlawful force extorts from them. Should a robber break into my house, and, with a dagger at my throat, make me seal deeds to convey my estate to him, would this give him any title? Just such a title by his sword has an unjust conqueror who forces me into submission. The injury and the crime is equal, whether committed by the wearer of a crown or some petty villain. The title of the offender and the number of his followers make no difference in the offense, unless it be to aggravate it. The only difference is, great robbers punish little ones to keep them in their obedience; but the great ones are rewarded with laurels and triumphs, because they are too big for the weak hands of justice in this world, and have the power in their own possession which should punish offenders. What is my remedy against a robber that so broke into my house? Appeal to the law for justice. But perhaps justice is denied, or I am crippled and cannot stir; robbed and have not the means to do it. If God has taken away all means of seeking remedy, there is nothing left but patience. But my son, when able, may seek the relief of the law, which I am denied; he or his son may renew his appeal till he recover his right. But the conquered, or their children, have no court—no arbitrator on earth to appeal to. Then they may appeal, as Jephtha did, to Heaven, and repeat their appeal till they have recovered the native right of their ancestors, which was to have such a legislative over them as the majority should approve and freely acquiesce in. If it be objected this would cause endless trouble, I answer, no more than justice does, where she lies open to all that appeal to her. He that troubles his neighbor without a cause is punished for it by the justice of the court he appeals to. And he that appeals to Heaven must be sure he has right on his side, and a right, too, that is worth the trouble and cost of the appeal, as he will answer at a tribunal that cannot be deceived, and will be sure to retribute to every one according to the mischiefs he hath created to his fellow-subjects—that is, any part of mankind. From whence it is plain that he that conquers in an unjust war can thereby have no title to the subjection and obedience of the conquered.

But supposing victory favors the right side, let us consider a conqueror in a lawful war, and see what power he gets, and over whom.

First, it is plain he gets no power by his conquest over those that conquered with him. They that fought on his side cannot suffer by the conquest, but must, at least, be as much free men as they were before. And most commonly they serve upon terms, and on condition to share with their leader, and enjoy a part of the spoil and other advantages that attend the conquering sword, or, at least, have a part of the subdued country bestowed upon them. And the conquering people are not, I hope, to be slaves by conquest, and wear their laurels only to show they are sacrifices to their leader's triumph. They that found absolute monarchy upon the title of the sword make their heroes, who are the founders of such monarchies, arrant "draw-can-sirs," and forget they had any officers and soldiers that fought on their side in the battles they won, or assisted them in the subduing, or shared in possessing the countries they mastered. We are told by some that the English monarchy is founded in the Norman Conquest, and that our princes have thereby a title to absolute dominion, which, if it were true (as by the history it appears otherwise), and that William had a right to make war on this island, yet his dominion by conquest could reach no farther than to the Saxons and Britons that were then inhabitants of this country. The Normans that came with him and helped to conquer, and all descended from them, are free men and no subjects by conquest, let that give what dominion it will. And if I or anybody else shall claim freedom as derived from them, it will be very hard to prove the contrary; and it is plain, the law that has made no distinction between the one and the other intends not there should be any difference in their freedom or privileges.

But supposing, which seldom happens, that the conquerors and conquered never incorporate into one people under the same laws and freedom; let us see next what power a lawful conqueror has over the subdued, and that I say is purely despotical. He has an absolute power over the lives of those who, by an unjust war, have forfeited them, but not over the lives or fortunes of those who engaged not in the war, nor over the possessions even of those who were actually engaged in it.

Secondly, I say, then, the conqueror gets no power but only over those who have actually assisted, concurred, or consented to that unjust force that is used against him. For the people having given to their governors no power to do an unjust thing, such as is to make an unjust war (for they never had such a power in themselves), they ought not to be charged as guilty of the violence and injustice that is committed in an unjust war any farther than they actually abet it, no more than they are to be thought guilty of any violence or oppression their governors should use upon the people themselves or any part of their fellow-subjects, they having empowered them no more to the one than to the other. Conquerors, it is true, seldom trouble themselves to make the distinction, but they willingly permit the confusion of war to sweep all together; but yet this alters not the right; for the conqueror's power over the lives of the conquered being only because they have used force to do or maintain an injustice, he can have that

power only over those who have concurred in that force; all the
rest are innocent, and he has no more title over the people of
that country who have done him no injury, and so have made no
forfeiture of their lives, than he has over any other who, without
any injuries or provocations, have lived upon fair terms with him.

Thirdly, the power a conqueror gets over those he overcomes
in a just war is perfectly despotical; he has an absolute power
over the lives of those who, by putting themselves in a state of
war, have forfeited them, but he has not thereby a right and title
to their possessions. This I doubt not but at first sight will seem
a strange doctrine, it being so quite contrary to the practice of
the world; there being nothing more familiar in speaking of the
dominion of countries than to say such an one conquered it, as if
conquest, without any more ado, conveyed a right of possession.
But when we consider that the practice of the strong and powerful, how universal soever it may be, is seldom the rule of right,
however it be one part of the subjection of the conquered not to
argue against the conditions cut out to them by the conquering
swords.

Though in all war there be usually a complication of force and
damage, and the aggressor seldom fails to harm the estate when
he uses force against the persons of those he makes war upon, yet
it is the use of force only that puts a man into the state of war. For
whether by force he begins the injury, or else having quietly and
by fraud done the injury, he refuses to make reparation, and by
force maintains it, which is the same thing as at first to have done
it by force; it is the unjust use of force that makes the war. For he
that breaks open my house and violently turns me out of doors,
or having peaceably got in, by force keeps me out, does, in effect,
the same thing; supposing we are in such a state that we have no
common judge on earth whom I may appeal to, and to whom we
are both obliged to submit, for of such I am now speaking. It is
the unjust use of force, then, that puts a man into the state of
war with another, and thereby he that is guilty of it makes a forfeiture of his life. For quitting reason, which is the rule given
between man and man, and using force, the way of beasts, he becomes liable to be destroyed by him he uses force against, as any
savage ravenous beast that is dangerous to his being.

But because the miscarriages of the father are no faults of the children, who may be rational and peaceable, notwithstanding the brutishness and injustice of the father, the father, by his miscarriages and violence, can forfeit but his own life, and involves not his children in his guilt or destruction. His goods which Nature, that willeth the preservation of all mankind as much as is possible, hath made to belong to the children to keep them from perishing, do still continue to belong to his children. For supposing them not to have joined in the war either through infancy or choice, they have done nothing to forfeit them, nor has the conqueror any right to take them away by the bare right of having subdued him that by force attempted his destruction, though, perhaps, he may have some right to them to repair the damages he has sustained by the war, and the defense of his own right, which how far it reaches to the possessions of the conquered we shall see by-and-by; so that he that by conquest has a right over a man's person, to destroy him if he pleases, has not thereby a right over his estate to possess and enjoy it. For it is the brutal force the aggressor has used that gives his adversary a right to take away his life and destroy him, if he pleases, as a noxious creature; but it is damage sustained that alone gives him title to another man's goods; for though I may kill a thief that sets on me in the highway, yet I may not (which seems less) take away his money and let him go; this would be robbery on my side. His force, and the state of war he put himself in, made him forfeit his life, but gave me no title to his goods. The right, then, of conquest extends only to the lives of those who joined in the war, but not to their estates, but only in order to make reparation for the damages received and the charges of the war, and that, too, with reservation of the right of the innocent wife and children.

Let the conqueror have as much justice on his side as could be supposed, he has no right to seize more than the vanquished could forfeit; his life is at the victor's mercy, and his service and goods he may appropriate to make himself reparation; but he cannot take the goods of his wife and children, they too had a title to the goods he enjoyed, and their shares in the estate he possessed. For example, I in the state of Nature (and all commonwealths are in the state of Nature one with another) have injured another man, and refusing to give satisfaction, it is come to a state of war wherein my defending by force what I had gotten unjustly makes me the aggressor. I am conquered; my life, it is true, as forfeit, is at mercy, but not my wife's and children's. They made not the war, nor assisted in it. I could not forfeit their lives, they were not mine to forfeit. My wife had a share in my estate, that neither could I forfeit. And my children also, being born of me, had a right to be maintained out of my labor or substance. Here then is the case: The conqueror has a title to reparation for damages received, and the children have a title to their father's estate for their subsistence. For as to the wife's share, whether her own labor or compact gave her a title to it, it is plain her husband could not forfeit what was hers. What must be done in the case? I answer: The fundamental law of Nature being that all, as much as may be, should be preserved, it follows that if there be not enough fully to satisfy both—viz., for the conqueror's losses and children's maintenance, he that hath and to spare must remit something of his full satisfaction, and give way to the pressing and preferable title of those who are in danger to perish without it.

But supposing the charge and damages of the war are to be made up to the conqueror to the utmost farthing, and that the children of the vanquished, spoiled of all their father's goods, are to be left to starve and perish, yet the satisfying of what shall, on this score, be due to the conqueror will scarce give him a title to any country he shall conquer. For the damages of war can scarce amount to the value of any considerable tract of land in any part of the world, where all the land is possessed, and none lies waste. And if I have not taken away the conqueror's land which, being vanquished, it is impossible I should, scarce any other spoil I have done him can amount to the value of mine, supposing it of an extent any way coming near what I had overrun of his, and equally cultivated too. The destruction of a year's product or two (for it seldom reaches four or five) is the utmost spoil that usually can be done. For as to money, and such riches and treasure taken away, these are none of Nature's goods, they have but a phantastical imaginary value; Nature has put no such upon them. They are of no more account by her standard than the Wampompeke of the Americans to an European prince, or the silver money of Europe would have been formerly to an American. And five years' product is not worth the perpetual inheritance of land, where all is possessed and none remains waste, to be taken up by him that is disseised, which will be easily granted, if one do but take away the imaginary value of money, the disproportion being more than between five and five thousand; though, at the same time, half a year's product is more worth than the inheritance where, there being more land than the inhabitants possess and make use of, any one has liberty to make use of the waste. But their conquerors take little care to possess themselves of the lands of the vanquished. No damage therefore that men in the state of Nature (as all princes and governments are in reference to one another) suffer from one another can give a conqueror power to dispossess the posterity of the vanquished, and turn them out of that inheritance which ought to be the possession of them and their descendants to all generations. The conqueror indeed will be apt to think himself master; and it is the very condition of the subdued not to be able to dispute their right. But, if that be all, it gives no other title than what bare force gives to the stronger over the weaker; and, by this reason, he that is strongest will have a right to whatever he pleases to seize on.

Over those, then, that joined with him in the war, and over those of the subdued country that opposed him not, and the posterity even of those that did, the conqueror, even in a just war, hath, by his conquest, no right of dominion. They are free from any subjection to him, and if their former government be dissolved, they are at liberty to begin and erect another to themselves.

The conqueror, it is true, usually by the force he has over them, compels them, with a sword at their breasts, to stoop to his conditions, and submit to such a government as he pleases to afford them; but the inquiry is, what right he has to do so? If it be said they submit by their own consent, then this allows their own consent to be necessary to give the conqueror a title to rule over them. It remains only to be considered whether promises, extorted by force, without right, can be thought consent, and how far they bind. To which I shall say, they bind not at all; because whatsoever another gets from me by force, I still retain the right of, and he is obliged presently to restore. He that forces my horse from me ought presently to restore him, and I have still a right to retake him. By the same reason, he that forced a promise from me ought presently to restore it—*i.e.,* quit me of the obligation of it; or I may resume it myself—*i.e.,* choose whether I will perform it. For the law of Nature laying an obligation on me, only by the rules she prescribes, cannot oblige me by the violation of her rules; such is the extorting anything from me by force. Nor does it at all alter the case, to say I gave my promise, no more than it excuses the force, and passes the right, when I put my hand in my pocket and deliver my purse myself to a thief who demands it with a pistol at my breast.

From all which it follows that the government of a conqueror, imposed by force on the subdued, against whom he had no right of war, or who joined not in the war against him, where he had right, has no obligation upon them.

But let us suppose that all the men of that community being all members of the same body politic, may be taken to have joined in that unjust war, wherein they are subdued, and so their lives are at the mercy of the conqueror.

I say this concerns not their children who are in their minority. For since a father hath not, in himself, a power over the life or liberty of his child, no act of his can possibly forfeit it; so that the children, whatever may have happened to the fathers, are free men, and the absolute power of the conqueror reaches no farther than the persons of the men that were subdued by him, and dies with them; and should he govern them as slaves, subjected to his absolute, arbitrary power, he has no such right of dominion over their children. He can have no power over them but by their own consent, whatever he may drive them to say or do, and he has no lawful authority, whilst force, and not choice, compels them to submission.

Every man is born with a double right. First, a right of freedom to his person, which no other man has a power over, but the free disposal of it lies in himself. Secondly, a right before any other man, to inherit, with his brethren, his father's goods.

By the first of these, a man is naturally free from subjection to any government, though he be born in a place under its jurisdiction. But if he disclaim the lawful government of the country he was born in, he must also quit the right that belonged to him, by the laws of it, and the possessions there descending to him from his ancestors, if it were a government made by their consent.

By the second, the inhabitants of any country, who are descended and derive a title to their estates from those who are subdued, and had a government forced upon them, against their free consents, retain a right to the possession of their ancestors, though they consent not freely to the government, whose hard conditions were, by force, imposed on the possessors of that country. For the first conqueror never having had a title to the land of that country, the people, who are the descendants of, or claim under those who were forced to submit to the yoke of a government by constraint, have always a right to shake it off, and free themselves from the usurpation or tyranny the sword hath brought in upon them, till their rulers put them under such a frame of government as they willingly and of choice consent to (which they can never be supposed to do, till either they are put in a full state of liberty to choose their government and governors, or at least till they have such standing laws to which they have, by themselves or their representatives, given their free consent, and also till they are allowed their due property, which is so to be proprietors of what they have that nobody can take away any part of it without their own consent, without which, men under any government are not in the state of free men, but are direct slaves under the force of war). And who doubts but the Grecian Christians, descendants of the ancient possessors of that country, may justly cast off the Turkish yoke they have so long groaned under, whenever they have a power to do it?

But granting that the conqueror, in a just war, has a right to the estates, as well as power over the persons of the conquered, which, it is plain, he hath not, nothing of absolute power will follow from hence in the continuance of the government. Because the descendants of these being all free men, if he grants them estates and possessions to inhabit his country, without which it would be worth nothing, whatsoever he grants them they have so far as it is granted property in; the nature whereof is, that, without a man's own consent, it cannot be taken from him.

Their persons are free by a native right, and their properties, be they more or less, are their own, and at their own dispose, and not at his; or else it is no property. Supposing the conqueror gives to one man a thousand acres, to him and his heirs for ever; to another he lets a thousand acres, for his life, under the rent of

£50 or £500 per annum. Has not the one of these a right to his thousand acres for ever, and the other during his life, paying the said rent? And hath not the tenant for life a property in all that he gets over and above his rent, by his labor and industry, during the said term, supposing it be double the rent? Can any one say, the king, or conqueror, after his grant, may, by his power of conqueror, take away all, or part of the land, from the heirs of one, or from the other during his life, he paying the rent? Or, can he take away from either the goods or money they have got upon the said land at his pleasure? If he can, then all free and voluntary contracts cease, and are void in the world; there needs nothing but power enough to dissolve them at any time, and all the grants and promises of men in power are but mockery and collusion. For can there be anything more ridiculous than to say, I give you and yours this for ever, and that in the surest and most solemn way of conveyance can be devised, and yet it is to be understood that I have right, if I please, to take it away from you again tomorrow?

I will not dispute now whether princes are exempt from the laws of their country, but this I am sure, they owe subjection to the laws of God and Nature. Nobody, no power can exempt them from the obligations of that eternal law. Those are so great and so strong in the case of promises, that Omnipotency itself can be tied by them. Grants, promises, and oaths are bonds that hold the Almighty, whatever some flatterers say to princes of the world, who, all together, with all their people joined to them, are, in comparison of the great God, but as a drop of the bucket, or a dust on the balance—inconsiderable, nothing!

The short of the case in conquest, is this: The conqueror, if he have a just cause, has a despotical right over the persons of all that actually aided and concurred in the war against him, and a right to make up his damage and cost out of their labor and estates, so he injure not the right of any other. Over the rest of the people, if there were any that consented not to the war, and over the children of the captives themselves or the possessions of either he has no power, and so can have, by virtue of conquest, no lawful title himself to dominion over them, or derive it to his posterity; but is an aggressor, and puts himself in a state of war against them, and has no better a right of principality, he, nor any of his successors, than Hingar, or Hubba, the Danes, had here in England, or Spartacus, had he conquered Italy, which is to have their yoke cast off as soon as God shall give those under their subjection courage and opportunity to do it. Thus, notwithstanding whatever title the kings of Assyria had over Judah, by the sword, God assisted Hezekiah to throw off the dominion of that conquering empire. "And the Lord was with Hezekiah, and he prospered; wherefore he went forth, and he rebelled against the king of Assyria, and served him not" (2 Kings xviii. 7). Whence it is plain that shaking off a power which force, and not right, hath set over any one, though it hath the name of rebellion, yet is no offense before God, but that which He allows and countenances, though even promises and covenants, when obtained by force, have intervened. For it is very probable, to any one that reads the story of Ahaz and Hezekiah attentively, that the Assyrians subdued Ahaz, and deposed him, and made Hezekiah king in his father's lifetime, and that Hezekiah, by agreement, had done him homage, and paid him tribute till this time.

Edmund Burke
(1729-1797)

THE FREQUENT American conception of Edmund Burke as the champion in the English Parliament of the independence of the thirteen colonies is not strictly accurate. He fought for their emancipation from unjust oppression, but not for their separation from England. Indeed, Burke's speeches against the unjust taxation of the Americans and in favor of conciliation with the colonies were but episodes in his battle against tyranny. He is to be thought of, however, as the defender of liberty and right. Edmund Burke was born in Dublin and educated at the university in his native city. In 1766 he entered Parliament as a Whig and was soon involved in a series of vigorous attacks on the Tory ministry of Lord North. His speech on American taxation was given in 1774 and his famous one on conciliation with the colonies in 1775, not long before the outbreak of hostilities between America and the mother country. His opposition to the excesses of the French revolutionists he expressed in 1790 in *Reflections on the French Revolution.*

In clarity of structure and vigor of expression Burke's speech on *Conciliation with America* is one of the most notable of eighteenth century documents. After having assailed the use of force against the colonies because it is temporary, uncertain, damaging to the object, and not based on experience, Burke then proceeded to analyze the temper and character of the Americans. It is this section of the famous address that is reprinted here. From this part, and, indeed, from the whole, it is apparent that Burke thought of the Americans as engaged in the same defense of liberty against oppression that he was engaged in carrying on in England. It is not to be wondered at, therefore, that Americans came to think of him as the English champion of their principles of democracy.

Temper and Character of the Americans (1775)

These, Sir, are my reasons for not entertaining that high opinion of untried force by which many gentlemen, for whose sentiments in other particulars I have great respect, seem to be so greatly captivated. But there is still behind a third consideration concerning this object, which serves to determine my opinion on the sort of policy which ought to be pursued in the management of America, even more than its population and its commerce—I mean its *temper and character.*

In this character of the Americans, a love of freedom is the predominating feature which marks and distinguishes the whole; and as an ardent is always a jealous affection, your colonies become suspicious, restive, and untractable whenever they see the least attempt to wrest from them by force or shuffle from them by chicane what they think the only advantage worth living for. This fierce spirit of liberty is stronger in the English colonies probably than in any other people of the earth; and this from a great variety of powerful causes, which, to understand the true temper of their minds and the direction which this spirit takes, it will not be amiss to lay open somewhat more largely.

First, the people of the colonies are descendants of Englishmen. England, Sir, is a nation which still I hope respects, and formerly adored, her freedom. The colonists emigrated from you when this part of your character was most predominant, and they took this bias and direction the moment they parted from your hands. They are therefore not only devoted to liberty, but to liberty according to English ideas and on English principles. Abstract liberty, like other mere abstractions, is not to be found. Liberty inheres in some sensible object; and every nation has formed to itself some favorite point, which by way of eminence becomes the criterion of their happiness. It happened you know, Sir, that the great contests for freedom in this country were from the earliest times chiefly upon the question of taxing. Most of the contests in the ancient commonwealths turned primarily on the right of election of magistrates, or on the balance among the several orders of the state. The question of money was not with them so immediate. But in England it was otherwise. On this point of taxes the ablest pens and most eloquent tongues have been exercised; the greatest spirits have acted and suffered. In order to give the fullest satisfaction concerning the importance of this point, it was not only necessary for those who in argument defended the excellence of the English constitution to insist on this privilege of granting money as a dry point of fact, and to prove that the right had been acknowledged in ancient parchments and blind usages to reside in a certain body called a House of Commons. They went much further; they attempted to prove, and they succeeded, that in theory it ought to be so, from the particular nature of a House of Commons, as an immediate representative of the people, whether the old records had delivered this oracle or not. They took infinite pains to inculcate, as a fundamental principle, that in all monarchies the people must in effect themselves, mediately or immediately, possess the power of granting their own money, or no shadow of liberty could subsist. The colonies draw from you, as with their life-blood, these ideas and principles. Their love of liberty, as with you, fixed and attached on this specific point of taxing. Liberty might be safe or might be endangered in twenty other particulars, without their being much pleased or alarmed. Here they felt its pulse, and as they found that beat they thought themselves sick or sound. I do not say whether they were right or wrong in applying your general arguments to their own case. It is not easy indeed to make a monopoly of theorems and corollaries. The fact is, that they did thus apply those general arguments; and your mode of governing them, whether through lenity or indolence, through wisdom or mistake, confirmed them in the imagination that they, as well as you, had an interest in these common principles.

They were further confirmed in this pleasing error by the form of their provincial legislative assemblies. Their governments are popular in a high degree, some are merely popular, in all the popular representative is the most weighty, and this share of the people in their ordinary government never fails to inspire them with lofty sentiments and with a strong aversion from whatever tends to deprive them of their chief importance.

If anything were wanting to this necessary operation of the form of government, religion would have given it a complete effect. Religion, always a principle of energy, in this new people is no way worn out or impaired, and their mode of professing it is also one main cause of this free spirit. The people are Protestants, and of that kind which is the most adverse to all implicit submission of mind and opinion. This is a persuasion not only favorable to liberty, but built upon it. I do not think, Sir, that the reason of this averseness in the dissenting churches, from all that looks like absolute government, is so much to be sought in their religious tenets as in their history. Every one knows that the Roman Catholic religion is at least coeval with most of the governments where it prevails, that it has generally gone hand in hand with them, and received great favor and every kind of support from authority. The Church of England, too, was formed from her cradle under the nursing care of regular government. But the dissenting interests have sprung up in direct opposition to all the ordinary powers of the world, and could justify that opposition only on a strong claim to natural liberty. Their very existence depended on the powerful and unremitted assertion of that claim. All Protestantism, even the most cold and passive, is a sort of dissent. But the religion most prevalent in our northern colonies is a refinement on the principle of resistance; it is the dissidence of dissent and the Protestantism of the Protestant religion. This religion, under a variety of denominations agreeing in nothing but in the communion of the spirit of liberty, is predominant in most of the northern provinces, where the Church of England, notwithstanding its legal rights, is in reality no more than a sort of private sect, not composing most probably the tenth of the people. The colonists left England when this spirit was high, and in the emigrants was the highest of all; and even that stream of foreigners, which has been constantly flowing into these colonies, has, for the greatest part, been composed of dissenters from the establishments of their several countries, and have brought with them a temper and character far from alien to that of the people with whom they mixed.

Sir, I can perceive by their manner that some gentlemen object to the latitude of this description; because in the southern colonies the Church of England forms a large body and has a regular establishment. It is certainly true. There is, however, a circumstance attending these colonies which, in my opinion, fully counterbalances this difference, and makes the spirit of liberty still more high and haughty than in those to the northward. It is, that in Virginia and the Carolinas they have a vast multitude of slaves. Where this is the case in any part of the world, those who are free are by far the most proud and jealous of their freedom. Freedom is to them not only an enjoyment, but a kind of rank and privilege. Not seeing there that freedom, as in countries where it is a common blessing and as broad and general as the air, may be united with much abject toil, with great misery, with all the exterior of servitude, liberty looks amongst them like something that is more noble and liberal. I do not mean, Sir, to commend the superior morality of this sentiment, which has at least as much pride as virtue in it; but I cannot alter the nature of man. The fact is so; and these people of the southern colonies are much more strongly, and with a higher and more stubborn spirit, attached to liberty than those to the northward. Such were all the ancient commonwealths, such were our Gothic ancestors, such in our days were the Poles, and such will be all masters of slaves who are not slaves themselves. In such a people, the haughtiness of domination combines with the spirit of freedom, fortifies it, and renders it invincible.

Permit me, Sir, to add another circumstance in our colonies, which contributes no mean part towards the growth and effect of this untractable spirit. I mean their education. In no country perhaps in the world is the law so general a study. The profession itself is numerous and powerful, and in most provinces it takes the lead. The greater number of the deputies sent to the congress were lawyers. But all who read, and most do read, endeavor to obtain some smattering in that science. I have been told by an eminent bookseller that in no branch of his business, after tracts of popular devotion, were so many books as those on the law exported to the plantations. The colonists have now fallen into the way of printing them for their own use. I hear that they have sold nearly as many of Blackstone's Commentaries in America as in

England. General Gage marks out this disposition very particularly in a letter on your table. He states that all the people in his government are lawyers, or smatterers in law, and that in Boston they have been enabled, by successful chicane, wholly to evade many parts of one of your capital penal constitutions. The smartness of debate will say, that this knowledge ought to teach them more clearly the rights of legislature, their obligations to obedience, and the penalties of rebellion. All this is mighty well. But my honorable and learned friend on the floor, who condescends to mark what I say for animadversion, will disdain that ground. He has heard, as well as I, that when great honors and great emoluments do not win over this knowledge to the service of the state, it is a formidable adversary to government. If the spirit be not tamed and broken by these happy methods, it is stubborn and litigious. *Abeunt studia in mores.* This study renders men acute, inquisitive, dexterous, prompt in attack, ready in defense, full of resources. In other countries, the people, more simple and of a less mercurial cast, judge of an ill principle in government only by an actual grievance; here they anticipate the evil and judge of the pressure of the grievance by the badness of the principle. They augur misgovernment at a distance, and snuff the approach of tyranny in every tainted breeze.

The last cause of this disobedient spirit in the colonies is hardly less powerful than the rest, as it is not merely moral, but laid deep in the natural constitution of things. Three thousand miles of ocean lie between you and them. No contrivance can prevent the effect of this distance in weakening government. Seas roll, and months pass, between the order and the execution, and the want of a speedy explanation of a single point is enough to defeat a whole system. You have, indeed, winged ministers of vengeance, who carry your bolts in their pounces to the remotest verge of the sea. But there a power steps in that limits the arrogance of raging passions and furious elements, and says, "So far shalt thou go, and no farther." Who are you, that should fret and rage and bite the chains of nature? Nothing worse happens to you than does to all nations who have extensive empire; and it happens in all the forms into which empire can be thrown. In large bodies, the circulation of power must be less vigorous at the extremities. Nature has said it. The Turk cannot govern

Egypt, and Arabia, and Curdistan, as he governs Thrace; nor has he the same dominion in Crimea and Algiers which he has at Brusa and Smyrna. Despotism itself is obliged to truck and huckster. The Sultan gets such obedience as he can. He governs with a loose rein that he may govern at all; and the whole of the force and vigor of his authority in his center is derived from a prudent relaxation in all his borders. Spain, in her provinces, is, perhaps, not so well obeyed as you are in yours. She complies too, she submits, she watches times. This is the immutable condition, the eternal law, of extensive and detached empire.

Then, Sir, from these six capital sources: of descent, of form of government, of religion in the northern provinces, of manners in the southern, of education, of the remoteness of situation from the first mover of government—from all these causes a fierce spirit of liberty has grown up. It has grown with the growth of the people in your colonies, and increased with the increase of their wealth; a spirit that unhappily meeting with an exercise of power in England which, however lawful, is not reconcilable to any ideas of liberty, much less with theirs, has kindled this flame that is ready to consume us.

Thomas Carlyle
(1795-1881)

THOMAS CARLYLE loved heroic leaders and hated "big, black democracy" and the rule of the many-headed multitude. His place here is justified, however, by his essential respect for liberty and his dislike for tyranny. He was born in Ecclefechan, Scotland, in 1795, the son of a mason. After a desultory and uncompleted education at the University of Edinburgh he gave up successively the professions of divinity and teaching, and took to writing. From his wife's farm at Craigenputtock he wrote his famous essay on Robert Burns and his astonishing *Sartor Resartus,* a sort of spiritual autobiography and philosophical miscellany. In 1834 he emerged from his retreat and moved to London. Here his first book was his *History of the French Revolution,* essentially an attack on this entire historical episode. Then followed his public lectures *On Heroes, Hero-Worship, and the Heroic in History,* delivered in 1840, his *Past and Present,* 1843, and his *Latter Day Pamphlets,* 1850. His tremendous *History of Frederick the Great* he wrote from 1858 to 1865. Carlyle's style is so elaborate and his denunciations are so unrestrained that he has been called the "moral brass-band" of the Victorian period.

Sartor Resartus, meaning "the tailor retailored," contains the "clothes philosophy" of Carlyle, in which he considered the universe as "a large suit of clothes which invests everything." *The Center of Indifference,* reprinted here, is Chapter VIII, Book II, of this treatise; it follows *The Everlasting No,* in which Carlyle denies the authority of Satan over him, and *The Everlasting Yea,* in which he finds himself and his place in the universe. *The Center of Indifference* is noted for its ironic attack upon the horrors and the wastage of war and upon the price that the poor common man must pay for the no-glory of carrying it on at the unfeeling behest of his governor.

Center of Indifference (1834)

Though, after this "Baphometic Fire-baptism" of his, our Wanderer signifies that his Unrest was but increased; as, indeed, "Indignation and Defiance," especially against things in general, are not the most peaceable inmates; yet can the Psychologist surmise that it was no longer a quite hopeless Unrest; that henceforth it had at least a fixed center to revolve round. For the fire-baptized soul, long so scathed and thunder-riven, here feels its own Freedom, which feeling is its Baphometic Baptism: the citadel of its whole kingdom it has thus gained by assault, and will keep inexpugnable; outwards from which the remaining dominions, not indeed without hard battling, will doubtless by degrees be conquered and pacificated. Under another figure, we might say, if in that great moment, in the *Rue Saint-Thomas de l'Enfer,* the old inward Satanic School was not yet thrown out of doors, it received peremptory judicial notice to quit;—whereby, for the rest, its howl-chantings, Ernulphus-cursings, and rebellious gnashings of teeth, might, in the meanwhile, become only the more tumultuous, and difficult to keep secret.

Accordingly, if we scrutinize these Pilgrimings well, there is perhaps discernible henceforth a certain incipient method in their madness. Not wholly as a Specter does Teufelsdröckh now storm through the world; at worst as a specter-fighting Man, nay who will one day be a Specter-queller. If pilgriming restlessly to so many "Saints' Wells," and ever without quenching of his thirst, he nevertheless finds little secular wells, whereby from time to time some alleviation is ministered. In a word, he is now, if not ceasing, yet intermitting to "eat his own heart"; and clutches round him outwardly on the NOT-ME for wholesomer food. Does not the following glimpse exhibit him in a much more natural state?

"Towns also and Cities, especially the ancient, I failed not to look upon with interest. How beautiful to see thereby, as through a long vista, into the remote Time! to have, as it were, an actual section of almost the earliest Past brought safe into the Present, and set before your eyes! There, in that old City, was a live ember of Culinary Fire put down, say only two thousand years ago; and there, burning more or less triumphantly, with such fuel as the region yielded, it has burnt, and still burns, and thou thyself seest the very smoke thereof. Ah! and the far more mysterious live ember of Vital Fire was then also put down there; and still miraculously burns and spreads; and the smoke and ashes thereof (in these Judgment-Halls and Church-yards), and its bellows-engines (in these Churches), thou still seest; and its name, looking out from every kind countenance, and every hateful one, still warms thee or scorches thee.

"Of Man's Activity and Attainment the chief results are aeriform, mystic, and preserved in Tradition only: such are his Forms of Government, with the Authority they rest on; his Customs, or Fashions both of Cloth-habits and of Soul-habits; much more his collective stock of Handicrafts, the whole Faculty he has acquired of manipulating Nature: all these things, as indispensable and priceless as they are, cannot in any way be fixed under lock and key, but must flit, spiritlike, on impalpable vehicles, from Father to Son; if you demand sight of them, they are nowhere to be met with. Visible Plowmen and Hammermen there have been, ever from Cain and Tubalcain downwards: but where does your accumulated Agricultural, Metallurgic, and other Manufacturing SKILL lie warehoused? It transmits itself on the atmospheric air, on the sun's rays (by Hearing and by Vision); it is a thing aeriform, impalpable, of quite spiritual sort. In like manner, ask me not, Where are the LAWS; where is the GOVERNMENT? In vain wilt thou go to Schönbrunn, to Downing Street, to the Palais Bourbon: thou findest nothing there but brick or stone houses, and some bundles of Papers tied with tape. Where, then, is that same cunningly-devised almighty GOVERNMENT of theirs to be laid hands on? Everywhere, yet nowhere: seen only in its works, this too is a thing aeriform, invisible; or if you will, mystic and miraculous. So spiritual (*geistig*) is our whole daily Life: all that we do springs out of Mystery, Spirit, invisible Force; only like a little

Cloud-image, or Armida's Palace, air-built, does the Actual body itself forth from the great mystic Deep.

"Visible and tangible products of the Past, again, I reckon-up to the extent of three: Cities, with their Cabinets and Arsenals; then tilled Fields, to either or to both of which divisions Roads with their Bridges may belong; and thirdly—Books. In which third truly, the last invented, lies a worth far surpassing that of the two others. Wondrous indeed is the virtue of a true Book. Not like a dead city of stones, yearly crumbling, yearly needing repair; more like a tilled field, but then a spiritual field: like a spiritual tree, let me rather say, it stands from year to year, and from age to age (we have Books that already number some hundred-and-fifty human ages); and yearly comes its new produce of leaves (Commentaries, Deductions, Philosophical, Political Systems; or were it only Sermons, Pamphlets, Journalistic Essays), every one of which is talismanic and thaumaturgic, for it can persuade men. O thou who art able to write a Book, which once in the two centuries or oftener there is a man gifted to do, envy not him whom they name City-builder, and inexpressibly pity him whom they name Conqueror or City-burner! Thou too art a Conqueror and Victor: but of the true sort, namely over the Devil: thou too hast built what will outlast all marble and metal, and be a wonder-bringing City of the Mind, a Temple and Seminary and Prophetic Mount, whereto all kindreds of the Earth will pilgrim.—Fool! why journeyest thou wearisomely, in thy antiquarian fervor, to gaze on the stone pyramids of Geeza, or the clay ones of Sacchara? These stand there, as I can tell thee, idle and inert, looking over the Desert, foolishly enough, for the last three-thousand years: but canst thou not open thy Hebrew BIBLE, then, or even Luther's Version thereof?"

No less satisfactory is his sudden appearance not in Battle, yet on some Battle-field; which, we soon gather, must be that of Wagram; so that here, for once, is a certain approximation to distinctness of date. Omitting much, let us impart what follows:

"Horrible enough! A whole Marchfeld strewed with shell-splinters, cannon-shot, ruined tumbrils, and dead men and horses: stragglers still remaining not so much as buried. And those red mold heaps: ay, there lie the Shells of Men, out of which all the Life and Virtue has been blown; and now are they swept to-

gether, and crammed-down out of sight, like blown Egg-shells!—
Did Nature, when she bade the Donau bring down his mold-
cargoes from the Carinthian and Carpathian Heights, and spread
them out here into the softest, richest level,—intend thee, O
Marchfeld, for a corn-bearing Nursery, whereon her children
might be nursed; or for a Cockpit, wherein they might the more
commodiously be throttled and tattered? Were thy three broad
Highways, meeting here from the ends of Europe, made for
Ammunition-wagons, then? Were thy Wagrams and Stillfrieds
but so many ready-built Casemates, wherein the house of Haps-
burg might batter with artillery, and with artillery be battered?
König Ottokar, amid yonder hillocks, dies under Rodolf's truncheon; here Kaiser Franz falls a-swoon under Napoleon's: within
which five centuries, to omit the others, how has thy breast, fair
Plain, been defaced and defiled! The greensward is torn-up and
trampled-down; man's fond care of it, his fruit-trees, hedge-rows,
and pleasant dwellings, blown-away with gun-powder; and the
kind seedfield lies a desolate, hideous Place of Skulls.—Nevertheless, Nature is at work; neither shall these Powder-Devilkins with
their utmost devilry gainsay her: but all that gore and carnage
will be shrouded-in, absorbed into manure; and next year the
Marchfeld will be green, nay greener. Thrifty unwearied Nature,
ever out of our great waste educing some little profit of thy own,
—how dost thou, from the very carcass of the Killer, bring Life
for the Living!

"What, speaking in quite unofficial language, is the net-purport
and upshot of war? To my own knowledge, for example, there
dwell and toil, in the British village of Dumdrudge, usually some
five-hundred souls. From these, by certain 'Natural Enemies' of
the French, there are successively selected, during the French war,
say thirty able-bodied men: Dumdrudge, at her own expense, has
suckled and nursed them: she has, not without difficulty and
sorrow, fed them up to manhood, and even trained them to
crafts, so that one can weave, another build, another hammer,
and the weakest can stand under thirty stone avoirdupois. Nevertheless, amid much weeping and swearing, they are selected; all
dressed in red; and shipped away, at the public charges, some two
thousand miles, or say only to the south of Spain; and fed there
till wanted. And now to that same spot, in the south of Spain,

are thirty similar French artisans, from a French Dumdrudge, in like manner wending: till at length, after infinite effort, the two parties come into actual juxtaposition; and Thirty stands fronting Thirty, each with a gun in his hand. Straightway the word 'Fire!' is given: and they blow the souls out of one another; and in place of sixty brisk useful craftsmen, the world has sixty dead carcasses, which it must bury, and anew shed tears for. Had these men any quarrel? Busy as the Devil is, not the smallest! They lived far enough apart; were the entirest strangers; nay, in so wide a Universe, there was even, unconsciously, by Commerce, some mutual helpfulness between them. How then? Simpleton! their Governors had fallen-out; and, instead of shooting one another, had the cunning to make these poor blockheads shoot.— Alas, so is it in Deutschland, and hitherto in all other lands; still as of old, 'what devilry soever Kings do, the Greeks must pay the piper!'—In that fiction of the English Smollett, it is true, the final Cessation of War is perhaps prophetically shadowed forth; where the two Natural Enemies, in person, take each a Tobacco-pipe, filled with Brimstone; light the same, and smoke in one another's faces, till the weaker gives in: but from such predicted Peace-Era, what blood-filled trenches, and contentious centuries, may still divide us!"

Thus can the Professor, at least in lucid intervals, look away from his own sorrows, over the many-colored world, and pertinently enough note what is passing there. We may remark, indeed, that for the matter of spiritual culture, if for nothing else, perhaps few periods of his life were richer than this. Internally, there is the most momentous instructive Course of Practical Philosophy, with Experiments, going on; towards the right comprehension of which his Peripatetic habits, favorable to Meditation, might help him rather than hinder. Externally, again, as he wanders to and fro, there are, if for the longing heart little substance, yet for the seeing eye sights enough: in these so boundless Travels of his, granting that the Satanic School was even partially kept down, what an incredible knowledge of our Planet, and its Inhabitants and their Works, that is to say, of all knowable things, might not Teufelsdröckh acquire!

"I have read in most Public Libraries," says he, "including those of Constantinople and Samarcand: in most Colleges, except the Chinese Mandarin ones, I have studied, or seen that there was no studying. Unknown Languages have I oftenest gathered from their natural repertory, the Air, by my organ of Hearing; Statistics, Geographics, Topographics came, through the Eye, almost of their own accord. The ways of Man, how he seeks food, and warmth, and protection for himself, in most regions, are ocularly known to me. Like the great Hadrian, I meted out much of the terraqueous Globe with a pair of Compasses that belonged to myself only.

"Of great Scenes why speak? Three summer days, I lingered reflecting, and even composing (*dichtete*), by the Pine-chasms of Vaucluse; and in that clear Lakelet moistened my bread. I have sat under the Palm-trees of Tadmor; smoked a pipe among the ruins of Babylon. The great Wall of China I have seen; and can testify that it is of gray brick, coped and covered with granite, and shows only second-rate masonry.—Great Events, also, have not I witnessed? Kings sweated-down (*ausgemergelt*) into Berlin-and-Milan Customhouse-Officers; the World well won, and the World well lost; oftener than once a hundred thousand individuals shot (by each other) in one day. All kindreds and peoples and nations dashed together and shifted and shoveled into heaps that they might ferment there, and in time unite. The birth-pangs of Democracy, wherewith convulsed Europe was groaning in cries that reached Heaven, could not escape me.

"For great Men I have ever had the warmest predilection; and can perhaps boast that few such in this era have wholly escaped me. Great Men are the inspired (speaking and acting) Texts of that divine BOOK OF REVELATIONS, whereof a Chapter is completed from epoch to epoch, and by some named HISTORY; to which inspired Texts your numerous talented men, and your innumerable untalented men, are the better or worse exegetic Commentaries, and wagonload of too-stupid, heretical or orthodox, weekly Sermons. For my study the inspired Texts themselves! Thus did not I, in very early days, having disguised me as tavern-waiter, stand behind the field-chairs, under that shady Tree at Treisnitz by the Jena Highway; waiting upon the great Schiller and greater Goethe; and hearing what I have not forgotten. For——"

—But at this point the Editor recalls his principle of caution, some time ago laid down, and must suppress much. Let not the sacredness of Laureled, still more, of Crowned Heads, be tampered with. Should we, at a future day, find circumstances altered, and the time come for Publication, then may these glimpses into the privacy of the Illustrious be conceded; which for the present were little better than treacherous, perhaps traitorous Eavesdroppings. Of Lord Byron, therefore, of Pope Pius, Emperor Tarakwang, and the "White Water-roses" (Chinese Carbonari) with their mysteries, no notice here! Of Napoleon himself we shall only, glancing from afar, remark that Teufelsdröckh's relation to him seems to have been of very varied character. At first we find our poor Professor on the point of being shot as a spy; then taken into private conversation, even pinched on the ear, yet presented with no money; at last indignantly dismissed, almost thrown out of doors, as an "Ideologist." "He himself," says the Professor, "was among the completest Ideologists, at least Ideopraxists: in the Idea (*in der Idee*) he lived, moved, and fought. The man was a Divine Missionary, though unconscious of it; and preached, through the cannon's throat, that great doctrine, *La carrière ouverte aux talens* (The Tools to him that can handle them), which is our ultimate Political Evangel, wherein alone can liberty lie. Madly enough he preached, it is true, as Enthusiasts and first Missionaries are wont, with imperfect utterance, amid much frothy rant; yet as articulately perhaps as the case admitted. Or call him, if you will, an American Backwoodsman, who had to fell unpenetrated forests, and battle with innumerable wolves, and did not entirely forbear strong liquor, rioting, and even theft; whom, notwithstanding, the peaceful Sower will follow, and, as he cuts the boundless harvest, bless."

More legitimate and decisively authentic is Teufelsdröckh's appearance and emergence (we know not well whence) in the solitude of the North Cape, on that June Midnight. He has "a light-blue Spanish cloak" hanging round him, as his "most commodious, principal, indeed sole upper garment"; and stands there, on the World-promontory, looking over the infinite Brine, like a little blue Belfry (as we figure), now motionless indeed, yet ready, if stirred, to ring quaintest changes.

"Silence as of death," writes he; "for Midnight, even in the Arctic latitudes, has its character: nothing but the granite cliffs ruddy-tinged, the peaceable gurgle of that slow-heaving Polar

Ocean, over which in the utmost North the great Sun hangs low
and lazy, as if he too were slumbering. Yet is his cloud-couch
wrought of crimson and cloth-of-gold; yet does his light stream
over the mirror of waters, like a tremulous fire-pillar, shooting
downwards to the abyss, and hide itself under my feet. In such
moments, Solitude also is invaluable; for who would speak, or be
looked on, when behind him lies all Europe and Africa, fast
asleep, except the watchmen; and before him the silent Immen-
sity, and Palace of the Eternal, whereof our Sun is but a porch-
lamp?

"Nevertheless, in this solemn moment comes a man, or monster, scrambling from among the rock-hollows; and, shaggy, huge
as the Hyperborean Bear, hails me in Russian speech: most probably, therefore, a Russian Smuggler. With courteous brevity, I
signify my indifference to contraband trade, my humane intentions, yet strong wish to be private. In vain: the monster, count-
ing doubtless on his superior stature, and minded to make sport
for himself, or perhaps profit, were it with murder, continues to
advance; ever assailing me with his importunate train-oil breath;
and now has advanced, till we stand both on the verge of the
rock, the deep Sea rippling greedily down below. What argument
will avail? On the thick Hyperborean, cherubic reasoning, seraphic eloquence were lost. Prepared for such extremity, I, deftly
enough, whisk aside one step; draw out, from my interior reser-
voirs, a sufficient Birmingham Horse-pistol, and say, 'Be so
obliging as retire, Friend (*Er ziehe sich zurück, Freund*), and with
promptitude!' This logic even the Hyperborean understands;
fast enough, with apologetic, petitionary growl, he sidles off; and,
except for suicidal as well as homicidal purposes, need not return.

"Such I hold to be the genuine use of Gunpowder: that it
makes all men alike tall. Nay, if thou be cooler, cleverer than I,
if thou have more *Mind,* though all but no Body whatever, then
canst thou kill me first, and art the taller. Hereby, at last, is the
Goliath powerless, and the David resistless; savage Animalism is
nothing, inventive Spiritualism is all.

"With respect to Duels, indeed, I have my own ideas. Few
things, in this so surprising world, strike me with more surprise.
Two little visual Spectra of men, hovering with insecure enough
cohesion in the midst of the UNFATHOMABLE, and to dissolve

therein, at any rate, very soon,—make pause at the distance of twelve paces asunder; whirl round; and, simultaneously by the cunningest mechanism, explode one another into Dissolution; and off-hand become Air, and Non-extant! Deuce on it *(ver-dammt)*, the little spitfires!—Nay, I think with old Hugo von Trimberg: 'God must needs laugh outright, could such a thing be, to see his wondrous Manikins here below.' "

But amid these specialties, let us not forget the great generality, which is our chief quest here: How prospered the inner man of Teufelsdröckh under so much outward shifting? Does Legion still lurk in him, though repressed; or has he exorcised that Devil's Brood? We can answer that the symptoms continue promising. Experience is the grand spiritual Doctor; and with him Teufelsdröckh has now been long a patient, swallowing many a bitter bolus. Unless our poor Friend belong to the numerous class of Incurables, which seems not likely, some cure will doubtless be effected. We should rather say that Legion, or the Satanic School, was now pretty well extirpated and cast out, but next to nothing introduced in its room; whereby the heart remains, for the while, in a quiet but no comfortable state.

"At length, after so much roasting," thus writes our Autobiographer, "I was what you might name calcined. Pray only that it be not rather, as is the more frequent issue, reduced to a *caput mortuum!* But in any case, by mere dint of practice, I had grown familiar with many things. Wretchedness was still wretched; but I could now partly see through it, and despise it. Which highest mortal, in this inane Existence, had I not found a Shadow-hunter, or Shadow-hunted; and, when I looked through his brave garnitures, miserable enough? Thy wishes have all been sniffed aside, thought I: but what, had they even been all granted! Did not the Boy Alexander weep because he had not two Planets to conquer; or a whole Solar System; or after that, a whole Universe? *Ach Gott,* when I gazed into these Stars, have they not looked down on me as if with pity, from their serene spaces; like Eyes glistening with heavenly tears over the little lot of man! Thousands of human generations, all as noisy as our own, have been swallowed-up of Time, and there remains no wreck of them any more; and Arcturus and Orion and Sirius and the Pleiades are still shining in their courses, clear and young, as when the Shepherd first noted them in the plain of Shinar. Pshaw! what is this paltry little Dog-cage of an Earth; what art thou that sittest whining there? Thou art still Nothing, Nobody: true; but who, then, is Something, Somebody? For thee the Family of Man has no use; it rejects thee; thou art wholly as a dissevered limb: so be it; perhaps it is better so!"

Too-heavy-laden Teufelsdröckh! Yet surely his bands are loosening; one day he will hurl the burden far from him, and bound forth free and with a second youth.

"This," says our Professor, "was the CENTER OF INDIFFERENCE I had now reached; through which whoso travels from the Negative Pole to the Positive must necessarily pass."

John Stuart Mill
(1806-1873)

JOHN STUART MILL had at once the advantage and the disadvantage of receiving from his famous father, the economist James Mill, a systematic educational discipline that was designed to make of his mind a clear, cold, logic machine. This system, described at length in his *Autobiography* (1873), made him extraordinarily clear in thought and incisive in expression but came perilously near to wrecking him mentally in his young manhood. From the danger of becoming merely apathetic in his attitudes toward life he was rescued, he said, by an intensive reading of Wordsworth's poetry. In addition to this debt to Wordsworth he owed much in his philosophical and economic thinking to Comte, Bentham, Ricardo, and Malthus. He early abandoned law for a clerkship in the East India House, which gave him abundant opportunity and leisure for his writing. In economics he followed at first his father's Utilitarianism but came later to modify his earlier views. His most famous works are: *A System of Logic* (1843), *Principles of Political Economy* (1848), *Essay on Liberty* (1859), *Representative Government* (1860), and *The Subjection of Women* (1869).

Throughout his life Mill was a noted liberal and a stanch defender of the right of free expression. "If all mankind minus one," he wrote in the second chapter of his essay *On Liberty*, "were of one opinion, and only one person were of the contrary opinion, mankind would be no more justified in silencing that one person, than he, if he had the power, would be justified in silencing mankind." The section from this same essay which is reprinted here comprises the whole of Chapter I, the Introduction to the five-chapter treatise.

On Liberty (1859)

The subject of this Essay is not the so-called Liberty of the Will, so unfortunately opposed to the misnamed doctrine of Philosophical Necessity; but Civil, or Social Liberty: the nature and limits of the power which can be legitimately exercised by society over the individual. A question seldom stated, and hardly ever discussed, in general terms, but which profoundly influences the practical controversies of the age by its latent presence, and is likely soon to make itself recognized as the vital question of the future. It is so far from being new, that, in a certain sense, it has divided mankind, almost from the remotest ages; but in the stage of progress into which the more civilized portions of the species have now entered, it presents itself under new conditions, and requires a different and more fundamental treatment.

The struggle between Liberty and Authority is the most conspicuous feature in the portions of history with which we are earliest familiar, particularly in that of Greece, Rome, and England. But in old times this contest was between subjects, or some classes of subjects, and the Government. By liberty, was meant protection against the tyranny of the political rulers. The rulers were conceived (except in some of the popular governments of Greece) as in a necessarily antagonistic position to the people whom they ruled. They consisted of a governing One, or a governing tribe or caste, who derived their authority from inheritance or conquest, who, at all events, did not hold it at the pleasure of the governed, and whose supremacy men did not venture, perhaps did not desire, to contest, whatever precautions might be taken against its oppressive exercise. Their power was regarded as necessary, but also as highly dangerous; as a weapon which they would attempt to use against their subjects, no less than against external enemies. To prevent the weaker members of the community from being preyed upon by innumerable vultures, it was needful that there should be an animal of prey stronger than the rest, commissioned to keep them down. But as the king of the vultures would be no less bent upon preying on the flock than any of the minor harpies, it was indispensable to be in a perpetual attitude of defense against his beak and claws. The aim, therefore, of patriots was to set limits to the power which the ruler should be suffered to exercise over the community; and this limitation was what they meant by liberty. It was attempted in two ways. First, by obtaining a recognition of certain immunities, called political liberties or rights, which it was to be regarded as a breach of duty in the ruler to infringe, and which, if he did infringe, specific resistance, or general rebellion, was held to be justifiable. A second, and generally a later expedient, was the establishment of constitutional checks, by which the consent of the community, or of a body of some sort, supposed to represent its interests, was made a necessary condition to some of the more important acts of the governing power. To the first of these modes of limitation, the ruling power, in most European countries, was compelled, more or less, to submit. It was not so with the second; and, to attain this, or when already in some degree possessed, to attain it more completely, became everywhere the principal object of the lovers of liberty. And so long as mankind were content to combat one enemy by another, and to be ruled by a master, on condition of being guaranteed more or less efficaciously against his tyranny, they did not carry their aspirations beyond this point.

A time, however, came, in the progress of human affairs, when men ceased to think it a necessity of nature that their governors should be an independent power, opposed in interest to themselves. It appeared to them much better that the various magistrates of the State should be their tenants or delegates, revocable at their pleasure. In that way alone, it seemed, could they have complete security that the powers of government would never be abused to their disadvantage. By degrees this new demand for elective and temporary rulers became the prominent object of the exertions of the popular party, wherever any such party existed; and superseded, to a considerable extent, the previous efforts to limit the power of rulers. As the struggle proceeded for making the ruling power emanate from the periodical choice of the ruled, some persons began to think that too much importance had been attached to the limitation of the power itself. *That* (it might seem) was a resource against rulers whose interests were habitually opposed to those of the people. What was now wanted was, that the rulers should be identified with the people; that their interest and will should be the interest and will of the nation. The nation did not need to be protected against its own will. There was no fear of its tyrannizing over itself. Let the rulers be effectually responsible to it, promptly removable by it, and it could afford to trust them with power of which it could itself dictate the use to be made. Their power was but the nation's own power, concentrated, and in a form convenient for exercise. This mode of thought, or rather perhaps of feeling, was common among the last generation of European liberalism, in the Continental section of which it still apparently predominates. Those who admit any limit to what a government may do, except in the case of such governments as they think ought not to exist, stand out as brilliant exceptions among the political thinkers of the Continent. A similar tone of sentiment might by this time have been prevalent in our own country, if the circumstances which for a time encouraged it, had continued unaltered.

But, in political and philosophical theories, as well as in persons, success discloses faults and infirmities which failure might have concealed from observation. The notion, that the people have no need to limit their power over themselves, might seem axiomatic, when popular government was a thing only dreamed about, or read of as having existed at some distant period of the past. Neither was that notion necessarily disturbed by such temporary aberrations as those of the French Revolution, the worst of which were the work of an usurping few, and which, in any case, belonged, not to the permanent working of popular institutions, but to a sudden and convulsive outbreak against monarchical and aristocratic despotism. In time, however, a democratic republic came to occupy a large portion of the earth's surface, and made itself felt as one of the most powerful members of the community of nations; and elective and responsible government became subject to the observations and criticisms which wait upon a great existing fact. It was now perceived that such phrases

as "self-government," and "the power of the people over themselves," do not express the true state of the case. The "people" who
exercise the power are not always the same people with those over
whom it is exercised; and the "self-government" spoken of is not
the government of each by himself, but of each by all the rest.
The will of the people, moreover, practically means the will of
the most numerous or the most active *part* of the people; the majority, or those who succeed in making themselves accepted as the
majority; the people, consequently, *may* desire to oppress a part
of their number; and precautions are as much needed against
this as against any other abuse of power. The limitation, therefore, of the power of government over individuals loses none of
its importance when the holders of power are regularly accountable to the community, that is, to the strongest party therein.
This view of things, recommending itself equally to the intelligence of thinkers and to the inclination of those important classes
in European society to whose real or supposed interests democracy is adverse, has had no difficulty in establishing itself; and in
political speculations "the tyranny of the majority" is now generally included among the evils against which society requires to
be on its guard.

Like other tyrannies, the tyranny of the majority was at first,
and is still vulgarly, held in dread, chiefly as operating through
the acts of the public authorities. But reflecting persons perceived
that when society is itself the tyrant—society collectively, over the
separate individuals who compose it—its means of tyrannizing are
not restricted to the acts which it may do by the hands of its political functionaries. Society can and does execute its own mandates: and if it issues wrong mandates instead of right, or any
mandates at all in things with which it ought not to meddle, it
practices a social tyranny more formidable than many kinds of
political oppression, since, though not usually upheld by such
extreme penalties, it leaves fewer means of escape, penetrating
much more deeply into the details of life, and enslaving the soul
itself. Protection, therefore, against the tyranny of the magistrate
is not enough: there needs protection also against the tyranny of
the prevailing opinion and feeling; against the tendency of society to impose, by other means than civil penalties, its own ideas
and practices as rules of conduct on those who dissent from them;

to fetter the development, and, if possible, prevent the formation, of any individuality not in harmony with its ways, and compel all characters to fashion themselves upon the model of its own. There is a limit to the legitimate interference of collective opinion with individual independence: and to find that limit, and maintain it against encroachment, is as indispensable to a good condition of human affairs, as protection against political despotism.

But though this proposition is not likely to be contested in ' general terms, the practical question, where to place the limit—how to make the fitting adjustment between individual independence and social control—is a subject on which nearly everything remains to be done. All that makes existence valuable to any one, depends on the enforcement of restraints upon the actions of other people. Some rules of conduct, therefore, must be imposed, by law in the first place, and by opinion on many things which are not fit subjects for the operation of law. What these rules should be, is the principal question in human affairs; but if we except a few of the most obvious cases, it is one of those which least progress has been made in resolving. No two ages, and scarcely any two countries, have decided it alike; and the decision of one age or country is a wonder to another. Yet the people of any given age and country no more suspect any difficulty in it, than if it were a subject on which mankind had always been agreed. The rules which obtain among themselves appear to them self-evident and self-justifying. This all but universal illusion is one of the examples of the magical influence of custom, which is not only, as the proverb says, a second nature, but is continually mistaken for the first. The effect of custom, in preventing any misgiving respecting the rules of conduct which mankind impose on one another, is all the more complete because the subject is one on which it is not generally considered necessary that reasons should be given, either by one person to others, or by each to himself. People are accustomed to believe, and have been encouraged in the belief by some who aspire to the character of philosophers, that their feelings, on subjects of this nature, are better than reasons, and render reasons unnecessary. The practical principle which guides them to their opinions on the regulation of human conduct, is the feeling in each person's mind that everybody should be required to act as he, and those with whom he sympathizes, would like them to act. No one, indeed, acknowledges to himself that his standard of judgment is his own liking; but an opinion on a point of conduct, not supported by reasons, can only count as one person's preference; and if the reasons, when given, are a mere appeal to a similar preference felt by other people, it is still only many people's liking instead of one. To an ordinary man, however, his own preference, thus supported, is not only a perfectly satisfactory reason, but the only one he generally has for any of his notions of morality, taste, or propriety, which are not expressly written in his religious creed; and his chief guide in the interpretation even of that. Men's opinions, accordingly, on what is laudable or blameable, are affected by all the multifarious causes which influence their wishes in regard to the conduct of others, and which are as numerous as those which determine their wishes on any other subject. Sometimes their reason—at other times their prejudices or superstitions: often their social affections, not seldom their antisocial ones, their envy or jealousy, their arrogance or contemptuousness: but most commonly, their desires or fears for themselves— their legitimate or illegitimate self-interest. Wherever there is an ascendant class, a large portion of the morality of the country emanates from its class interests, and its feelings of class superiority. The morality between Spartans and Helots, between planters and negroes, between princes and subjects, between nobles and roturiers, between men and women, has been for the most part the creation of these class interests and feelings: and the sentiments thus generated, react in turn upon the moral feelings of the members of the ascendant class, in their relations among themselves. Where, on the other hand, a class, formerly ascendant, has lost its ascendancy, or where its ascendancy is unpopular, the prevailing moral sentiments frequently bear the impress of an impatient dislike of superiority. Another grand determining principle of the rules of conduct, both in act and forbearance, which have been enforced by law or opinion, has been the servility of mankind towards the supposed preferences or aversions of their temporal masters, or of their gods. This servility, though essentially selfish, is not hypocrisy; it gives rise to perfectly genuine sentiments of abhorrence; it made men burn magicians and heretics. Among so many baser influences, the general and obvious interests of society have of course had a share, and a large one, in the direction of the moral sentiments: less, however, as a matter of reason, and on their own account, than as a consequence of the sympathies and antipathies which grew out of them: and sympathies and antipathies which had little or nothing to do with the interests of society, have made themselves felt in the establishment of moralities with quite as great force.

The likings and dislikings of society, or of some powerful portion of it, are thus the main thing which has practically determined the rules laid down for general observance, under the penalties of law or opinion. And in general, those who have been in advance of society in thought and feeling, have left this condition of things unassailed in principle, however they may have come into conflict with it in some of its details. They have occupied themselves rather in inquiring what things society ought to like or dislike, than in questioning whether its likings or dislikings should be a law to individuals. They preferred endeavoring to alter the feelings of mankind on the particular points on which they were themselves heretical, rather than make common cause in defense of freedom, with heretics generally. The only case in which the higher ground has been taken on principle and maintained with consistency, by any but an individual here and there, is that of religious belief: a case instructive in many ways, and not least so as forming a most striking instance of the fallibility of what is called the moral sense: for the *odium theologicum,* in a sincere bigot, is one of the most unequivocal cases of moral feeling. Those who first broke the yoke of what called itself the Universal Church, were in general as little willing to permit difference of religious opinion as that church itself. But when the heat of the conflict was over, without giving a complete victory to any party, and each church or sect was reduced to limit its hopes to retaining possession of the ground it already occupied; minorities, seeing that they had no chance of becoming majorities, were under the necessity of pleading to those whom they could not convert, for permission to differ. It is accordingly on this battlefield, almost solely, that the rights of the individual against society have been asserted on broad grounds of principle, and the claim of society to exercise authority over dissentients, openly controverted. The great writers to whom the world owes what religious liberty it possesses, have mostly asserted freedom of conscience as an indefeasible right, and denied absolutely that a human being is accountable to others for his religious belief. Yet so natural to mankind is intolerance in whatever they really care about, that religious freedom has hardly anywhere been practically realized, except where religious indifference, which dislikes to have its peace disturbed by theological quarrels, has added its weight to the scale. In the minds of almost all religious persons, even in the most tolerant countries, the duty of toleration is admitted with tacit reserves. One person will bear with dissent in matters of church government, but not of dogma; another can tolerate everybody, short of a Papist or a Unitarian; another, every one who believes in revealed religion; a few extend their charity a little further, but stop at the belief in a God and in a future state. Wherever the sentiment of the majority is still genuine and intense, it is found to have abated little of its claim to be obeyed.

In England, from the peculiar circumstances of our political history, though the yoke of opinion is perhaps heavier, that of law is lighter, than in most other countries of Europe; and there is considerable jealousy of direct interference, by the legislative or the executive power, with private conduct; not so much from any just regard for the independence of the individual, as from the still subsisting habit of looking on the government as representing an opposite interest to the public. The majority have not yet learnt to feel the power of the government their power, or its opinions their opinions. When they do so, individual liberty will probably be as much exposed to invasion from the government, as it already is from public opinion. But, as yet, there is a considerable amount of feeling ready to be called forth against any attempt of the law to control individuals in things in which they have not hitherto been accustomed to be controlled by it; and this with very little discrimination as to whether the matter is, or is not, within the legitimate sphere of legal control; insomuch that the feeling, highly salutary on the whole, is perhaps quite as often misplaced as well grounded in the particular instances of its application. There is, in fact, no recognized principle by which the propriety or impropriety of government interference is customarily tested. People decide according to their personal preferences. Some, whenever they see any good to be done, or evil to be remedied, would willingly instigate the government to undertake the business; while others prefer to bear almost any amount of social evil, rather than add one to the departments of human interests amenable to governmental control. And men range themselves on one or the other side in any particular case, according to this general direction of their sentiments; or according to the degree of interest which they feel in the particular thing which it is proposed that the government should do, or according to the belief they entertain that the government would, or would not, do it in the manner they prefer; but very rarely on account of any opinion to which they consistently adhere, as to what things are fit to be done by a government. And it seems to me that in consequence of this absence of rule or principle, one side is at present as often wrong as the other; the interference of government is, with about equal frequency, improperly invoked and improperly condemned.

The object of this Essay is to assert one very simple principle, as entitled to govern absolutely the dealings of society with the individual in the way of compulsion and control, whether the means used be physical force in the form of legal penalties, or the moral coercion of public opinion. That principle is, that the sole end for which mankind are warranted, individually or collectively, in interfering with the liberty of action of any of their number, is self-protection. That the only purpose for which power can be rightfully exercised over any member of a civilized community, against his will, is to prevent harm to others. His own good, either physical or moral, is not a sufficient warrant. He cannot rightfully be compelled to do or forbear because it will be better for him to do so, because it will make him happier, because, in the opinions of others, to do so would be wise, or even right. These are good reasons for remonstrating with him, or reasoning with him, or persuading him, or entreating him, but not for compelling him, or visiting him with any evil in case he do otherwise. To justify that, the conduct from which it is desired to deter him, must be calculated to produce evil to some one else. The only part of the conduct of any one, for which he is amenable to society, is that which concerns others. In the part which merely concerns himself, his independence is, of right, absolute. Over himself, over his own body and mind, the individual is sovereign.

It is, perhaps, hardly necessary to say that this doctrine is meant to apply only to human beings in the maturity of their faculties. We are not speaking of children, or of young persons below the age which the law may fix as that of manhood or womanhood. Those who are still in a state to require being taken care of by others, must be protected against their own actions as well as against external injury. For the same reason, we may leave out of consideration those backward states of society in which the race itself may be considered as in its nonage. The early difficulties in the way of spontaneous progress are so great, that there is seldom any choice of means for overcoming them; and a ruler full of the spirit of improvement is warranted in the use of any expedients that will attain an end, perhaps otherwise unattainable. Despotism is a legitimate mode of government in dealing with barbarians, provided the end be their improvement, and the means justified by actually effecting that end. Liberty, as a principle, has no application to any state of things anterior to the time when mankind have become capable of being improved by free and equal discussion. Until then, there is nothing for them but implicit obedience to an Akbar or a Charlemagne, if they are so fortunate as to find one. But as soon as mankind have attained the capacity of being guided to their own improvement by conviction or persuasion (a period long since reached in all nations with whom we need here concern ourselves), compulsion, either in the direct form or in that of pains and penalties for non-compliance, is no longer admissible as a means to their own good, and justifiable only for the security of others.

It is proper to state that I forgo any advantage which could be derived to my argument from the idea of abstract right, as a thing independent of utility. I regard utility as the ultimate appeal on all ethical questions; but it must be utility in the largest sense, grounded on the permanent interests of man as a progressive being. Those interests, I contend, authorize the subjection of individual spontaneity to external control, only in respect to those actions of each, which concern the interest of other people. If any one does an act hurtful to others, there is a prima facie case for punishing him, by law, or, where legal penalties are not safely applicable, by general disapprobation. There are also many positive acts for the benefit of others, which he may rightfully be compelled to perform; such as, to give evidence in a court of justice; to bear his fair share in the common defense, or in any other joint work necessary to the interest of the society of which he enjoys the protection; and to perform certain acts of individual beneficence, such as saving a fellow creature's life, or interposing to protect the defenseless against ill-usage, things which whenever it is obviously a man's duty to do, he may rightfully be made responsible to society for not doing. A person may cause evil to others not only by his actions but by his inaction, and in either case he is justly accountable to them for the injury. The latter case, it is true, requires a much more cautious exercise of compulsion than the former. To make any one answerable for doing evil to others, is the rule; to make him answerable for not preventing evil, is, comparatively speaking, the exception. Yet there are many cases clear enough and grave enough to justify that exception. In all things which regard the external relations of the individual, he is *de jure* amenable to those whose interests are concerned, and if need be, to society as their protector. There are often good reasons for not holding him to the responsibility; but these reasons must arise from the special expediencies of the case: either because it is a kind of case in which he is on the whole likely to act better, when left to his own discretion, than when controlled in any way in which society have it in their power to control him; or because the attempt to exercise control would produce other evils, greater than those which it would prevent. When such reasons as these preclude the enforcement of responsibility, the conscience of the agent himself should step into the vacant judgment-seat, and protect those interests of others which have no external protection; judging himself all the more rigidly, because the case does not admit of his being made accountable to the judgment of his fellow creatures.

But there is a sphere of action in which society, as distinguished from the individual, has, if any, only an indirect interest; comprehending all that portion of a person's life and conduct which affects only himself, or if it also affects others, only with their free, voluntary, and undeceived consent and participation.

When I say only himself, I mean directly, and in the first instance: for whatever affects himself, may affect others through himself; and the objection which may be grounded on this contingency will receive consideration in the sequel. This, then, is the appropriate region of human liberty. It comprises, first, the inward domain of consciousness; demanding liberty of conscience, in the most comprehensive sense; liberty of thought and feeling; absolute freedom of opinion and sentiment on all subjects, practical or speculative, scientific, moral, or theological. The liberty of expressing and publishing opinions may seem to fall under a different principle, since it belongs to that part of the conduct of an individual which concerns other people; but, being almost of as much importance as the liberty of thought itself, and resting in great part on the same reasons, is practically inseparable from it. Secondly, the principle requires liberty of tastes and pursuits; of framing the plan of our life to suit our own character; of doing as we like, subject to such consequences as may follow: without impediment from our fellow creatures, so long as what we do does not harm them, even though they should think our conduct foolish, perverse, or wrong. Thirdly, from this liberty of each individual, follows the liberty, within the same limits, of combination among individuals; freedom to unite, for any purpose not involving harm to others: the persons combining being supposed to be of full age, and not forced or deceived.

No society in which these liberties are not, on the whole, respected, is free, whatever may be its form of government; and none is completely free in which they do not exist absolute and unqualified. The only freedom which deserves the name, is that of pursuing our own good in our own way, so long as we do not attempt to deprive others of theirs, or impede their efforts to obtain it. Each is the proper guardian of his own health, whether bodily, or mental and spiritual. Mankind are greater gainers by suffering each other to live as seems good to themselves, than by compelling each to live as seems good to the rest.

Though this doctrine is anything but new, and, to some persons, may have the air of a truism, there is no doctrine which stands more directly opposed to the general tendency of existing opinion and practice. Society has expended fully as much effort in the attempt (according to its lights) to compel people to conform to its notions of personal, as of social excellence. The ancient commonwealths thought themselves entitled to practice, and the ancient philosophers countenanced, the regulation of every part of private conduct by public authority, on the ground that the State had a deep interest in the whole bodily and mental discipline of every one of its citizens; a mode of thinking which may have been admissible in small republics surrounded by powerful enemies, in constant peril of being subverted by foreign attack or internal commotion, and to which even a short interval of relaxed energy and self-command might so easily be fatal, that they could not afford to wait for the salutary permanent effects of freedom. In the modern world, the greater size of political communities, and, above all, the separation between spiritual and temporal authority (which placed the direction of men's consciences in other hands than those which controlled their worldly affairs), prevented so great an interference by law in the details of private life; but the engines of moral repression have been wielded more strenuously against divergence from the reigning opinion in self-regarding, than even in social matters; religion, the most powerful of the elements which have entered into the formation of moral feeling, having almost always been governed either by the ambition of a hierarchy, seeking control over every department of human conduct, or by the spirit of Puritanism. And some of those modern reformers who have placed themselves in strongest opposition to the religions of the past, have been no way behind either churches or sects in their assertion of the right of spiritual domination: M. Comte, in particular, whose social system, as unfolded in his *Système de Politique Positive,* aims at establishing (though by moral more than by legal appliances) a despotism of society over the individual, surpassing anything contemplated in the political ideal of the most rigid disciplinarian among the ancient philosophers.

Apart from the peculiar tenets of individual thinkers, there is also in the world at large an increasing inclination to stretch unduly the powers of society over the individual, both by the force of opinion and even by that of legislation: and as the tendency of all the changes taking place in the world is to strengthen society, and diminish the power of the individual, this encroachment is not one of the evils which tend spontaneously to disappear, but, on the contrary, to grow more and more formidable. The disposition of mankind, whether as rulers or as fellow citizens, to impose their own opinions and inclinations as a rule of conduct on others, is so energetically supported by some of the best and by some of the worst feelings incident to human nature, that it is hardly ever kept under restraint by anything but want of power; and as the power is not declining, but growing, unless a strong barrier of moral conviction can be raised against the mischief, we must expect, in the present circumstances of the world, to see it increase.

It will be convenient for the argument, if, instead of at once entering upon the general thesis, we confine ourselves in the first instance to a single branch of it, on which the principle here stated is, if not fully, yet to a certain point, recognized by the current opinions. This one branch is the Liberty of Thought: from which it is impossible to separate the cognate liberty of speaking and of writing. Although these liberties, to some considerable amount, form part of the political morality of all countries which profess religious toleration and free institutions, the grounds, both philosophical and practical, on which they rest, are perhaps not so familiar to the general mind, nor so thoroughly appreciated by many even of the leaders of opinion, as might have been expected. Those grounds, when rightly understood, are of much wider application than to only one division of the subject, and a thorough consideration of this part of the question will be found the best introduction to the remainder. Those to whom nothing which I am about to say will be new, may therefore, I hope, excuse me, if on a subject which for now three centuries has been so often discussed, I venture on one discussion more.

John Bright
(1811-1889)

FROM the point of view of the Americans of his time John Bright, brilliant orator and defender of freedom and justice, was to the United States of the Civil War what Edmund Burke was to the colonies of the Revolutionary War. The son of a Quaker cotton-spinner of Rochdale he grew up with a hatred of war and a persistent eagerness to defend the oppressed whenever he could. He entered Parliament as a Liberal for Durham and later represented Manchester and Birmingham. In 1854 he denounced the Crimean War vigorously; he supported the Reform Bill of 1867 and the Irish Land Act in favor of the oppressed tenants in 1870. This last act of justice came early in Gladstone's administration, and Bright continued to support the prime minister until 1882. From the American point of view his most important activity in Parliament was his espousal of the cause of the North in what the British called "The Planters' War." In spite of Bright's financial losses from the blockade of the ports of the Confederate states and the consequent stoppage of cotton shipments to keep English mills running, he took the long view that a nation founded on the principles of liberty and freedom for all should not be divided.

The following expressions of Bright's attitude toward the American Civil War are taken from his *Speeches on Questions of Public Policy,* selected and edited by James E. Thorold Rogers in 1868. The general title which heads this note was chosen by the present editors. The first extract, from Volume I, America I, comes from an address on *The Trent Affair,* delivered on December 4, 1861, in his native city of Rochdale. The second extract, from Volume I, America VI, is part of a reply which he made in the House of Commons on June 30, 1863, to Mr. Roebuck's motion for Recognition of the Southern Confederacy.

The Defense of Liberty
in America (1861, 1863)

[I] Now, then, before I sit down, let me ask you what is this people, about which so many men in England at this moment are writing, and speaking, and thinking, with harshness, I think with injustice, if not with great bitterness? Two centuries ago, multitudes of the people of this country found a refuge on the North American continent, escaping from the tyranny of the Stuarts and from the bigotry of Laud. Many noble spirits from our country made great experiments in favor of human freedom on that continent. Bancroft, the great historian of his own country, has said, in his own graphic and emphatic language, "The history of the colonization of America is the history of the crimes of Europe." From that time down to our own period, America has admitted the wanderers from every clime. Since 1815, a time which many here remember, and which is within my lifetime, more than three millions of persons have emigrated from the United Kingdom to the United States. During the fifteen years from 1845 or 1846 to 1859 or 1860—a period so recent that we all remember the most trivial circumstances that have happened in that time— during those fifteen years more than two million three hundred and twenty thousand persons left the shores of the United Kingdom as emigrants for the States of North America.

At this very moment, then, there are millions in the United States who personally, or whose immediate parents, have at one time been citizens of this country. They found a home in the Far West; they subdued the wilderness; they met with plenty there, which was not afforded them in their native country; and they have become a great people. There may be persons in England who are jealous of those States. There may be men who dislike democracy, and who hate a republic; there may be even those whose sympathies warm towards the slave oligarchy of the South. But of this I am certain, that only misrepresentation the most gross or calumny the most wicked can sever the tie which unites the great mass of the people of this country with their friends and brethren beyond the Atlantic.

Now, whether the Union will be restored or not, or the South achieve an unhonored independence or not, I know not, and I predict not. But this I think I know—that in a few years, a very few years, the twenty millions of freemen in the North will be thirty millions, or even fifty millions—a population equal to or exceeding that of this kingdom. When that time comes, I pray that it may not be said amongst them, that, in the darkest hour of their country's trials, England, the land of their fathers, looked on with icy coldness and saw unmoved the perils and calamities of their children. As for me, I have but this to say: I am but one in this audience, and but one in the citizenship of this country; but if all other tongues are silent, mine shall speak for that policy which gives hope to the bondsmen of the South, and which tends to generous thoughts, and generous words, and generous deeds, between the two great nations who speak the English language, and from their origin are alike entitled to the English name.

[II] I now come to the proposition which the hon. and learned Gentleman has submitted to the House, and which he has already submitted to a meeting of his constituents at Sheffield. At that meeting, on the 27th of May, the hon. and learned Gentleman used these words: "What I have to consider is, what are the interests of England: what is for her interests I believe to be for the interests of the world." Now, leaving out of consideration the latter part of that statement, if the hon. and learned Gentleman will keep to the first part of it, then what we have now to consider in this question is, what is for the interest of England. But the hon. and learned Gentleman has put it tonight in almost as offensive a way as he did before at Sheffield, and has said that the United States would not bully the world if they were divided and sub-divided; for he went so far as to contemplate division into more than two independent sections. I say that the whole of his case rests upon a miserable jealousy of the United States, or on what I may term a base fear. It is a fear which appears to me just as groundless as any of those panics by which the hon. and learned Gentleman has attempted to frighten the country.

There never was a State in the world which was less capable of aggression with regard to Europe than the United States of America. I speak of its government, of its confederation, of the peculiarities of its organization; for the House will agree with me, that nothing is more peculiar than the fact of the great power which the separate States, both of the North and South, exercise upon the policy and course of the country. I will undertake to say, that, unless in a question of overwhelming magnitude, which would be able to unite any people, it would be utterly hopeless to expect that all the States of the American Union would join together to support the central Government in any plan of aggression on England or any other country of Europe.

Besides, nothing can be more certain than this, that the Government which is now in power, and the party which have elected Mr. Lincoln to office, is a moral and peaceable party, which has been above all things anxious to cultivate the best possible state of feeling with regard to England. The hon. and learned Gentleman, of all men, ought not to entertain this fear of United States aggression, for he is always boasting of his readiness to come into the field himself. I grant that it would be a great necessity indeed which would justify a conscription in calling out the hon. and learned Gentleman, but I say he ought to consider well before he spreads these alarms among the people. For the sake of this miserable jealousy, and that he may help to break up a friendly nation, he would depart from the usages of nations, and create an everlasting breach between the people of England and the people of the United States of America. He would do more; and notwithstanding what he has said tonight, I may put this as my strongest argument against his case—he would throw the weight of England into the scale in favor of the cause of slavery.

I want to know, to ask you, the House of Commons, whether you have turned back to your own proceedings in 1834, and traced the praises which have been lavished upon you for thirty years by the great and good men of other countries,—and whether, after what you did at that time, you believe that you will meet the views of the thoughtful, moral, and religious people of England, when you propose to remit to slavery three millions of negroes in the Southern States, who in our views, and regarding the Proclamation of the only President of the United

States as a legal document, are certainly and to all intents and purposes free? ["Oh!"] The hon. and learned Gentleman may say "Oh!" and shake his head lightly, and be scornful at this. He has managed to get rid of all those feelings under which all men, black and white, like to be free. He has talked of the cant and hypocrisy of these men. Was Wilberforce, was Clarkson, was Buxton,—I might run over the whole list,—were these men hypocrites, and had they nothing about them but cant?

I could state something about the family of my hon. Friend below me (Mr. Forster), which I almost fear to state in his presence; but his revered father—a man unsurpassed in character, not equaled by many in intellect, and approached by few in service— laid down his life in a Slave State in America, while carrying to the governors and legislatures of every Slave State the protest of himself and his sect against the enormity of that odious system.

In conclusion, Sir, I have only this to say,—that I wish to take a generous view of this question,—a view, I say, generous with regard to the people with whom we are in amity, whose Minister we receive here, and who receive our Minister in Washington. We see that the Government of the United States has for two years past been contending for its life, and we know that it is contending necessarily for human freedom. That Government affords the remarkable example—offered for the first time in the history of the world—of a great Government coming forward as the organized defender of law, freedom, and equality.

Surely the hon. Gentlemen opposite cannot be so ill-informed as to say that the revolt of the Southern States is in favor of freedom and equality. In Europe often, and in some parts of America, when there has been insurrection, it has generally been of the suffering against the oppressor, and rarely has it been found, and not more commonly in our history than in the history of any other country, that the Government has stepped forward as the organized defender of freedom—of the wide and general freedom of those under its rule. With such a Government, in such a contest, with such a foe, the hon. and learned Gentleman the Member for Sheffield, who professes to be more an Englishman than most Englishmen, asks us to throw into the scale against it the weight of the hostility of England.

I have not said a word with regard to what may happen to

England if we go into war with the United States. It will be a war upon the ocean,—every ship that belongs to the two nations will, as far as possible, be swept from the seas. But when the troubles in America are over,—be they ended by the restoration of the Union, or by separation,—that great and free people, the most instructed in the world,—there is not an American to be found in the New England States who cannot read and write, and there are not three men in one hundred in the whole Northern States who cannot read and write,—and those who cannot read and write are those who have recently come from Europe,— I say the most instructed people in the world, and the most wealthy,—if you take the distribution of wealth among the whole people,—will have a wound in their hearts by your act which a century may not heal; and the posterity of some of those who now hear my voice may look back with amazement, and I will say with lamentation, at the course which was taken by the hon. and learned Gentleman, and by such hon. Members as may choose to follow his leading. ["No! No!"] I suppose the hon. Gentlemen who cry "No!" will admit that we sometimes suffer from the errors of our ancestors. There are few persons who will not admit that, if their fathers had been wiser, their children would have been happier.

We know the cause of this revolt, its purposes, and its aims. Those who made it have not left us in darkness respecting their intentions, but what they are to accomplish is still hidden from our sight; and I will abstain now, as I have always abstained with regard to it, from predicting what is to come. I know what I hope for,—and what I shall rejoice in,—but I know nothing of future facts that will enable me to express a confident opinion. Whether it will give freedom to the race which white men have trampled in the dust, and whether the issue will purify a nation steeped in crimes committed against that race, is known only to the Supreme. In His hands are alike the breath of man and the life of States. I am willing to commit to Him the issue of this dreaded contest; but I implore of Him, and I beseech this House, that my country may lift nor hand nor voice in aid of the most stupendous act of guilt that history has recorded in the annals of mankind.

James Bryce
(1838-1922)

OF ALL the British ambassadors to America probably the one most acceptable to the Americans and certainly the one who had the best understanding of their characters, ideologies, and ways of living, was Viscount Bryce, distinguished diplomat and historian. He was born in Belfast, Ireland, in 1838, and educated at the University of Glasgow and at Trinity College, Oxford. After practicing law for some years in London, he became regius professor of civil law at Oxford, a place which he held with distinction from 1870 to 1893. He entered Parliament as a Liberal and took an active part in governmental problems. Among the important posts which he occupied were those of undersecretary for foreign affairs (1886), chancellor of the duchy of Lancaster (1892), president of the Board of Trade (1894), and chief secretary for Ireland (1905–06). When he was sent to Washington in 1907 as ambassador, he was already widely known in this country through his *American Commonwealth* (1888); for six years he did his utmost to improve relations between England and America. Among his more important historical and political studies are his classic *Holy Roman Empire* (1864) and his *Modern Democracies* (1921). This last considerable literary work of his long and useful career is a study of the democratic principles in government and of the form, characteristics, and operations of all the notable democracies of the world. He devoted a considerable portion of the book, as was natural, to the democracy in the west in which he served for so many years as ambassador.

The first of the three selections from Viscount Bryce's *Modern Democracies* reprinted here comprises Chapter III of Volume I, Part I of the book. Together with the two selections that follow, it reveals Bryce's clarity of thought and restrained simplicity of style.

The Definition of Democracy (1921)

The word Democracy has been used ever since the time of Herodotus to denote that form of government in which the ruling power of a State is legally vested, not in any particular class or classes, but in the members of the community as a whole. This means, in communities which act by voting, that rule belongs to the majority, as no other method has been found for determining peaceably and legally what is to be deemed the will of a community which is not unanimous. Usage has made this the accepted sense of the term, and usage is the safest guide in the employment of words.

Democracy, as the rule of the Many, was by the Greeks opposed to Monarchy, which is the rule of One, and to Oligarchy, which is the rule of the Few, *i.e.* of a class privileged either by birth or by property. Thus it came to be taken as denoting in practice that form of government in which the poorer class, always the more numerous, did in fact rule; and the term *Demos* was often used to describe not the whole people but that particular class as distinguished from the wealthier and much smaller class. Moderns sometimes also use it thus to describe what we call "the masses" in contradistinction to "the classes." But it is better to employ the word as meaning neither more nor less than the Rule of the Majority, the "classes and masses" of the whole people being taken together.

So far there is little disagreement as to the sense of the word. But when we come to apply this, or indeed any broad and simple definition, to concrete cases, many questions arise. What is meant by the term "political community"? Does it include all the inhabitants of a given area or those only who possess full civic

From James Bryce, *Modern Democracies* (1921). By permission of The Macmillan Company, publishers.

rights, the so-called "qualified citizens"? Can a community such as South Carolina, or the Transvaal, in which the majority of the inhabitants, because not of the white race, are excluded from the electoral suffrage, be deemed a democracy in respect of its vesting political power in the majority of qualified citizens, the "qualified" being all or nearly all white? Is the name to be applied equally to Portugal and Belgium, in which women do not vote, and to Norway and Germany, in which they do? Could anybody deny it to France merely because she does not grant the suffrage to women? Or if the electoral suffrage, instead of being possessed by all the adult, or adult male, citizens, is restricted to those who can read and write, or to those who possess some amount of property, or pay some direct tax, however small, does that community thereby cease to be a democracy?

So again, what difference is made by such limitations on the power of the majority as a Constitution may impose? There are communities in which, though universal suffrage prevails, the power of the voters is fettered in its action by the rights reserved to a king or to a non-elective Upper House. Such was the German Empire, such was the Austrian Monarchy, such are some of the monarchies that still remain in Europe. Even in Britain and in Canada, a certain, though now very slender, measure of authority has been left to Second Chambers. In all the last-mentioned cases must we not consider not only who possess the right of voting, but how far that right carries with it a full control of the machinery of government? Was Germany, for instance, a democracy in 1913 because the Reichstag was elected by manhood suffrage?

Another class of cases presents another difficulty. There are countries in which the Constitution has a popular quality in respect of its form, but in which the mass of the people do not in fact exercise the powers they possess on paper. This may be because they are too ignorant or too indifferent to vote, or because actual supremacy belongs to the man or group in control of the government through a control of the army. Such are most of the so-called republics of Central and South America. Such have been, at particular moments, some of the new kingdoms of south eastern Europe, where the bulk of the population has not yet learnt how to exercise the political rights which the Constitution gives. Bulgaria and Greece were nominally democratic in 1915, but the king of the former carried the people into the Great War, as the ally of Germany, against their wish, and the king of the latter would have succeeded in doing the same thing but for the fact that the Allied fleets had Athens under their guns.

All these things make a difference to the truly popular character of a government. It is the facts that matter, not the name. People used to confound—some persons in some countries still confound—a Republic with a Democracy, and suppose that a government in which one person is the titular and permanent head of the State cannot be a government by the people. It ought not to be necessary nowadays to point out that there are plenty of republics which are not democracies, and some monarchies, like those of Britain and Norway, which are. I might multiply instances, but it is not worth while. Why spend time on what is a question of words? No one has propounded a formula which will cover every case, because there are governments which are "on the line," too popular to be called oligarchies, and scarcely popular enough to be called democracies. But though we cannot define either Oligarchy or Democracy, we can usually know either the one or the other when we see it. Where the will of the whole people prevails in all important matters, even if it has some retarding influences to overcome, or is legally required to act for some purposes in some specially provided manner, that may be called a Democracy. In this book I use the word in its old and strict sense, as denoting a government in which the will of the majority of qualified citizens rules, taking the qualified citizens to constitute the great bulk of the inhabitants, say, roughly, at least three-fourths, so that the physical force of the citizens coincides (broadly speaking) with their voting power. Using this test, we may apply the name to the United Kingdom and the British self-governing Dominions, to France, Italy, Portugal, Belgium, Holland, Denmark, Sweden, Norway, Greece, the United States, Argentina, and possibly Chile and Uruguay. Of some of the newer European States it is too soon to speak, and whatever we may call the republics of Central America and the Caribbean Sea, they are not democracies.

Although the words "democracy" and "democratic" denote nothing more than a particular form of government, they have, particularly in the United States, Canada, and Australia, acquired attractive associations of a social and indeed almost of a moral character. The adjective is used to describe a person of a simple and friendly spirit and genial manners, "a good mixer," one who, whatever his wealth or status, makes no assumption of superiority, and carefully keeps himself on the level of his poorer or less eminent neighbors. I have heard a monarch described as "a democratic king." Democracy is supposed to be the product and the guardian both of Equality and of Liberty, being so consecrated by its relationship to both these precious possessions as to be almost above criticism. Historically no doubt the three have been intimately connected, yet they are separable in theory and have sometimes been separated in practice, as will appear from the two following chapters.

The Beginnings of Democracy
in North America (1921)

Of all modern countries the United States supplies the most abundant data for the study of popular government. It has been a democracy for a century and a quarter, and is now by far the largest of the nations that live under self-governing institutions. It shows the working of these institutions, on a great scale in its Federal Government and in the governments of the most populous States, on a smaller scale in the lesser States, as well as in counties, townships, and cities, some of which latter have a frame of government that makes them resemble autonomous republics. It has exerted an immense influence on other countries, for its example fired the French people at the outbreak of the Revolution of 1789, and its constitution has been taken as a model by the new republics of the western hemisphere. Since Tocqueville published in 1832 his memorable book on American democracy, the United States has stood before the minds of European thinkers and statesmen not only as the land to which the races of the Old World are drawn by hopes of happiness and freedom, but also as the type of what the rule of the people means when the people are left to themselves, and as the pattern of what other peoples are likely to become as they in their turn move along the fateful path to democratic institutions. Whoever in Europe has wished to commend or to disparage those institutions has pointed to the United States, and has found plenty of facts to warrant either praise or blame.

No nation ever embarked on its career with happier auguries for the success of popular government. The friends of liberty in Europe indulged the highest hopes of what Liberty could accomplish in a new land, exempt from the evils which the folly or selfishness of monarchs and nobles had inflicted on the countries

From Bryce's *Modern Democracies* (1921), Volume II, Part II, Chapter XXXVIII. By permission of The Macmillan Company, publishers.

of Europe. The Americans themselves, although the Revolutionary War left them impoverished as well as vexed by local jealousies, were full of pride and confidence. There was much to justify this confidence. Their own racial quality and the traditions they inherited, the favoring features of their physical environment and the security from external dangers which isolation promised, made up, taken in conjunction, a body of conditions for a peaceful and prosperous political life such as no other people had ever enjoyed. Those who settled Spanish America had an equally vast and rich territory open before them. Those who settled Australia and New Zealand had an equally noble inheritance of freedom behind them. But in neither of these cases were the gifts of Nature and those of a splendid Past bestowed together in such ample measure on the founders of a State.

Let us pass these gifts in brief review.

Temperate North America was a vast country fit to be the home of a North European race, and a practically unoccupied country, for the aboriginal tribes, though most of them fierce and brave, were too few to constitute an obstacle to settlement. There was land for everybody; and nearly all of it, as far as the Rocky Mountains, available for cultivation. It is only today, three centuries after the first English colonists settled in Virginia and on the shores of Massachusetts Bay, nearly a century and a half after the Declaration of Independence, that the unappropriated arable areas have become scarce. Besides the immense stretches of rich soil, there were superb forests and mineral deposits it will take many centuries to exhaust.

In such a country everybody could find means of sustenance. Among the earlier settlers and almost down to our own time there was no economic distress, no pauperism nor ground for apprehending it. Nobody was rich, nobody very poor. Neither were there any class antagonisms. Though the conditions of colonial life had created a kind of equality unknown to old countries, certain distinctions of rank existed, but they were not resented, and caused no friction, either social or political. The people were nearly all of English or (in the Middle States) of Dutch or Scotch-Irish stock, stocks that had already approved themselves industrious in peace, valiant in war, adventurous at sea. All were practically English in their ways of thinking, their beliefs, their social usages, yet with an added adaptability and resourcefulness such as the simpler or rougher life in a new country is fitted to implant. In the northern colonies they were well educated, as education was understood in those days, and mentally alert. The habit of independent thinking and a general interest in public affairs had been fostered both by the share which the laity of the northern colonies took in the management of the Congregational churches and by the practice of civil self-government, brought from England, while the principles of the English Common Law, exact yet flexible, had formed the minds of their leading men. Respect for law and order, a recognition both of the rights of the individual and of the authority of the duly appointed magistrate, were to them the foundations of civic duty.

Though there were wide economic and social differences between the Northern colonies, where the farmers and seafaring men constituted the great bulk of the population and the Southern, in which large plantations were worked by slave labor, these differences did not yet substantially affect the unity of the nation: for the racial distinctions were negligible, and no language but English was spoken, except by some Germans in Pennsylvania. Such divergences in religious doctrine and church government as existed were too slight to be a basis for parties or to create political acrimony. Finally, it was their good fortune to be safe from any external dangers. The power of France had, since 1759, ceased to threaten them on the side of Canada, and on the south neither from Florida nor from Louisiana, both then in the hands of Spain, was there anything to fear.

With conditions so favorable to peace only a small navy and still smaller army were needed, circumstances which promised security against the growth of a military caste or the ascendancy of a successful general. These fortunate conditions continued to exist for many years. Once, however, the unity of the nation was imperiled. The maintenance of Negro slavery, which wise statesmen had hoped to see disappear naturally, and the attempt to extend its area so as to retain for the Slave States an equal power in the government, led to a long struggle between the Free and the Slave States which ended in the War of Secession, a war that retarded the progress of the South and has left behind it a still unsolved internal problem. Nevertheless, the cohesive forces proved strong enough to reassert themselves when the fight was over. The present generation knows no animosities, and honors alike those who, between 1860 and 1865, fought on one or other side. The old Slavery issues belong to a dead past, and need seldom be referred to in the pages that follow, for the tendencies that characterize popular government have developed themselves upon lines with which slavery had little to do, so the phenomena which we have today to study would (except as respects the suffrage in, and the political attitude of, the Southern States) have been much the same if no slave-ship had ever brought a Negro from Africa.

What were the tendencies of thought and feeling wherewith the nation started on its course and which constituted the main lines of its political character? Some were inherited, some the outcome of colonial conditions.

There was a strong religious sense, present everywhere, but strongest in New England, and there fostering a somewhat stern and almost grim view of duty. This has continued to be a feature which sharply distinguishes native American thought and conduct from all revolutionary and socialistic movements on the European continent. There has never been any anti-Christian or anti-clerical sentiment, such as has embittered politics and disrupted parties in France, Italy, Spain, and Mexico.

There was a vehement passion for liberty, dating, in embryo, from the early Puritan settlements in New England and keen also among the Scotch-Irish of Virginia, the Carolinas and Pennsylvania, who had fled from the oppressions suffered by the Presbyterians of Ulster. Intensified by the long struggle against King George III., this passion ran to excess when it induced the belief that with Liberty in the van all other good things would follow. During the War of Independence the men of conservative opinions, branded as enemies of freedom, had been mostly silenced or expelled. The victory of the People over arbitrary power had glorified both Liberty and the People. It was natural to assume that the one would be always victorious and the other always wise.

With the love of Liberty there went a spirit of individualistic self-reliance and self-help, not indeed excluding associated action, for that they possessed in their town meetings and colonial assemblies, but averse to official control or supervision. In the great

majority of the people these tendencies coexisted with a respect
for law and a sense of the value of public order. But there were,
especially in the wilder districts, restive elements which gave
trouble to the Federal Government in its early days and obliged
it to use military force to overcome resistance to the enforcement
of revenue statutes. Lawlessness has never been extinguished in
the mountainous regions of East Kentucky and East Tennessee.

Neither did the respect for constituted authority, general in
the older and best-settled parts of the country, prevent a suspicious attitude towards officials, including even members of the
legislatures. Here the individualism characteristic of the Puritan
and of the settler asserted itself. Any assumption of power was
watched with a jealousy which kept strictly within the range of
their functions those whom the people had chosen for public
service.

Lastly, there was a spirit of localism which showed itself in the
desire to retain as much public business as possible under local
control and entrust as little as possible to a central authority.
The attachment to self-government in each small community was
rooted, not in any theory, but rather in instinct and habit. Nobody thought of choosing any one but a neighbor to represent
him in an elected body. This showed itself especially in the northern colonies which had grown up out of little rural Towns. The
Town was not a mere electoral area but a community, which
thought that no one but a member of the community could
represent it or deal with its affairs.

These tendencies were fundamentally English, though more
fully developed in America, as an orchard tree grown for centuries in one country may, when placed in a new soil under a
new sun, put forth more abundant foliage and fruit of richer
flavor. The Americans, however, began soon after the Revolution
to think of themselves, and the less instructed sections among
them have continued so to think, as a new people. They fancied
their history to have begun from 1776, or at earliest from 1607
and 1620, forgetting, in the pride of their new nationalism, that
both their character and their institutions were due to causes
that had been at work centuries before, as far back as Magna
Carta and even as the Folk Moots of their primitive ancestors in
the days of Ecghbert and Alfred. Rather were they an old people,

the heirs of many ages, though under the stimulus of a new nature and an independent life renewing their youth even as the
age of an eagle.

Such was the land and such the people in which the greatest of
modern democracies began to build up its frame of government.
On what foundations of doctrine was the structure made to rest?

The Americans of the Revolution started from two fundamental principles or dogmas. One was Popular Sovereignty. From
the People all power came: at their pleasure and under their
watchful supervision it was held: for their benefit and theirs
alone was it to be exercised. The other principle was Equality.
This had from the first covered the whole field of private civil
rights with no distinctions of privilege. Equality of political rights
was for a time incomplete, voting power being in some States
withheld from the poorest as not having a permanent stake in
the community, but in course of time all the States placed all
their citizens on the same footing.

Along with these two principles certain other doctrines were so
generally assumed as true that men did not stop to examine,
much less to prove them. Nearly all believed that the possession
of political rights, since it gives self-respect and imposes responsibility, does of itself make men fit to exercise those rights, so that
citizens who enjoy liberty will be sure to value it and guard it.
Their faith in this power of liberty, coupled with their love of
equality, further disposed them to regard the differences between
one citizen and another as so slight that almost any public functions may be assigned to any honest man, while fairness requires
that such functions should go round and be enjoyed by each in
turn. These doctrines, however, did not exclude the belief that in
the interest of the people no one chosen to any office must enjoy
it long or be allowed much discretion in its exercise, for they held
that though the private citizen may be good while he remains the
equal of others, power is a corrupting thing, so the temptation to
exceed or misuse functions must be as far as possible removed.

The Results Democratic Government Has Given (1921)

To test democracy by its results as visible in the six countries examined, it will be convenient to consider how far in each of them the chief ends for which government exists have been attained, taking these ends to include whatever the collective action of men associated for the common good can do for the moral and material welfare of a community and the individual citizens who compose it, helping them to obtain the maximum that life can afford of enjoyment and to suffer the minimum life may bring of sorrow.

These ends may be summed up as follows:

Safety against attack on the community from without.

Order within the community—prevention of violence and creation of the consequent sense of security.

Justice, the punishment of offenses and the impartial adjustment of disputes on principles approved by the community.

Efficient administration of common affairs, so as to obtain the largest possible results at the smallest possible cost.

Assistance to the citizens in their several occupations, as, for example, by the promotion of trade or the regulation of industry, in so far as this can be done without checking individual initiative or unduly restricting individual freedom.

These may be called the primary and generally recognized functions of government in a civilized country. Other results, needing a fuller explanation, will be presently adverted to. I take first the five ends above named.

1. *Safety against External Attack.*—In all the Six Democracies this end has been attained as fully as in most non-democratic governments, and in one respect better attained, because the neces-

From Bryce's *Modern Democracies* (1921), Part III, Chapter LXXIII. By permission of The Macmillan Company, publishers.

sary preparations for defense have not given reasonable ground to other nations to fear that armaments were being increased with a view to hostile aggression.

2. In most of the Six internal order has been well maintained, best perhaps in Switzerland, least perhaps in parts of the United States, where, although the Federal Government has done its duty faithfully, some State Governments have tolerated lynching and failed to check other breaches of the law. Rioting in connection with Labor disputes has occurred everywhere, but except in some Australian cases the constituted authorities have shown themselves able to deal with it.

3. Justice has been honestly and capably administered, quite as well as under other forms of government, in Switzerland, Canada, Australia, and New Zealand, and in France also, though perhaps with not so full a confidence of the people in the perfect honor of all the Courts. In the United States the Federal Courts are staffed (with few exceptions) by upright and capable men, and the same is true of certain States. In others, however, the Judiciary is below the level of its functions, and in a few it is not trusted, while criminal procedure is cumbrous and regrettably ineffective.

4. Civil administration has long been conducted with efficiency in France and Switzerland, and is now, since the partial abolition of the "Spoils System," beginning to be so conducted in the United States Federal Government and in many of the State Governments. A similar improvement is visible in Canada. Australia and New Zealand have permanent services which are honest but as yet not more than fairly competent. Still possessed by the notion that one man is as good as another, the new democracies have not yet duly recognized the increased call for thorough knowledge and trained skill in handling the widened functions now imposed on governments, both in determining the principles of economic and social policy to be adopted and in carrying them out in a scientific spirit. That the management of national finances has, in every country except Switzerland, been lavish and frequently wasteful is the fault not of the civil services but of Ministers and legislatures who have spent vast sums in that form of electioneering bribery which consists in making grants of money to particular classes (as in the United States to those who professed to be Civil War Veterans), or to constituencies under

the pretense of executing public works. This kind of bribery, like the indulgence extended to law-breakers whose displeasure can be shown at elections, is directly attributable to democracy.

5. What further services, beyond those already mentioned, Government may render to a community or to any class of its citizens by acquiring property to be used for the common benefit, or by embarking on industries or trading enterprises, or by aiding individuals to do so, is a question on which opinions differ so widely that no standard exists whereby to estimate the merits or defaults of governments. The only two countries that have gone far in this direction are New Zealand and Australia, with results (described already) which raise doubts whether democracy is a form of government fitted for such enterprises. Other matters, however, which are now generally deemed to fall within the sphere of legislation, such as public health and the conditions of labor and the regulation of the means of transportation, have received in all the Six countries due attention, the newer democracies being in no wise behind their elder sisters.

Of the conduct of foreign policy, once deemed a department in which popular governments were inconstant and incompetent, nothing need be added to what has been said in a preceding chapter except that the errors of the peoples have been no greater than those committed by monarchs, or by oligarchies, or in democracies themselves by the small groups, or the individual Ministers, to whose charge foreign relations had been entrusted.

Outside and apart from these definite duties, legally assigned to and discharged by government, there is a sphere in which its action can be felt and in which both its form and its spirit tell upon the individual citizen. When political institutions call upon him to bear a part in their working, he is taken out of the narrow circle of his domestic or occupational activities, admitted to a larger life which opens wider horizons, associated in new ways with his fellows, forced to think of matters which are both his and theirs. Self-government in local and still more in national affairs becomes a stimulant and an education. These influences may be called a by-product of popular government, incidental, but precious. Whoever has grown up in a household where public affairs were followed with interest and constantly discussed by the elders and friends of the family knows how much the boy gains by listening, asking questions, trying to understand the answers given; and the gain to the budding mind is greatest when the differences of opinion he hears expressed are most frequent. In Britain and America every general Parliamentary or Presidential Election marked for many a boy an epoch in the development of his thought, leading him to reflect thenceforth on events as they followed one another. In the Six Democracies described this kind of education is always going on, and the process is continued in an even more profitable form where the citizen, when he has reached the voting age, is required to vote not only at elections, but also, as in Switzerland and some of the American States, on laws submitted to the people by Referendum and Initiative.

Could this examination be extended to six other European countries, Italy, Holland, Belgium, Denmark, Sweden, Norway, the results to be described would not differ materially from those set forth as attained in the Six countries examined in Part II. In none has justice or order or the efficiency of civil administration suffered in the process of democratization which all have undergone within the last ninety years, and in most these primary duties of government are better discharged. We may accordingly treat the results our inquiry has given for the Six as substantially true for European democracies in general.

Here, however, a wider question arises. Some one may say: "These attempts to estimate what government has done or failed to do for the citizen do not convey a definite impression of what is after all the thing of most worth, viz. the amount of satisfaction, be it greater or less, with life and in life which democracy has brought to the modern world. What has it done for human happiness? Is it discredited, as some argue, by the fact that, after its long and steady advance, those civilized peoples which had hoped so much from popular government have seen in these latest years the most awful calamities which history records? Has it, if we think of the individual man, made him more or less disposed to say, taking the common test, "If I could, I would live my life over again," or does it leave him still in the frame of mind expressed twenty-three centuries ago by the Greek poet, who wrote, "The best thing for a man is never to have been born at all, and the next best to return swiftly to that darkness whence he came"?

Shall we say, in the familiar lines of a later poet, that the

question is idle, because governments have infinitesimally little to
do with the matter?

> How small of all that human hearts endure,
> That part which laws or kings can cause or cure.

What is Happiness? Nations as well as men have shown by
their acts how differently they conceive it. Some, like Albanians
and Afghans, cannot be happy without fighting, and the exploits
of the heroes recorded in the Icelandic sagas as well as the feats of
warlike prowess which fill the *Iliad* seem to show that the first
European peoples to produce great literatures cherished the same
ideals. Yet the ideals of peace also were never absent. Eris and
Atē, Strife, and Sin the parent of Strife, loom large in the Homeric
poems as figures to be hated, because they are sources of misery.
That impassioned little poem, the hundred and forty-fourth
Psalm, begins with the stern joy of battle in the verses:

> Blessed be Jehovah my Strength who teacheth my hands to war and
> my fingers to fight.
> My goodness and my fortress, my high tower and my deliverer, my
> shield and he in whom I trust.

And ends with a prayer for the blessedness of peaceful prosperity
which the Almighty bestows:

> That our sons may grow up like young plants and our daughters be
> as the polished corners of the temple:
> That our garners may be full affording all manner of stores:
> That our oxen may be strong to labor, that there may be no break-
> ing in nor going out, that there be no complaining in our streets.
> Happy is the people that is in such a case; happy the people whose
> God is Jehovah.

So peace is for Dante the supreme good, which the government
of an Emperor commissioned from on high is to confer upon an
Italy distracted by internal strife, leading men to the practice on
earth of active virtue in this world, according to the precepts of
philosophy, as the successor of Peter is to lead them to celestial
felicity in the world to come. The Greek philosophers, however,

and the Eastern mystics and the Christian theologians agree in regarding Happiness as a thing which governments can neither make nor mar, since it is unaffected by the possession or the lack of earthly goods. From this exalted view there is a long downward scale, for the pleasures of sense must not be forgotten: many Europeans would deem Happiness unattainable in a land where alcoholic stimulants were unprocurable; and among the various ideals of different modern countries there is that of the maximum of amusement with the minimum of toil, high wages and leisure for bull-fights or horse races and athletic sports, in which many, and that not in Spain or Australia only, place their *Summum bonum*.

Of Democracy and Happiness can more be said than this, that whatever governments can do to increase the joy of life is so slight in comparison with the other factors that tell on life for good and evil as to make the question not worth discussing on its positive side? With the negative side it is otherwise. The establishment of popular freedom has removed or at least diminished sources of fear or suffering which existed under more arbitrary forms of government. France has never returned to the oppressions and injustices, even the religious persecutions which had lasted down to the days of Louis XV. In England, under the dawning light of popular power, the Slave Trade and the pillory and the cruel penal code and the oppressive restrictions on industry had begun to disappear even before the peaceful revolution of 1832; and slavery in every British dominion fell at once thereafter. In Germany, Switzerland, and Spain torture-chambers had remained till the advent of the armies of republican France. Russia is the only country in which the overthrow of an old-established tyranny has not been followed by the extinction of administrative cruelty. Freedom of thought and speech, if not everywhere the gift of popular government, has found its best guarantee in democratic institutions.

It remains to see which among the things expected from it by its sanguine apostles of a century ago Democracy has so far failed to bestow upon the people. To Mazzini and his disciples, as to Jefferson and many another fifty years before, Democracy was a Religion, or the natural companion of a religion, or a substitute for religion, from which effects on morals and life were hoped similar to those which the preachers of new creeds have so often seen with the eyes of faith.

What, then, has democracy failed to accomplish? It has brought no nearer friendly feeling and the sense of human brotherhood among the peoples of the world towards one another. Freedom has not been a reconciler.

Neither has it created goodwill and a sense of unity and civic fellowship within each of these peoples. Though in earlier days strife between classes had arisen, it is only in these later days that what is called Class War has become recognized as a serious menace to the peace of States, and in some countries the dominant factor in political and economic conflicts. Liberty and Equality have not been followed by Fraternity. Not even far off do we see her coming shine.

It has not enlisted in the service of the State nearly so much of the best practical capacity as each country possesses and every country needs for dealing with the domestic and international questions of the present age.

It has not purified or dignified politics, nor escaped the pernicious influence which the Money Power can exert. In some states corruption has been rife, and the tone of public life no better than it was under the monarchies or oligarchies of the eighteenth century.

Lastly, Democracy has not induced that satisfaction and contentment with itself as the best form of government which was expected, and has not exorcised the spirit that seeks to attain its aims by revolution. One of the strongest arguments used to recommend Universal Suffrage was that as it gave supreme power to the numerical majority, every section of the people would bow to that majority, realizing that their aims must be sought by constitutional methods, since a resort to violence would be treason against the People and their legal sovereignty. Nevertheless, in many a country revolutionary methods are now being either applied or threatened just as they were in the old days of tyrannical kings or oligarchies. If Democracy is flouted, what remains? There was a Greek proverb, "If water chokes, what can one drink to stop choking?" If the light of Democracy be turned to darkness, how great is that darkness!

Any one can see that these things which have not been attained ought not to have been expected. No form of government, nothing less than a change in tendencies of human nature long known and recognized as permanent, could have accomplished what philosophies and religions and the spread of knowledge and progress in all the arts of life had failed to accomplish. Christianity—a far more powerful force than any political ideas or political institutions, since it works on the inmost heart of man —has produced nearly all the moral progress that has been achieved since it first appeared, and can in individual men transmute lead into gold, yet Christianity has not done these things for peoples, because, checked or perverted by the worse propensities of human nature, it has never been applied in practice. It has not abolished oppression and corruption in governments, nor extinguished international hatreds and wars, has not even prevented the return of hideous cruelties in war which were believed to have been long extinct.

Yet the right way to judge Democracy is to try it by a concrete standard, setting it side by side with other governments. If we look back from the world of today to the world of the sixteenth century, comfort can be found in seeing how many sources of misery have been reduced under the rule of the people and the recognition of the equal rights of all. If it has not brought all the blessings that were expected, it has in some countries destroyed, in others materially diminished, many of the cruelties and terrors, injustices and oppressions that had darkened the souls of men for many generations.

Part Two

Democracy in America

Democracy is better than tyranny.
DIOGENES LAERTIUS: Periander 4.

Liberty has still a continent to live in.
HORACE WALPOLE: Letter, *February* 17, 1779.

Our country has liberty without license and authority without despotism. JAMES, CARDINAL GIBBONS: Address, *Rome, March* 25, 1887.

I believe in Democracy because it releases the energies of every human being. WOODROW WILSON: Address, *New York, September* 4, 1912.

He who would save liberty must put his trust in Democracy. NORMAN THOMAS, Saturday Review of Literature, *June* 7, 1930.

Democracy is on trial in the world, on a more colossal scale than ever before. C. F. DOLE: The Spirit of Democracy.

Daniel Webster
(1782-1852)

"NOT MANY days ago I saw at breakfast the notablest of your notabilities, Daniel Webster. He is a magnificent specimen. You might say to all the world, 'This is our Yankee Englishman; such limbs we make in Yankee land!' As a logic fencer, or parliamentary Hercules, one would be inclined to back him at first sight against the extant world. The tanned complexion, that amorphous crag-like face; the dull black eyes under the precipice of brows, like dull anthracite furnaces, needing only to be blown; the mastiff mouth accurately closed; I have not traced so much of *silent Berserker rage* that I remember in any man." Thus Thomas Carlyle (see p. 86) described America's Demosthenes in 1839. Foremost orator of America, great statesman, liberal and just thinker, he earned the respect and admiration of England and America, North and South. His address at the laying of the cornerstone of the Bunker Hill Monument on June 17, 1825 (see p. 334) is the clearest and most eloquent statement ever made of the principles underlying the American War of Independence; his famous debate with Hayne, in which he defended the supremacy of the Union against the claims for states' rights, every one knows; his argument before the Supreme Court in the Dartmouth College Case resulted in one of the most notable and far-reaching decisions ever handed down by that body. His services as Senator, as Secretary of State under William Henry Harrison, and as international arbiter in the settlement with England of the Northeastern Boundary Dispute all justify Carlyle's praise of him, a tribute by a "crag-like" Scotchman to a "crag-like" American nursed in the New England hills.

The Revolution in Greece Webster delivered in the House of Representatives in 1824 while the Greeks were fighting the Turks for their freedom.

The Revolution in Greece (1824)

The House of Representatives having, on the 19th of January, resolved itself into a committee of the whole, and this resolution being taken into consideration, Mr. Webster spoke to the following effect.

I am afraid, Mr. Chairman, that, so far as my part in this discussion is concerned, those expectations which the public excitement existing on the subject, and certain associations easily suggested by it, have conspired to raise, may be disappointed. An occasion which calls the attention to a spot so distinguished, so connected with interesting recollections, as Greece, may naturally create something of warmth and enthusiasm. In a grave, political discussion, however, it is necessary that those feelings should be chastised. I shall endeavor properly to repress them, although it is impossible that they should be altogether extinguished. We must, indeed, fly beyond the civilized world; we must pass the dominion of law and the boundaries of knowledge; we must, more especially, withdraw ourselves from this place, and the scenes and objects which here surround us,—if we would separate ourselves entirely from the influence of all those memorials of herself which ancient Greece has transmitted for the admiration and the benefit of mankind. This free form of government, this popular assembly, the common council held for the common good,—where have we contemplated its earliest models? This practice of free debate and public discussion, the contest of mind with mind, and that popular eloquence, which, if it were now here, on a subject like this, would move the stones of the Capitol, —whose was the language in which all these were first exhibited? Even the edifice in which we assemble, these proportioned columns, this ornamented architecture, all remind us that Greece has existed, and that we, like the rest of mankind, are greatly her debtors.

But I have not introduced this motion in the vain hope of discharging anything of this accumulated debt of centuries. I have not acted upon the expectation, that we, who have inherited this obligation from our ancestors, should now attempt to pay it to those who may seem to have inherited from *their* ancestors a right to receive payment. My object is nearer and more immediate. I wish to take occasion of the struggle of an interesting and gallant people, in the cause of liberty and Christianity, to draw the attention of the House to the circumstances which have accompanied that struggle, and to the principles which appear to have governed the conduct of the great states of Europe in regard to it; and to the effects and consequences of these principles upon the independence of nations, and especially upon the institutions of free governments. What I have to say of Greece, therefore, concerns the modern, not the ancient; the living, and not the dead. It regards her, not as she exists in history, triumphant over time, and tyranny, and ignorance; but as she now is, contending, against fearful odds, for being, and for the common privileges of human nature.

As it is never difficult to recite commonplace remarks and trite aphorisms, so it may be easy, I am aware, on this occasion, to remind me of the wisdom which dictates to men a care of their own affairs, and admonishes them, instead of searching for adventures abroad, to leave other men's concerns in their own hands. It may be easy to call this resolution *Quixotic,* the emanation of a crusading or propagandist spirit. All this, and more, may be readily said; but all this, and more, will not be allowed to fix a character upon this proceeding, until that is proved which it takes for granted. Let it first be shown, that in this question there is nothing which can affect the interest, the character, or the duty of this country. Let it be proved, that we are not called upon, by either of these considerations, to express an opinion on the subject to which the resolution relates. Let this be proved, and then it will indeed be made out, that neither ought this resolution to pass, nor ought the subject of it to have been mentioned in the communication of the President to us. But, in my opinion, this cannot be shown. In my judgment, the subject is interesting to the people and the government of this country, and we are called upon, by considerations of great weight and moment, to express our opinions upon it. These considerations, I think, spring from a sense of our own duty, our character, and our own interest. I wish to treat the subject on such grounds, exclusively, as are truly *American;* but then, in considering it as an American question, I cannot forget the age in which we live, the prevailing spirit of the age, the interesting questions which agitate it, and our own peculiar relation in regard to these interesting questions. Let this be, then, and as far as I am concerned I hope it will be, purely an American discussion; but let it embrace, nevertheless, everything that fairly concerns America. Let it comprehend, not merely her present advantage, but her permanent interest, her elevated character as one of the free states of the world, and her duty towards those great principles which have hitherto maintained the relative independence of nations, and which have, more especially, made her what she is.

At the commencement of the session, the President, in the discharge of the high duties of his office, called our attention to the subject to which this resolution refers. "A strong hope," says that communication, "has been long entertained, founded on the heroic struggle of the Greeks, that they would succeed in their contest, and resume their equal station among the nations of the earth. It is believed that the whole civilized world takes a deep interest in their welfare. Although no power has declared in their favor, yet none, according to our information, has taken part against them. Their cause and their name have protected them from dangers which might ere this have overwhelmed any other people. The ordinary calculations of interest, and of acquisition with a view to aggrandizement, which mingle so much in the transactions of nations, seem to have had no effect in regard to them. From the facts which have come to our knowledge, there is good cause to believe that their enemy has lost forever all dominion over them; that Greece will become again an independent nation."

It has appeared to me that the House should adopt some resolution reciprocating these sentiments, so far as it shall approve them. More than twenty years have elapsed since Congress first ceased to receive such a communication from the President as could properly be made the subject of a general answer. I do not mean to find fault with this relinquishment of a former and an ancient practice. It may have been attended with inconveniences which justified its abolition. But, certainly, there was one advantage belonging to it; and that is, that it furnished a fit opportunity for the expression of the opinion of the houses of Congress upon those topics in the executive communication which were not expected to be made the immediate subjects of direct legislation. Since, therefore, the President's message does not now receive a general answer, it has seemed to me to be proper that, in some mode, agreeable to our own usual form of proceeding, we should express our sentiments upon the important and interesting topics on which it treats.

If the sentiments of the message in respect to Greece be proper, it is equally proper that this House should reciprocate those sentiments. The present resolution is designed to have that extent, and no more. If it pass, it will leave any future proceeding where it now is, in the discretion of the executive government. It is but an expression, under those forms in which the House is accustomed to act, of the satisfaction of the House with the general sentiments expressed in regard to this subject in the message, and of its readiness to defray the expense incident to any inquiry for the purpose of further information, or any other agency which the President, in his discretion, shall see fit, in whatever manner and at whatever time, to institute. The whole matter is still left in his judgment, and this resolution can in no way restrain its unlimited exercise.

I might well, Mr. Chairman, avoid the responsibility of this measure, if it had, in my judgment, any tendency to change the policy of the country. With the general course of that policy I am quite satisfied. The nation is prosperous, peaceful, and happy; and I should very reluctantly put its peace, prosperity, or happiness at risk. It appears to me, however, that this resolution is strictly conformable to our general policy, and not only consistent with our interests, but even demanded by a large and liberal view of those interests.

It is certainly true that the just policy of this country is, in the first place, a peaceful policy. No nation ever had less to expect from forcible aggrandizement. The mighty agents which are working out our greatness are time, industry, and the arts. Our augmentation is by growth, not by acquisition; by internal development, not by external accession. No schemes can be suggested to us so magnificent as the prospects which a sober contemplation of our own condition, unaided by projects, uninfluenced by ambition, fairly spreads before us. A country of such vast extent, with such varieties of soil and climate, with so much public spirit and private enterprise, with a population increasing so much beyond former example, with capacities of improvement not only unapplied or unexhausted, but even, in a great measure, as yet unexplored,—so free in its institutions, so mild in its laws, so secure in the title it confers on every man to his own acquisitions,—needs nothing but time and peace to carry it forward to almost any point of advancement.

In the next place, I take it for granted that the policy of this country, springing from the nature of our government and the spirit of all our institutions, is, so far as it respects the interesting questions which agitate the present age, on the side of liberal and enlightened sentiments. The age is extraordinary; the spirit that actuates it is peculiar and marked; and our own relation to the times we live in, and to the questions which interest them, is equally marked and peculiar. We are placed, by our good fortune and the wisdom and valor of our ancestors, in a condition in which we *can* act no obscure part. Be it for honor, or be it for dishonor, whatever we do is sure to attract the observation of the world. As one of the free states among the nations, as a great and rapidly rising republic, it would be impossible for us, if we were so disposed, to prevent our principles, our sentiments, and our example from producing some effect upon the opinions and hopes of society throughout the civilized world. It rests probably with ourselves to determine whether the influence of these shall be salutary or pernicious.

It cannot be denied that the great political question of this age is that between absolute and regulated governments. The substance of the controversy is whether society shall have any part in its own government. Whether the form of government shall be that of limited monarchy, with more or less mixture of hereditary power, or wholly elective or representative, may perhaps be considered as subordinate. The main controversy is between that absolute rule, which, while it promises to govern well, means, nevertheless, to govern without control, and that constitutional system which restrains sovereign discretion, and asserts that society may claim as matter of right some effective power in the establishment of the laws which are to regulate it. The spirit of the times sets with a most powerful current in favor of these last-mentioned opinions. It is opposed, however, whenever and wherever it shows itself, by certain of the great potentates of Europe; and it is opposed on grounds as applicable in one civilized nation as in another, and which would justify such opposition in relation to the United States, as well as in relation to any other state or nation, if time and circumstances should render such opposition expedient.

What part it becomes this country to take on a question of this sort, so far as it is called upon to take any part, cannot be doubtful. Our side of this question is settled for us, even without our own volition. Our history, our situation, our character, necessarily decide our position and our course, before we have even time to ask whether we have an option. Our place is on the side of free institutions. From the earliest settlement of these States, their inhabitants were accustomed, in a greater or less degree, to the enjoyment of the powers of self-government; and for the last half-century they have sustained systems of government entirely representative, yielding to themselves the greatest possible prosperity, and not leaving them without distinction and respect among the nations of the earth. This system we are not likely to abandon; and while we shall no farther recommend its adoption to other nations, in whole or in part, than it may recommend itself by its visible influence on our own growth and prosperity, we are, nevertheless, interested to resist the establishment of doctrines which deny the legality of its foundations. We stand as an equal among nations, claiming the full benefit of the established international law; and it is our duty to oppose, from the earliest to the latest moment, any innovations upon that code which shall bring into doubt or question our own equal and independent rights.

I will now, Mr. Chairman, advert to those pretensions put forth by the allied sovereigns of Continental Europe, which seem to me calculated, if unresisted, to bring into disrepute the principles of our government, and, indeed, to be wholly incompatible with any degree of national independence. I do not introduce these considerations for the sake of topics. I am not about to declaim against crowned heads, nor to quarrel with any country for preferring a form of government different from our own. The right of choice that we exercise for ourselves, I am quite willing to leave also to others. But it appears to me that the pretensions to which I have alluded are wholly inconsistent with the independence of nations generally, without regard to the question whether their governments be absolute, monarchical and limited, or purely popular and representative. I have a most deep and thorough conviction, that a new era has arisen in the world, that new and dangerous combinations are taking place, promulgating doctrines and fraught with consequences wholly subversive in their tendency of the public law of nations and of the general liberties of mankind. Whether this be so, or not, is the question which I now propose to examine, upon such grounds of information as are afforded by the common and public means of knowledge.

Everybody knows that, since the final restoration of the Bourbons to the throne of France, the Continental powers have entered into sundry alliances, which have been made public, and have held several meetings or congresses, at which the principles of their political conduct have been declared. These things must necessarily have an effect upon the international law of the states of the world. If that effect be good, and according to the principles of that law, they deserve to be applauded. If, on the contrary, their effect and tendency be most dangerous, their principles wholly inadmissible, their pretensions such as would abolish every degree of national independence, then they are to be resisted.

I begin, Mr. Chairman, by drawing your attention to the treaty concluded at Paris in September, 1815, between Russia, Prussia, and Austria, commonly called the Holy Alliance. This singular alliance appears to have originated with the Emperor of Russia; for we are informed that a draft of it was exhibited by him, personally, to a plenipotentiary of one of the great powers of Europe, before it was presented to the other sovereigns who ultimately signed it.* This instrument professes nothing, certainly, which is not extremely commendable and praiseworthy. It promises only that the contracting parties, both in relation to other states, and in regard to their own subjects, will observe the rules of justice and Christianity. In confirmation of these promises, it makes the most solemn and devout religious invocations. Now, although such an alliance is a novelty in European history, the world seems to have received this treaty, upon its first promulgation, with general charity. It was commonly understood as little or nothing more than an expression of thanks for the successful termination of the momentous contest in which those sovereigns had been engaged. It still seems somewhat unaccountable, however, that these good resolutions should require to be confirmed by treaty. Who doubted that these august sovereigns would treat each other with justice, and rule their own subjects in mercy? And what necessity was there for a solemn stipulation by treaty, to insure the performance of that which is no more than the ordinary duty of every government? It would hardly be admitted by these sovereigns, that by this compact they consider themselves bound to introduce an entire change, or any change, in the course of their own conduct. Nothing substantially new, certainly, can be supposed to have been intended. What principle, or what practice, therefore, called for this solemn declaration of the intention of the parties to observe the rules of religion and justice?

It is not a little remarkable, that a writer of reputation upon the Public Law, described, many years ago, not inaccurately, the character of this alliance. I allude to Puffendorf. "It seems useless," says he, "to frame any pacts or leagues, barely for the defense and support of universal peace; for by such a league nothing is superadded to the obligation of natural law, and no agreement is made for the performance of anything which the parties were not previously bound to perform; nor is the original obligation rendered firmer or stronger by such an addition. Men of any tolerable culture and civilization might well be ashamed of entering into any such compact, the conditions of which imply only that the parties concerned shall not offend in any clear point of

* See Lord Castlereagh's speech in the House of Commons, February 3, 1816. Debates in Parliament, Vol. XXXVI. p. 355; where also the treaty may be found at length.

duty. Besides, we should be guilty of great irreverence towards God, should we suppose that his injunctions had not already laid a sufficient obligation upon us to act justly, unless we ourselves voluntarily consented to the same engagement; as if our obligation to obey his will depended upon our own pleasure.

"If one engage to serve another, he does not set it down expressly and particularly among the terms and conditions of the bargain, that he will not betray nor murder him, nor pillage nor burn his house. For the same reason, that would be a dishonorable engagement, in which men should bind themselves to act properly and decently, and not break the peace." *

Such were the sentiments of that eminent writer. How nearly he had anticipated the case of the Holy Alliance will appear from the preamble to that alliance. After stating that the allied sovereigns had become persuaded, by the events of the last three years, that "their relations with each other ought to be regulated exclusively by the sublime truths taught by the eternal religion of God the Saviour," they solemnly declare their fixed resolution "to adopt as the sole rule of their conduct, both in the administration of their respective states, and in their political relations with every other government, the precepts of that holy religion, namely, the precepts of justice, charity, and peace, which, far from being applicable to private life alone, ought, on the contrary, to have a direct influence upon the counsels of princes, and guide all their steps, as being the only means of consolidating human institutions, and remedying their imperfections." †

This measure, however, appears principally important, as it was the first of a series, and was followed afterwards by others of a more marked and practical nature. These measures, taken together, profess to establish two principles, which the Allied Powers would introduce as a part of the law of the civilized world; and the establishment of which is to be enforced by a million and a half of bayonets.

The first of these principles is, that all popular or constitutional rights are held no otherwise than as grants from the crown. Society, upon this principle, has no rights of its own; it takes good government, when it gets it, as a boon and a concession,

* Law of Nature and Nations, Book II. cap. 2, § 11.
† Martens, Recueil des Traités, Tome XIII. p. 656.

but can demand nothing. It is to live by that favor which emanates from royal authority, and if it have the misfortune to lose that favor, there is nothing to protect it against any degree of injustice and oppression. It can rightfully make no endeavor for a change, by itself; its whole privilege is to receive the favors that may be dispensed by the sovereign power, and all its duty is described in the single word *submission*. This is the plain result of the principal Continental state papers; indeed, it is nearly the identical text of some of them.

The circular despatch addressed by the sovereigns assembled at Laybach, in the spring of 1821, to their ministers at foreign courts, alleges, "that useful and necessary changes in legislation and in the administration of states ought only to emanate from the free will and intelligent and well-weighed conviction of those whom God has rendered responsible for power. All that deviates from this line necessarily leads to disorder, commotions, and evils far more insufferable than those which they pretend to remedy." * Now, Sir, this principle would carry Europe back again, at once, into the middle of the Dark Ages. It is the old doctrine of the Divine right of kings, advanced now by new advocates, and sustained by a formidable array of power. That the people hold their fundamental privileges as matter of concession or indulgence from the sovereign power, is a sentiment not easy to be diffused in this age, any farther than it is enforced by the direct operation of military means. It is true, certainly, that some six centuries ago the early founders of English liberty called the instrument which secured their rights a *charter*. It was, indeed, a concession; they had obtained it sword in hand from the king; and in many other cases, whatever was obtained, favorable to human rights, from the tyranny and despotism of the feudal sovereigns, was called by the names of *privileges* and *liberties,* as being matter of special favor. Though we retain this language at the present time, the principle itself belongs to ages that have long passed by us. The civilized world has done with "the enormous faith, of many made for one." Society asserts its own rights, and alleges them to be original, sacred, and unalienable. It is not satisfied with having kind masters; it demands a participation in its own government; and in states much advanced in civilization,

* Annual Register for 1821, p. 601.

it urges this demand with a constancy and an energy that cannot well nor long be resisted. There are, happily, enough of regulated governments in the world, and those among the most distinguished, to operate as constant examples, and to keep alive an unceasing panting in the bosoms of men for the enjoyment of similar free institutions.

When the English Revolution of 1688 took place, the English people did not content themselves with the example of Runnymede; they did not build their hopes upon royal charters; they did not, like the authors of the Laybach circular, suppose that all useful changes in constitutions and laws must proceed from those only whom God has rendered responsible for power. They were somewhat better instructed in the principles of civil liberty, or at least they were better lovers of those principles than the sovereigns of Laybach. Instead of petitioning for charters, they declared their rights, and while they offered to the Prince of Orange the crown with one hand, they held in the other an enumeration of those privileges which they did not profess to hold as favors, but which they demanded and insisted upon as their undoubted rights.

I need not stop to observe, Mr. Chairman, how totally hostile are these doctrines of Laybach to the fundamental principles of our government. They are in direct contradiction; the principles of good and evil are hardly more opposite. If these principles of the sovereigns be true, we are but in a state of rebellion or of anarchy, and are only tolerated among civilized states because it has not yet been convenient to reduce us to the true standard.

But the second, and, if possible, the still more objectionable principle, avowed in these papers, is the right of forcible interference in the affairs of other states. A right to control nations in their desire to change their own government, wherever it may be conjectured, or pretended, that such change might furnish an example to the subjects of other states, is plainly and distinctly asserted. The same Congress that made the declaration at Laybach had declared, before its removal from Troppau, "that the powers have an undoubted right to take a hostile attitude in regard to those states in which the overthrow of the government may operate as an example."

There cannot, as I think, be conceived a more flagrant viola-

tion of public law, or national independence, than is contained
in this short declaration.

No matter what be the character of the government resisted;
no matter with what weight the foot of the oppressor bears on
the neck of the oppressed; if he struggle, or if he complain, he
sets a dangerous example of resistance,—and from that moment
he becomes an object of hostility to the most powerful potentates
of the earth. I want words to express my abhorrence of this abominable principle. I trust every enlightened man throughout the
world will oppose it, and that, especially, those who, like ourselves, are fortunately out of the reach of the bayonets that enforce it, will proclaim their detestation of it, in a tone both loud
and decisive. The avowed object of such declarations is to preserve the peace of the world. But by what means is it proposed to
preserve this peace? Simply, by bringing the power of all governments to bear against all subjects. Here is to be established a sort
of double, or treble, or quadruple, or, for aught I know, quin-
tuple allegiance. An offense against one king is to be an offense
against all kings, and the power of all is to be put forth for the
punishment of the offender. A right to interfere in extreme cases,
in the case of contiguous states, and where imminent danger is
threatened to one by what is occurring in another, is not without
precedent in modern times, upon what has been called the law
of vicinage; and when confined to extreme cases, and limited to
a certain extent, it may perhaps be defended upon principles of
necessity and self-defense. But to maintain that sovereigns may
go to war upon the subjects of another state to repress an example, is monstrous indeed. What is to be the limit to such a principle, or to the practice growing out of it? What, in any case, but
sovereign pleasure, is to decide whether the example be good or
bad? And what, under the operation of such a rule, may be
thought of our example? Why are we not as fair objects for the
operation of the new principle, as any of those who may attempt
a reform of government on the other side of the Atlantic?

The ultimate effect of this alliance of sovereigns, for objects
personal to themselves, or respecting only the permanence of
their own power, must be the destruction of all just feeling, and
all natural sympathy, between those who exercise the power of
government and those who are subject to it. The old channels of

mutual regard and confidence are to be dried up, or cut off. Obedience can now be expected no longer than it is enforced. Instead of relying on the affections of the governed, sovereigns are to rely on the affections and friendship of other sovereigns. There are, in short, no longer to be nations. Princes and people are no longer to unite for interests common to them both. There is to be an end of all patriotism, as a distinct national feeling. Society is to be divided horizontally; all sovereigns above, and all subjects below; the former coalescing for their own security, and for the more certain subjection of the undistinguished multitude beneath. This, Sir, is no picture drawn by imagination. I have hardly used language stronger than that in which the authors of this new system have commented on their own work. M. de Chateaubriand, in his speech in the French Chamber of Deputies, in February last, declared that he had a conference with the Emperor of Russia at Verona, in which that august sovereign uttered sentiments which appeared to him so precious, that he immediately hastened home, and wrote them down while yet fresh in his recollection. "The Emperor declared," said he, "that there can no longer be such a thing as an English, French, Russian, Prussian, or Austrian policy; there is henceforth but one policy, which, for the safety of all, should be adopted both by people and kings. It was for me first to show myself convinced of the principles upon which I founded the alliance; an occasion offered itself,—the rising in Greece. Nothing certainly could occur more for my interests, for the interests of my people; nothing more acceptable to my country, than a religious war in Turkey. But I have thought I perceived in the troubles of the Morea the sign of revolution, and I have held back. Providence has not put under my command eight hundred thousand soldiers to satisfy my ambition, but to protect religion, morality, and justice, and to secure the prevalence of those principles of order on which human society rests. It may well be permitted, that kings may have public alliances to defend themselves against secret enemies."

These, Sir, are the words which the French minister thought so important that they deserved to be recorded; and I, too, Sir, am of the same opinion. But if it be true that there is hereafter to be neither a Russian policy, nor a Prussian policy, nor an

Austrian policy, nor a French policy, nor even, which yet I will not believe, an English policy, there will be, I trust in God, an American policy. If the authority of all these governments be hereafter to be mixed and blended, and to flow, in one augmented current of prerogative, over the face of Europe, sweeping away all resistance in its course, it will yet remain for us to secure our own happiness by the preservation of our own principles; which I hope we shall have the manliness to express on all proper occasions, and the spirit to defend in every extremity. The end and scope of this amalgamated policy are neither more nor less than this, to interfere, by force, for any government, against any people who may resist it. Be the state of the people what it may, they shall not rise; be the government what it will, it shall not be opposed.

The practical commentary has corresponded with the plain language of the text. Look at Spain, and at Greece. If men may not resist the Spanish Inquisition, and the Turkish scimitar, what is there to which humanity must not submit? Stronger cases can never arise. Is it not proper for us, at all times, is it not our duty, at this time, to come forth, and deny, and condemn, these monstrous principles? Where, but here, and in one other place, are they likely to be resisted? They are advanced with equal coolness and boldness; and they are supported by immense power. The timid will shrink and give way, and many of the brave may be compelled to yield to force. Human liberty may yet, perhaps, be obliged to repose its principal hopes on the intelligence and the vigor of the Saxon race. As far as depends on us, at least, I trust those hopes will not be disappointed; and that, to the extent which may consist with our own settled, pacific policy, our opinions and sentiments may be brought to act on the right side, and to the right end, on an occasion which is, in truth, nothing less than a momentous question between an intelligent age, full of knowledge, thirsting for improvement, and quickened by a thousand impulses, on one side, and the most arbitrary pretensions, sustained by unprecedented power, on the other.

This asserted right of forcible intervention in the affairs of other nations is in open violation of the public law of the world. Who has authorized these learned doctors of Troppau to establish new articles in this code? Whence are their diplomas? Is the whole world expected to acquiesce in principles which entirely subvert the independence of nations? On the basis of this independence has been reared the beautiful fabric of international law. On the principle of this independence, Europe has seen a family of nations flourishing within its limits, the small among the large, protected not always by power, but by a principle above power, by a sense of propriety and justice. On this principle, the great commonwealth of civilized states has been hitherto upheld. There have been occasional departures or violations, and always disastrous, as in the case of Poland; but, in general, the harmony of the system has been wonderfully preserved. In the production and preservation of this sense of justice, this predominating principle, the Christian religion has acted a main part. Christianity and civilization have labored together; it seems, indeed, to be a law of our human condition, that they can live and flourish only together. From their blended influence has arisen that delightful spectacle of the prevalence of reason and principle over power and interest, so well described by one who was an honor to the age;—

> "And sovereign Law, the state's collected will,
>   O'er thrones and globes elate,
> Sits empress,—crowning good, repressing ill:
>   Smit by her sacred frown,
> The fiend, Discretion, like a vapor, sinks,
>   And e'en the all-dazzling crown
> Hides his faint rays, and at her bidding shrinks."

But this vision is past. While the teachers of Laybach give the rule, there will be no law but the law of the strongest.

It may now be required of me to show what interest *we* have in resisting this new system. What is it to *us,* it may be asked, upon what principles, or what pretenses, the European governments assert a right of interfering in the affairs of their neighbors? The thunder, it may be said, rolls at a distance. The wide Atlantic is between us and danger; and, however others may suffer, *we* shall remain safe.

I think it is a sufficient answer to this to say, that we are one of the nations of the earth; that we have an interest, therefore, in the preservation of that system of national law and national intercourse which has heretofore subsisted, so beneficially for all. Our system of government, it should also be remembered, is, throughout, founded on principles utterly hostile to the new code; and if we remain undisturbed by its operation, we shall owe our security either to our situation or our spirit. The enterprising character of the age, our own active, commercial spirit, the great increase which has taken place in the intercourse among civilized and commercial states, have necessarily connected us with other nations, and given us a high concern in the preservation of those salutary principles upon which that intercourse is founded. We have as clear an interest in international law, as individuals have in the laws of society.

But apart from the soundness of the policy, on the ground of direct interest, we have, Sir, a duty connected with this subject, which I trust we are willing to perform. What do *we* not owe to the cause of civil and religious liberty? to the principle of lawful resistance? to the principle that society has a right to partake in its own government? As the leading republic of the world, living and breathing in these principles, and advanced, by their operation, with unequaled rapidity in our career, shall we give *our* consent to bring them into disrepute and disgrace? It is neither ostentation nor boasting to say, that there lies before this country, in immediate prospect, a great extent and height of power. We are borne along towards this, without effort, and not always even with a full knowledge of the rapidity of our own motion. Circumstances which never combined before have co-operated in our favor, and a mighty current is setting us forward which we could not resist even if we would, and which, while we would stop to make an observation, and take the sun, has set us, at the end of the operation, far in advance of the place where we commenced it. Does it not become us, then, is it not a duty imposed on us, to give our weight to the side of liberty and justice, to let mankind know that we are not tired of our own institutions, and to protest against the asserted power of altering at pleasure the law of the civilized world?

But whatever we do in this respect, it becomes us to do upon clear and consistent principles. There is an important topic in the message to which I have yet hardly alluded. I mean the rumored combination of the European Continental sovereigns against the newly established free states of South America. Whatever position this government may take on that subject, I trust it will be one which can be defended on known and acknowledged grounds of right. The near approach or the remote distance of danger may affect policy, but cannot change principle. The same reason that would authorize us to protest against unwarrantable combinations to interfere between Spain and her former colonies, would authorize us equally to protest, if the same combination were directed against the smallest state in Europe, although our duty to ourselves, our policy, and wisdom, might indicate very different courses as fit to be pursued by us in the two cases. We shall not, I trust, act upon the notion of dividing the world with the Holy Alliance, and complain of nothing done by them in their hemisphere if they will not interfere with ours. At least this would not be such a course of policy as I could recommend or support. We have not offended, and I hope we do not intend to offend, in regard to South America, against any principle of national independence or of public law. We have done nothing, we shall do nothing, that we need to hush up or to compromise by forbearing to express our sympathy for the cause of the Greeks, or our opinion of the course which other governments have adopted in regard to them.

It may, in the next place, be asked, perhaps, Supposing all this to be true, what can *we* do? Are we to go to war? Are we to interfere in the Greek cause, or any other European cause? Are we to endanger our pacific relations? No, certainly not. What, then, the question recurs, remains for us? If we will not endanger our own peace, if we will neither furnish armies nor navies to the cause which we think the just one, what is there within our power?

Sir, this reasoning mistakes the age. The time has been, indeed, when fleets, and armies, and subsidies, were the principal reliances even in the best cause. But, happily for mankind, a great change has taken place in this respect. Moral causes come into consideration, in proportion as the progress of knowledge is advanced; and the public opinion of the civilized world is rapidly gaining an ascendency over mere brutal force. It is already able to oppose the most formidable obstruction to the progress of injustice and oppression; and as it grows more intelligent and more intense, it will be more and more formidable. It may be silenced by military power, but it cannot be conquered. It is elastic, irrepressible, and invulnerable to the weapons of ordinary warfare. It is that impassible, unextinguishable enemy of mere violence and arbitrary rule, which, like Milton's angels,

> "Vital in every part, ...
> Cannot, but by annihilating, die."

Until this be propitiated or satisfied, it is vain for power to talk either of triumphs or of repose. No matter what fields are desolated, what fortresses surrendered, what armies subdued, or what provinces overrun. In the history of the year that has passed by us, and in the instance of unhappy Spain, we have seen the vanity of all triumphs in a cause which violates the general sense of justice of the civilized world. It is nothing that the troops of France have passed from the Pyrenees to Cadiz; it is nothing that an unhappy and prostrate nation has fallen before them; it is nothing that arrests, and confiscation, and execution, sweep away the little remnant of national resistance. There is an enemy that still exists to check the glory of these triumphs. It follows the conqueror back to the very scene of his ovations; it calls upon him to take notice that Europe, though silent, is yet indignant; it shows him that the scepter of his victory is a barren scepter; that it shall confer neither joy nor honor, but shall molder to dry ashes in his grasp. In the midst of his exultation, it pierces his ear with the cry of injured justice; it denounces against him the indignation of an enlightened and civilized age; it turns to bitterness the cup of his rejoicing, and wounds him with the sting which belongs to the consciousness of having outraged the opinion of mankind.

In my opinion, Sir, the Spanish nation is now nearer, not only in point of time, but in point of circumstance, to the acquisition of a regulated government, than at the moment of the French invasion. Nations must, no doubt, undergo these trials in their progress to the establishment of free institutions. The very trials benefit them, and render them more capable both of obtaining and of enjoying the object which they seek.

I shall not detain the committee, Sir, by laying before it any statistical, geographical, or commercial account of Greece. I have no knowledge on these subjects which is not common to all. It is universally admitted, that, within the last thirty or forty years, the condition of Greece has been greatly improved. Her marine is at present respectable, containing the best sailors in the Mediterranean, better even, in that sea, than our own, as more accustomed to the long quarantines and other regulations which prevail in its ports. The number of her seamen has been estimated as high as 50,000, but I suppose that estimate must be much too large. She has, probably, 150,000 tons of shipping. It is not easy to ascertain the amount of the Greek population. The Turkish government does not trouble itself with any of the calculations of political economy, and there has never been such a thing as an accurate census, probably, in any part of the Turkish empire. In the absence of all official information, private opinions widely differ. By the tables which have been communicated, it would seem that there are 2,400,000 Greeks in Greece proper and the islands; an amount, as I am inclined to think, somewhat overrated. There are, probably, in the whole of European Turkey, 5,000,000 Greeks, and 2,000,000 more in the Asiatic dominions of that power.

The moral and intellectual progress of this numerous population, under the horrible oppression which crushes it, has been such as may well excite regard. Slaves, under barbarous masters, the Greeks have still aspired after the blessings of knowledge and civilization. Before the breaking out of the present revolution, they had established schools, and colleges, and libraries, and the press. Wherever, as in Scio, owing to particular circumstances, the weight of oppression was mitigated, the natural vivacity of the Greeks, and their aptitude for the arts, were evinced. Though certainly not on an equality with the civilized and Christian states of Europe,—and how is it possible, under such oppression as they endured, that they should be?—they yet furnished a striking contrast with their Tartar masters. It has been well said that it is not easy to form a just conception of the nature of the despotism exercised over them. Conquest and subjugation, as known among European states, are inadequate modes of expression by which to denote the dominion of the Turks. A conquest in the civilized world is generally no more than an acquisition of a new dominion to the conquering country. It does not imply a never-ending bondage imposed upon the conquered, a perpetual mark, —an opprobrious distinction between them and their masters; a bitter and unending persecution of their religion; an habitual violation of their rights of person and property, and the unre-strained indulgence towards them of every passion which belongs to the character of a barbarous soldiery. Yet such is the state of Greece. The Ottoman power over them, obtained originally by the sword, is constantly preserved by the same means. Wherever it exists, it is a mere military power. The religious and civil code of the state being both fixed in the Koran, and equally the object of an ignorant and furious faith, have been found equally inca-pable of change. "The Turk," it has been said, "has been *en-camped* in Europe for four centuries." He has hardly any more participation in European manners, knowledge, and arts, than when he crossed the Bosphorus. But this is not the worst. The power of the empire is fallen into anarchy, and as the principle which belongs to the head belongs also to the parts, there are as many despots as there are pachas, beys, and viziers. Wars are almost perpetual between the Sultan and some rebellious gov-ernor of a province; and in the conflict of these despotisms, the people are necessarily ground between the upper and the nether millstones. In short, the Christian subjects of the Sublime Porte feel daily all the miseries which flow from despotism, from an-archy, from slavery, and from religious persecution. If anything yet remains to heighten such a picture, let it be added, that every office in the government is not only actually, but professedly, venal; the pachalics, the vizierates, the cadiships, and whatso-ever other denomination may denote the depositary of power. In the whole world, Sir, there is no such oppression felt as by the Christian Greeks. In various parts of India, to be sure, the government is bad enough; but then it is the government of bar-barians over barbarians, and the feeling of oppression is, of course, not so keen. There the oppressed are perhaps not better than their oppressors; but in the case of Greece, there are mil-lions of Christian men, not without knowledge, not without refinement, not without a strong thirst for all the pleasures of civilized life, trampled into the very earth, century after century, by a pillaging, savage, relentless soldiery. Sir, the case is unique.

There exists, and has existed, nothing like it. The world has no such misery to show; there is no case in which Christian communities can be called upon with such emphasis of appeal.

But I have said enough, Mr. Chairman, indeed I need have said nothing, to satisfy the House, that it must be some new combination of circumstances, or new views of policy in the cabinets of Europe, which have caused this interesting struggle not merely to be regarded with indifference, but to be marked with opprobrium. The very statement of the case, as a contest between the Turks and Greeks, sufficiently indicates what must be the feeling of every individual, and every government, that is not biased by a particular interest, or a particular feeling, to disregard the dictates of justice and humanity.

And now, Sir, what has been the conduct pursued by the Allied Powers in regard to this contest? When the revolution broke out, the sovereigns were assembled in congress at Laybach; and the papers of that assembly sufficiently manifest their sentiments. They proclaimed their abhorrence of those "criminal combinations which had been formed in the eastern parts of Europe"; and, although it is possible that this denunciation was aimed, more particularly, at the disturbances in the provinces of Wallachia and Moldavia, yet no exception is made, from its general terms, in favor of those events in Greece which were properly the commencement of her revolution, and which could not but be well known at Laybach, before the date of these declarations. Now, it must be remembered that Russia was a leading party in this denunciation of the efforts of the Greeks to achieve their liberation; and it cannot but be expected by Russia that the world should also remember what part she herself has heretofore acted in the same concern. It is notorious that within the last half-century she has again and again excited the Greeks to rebellion against the Porte, and that she has constantly kept alive in them the hope that she would, one day, by her own great power, break the yoke of their oppressor. Indeed, the earnest attention with which Russia has regarded Greece goes much farther back than to the time I have mentioned. Ivan the Third, in 1482, having espoused a Grecian princess, heiress of the last Greek Emperor, discarded St. George from the Russian arms, and adopted the Greek two-headed black eagle, which has continued in the

Russian arms to the present day. In virtue of the same marriage, the Russian princes claim the Greek throne as their inheritance.

Under Peter the Great, the policy of Russia developed itself more fully. In 1696, he rendered himself master of Azof, and in 1698, obtained the right to pass the Dardanelles, and to maintain, by that route, commercial intercourse with the Mediterranean. He had emissaries throughout Greece, and particularly applied himself to gain the clergy. He adopted the *Labarum* of Constantine, "In hoc signo vinces"; and medals were struck, with the inscription, "Petrus I. Russo-Græcorum Imperator." In whatever new direction the principles of the Holy Alliance may now lead the politics of Russia, or whatever course she may suppose Christianity now prescribes to her, in regard to the Greek cause, the time has been when she professed to be contending for that cause, as identified with Christianity. The white banner under which the soldiers of Peter the First usually fought, bore, as its inscription, "In the name of the Prince, and for our country." Relying on the aid of the Greeks, in his war with the Porte, he changed the white flag to red, and displayed on it the words, "In the name of God, and for Christianity." The unfortunate issue of this war is well known. Though Anne and Elizabeth, the successors of Peter, did not possess his active character, they kept up a constant communication with Greece, and held out hopes of restoring the Greek empire. Catharine the Second, as is well known, excited a general revolt in 1769. A Russian fleet appeared in the Mediterranean, and a Russian army was landed in the Morea. The Greeks in the end were disgusted at being expected to take an oath of allegiance to Russia, and the Empress was disgusted because they refused to take it. In 1774, peace was signed between Russia and the Porte, and the Greeks of the Morea were left to their fate. By this treaty the Porte acknowledged the independence of the khan of the Crimea; a preliminary step to the acquisition of that country by Russia. It is not unworthy of remark, as a circumstance which distinguished this from most other diplomatic transactions, that it conceded to the cabinet of St. Petersburg the right of intervention in the interior affairs of Turkey, in regard to whatever concerned the religion of the Greeks. The cruelties and massacres that happened to the Greeks after the peace between Russia and the Porte, notwithstanding the general pardon which had been stipulated for them, need not now be recited. Instead of retracing the deplorable picture, it is enough to say, that in this respect the past is justly reflected in the present. The Empress soon after invaded and conquered the Crimea, and on one of the gates of Kerson, its capital, caused to be inscribed, "The road to Byzantium." The present Emperor, on his accession to the throne, manifested an intention to adopt the policy of Catharine the Second as his own, and the world has not been right in all its suspicions, if a project for the partition of Turkey did not form a part of the negotiations of Napoleon and Alexander at Tilsit.

All this course of policy seems suddenly to be changed. Turkey is no longer regarded, it would appear, as an object of partition or acquisition, and Greek revolts have all at once become, according to the declaration of Laybach, "criminal combinations." The recent congress at Verona exceeded its predecessor at Laybach in its denunciations of the Greek struggle. In the circular of the 14th of December, 1822, it declared the Grecian resistance to the Turkish power to be rash and culpable, and lamented that "the firebrand of rebellion had been thrown into the Ottoman empire." This rebuke and crimination we know to have proceeded on those settled principles of conduct which the Continental powers had prescribed for themselves. The sovereigns saw, as well as others, the real condition of the Greeks; they knew as well as others that it was most natural and most justifiable, that they should endeavor, at whatever hazard, to change that condition. They knew that they themselves, or at least one of them, had more than once urged the Greeks to similar efforts; that they themselves had thrown the same firebrand into the midst of the Ottoman empire. And yet, so much does it seem to be their fixed object to discountenance whatsoever threatens to disturb the actual government of any country, that, Christians as they were, and allied, as they professed to be, for purposes most important to human happiness and religion, they have not hesitated to declare to the world that they have wholly forborne to exercise any compassion to the Greeks, simply because they thought that they saw, in the struggles of the Morea, the sign of revolution. This, then, is coming to a plain, practical result. The Grecian revolution has been discouraged, discountenanced, and denounced, solely because it *is* a revolution. Independent of all inquiry into the reasonableness of its causes or the enormity of the oppression which produced it; regardless of the peculiar claims which Greece possesses upon the civilized world; and regardless of what has been their own conduct towards her for a century; regardless of the interest of the Christian religion,—the sovereigns at Verona seized upon the case of the Greek revolution as one above all others calculated to illustrate the fixed principles of their policy. The abominable rule of the Porte on one side, the value and the sufferings of the Christian Greeks on the other, furnished a case likely to convince even an incredulous world of the sincerity of the professions of the Allied Powers. They embraced the occasion with apparent ardor; and the world, I trust, is satisfied.

We see here, Mr. Chairman, the direct and actual application of that system which I have attempted to describe. We see it in the very case of Greece. We learn, authentically and indisputably, that the Allied Powers, holding that all changes in legislation and administration ought to proceed from kings alone, were wholly inexorable to the sufferings of the Greeks, and entirely hostile to their success. Now it is upon this practical result of the principle of the Continental powers that I wish this House to intimate its opinion. The great question is a question of principle. Greece is only the signal instance of the application of that principle. If the principle be right, if we esteem it conformable to the law of nations, if we have nothing to say against it, or if we deem ourselves unfit to express an opinion on the subject, then, of course, no resolution ought to pass. If, on the other hand, we see in the declarations of the Allied Powers principles not only utterly hostile to our own free institutions, but hostile also to the independence of all nations, and altogether opposed to the improvement of the condition of human nature; if, in the instance before us, we see a most striking exposition and application of those principles, and if we deem our opinions to be entitled to any weight in the estimation of mankind,—then I think it is our duty to adopt some such measure as the proposed resolution.

It is worthy of observation, Sir, that as early as July, 1821, Baron Strogonoff, the Russian minister at Constantinople, represented to the Porte, that, if the undistinguished massacres of the Greeks, both of such as were in open resistance and of those who remained patient in their submission were continued, and should become a settled habit, they would give just cause of war against the Porte to all Christian states. This was in 1821. It was followed, early in the next year, by that indescribable enormity, that appalling monument of barbarian cruelty, the destruction of Scio; a scene I shall not attempt to describe; a scene from which human nature shrinks shuddering away; a scene having hardly a parallel in the history of fallen man. This scene, too, was quickly followed by the massacres in Cyprus; and all these things were perfectly known to the Christian powers assembled at Verona. Yet these powers, instead of acting upon the case supposed by Baron Strogonoff, and which one would think had been then fully made out,—instead of being moved by any compassion for the sufferings of the Greeks,—these powers, these Christian powers, rebuke their gallantry and insult their sufferings by accusing them of "throwing a firebrand into the Ottoman empire." Such, Sir, appear to me to be the principles on which the Continental powers of Europe have agreed hereafter to act; and this, an eminent instance of the application of those principles.

I shall not detain the committee, Mr. Chairman, by any attempt to recite the events of the Greek struggle up to the present time. Its origin may be found, doubtless, in that improved state of knowledge which, for some years, has been gradually taking place in that country. The emancipation of the Greeks has been a subject frequently discussed in modern times. They themselves are represented as having a vivid remembrance of the distinction of their ancestors, not unmixed with an indignant feeling that civilized and Christian Europe should not ere now have aided them in breaking their intolerable fetters.

In 1816 a society was founded in Vienna for the encouragement of Grecian literature. It was connected with a similar institution at Athens, and another in Thessaly, called the "Gymnasium of Mount Pelion." The treasury and general office of the institution were established at Munich. No political object was avowed by these institutions, probably none contemplated. Still, however, they had their effect, no doubt, in hastening that condition of things in which the Greeks felt competent to the establishment of their independence. Many young men have been for years annually sent to the universities in the western states of

Europe for their education; and, after the general pacification of Europe, many military men, discharged from other employment, were ready to enter even into so unpromising a service as that of the revolutionary Greeks.

In 1820, war commenced between the Porte and Ali, the well-known Pacha of Albania. Differences existed also with Persia and with Russia. In this state of things, at the beginning of 1821, an insurrection broke out in Moldavia, under the direction of Alexander Ypsilanti, a well-educated soldier, who had been major-general in the Russian service. From his character, and the number of those who seemed inclined to join him, he was supposed to be countenanced by the court of St. Petersburg. This, however, was a great mistake, which the Emperor, then at Laybach, took an early opportunity to rectify. The Turkish government was alarmed at these occurrences in the northern provinces of European Turkey, and caused search to be made of all vessels entering the Black Sea, lest arms or other military means should be sent in that manner to the insurgents. This proved inconvenient to the commerce of Russia, and caused some unsatisfactory correspondence between the two powers. It may be worthy of remark, as an exhibition of national character, that, agitated by these appearances of intestine commotion, the Sultan issued a proclamation, calling on all true Mussulmans to renounce the pleasures of social life, to prepare arms and horses, and to return to the manner of their ancestors, the life of the plains. The Turk seems to have thought that he had, at last, caught something of the dangerous contagion of European civilization, and that it was necessary to reform his habits, by recurring to the original manners of military roving barbarians.

It was about this time, that is to say, at the commencement of 1821, that the revolution burst out in various parts of Greece and the isles. Circumstances, certainly, were not unfavorable to the movement, as one portion of the Turkish army was employed in the war against Ali Pacha in Albania, and another part in the provinces north of the Danube. The Greeks soon possessed themselves of the open country of the Morea, and drove their enemy into the fortresses. Of these, that of Tripolitza, with the city, fell into their hands, in the course of the summer. Having after these first movements obtained time to breathe, it became, of course, an early object to establish a government. For this purpose delegates of the people assembled, under that name which describes the assembly in which we ourselves sit, that name which "freed the Atlantic," a *Congress.* A writer, who undertakes to render to the civilized world that service which was once performed by Edmund Burke, I mean the compiler of the English Annual Register, asks, by what authority this assembly could call itself a Congress. Simply, Sir, by the same authority by which the people of the United States have given the same name to their own legislature. We, at least, should be naturally inclined to think, not only as far as names, but things also, are concerned, that the Greeks could hardly have begun their revolution under better auspices; since they have endeavored to render applicable to themselves the general principles of our form of government, as well as its name. This constitution went into operation at the commencement of the next year. In the meantime, the war with Ali Pacha was ended, he having surrendered, and being afterwards assassinated, by an instance of treachery and perfidy, which, if it had happened elsewhere than under the government of the Turks, would have deserved notice. The negotiation with Russia, too, took a turn unfavorable to the Greeks. The great point upon which Russia insisted, beside the abandonment of the measure of searching vessels bound to the Black Sea, was, that the Porte should withdraw its armies from the neighborhood of the Russian frontiers; and the immediate consequence of this, when effected, was to add so much more to the disposable force ready to be employed against the Greeks. These events seemed to have left the whole force of the Ottoman empire, at the commencement of 1822, in a condition to be employed against the Greek rebellion; and, accordingly, very many anticipated the immediate destruction of the cause. The event, however, was ordered otherwise. Where the greatest effort was made, it was met and defeated. Entering the Morea with an army which seemed capable of bearing down all resistance, the Turks were nevertheless defeated and driven back, and pursued beyond the isthmus, within which, as far as it appears, from that time to the present, they have not been able to set their foot.

It was in April of this year that the destruction of Scio took place. That island, a sort of appanage of the Sultana mother, enjoyed many privileges peculiar to itself. In a population of 130,000 or 140,000, it had no more than 2,000 or 3,000 Turks; indeed, by some accounts, not near as many. The absence of these ruffian masters had in some degree allowed opportunity for the promotion of knowledge, the accumulation of wealth, and the general cultivation of society. Here was the seat of modern Greek literature; here were libraries, printing-presses, and other establishments, which indicate some advancement in refinement and knowledge. Certain of the inhabitants of Samos, it would seem, envious of this comparative happiness of Scio, landed upon the island in an irregular multitude, for the purpose of compelling its inhabitants to make common cause with their countrymen against their oppressors. These, being joined by the peasantry, marched to the city and drove the Turks into the castle. The Turkish fleet, lately reinforced from Egypt, happened to be in the neighboring seas, and, learning these events, landed a force on the island of fifteen thousand men. There was nothing to resist such an army. These troops immediately entered the city and began an indiscriminate massacre. The city was fired; and in four days the fire and sword of the Turk rendered the beautiful Scio a clotted mass of blood and ashes. The details are too shocking to be recited. Forty thousand women and children, unhappily saved from the general destruction, were afterwards sold in the market of Smyrna, and sent off into distant and hopeless servitude. Even on the wharves of our own cities, it has been said, have been sold the utensils of those hearths which now exist no longer. Of the whole population which I have mentioned, not above nine hundred persons were left living upon the island. I will only repeat, Sir, that these tragical scenes were as fully known at the Congress of Verona, as they are now known to us; and it is not too much to call on the powers that constituted that congress, in the name of conscience and in the name of humanity, to tell us if there be nothing even in these unparalleled excesses of Turkish barbarity to excite a sentiment of compassion; nothing which they regard as so objectionable as even the very idea of popular resistance to power.

The events of the year which has just passed by, as far as they have become known to us, have been even more favorable to the Greeks than those of the year preceding. I omit all details, as being as well known to others as to myself. Suffice it to say, that with no other enemy to contend with, and no diversion of his force to other objects, the Porte has not been able to carry the war into the Morea; and that, by the last accounts, its armies were acting defensively in Thessaly. I pass over, also, the naval engagements of the Greeks, although that is a mode of warfare in which they are calculated to excel, and in which they have already performed actions of such distinguished skill and bravery, as would draw applause upon the best mariners in the world. The present state of the war would seem to be, that the Greeks possess the whole of the Morea, with the exception of the three fortresses of Patras, Coron, and Modon; all Candia, but one fortress; and most of the other islands. They possess the citadel of Athens, Missolonghi, and several other places in Livadia. They have been able to act on the offensive, and to carry the war beyond the isthmus. There is no reason to believe their marine is weakened; more probably, it is strengthened. But, what is most important of all, they have obtained time and experience. They have awakened a sympathy throughout Europe and throughout America; and they have formed a government which seems suited to the emergency of their condition.

Sir, they have done much. It would be great injustice to compare their achievements with our own. We began our Revolution, already possessed of government, and, comparatively, of civil liberty. Our ancestors had from the first been accustomed in a great measure to govern themselves. They were familiar with popular elections and legislative assemblies, and well acquainted with the general principles and practice of free governments. They had little else to do than to throw off the paramount authority of the parent state. Enough was still left, both of law and of organization, to conduct society in its accustomed course, and to unite men together for a common object. The Greeks, of course, could act with little concert at the beginning; they were unaccustomed to the exercise of power, without experience, with limited knowledge, without aid, and surrounded by nations which, whatever claims the Greeks might seem to have upon them, have afforded them nothing but discouragement and reproach. They have held out, however, for three campaigns; and that, at least, is something. Constantinople and the northern provinces have sent forth thousands of troops;—they have been defeated. Tripoli, and Algiers, and Egypt, have contributed their marine contingents;—they have not kept the ocean. Hordes of Tartars have crossed the Bosphorus;—they have died where the Persians died. The powerful monarchies in the neighborhood have denounced their cause, and admonished them to abandon it and submit to their fate. They have answered them, that, although two hundred thousand of their countrymen have offered up their lives, there yet remain lives to offer; and that it is the determination of *all*, "yes, of ALL," to persevere until they shall have established their liberty, or until the power of their oppressors shall have relieved them from the burden of existence.

It may now be asked, perhaps, whether the expression of our own sympathy, and that of the country, may do them good? I hope it may. It may give them courage and spirit, it may assure them of public regard, teach them that they are not wholly forgotten by the civilized world, and inspire them with constancy in the pursuit of their great end. At any rate, Sir, it appears to me that the measure which I have proposed is due to our own character, and called for by our own duty. When we shall have discharged that duty, we may leave the rest to the disposition of Providence.

I do not see how it can be doubted that this measure is entirely *pacific*. I profess my inability to perceive that it has any possible tendency to involve our neutral relations. If the resolution pass, it is not of necessity to be immediately acted on. It will not be acted on at all, unless, in the opinion of the President, a proper and safe occasion for acting upon it shall arise. If we adopt the resolution today, our relations with every foreign state will be tomorrow precisely what they now are. The resolution will be sufficient to express our sentiments on the subjects to which I have adverted. Useful for that purpose, it can be mischievous for no purpose. If the topic were properly introduced into the message, it cannot be improperly introduced into discussion in this House. If it were proper, which no one doubts, for the President to express his opinions upon it, it cannot, I think, be improper for us to express ours. The only certain effect of this resolution is to signify, in a form usual in bodies constituted like this, our approbation of the general sentiment of the message. Do we wish to withhold that approbation? The resolution confers on the President no new power, nor does it enjoin on him the exercise of any new duty; nor does it hasten him in the discharge of any existing duty.

I cannot imagine that this resolution can add anything to those excitements which it has been supposed, I think very causelessly, might possibly provoke the Turkish government to acts of hostility. There is already the message, expressing the hope of success to the Greeks and disaster to the Turks, in a much stronger manner than is to be implied from the terms of this resolution. There is the correspondence between the Secretary of State and the Greek Agent in London, already made public, in which similar wishes are expressed, and a continuance of the correspondence apparently invited. I might add to this, the unexampled burst of feeling which this cause has called forth from all classes of society, and the notorious fact of pecuniary contributions made throughout the country for its aid and advancement. After all this, whoever can see cause of danger to our pacific relations from the adoption of this resolution has a keener vision than I can pretend to. Sir, there is no augmented danger; there is no danger. The question comes at last to this, whether, on a subject of this sort, this House holds an opinion which is worthy to be expressed.

Even suppose, Sir, an agent or commissioner were to be immediately sent,—a measure which I myself believe to be the proper one,—there is no breach of neutrality, nor any just cause of offense. Such an agent, of course, would not be accredited; he would not be a public minister. The object would be inquiry and information; inquiry which we have a right to make, information which we are interested to possess. If a dismemberment of the Turkish empire be taking place, or has already taken place; if a new state be rising, or be already risen, in the Mediterranean,—who can doubt, that, without any breach of neutrality, we may inform ourselves of these events for the government of our own concerns? The Greeks have declared the Turkish coasts in a state of blockade; may we not inform ourselves whether this blockade be *nominal* or *real?* and, of course, whether it shall be regarded or disregarded? The greater our trade may happen to be with Smyrna, a consideration which seems to have alarmed some gentlemen, the greater is the reason, in my opinion, why we should seek to be accurately informed of those events which may affect its safety. It seems to me impossible, therefore, for any reasonable man to imagine that this resolution can expose us to the resentment of the Sublime Porte.

As little reason is there for fearing its consequences upon the conduct of the Allied Powers. They may, very naturally, dislike our sentiments upon the subject of the Greek revolution; but what those sentiments are they will much more explicitly learn in the President's message than in this resolution. They might, indeed, prefer that we should express no dissent from the doctrines which they have avowed, and the application which they have made of those doctrines to the case of Greece. But I trust we are not disposed to leave them in any doubt as to our sentiments upon these important subjects. They have expressed their opinions, and do not call that expression of opinion an interference; in which respect they are right, as the expression of opinion in such cases is not such an interference as would justify the Greeks in considering the powers at war with them. For the same reason, any expression which we may make of different principles and different sympathies is no interference. No one would call the President's message an interference; and yet it is much stronger in that respect than this resolution. If either of them could be construed to be an interference, no doubt it would be improper, at least it would be so according to my view of the subject; for the very thing which I have attempted to resist in the course of these observations is the right of foreign interference. But neither the message nor the resolution has that character. There is not a power in Europe which can suppose, that, in expressing our opinions on this occasion, we are governed by any desire of aggrandizing ourselves or of injuring others. We do no more than to maintain those established principles in which we have an interest in common with other nations, and to resist the introduction of new principles and new rules, calculated to destroy the relative independence of states, and particularly hostile to the whole fabric of our government.

I close, then, Sir, with repeating, that the object of this resolution is to avail ourselves of the interesting occasion of the Greek revolution to make our protest against the doctrines of

the Allied Powers, both as they are laid down in principle and
as they are applied in practice. I think it right, too, Sir, not to
be unseasonable in the expression of our regard, and, as far as
that goes, in a manifestation of our sympathy with a long oppressed and now struggling people. I am not of those who would,
in the hour of utmost peril, withhold such encouragement as
might be properly and lawfully given, and, when the crisis should
be past, overwhelm the rescued sufferer with kindness and ca-
resses. The Greeks address the civilized world with a pathos not
easy to be resisted. They invoke our favor by more moving considerations than can well belong to the condition of any other
people. They stretch out their arms to the Christian communities
of the earth, beseeching them, by a generous recollection of their
ancestors, by the consideration of their desolated and ruined
cities and villages, by their wives and children sold into an accursed slavery, by their blood, which they seem willing to pour
out like water, by the common faith, and in the name, which
unites all Christians, that they would extend to them at least
some token of compassionate regard.

Francis Lieber
(1800-1872)

IN THE first century of America's national growth the country profited, as it still does, by offering an asylum to European intellectuals whose liberalism brought them into difficulties in their own lands. So it was with Francis Lieber, brilliant political philosopher who contributed richly to American culture. He was born in Berlin, wounded at Waterloo when a boy of fifteen, educated at Jena, and twice imprisoned in Germany for the liberal principles that had led him to fight for Greek independence against the Turks (see p. 139). He came to the United States in 1827 and within six years had won fame for his achievement in originating and publishing the thirteen-volume *Encyclopaedia Americana.* While serving as professor of history and political economy at South Carolina College from 1835 to 1856, he wrote *A Manual of Political Ethics* (1838) and *On Civil Liberty and Self-Government.* In 1857 he became professor first of history and later of law at Columbia University. During the American Civil War he prepared for the Union government a widely used *Code for the Government of Armies.* In these and many other ways Lieber repaid the land of his adoption for providing a refuge for him in his young manhood.

Francis Lieber's logical, closely reasoned, and clearly written treatise *On Civil Liberty and Self-Government* was the first systematic work on political science to be published in the United States. The selection reprinted here is a chapter taken from his revised edition of this work made in 1859.

In What Civil Liberty Consists, Proved by Contraries (1859)

I have endeavored to give a sketch of Anglican liberty. It is the liberty we prize and love for a hundred reasons, and which we would love if there were no other reason than that it *is* liberty. We know that it is the political state most befitting to conscious man. History as well as our own pregnant times proves to us the value of those guarantees, their necessity if we wish to see our political dignity secure, and their effect upon the stability of government, as well as on the energies of the people. We are proud of our self-government and our love of the law as our master, and we cling the faster to all these ancient and modern guarantees, the more we observe that, wherever the task which men have proposed to themselves is the suppression of liberty, these guarantees are sure to be the first objects of determined and persevering attack. It is instructive for the friend of freedom to observe how uniformly and instinctively the despots of all ages and countries have assailed the different guarantees enumerated in the preceding pages. We can learn much in all practical matters by the rule of contraries. As the arithmetician proves his multiplication by division, and his subtraction by addition, so may we learn what those who love liberty ought to prize, by observing what those who hate freedom suppress or war against. This process is made peculiarly easy as well as interesting at this very period, when the government of a large nation is avowedly engaged in suppressing all liberty and in establishing the most uncompromising monarchical absolutism.

I do not know a single guarantee contained in the foregoing pages, which might not be accompanied by a long historical commentary showing how necessary it is, from the fact that it has been attacked by those who are plainly and universally acknowledged as having oppressed liberty or as having been at least guilty of the inchoate crime. It is a useful way to turn the study of history to account, especially for the youth of free nations. It turns their general ardor to distinct realities, and furnishes the student with confirmations by facts. We ought always to remember that one of the most efficient modes of learning the healthful state of our body and the normal operation of its various organs consists in the study of their diseased states and abnormal conditions. The pathologic method is an indispensable one in all philosophy and in politics. The imperial time of Rome is as replete with pathetic lessons for the statesman as the republican epoch.

It would lead me far beyond the proper limits of this work, were I to select all the most noted periods of usurpation, or those times in which absolutism, whether monarchical or democratic, has assumed the sway over liberty, and thus to try the gauge of our guarantees. It may be well, however, to select a few instances.

In doing so I shall restrict myself to instances taken from the transactions of modern nations of our own race; but the student will do well to compare the bulk of our liberty with the characteristics of ancient and modern despotism in Asia, and see how the absence of our safeguards has there always prevented the development of humanity which we prize so highly. He ought then to compare this our own modern liberty with what is more particularly called antiquity, and see in what we excel the ancients or fall behind them, and in what that which they revered as liberty differed from ours. He ought to keep in mind our guarantees in reading the history of former free states, and of the processes by which they lost their liberty, or of the means to which the enemies of liberty have resorted, from those so masterly delineated by Aristotle, down to Dr. Francia and those of the present time, and he ought again to compare our broadcast national liberty with the liberties of the feudal age. He ought, lastly, to present clearly to his mind the psychologic processes by which liberty has been lost—by gratitude, hero-worship, impatience, indolence, permitting great personal popularity to overshadow institutions and laws, hatred against opposite parties or classes, denial of proper power to government, the arrogation of more and more power, and the gradual transition into absolutism; by local jealousies, by love of glory and conquest, by passing unwise laws against a magnified and irritating evil—laws which afterwards serve to oppress all, by recoiling oppression of a part, by poverty and by worthless use of wealth, by sensuality and that indifference which always follows in its train.

Liberty of communion is one of the first requisites of freedom. Wherever, therefore, a government struggles against liberty, this communion forms a subject of peculiar attention. Not only is liberty of the press abolished, but all communion is watched over by the power-holder, or suppressed as far as possible. The spy, the mouchard, the delator, the informer, the sycophant, are sure accompaniments of absolutism. The British administration under Charles II and James II looked with a jealous eye on the "coffee-houses," and occasionally suppressed them. One of the first things done by the French minister of police, after the second of December, was to close a number of "cabarets" in Paris, and to put all France under surveillance. This may become necessary for a time under pressing circumstances, which may place a government in the position of a general in a beleaguered city, but it is not liberty; it is the contrary, and if the measure is adopted as a permanent one it becomes sheer despotism. So soon as Louis Napoleon had placed himself at the head of an absolute government, he not only abolished the liberty of the press, but he went much farther, as we have seen; he placed the printing-presses themselves and the sale of type under the police, and ordered that no press with the necessary printing materials should be sold or change hands without previous information being given to the police.

While it is a characteristic of our liberty that the public funds are under the peculiar guardianship of the popular house of the legislature, and that short appropriations are made for distinct purposes, especially for the army and navy, all governments hostile to liberty endeavor to rule without appropriations, or, if this is not feasible, by having the appropriations made for a long term and not for detailed purposes. The last decree of Napoleon III, relating to this subject, is that the legislative corps must vote the budget of each department *en bloc,* that is, in a lump, and either wholly reject or adopt it, without amendment. English history furnishes a long commentary on this point of appropriations. Charles I lost his head in his struggle for a government without parliament, which then meant, in a great measure, without regular appropriations, or the assumption of ruling by taxation on royal authority. Wherever on the European continent it has been the endeavor to establish a constitutional government, the absolutists have complained of the "indecency" of making governments annually "beg" for supplies.

Liberty requires the supremacy of the law; the supremacy of the law requires the subordination of the army to the legislature and the whole civil government. The Declaration of Rights enumerates the raising and keeping a standing army without consent of parliament, as one of the proofs that James II had endeavored "to subvert and extirpate the laws and liberties" of England; while all governments reluctantly yielding to the demands of liberty have struggled to prevent at least the obligation of the army to take the oath of fidelity to the constitution. The army is studiously separated from the people, and courted as peculiarly allied to the prince. Napoleon I treated the army as the church was often treated in the middle ages—the main body in the state; and Napoleon III lately said in a solemn speech that he desired to present the new empress to the people and the army, as if it formed at least one-half of the state and were a body separate from the people. When he gave eagles to the whole army at what is called the fête of the eagles, in 1852, he said: "The history of nations is in a great measure the history of armies," and continued in a strain sounding as if it belonged to the times of the migration of nations.*

* I quote the whole passage of this stupendous allocution, which no historian or political philosopher, had he discovered it, as Cuvier found and construed remains of animals, would have assigned to the middle of the nineteenth century. What becomes of England and the United States if the essence of history does not lie in the development of the nation and especially of its institutions? The following are the exact words:

"Soldiers, the history of nations is in great part the history of armies. On their success, or on their reverses, depends the fate of civilization and of the country. When they are vanquished, there is either invasion or anarchy; when victorious, glory or order.

"In consequence, nations, like armies, pay a religious veneration to the emblems of military honor, which sum up in themselves a whole past existence of struggles and of triumphs.

"The Roman eagle, adopted by the Emperor Napoleon at the commencement of the present century, was the most striking signification of the regeneration and grandeur of France;" and so on.

When the democratic Cæsar reviewed the guards, before they started for the Crimea, in 1855, he called the army the nobility of the French nation.

But English and American freemen will never forget that the highest glory of a great people, and that by which it most signally performs the task assigned to it in the furtherance of our race, are its literature and its law, if this consists in a wise system founded on justice, humanity, and freedom.

The supremacy of the law is an elementary requisite of liberty. All absolutism spurns, and has a peculiar dislike of, the idea of fundamental laws. Aristotle enumerates as the fourth species of government that in which the multitude and not the law is the supreme master; James II claimed the dispensing power, and Louis Napoleon affirmed, when yet president under the republican constitution which prohibited his re-election, that if the people wanted him to continue in office he should do it nevertheless, and all his adherents declared that the people being the masters could do as they liked, which reminds us of the Athenians who impatiently exclaimed: "Can we not do what we list?" when told that there was a law forbidding what they intended to do.

The division of power, which was already observed as an important point in government by "the master of all that know," is invariably broken down as far as possible by the absolutists. The judiciary is interfered with whenever its slow procedure or its probable results irritate the power-holder. The history of all nations, from the earliest times to Napoleon III's taking the trial on the legality of the Orleans spoliation out of the hands of the judiciary, proves it on every page.

Self-government, general as well as local, is indispensable to our liberty, but interference and dictation are the essence of absolutism. Monarchical absolutisms presume to do everything and to provide for everything, and Robespierre, in his "great speech" for the restoration of the Supreme Being, said: "The function of government is to direct the moral and physical forces of the nation. For this purpose the aim of a constitutional government is the republic.*

Liberty requires that every one should be judged by his common court. All despots insist on extraordinary courts, courts of commission, and an easy application of martial law.

* The words of Robespierre are sufficiently clear, if taken as an illustration of what has been stated in the text; otherwise, I own, the sense is not perfectly apparent.

Forcible expatriation or deportation "beyond the seas" by the executive is looked upon with peculiar horror by all freemen. The English were roused by it to resistance; Napoleon III began his absolute reign with exile and deportation. So did the Greek factions banish their opponents when they had the power of doing so, because no "opposition" in the modern sense was known to them. With them it was the blundering business of factions; moderns know better, and if they return to it, it is because despotism is a thing full of fear and love of show.

How great an offense it is to deprive a man of his lawful court and to judge him by aught else than by the laws of the land, now in the middle of the nineteenth century, will appear the more forcibly if the reader will bring to his mind that passage of Magna Carta which appeared to Chatham worth all the classics, and if he will remember the year when the Great Charter was carried. The passage, so pregnant to the mind of Chatham, is this:

"No freeman shall be taken, or imprisoned, or be disseised of his freehold or liberties, or free customs, or be outlawed or exiled, or any otherwise destroyed, nor will we (the king) pass upon him, nor condemn him, but by lawful judgement of his peers, or by the law of the land. We will sell to no man, we will not deny or defer to any man, justice or right." *

Publicity is a condition without which liberty cannot live. The moment it had been concluded by the present government of France to root out civil freedom, it was ordained that neither the remarks of the members of the legislative corps, nor the pleadings in the courts of justice, should be reported in the papers. Modern political publicity, however, consists chiefly in publication through the journals. We acknowledge this practically by the fact that, although our courts are never closed,† yet, for particular reasons arising out of the case under consideration, the publication of the proceedings is sometimes prohibited by the judge until the close of the trial, but never beyond it.

Liberty stands in need of the legal precedent, and Charles I

* [*I.e.*, chap. xxix. of the Charter of 9 Henry III confirmed by Edward I in the twenty-fifth year of his reign, and nearly agreeing with chapters xlvi. and xlvii. of John's Charter, as given in Appendix IV.]

† Very scandalous judicial cases, offensive to public morals, are, in France, conducted with closed doors.

pursued Cotton because he furnished Pym and other patriots with precedents, while the present French government has excluded instruction in history from the plan of general education. History, in a certain point of view, may be called the great precedent. History is of all branches the most nourishing for public life and liberty. It furnishes a strong pabulum and incites by great examples removed beyond all party or selfish views. The favorite book of Chatham was Plutarch, and his son educated himself upon Thucydides.* The best historians have been produced by liberty, and the despot is consistent when he wishes to shackle the noble muse.

Sincere civil liberty requires that the legislature should have the initiative. All governments reluctant to grant full liberty have withheld it, and one of the first things decreed by Louis Napoleon after the second of December was that the "legislative corps" should discuss such propositions of laws only as the council of state should send to it. The council of state, however, is a mere body of officers appointed and discharged at the will of the ruler.

Liberty requires that government do not form a body permanently and essentially separated from the people; all modern absolute rulers have resorted to a number of distinctions—titles, ribbons, orders, peacock-feathers and buttons, uniforms, or whatever other means of separating individuals from the people at large may seem expedient.

Liberty requires the trial by jury. Consequently, one of the first attacks which arbitrary power makes upon freedom is regularly directed against that trial. There is now a law in preparation in France, of which the outlines have been published, and which will place the jurors under the almost exclusive influence of the government.

Liberty requires, as we have seen, a candid and well-guaranteed trial for treason; all despotic governments, on the contrary, endeavor to break down these guarantees in particular. They arrogate the power of condemning political offenders without trial, or strip the trial for treason of its best guarantees.

But we might go through the whole list of safeguards and principles of liberty, and find that in each case absolutism does the opposite.

* So Bishop Tomlinson tells us in the Life of his pupil.

If the American peruses the Declaration of Independence, he will find there, in the complaints of our forefathers, almost a complete list of those rights, privileges, and guarantees which they held dearest and most essential to liberty; for they believed that nearly every guarantee had been assailed.

Abraham Lincoln
(1809-1865)

ABRAHAM LINCOLN'S birth in a log cabin in Kentucky and his self-education are in the best traditions of American democracy, which has always insisted that American leaders be "of the people," simple and unassuming but capable through self-development of attaining a high capacity for leadership. Lincoln was "self-made" in the most acceptable sense of that over-used term. He studied between intervals of hard toil and became, at length, a practicing lawyer in Illinois and, in 1847, a member of the House of Representatives at Washington. Although defeated by Stephen A. Douglas for the senatorship in 1858, he had become nationally known as the result of his campaign, and he was elected to the presidency in 1860. He was re-elected in 1864, and at the time of his assassination in April of the following year he had come to be recognized both in America and in an England that had once reviled him as one of the truly great ones of the world. It is Lincoln rather than the first President of the United States who is the incarnation of the spirit of America, rugged, somewhat uncouth, but essentially honest, direct, and righteous.

Lincoln's speeches and writings were like himself direct and unadorned. It can hardly be said that he was as great an orator as the massive Webster (see p. 139); nevertheless, his debates with Douglas were as remarkable as were Webster's with Hayne. His Second Inaugural is classic. So also is the Gettysburg address, undoubtedly the most famous short speech in American history. It was delivered at the dedication of the National Cemetery at Gettysburg, Pennsylvania, on November 19, 1863, five months after the defeat there of the Confederate army. Only an incident in a program of much longer speeches, because of its perfection of style, its restraint, and its clear summation of the spirit of American democracy, it has outlived them all.

Address at the Dedication
of the Gettysburg National Cemetery (1863)

Fourscore and seven years ago our fathers brought forth on this continent a new nation, conceived in liberty, and dedicated to the proposition that all men are created equal.

Now we are engaged in a great civil war, testing whether that nation, or any nation so conceived and so dedicated, can long endure. We are met on a great battlefield of that war. We have come to dedicate a portion of that field as a final resting-place for those who here gave their lives that that nation might live. It is altogether fitting and proper that we should do this.

But, in a larger sense, we cannot dedicate—we cannot consecrate—we cannot hallow—this ground. The brave men, living and dead, who struggled here, have consecrated it far above our poor power to add or detract. The world will little note nor long remember what we say here, but it can never forget what they did here. It is for us, the living, rather, to be dedicated here to the unfinished work which they who fought here have thus far so nobly advanced. It is rather for us to be here dedicated to the great task remaining before us—that from these honored dead we take increased devotion to that cause for which they gave the last full measure of devotion; that we here highly resolve that these dead shall not have died in vain; that this nation under God shall have a new birth of freedom; and that government of the people, by the people, for the people, shall not perish from the earth.

James Russell Lowell
(1819-1891)

JAMES RUSSELL LOWELL is one of that distinguished group of American writers and philosophers who combined diplomacy with letters and so became in various European countries the representatives not only of their government but also of American culture. He studied law but devoted his life mainly to writing. The wide range of his interests produced much good poetry and many essays on social and political themes. In 1855 he succeeded Longfellow as professor of belles-lettres at Harvard, and maintained this post until 1886. During this time he was editor, moreover, of *The Atlantic Monthly* for five years and of *The North American Review* for nine years. In 1877 he went to Madrid as Minister to Spain, but was transferred the same year to London, where for eight years he served his government faithfully and did much to promote good understanding between the two countries. His *Commemoration Ode,* read at Harvard in 1865 (see p. 412), is probably his best poem, although his *Vision of Sir Launfal* is more popular, perhaps because of its sentimentality. His rhymed *Biglow Papers,* first series published in the *Boston Courier* (1846) and second series in *The Atlantic Monthly* (1862-66), are delightfully dry, humorous, and satirical comments on matters political; in these verses Lowell speaks through the mouth and in the New England dialect of "Hosea Biglow," a valiant opponent of slavery. Lowell's literary papers were collected in *Among My Books* (1870) and *My Study Windows* (1871), and many of his political and social speeches appeared in *Democracy and Other Addresses* (1886). All these utterances are characterized by a combination of New England culture and Yankee simplicity and common sense.

The following address is one of the many delivered during his residence in England as American ambassador.

Democracy (1884)

INAUGURAL ADDRESS ON ASSUMING THE PRESIDENCY
OF THE BIRMINGHAM AND MIDLAND INSTITUTE,
BIRMINGHAM, ENGLAND, OCTOBER 6, 1884

He must be a born leader or misleader of men, or must have been sent into the world unfurnished with that modulating and restraining balance-wheel which we call a sense of humor, who, in old age, has as strong confidence in his opinions and in the necessity of bringing the universe into conformity with them as he had in youth. In a world the very condition of whose being is that it should be in perpetual flux, where all seems mirage, and the one abiding thing is the effort to distinguish realities from appearances, the elderly man must be indeed of a singularly tough and valid fiber who is certain that he has any clarified residuum of experience, any assured verdict of reflection, that deserves to be called an opinion, or who, even if he had, feels that he is justified in holding mankind by the button while he is expounding it. And in a world of daily—nay, almost hourly—journalism, where every clever man, every man who thinks himself clever, or whom anybody else thinks clever, is called upon to deliver his judgment point-blank and at the word of command on every conceivable subject of human thought, or, on what sometimes seems to him very much the same thing, on every inconceivable display of human want of thought, there is such a spendthrift waste of all those commonplaces which furnish the permitted staple of public discourse that there is little chance of beguiling a new tune out of the one-stringed instrument on which we have been thrumming so long. In this desperate necessity one is often tempted to think that, if all the words of the dictionary were tumbled down in a heap and then all those fortuitous juxtapositions and combinations that made tolerable sense were picked out and pieced together, we might find among them some poignant suggestions towards novelty of thought or expression.

Reprinted by permission of and special arrangement with Houghton Mifflin Company.

But, alas! it is only the great poets who seem to have this un-solicited profusion of unexpected and incalculable phrase, this infinite variety of topic. For everybody else everything has been said before, and said over again after. He who has read his Aristotle will be apt to think that observation has on most points of general applicability said its last word, and he who has mounted the tower of Plato to look abroad from it will never hope to climb another with so lofty a vantage of speculation. Where it is so simple if not so easy a thing to hold one's peace, why add to the general confusion of tongues? There is some-thing disheartening, too, in being expected to fill up not less than a certain measure of time, as if the mind were an hour-glass, that need only be shaken and set on one end or the other, as the case may be, to run its allotted sixty minutes with decorous exactitude. I recollect being once told by the late eminent naturalist, Agassiz, that when he was to deliver his first lecture as professor (at Zürich, I believe) he had grave doubts of his ability to occupy the prescribed three quarters of an hour. He was speaking without notes, and glancing anxiously from time to time at the watch that lay before him on the desk. "When I had spoken a half hour," he said, "I had told them everything I knew in the world, every-thing! Then I began to repeat myself," he added, roguishly, "and I have done nothing else ever since." Beneath the humorous ex-aggeration of the story I seemed to see the face of a very serious and improving moral. And yet if one were to say only what he had to say and then stopped, his audience would feel defrauded of their honest measure. Let us take courage by the example of the French, whose exportation of Bordeaux wines increases as the area of their land in vineyards is diminished.

To me, somewhat hopelessly revolving these things, the un-delayable year has rolled round, and I find myself called upon to say something in this place, where so many wiser men have spoken before me. Precluded, in my quality of national guest, by motives of taste and discretion, from dealing with any question of immediate and domestic concern, it seemed to me wisest, or at any rate most prudent, to choose a topic of comparatively abstract interest, and to ask your indulgence for a few somewhat general-ized remarks on a matter concerning which I had some experi-mental knowledge, derived from the use of such eyes and ears as

Nature had been pleased to endow me withal, and such report as I had been able to win from them. The subject which most readily suggested itself was the spirit and the working of those conceptions of life and polity which are lumped together, whether for reproach or commendation, under the name of Democracy. By temperament and education of a conservative turn, I saw the last years of that quaint Arcadia which French travelers saw with delighted amazement a century ago, and have watched the change (to me a sad one) from an agricultural to a proletary population. The testimony of Balaam should carry some conviction. I have grown to manhood and am now growing old with the growth of this system of government in my native land, have watched its advances, or what some would call its encroachments, gradual and irresistible as those of a glacier, have been an ear-witness to the forebodings of wise and good and timid men, and have lived to see those forebodings belied by the course of events, which is apt to show itself humorously careless of the reputation of prophets. I recollect hearing a sagacious old gentleman say in 1840 that the doing away with the property qualification for suffrage twenty years before had been the ruin of the State of Massachusetts; that it had put public credit and private estate alike at the mercy of demagogues. I lived to see that Commonwealth twenty odd years later paying the interest on her bonds in gold, though it cost her sometimes nearly three for one to keep her faith, and that while suffering an unparalleled drain of men and treasure in helping to sustain the unity and self-respect of the nation.

If universal suffrage has worked ill in our larger cities, as it certainly has, this has been mainly because the hands that wielded it were untrained to its use. There the election of a majority of the trustees of the public money is controlled by the most ignorant and vicious of a population which has come to us from abroad, wholly unpracticed in self-government and incapable of assimilation by American habits and methods. But the finances of our towns, where the native tradition is still dominant and whose affairs are discussed and settled in a public assembly of the people, have been in general honestly and prudently administered. Even in manufacturing towns, where a majority of the voters live by their daily wages, it is not so often the recklessness as the moderation of public expenditure that surprises an old-fashioned observer. "The beggar is in the saddle at last," cries Proverbial Wisdom. "Why, in the name of all former experience, doesn't he ride to the Devil?" Because in the very act of mounting he ceased to be a beggar and became part owner of the piece of property he bestrides. The last thing we need be anxious about is property. It always has friends or the means of making them. If riches have wings to fly away from their owner, they have wings also to escape danger.

I hear America sometimes playfully accused of sending you all your storms, and am in the habit of parrying the charge by alleging that we are enabled to do this because, in virtue of our protective system, we can afford to make better bad weather than anybody else. And what wiser use could we make of it than to export it in return for the paupers which some European countries are good enough to send over to us who have not attained to the same skill in the manufacture of them? But bad weather is not the worst thing that is laid at our door. A French gentleman, not long ago, forgetting Burke's monition of how unwise it is to draw an indictment against a whole people, has charged us with the responsibility of whatever he finds disagreeable in the morals or manners of his countrymen. If M. Zola or some other competent witness would only go into the box and tell us what those morals and manners were before our example corrupted them! But I confess that I find little to interest and less to edify me in these international bandyings of "You're another."

I shall address myself to a single point only in the long list of offenses of which we are more or less gravely accused, because that really includes all the rest. It is that we are infecting the Old World with what seems to be thought the entirely new disease of Democracy. It is generally people who are in what are called easy circumstances who can afford the leisure to treat themselves to a handsome complaint, and these experience an immediate alleviation when once they have found a sonorous Greek name to abuse it by. There is something consolatory also, something flattering to their sense of personal dignity, and to that conceit of singularity which is the natural recoil from our uneasy consciousness of being commonplace, in thinking ourselves victims of a malady by which no one had ever suffered before. Accordingly they find it simpler to class under one comprehensive heading whatever they find offensive to their nerves, their tastes, their interests, or what they suppose to be their opinions, and christen it Democracy, much as physicians label every obscure disease gout, or as cross-grained fellows lay their ill-temper to the weather. But is it really a new ailment, and, if it be, is America answerable for it? Even if she were, would it account for the phylloxera, and hoof-and-mouth disease, and bad harvests, and bad English, and the German bands, and the Boers, and all the other discomforts with which these later days have vexed the souls of them that go in chariots? Yet I have seen the evil example of Democracy in America cited as the source and origin of things quite as heterogeneous and quite as little connected with it by any sequence of cause and effect. Surely this ferment is nothing new. It has been at work for centuries, and we are more conscious of it only because in this age of publicity, where the newspapers offer a rostrum to whoever has a grievance, or fancies that he has, the bubbles and scum thrown up by it are more noticeable on the surface than in those dumb ages when there was a cover of silence and suppression on the cauldron. Bernardo Navagero, speaking of the Provinces of Lower Austria in 1546, tells us that "in them there are five sorts of persons, Clergy, Barons, Nobles, Burghers, and Peasants. Of these last no account is made, *because they have no voice in the Diet.*"

Nor was it among the people that subversive or mistaken doctrines had their rise. A Father of the Church said that property was theft many centuries before Proudhon was born. Bourdaloue reaffirmed it. Montesquieu was the inventor of national workshops, and of the theory that the State owed every man a living. Nay, was not the Church herself the first organized Democracy? A few centuries ago the chief end of man was to keep his soul alive, and then the little kernel of leaven that sets the gases at work was religious, and produced the Reformation. Even in that, far-sighted persons like the Emperor Charles V saw the germ of political and social revolution. Now that the chief end of man seems to have become the keeping of the body alive, and as comfortably alive as possible, the leaven also has become wholly political and social. But there had also been social upheavals before the Reformation and contemporaneously with it, especially among men of Teutonic race. The Reformation gave outlet and direction to an unrest already existing. Formerly the immense majority of men—our brothers—knew only their sufferings, their wants, and their desires. They are beginning now to know their opportunity and their power. All persons who see deeper than their plates are rather inclined to thank God for it than to bewail it, for the sores of Lazarus have a poison in them against which Dives has no antidote.

There can be no doubt that the spectacle of a great and prosperous Democracy on the other side of the Atlantic must react powerfully on the aspirations and political theories of men in the Old World who do not find things to their mind; but, whether for good or evil, it should not be overlooked that the acorn from which it sprang was ripened on the British oak. Every successive swarm that has gone out from this *officina gentium* has, when left to its own instincts—may I not call them hereditary instincts?—assumed a more or less thoroughly democratic form. This would seem to show, what I believe to be the fact, that the British Constitution, under whatever disguises of prudence or decorum, is essentially democratic. England, indeed, may be called a monarchy with democratic tendencies, the United States a democracy with conservative instincts. People are continually saying that America is in the air, and I am glad to think it is, since this means only that a clearer conception of human claims and human duties is beginning to be prevalent. The discontent with the existing order of things, however, pervaded the atmosphere wherever the conditions were favorable, long before Columbus, seeking the back door of Asia, found himself knocking at the front door of America. I say wherever the conditions were favorable, for it is certain that the germs of disease do not stick or find a prosperous field for their development and noxious activity unless where the simplest sanitary precautions have been neglected. "For this effect defective comes by cause," as Polonius said long ago. It is only by instigation of the wrongs of men that what are called the Rights of Man become turbulent and dangerous. It is then only that they syllogize unwelcome truths. It is not the insurrections of ignorance that are dangerous, but the revolts of intelligence:

> The wicked and the weak rebel in vain,
> Slaves by their own compulsion.

Had the governing classes in France during the last century paid as much heed to their proper business as to their pleasures or manners, the guillotine need never have severed that spinal marrow of orderly and secular tradition through which in a normally constituted state the brain sympathizes with the extremities and sends will and impulsion thither. It is only when the reasonable and practicable are denied that men demand the unreasonable and impracticable; only when the possible is made difficult that they fancy the impossible to be easy. Fairy tales are made out of the dreams of the poor. No; the sentiment which lies at the root of democracy is nothing new. I am speaking always of a sentiment, a spirit, and not of a form of government; for this was but the outgrowth of the other and not its cause. This sentiment is merely an expression of the natural wish of people to have a hand, if need be a controlling hand, in the management of their own affairs. What is new is that they are more and more gaining that control, and learning more and more how to be worthy of it. What we used to call the tendency or drift—what we are being taught to call more wisely the evolution of things—has for some time been setting steadily in this direction. There is no good in arguing with the inevitable. The only argument available with an east wind is to put on your overcoat. And in this case, also, the prudent will prepare themselves to encounter what they cannot prevent. Some people advise us to put on the brakes, as if the movement of which we are conscious were that of a railway train running down an incline. But a metaphor is no argument, though it be sometimes the gunpowder to drive one home and imbed it in the memory. Our disquiet comes of what nurses and other experienced persons call growing-pains, and need not seriously alarm us. They are what every generation before us—certainly every generation since the invention of printing—has gone through with more or less good fortune. To the door of every generation there comes a knocking, and unless the household, like the Thane of Cawdor and his wife, have been doing some deed without a name, they need not shudder. It turns out at worst to be a poor relation who wishes to come in out of the cold. The porter always grumbles and is slow to open. "Who's there, in the name of Beelzebub?" he mutters. Not a change for the better in our human housekeeping has ever taken place that wise and good men have not opposed it,—have not prophesied with the alderman that the world would wake up to find its throat cut in consequence of it. The world, on the contrary, wakes up, rubs its eyes, yawns, stretches itself, and goes about its business as if nothing had happened. Suppression of the slave trade, abolition of slavery, trade unions,—at all of these excellent people shook their heads despondingly, and murmured "Ichabod." But the trade unions are now debating instead of conspiring, and we all read their discussions with comfort and hope, sure that they are learning the business of citizenship and the difficulties of practical legislation.

One of the most curious of these frenzies of exclusion was that against the emancipation of the Jews. All share in the government of the world was denied for centuries to perhaps the ablest, certainly the most tenacious, race that had ever lived in it—the race to whom we owed our religion and the purest spiritual stimulus and consolation to be found in all literature—a race in which ability seems as natural and hereditary as the curve of their noses, and whose blood, furtively mingling with the bluest bloods in Europe, has quickened them with its own indomitable impulsion. We drove them into a corner, but they had their revenge, as the wronged are always sure to have it sooner or later. They made their corner the counter and banking-house of the world, and thence they rule it and us with their ignobler scepter of finance. Your grandfathers mobbed Priestley only that you might set up his statue and make Birmingham the headquarters of English Unitarianism. We hear it said sometimes that this is an age of transition, as if that made matters clearer; but can any one point us to an age that was not? If he could, he would show us an age of stagnation. The question for us, as it has been for all before us, is to make the transition gradual and easy, to see that our points are right so that the train may not come to grief. For we should remember that nothing is more natural for people whose education has been neglected than to spell evolution with an initial "r." A great man struggling with the storms of fate has been called a sublime spectacle; but surely a great man wrestling with these new forces that have come into the world, mastering them and controlling them to beneficent ends, would be a yet sublimer. Here is not a danger, and if there were it would be only a better school of manhood, a nobler scope for ambition. I have hinted that what people are afraid of in democracy is less the thing itself than what they conceive to be its necessary adjuncts and consequences. It is supposed to reduce all mankind to a dead level of mediocrity in character and culture, to vulgarize men's conceptions of life, and therefore their code of morals, manners, and conduct—to endanger the rights of property and possession. But I believe that the real gravamen of the charges lies in the habit it has of making itself generally disagreeable by asking the Powers that Be at the most inconvenient moment whether they are the powers that ought to be. If the powers that be are in a condition to give a satisfactory answer to this inevitable question, they need feel in no way discomfited by it.

Few people take the trouble of trying to find out what democracy really is. Yet this would be a great help, for it is our lawless and uncertain thoughts, it is the indefiniteness of our impressions, that fill darkness, whether mental or physical, with specters and hobgoblins. Democracy is nothing more than an experiment in government, more likely to succeed in a new soil, but likely to be tried in all soils, which must stand or fall on its own merits as others have done before it. For there is no trick of perpetual motion in politics any more than in mechanics. President Lincoln defined democracy to be "the government of the people by the people for the people." This is a sufficiently compact statement of it as a political arrangement. Theodore Parker said that "Democracy meant not 'I'm as good as you are,' but 'You're as good as I am.'" And this is the ethical conception of it, necessary as a complement of the other; a conception which, could it be made actual and practical, would easily solve all the riddles that the old sphinx of political and social economy who sits by the roadside has been proposing to mankind from the beginning, and which mankind have shown such a singular talent for answering wrongly. In this sense Christ was the first true democrat that ever breathed, as the old dramatist Dekker said he was the first true gentleman. The characters may be easily doubled, so strong is the likeness between them. A beautiful and profound parable of the Persian poet Jellaladeen tells us that "One knocked at the Beloved's door, and a voice asked from within 'Who is there?' and he answered 'It is I.' Then the voice said, 'This house will not hold me and thee'; and the door was not opened. Then went the lover into the desert and fasted and prayed in solitude, and after a year he returned and knocked again at the door; and again the voice asked 'Who is there?' and he said 'It is thyself'; and the door was opened to him." But that is idealism, you will say, and this is an only too practical world. I grant it; but I am one of those who believe that the real will never find an irremovable basis till it rests on the ideal. It used to be thought that a democracy was possible only in a small territory, and this is doubtless true of a democracy strictly defined, for in such all the citizens decide directly upon every question of public concern in a general assembly. An example still survives in the tiny Swiss canton of Appenzell. But this immediate intervention of the people in their own affairs is not of the essence of democracy; it is not necessary, nor indeed, in most cases, practicable. Democracies to which Mr. Lincoln's definition would fairly enough apply have existed, and now exist, in which, though the supreme authority reside in the people, yet they can act only indirectly on the national policy. This generation has seen a democracy with an imperial figurehead, and in all that have ever existed the body politic has never embraced all the inhabitants included within its territory, the right to share in the direction of affairs has been confined to citizens, and citizenship has been further restricted by various limitations, sometimes of property, sometimes of nativity, and always of age and sex.

The framers of the American Constitution were far from wishing or intending to found a democracy in the strict sense of the word, though, as was inevitable, every expansion of the scheme of government they elaborated has been in a democratical direction. But this has been generally the slow result of growth, and not the sudden innovation of theory; in fact, they had a profound disbelief in theory, and knew better than to commit the folly of breaking with the past. They were not seduced by the French fallacy that a new system of government could be ordered like a new suit of clothes. They would as soon have thought of ordering a new suit of flesh and skin. It is only on the roaring loom of time that the stuff is woven for such a vesture of their thought and experience as they were meditating. They recognized fully the value of tradition and habit as the great allies of permanence and stability. They all had that distaste for innovation which belonged to their race, and many of them a distrust of human nature derived from their creed. The day of sentiment was over, and no dithyrambic affirmations or fine-drawn analyses of the Rights of Man would serve their present turn. This was a practical question, and they addressed themselves to it as men of knowledge and judgment should. Their problem was how to adapt English principles and precedents to the new conditions of American life, and they solved it with singular discretion. They put as many obstacles as they could contrive, not in the way of the people's will, but of their whim. With few exceptions they probably admitted the logic of the then accepted syllogism,—democracy, anarchy, despotism. But this formula was framed upon the experience of small cities shut up to stew within their narrow walls where the number of citizens made but an inconsiderable fraction of the inhabitants, where every passion was reverberated from house to house and from man to man with gathering rumor till every impulse became gregarious and therefore inconsiderate, and every popular assembly needed but an infusion of eloquent sophistry to turn it into a mob, all the more dangerous because sanctified with the formality of law.

Fortunately their case was wholly different. They were to legislate for a widely scattered population and for States already practiced in the discipline of a partial independence. They had an unequaled opportunity and enormous advantages. The material they had to work upon was already democratical by instinct and habitude. It was tempered to their hands by more than a century's schooling in self-government. They had but to give permanent and conservative form to a ductile mass. In giving impulse and direction to their new institutions, especially in supplying them with checks and balances, they had a great help and safeguard in their federal organization. The different, sometimes conflicting, interests and social systems of the several States made existence as a Union and coalescence into a nation conditional on a constant practice of moderation and compromise. The very

elements of disintegration were the best guides in political training. Their children learned the lesson of compromise only too
well, and it was the application of it to a question of fundamental
morals that cost us our civil war. We learned once for all that
compromise makes a good umbrella but a poor roof; that it is a
temporary expedient, often wise in party politics, almost sure to
be unwise in statesmanship.

Has not the trial of democracy in America proved, on the
whole, successful? If it had not, would the Old World be vexed
with any fears of its proving contagious? This trial would have
been less severe could it have been made with a people homogeneous in race, language, and traditions, whereas the United
States have been called on to absorb and assimilate enormous
masses of foreign population heterogenous in all these respects,
and drawn mainly from that class which might fairly say that the
world was not their friend, nor the world's law. The previous
condition too often justified the traditional Irishman, who, landing in New York and asked what his politics were, inquired if
there was a Government there, and on being told that there was,
retorted, "Thin I'm agin it!" We have taken from Europe the
poorest, the most ignorant, the most turbulent of her people, and
have made them over into good citizens, who have added to our
wealth, and who are ready to die in defense of a country and of
institutions which they know to be worth dying for. The exceptions have been (and they are lamentable exceptions) where
these hordes of ignorance and poverty have coagulated in great
cities. But the social system is yet to seek which has not to look
the same terrible wolf in the eyes. On the other hand, at this very
moment Irish peasants are buying up the worn-out farms of
Massachusetts, and making them productive again by the same
virtues of industry and thrift that once made them profitable to
the English ancestors of the men who are deserting them. To
have achieved even these prosaic results (if you choose to call
them so), and that out of materials the most discordant,—I might
say the most recalcitrant,—argues a certain beneficent virtue in
the system that could do it, and is not to be accounted for by
mere luck. Carlyle said scornfully that America meant only roast
turkey every day for everybody. He forgot that States, as Bacon
said of wars, go on their bellies. As for the security of property,

it should be tolerably well secured in a country where every other man hopes to be rich, even though the only property qualification be the ownership of two hands that add to the general wealth. Is it not the best security for anything to interest the largest possible number of persons in its preservation and the smallest in its division? In point of fact, far-seeing men count the increasing power of wealth and its combinations as one of the chief dangers with which the institutions of the United States are threatened in the not distant future. The right of individual property is no doubt the very cornerstone of civilization as hitherto understood, but I am a little impatient of being told that property is entitled to exceptional consideration because it bears all the burdens of the State. It bears those, indeed, which can most easily be borne, but poverty pays with its person the chief expenses of war, pestilence, and famine. Wealth should not forget this, for poverty is beginning to think of it now and then. Let me not be misunderstood. I see as clearly as any man possibly can, and rate as highly, the value of wealth, and of hereditary wealth, as the security of refinement, the feeder of all those arts that ennoble and beautify life, and as making a country worth living in. Many an ancestral hall here in England has been a nursery of that culture which has been of example and benefit to all. Old gold has a civilizing virtue which new gold must grow old to be capable of secreting.

I should not think of coming before you to defend or to criticize any form of government. All have their virtues, all their defects, and all have illustrated one period or another in the history of the race, with signal services to humanity and culture. There is not one that could stand a cynical cross-examination by an experienced criminal lawyer, except that of a perfectly wise and perfectly good despot, such as the world has never seen, except in that white-haired king of Browning's, who

> Lived long ago
> In the morning of the world,
> When Earth was nearer Heaven than now.

The English race, if they did not invent government by discussion, have at least carried it nearest to perfection in practice. It seems a very safe and reasonable contrivance for occupying the attention of the country, and is certainly a better way of settling questions than by push of pike. Yet, if one should ask it why it should not rather be called government by gabble, it would have to fumble in its pocket a good while before it found the change for a convincing reply. As matters stand, too, it is beginning to be doubtful whether Parliament and Congress sit at Westminster and Washington or in the editors' rooms of the leading journals, so thoroughly is everything debated before the authorized and responsible debaters get on their legs. And what shall we say of government by a majority of voices? To a person who in the last century would have called himself an Impartial Observer, a numerical preponderance seems, on the whole, as clumsy a way of arriving at truth as could well be devised, but experience has apparently shown it to be a convenient arrangement for determining what may be expedient or advisable or practicable at any given moment. Truth, after all, wears a different face to everybody, and it would be too tedious to wait till all were agreed. She is said to lie at the bottom of a well, for the very reason, perhaps, that whoever looks down in search of her sees his own image at the bottom, and is persuaded not only that he has seen the goddess, but that she is far better looking than he had imagined.

The arguments against universal suffrage are equally unanswerable. "What," we exclaim, "shall Tom, Dick, and Harry have as much weight in the scale as I?" Of course, nothing could be more absurd. And yet universal suffrage has not been the instrument of greater unwisdom than contrivances of a more select description. Assemblies could be mentioned composed entirely of Masters of Arts and Doctors in Divinity which have sometimes shown traces of human passion or prejudice in their votes. Have the Serene Highnesses and Enlightened Classes carried on the business of Mankind so well, then, that there is no use in trying a less costly method? The democratic theory is that those Constitutions are likely to prove steadiest which have the broadest base, that the right to vote makes a safety-valve of every voter, and that the best way of teaching a man how to vote is to give him the chance of practice. For the question is no longer the academic one, "Is it wise to give every man the ballot?" but rather the practical one, "Is it prudent to deprive whole classes of it any longer?" It may be conjectured that it is cheaper in the long run to lift men up than to hold them down, and that the ballot in their hands is less dangerous to society than a sense of wrong in their heads. At any rate this is the dilemma to which the drift of opinion has been for some time sweeping us, and in politics a dilemma is a more unmanageable thing to hold by the horns than a wolf by the ears. It is said that the right of suffrage is not valued when it is indiscriminately bestowed, and there may be some truth in this, for I have observed that what men prize most is a privilege, even if it be that of chief mourner at a funeral. But is there not danger that it will be valued at more than its worth if denied, and that some illegitimate way will be sought to make up for the want of it? Men who have a voice in public affairs are at once affiliated with one or other of the great parties between which society is divided, merge their individual hopes and opinions in its safer, because more generalized, hopes and opinions, are disciplined by its tactics, and acquire, to a certain degree, the orderly qualities of an army. They no longer belong to a class, but to a body corporate. Of one thing, at least, we may be certain, that, under whatever method of helping things to go wrong man's wit can contrive, those who have the divine right to govern will be found to govern in the end, and that the highest privilege to which the majority of mankind can aspire is that of being governed by those wiser than they. Universal suffrage has in the United States sometimes been made the instrument of inconsiderate changes, under the notion of reform, and this from a misconception of the true meaning of popular government. One of these has been the substitution in many of the states of popular election for official selection in the choice of judges. The same system applied to military officers was the source of much evil during our civil war, and, I believe, had to be abandoned. But it has been also true that on all great questions of national policy a reserve of prudence and discretion has been brought out at the critical moment to turn the scale in favor of a wiser decision. An appeal to the reason of the people has never been known to fail in the long run. It is, perhaps, true that, by effacing the principle of passive obedience, democracy, ill understood, has slackened the spring of that ductility to discipline which is essential to "the unity and married calm of States." But I feel assured that experience and necessity will cure this evil, as they have shown their power to cure others. And under what frame of policy have evils ever been remedied till they became intolerable, and shook men out of their indolent indifference through their fears?

We are told that the inevitable result of democracy is to sap the foundations of personal independence, to weaken the principle of authority, to lessen the respect due to eminence, whether in station, virtue, or genius. If these things were so, society could not hold together. Perhaps the best forcing-house of robust individuality would be where public opinion is inclined to be most overbearing, as he must be of heroic temper who should walk along Piccadilly at the height of the season in a soft hat. As for authority, it is one of the symptoms of the time that the religious reverence for it is declining everywhere, but this is due partly to the fact that statecraft is no longer looked upon as a mystery, but as a business, and partly to the decay of superstition, by which I mean the habit of respecting what we are told to respect rather than what is respectable in itself. There is more rough and tumble in the American democracy than is altogether agreeable to people of sensitive nerves and refined habits, and the people take their political duties lightly and laughingly, as is, perhaps, neither unnatural nor unbecoming in a young giant. Democracies can no more jump away from their own shadows than the rest of us can. They no doubt sometimes make mistakes and pay honor to men who do not deserve it. But they do this because they believe them worthy of it, and though it be true that the idol is the measure of the worshiper, yet the worship has in it the germ of a nobler religion. But is it democracies alone that fall into these errors? I, who have seen it proposed to erect a statue to Hudson, the railway king, and have heard Louis Napoleon hailed as the savior of society by men who certainly had no democratic associations or leanings, am not ready to think so. But democracies have likewise their finer instincts. I have also seen the wisest statesman and most pregnant speaker of our generation, a man of humble birth and ungainly manners, of little culture beyond what his own genius supplied, become more absolute in power than any monarch of modern times through the reverence of his countrymen for his honesty, his wisdom, his sincerity, his faith in God and man, and the nobly humane simplicity of his character. And I remember another whom popular respect enveloped as with a halo, the least vulgar of men, the most austerely genial, and the most independent of opinion. Wherever he went he never met a stranger, but everywhere neighbors and friends proud of him as their ornament and decoration. Institutions which could bear and breed such men as Lincoln and Emerson had surely some energy for good. No, amid all the fruitless turmoil and miscarriage of the world, if there be one thing steadfast and of favorable omen, one thing to make optimism distrust its own obscure distrust, it is the rooted instinct in men to admire what is better and more beautiful than themselves. The touchstone of political and social institutions is their ability to supply them with worthy objects of this sentiment, which is the very tap-root of civilization and progress. There would seem to be no readier way of feeding it with the elements of growth and vigor than such an organization of society as will enable men to respect themselves, and so to justify them in respecting others.

Such a result is quite possible under other conditions than those of an avowedly democratical Constitution. For I take it that the real essence of democracy was fairly enough defined by the First Napoleon when he said that the French Revolution meant "la carrière ouverte aux talents"—a clear pathway for merit of whatever kind. I should be inclined to paraphrase this by calling democracy that form of society, no matter what its political classification, in which every man had a chance and knew that he had it. If a man can climb, and feels himself encouraged to climb, from a coalpit to the highest position for which he is fitted, he can well afford to be indifferent what name is given to the government under which he lives. The Bailli of Mirabeau, uncle of the more famous tribune of that name, wrote in 1771: "The English are, in my opinion, a hundred times more agitated and more unfortunate than the very Algerines themselves, because they do not know and will not know till the destruction of their overswollen power, which I believe very near, whether they are monarchy, aristocracy, or democracy, and wish to play the part of all three." England has not been obliging enough to fulfill the Bailli's prophecy, and perhaps it was this very carelessness about the name, and concern about the substance of popular government, this skill in getting the best out of things as they are, in utilizing all the motives which influence men, and in giving one direction to many impulses, that has been a principal factor of her greatness and power. Perhaps it is fortunate to have an unwritten constitution, for men are prone to be tinkering the work of their own hands, whereas they are more willing to let time and circumstance mend or modify what time and circumstances have made. All free governments, whatever their name, are in reality governments by public opinion, and it is on the quality of this public opinion that their prosperity depends. It is, therefore, their first duty to purify the element from which they draw the breath of life. With the growth of democracy grows also the fear, if not the danger, that this atmosphere may be corrupted with poisonous exhalations from lower and more malarious levels, and the question of sanitation becomes more instant and pressing. Democracy in its best sense is merely the letting in of light and air. Lord Sherbrooke, with his usual epigrammatic terseness, bids you educate your future rulers. But would this alone be a sufficient safeguard? To educate the intelligence is to enlarge the horizon of its desires and wants. And it is well that this should be so. But the enterprise must go deeper and prepare the way for satisfying those desires and wants in so far as they are legitimate. What is really ominous of danger to the existing order of things is not democracy (which, properly understood, is a conservative force), but the Socialism, which may find a fulcrum in it. If we cannot equalize conditions and fortunes any more than we can equalize the brains of men—and a very sagacious person has said that "where two men ride of a horse one must ride behind"—we can yet, perhaps, do something to correct those methods and influences that lead to enormous inequalities, and to prevent their growing more enormous. It is all very well to pooh-pooh Mr. George and to prove him mistaken in his political economy. I do not believe that land should be divided because the quantity of it is limited by nature. Of what may this not be said? *A fortiori,* we might on the same principle insist on a division of human wit, for I have observed that the quantity of this has been even more inconveniently limited. Mr.

George himself has an inequitably large share of it. But he is right in his impelling motive; right, also, I am convinced, in insisting that humanity makes a part, by far the most important part, of political economy; and in thinking man to be of more concern and more convincing than the longest columns of figures in the world. For unless you include human nature in your addition, your total is sure to be wrong and your deductions from it fallacious. Communism means barbarism, but Socialism means, or wishes to mean, co-operation and community of interests, sympathy, the giving to the hands not so large a share as to the brains, but a larger share than hitherto in the wealth they must combine to produce—means, in short, the practical application of Christianity to life, and has in it the secret of an orderly and benign reconstruction. State Socialism would cut off the very roots in personal character—self-help, forethought, and frugality—which nourish and sustain the trunk and branches of every vigorous Commonwealth.

I do not believe in violent changes, nor do I expect them. Things in possession have a very firm grip. One of the strongest cements of society is the conviction of mankind that the state of things into which they are born is a part of the order of the universe, as natural, let us say, as that the sun should go round the earth. It is a conviction that they will not surrender except on compulsion, and a wise society should look to it that this compulsion be not put upon them. For the individual man there is no radical cure, outside of human nature itself, for the evils to which human nature is heir. The rule will always hold good that you must

Be your own palace or the world's your jail.

But for artificial evils, for evils that spring from want of thought, thought must find a remedy somewhere. There has been no period of time in which wealth has been more sensible of its duties than now. It builds hospitals, it establishes missions among the poor, it endows schools. It is one of the advantages of accumulated wealth, and of the leisure it renders possible, that people have time to think of the wants and sorrows of their fellows. But all these remedies are partial and palliative merely. It is as if we should apply plasters to a single pustule of the smallpox with a view of driving out the disease. The true way is to discover and to extirpate the germs. As society is now constituted these are in the air it breathes, in the water it drinks, in things that seem, and which it has always believed, to be the most innocent and healthful. The evil elements it neglects corrupt these in their springs and pollute them in their courses. Let us be of good cheer, however, remembering that the misfortunes hardest to bear are those which never come. The world has outlived much, and will outlive a great deal more, and men have contrived to be happy in it. It has shown the strength of its constitution in nothing more than in surviving the quack medicines it has tried. In the scales of the destinies brawn will never weigh so much as brain. Our healing is not in the storm or in the whirlwind, it is not in monarchies, or aristocracies, or democracies, but will be revealed by the still small voice that speaks to the conscience and the heart, prompting us to a wider and wiser humanity.

Woodrow Wilson
(1856-1924)

THE HISTORY of the United States does not show that college professors are usually regarded as possible timber for the presidency, but Woodrow Wilson was an exception. From 1890 to 1902 he was Professor of Jurisprudence and Political Economy at Princeton University, his alma mater, and in 1902 he became president of that institution. Eight years later he was elected to the governorship of New Jersey, and in 1912, when Taft and Theodore Roosevelt split the Republican party, Wilson became President of the United States. Just before America joined Great Britain and France in the war against Germany he was re-elected, rather ironically under the party slogan "he kept us out of war." Trained thinkers do not always make good war presidents, but Wilson's direction of an embattled commonwealth was vigorous. When the Germans collapsed, however, in the fall of 1918, he found it difficult to square his own ideals of peace and justice with the more practical demands of the statesmen of the allied powers, or even to get his own countrymen to give up their isolationism for a place in the League of Nations. He hastened his death by his over-exertions for his high cause and left posterity to justify his visions.

Woodrow Wilson was one of the most able and finished speakers and writers ever in the White House. He was the author of several books, including *A History of the American People* (1901) and *Constitutional Government in the United States* (1908). His style has distinction; moreover, he had the knack of creating telling aphorisms, and such phrases as "ultimate peace of the world," and "make the world safe for democracy" were rallying cries until slain by post-war disillusionment and cynicism. *The New Freedom* (1913), from which the following selection is taken, consists of excerpts from his campaign speeches.

The Liberation of a People's
Vital Energies (*1913*)

No matter how often we think of it, the discovery of America must each time make a fresh appeal to our imaginations. For centuries, indeed from the beginning, the face of Europe had been turned toward the east. All the routes of trade, every impulse and energy, ran from west to east. The Atlantic lay at the world's back-door. Then, suddenly, the conquest of Constantinople by the Turk closed the route to the Orient. Europe had either to face about or lack any outlet for her energies; the unknown sea at the west at last was ventured upon, and the earth learned that it was twice as big as it had thought. Columbus did not find, as he had expected, the civilization of Cathay; he found an empty continent. In that part of the world, upon that new-found half of the globe, mankind, late in its history, was thus afforded an opportunity to set up a new civilization; here it was strangely privileged to make a new human experiment.

Never can that moment of unique opportunity fail to excite the emotion of all who consider its strangeness and richness; a thousand fanciful histories of the earth might be contrived without the imagination daring to conceive such a romance as the hiding away of half the globe until the fullness of time had come for a new start in civilization. A mere sea captain's ambition to trace a new trade route gave way to a moral adventure for humanity. The race was to found a new order here on this delectable land, which no man approached without receiving, as the old voyagers relate, you remember, sweet airs out of woods aflame with flowers and murmurous with the sound of pellucid waters. The hemisphere lay waiting to be touched with life,—life from the old centers of living, surely, but cleansed of defilement, and

From *The New Freedom*, by Woodrow Wilson, copyright, 1913, 1933, by Doubleday, Doran and Company, Inc.

cured of weariness, so as to be fit for the virgin purity of a new bride. The whole thing springs into the imagination like a wonderful vision, an exquisite marvel which once only in all history could be vouchsafed.

One other thing only compares with it; only one other thing touches the springs of emotion as does the picture of the ships of Columbus drawing near the bright shores,—and that is the thought of the choke in the throat of the immigrant of today as he gazes from the steerage deck at the land where he has been taught to believe he in his turn shall find an earthly paradise, where, a free man, he shall forget the heartaches of the old life, and enter into the fulfillment of the hope of the world. For has not every ship that has pointed her prow westward borne hither the hopes of generation after generation of the oppressed of other lands? How always have men's hearts beat as they saw the coast of America rise to their view! How it has always seemed to them that the dweller there would at last be rid of kings, of privileged classes, and of all those bonds which had kept men depressed and helpless, and would there realize the full fruition of his sense of honest manhood, would there be one of a great body of brothers, not seeking to defraud and deceive one another, but seeking to accomplish the general good!

What was in the writings of the men who founded America,— to serve the selfish interests of America? Do you find that in their writings? No; to serve the cause of humanity, to bring liberty to mankind. They set up their standards here in America in the tenet of hope, as a beacon of encouragement to all the nations of the world; and men came thronging to these shores with an expectancy that never existed before, with a confidence they never dared feel before, and found here for generations together a haven of peace, of opportunity, of equality.

God send that in the complicated state of modern affairs we may recover the standards and repeat the achievements of that heroic age!

For life is no longer the comparatively simple thing it was. Our relations one with another have been profoundly modified by the new agencies of rapid communication and transportation, tending swiftly to concentrate life, widen communities, fuse interests, and complicate all the processes of living. The individual

is dizzily swept about in a thousand new whirlpools of activities.
Tyranny has become more subtle, and has learned to wear the
guise of mere industry, and even of benevolence. Freedom has
become a somewhat different matter. It cannot,—eternal principle that it is,—it cannot have altered, yet it shows itself in new
aspects. Perhaps it is only revealing its deeper meaning.

What is liberty?

I have long had an image in my mind of what constitutes liberty. Suppose that I were building a great piece of powerful machinery, and suppose that I should so awkwardly and unskillfully
assemble the parts of it that every time one part tried to move it
would be interfered with by the others, and the whole thing
would buckle up and be checked. Liberty for the several parts
would consist in the best possible assembling and adjustment of
them all, would it not? If you want the great piston of the engine
to run with absolute freedom, give it absolutely perfect alignment
and adjustment with the other parts of the machine, so that it
is free, not because it is let alone or isolated, but because it has
been associated most skillfully and carefully with the other parts
of the great structure.

What is liberty? You say of the locomotive that it runs free.
What do you mean? You mean that its parts are so assembled
and adjusted that friction is reduced to a minimum, and that it
has perfect adjustment. We say of a boat skimming the water
with light foot, "How free she runs," when we mean, how perfectly she is adjusted to the force of the wind, how perfectly she
obeys the great breath out of the heavens that fills her sails.
Throw her head up into the wind and see how she will halt and
stagger, how every sheet will shiver and her whole frame be
shaken, how instantly she is "in irons," in the expressive phrase
of the sea. She is free only when you have let her fall off again
and have recovered once more her nice adjustment to the forces
she must obey and cannot defy.

Human freedom consists in perfect adjustments of human interests and human activities and human energies.

Now, the adjustments necessary between individuals, between
individuals and the complex institutions amidst which they live,
and between those institutions and the government, are infinitely

more intricate today than ever before. No doubt this is a tiresome and roundabout way of saying the thing, yet perhaps it is worth while to get somewhat clearly in our mind what makes all the trouble today. Life has become complex; there are many more elements, more parts, to it than ever before. And, therefore, it is harder to keep everything adjusted,—and harder to find out where the trouble lies when the machine gets out of order.

You know that one of the interesting things that Mr. Jefferson said in those early days of simplicity which marked the beginnings of our government was that the best government consisted in as little governing as possible. And there is still a sense in which that is true. It is still intolerable for the government to interfere with our individual activities except where it is necessary to interfere with them in order to free them. But I feel confident that if Jefferson were living in our day he would see what we see: that the individual is caught in a great confused nexus of all sorts of complicated circumstances, and that to let him alone is to leave him helpless as against the obstacles with which he has to contend; and that, therefore, law in our day must come to the assistance of the individual. It must come to his assistance to see that he gets fair play; that is all, but that is much. Without the watchful interference, the resolute interference, of the government, there can be no fair play between individuals and such powerful institutions as the trusts. Freedom today is something more than being let alone. The program of a government of freedom must in these days be positive, not negative merely.

Well, then, in this new sense and meaning of it, are we preserving freedom in this land of ours, the hope of all the earth? Have we, inheritors of this continent and of the ideals to which the fathers consecrated it,—have we maintained them, realizing them, as each generation must, anew? Are we, in the consciousness that the life of man is pledged to higher levels here than elsewhere, striving still to bear aloft the standards of liberty and hope, or, disillusioned and defeated, are we feeling the disgrace of having had a free field in which to do new things and of not having done them?

The answer must be, I am sure, that we have been in a fair way of failure,—tragic failure. And we stand in danger of utter failure yet except we fulfill speedily the determination we have reached, to deal with the new and subtle tyrannies according to their deserts. Don't deceive yourselves for a moment as to the power of the great interests which now dominate our development. They are so great that it is almost an open question whether the government of the United States can dominate them or not. Go one step further, make their organized power permanent, and it may be too late to turn back. The roads diverge at the point where we stand. They stretch their vistas out to regions where they are very far separated from one another; at the end of one is the old tiresome scene of government tied up with special interests; and at the other shines the liberating light of individual initiative, of individual liberty, of individual freedom, the light of untrammeled enterprise. I believe that that light shines out of the heavens itself that God has created. I believe in human liberty as I believe in the wine of life. There is no salvation for men in the pitiful condescensions of industrial masters. Guardians have no place in a land of freemen. Prosperity guaranteed by trustees has no prospect of endurance. Monopoly means the atrophy of enterprise. If monopoly persists, monopoly will always sit at the helm of the government. I do not expect to see monopoly restrain itself. If there are men in this country big enough to own the government of the United States, they are going to own it; what we have to determine now is whether we are big enough, whether we are men enough, whether we are free enough, to take possession again of the government which is our own. We haven't had free access to it, our minds have not touched it by way of guidance, in half a generation, and now we are engaged in nothing less than the recovery of what was made with our own hands, and acts only by our delegated authority.

I tell you, when you discuss the question of the tariffs and of the trusts, you are discussing the very lives of yourselves and your children. I believe that I am preaching the very cause of some of the gentlemen whom I am opposing when I preach the cause of free industry in the United States, for I think they are slowly girding the tree that bears the inestimable fruits of our life, and that if they are permitted to gird it entirely nature will take her revenge and the tree will die.

I do not believe that America is securely great because she has great men in her now. America is great in proportion as she can make sure of having great men in the next generation. She is rich in her unborn children; rich, that is to say, if those unborn children see the sun in a day of opportunity, see the sun when they are free to exercise their energies as they will. If they open their eyes in a land where there is no special privilege, then we shall come into a new era of American greatness and American liberty; but if they open their eyes in a country where they must be employees or nothing, if they open their eyes in a land of merely regulated monopoly, where all the conditions of industry are determined by small groups of men, then they will see an America such as the founders of this Republic would have wept to think of. The only hope is in the release of the forces which philanthropic trust presidents want to monopolize. Only the emancipation, the freeing and heartening of the vital energies of all the people will redeem us. In all that I may have to do in public affairs in the United States I am going to think of towns such as I have seen in Indiana, towns of the old American pattern, that own and operate their own industries, hopefully and happily. My thought is going to be bent upon the multiplication of towns of that kind and the prevention of the concentration of industry in this country in such a fashion and upon such a scale that towns that own themselves will be impossible. You know what the vitality of America consists of. Its vitality does not lie in New York, nor in Chicago; it will not be sapped by anything that happens in St. Louis. The vitality of America lies in the brains, the energies, the enterprise of the people throughout the land; in the efficiency of their factories and in the richness of the fields that stretch beyond the borders of the town; in the wealth which they extract from nature and originate for themselves through the inventive genius characteristic of all free American communities.

That is the wealth of America, and if America discourages the locality, the community, the self-contained town, she will kill the nation. A nation is as rich as her free communities; she is not as rich as her capital city or her metropolis. The amount of money in Wall Street is no indication of the wealth of the American people. That indication can be found only in the fertility of the American mind and the productivity of American industry everywhere throughout the United States. If America were not rich and fertile, there would be no money in Wall Street. If Americans were not vital and able to take care of themselves, the great money exchanges would break down. The welfare, the very existence of the nation, rests at last upon the great mass of the people; its prosperity depends at last upon the spirit in which they go about their work in their several communities throughout the broad land. In proportion as her towns and her countrysides are happy and hopeful will America realize the high ambitions which have marked her in the eyes of all the world.

The welfare, the happiness, the energy and spirit of the men and women who do the daily work in our mines and factories, on our railroads, in our offices and ports of trade, on our farms and on the sea, is the underlying necessity of all prosperity. There can be nothing wholesome unless their life is wholesome; there can be no contentment unless they are contented. Their physical welfare affects the soundness of the whole nation. How would it suit the prosperity of the United States, how would it suit business, to have a people that went every day sadly or sullenly to their work? How would the future look to you if you felt that the aspiration had gone out of most men, the confidence of success, the hope that they might improve their condition? Do you not see that just so soon as the old self-confidence of America, just so soon as her old boasted advantage of individual liberty and opportunity, is taken away, all the energy of her people begins to subside, to slacken, to grow loose and pulpy, without fiber, and men simply cast about to see that the day does not end disastrously with them?

So we must put heart into the people by taking the heartlessness out of politics, business, and industry. We have got to make politics a thing in which an honest man can take his part with satisfaction because he knows that his opinion will count as much as the next man's, and that the boss and the interests have been dethroned. Business we have got to untrammel, abolishing tariff favors, and railroad discrimination, and credit denials, and all forms of unjust handicaps against the little man. Industry we have got to humanize,—not through the trusts,—but through the direct action of law guaranteeing protection against dangers and compensation for injuries, guaranteeing sanitary conditions, proper hours, the right to organize, and all the other things which the conscience of the country demands as the workingman's right. We have got to cheer and inspirit our people with the sure prospects of social justice and due reward, with the vision of the open gates of opportunity for all. We have got to set the energy and the initiative of this great people absolutely free, so that the future of America will be greater than the past, so that the pride of America will grow with achievement, so that America will know as she advances from generation to generation that each brood of her sons is greater and more enlightened than that which preceded it, know that she is fulfilling the promise that she has made to mankind.

Such is the vision of some of us who now come to assist in its realization. For we Democrats would not have endured this long burden of exile if we had not seen a vision. We could have traded; we could have got into the game; we could have surrendered and made terms; we could have played the role of patrons to the men who wanted to dominate the interests of the country,—and here and there gentlemen who pretended to be of us did make those arrangements. They couldn't stand privation. You never can stand it unless you have within you some imperishable food upon which to sustain life and courage, the food of those visions of the spirit where a table is set before us laden with palatable fruits, the fruits of hope, the fruits of imagination, those invisible things of the spirit which are the only things upon which we can sustain ourselves through this weary world without fainting. We have carried in our minds, after you had thought you had obscured and blurred them, the ideals of those men who first set their foot upon America, those little bands who came to make a foothold in the wilderness, because the great teeming nations that they had left behind them had forgotten what human liberty was, liberty of thought, liberty of religion, liberty of residence, liberty of action.

Since their day the meaning of liberty has deepened. But it has not ceased to be a fundamental demand of the human spirit, a fundamental necessity for the life of the soul. And the day is at hand when it shall be realized on this consecrated soil,—a New Freedom,—a Liberty widened and deepened to match the broadened life of man in modern America, restoring to him in very truth the control of his government, throwing wide all gates of lawful enterprise, unfettering his energies, and warming the generous impulses of his heart,—a process of release, emancipation, and inspiration, full of a breath of life as sweet and wholesome as the airs that filled the sails of the caravels of Columbus and gave the promise and boast of magnificent Opportunity in which America *dare not fail.*

Arthur Meier Schlesinger
(1888-   )

ARTHUR MEIER SCHLESINGER is one of the notable American historians who has devoted himself to analyzing the American patterns of living and to interpreting American history and American life in classroom, lecture hall, and book. He was educated at Ohio State University and at Columbia, and has taught at Ohio State and at the State University of Iowa. He has also lectured, as Visiting Professor, at the University of London and the University of Edinburgh. One of his recent notable services has been as technical adviser to Colonial Williamsburg. At present he is Francis Lee Higginson Professor of History at Harvard. Among his books are *The Colonial Merchants and the American Revolution 1763–1776* (1918) and *New Viewpoints in American History* (1922). With Dr. D. R. Fox, he is also co-editor of the significant *A History of American Life,* begun in 1927 and to be completed in twelve volumes.

The following essay is taken from *New Viewpoints in American History* and represents the new trend in historical writing. Professor Schlesinger writes in his *Preface:* "The object of the present work is to bring together and summarize, in non-technical language, some of the results of the researches of the present era of historical study and to show their importance to a proper understanding of American history." From a literary point of view, this essay is an excellent example of the art of definition.

Radicalism and Conservatism
in American History (1922)

The heated discussion conducted in recent years by press and platform on the merits and demerits of radicalism and conservatism causes the student of American history to search his mind concerning the effects of these opposing types of thought on the past history of the United States. In such an inquiry, an initial difficulty presents itself: what do the terms, "conservative" and "radical," mean? Popular usage has tended to rob these expressions of exact meaning and to convert them into epithets of opprobrium and adulation which are used as the bias or interest of the person may dictate. The conservative, having mapped out the confines of truth to his own satisfaction, judges the depravity and errors of the radical by the extent of his departure from the boundaries thus established. Likewise the radical, from his vantage-point of truth, measures the knavery and infirmities of his opponents by the distance they have yet to travel to reach his goal. Neither conservative nor radical regards the other with judicial calm or "sweet reasonableness." Neither is willing to admit that the other has a useful function to perform in the progress of society. Each regards the other with deep feeling as the enemy of everything that is fundamentally good in government and society.

In seeking a workable definition of these terms, the philosophic insight of Thomas Jefferson is a beacon light to the inquirer. When Jefferson withdrew from active political life at the close of his presidency in 1809, he left behind him the heat and smoke of partisan strife and retired to a contemplative life on his Virginia estate, where his fellow countrymen learned to revere him as the "Sage of Monticello." The voluminous correspondence

From Arthur Meier Schlesinger, *New Viewpoints in American History.* By permission of the Macmillan Company, publishers.

of these twilight years of his life is full of instruction for the student of history and politics. His tremendous curiosity caused him to find an unfailing source of speculation in the proclivity of mankind to separate into contrasting schools of opinion. In one luminous passage, representative of the bent of his thought, he declared: "Men, according to their constitutions, and the circumstances in which they are placed, differ honestly in opinion. Some are Whigs, Liberals, Democrats, call them what you please. Others are Tories, Serviles, Aristocrats, etc. The latter fear the people, and wish to transfer all power to the higher classes of society; the former consider the people as the safest depository of power in the last resort; they cherish them, therefore, and wish to leave in them all the powers to the exercise of which they are competent."

In this passage Jefferson does not use the expressions "conservative" and "radical"—indeed, those words had no place in the American political vocabulary until Civil War times—but his penetrating analysis throws a flood of light on the significance of those terms nevertheless. The Tory who fears the people and the Whig who trusts them are equivalent to our own categories of "conservative" and "radical." Thus Jefferson finds the vital distinction between the two schools of opinion in their respective attitudes toward popular government.

But before accepting Jefferson's classification as correct, what shall we do with the common notion that the conservative is a person who opposes change and that the ear-mark of the radical is his liking for innovation? This does not seem to be a fundamental distinction. If a difference of opinion concerning the need of change were the basic difference between the two, then Americans who advocate a limitation of the suffrage to male property-owners may properly be regarded as radicals, for they advocate an alteration in the established order; and French patriots of today opposing the re-establishment of the Orleanist monarchy are to be classed as conservatives, for they would keep things unchanged. Few people would be willing to follow the logic of their premises to such conclusions. On the other hand, it cannot be denied that history has generally shown the radical in the role of an active proponent of change and has cast the conservative for the part of the stalwart defender of things as they are. Is such evidence to be dismissed as a coincidence oft-repeated, or has there been behind the actions of both radical and conservative some self-interested purpose which has determined their respective attitudes toward the established order?

The very question perhaps suggests the answer. Broadly speaking, all history has been an intermittent contest on the part of the more numerous section of society to wrest power and privilege from the minority which had hitherto possessed it. The group which at any period favored broader popular rights and liberties was therefore likely to find itself as a contender for the new and untried, leaving to its antagonists the comfortable repute of being the conservators of the *status quo* and the foes of change. But, though the historical conditions influenced the character of the contest, such conditions were, after all, merely the stage setting of the struggle. Advocacy of change should, under such circumstances, be regarded merely as the means employed to attain an end and, in no sense, as an end in itself. Recurring now to Jefferson's definition, the goal sought by each group—whether it be in the direction of greater or less democracy—would appear to constitute the real difference between the two.

It should be clear, then, that the radical is a person who, in contrast to the conservative, favors a larger participation of the people in the control of government and society and in the benefits accruing from such control. To attain his ideal the radical may become a protagonist of change; he usually has been one, as a matter of history, but this fact is a mere incident to, and not the touchstone of, his radicalism. The temperament of the radical is sanguine. He can say with Jefferson: "I steer my bark with Hope in the head, leaving Fear astern. My hopes, indeed, sometimes fail; but not oftener than the forebodings of the gloomy." The conservative, on the other hand, is skeptical of the capacity of the mass of the people to protect their own interests intelligently; and believing that social progress in the past has always come from the leadership of wealth and ability, he is the consistent opponent of the unsettling plans of the radical. If the old saw is true that a pessimist is the wife of an optimist, perhaps the cynicism of the conservative is amply accounted for by his enforced association with the radical. The radical regards himself

as a man of vision; but the conservative sees him only as a vision-
ary. The radical as a type is likely to be broad-minded and
shallow-minded; the disinterested conservative is inclined to be
high-minded and narrow-minded.

Of course, the expressions "radical" and "conservative" are
relative terms, for at any given time the lines are drawn by the
opposing forces upon the basis of the circumstances then existing.
It is a truism that the radical of today may become the conservative of tomorrow. This does not necessarily argue inconsistency.
It may indicate rather that, when the specific measures which the
radical has advocated have been adopted, he believes that the supreme aim of public policy has been attained and he becomes a
defender of the new *status quo* against any further extensions of
popular rights. This is perhaps the same as saying that the conservative of today, had he held the same opinions on political
and social questions a generation ago, would have been looked
upon then as a radical. The movement of history has been from
radicalism to conservatism so far as the attitude of individuals is
concerned, but from conservatism to radicalism so far as the trend
of public policy is concerned.

Not only are the terms relative in the sense just indicated, but
they are comparative as applied to variations of opinion that exist
within each school of thought. In the conservative camp are to
be found different degrees of distrust of popular rule, varying
from the purblind reactionaries on the extreme right to the moderates on the extreme left. Similarly the radical camp has its sub-
divisions, comprising all grades of confidence in popular government from a left wing of ultra-radicals to a wing at the opposite
extreme composed of progressives or liberals. The apostles of lawlessness—those who would accomplish their ends through a defiance of, or assault on, the law—are to be found in the exterior
wings of both camps. In this sense the reactionaries who seek to
gain their purposes through the corruption or intimidation of
the courts are to be regarded as much the enemies of law and
order as the followers of Daniel Shays in 1786 when they tried to
disperse the courts with violence. On the other hand, the moderates of the conservative camp tend to fraternize with the liberals of the radical camp without, however, completely merging

their identity because of deep-grained prepossessions and habits of thought. It is in this middle zone or "No Man's Land" between the camps that there occurs the only true meeting of minds; and in democratic countries, advances can be made, under legal forms and proper safeguards, only through the temporary union of these groups for common purposes.

No attempt need be made here to idealize or glorify either the radical or the conservative. Adherents of each are constantly engaged in constructing traditions which would ascribe superhuman attributes to the great leaders and spokesmen of their respective schools of opinion in the past. In this myth-making process the radicals inevitably suffer a serious handicap, for the audacious reformer of a century ago is likely to appear today as a man of orthodox ideas, and latter-day conservatives, without any appreciation of the earlier clash of ideas, are likely to claim him as their very own. For example, the average American citizen who values property rights as superior to human rights easily imagines himself in the forefront of the riot that led to the Boston Massacre, for through the mellow haze of time he forgets the real character of that street brawl with its raucous mob of blatant, missile-hurling roughs and halfbreeds.*

Whatever may be said in praise of either the conservative or the radical, both find themselves in bad company, for each makes his appeal to some of the basest as well as to some of the most ennobling qualities of human nature. The thinking conservative finds his chief allies in the self-complacency of comfortable mediocrity, in the apathy and stupidity of the toil-worn multitudes, and in the aggressive self-interest of the privileged classes. All those who dread uncertainty either because of timidity or from conventional-mindedness or for fear of material loss are enlisted under the conservative standard. The honest radical draws much of his support from self-seeking demagogues and reckless experimenters, from people who want the world changed because they cannot get along in it as it is, from *poseurs* and *dilettanti,* and from malcontents who love disturbance for its own sake. The two schools have more in common than either would admit; both

---

* The reader, of a conservative turn of mind, should not fail to read A. P. Peabody's article, "Boston Mobs before the Revolution" in *The Atlantic Monthly,* vol. lxii, pp. 321-333.

have their doctrinaires and dogmatists; both tend toward a stiffening of intellectual creeds; and who can deny that each has its share of mental defectives and the criminal-minded?

2

There are special reasons why radical thought and aspiration should have attained fertile growth in American soil. From our earliest history a process of social selection has been going on which has served to separate the radical from the conservative elements of the population and has given to the former unique opportunities for impressing their philosophy upon the population in general. As Professor Van Tyne has pointed out in a notable passage, the tendency of colonization was to stock the American colonies with radicals and dissenters and to leave behind in England the conservatives and conformists, thereby rendering inevitable sharp contrasts in temperament and outlook between the colonists and the mother country. This process has repeated itself with endless variation in the later history of our country. The incoming tides of foreign immigration have deposited upon our shores many of the restless and rebellious spirits of the Old World civilizations. The periodic flow of westward settlement in this country has tended to carry the adventurous and the discontented forward into new lands of opportunity, leaving the older settlements to the control of timid and conservative people. Thus the radical spirit has constantly been fed and refreshed by contributions from abroad; and in our own land the processes of social integration have tended to segregate the radical-minded geographically and to permit them to develop without the restraining influences of a long-established conservative class.

Under such favoring circumstances radicalism might have been expected to attain its most extreme expression in America. The result, however, has been neither a reign of overbearing individualism nor the establishment of a co-operative commonwealth, although both forms of social organization had their advocates and were given sporadic trial. The acquisition of property on easy terms in the newer parts of the country made the settlers quickly forget the bitter injustices and oppressions of the older civilizations and, without sapping their interest in democratic progress, gave them a personal stake in the orderly advance of the community. Indeed, the very freedom which they enjoyed to experiment as they wished with their own lives and property exercised a moderating influence on their conduct. So it has happened that, while progress along liberal lines has been rapid in the newer parts of America, it has been accomplished through the acts of legislatures and the amending of constitutions. In the older sections such advances have been made slowly and have often been attended by severe political struggles, sometimes culminating in armed conflict, as in the case of the Dorr Rebellion in Rhode Island in 1842–1843.

It is not surprising that, as a result of this continuing process of social differentiation, one of the outstanding characteristics of American national development should be the constant interest of the people in movements for democratic and humanitarian reform. Every movement of radical tendency has developed through certain clearly-defined stages, as if in obedience to some immutable law of social dynamics. These phases can generally be reduced to three. At the outset there occurs a period of violent propaganda conducted by a small group of agitators. These pioneers resort to picturesque and sensational methods of propaganda in order to awaken the apathetic public to the presence of evil conditions and the need for change. They constitute a flying wedge of protest and moral indignation. The late ex-President Roosevelt referred to this vanguard when he declared in his autobiography: "Every reform movement has a lunatic fringe." It is indeed a "lunatic fringe," in the sense that these trumpeters of reform act irrationally according to the standards of the majority of the people, and must expect to suffer their ridicule or ostracism or persecution. In this advanced group may ordinarily be found the "soap-boxer," the "muckraker," the idealist, the doctrinaire, the fanatic, the would-be revolutionist and, at times even in American history, the martyr. These agitators, irrespective of individual peculiarities, share a bitter disregard of existing public opinion, a passion for destructive criticism, and an emotional conviction that in their proposal is to be found a panacea for human ills.

Some movements never advance beyond this first ultra-radical stage, for they fail to gain converts outside of the group immediately engaged in furthering the cause. The second stage arrives when the pioneer reformers succeed in arousing interest and approval among the soberer elements of the population. The ideas long regarded as "queer" or "dangerous" are now on the point of gaining the sanction of respectability; and the assurance of a growing popular favor enlists the support of some of the experienced leaders of the people—the "practical statesmen." These men possess the constructive ability, the organizing genius and the knowledge of political strategy which are necessary in order to carry into execution the ideas of the agitators. Less agile of imagination and frequently less pure of purpose, they know better the temper and limitations of the average man; and under their direction the new policies and doctrines, perhaps in modified form, become the law of the land. Thus the actual achievers of the reform are the liberals or progressives, aided perhaps by those moderates of the conservative camp who favor the proposed change as the best preventive of more basic changes. If, as sometimes happens, some of the abler leaders of the first period survive into the second and are placed in positions of power by a surge of popular feeling, they usually become sobered and moderated by responsibility and experience, and their conduct is scarcely distinguishable from that of the practical statesmen.

The third and final stage of the reform is reached when the new doctrines, having lost their air of strangeness and demonstrated either their utility or harmlessness, become imbedded in the conscience and philosophy of the people at large. The public becomes adjusted to practices and policies that were altogether unacceptable a few years earlier; indeed most of the people have already forgotten that these reforms were not always a part of the commonly accepted stock of ideas. The cycle of reform has about completed itself; for public opinion hardens into a new conservatism and forms a crust that toughly resists any further efforts for change. Advocates for new advances must employ the militant and fantastic methods which mark the "lunatic fringe" of a new crusade for reform.

3

Examples of reform movements abound in American history. These have been multifarious in their objects and reflect the diversified interests and social outlook of the ages in which they flourished. Some of the most significant of these enterprises have been concerned with improving the lot of the average man or the condition of society's wards—the dependent and the criminal. From many points of view such movements would appear to merit more careful study by the youth in our schools than most reforms of a purely political type; but, the anti-slavery movement excepted, reformative movements of a humanitarian character receive little or no attention in the orthodox histories. Yet what thoughtful American can deny the superb courage and inestimable service of the men and women (unknown to most of us) whose efforts made possible religious liberty, free public education, scientific care of the deaf, the dumb and the blind, a more humane criminal code, the abolition of child labor, reformative treatment of criminals, statutory reduction of the workday, governmental protection of the public health, and the abolition of the saloon?

The reforming activities of political parties and party factions are better known. Jefferson advanced the proposition that a people should never pass legislation binding for a period longer than the lifetime of their own generation, for, as conditions change, men change, and every fresh generation should have a free opportunity to fashion its own laws and constitutions according to its special circumstances. Using certain tables compiled by M. de Buffon, he went so far as to fix the average duration of a generation at nineteen years. Looking back over the annals of the United States, we can see that the course of our national development has, in a large degree, mirrored the changing needs and interests of the procession of generations. From one point of view, American history may be regarded as a succession of eager new generations ruthlessly elbowing aside older and effete generations; and although lacking the automatic modes of expression that Jefferson would have provided, each fresh accession of leadership has wrought a transformation of party creeds, and represented new policies, practices and ethical conceptions, better adapted to the changed economic and social conditions of the time. It is scarcely necessary to set forth the history of each of these generations in detail, for the results of their labors are recorded in the achievements of the nation. Each fresh generation experienced the usual difficulties of a group advocating unaccustomed ideas; and the following sketch should yield, among other things, many illustrations of the familiar cycle by which novel ideas become acceptable maxims of policy and then are consecrated as the truisms of statesmen.

Without going back into the period of our colonial beginnings, it is plain to see that the Declaration of Independence signalized the accession of the first generation to power in our national history. No spirit of decrepit age or feeble counsel stalked through the scintillant passages of that immortal document. Strong medicine though it was for the American subjects of George III, their minds had been prepared for the event by a long period of violent propaganda conducted by such skilled masters of the art as James Otis, Patrick Henry, Samuel Adams, Alexander McDougall, Charles Thomson, Christopher Gadsden and Tom Paine. The methods of these patriot-agitators were thoroughly demagogic and sensational, characterized by unlawful assemblages and mob violence as well as by legislative memorials and pamphleteering of unusual merit; and gradually they succeeded in arousing the colonial population to a realization of the injustices which they decried. They sought radical reform, for it was their object to destroy the autocratic power of the British king and to establish in America an untried form of government based upon the principle of popular rule.

Due to the unusual conditions existing in a country torn by revolutionary conflict, the influence of the orginal agitators continued beyond the time when their chief usefulness had expired. Independence proclaimed, the task fell to them of establishing a federal government for the thirteen new-fledged states, a task demanding constructive genius of a high order. Their effort at a solution, offered in the form of the Articles of Confederation, precipitated the "Critical Period" of American history and revealed the poverty of their organizing ability. Under the circumstances they were compelled to surrender leadership not to a new generation but to a different element of their own generation—to men who thought less in terms of theories and emotions, and more in terms of realities, men who did not despise bargain and compromise if they might thereby gain the end they had in view. The accession of these men inaugurated a period of conservative reaction. Hamilton, John Adams, Washington, John Jay and their

Federalist associates accepted the liberal philosophy of their predecessors with mental reservations; but they brought about the
adoption of the Constitution and created under it a national government which not only worked successfully at the time but
which stands today as one of the oldest continuous constitutional
governments in the world.

When the Federalists were yet at the height of their power, the
sappers and miners of a new age were passionately devoting their
energies to the subversion of the existing régime. Led by such
men as Jefferson, Madison, Aaron Burr, William Duane, Thomas
Callender and Philip Freneau, the object of these crusaders was
radical reform. They wished to replace what they considered to
be a centralized government of pseudo-monarchical tendencies
with a truly republican government based upon the principle of
decentralization of authority. The presidential election of 1800
brought the new leaders into control, and Jefferson's inauguration may be regarded as the beginning of the second generation
of American statesmanship. The new rulers consisted in part of
the abler figures among the group of agitators; and the leaders
of the supplanted generation formed the dwindling nucleus of an
intransigeant opposition. Jefferson and his successors in the presidency, Madison and Monroe, were sobered by the responsibility
of holding office and found themselves forced to modify in practice many views that had seemed unassailable in speculation. Notwithstanding a flabbiness of administration characteristic of a
liberal government in power, the Jeffersonian Republicans succeeded in proving the practicability of liberal principles as the
guide of public policy.

While the Jeffersonian Republicans were still holding the seats
of authority, a growing discontent against their control began to
find expression under the skillful direction of a younger generation of leaders aspiring for power. The pacifistic foreign policy
of the elder statesmen in face of the aggressions of England and
France furnished the issue upon which the new group succeeded
in attaining national prominence. Henry Clay, John C. Calhoun,
Richard M. Johnson, Felix Grundy, Langdon Cheves, Peter B.
Porter and other "War Hawks" entered Congress in 1811 and
plunged the nation into an unprofitable war contrary to the best
judgment of many of the seasoned statesmen of the time. By the

close of the war, the new generation had formulated their plan of legislative reform and were definitely in command of the situation, although their measures were looked on askance by Madison and Monroe and bitterly opposed by Daniel Webster, a young man of the new age still lingering under the influence of the discredited Federalist leadership. Their program of legislation, presented to Congress in 1816–1817, was essentially conservative in its tendency, containing as its main features a protective tariff, a new and greater United States Bank, the construction of internal improvements at national expense, and adequate military preparedness. Before they yielded to the onrush of the next generation most of these reforms had been passed into federal statutes; indeed, their chief policies gained such general acceptance that party lines disappeared entirely about 1820.

Shortly thereafter began the inevitable agitation which presaged the accession of a new generation to the control of public policy. The forerunners of the new leadership raised their voices in protest against the political philosophy that controlled the times —the right of the well-born to rule—rather than against any specific measures which the dominant group had enacted. The first attempt at revolt resulted in the indecisive election of 1824; but thereafter a veritable hue and cry was raised against the Adams-Clay administration and all their works and doctrines, and the forces of discontent became well organized under the direction of such men as William B. Lewis, Thomas H. Benton, Amos Kendall, Duff Green and Martin Van Buren. The inauguration of Andrew Jackson in 1829 marked the entrance of the new political generation, the fourth in order of succession, into command of the government. The practical statesmen of the new order were Jackson himself, Thomas H. Benton and Martin Van Buren, each of whom, in his own way, embodied the liberal ideals of the new time. Their principles called for increased control of the common people in all departments of government and politics; or, in other words, for the abolition of special privilege in appointments to office, in the federal banking system (the United States Bank), in internal improvements, and in the disposition of western lands. Before they were retired from power, the Jacksonian Democrats succeeded in translating their doctrines into governmental practice though challenged at every turn by the brilliant and versatile opposition of the leaders whom they had supplanted. Many of the details of their program were modified by later generations, but the basic principles of government which they established are to this day accepted as the foundations of the American democratic structure.

While the generation of Jackson was still strongly entrenched in power, the portents that foretold the oncoming of a new statesmanship were beginning to display themselves in the political heavens. The heralds of the coming era were deeply convinced that the pivotal issue in national affairs was one which the elder leaders had carefully ignored and evaded—the slavery question. To a consideration of this issue the new generation brought all the energy and arrogant assurance with which fresh generations have always approached weighty problems of public policy. Unfortunately for the orderly evolution of national institutions, the new leadership brought conflicting viewpoints to bear upon the great problem of the time, one portion of the new statesmen hailing from the South and the other portion from the free states of the North. The great conflict of the new era was not, as so often before, a contest between a superannuated statesmanship and the buoyant, resistless vanguard of a new leadership, but a struggle between men of the same generation, equally sure of themselves, equally determined to attain dominance and establish their policies in governmental practice.

With the accession of John Tyler to the presidency in 1841 the new generation assumed direction of the government with the conservative pro-slavery contingent in the ascendant, a position which they succeeded in retaining for nearly twenty years. From the outset they had to contend with the ceaseless and growing agitation of the abolitionists, led by such men as Garrison, Giddings, Wendell Phillips, Gerrit Smith and John Greenleaf Whittier; and all their guile and power availed them nothing against zealots who were inspired only to greater effort by "gag resolutions" and mob attacks. Nevertheless the mass of the people were slow to accept the teachings of the abolitionists; and in the meantime the conservative ideas of the pro-slavery group were in large part carried into force. Under the skillful guidance of men like James K. Polk, Jefferson Davis, Stephen A. Douglas and Alexander H. Stephens, half of the Republic of Mexico was annexed, the federal territories were opened to slavery, and a stricter fugitive slave law was enacted.

But gradually the anti-slavery agitation began to bear fruit. Leadership in the movement, originally held by ultra-radical abolitionists like Garrison and Phillips, passed to anti-slavery liberals like Chase and Seward and Lincoln. The propaganda of emotionalism was succeeded by appeals to reason and organized political activity culminating in the Republican party. Division within the ranks of the Democratic leaders early in 1860 gave the anti-slavery forces their opportunity; and in the presidential election of that year they elected their candidate Abraham Lincoln to the presidency on a platform pledging the party to the non-extension of slavery. The southerners believed that behind this moderate program lay the uncompromising purposes of men like Garrison and John Brown; and they chose to shift any subsequent controversy from legislative halls to the battlefield.

The processes of orderly social growth are always unsettled by military conflict; and in the case of the Civil War the high passions aroused by the struggle made it possible for the anti-slavery radicals to gain ascendency in Congress although under other circumstances their period of influence would have expired when the anti-slavery cause was taken up by the practical statesmen. Such men as Thaddeus Stevens, Charles Sumner and Ben Wade gloried in the name Radical as distinguished from Conservative or Administration Republican; and under their propulsion, abolition measures of increasing severity were enacted by Congress, and the president was given no peace until he had issued the Emancipation Proclamation. When victory crowned the Union arms, the task fell to the Radicals, unsuited to their genius, of reconstructing the South; and this they undertook with the same energy and singleness of purpose with which they had fought the war. Applying their doctrinaire preconceptions to the solution of the Negro problem, they raised the slaves to the level of white citizens and conferred upon the black men the right to vote. But by these last measures the generation had over-reached itself in its radicalism; reforms enacted under such auspices and at such a juncture were not likely to be enduring in effect. Although the changes were solemnly embodied in the federal Constitution in the fourteenth and fifteenth amendments, they were so far in advance of public opinion that to this day they remain a dead letter so far as the great majority of the Negroes are concerned.

The reconstruction statesmen began rapidly to pass away early in the seventies as if burnt out by the very intensity of their zeal, and their places were soon taken by new men whose minds dwelt on matters far removed from the idealistic and humanitarian interests of the earlier period. The new leaders were concerned primarily with the economic and industrial exploitation of the nation's resources and with governmental policies that would assist material development at every turn. Under their direction the energies of the government were, in the sixth generation of American politics, turned to conservative purposes—to land-grants for railroads, the protective tariff system, "sound money" finance and a policy of non-interference in the methods and management of industry. Men like Roscoe Conkling, Blaine, Garfield, Levi P. Morton, Samuel J. Randall and "Czar" Reed came into charge of public affairs. Even such spokesmen as Schurz, Curtis and Cleveland, whose voices were raised in protest against some of the more obnoxious practices of the dominant leadership, did not differ fundamentally from them in their conception of the functions of government. While this generation was in power, the United States made the transition to the modern era and the foundations were laid for the stupendous business development of the present time.

The note of dissent was early sounded against the domination of the government by the great corporate interests; but the protestants were for many years in a hopeless minority. They spent their energies, with little effect, in launching radical minor parties and in organizing radical agrarian and workingman associations. In the decade of the nineties the movement of protest against the existing order reached threatening proportions in the Populist movement and the "free silver" campaign of 1896. In the opening years of the new century the work of propaganda was taken up with missionary zeal by the "muckrakers," a group of publicists and writers whose object it was to inflame public opinion against corruption and abuses in government and "big business."

On the crest of the wave of popular resentment thus raised up, the leaders of the new generation came into power, the seventh political generation since the natal days of the republic. Unlike the elder leaders, the new statesmen were animated with liberal ideals; without regard to party affiliations they labored for "progressive" legislation and strove for the advent of a "new democracy." Under the inspiration of such men as Bryan, Roosevelt, Wilson, La Follette, Hughes and Hiram Johnson, they brought about the enactment of laws for the restraint of trusts, railroads, land-grabbing corporations and the financial interests; the working conditions of employees were greatly improved by the enactment of a wide variety of welfare legislation; and an effort was made to rejuvenate the power of the people in governmental affairs through direct nominations and direct legislation, the granting of woman suffrage and the popular election of senators. The new measures were carried through in face of the embittered opposition of the survivors of the departed epoch.

When the United States entered the World War in 1917, the signs of the times indicated that the generation had about run its course. Its program of domestic reform had been enacted; Roosevelt passed away in 1919, Wilson, La Follette and other vigorous reformers of an earlier day were beginning to show signs of physical decline; the adoption of federal suffrage for women suggested a point of departure for a new era. An unceasing criticism directed against the foundations of the existing order had been conducted by the Socialists and other radical groups and was apparently preparing the way for the transfer of power to fresh hands. New and lively issues were already looming up which had received little serious consideration by those in power, questions concerned with the application of democratic principles to industrial organization and with the relations of the United States to the world order. A leadership representative of the new day seemed slow in making its appearance, and the presidential campaign of 1920 showed the country in a condition of drift awaiting the coming of new pilots. Future events alone can supply the confirmatory evidence to show whether, as at present seems likely, we are today standing on the threshold of the eighth generation of American statesmanship.

4

For confirmed radicals and orthodox conservatives this survey of the successive generations of American history will serve merely to reinforce their preconceptions as to the importance of their respective theories of progress to national development. The one group will find in the evidence sufficient reason for maintaining that the American people would have fared better if statesmen of the Jeffersonian school had always been at the helm. The other will discover justification for the conviction that the nation made its chief advances under the guidance of statesmen of the Hamiltonian school. The former group will be likely to stress the dynamic quality of democratic and humanitarian ideals as the motive force of national progress. The latter will point to administrative efficiency and the stimulation of economic enterprise as supplying the chief impulse to national achievement.

But to the candid student of social tendencies it is not likely that either conclusion will prove wholly acceptable. Beyond question the foregoing review yields two generalizations which would seem to be pregnant with significance. In the first place, epochs of radicalism and conservatism have followed each other in alternating order; and, secondly, with the changing of epochs, leadership in public affairs has passed from the liberals of the one division to the moderates of the other and *vice versa,* except in times of war and after-war readjustment when the extremists of the one group or the other have ordinarily been in the saddle. Whatever fallacies or losses may be apparent to the logician in such a zigzag scheme of progress, it nevertheless remains that in America social development has never followed a straight line, but, within limits, has been the result of the unconscious employment by the people of the trial-and-error method. Experimentation and opportunism, rather than preconceived theories, have been the animating spirit of American progress.

To the working out of this vital social process, both the radical and the conservative have made important and essential contributions. Their mutual criticism and vigilant antagonism have served to keep America abreast the most enlightened nations of the world without the periodic recourse to revolutionary violence characteristic of continental European countries. The functioning of these crosscurrents and countercurrents of opinion has been made possible by the solemn guarantees, in the state and federal constitutions, of free speech and a free press. If the experience of the past is a dependable guide to the future, the best assurance of the peaceful and orderly advance of the people in the future would seem to lie in a jealous regard for the right of free exchanges and comparisons of opinion.

In conclusion, this survey of the procession of generations suggests a criterion for analyzing the elusive quality of *greatness,* which by general consent attaches to certain characters in American history. Restricting our inquiry to the incumbents of the presidency, a consensus of opinion among historians and publicists ascribes pre-eminence to Washington, Jefferson, Jackson and Lincoln, and, in a preliminary way, to Roosevelt and Wilson. But what were the tests and standards that were applied in making this selection? It is not to be denied that this group of foremost presidents differed from each other in many conventional respects —in education, temperament, training, personality, party affiliation, and attachment to specific public policies. Furthermore, Washington as president was swayed by conservative ideals whereas the other presidents were exponents of the doctrines of liberalism as understood by the men of their own generation. Evidently their title to fame is not derived from any of the aptitudes or qualities that have been noted.

The answer to our query has perhaps been reached by this process of elimination. These statesmen enjoyed one attribute, and one only, in common: they were men of elastic mind, sensitive to the quickening impulses of a new time, swift to grasp a fresh vision of public duty and to present their solution in a form capable of rallying public opinion to its support. Their ability to marshal the energies of the nation to meet the new situation assured them of their historic position among the great leaders of the nation. Thus the essence of greatness, as viewed in the perspective of history, does not consist in the ability to hold back or even to mark time but in the capacity for adaptability to change, in the quality of leading the nation to the acceptance of new responsibilities and larger opportunities.

Ralph Barton Perry
(1876-   )

RALPH BARTON PERRY is Professor of Philosophy at Harvard
University. He received his education at Princeton and Harvard
and has taught at Williams and Smith colleges as well as on the
Hyde lectureship in French universities in 1921–1922. During the
first World War he served as major and as Secretary of the War
Department Commission on Education and Special Training. He
is a Chevalier of the French Legion of Honor. His books reveal
the broad scope of his philosophical and social interests: *The
Approach to Philosophy* (1905); *The New Realism* (1912); *The
Free Man and the Soldier* (1916); *The Present Conflict of Ideals*
(1918); *The Thought and Character of William James* (1935)—
the Pulitzer Prize biography for that year; *The Meaning of the
Humanities* (1938).

The essay reprinted here is a careful analysis of the problems
of democracy in the face of a crisis and a proposal that they be
solved not by emotion but by reason. Although recent events
have affected some of the statements in this essay, the general
argument still has force.

The Alleged Failure of Democracy (1934)

The rejection of democracy is nowadays regarded as evidence of superior wisdom. Although it is still customary, for political purposes, to pay it lip service, "between friends," or in the judgment of the hard-boiled fact finder, it is often supposed to be an exploded myth—a practical failure as well as a theoretical fallacy. Opinion has been veering so swiftly in this direction that while a few years ago the defense of democracy would have been condemned as hackneyed and banal, one who undertakes it now is suspected of seeking notoriety.

The beginning of wisdom in this matter is to state the question. What does it mean to say or to believe that democracy is a failure? There are two judgments of this sort that clearly beg the question. They need to be disposed of first lest they become sources of confusion. There is the judgment which condemns democracy because it is too democratic, and there is the judgment which condemns it because it is not democratic enough.

What does it mean to condemn democracy as too democratic? People do not as a rule beg a question explicitly: they do not say in so many words that democracy is a bad thing because democracy is a bad thing. But there are those who argue against democracy in theory from their dislike of it in practice. Since the practice is precisely what the theory means, these critics are really not arguing at all, but are only expressing a prejudice.

It sometimes happens that those who express a dislike for democracy in proximity were once loud in their praise of it or hot in its pursuit. Such a reversal is not at all unusual, for goals which exert an attractive force at a distance often exert a repulsive force when they are approached more closely. When I was a boy I had

Reprinted from the Autumn, 1934, *Yale Review*, Copyright Yale University Press, by permission of the Editor.

a dog whose favorite pastime was chasing cats. Ordinarily this furnished agreeable and harmless exhilaration both to the dog and to the cats. But every once in a while, owing to some unnatural burst of speed or accident of topography, the dog would overtake a cat. Then he promptly sat down and scratched a flea or suddenly thought of some other engagement. Cats were good to chase, but catching them was a very different matter, for which he had neither the appetite nor the technique. You could see, too, that he was somewhat disgusted with the cat because it refused to go on escaping. Now, one of the dangers of pursuing ideals is that some day, owing to prodigious exertions, you may, the first thing you know, overtake one. Or you may, at any rate, gain on it. And then, as you come to close quarters, it is possible that you will experience a sudden revulsion of feeling. If we look about us, I think we shall find here and there ardent pursuers of democracy who have assumed the posture of that dog—trying to appear as irrelevant as possible.

For a long time, feebly and intermittently since the beginning of the Christian era, vigorously and continuously since the beginning of our own national existence, we have been trying to improve the condition of the masses. It is a great end to pursue, and it has given us a great run. But recently we have been gaining on it; and, instead of celebrating the victory, the fastidious withdraw their skirts, anxious housewives deplore the passing of "the good old-fashioned servant," and uneasy employers complain of the increase of wages and the standard of living. American reformers, beginning with Thomas Jefferson, have eloquently preached the gospel of universal salvation by education. Now that their eloquence has borne fruit, and the youth of the land are thronging to the colleges, many leaders of education are barricading their doors and posting sentries to keep back the crowd. They are remarking with an air of perfect innocence, as though they had never said anything on the subject before, that, after all, the value of formal education has been much exaggerated—and that for most men there is nothing so good as that great public school of *experience,* which was opened some time ago by the Creator in the Garden of Eden and which it costs nothing to operate.

The second kind of question-begging critic objects to democracy because it is not democratic enough. While critics of the first kind profess the theory but shrink from its execution, these complain that it has in fact never been executed. They beg the question because although they seem to be advancing arguments against democratic institutions they are really assuming democracy as their standard of criticism. They are in their hearts its most radical and dogmatic partisans. When such a critic argues that public education does not really emancipate the mind, or that the people do not really rule, or that genuine equality is inconsistent with a capitalistic system, or that the American democracy does not in fact permit those liberties of speech and press which it is pledged to secure, the very bitterness of his lament reveals the depth of his passion for emancipation, popular government, equality, and liberty. An analogy is afforded by the case of Christianity. There are those who, like the first opponent of democracy, do not like Christianity at close range, or prefer the profession to the practice. They feel, like Nietzsche, that there is already too much Christianity in the world. Radical Christians, on the other hand, condemn Christendom for being too little Christian, and by this condemnation affirm the rigorous and uncompromising quality of their adherence to Christian principles.

These two sets of critics, then, we may ignore; neither has fairly examined the fundamental question. But today they are being joined by critics of a more thoroughgoing sort, who profess to have considered democracy on its merits and to have rejected it deliberately. They would have us reopen a question that was supposed to have been settled. They would have us reverse the main current of political change during the last two centuries. They would have America, instead of moving forward in the direction of her original impulse and towards her supposed historic destiny, go back and begin over again, modeling her institutions on those very forms which were once denounced as tyrannical abuses.

Those who thus reject democracy advisedly and explicitly may also be divided into two groups, namely, those who reject it for practical reasons and those who reject it for reasons of theory. Critics of the first sort claim that democracy does not work, while critics of the second sort contend that, being based on false assumptions and bad logic, it should never have been tried.

We are here concerned primarily with the charge that democracy has broken down—that, owing to human nature and the complexities of life, it has proved a failure. In replying to this form of attack I would not for a moment argue, or seem to argue, that democracy has been an unqualified success. That it has in some measure failed is indisputable, and this partial failure has been, no doubt, in some measure due to the complacent assumption of success. Sound criticism, however, will know how to pass beyond complacency or rhetorical eulogy without leaping to the other and equally futile extreme of reckless despair.

The adverse judgment which the present age is disposed to pronounce on the success of democracy has, in the first place, to be qualified by the reflection that all human institutions are failures as judged by standards of perfection. They all leave room for improvement. There is what may be called a constant of failure in all great enterprises, arising out of the complexity of the problem, the weaknesses of mankind, and the weight of the obstacles to be overcome. Marriage is a failure, agriculture and industry are failures, religion is a failure, education is a failure. Government, being peculiarly difficult, is perhaps the greatest failure of all. But it would be equally true to say that government is a remarkable achievement. It all depends upon the height of your expectation; and if it be legitimate to remark how badly it is done, it is equally legitimate and sometimes more wholesome to wonder that it should be done at all. From time to time some particular institution becomes the symbol of human failure in general and has to bear the brunt of human discontent. There are signs that economic institutions are taking their turn as such a symbol and that the sins of government may soon be deemed less scandalous.

In fairness, then, we should admit this constant of human failure, and at the same time eliminate it from the specific bill of indictment brought against democracy. Besides this ordinary failure, to be seen in every phase of human development, there is also an extraordinary failure peculiar to the times in which we live. It seems safe to predict that when the curve of human fortunes is charted by the historians of the future, it will show a pronounced dip between 1914 and some year later than 1934. Here again, we are likely to charge the whole account against some single factor such as democracy on which attention happens at the moment to be focused. But nobody, so far as I know, has proved that democracy was responsible for the Great War, or for the economic prostration and lowered morale which have followed it; for the price of raw materials, or technological unemployment, or economic nationalism, or bank failures, or the increase of divorce, or the decline of religion and the arts. The fact is that with few exceptions everything has worked badly since 1914; and it is just as unnatural and unreasonable to hold a particular political institution wholly responsible for this as it is to charge every evil against the political party that happens to be in power. Thus so much of the failure of democracy as is shared by other institutions, whether it be the normal failure which attends all human affairs or the abnormal failure of this particular historic crisis, should be discounted. Let us now examine the evidence.

First, precisely what is it that is supposed to have failed? The answer is that it is *political democracy*. Social democracy has not failed, for the good and sufficient reason that it has never had the chance. The point is this: political democracy is a form of government designed to produce a desirable social result. According to Aristotle the state exists for the sake of "the good life," and all parties to the discussion would doubtless agree upon the truth of that saying. Most proponents of political democracy believe that the good life, or desirable social result, which the state should promote, is an individualistic, free, and, in some sense, equalitarian society. The name we usually give to this standard is social democracy. It is not this which has failed, for social democracy is itself the ideal. By what shall it be judged a failure? To say that it has failed would be like saying that justice, goodness, or happiness has failed. The fact is that critics of democracy have not, as a rule, distinguished between democracy as a political means and democracy as a social end. Making the charitable assumption that they know what they mean, they probably mean that political democracy has failed to provide that minimum of security and order which conditions *any* form of the good life, including social democracy. Is this charge well founded? Or, if it be conceded that mankind has recently suffered from insecurity and disorder, is this the fault of political democracy?

There is here, I think, at least that degree of reasonable doubt which is supposed to justify acquittal. Writing in 1929 about the Great War, Professor G. G. Benjamin put the question, "What, then, do the source materials, the memoirs and monographs produced since the armistice, prove?" The third of the five summary conclusions with which he answers his question is that "the failure of Germany was the failure of absolute power." I do not see how anybody who reads the history of Europe during the years immediately preceding the war can fail to be impressed by the stupidity and feebleness of the three great military monarchies, Germany, Russia, Austria. It is to be observed, furthermore, that these three governments were swept away by the war, and that the three nations which emerged victorious and are now the most powerful, England, France, and the United States, are all political democracies.

If we examine the charge more closely, we find that what is supposed to have failed is not political democracy in general, but only parliamentary government of a specific kind. Political democracy has a good many more tricks in its bag. There is, for example, representative government in the old-fashioned sense intended by the framers of the federal Constitution. There are alternative electoral and party methods, alternative forms of the legislative body and of its relation to the executive. I am not qualified to propose a remedy, but I do not for a moment believe that therapeutic invention is exhausted or that institutional development is at a standstill. The failures of political democracy, even if they be granted, would suggest not that democracy in general be abandoned but that in respect of certain specific mechanisms it be varied and improved.

It is true that outside of England, France, and the United States there has been a very general abandonment or rejection of democratic institutions. The general trend towards political democracy that was so clearly marked in the last century has lately been checked or diverted. The most notable governments that have arisen since the war, communistic Russia, Fascist Italy, and Nazist Germany, are blatant dictatorships. Turkey, Yugoslavia, Poland, Hungary, and Austria are dictatorships in substance if not in form. Japan is in the throes of political reaction. The facts are indisputable. How shall they be interpreted? I submit that

they are the effects of emergency rather than of constructive development.

In times of stress or national calamity, when heroic measures
are necessary, when swift, remedial action is important at all costs
—in times of civil war, actual or threatening, and in times of
panic or desperation—in such times political procedure must be
temporarily altered. A demand arises for unified and authoritative control. Liberty of action must give way for the term of the
emergency to discipline, and discussion to obedience. There is
nothing new in this. It happens in every country in event of war,
in every community in case of flood or earthquake, in every
family in case of accident or illness, in every individual in moments of crisis. There is then a temporary stripping for action and
a massing of energies where the danger threatens, with sacrifice,
abridgments, paralysis elsewhere. There are, in other words, peculiar modes of organization and control which are required for
emergencies. But it would be a grave mistake to define our norms
and ideals by such requirements. An emergency is by definition
something out of the ordinary, requiring extraordinary measures.
Their use is to keep one alive until the better life can be resumed.
When one's leg is broken one puts it in a plaster cast, but one
does not therefore conclude that freely moving limbs are a failure
and should be permanently abolished. The ultimate purpose of
the rigid cast is to restore the usual freedom of movement.

Temporary or urgent measures may be very different from the
desired eventuality. Suppose a party to be trekking West in a
covered wagon to settle in a new part of the country. Although
they have a definite goal, they are compelled, on their way, to
meet emergencies. They are overtaken by storms, attacked by
Indians, threatened by hunger and drought, impeded by rivers,
mountains, heat, and cold. Each emergency has to be met on its
own terms. It dictates the weapons which shall be used, and forces
the travelers to do things which are not in the direct line of their
project. They may be compelled to halt, to make a wide detour,
or even to retrace their steps. They may be compelled to burn
their supplies for heat, or slaughter their draft animals for food,
or abandon their tools to lighten their load. For the moment they
are not behaving in a manner that at all suggests the settlement
of a new country in the West. But that is their destination, none

the less; and if they are wise they will cling to their map, their instruments of observation, and the directions for their route, in order that their journey may be resumed when the emergency is over.

What a political society does in time of emergency is not, therefore, a safe indication of its destination. What it is compelled to do in this or that crisis may be very different from what it means to do, or what is best for it to do in the long run. Granting this to be the case, there remain two alternatives. It may be necessary during a time of great emergency that the processes of political democracy should be abandoned altogether, as a sailing vessel in heavy weather may proceed under power or be towed to port. I do not deny, in other words, that democracy may sometimes be unworkable, and that some other political device may then be necessary in order to obtain that minimum of security and order which must be had at any price. In that case, I should still reserve the judgment that such a substitution would be a misfortune, at best a lesser of two evils, and a remedy to be discontinued with the return of more favorable weather. There is, however, an alternative. As ships may reef their sails or heave to and ride out the storm, so a political democracy may in emergencies find the necessary readjustments within its own constitution.

Recent political changes in America are interesting because they are not revolutionary. Two experiments are being carried on simultaneously. One of these is the attempt to modify the capitalistic economy so that it may save *itself* from shipwreck. The other is the attempt to introduce into democracy such flexibility as will enable it to meet the most severe tests without rejecting its own essential principle. The first is, I venture to say, a more constructive economic experiment than communism, and the second a more constructive experiment than dictatorship.

What, then, is the essential principle of political democracy? Defined in general terms, political democracy is government by consent. Government is conceived as an expression of popular judgment. To understand the operation of this principle it is necessary to consider two subordinate questions: how popular judgment is to be formed; and how the government is to express it.

As to the first of these questions, democracy requires that popular judgment shall be formed freely, thoughtfully, and intelligently, or as freely, thoughtfully, and intelligently as possible. By freedom of judgment I mean the opportunity of reaching a conclusion for oneself on the merits of the question. By thoughtfulness I mean the use of those methods of observation, inference, and generalization by which knowledge is distinguished from mere opinion. By intelligence I mean appeal to the evidence which is relevant to the issue. In other words, it is not enough that there should be an agreement between the government and public opinion, even if there should be something approaching unanimity of opinion. Democracy is concerned with the processes by which opinion is formed. An ignorant, apathetic, or sullen acquiescence will not do. A manufactured public opinion is only a technique by which arbitrary authority is stabilized, and opinion is manufactured by preventing or destroying those qualities of judgment on which democracy depends. Freedom is destroyed by intimidation and bribery; thoughtfulness, by hysteria; intelligence, by censorship.

If the state thus manufactures the obedience on which it rests, or the agreement or unanimity of its support, there is no democracy. In order to be democratic the state must rest not upon a political will which expresses merely its own interest but upon a nonpolitical will which expresses the cultural, moral, economic, religious, and other special interests of its members. For it is a part of the democratic idea that the state, instead of being an end in itself, worshiped either abjectly or enthusiastically by its members, shall be an instrument which they support and control for the sake of the human goods and satisfactions that it promotes. The condemnation of Hitler is sometimes qualified by the observation that, after all, he has "unified" Germany. But there is no virtue in unity as such. A lynching party is unified. There is unity in death and in silence—in the sameness of mind achieved by suppression or intoxication. The only kind of unity that is consistent with the democratic principle is a unity that harbors differences and renders them benign. The supreme test of democratic society is its power to thrive on spontaneity and dissent.

There remains the question of the manner in which government shall express the popular will. In proportion as a democracy is complex it is necessary that its official agents, whether

legislative, executive, or judicial, shall be authorized to use their
own discretion. It is unthinkable that government should at all
times express the desire and opinion of all the people; unthinkable because all the people never desire and think the same thing
at the same time, and because it is impossible that all the people
should concern themselves with every act of government. Government involves, then, the submission of dissenting minorities and
the delegation of authority. The submission of dissenting minorities is reconciled with democratic principles by the fact that he
who is in the minority on one issue may be in the majority on
another. His submission may be described as provisional, and is
part of a system in which in the long run he has his chance or
takes his turn. The delegation of authority is reconciled with
democratic principles by the fact that the persons to whom authority is delegated are chosen for what they are, and are given
a mandate which is both limited in time and defined by broad
principles of polity. And it is to such a system as a whole, involving its disagreements as well as its agreements with their momentary and individual wills, that the people as a whole consent.

A certain amount of confusion arises from the use of the expression "self-government." If this were taken to mean that any
given individual submitted only to his own decisions, there
would, of course, be no government at all, but rather anarchy.
There can be self-government only in so far as there are in each
citizen two selves—the self that exercises the ultimate sovereignty,
and the self that is called upon for some immediate act of obedience. What I in a more general sense approve, I am called upon
in a more particular sense to obey. And when the moment for
obedience arises, there may be not only a duality but a conflict
between these two selves.

But this is a conflict only in the most superficial sense. One may
not only need to be protected against oneself, one may actually
desire to be protected against oneself. I may say to my friend, "If
ever you are trying to rescue me from drowning and I struggle,
knock me on the head"; then if my friend, upon occasion, carries
out this commission, he is obeying my will in a true sense despite
his momentary obligation to coerce me. It is the appeal from
Philip drunk to Philip sober. There is my long-range judgment,
and there is my narrower view; there is the judgment which ex-

presses the fundamental needs, perhaps for order and economy, which I share with the larger group to which I belong, and there is the greed or impulse of the moment. A government which protects the first against the second is not only expressing my will but is doing so in precisely that manner for which the function of government is instituted.

We can now understand how a democracy may adjust itself to emergencies without ceasing to be democratic. At such times there is a prior demand for promptness of action and for attention to fundamental common needs. Popular judgment always gives some rope to the government of its choice. It is only a question of how long the rope shall be. It is desirable that government shall be flexible enough so that the rope may be lengthened or shortened as the situation changes. Sometimes it is desirable for popular opinion to drive with taut reins and sometimes with loose. In a crisis it may be well to give the official horse his head. Provided there is no concealment of facts, suppression of opposition, or deliberate confusion of the public mind, this does not imply that the driver has abandoned either his control or his guidance; he is merely adopting the method most likely to bring him to his destination.

It is a mistake to describe such a method as dictatorship—as if it amounted to an abandonment of democracy. I admit that a real dictatorship is sometimes excused on precisely the same grounds, and there may be situations in which it affords the only line of escape from political chaos. But a dictatorship—founded on intimidation, censorship, hysteria, or ignorance—and a temporary increase of the discretionary powers of government based on free discussion and general consent, are poles asunder. The latter is not an abandonment of democracy, but its skillful adaptation to special conditions. It is consistent with the political ideal of government which shall express, on the whole and in the long run, the interested and more or less intelligent judgment of those who live under it and are its supposed beneficiaries.

The rejection of democracy as a practical failure implies a willingness to accept some alternative. What are the alternatives to democracy? There should be a law compelling every destructive critic to provide an alternative. The alternatives to political democracy have been tried, and it was because they had been

tried unsuccessfully that political evolution up to 1914 moved in
the direction of democracy. Jefferson remarked in his First Inaugural Address:

> Sometimes it is said that man cannot be trusted with the government
> of himself. Can he, then, be trusted with the government of others? Or
> have we found angels in the forms of kings to govern him? Let history
> answer this question.

I, for one, if I should withdraw my support from democracy,
should not know where to find any other political investment that
I would not distrust more, unless, as seems unlikely, an Almighty,
All-wise, and All-benevolent God could be induced to assume the
government himself.

It is a curious thing that those who turn in their thoughts from
democracy to dictatorship forget that dictatorship consists to a
large extent in the evils of a democracy without its merits. If anyone who is weary of democracy were asked to name its most intolerable abuse, he would no doubt name the demagogue. But, as
Plato pointed out a good many years ago, the tyrant is essentially
a great demagogue, who is so artful and unscrupulous in his
demagoguery that he drives out all the little demagogues and
monopolizes the business for himself.

An editorial writer in the *Manchester Guardian* recently recalled Bismarck's saying that "any fool can govern by martial or
semimartial law. . . ."

> It is a mistake [the writer continued] to suppose that a dictatorship
> brings the able men to the top. The exact opposite is true—it eliminates
> the courageous, the critical, the intelligent. . . . No premier in any
> European democracy has so many catch phrases as Mussolini or Pilsud-
> ski [and he might have added Hitler] to call forth popular applause so
> blind and hysterical.

There is no commoner form of sentimentalism than that with
which we color those forms of government under which we are
not obliged to live. The man who longs for a dictatorship usually
imagines that *he* is the dictator, or at any rate that he is the dictator's best friend and most trusted counselor. He thinks of the
system as a means of getting done, promptly and thoroughly,

what he himself believes ought to be done. But the fact is that for most people most of the time dictatorship consists not in dictating but in being dictated to; not in getting done what one thinks ought to be done, but in being compelled to submit helplessly to what one thinks ought not to be done. It is true that we are living in an age when nondemocratic forms of government are being revived and modernized. But instead of weakening our allegiance to democratic institutions this should rather confirm our faith by presenting the odious alternatives in their stark reality.

Any government has in the last analysis to be justified by the quality of the life which it promotes. A political democracy claims to secure more than that bare minimum of security and order which may be rightly demanded of any social system. Those who adhere to it as a political creed commonly do so because of an equalitarian social ideal.

This ideal means that a man should have his chance to rise as high in attainment as his energy and natural capacity will carry him. It is not implied that attainment shall be equal. There is only one way by which this could be brought about—by penalizing superiority and so reducing life to the level of the least competent. The ideal of social democracy implies a spirit that is rarer and more generous—a magnanimity which will respect genuine superiority wherever it appears, and prefer a pyramid of excellence to a plane of mediocrity. It will recognize the unalterable inequalities of endowment, and the inevitable inequalities of attainment; and will encourage eminence for the enrichment of the common life.

But the cult of social democracy is not satisfied with a vicarious equality, a merely theoretical equality of rights, or an unattainable equality of aspiration. In the common human faculties and the common human lot it discovers actual equalities. It focuses attention on these equalities, and from them it proposes to form the essential bond between man and man, believing that a society founded on mutual respect is the fundamental condition of the best life. Political democracy is both a means to this social end and one of its chief embodiments.

Walter James Shepard
(1876-1936)

AFTER undergraduate work at Harvard University and further
study at Heidelberg, London, and Berlin, Walter James Shepard
began his college teaching in the field of political science at the
University of Wisconsin, and then took posts in the same departments at the University of Missouri and Ohio State University.
In 1924–1928 he was connected with the Robert Brookings Graduate School of Economics and Government at Washington, D. C.
His last academic position was that of Dean of the College of
Arts and Science at Ohio State University.

The essay reprinted here is an analytical definition of the idea
of *democracy*. Into it are woven not only the abstract and current
thinking about the meaning of the term but also something of
the historical background which is necessary for its understanding. Because of his broad knowledge and his wide professional
training, Shepard's definition and interpretation are based on
general principles; they should be compared, therefore, with those
of the more journalistic writers, such as Mr. Johnson's on p. 261.

Democracy Today (1935)

The term "democracy" is a perfect example of a verbal stereotype. It arouses at once a favorable reaction in the popular mind. It is surrounded with an aura of sanctity. It immediately suggests the glorious achievement of independence by the American patriots of 1776. It calls forth visions of heroes such as Jefferson and Lincoln. It evokes as its antithesis concepts of despotism, of dictatorship, of absolute monarchy. To be a democrat is to be on the side of the angels. Since the latter part of the eighteenth century, democracy has assumed a transcendental position in the thought of the Western world, and particularly in that of the people of the United States. It has constituted a basic faith which has oriented our thought and action in every direction. It has been the religion by which we have lived and for which we have been willing to die. To question the sacred principle of democracy has been to lay a profane hand upon the Ark of the Covenant.

This idealization of democracy was the natural product of the circumstances and conditions of the eighteenth century. It was necessary that democracy should be conceived as a fundamental creed in order effectively to oppose and overthrow the established order of monarchical and aristocratic rule. The eighteenth-century theory of democracy was not based upon an exhaustive, historical, and inductive examination of the results and consequences of democratic government as compared with other forms, but was accepted as a self-evident principle, springing from assumptions of natural law, human equality, and social contract. The Declaration of Independence is the classic formulation of these assumed premises and of the consequent and incontestable principle that government should be an expression of the will of the people.

Reprinted by permission from *Annals of the American Academy of Political and Social Science,* July, 1935.

An essential corollary of the democratic dogma was the doctrine of economic individualism. Adam Smith's *Wealth of Nations* appeared in the same year as the Declaration of Independence, and promulgated the theory of laissez faire as the Declaration pronounced the basic doctrines of democracy. Both ideas were the product of a particular time and constellation of circumstances. They were closely related and interdependent in their origin. The monarchical and aristocratic political order had become intolerable; democracy was the God-given principle upon which reformers sought to construct a better world. Mercantilism likewise embodied a system of restraints and limitations upon the free spirit of the individual, and was attacked by the principle of laissez faire, justified by the assumptions of natural law and human equality.

Both the theory of democracy and that of laissez faire were highly individualistic. The eighteenth-century intellectual climate was conducive to their spread and general acceptance. In their basic assumptions, in the circumstances which occasioned their rise and growth, in their impact upon the existing social order, and in their subsequent history, the ideas of democracy and laissez faire are counterparts, complementary aspects of one fundamental ideology.

The present discrediting of laissez faire involves a serious challenge to democracy. In anticipating a new economic regime in which free and unrestricted competition shall give way to some form of extensive and intensive social control of industry and business, we must likewise perceive that democratic government, as we have known it, is destined to undergo fundamental alteration. As we have generally abandoned our faith in any divinely established system of economic laws which can be trusted, so long as there is no human interference, to operate automatically to the achievement of the greatest possible general welfare, so we must surrender our sublime confidence in the supreme virtue and merit of democratic government. Indeed, we are already experiencing a considerable political disillusionment. We are becoming increasingly a nation of political skeptics. The bright and glorious dream of government by the people has dimmed to the point of disappearance in Europe.

Any critical examination of the use of the term "democracy"

immediately discovers its ambiguity and the multiplicity of meanings which it carries. Originally and etymologically, it merely
means government by the people. But to this original meaning
there have been added extensions, such as social or legal equality,
individual liberty, economic opportunity, simplicity of conduct,
and the equal rights of all in every relationship of life. It frequently implies a denial of intellectual or moral superiority. It is
conceived as opposing the claims of experts, of special qualifications, of higher intelligence. It has been seized upon and made
an essential term in the vocabularies of economics, sociology, education, philosophy, and religion.

Even when confined to the realm of government, the idea of
democracy is far from distinct and definite. At times the system of
government in England is described as democratic. Frequently it
is denounced, at least by demagogues, as expressing the opposing
principles of monarchy and aristocracy. Witness the fulminations
of Mayor William Hale Thompson of Chicago against England
and the English government. A representative system of government is usually thought of as democratic, but the Swiss Constitution distinguishes between representative government and democracy in providing that the governments of the several cantons
shall be republican, either representative or democratic. The
political implications of democracy include the principles of universal suffrage, majority rule, rotation in office, popular election
of all officials, the initiative, referendum, and recall, and direct
primaries.

It is the province of political science to clarify political terminology, and no single term demands clarification more than
the term "democracy."

The first step in such clarification is to return to the original
meaning of the word as government by the people, and to strip it
of all other meanings and connotations. It was in this sense that
it was used by the Greeks in contrast with the two other primary
forms of government, aristocracy and monarchy. We should likewise regain the Greek attitude toward democracy, which was simply one of weighing the advantages and the disadvantages inherent in this type as compared with those inherent in the other
two primary forms. The Greeks did not conceive of democracy
as a final end and goal of human existence. They thought of it

merely as one means by which the necessary purposes of society might be achieved, and they were open-minded with regard to whether and under what circumstances democratic government might be superior to aristocratic or monarchical government. Aristotle, the philosopher of the golden mean, reached the conclusion that the best form of government was one which embodied elements from all three of the primary types. Thus the study of government was kept strictly upon the plane of relative values. There was nothing final or teleological in the concept.

Democracy must be considered both as a system of ideas, an ideology, and as a system of institutions, of collective behavior patterns, of ways and means by which a community seeks to achieve certain results. As an ideology, democracy asserts the principle that government must rest upon the consent of the governed, that all political authority is derived from the people. Democracy is essentially a doctrine of popular sovereignty. But even this statement embodies a fundamental ambiguity. What do we mean by the people to whom we attribute supreme authority? Do we mean the entire mass of the people of a country? If so, how is their authority expressed and exercised? Certainly not through the formal instruments of law. Even under the most extended suffrage, only a minority are permitted to vote, and only a part of the voters, often no more than half, actually cast their ballots at elections.

It is important that we distinguish between the terms "people" and "electorate." The former is an amorphous, unorganized, discrete mass; the latter is a legally constituted, organized group. When we speak of government by the people, do we mean merely government by the voters, or do we have the idea of a transcendental entity which expresses and enforces a *volonté générale?* Our thinking will be muddy and illogical if we are not particularly careful to distinguish sharply between the people in the mass and the electorate. It has been the failure to make this distinction, not only by political orators and newspapers but even by political scientists, that has occasioned much of our confusion in discussions of democracy.

If we conceive the people as the entire population of a country, the expression of authoritative will is equivalent to public opinion, and democracy in consequence is government by public opinion. This implies a denial of the principle of equality in the participation in government of all the individuals of the community. The contribution of some individuals to the public opinion on any question of policy is a thousand times as great as that of others; many make no contribution at all. Furthermore, those who contribute substantially to the public opinion on any particular question are quite different from those who contribute on any other question. We are becoming increasingly aware of, if not alarmed at, the methods and means by which public opinion is manufactured. The radio as an instrument of creating and mobilizing public opinion has in recent years become portentous. Propaganda and ballyhoo play upon the minds of the populace with really terrific results. Is this democracy? And if so, can we still entertain our profound faith in its wisdom and efficacy? Is the voice of the people the voice of God?

But let us examine the alternative definition of "the people" which makes it equivalent to the electorate. Certainly the electorate is not and never has been the sovereign authority in the state. So far from being above the law, *legibus solutus,* the electorate has always been subject to definite legal restraints. Who may vote and what functions the body of voters may perform are definitely determined by law. The electorate is merely one of the numerous organs of government which, like legislature, governor, president, administrative commission, and court, perform certain prescribed and limited functions.

The act of choosing governmental officials is of the same character whether the act of choice rests with the governor of a state, with a legislative body, or with the electorate. The enactment of a law is legislation, whether the instrument by which it is placed upon the statute book be a bicameral assembly or the electorate voting on a referendum. And the question of what organ of government is most competent to perform a particular function is not a matter of a fundamental right of a sovereign authority, but one of practical expediency. Whether the electorate should choose the judges or whether they should be appointed by the governor involves no doctrine of popular sovereignty, but only the principle of the most effective utilization of governmental agencies.

In the great symphony of government, the electorate, as well as legislatures, executives, and courts, has played a significant, perhaps an indispensable, part. It has indeed been intrusted with roles beyond its capacity. The weight of the long ballot has been too heavy for it to bear. The function of legislation, through the initiative and referendum, it has only indifferently performed. The expansion of its duties has resulted from the naïve acceptance of the democratic dogma, and the unconscious identification of the electorate with the popular sovereign. The slogan of Theodore Roosevelt's campaign in 1912, "Shall the People Rule?" found its response in the platform of the Progressive Party, which demanded the extended use of the initiative, the referendum, the recall, and the recall of judicial decisions.

Democracy as an idea must be brought down from the pinnacle of faith and sentiment which it has occupied as an ultimate and absolute, and given its proper place on the level of relative values. We must approach the problem of government, as did the Greeks, as a highly empirical science, comparing the advantages and the disadvantages of various forms. We shall probably then conclude, as did Aristotle, that a system which finds a place for the one, the few, and the many, offers the best prospect of permanence and efficiency. Our judgment of what particular role each shall play must be based upon the practical considerations of time, place, and circumstance.

2

If we examine the system of political institutions which have existed in the United States since the founding of our government, and to which we have given the name "democracy," we must frankly admit that at no time have the people, defined either as the mass of the people or as the electorate, actually occupied the seat of sovereign authority. From the beginning, control has been in the hands of powerful special economic and social groups. Those who had loaned money to the states, those who held claims upon the public domain, those who possessed slaves, those who had fought in the wars, made the laws and directed the policy of government in the earlier periods of our history. More recently the "invisible government" of bankers, great industrialists, and powerful business men has dominated the course of our national life, though subject to constant attack by agrarian and labor groups.

The gradual broadening of the suffrage in no sense ushered in "the rule of the people." The voters have throughout been the prey of politicians, who have been time-serving tools of the interests. If occasional instances can be cited where the interest of the people as such has triumphed, they have only emphasized the general rule that ours has been a government "of the interests, by the interests, and for the interests."

Perhaps this is no more than we should have expected. The concept of "general welfare" is indeed a very tenuous one. Even such a primary purpose of government as national defense, we have recently learned, has been pursued under the baleful influence of munition makers and international bankers. The major issues of American politics—the tariff, the money question, the use of the land and natural resources of the country, the control of the railways, the limitation of great industrial combinations, protection of labor, the soldiers' bonus, and prohibition—have been fought out between powerful organized interests and pressure groups. The multiplication of lobbies in Washington evidences the fact that special interests and pressure groups, rather than the general welfare, largely determine the course of national policy.

The state governments are even less an expression of real democracy. Political bosses and machines dominate legislation and administration. If, in spite of the myriad of interest groups that influence and control the agencies of government, the public interest is at times served, it is generally only because it is in a measure identified with some powerful group.

Is this democracy? Is this in fact government of the people, by the people, and for the people? As the technological and industrial revolution has progressed, the complexity and heterogeneity of our social order have greatly increased. The chasm between the facts and the fiction of government has correspondingly widened. Neither as a system of ideas nor of institutions is democracy veritably present in the America of today.

3

The realist in politics must recognize that ours is in fact a mixed form of government. Furthermore, the line of progress does not lie in an attempt to restore a primitive and pure democracy, but in the reorganization of political institutions so that a real and vital place shall be found for the one, the few, and the many. The veil of obsolete political theory must be torn asunder; we must look at the facts squarely, and objectively appraise the tendencies that are present in our changing social order.

The danger of dictatorship is one which we cannot neglect. But we shall not avert this danger by attempting to hamper and restrain the effective use of power by president or governor. A system of checks and balances, of separation of powers, is ill-adapted to a highly complex economic society, where instant action is frequently imperative and where a vast system of rules and regulations, indistinguishable in their effect and importance from law, must be constantly promulgated. "The intervening state" is a present actuality. Only by centralizing power in the hands of a single authority can we secure that flexibility, co-ordination, and effectiveness in government which our highly industrialized and technological society requires.

Certainly there must be responsibility; we will not tolerate a dictator. But the traditional suspicion and distrust with which the American people have viewed their governors and presidents must give way to a frank acceptance of the principle of concentration of power under definite responsibility. We must abandon our time-worn doctrine of "a government of laws and not of men."

A chief magistrate, however able and powerful, is incapable alone of administering the widely extended and intricate mechanism of government or of formulating the policy of the state in all particulars. Public services have expanded beyond the compass of any single human mind. They are destined to still greater expansion. A corps of highly trained and competent administrators, investigators, technical specialists, and advisers, operating in every branch and division of government, free from all political attachments and secure in their positions against political upheavals, is already taking shape and form.

This element in government must be greatly increased. The

traditional American prejudice against bureaucracy is still strong. The Brain Trust has been the target of widespread and bitter denunciation. We have not yet escaped from the frontier, egalitarian ideas of the Jacksonian period. But a government constituted according to the simple pattern of the early nineteenth century no longer suffices. Today government must command the best brains, the highest intelligence, the most expert ability, and the noblest character that the Nation can produce. An aristocracy of intelligence and character has an essential role to play in contemporary government. The Nation must learn to trust its intellectual leaders. The knowledge, the institutions of learning, must be given scope and opportunity. For if the light of reason and intelligence are not to guide and direct our course, the blind forces of ignorance, fear, and lust for power will speedily drive us over the abyss.

What may we forecast as the role of the electorate in the government of the future? Our experience with popular government has certainly not been an unqualified success. An unbiased and scientific historical examination of the electoral institution and the way it has performed its function is a pressing need which critical scholarship should undertake. We shall probably agree that there will always be an important place for the electorate, but not a position of supreme and transcendent authority. The doctrine of popular sovereignty is untrue and misleading. The electorate is merely one among the various organs which share the authority of the state. There is no hierarchy of authorities culminating in some sovereign power. Organs of government are rather like the tumblers in a lock, each affecting and being affected by all the others.

The restriction of the electoral function to a very few, simple, and very significant acts of choosing representative officials and sanctioning alterations in the fundamental law would seem desirable. We cannot much longer tolerate the impossible burden of the long ballot. Universal suffrage must lose the sanctity with which it has been clothed. Positive qualifications of competence and interest must be established for participation in elections.

We must likewise give serious consideration to a reorganization of the electoral body along functional or occupational lines. The present geographical basis of constituencies is a relic of a simple, undifferentiated, homogeneous, and largely agricultural society. The present lines of social cleavage are economic and occupational. If the principle of representation in government is to have any significant meaning, constituencies must be organized so that the representative shall really reflect and *represent* the interests of the group which has chosen him.

This is not a simple matter. But unless the problem is solved, the theory of representative government will become increasingly a travesty and a delusion. Members of Congress and of the state legislatures today cannot represent the generalized public interest of their constituencies, because of its extreme generality and tenuousness. They cannot in any true sense represent all the numerous, varied, and conflicting interests found within the geographical areas which they are supposed to represent. The inevitable result is that they become representatives of certain special interests—labor, agriculture, industry, banking, the Anti-Saloon League, the public utilities, the veterans. They are less and less representatives of the people, since the interests of the people, as such, are submerged and lost in the welter of special interests which are effectively organized and articulate. Indeed, upon analysis, the concept of public interest tends to fade and disappear.

The interests of the individual of which government must take cognizance are largely economic and are shared with others of his group or class. An organization of the voters along the essential lines of group interest, conforming to the actual structure of society, would vitalize the electorate and give to our lawmaking bodies the character of real representative institutions.

The theory of democracy implies the use of the instruments of discussion and reason in reaching decisions. The Greek agora, the New England town meeting, the English House of Commons before the stress and storm of our present time, the American Senate in the era of Webster, Clay, and Calhoun, exemplified something approaching the ideal of government by deliberation and discussion, with reason holding the scales of judgment. Today the debates of Congress count for little. Far more effective are the hundreds of thousands of telegrams that fall like the leaves of Vallombrosa upon the devoted heads of our lawmakers whenever an issue of widespread interest appears upon the calendar. Serious and rational discussion has given place to the nation-wide voice of the radio. Emotional appeal, ballyhoo, and pressure politics are today apparently the most effective means for determining the course of public affairs. They have been used with success in Italy and Germany to crush constitutional government and destroy every aspect of democracy. How shall we meet the menace of these newer forms of propaganda?

4

Whatever be our final judgment with respect to the history of democracy in this country, there can be no doubt that we have cherished the tradition of freedom, the precious heritage of a thousand years of conflict. Freedom of speech, freedom of the press, freedom of assembly, freedom of religion, a fair and impartial trial of those accused of crime, have been wrought into the very spirit of America. They are being challenged today as perhaps never before in our national history. They must not be surrendered. Propaganda and pressure politics must be met—can only be countered—by the undefiled and aseptic influence of education.

In the social order of the future, education must occupy the central and dominant position. It must supply the scheme of values, the basic faith of our civilization. It alone can give a new meaning and purpose to life. Education, conceived as an end and not as a means, interpreted in its broadest sense as the emancipation of the human spirit, the unleashing of all the capacities and potentialities of the individual, must command the supreme devotion and allegiance which we have hitherto given to democracy. Man cannot live by bread alone. There must be a vision, for "where there is no vision the people perish." To the baffled, thwarted, and distracted millions of our people there must come the promise of a new and better world. That promise lies not in a transient and deceptive economic recovery. It does not lie in the false doctrines and false hopes of communism or fascism. It lies only in a new vision of education, which, accepted by the people, shall become the driving force of government. With a profound and compelling faith in education in the minds and hearts of the people, the government of the one and of the few—the aristocracy of intellect and character—will be accepted and supported by the many. Then may the wild winds of doctrine blow freely, for the structure of our government will rest upon a foundation that cannot be shaken.

Gerald White Johnson
(1890-   )

THE PRACTICING journalist and editorial writer, coming, as
he does, into immediate contact with the world, is likely to have
a different point of view from that of the cloistered scholar. Mr.
Johnson's comments are thus of particular interest, especially
when they are compared with those of the college professors. He
was born in Riverton, North Carolina, and educated at Wake
Forest College in that state. His high qualifications as a newspaper man have brought him honorary degrees from a number
of colleges. After having served the University of North Carolina
as Professor of Journalism from 1924 to 1926, he became editorial writer for the *Baltimore Evening Sun*. Since 1939 he has
been with *The Sun* (Baltimore). Among his many books are:
What is News? (1926); *Andrew Jackson—An Epic in Homespun*
(1927); *Randolph of Roanoke—A Political Fantastic* (1929); *The
Secession of the Southern States* (1933); *America's Silver Age*
(1939).

The following essay was published in *Harper's Magazine* in
1938 as one of a series of discussions of The American Way. It
presents the problem of American life today as influenced by its
historical background and as subject to the practical realities of
life.

The American Way (1938)

THE TWO FUNDAMENTALS

While he was President of the United States Woodrow Wilson made a speech at Charlotte, North Carolina, in which he astonished and outraged the Tarheels by pointing out that they are not typical Americans. North Carolina had then, and doubtless still has, a smaller foreign-born population than any other State. The census of 1910—the latest one at the time of Mr. Wilson's speech—showed that 99.4 per cent of the residents in the Old North State were native-born of native parents, while many thousands of them were Americans of the fifth to the tenth generation. What, asked the bewildered and resentful audience, could be more American than that?

Yet the President's words were true and they remain true today. The census of 1930 showed that Americans of foreign birth, or with at least one foreign-born parent, number 40,286,278 in a total population of 122,775,046. Move the inquiry back a generation—that is, include grandparents as well as parents—and the number would certainly double. Racial stock as anciently American as the North Carolinian is anything but typical of the country. Most of the population consists of people most of whose progenitors were living in other countries when Lee surrendered to Grant.

Obviously, the ideas and ideals of this population must be taken into account in any effort to determine what is the American way of doing anything. It is idle to expect to find in the writings of the founders of the republic a complete expression of the beliefs of families that did not even learn the language of the founders until the founders had been dead for many years.

It is this vast displacement of tradition—unique, so far as I am

From *The American Way*, by David Cushman Coyle and Others; reprinted by permission of Harper & Brothers, publishers.

aware, in the history of nations—that has given an aura of un-
reality and frequently a tinge of cant to modern expression of
ideas that in earlier days were unquestionably valid. When President Hoover, for instance, during the political campaign of 1932
expressed his faith in "rugged individualism" as an essential part
of the American tradition he incurred the suspicion of thousands
who refused to credit his sincerity. Yet Mr. Hoover would have
no difficulty in citing a tremendous amount of highly respectable
authority in support of his position. Why, indeed, should he do
more than mention the name of Benjamin Franklin? By his con-
temporaries, and for some generations later, Franklin was accepted without question as an authentic voice of America; and
he was the greatest of all exponents of rugged individualism.

It is hardly credible though that any rational man would argue
seriously that the philosophy of Benjamin Franklin embodies the
prevailing trend of thought in the United States of 1937. It is a
philosophy empirical in the extreme; and it was based on observation of an environment that exists no longer even as a family
tradition in the minds of the greater part of the nation. The
older American stock may have heard from their grandfathers
tales of an America identifiable with the one of which Franklin
wrote; but the older American stock is now a minority of the nation. Most Americans are sprung from ancestors who lived in an
entirely different environment and who thought in widely different ways.

Various institutions, most important among them being the
American public school, have operated to implant the old tradition in the new population, but not with unqualified success. In
some measure the effect has been partially to erase the traditions
the newcomers brought from Europe without entirely supplanting them with those developed in America. The plate is fogged.
The picture is cloudy and uncertain. A natural and inevitable
conflict of ideals sometimes results in concepts of Americanism so
bizarre as to seem, to those whose traditions are clear and definite,
beyond the bounds of sanity. Unquestionably there are men, and
thousands of them, not insane by any legal or medical standard,
who really believe that the programs of the Ku Klux Klan and
the Black Legion are in line with the true American tradition;
and there are scores of less extreme movements whose supporters

are firmly convinced that they are upholding the ideals of the
founders of this republic.

2

One of these movements is democracy. Strong faith in democracy emphatically was not characteristic of the men who set up
this republic. Hardly anyone will question this statement as regards Washington and Hamilton; but it applies as well to the
man who is commonly regarded as the very high priest of democratic dogma, Thomas Jefferson. His enemies understood this
clearly. One of their favorite methods of denouncing him was to
fling the word "democrat" in his face; they never doubted that
this was the insult that would sting him worst, and they were
right.

A certain measure, but by modern standards a narrowly limited
measure, of democracy was indeed regarded by Jefferson as inevitable and was, therefore, accepted by him with what grace he
could muster. He envisaged the gradual extension of democracy
too as probably necessary, and was prepared to countenance it.
But for all that, he reserved doubts as to the political competence
of the masses, except as they were directed by men of skill and
integrity; and he dreaded above all the participation in politics
of an urban proletariat.

With such an attitude taken by the most eminent radical of the
time it is hardly necessary to examine in detail the recorded sentiments of the rest. They did not all go so far as to proclaim, like
Hamilton, that "the rich and well born" should control the destinies of the republic; but even those who did not agree with this
assertion saw nothing really scandalous in it.

Democracy was no religion, no sacred article of faith with the
men who founded the republic. They accepted it, in limited form
—there was a property qualification for suffrage and at that the
people voted directly on very few offices in most of the States—
but they accepted it as a makeshift and a pretty doubtful one.
They took democracy, not because they thought it was good, but
because everything else offered was obviously much worse. They
took it very much in the spirit in which they took the Constitution; for Franklin was speaking for nearly every member of the

Convention when he said, "I consent to this Constitution because I expect no better, and I am not sure it is not the best."

Worship of democracy and the Constitution is a later accretion to the American tradition. It was not the American way in the beginning, nor is there any very compelling reason to suppose that it will remain the American way until the end.

Even liberty, the one abstraction on which there was widest agreement, had its limitations in the minds of the makers of the republic. The very man who wrote in the Declaration of Independence, "We hold these truths to be self-evident, that all men are created equal, that they are endowed by their Creator with certain inalienable Rights, that among these are Life, Liberty, and the pursuit of Happiness," was at the moment when he penned the words the owner of slaves. It did not occur to him at the time that his words could possibly have any application to slaves, because the word "men" carried in his mind a special significance; it meant, if not gentlemen, at least white men and Englishmen. Even twenty years later Jefferson's comments on the French Revolution are eloquent of his delighted surprise at discovering that Frenchmen too are actually men.

Independence was not at all to the taste of the signers of the Declaration. They exhausted every resource in their efforts to avoid it, and the document itself is a long protestation that they did not approve of it, that they had sought desperately to escape it, and that they accepted it only because they were driven to do so.

If the peculiar sanctity now attaching to democracy, liberty, and the Constitution is an addition to the American tradition, originating not with the founders of the government, but long afterward, there were, on the other hand, certain concepts which they undoubtedly regarded as essential components of the American tradition, but which have long since been discarded. One was the notion that the United States was and must forever remain essentially a society of husbandmen. Jefferson was the great protagonist of this delusion, but even Hamilton admitted that the United States must always remain primarily agrarian. In view of the fact that the first census after adoption of the Constitution, that of 1790, showed a population 96.7 per cent rural, this assumption is understandable; but the fact remains that in 1930 the population was only 43.8 per cent rural—well over half urban. The tradition of the agrarian nation has been compelled to yield to the contrary fact.

With it has gone the aristocratic concept of politics accepted so implicitly by the makers of the republic that it never entered their minds to write it into the organic law. The Declaration of Independence and the Constitution, the two documents generally regarded as the embodiment of the essential American tradition, are products of the eighteenth century. The aristocratic theory had been challenged by countless philosophers in earlier times, but its actual demolition began with the French Revolution, when the Constitution had been in force for years.

Actual participation in government by the poor and ignorant was simply not a part of eighteenth-century thought. A few advanced thinkers, especially in France, toyed with the idea of universal participation, to be sure, but always in vague and ill-defined terms. At the time of the American Revolution universal suffrage was an idea as strange and radical as companionate marriage and euthanasia are today—that is to say, it had been suggested, but hardly taken seriously.

The men who established this country took it for granted that the conduct of public affairs would always remain in the hands of an upper class. They envisaged an aristocracy whose members would be qualified by brains and character, not by lineage; but they unquestionably envisaged an aristocracy, because any other form of political organization was beyond their imagining. "Let us erect a standard," said Washington, "to which the wise and honest may repair." No others were invited. If no effective barriers were raised to bar the silly and crooked, it was because the founders had such faith in the potency of aristocracy that they could not imagine its subjugation, not to mention its abolition.

The twentieth century finds that the facts are quite different. Science and technology, rather than philosophy, have made such radical changes in the world that eighteenth-century reasoning no longer applies. For one thing, the dense ignorance in which the masses of mankind were sunk in the eighteenth century has been partially removed. Not only are ordinary men now able to read, but the barriers of time and distance have been so far swept away that it is possible for an artisan in California to have reasonably accurate and virtually instant information of every important event that occurs in Washington. When Madison was drawing up the organic law of the Union it was physically possible for only a small number of minds to operate on the problems of government; the vastly greater number had neither the information nor the education requisite to making even the simplest of judgments. Lacking the gift of prophecy that might have foretold the railway and the telegraph, Madison and his friends inevitably supposed that it would always be so. They had every reason to regard the rule of the select few as an ineradicable part of the American way; but it has not remained.

Any student of American history can multiply these examples, but it is useless to labor the point. Our concept of what we call Americanism has been protean in the past, and there is no convincing reason to believe that it has lost this character. The odds are heavy that some things which most of us now look upon as fundamental to our tradition and culture within fifty years will be altered or abolished. Shall one assert then that the question of what is the American way cannot be answered until one has been told what American, and when, and where?

This does not necessarily follow. In the first place, no rational man would ask such a question without implying a certain selectivity. The American way is certainly not the way of the villains and fools that have afflicted the country, but rather of its best and wisest men. Washington, Franklin, Hamilton, Jefferson were highly exceptional, far indeed from being average Americans; yet when one speaks of the American way he certainly means theirs rather than the way of Benedict Arnold and Jesse James.

In the second place, there are a few principles held to be true by the founders of the republic that are still held to be true, in exactly the same way, by the wisest and best Americans of the twentieth century. These surviving ideas are very few and very simple; but if it can be established that they have remained unaltered during all the changing fortunes of the republic and are, at bottom, unaltered today, one is fairly safe in describing them as the essential American tradition.

3

For my part, I hesitate to pronounce positively genuine more than two. The first of these is the dignity of the individual. The second, a reasonable measure of respect for reality in politics.

Let Jefferson state them both in more seemly language: "All men are created equal . . . endowed by their Creator with certain inalienable Rights." For the moment, never mind what the rights are; the essential point is that all men are created equal and endowed with rights. This is the dignity of the individual.

Then for the second: "I am not for awing the human mind by stories of rawhead and bloody bones to a distrust of its own vision, and to rely implicitly on that of others." This, after all, is but "no nonsense" writ large.

Upon these two concepts, it seems to me, is erected the whole structure of American ideals and institutions. No matter what program a man may propose, if he can make it square with these two principles I, for one, hesitate to declare it positively un-American. On the other hand, any program that obviously violates either of these is not in line with American tradition.

The implications of these ideas are sweeping. For example, on the first one the totalitarian state goes to wreck. If a man, created equal with all his fellows, is endowed with "inalienable Rights" and endowed by his Creator, then the first of these rights must of necessity be the right to think; for without liberty of mind he cannot be aware of his possession. This right, according to the American tradition, canot be invaded by any earthly power, not even that of the State. But to restrict men's opportunity to learn, whether by reading, or by listening, or by discussion, is to restrict their thoughts, which is a right not transferred and not transferable to any state or king or dictator.

Jefferson wrote down "Life, Liberty and the pursuit of Happiness" as among the "inalienable Rights," but this is not absolutely true. All three a man may alienate by his own act. He may commit a crime that will compel society to restrain him, or even to destroy him, for the protection of its other members; but not even crime, except the sort of crime by which he forfeits his life, can deprive a man of the right upon which all others rest, the right to do his own thinking.

But if the individual, including the humblest, is inviolate in his personality, then the state cannnot be entirely sovereign, that is to say, it cannot be totalitarian. "Thus far shalt thou go and no farther" cannot be said, even at the border of the realm of the spirit, to a genuinely totalitarian state. Other rights are qualified, even the right to life itself; hence a policy that seems to invade, or in fact does invade, other rights may, or may not, be basically American. But any policy based on the assumption that the citizen is, or ever may become, merely a tool of the state, under an obligation not merely to act, but also to think for the good of the state, is a denial of every moment of the existence of this republic from 1776 to the present.

If the doctrine of the dignity of the individual embodies the principle of permanence which has maintained the identity of our country, the doctrine of respect for reality embodies the principle of development which has made the country great.

The earlier American historians strove manfully—as the writers of elementary school texts do still—to inculcate the idea that the revolutionaries of 1776 were inspired to fight a seven years' war by pure love of liberty, religious and political. Later and more cynical historians, revolting against an impossible idealism, have almost subscribed to the idea that they fought for unadulterated—since one hesitates to call it pure—love of money. But I am not aware that any historian, early or late, has suggested that they fought out of sheer annoyance at being continually told that the moon is made of green cheese. Yet a pretty good case can be made out in suport of some such theory.

For nearly two centuries before the outbreak of the Revolution the colonists had been facing a very stern reality. They had brought from Europe a highly developed system of political ideas and an equally highly developed system of political organization. But they found that neither worked. That "divinity doth hedge a king" was a pretty theory, but the scarcity of corn in Jamestown was an ugly fact; therefore gentlemen who had obtained from the king, as the fountain of honor, exemption from menial tasks nevertheless were compelled to bend their backs to the shovel and the hoe. If the rights and privileges of gentlemen did not apply in the new land, why should any of the rest of the old order that was obviously inapplicable to the new conditions?

Slowly the colonists were driven to realize that "a distrust of its own vision" is a fatal handicap to a nation. Oglethorpe came with a marvelous scheme of political organization; but if it had not sacrificed Oglethorpe's scheme and trusted its own vision, Georgia must have perished. Braddock came, bearing the king's commission and skilled in the rules of warfare; he brushed aside with contempt the facts of border warfare and died, with most of his army, as a result. Governor after governor came, honored with the confidence of the king and his ministers; but proved, in fact, incompetent.

After a century and three-quarters of such lessons, Americans at last firmly grasped the idea that any government which persistently ignores the facts is a villainously bad government. Underlying the libertarian philosophy of 1776; underlying the desire for religious liberty; underlying the motive of economic advantage—underlying all else was a keen realization of the absurdity of government by an authority distant three thousand miles, geographically, and six weeks temporally. It would be folly to deny the philosophical, religious, and economic motives behind the American Revolution; but a sense of humor, which is basically a sense of reality, had somewhat to do with it too.

This pragmatic view of the state has survived throughout our history. We began with a Constitution that satisfied nobody except in one particular, to wit, that it was less extremely objectionable than the worst proposed. Maybe it was, as Gladstone said, the greatest work ever struck off by the hand and brain of man at one time, but it certainly was not so regarded by the men who made it and in a hundred and fifty years their successors have altered it twenty-one times.

But the mere adoption of the Constitution is evidence of the fact that the Americans of 1787 regarded it as the first duty of the government to cope with the realities of the situation. This opinion was not unanimous; it took three years to bring the last of the thirteen members of the Confederation into the new Union. But it was the prevailing American doctrine, and it has been the prevailing doctrine ever since. Only once has it been resolutely challenged. In 1861 eleven Southern States went beyond the point at which New England had faltered forty-five years earlier and supported with arms the theory of States' Rights against the emerging fact of nationality. On that occasion the fact triumphed and the theory was drowned in blood; and the effort has not been repeated.

When the basic doctrine of any society, political or other, is so loose and vaguely defined, many of its members are doomed to perpetual mental suffering. This has certainly been true of the American republic. There has never been a moment since its establishment when it did not seem, to a considerable number of its citizens, to be tottering to its fall. Indeed, the Constitution itself was regarded by some men in every State as a denial of everything America stood for. In Massachusetts they called it "the great Leviathan," in New York "The Gilded Trap," in Virginia "pernicious, impolitic, dangerous." Nor were these sentiments the mouthings of irresponsible demagogues; they expressed the considered opinion of honest men, some of them able men.

Since then emotion has swung to the other extreme, and the terrified are afraid, not of the Constitution, but for it. The great exemplar of this attitude was John C. Calhoun, who devoted his time for thirty years to mourning the evident reshaping of the Constitution. His error was in supposing that altering or even abolishing the Constitution would necessarily change the nature of the republic. History has demonstrated the falsity of this view. We have actually changed the Constitution in no less than twenty-one particulars; but the republic survives, and it is essentially the same as the republic over which George Washington presided. The reason is that all the changes, with a single exception, have recognized, first, the dignity of the individual, and, second, that the law must be in agreement with the facts. The one exception was the Eighteenth Amendment, which has been repealed.

The Constitutionality of an idea, or an act, is therefore an uncertain test of its Americanism. Jefferson himself believed that the Louisiana Purchase was flatly unconstitutional. So, in the estimation of many able lawyers, were the Emancipation Proclamation and the recognition of the revolutionary government of Panama; but they met the facts of the existing situation when the Constitution did not, so they were profoundly American. Prohibition, on the other hand, like the Fugitive Slave law, stood the test of the courts; but both of these incontestably constitutional enactments denied both the dignity of the individual and the plain facts of the situation. Both were un-American and both collapsed.

4

Heretical as it may sound, I do not believe that either democracy or liberty is a fundamental part of Americanism, much less that "equality of opportunity" which is supplanting universal suffrage as the theoretical expression of liberty. Democracy and liberty are not bases, but logical outgrowths of the American tradition. They are inescapable deductions from the fundamental ideas but, as a philosophical proposition, might conceivably be supplanted by something else without touching the fundamentals.

Mind you, I cannot imagine how it could be done. In fact the American people have never been able to imagine how it could be done, so they have not tried it.

Democracy and liberty are the outgrowth of the combination of the two American ideas. The concept of the dignity of the individual may be entertained without the concept of democracy as an inevitable result. Indeed its finest statement as a political policy is Chatham's famous rhetorical description of the poor man's cottage: "It may be frail; its roof may shake; the wind may blow through it; the storms may enter, the rain may enter—but the King of England cannot enter!" Chatham was no democrat. He was an earl; but the government he headed did recognize, if it did not always respect, the dignity of the individual. That benevolent despotism beloved of political theorists might recognize this element of Americanism without admitting the validity of democracy.

But to this theorem add the other, that political organization must conform fairly closely to reality, and escape from democracy becomes impossible. To accept any other theory it is necessary to assume that there is a test, other than experience, that will reveal the superior man. Whether it is the test of genealogy, as in the case of legitimist monarchs, or of theology, as in the case of the selection of the Dalai Lama, or of force, as in the case of dictators, or of thaumaturgy, as in the cases of various primitive tribes, there must be a test that will reveal the true sovereign. But there is no test except experience. Nothing else can prove a man's capacity to be the head of the state. Recently we have seen an amiable gentleman, but no philosopher, God knows, proclaimed as "the high and mighty prince Edward . . . our rightful lord," and then reduced within twelve months to the level of a simple subject, without even a title until his successor granted him one. Well, I have always cherished a decided partiality for the Duke of Windsor; but the notion that Eddie, for all his good qualities, ever was a high and mighty prince, much less the rightful lord of several hundred million people, is one that I can't swallow.

Of course, I understand that it is all symbolical. I am aware that no intelligent Englishman ever dreams of taking all the ritual literally, and that, far from being ruled, he asserts the right to rule the most intimate affairs, even to the marriage, of his so-called sovereign. But that is just it. There is no deep-seated conviction among the British that their political organization must conform, with reasonable fidelity, to reality; therefore, they can—and to a large extent do—accept democracy, but they are by no means driven to it. For us though there is no escape; believing in reality as well as in individualism, we have found no workable method of government other than the rule of the people. Then, if you set up rule of the people, liberty follows as a matter of course. If the people have the power, they are politically a free people. They can't be anything else.

The dualism of the American tradition seems, as it is set down on paper, simple enough, but it is in reality a subtle and difficult concept. Many Americans, among them some very distinguished men, have been quite unable to grasp it. For one thing, it definitely limits the power of democracy. "Though the will of the majority is in all cases to prevail," observed Jefferson, "that will, to be rightful, must be reasonable." It is not reasonable if it denies that every man is endowed by his Creator with rights; nor is it reasonable if it writes into the law some such principle as that adopted by the Middle Western State whose legislature enacted that *pi* should thereafter be equal to 3, instead of 3.1416 plus. Thus any law that seeks to control the minds of men, or that denies the plain facts of existence, is profoundly un-American, though it were upheld by fifty Supreme Courts.

The will of the majority is no more divinely inspired than is the will of an absolute monarch, and there is nothing essentially righteous in its establishment as the final arbiter. The reasons for accepting it are based on no consideration more exalted than expediency. The majority presumably can present more bayonets than the minority; hence it is expedient to permit the majority to prevail, lest it resort to bayonets. In that case it would prevail anyhow, and the minority would be underground.

Whenever and wherever a question is capable of settlement by force, there the rule of the majority should be accepted simply as a method of avoiding bloodshed. The problem of who shall occupy the White House is capable of solution by force; not so the problem of the origin of the human species. An ablebodied policeman with a club can make me pay taxes; therefore a decision by the majority as to what taxes shall be levied is binding. But all the policemen between Sandy Hook and the Golden Gate cannot make me revere the Constitution; therefore a majority decision that I shall be compelled to revere it is idiotic and profoundly un-American. It violates both principles of Americanism —in the first place, it invades my human dignity by denying that I have a right to think for myself, about the Constitution as about all other things; and, in the second place, it ignores the stern reality that the thing can't be done.

This is why the wildest economic theory ever germinated in Moscow is by no means as thoroughly un-American as the teachers' oath laws that have been sustained by the courts in a number of States. The un-American element in Communism, in Fascism, and in Nazism is precisely the same: it is the theory that a man has no rights as a man, but only as a member of society. The teachers' oath laws seem to assume that an American has no right to think about hating the United States. But he has. He has a right to think about anything. More than that, it is an innate right that the United States cannot take away and has no right to try to take away. Our property and our bodies may be in the hands of the government and subject to control by majority rule. But our manhood is our own, and truth is neither our property nor that of the government; hence Americans have always believed that when the government presumes to lay its hands on these things, "it is their right, it is their duty, to throw off such government and to provide new guards for their future security."

5

What is the evidence of the truth of the two basic American beliefs? As far as I know, there is none at all. The evidence of experience is not conclusive, as other nations have existed well enough without either. Yet, while it may not constitute absolute proof of the truth of our fundamental assumptions, this evidence is impressive. The United States is the only great nation in the world today that is still operating under the same political ideas that controlled it in 1787. All the others have experienced at least one revolution, most of them several, with the exception of Great Britain, which escaped revolution by adopting a modification of our democracy.

Furthermore, these hundred and fifty years have constituted a period during which all political systems were subjected to stresses far more numerous and more powerful than have occurred in any other period of equal length in all history. The whole world has been made over since the Constitutional Convention finished its labors and adjourned, but the organization it set up, based on these two principles, is still doing business at the old stand. It has survived, not merely wars, including one frightful civil convulsion, but the worse strain of enormous expansion, in area, in population, and in wealth. It has survived the conversion of its population from a rural into an urban people. It has survived the abolition of time and distance as regards communication, and their immense reduction as regards transportation. It has survived the invasion of the electorate by forty-three million poor voters. It has survived the worst economic cataclysm of modern times with only one shot fired against the government, and that by a crazy man. Surely, this is enough to prove that the American way, whether true or not, is amazingly flexible and strong.

Since all is change, doubtless in time this too will pass away. But never believe that you and I shall be here to see it go. There are those who cry that the republic even now is crumbling into ruin. And why not? Cassandra, bless her, is a permanent feature of the American pageant. Her wails are the antistrophe in the great national chorus, and were they to be hushed we might infer that things were abnormal indeed. She cried out when the Constitution was adopted, and again when John Adams reduced the republic to a tyranny, and again when Thomas Jefferson delivered it over to anarchy. She had convulsions when Andrew Jackson, and, later, Abraham Lincoln, tore the Constitution to shreds and tatters. She foretold impending doom when Ulysses S. Grant accepted the carriage and pair and when Grover Cleveland bluntly demanded gold. Theodore Roosevelt destroyed the country, and so did Woodrow Wilson.

Oh, well, some day no doubt Cassandra will be right. But the country has been destroyed so often that the present attitude of the typical American seems to be

> When people all around are making faces
> And all the world's a-jangle and ajar,
> I meditate on interstellar spaces
> And smoke a mild segar.

After all, terrific excitement over nonessentials is also a characteristic American way. But however high the income tax may run, and however far the alphabetical agencies may go toward converting the country into the Utopia of tramps, these things do not affect the country's real tradition. As long as no "tyranny over the mind of man" is erected here, George Washington, or any man who sat with him, might return to this strange country and, in spite of all the changes, exclaim without hesitation, "This is my own, my native land!"

Stoyan Pribichevich
(1905-   )

THE EXPERIENCES in America and the points of view of recent immigrants are always interesting because fresh and different from those of writers who were born Americans. So the following narrative and analysis presents the impingement upon the American way of living and working of an industrial and social pattern that is quite different. Stoyan Pribichevich has summed up his life and indicated his point of view in the first paragraph of his essay; thus he has furnished a background for the reader's understanding of his experiences. Moreover, the author has given his readers an excellent insight into the problems of a European intellectual upon his arrival in the United States, problems that arise from the necessity of his making a living and an adjustment to a new environment. By using a narrative form, the author has presented his analysis of the American workman and of his position in a democratic society. The essay should be compared with similar expositions and narratives in the present anthology.

In an American Factory (1938)

I came to America in 1934 as a political exile who could hardly speak English. In 1932 I had become involved in Yugoslav university students' riots and in printing pamphlets against King Alexander's dictatorship. I was twenty-seven years of age then, a doctor of political science and a practicing lawyer in Belgrade. Before the political police could seize me I managed to cross the Yugoslav frontier disguised as a peasant. I went to Paris where I spent two years, helping my father—a former member of the Yugoslav cabinet and also an exile—to write a book on democracy. I quarreled with the painters of Montparnasse on art, played the violin, and argued with my exiled countrymen in cafés clouded with tobacco smoke about the perfect democratic society. Then I thought I would visit a relative of mine in New York. I signed under oath a long printed paper in English declaring that I was not a bomb thrower, lunatic, or venereal patient, and landed in Manhattan.

Coming from France, which to me seemed a thoroughly logical country, I was confused by the many incomprehensible contradictions of American life. Yet I found to my astonishment that my American friends thought the French were a crazy people. When they asked me why France has more than twenty political parties, I countered: "Why do you jam Roosevelt, Glass, and Hague all in one party, and Hoover, Borah, and La Guardia together in the other?" I could not understand why the country with the largest workers' population in the world should have no labor party; why centralization should be advocated by liberals, and States' Rights defended by big corporations; why Tom Mooney should be in jail for murder and Al Capone for tax evasion; why aliens should be regarded with contempt by the sons

From *Harpers Magazine*, September, 1938. Reprinted by permission of the author.

of aliens; why religion should be separated from the state, and Darwin's theory of evolution banned by one State in the name of the Bible; why bishops should oppose child-labor regulation; why gangsters and kidnapers should grow up next door to the strange prophets and utopians of the Share-the-Wealth, Epic, Social Justice, and Old-Age-Pension plans; why the dictatorships of Louisiana and Jersey City should flourish under a democratic federal Constitution.

Only gradually did I begin to grasp the deep significance of American inconsistencies which so strike the set, static mind of a European: to realize that they were mere symptoms of growth, showing a slow trend of the nation toward ever-increasing democracy.

In this country I experienced for the first time the magnificent feeling of absolute personal freedom. No policeman could stop me in the street or in a restaurant and ask me to show him my papers. I could walk about without carrying an identity card in my pocket, change my address without reporting to the police, and slap a cop on the shoulder just because I was feeling fine. Only a European can appreciate the personal freedom a man enjoys in this country.

I decided to stay here—and went back to France to change my legal clothes. I obtained an immigration visa and, toward the end of 1935, returned to America as an immigrant.

I began to look for work. When I had tried to get a job in Europe either I could get no appointment or I was treated rudely. Here I was received very politely by bank directors or the heads of law firms. I was helped out of my overcoat, shown a chair, and offered a cigar. Then I would tell my story to an attentive listener. "Right now there is very little I can do for you," the man behind the desk would say apologetically, "but I shall certainly be glad to get in touch with you if anything should come up." Then he would take my address and telephone number and escort me to the door. It was not until I reached the street that I realized I had not got the job. It is almost a pleasure to be turned down in this country.

Finally I secured work. Despite my four languages and legal training, it was the job of a worker in an Ohio machine shop. It happened this way. Three and a half years ago I met a manufac-

turer from Cleveland at a party in New York. He teased me, saying that as a newcomer to America I should learn about American life by spending a few months as a worker in his shop. I did
not see him again. When, in 1936, I was unable to find a job in
New York and found myself penniless, I wrote to him and asked
whether he remembered me and his invitation. He replied that
he did and renewed his offer. I packed my things and went. Instead of a few months, I spent a whole year in his shop.

2

When, one gray, foggy morning in the beginning of 1937, I got
off the train in Cleveland, I became dismayed at the thought of
what lay before me. I did not know a soul in this city. I had
never done physical work before. I wanted to return to New
York where I had friends. But there was no more money for
another train fare and no way out. As I stood in the cold, damp
mist, I felt weak for a moment.

"Which is the way to the X Company?" I asked a passer-by.
He pointed to a waiting trolley car.

Rolling along the dingy, interminable avenue, I began to
whistle. The morning sun pierced through the torn rags of dirty
fog, and slowly a feeling of glory descended upon me. I was following the old trail that for forty years before me had been trod-
den by those countless thousands of immigrants from Yugoslavia
who had helped to build America. With a few borrowed dollars
in my pocket I was on my way to work in an American factory.
"It's a great thing," I said to myself.

It was bitter cold and a heavy snowfall set in as I walked
through the gloomy, smoky industrial district to put on overalls
for the first time. The huge plant, covering two blocks, all in steel
and concrete, was run by electricity. Passing through enormous
rooms, I saw countless machines swinging their metal arms
through the air like fantastic octopuses, hissing furiously, and
drowning in their roar the voices of men. Over them were bending rough, athletic-looking workers, with rolled-up sleeves and
black caps, their faces grim and smeared with oil and grease,
their eyes intent.

The so-called "turret lathe" was manufactured in this shop.
This is a machine which in its turn makes tools and machine

parts. You can fabricate almost anything with it, from automobile parts to bullets.

The factory itself was spotless. I had seen orderly European shops, but they had not gleamed with such beautiful cleanliness.

I was assigned to the second shift. Through underground passages I was led to the Assembly, another huge room where the finished parts of turret lathe machines were put together, tested, and taken apart for shipment. The workers cast curious glances at the newcomer. They were amused at my clumsy attempts to punch the clock and showed me a vacant locker along the left wall where I changed clothes. Then, at four o'clock, the note of the factory bell sounded in my ears, and our shift started off like a regiment toward the machines in the center. Holding our tool boxes in our hands, we waited in line for the foreman to assign us our jobs.

I did rough work on that first night. I swept the floor and picked up waste and dirt with my bare hands. I carried heavy machine parts in my arms or on my shoulders. I screwed big pipes together. A compassionate worker showed me how to hold a file, and with it I smoothed off the edges of five push-button plates. Within fifteen minutes my hands were blistered, my arms impregnated with black metal dust and machine oil, and my mouth full of grease. When I was through at midnight the muscles of my feet, legs, fingers, hands, arms, and back ached terribly. I dragged myself home and slept like a dead man. "How do you feel?" the foreman asked me as we washed up the following night. I shrugged my shoulders. He winked at another worker and laughed: "It'll do him good; in three weeks he'll have muscles like Popeye the Sailor."

The factory reminded me of a European dictatorial state, where bureaucrats plan and order and citizens work and obey. The board of the Company was the government, and the workers were the people, ruled through a centralized hierarchy of officials and controlled by a mechanized system of registration, bookkeeping, time cards, and punch clocks. Like citizens of authoritarian states, we did our individual assignments without knowing their purpose or the general plan of work. I met a worker whose specialty was to assemble gear boxes to the turret lathe machines and who had no idea what the machines were for. The foreman was our

supreme visible authority. With his superiors we could not communicate. And the president, with his board members and directors, sat high above us like an invisible, unapproachable god.
Watchmen were stationed inside and outside the building to let
nobody in or out except on a special permit. We even had our
numbers. Mine was 1941.

I was struck by the contrast between the American worker's
political freedom and the rigid regimentation of his forty-hour
week. The French worker cannot conceive a personal freedom
which does not include a certain leisureliness at work. So he must
work six days a week if the production is not to lag and the production costs to rise. The American worker pays for his two free
days by straining his energies under a mechanized discipline during the other five. A German-American worker, who previously
had been employed in an automobile plant, said to me: "What
are you talking about? This machine shop is a fine place to work.
On my last job, after we'd won the sit-down strike, the Company
made us punch our cards even when we went to the toilet!" I
have often wondered whether the willingness of the American
worker to submit to such regimentation might not be due, not
only to his sense of efficiency but also to a general American trait.
In spite of their fundamental belief in the democratic form of
government, Americans show a certain predilection for personal
rule and the "one man" system in their group and business activities. In no other free country are the significant terms "chief" and
"boss" so frequently heard.

We were only twenty in our group in the Assembly Room,
but we were of fourteen different nationalities: Serbs, Slovenes,
Croats, Italians, Hungarians, Rumanians, Czechs, Germans,
Poles, Swedes, Englishmen, Scotchmen, Irishmen—even Americans. When, later, I was transferred to other departments, I
found Slovaks and Lithuanians in addition. Of course only the
older men were foreign-born. The young workers were born in
this country, mostly of foreign parentage at least on one side.
They hardly spoke the native languages of their parents and
cared little about their old countries. During an entire year I
never witnessed a nationalistic dispute among these people. There
was something humorous about our racial differences in this

American shop. We cracked jokes at one another and imitated the various foreign accents in our English speech. There was an Italian who never took offense when called "Spaghetti." A pro-Hitler German laughed every time we grotesqued the Nazi salute and yelled "Heil Hitler!" at him. "Hey, you! You took our country!" shouted a Hungarian at me from his machine one day, referring to Yugoslavia's annexation of southern Hungarian provinces after the World War. "Sure!" I retorted, swinging my hammer; "you had us for a thousand years, and it's our turn now!" We both laughed. And yet I knew that in Europe, or even in their native-quarter saloons, these same fellows would fight bitterly on less provocation.

International politics were a daily topic. Most foreign-born workers thought they were safer and better off here than they would be overseas. Some Italians were pro-Mussolini, and of course had to take a lot of chaffing. The anti-Fascist Italians did not speak to them. The Germans were rather silent about their beliefs, and it was difficult to find out whether they were for or against Hitler. The reasonable guess was that those who would not divulge their opinions intimately disapproved of the Nazi regime. All workers regardless of nationality sympathized with China. And, almost without exception, they hated General Franco intensely. Most were anti-Communist, but many expressed interest in Soviet Russia's economic experiment.

At first my fellow-workers showed annoyance at my ignorance of a mechanic's work, but when they realized I had never been in a shop before they were eager to help me. They showed me how to file, hammer, and scrape. They let me use their tools, air hoses, and trucks. They pulled heavy crane chains for me—and fixed up my mistakes. Their sense of comradeship and co-operation was genuine and magnificent. I profited by it greatly—and so did the Company. A robust Rumanian, after having loaded some eighty pounds on my back one day, said: "So you never work before? I work when I was sixteen!" He obviously considered intellectual occupation as just fooling around. Naturally, they were all curious about my background. No matter how hard I tried to conceal it, I would repeatedly give myself away by some such form of address as "Please," "May I?" or "Thank you." They instinctively regarded such politenesses as the social affectation of an upper class. Correct grammar was also a high-hat pretense to them, and I soon caught myself saying "He don't" or "I says."

Like school children, they loved to throw paper balls and orange peels at one another or to pinch an unsuspecting posterior. After my transfer to the small-tool department I was solemnly escorted to a "weight guesser" who held me on his back, while, surrounded by a roaring crowd of the "brotherhood," I unexpectedly received three burning slaps on my rear. My unpronounceable last name was a cause of great fun. Everybody practiced it with comical variations. My stern-faced foreman was greeted with loud cheers one night when he gave it up and shouted in desperation: "Where's that new fellow, what's his name, Pepperbitch?" Most of my fellow-workers disapproved of drinking but chewed tobacco enthusiastically. Every night in the Assembly I watched, fascinated, a machinist who at regular intervals spat streams of coffee-brown liquid in an arc over his machine and never missed the spittoon.

The stories of some of the immigrant workers were tragic. There was an emaciated Scotchman with a finely chiseled face and trembling hands, who collapsed nearly every week and had to be sent home, his eyes glassy. Years before he had contracted tropical malaria working for a British company in India. A Swede, with all the symptoms of stomach ulcers, lips tightened, skin earthen, drilled and hammered doggedly. From time to time he crouched down behind his machine to endure silently an intolerable pain. A poor Italian, his wife long dead, had to leave his children without supervision while he worked at night in the shop. Almost every year his eldest daughter brought him an illegitimate child. She had been only sixteen when she had the first one.

A Croat with an ambassador's face had been worth fifty thousand dollars before the depression. Left without a cent, he was prevented by his children from committing suicide, and went to work in the shop. Another Croat was picked up in 1903 at the age of nineteen in a desolate mountain region of Croatia by the agents of an American railroad company, who took him away from his sheep and shipped him off to America. On his arrival in Pennsylvania he was lined up with many others in an open field.

The foremen stripped off their coats and examined their muscles as if they had been cattle or African slaves. Still another country-man of mine told me that he came here at the age of thirteen to fell trees with the Negroes in the forests of Virginia. He is a fine machinist now and speaks good English. He made a very signifi-cant statement to me: "Nobody knows how many dramas are buried in American shops. Most of our people do not prosper in America because they do not take the trouble to learn English. And they never will as long as they live in racial colonies."

Yet most of the immigrants loved America with a peculiar sense of pride. "We are told to go back where we came from," exclaimed a Serbian worker from California. "No, sir! This is our country. And our affection for it is all the more deep for having watered it with the sweat of our labor. We made this country what it is today."

I often hear about the unemployment of men over forty. But in this machine shop wherever skill or experience was needed most men were over forty. And even physically many of them had more resistance than the young fellows.

3

I did not really mind being ignorant of a mechanic's work, I could always ask for help or advice. But unfortunately I belong to that class of persons who become panicky every time they have to hammer a nail or open a stubborn lock. Every worker knew, for instance, how to sharpen a drill on the automatic stone wheel. But in my hands the thing invariably went crooked, and I left part of my skin on the whirling grinder. Stamping numbers on a machine part, I would first hit gently; the number would not come out; then I would gather myself for a terrific whack which, of course, would land right on my knuckles. And the holes I drilled were always cock-eyed. Irritated and impatient, I tried to overcome my subconscious fear of mechanical things by the use of physical force and, naturally, ruined both my work and my hands.

It took me a long time to realize that a mechanic's ability resides in a careful deliberation and calculation of movements rather than in brute strength. I began to observe that my fellow-workers used their hands with caution, sized up every load before lifting it, took care to place their fingers in the right places, and then pushed or pulled with just the required physical energy. When their efforts were unsuccessful they repeated them slowly over and over again. It was a superb lesson in self-control and patience. Like a fine racehorse, a machine wants to be treated firmly, but with kindness and intelligence. "Take your time, my boy," remarked an old Slovene, watching me tighten some screws, "you are going to waste a lot of time hurrying."

I was amazed by the tenderness which the workers showed toward the inanimate objects of their labor. "Oh, she'll be all right again," said a youngster of a machine he was repairing, and patted it as though it were a sick person. After "tapping"—cutting screw threads in—a big turret one night, I left it dripping with oil on the bench and turned to my next job. Immediately a bushy-haired fellow ran up to me and shouted angrily: "You can't leave her like that! Are you a machinist?" And he neatly wiped it off with his rag. "See?" he said and looked fondly at the shining metal.

I took such rude reprimands without resentment, learning that these men did work of fine quality and that infinite care was the first requirement. Helping to take complicated parts out of the machine "heads" and to replace them, I always had the vivid impression of assisting at an operation on a human body. Even their tools—wrenches, pincers, scrapers, pliers, drills—were similar to a surgeon's or dentist's instruments. A mechanic's work is surgery on metal. In spite of scale and micrometer, the human eye and hand have the final control. No mechanical device can supplant the craftsman's sensitive fingers in fitting a bar to a hole, in feeling the evenness of a slide, or in the finishing touch of smoothing and polishing.

Whenever I got stuck and called for help, unable to find the cause of trouble, my neighbor would shout over the noise: "Find out! Think!" Then he would come closer, look the machine over, and adjust something at the far opposite end which had made my bar in front fit badly. It was this power of quick mechanical diagnosis that my legally, abstractly trained mind could not grasp. But no worker or instructor ever troubled to give me a theoretical explanation of a job. They would say: "Watch me!" then pull a lever, push a button, turn a wheel, and stand back for me to repeat their movements. They would tell me how, but never why.

The invisible control of the worker's activities through book-keeping and job cards was so ubiquitous and inexorable that the office could at any time find out which worker had put which screw on which part, and on what day. Once I broke a small handle. "You can't get away with that; they'll find it out," said a man who saw me do the damage. "You'd better go to the foreman and report." Every operation, no matter how small, had to be accomplished within the prescribed standard time, marked on special cards. On my first day in the shop I was warned by fellow-workers not to "ring out" my cards before the allotted time was up, or the office would cut down the standard norm for everybody. This had been tacitly agreed by them all to prevent the management from speeding us up. Whoever "rang" less than one hundred per cent time was a scab. Intelligently, the management took no steps against this. But the collective work of a shift could sometimes be speeded up imperceptibly. One week we were told we were to work six days and be paid time and a half for overtime. When Friday came the foreman said he had changed his mind. Asked why, he answered: "The department has caught up." In other words, under his continual gentle urging during that week we had all worked slightly faster, with the result that the shift accomplished six days' work in five days for five days' pay.

Most men disliked the time-card system. "I like to do a good job but I hate to have a time limit for it," said a German scraper to me. It was easy to keep to time norms either in very simple or in very mechanized jobs; but when the quality of each piece depended on the skill of the worker's hands, the uniform time rules became meaningless bureaucratic measures. Once I took three hours and a half to scrape the slides properly and ream the holes on eight parts. Another time I took nine hours. In spite of the time cards the foremen had to give us individual allowances on all quality jobs.

One night as the "pay man" distributed our checks, a bad-tempered Swede flung his on the floor and spat on it. Shaking his fists he roared: "They deduct money for social security, for the community fund, for hospital insurance, and I have to pay my union dues and the income tax. God damn it, I work for everybody except myself!" "I am afraid," I tried to pacify him, "you'll have to pick up your check anyway."

The workers work hard all their lives and get enough for a living, sometimes a comfortable living, but never enough to stop working. "Once in a shop, always in a shop," was the gloomy refrain in every department. Sitting on wooden boxes or machine levers at lunch or dinner time, we often exchanged confidences and talked about our intimate ambitions. The old workers would shake their heads telling of twenty, thirty years spent in shops. The young ones would dreamingly speak of their hopes for the future. A fine machine operator said bitterly: "I get sick looking at this machine. Shall I run it when I am fifty? What a life!" Another hoped to get an office job some day. Still another dreamed of becoming a schoolteacher. He had finished high school; then he had got married, had had two children, and had gone into the shop instead of to college. Most wanted to go into "business for themselves" some day. Not one wished to remain a shop worker.

Discussing the reasons for the complete failure of the Marxist class ideology in this country, Mr. George Sokolsky said once that the American worker is merely a capitalist without money. I do not think that this is quite correct. My fellow-workers did not like being laborers but they also had no desire to become employers. They wanted to be on their own, neither hired nor hiring. Their attitude toward life was not proletarian nor was it capitalist; it was typically middle-class.

4

We had an "open shop." Most men were unorganized. Of the rest, a larger part belonged to the AFL, and a smaller to the CIO. The organized workers were not always ready to divulge their affiliations, so that the exact strength of these groups could not be ascertained. Once I met a man who pretended to be a CIO sympathizer and later admitted AFL membership. Some workers actually signed up for both organizations. It was particularly hard to tell whether the unorganized workers were really indifferent or had secret leanings. Only a few expressed themselves outspokenly. Sometimes when I was going to the factory I would pass a couple of men at the gates distributing CIO leaflets. The mimeographed handbills did not assail the rival union directly, but attacked the Company and called upon the workers to join "the only powerful, militant union." Then in all departments AFL notices would appear calling the members to a meeting to discuss "important questions." So it went during my whole year. There was no disturbance, except that one afternoon when I arrived at work I found the day men sitting on the floor smoking. The first shift of the entire plant had gone on a sit-down strike to force the Company to fire a man. Some said that he was a CIO committee man who had gone over to the AFL. Some, that he was a Communist. Some, that he was a Company spy. Some, that they did not know. Whatever the charge against him may have been, he was fired, and the second shift resumed work.

Many unorganized workers felt apathetic toward unionism. They either saw no reason to pay the dues or resented the AFL-CIO strife. "When two unions fight each other," said an old workingman, "it is the Company which profits, not the workers; until they settle their affairs I won't join either of them." But a union member was quick to reply: "*You* are helping the Company if you don't join us to help us fight it out." In the Assembly the CIO seemed to have more sympathizers than the AFL. The Assembly workers were mostly common laborers. They did not know much about "vertical" and "horizontal" unionism, but disliked the upper labor crust and looked upon the CIO as an organization of commoners.

One day I was transferred to the Small Tool Department. Here most of the workers looked like real artisans, distinguished, middle-aged, or elderly. Everybody worked at his own machine or bench, quite for himself. There was no such collective activity as in the Assembly. The men had a contempt for "mass psychology." They were not too familiar with one another, did not swear or laugh loudly, and seemed to dislike common manners as well as common labor. They were almost all members of the AFL. An officer of the AFL Local took the trouble to explain to me at length that social distinction between the skilled and unskilled workers was necessary. "We can't mix with those guys; we're a different class of people."

One Saturday the Company took us, a group of young workers, to see an Ohio foundry some forty miles away in the country. In

the humid, suffocating air of what looked to me like a subterra-
nean prison, I watched workers covered with dirt and shining
with sweat struggling with heavy molds of cast iron. Others,
stripped to their waists in the unbearable heat, tended the huge
blazing furnace. Horrified that there should be people who spent
all their lives doing such work, I spoke to a youthful mechanic.
He shrugged his shoulders and replied dryly: "Somebody's got to
do it. These fellows are no good for anything else." It dawned
upon me that there are as many class differences within American
Labor as exist within the nation.

We all believe that youth is by nature revolutionary, and old
age conservative. I was surprised, therefore, to observe that social
discontent was more frequent among the old than among the
young generation in the shop. While the older men attended the
union meetings, discussed labor politics, or condemned employers, the young ones talked sports, movies, dancing, and, eventually, Japan. The older fellows were bitter because they had
gone through the depression and had no more hope of recovering. They were interested in unionism because they felt a need
for protection.

On the whole my fellow-workers were less interested in politics than are European workers. I heard no ideological arguments. While in Europe unionism plays an important part as an
instrument of the labor parties in their struggle for political
power and control of government, here it was presented to me
merely as a paying proposition. "The union," I was told by an
AFL man, "will fight for your raise. Therefore the dues you pay
are sort of an investment." Questioned about the reasons for the
heavy dues in the AFL, an officer explained: "Members don't
quit easily an organization to which they have paid large sums of
money."

Yet in spite of the complete absence of a Marxian point of
view, there was a deep psychological gulf between the labor and
the management, that atmosphere of mutual mistrust which is at
the bottom of every class antagonism. The office people were inclined to assume that the workers would naturally like to do as
little work as possible for as much money as they could get. The
workers, on the other hand, were convinced that the management
made profits by obtaining the maximum of work for a minimum

of pay. In every move of the Company they suspected a trick. Their mental attitude unconsciously adopted the doctrine of class exploitation.

In November, 1937, the management announced a bonus for all the workers then in their employ—and laid off a number of men a few days later. The "lay-offs" continued. Every two or three weeks the foremen made the rounds of their departments. We knew that the fellows by whom they stopped to say a few words were working that night for the last time. Within some three months the labor force was cut down to two thirds, and the three-day week became a rule. It was the firm and unanimous belief of all the men that the new depression was caused by a "business sit-down" and forced by the "big shots" to sabotage the President. Indignation and fear grew every day. Fighting for existence, the workers began to mistrust not only the Company but one another. They lied to one another about their wages. The more skilled resented the less skilled staying on the job. The older ones wanted the younger ones to get out first. Everybody was anxious to punch his time cards one hundred per cent. And many jealously kept their time-saving tricks from others. Yet there was no general feeling of panic. Last January they still believed that the recession was temporary. Then there was the Relief. And those who had savings in banks knew they were safe.

I had been told that before the great depression American workers, like all Americans, were encouraged by the current business philosophy to be spendthrifts and to live like millionaires on the installment plan. On my first day of work I had been amazed at the hundreds of workers' automobiles in the factory parking place—like a bankers' convention. But the American worker's economic psychology is undergoing a great change. Time and again I was warned by the older workmen: "My son, save every cent! You don't know how long you're going to keep your job."

Never in my life have I so often been asked whether I was married and why I was not. Practically everybody in the shop had a wife. The fact that I was a bachelor did not please my fellow-workers and counted definitely against my character. Once I said I did not want to get married. "What are you living for?" a young worker asked me contemptuously. "I was married when I was eighteen," he added defiantly and turned his back on me. Another youngster, who at twenty-four had a six-year-old child, wondered: "What the hell are you waiting for?" This was strange to me, for in Europe I had been brought up to believe that industrialism has a destructive effect on the family life of the working masses. And yet swear words, dirty jokes, and foul expressions were in common use all over the shop. Some fellows kept pornographic booklets and pictures and enjoyed showing them secretly to one another. The rear of the factory bordered on a Negro district, and on sunny afternoons black women—or "brown peachies," as the workers called them—leaned over the window sills or stood on their wooden balconies. Gathered at the factory windows across the street, the workers complimented them with bawdy invitations. But I soon sensed that their obscenity was only an emotional release. Divorce and adultery were rare among them. They just liked to pretend to be oversexed.

On winter nights lonely pedestrians were exposed to frequent hold-ups in the deserted streets between the plant and my living quarters. Walking home once after midnight in the dim light of the avenue, I saw the slim figure of a young blonde woman emerge from a restaurant ahead of me. A man, rather unsteady on his feet, followed her. I passed them and turned into a dark, narrow street. Soon I heard the light steps of the woman running behind me. Catching up with me, she said, panting: "Would you mind taking me to the next avenue? I'm afraid of this man." She was pretty. "All right," I replied, smiling and wary of a frame-up at the same time, "but this is not the place nor the hour for pretty girls to be." She shivered and said nothing. The man, muttering, was close on our heels, and I carefully watched his shadow on the pavement in front of me. As we reached the corner a black car came swinging round and stopped. There was a man behind the wheel. The young woman hesitated for a moment, whispered: "Thank you!" and rushed into the car. The drunk on the sidewalk swore, I bowed like a disappointed cavalier, and the automobile dashed off in the dark.

The following night I again heard steps behind me—a man's steps. "Do you work for the X Company?" he asked me brusquely. There had been labor troubles in the city, unrest among the workers, and a half-day sit-down strike in our plant.

"Yes," I said, bracing myself.

"Did you pick up the girl last night?" The dark fellow looked searchingly into my eyes.

"Yes," I repeated more defiantly, ready for a fight.

"I was in that car," he continued more softly and looked away. "I also work for the X Company, and she's my wife. You see, she works nights near here, and I usually meet her with the car after work. Last night I was late. She told me you protected her from a man who annoyed her. Thank you."

I relaxed. We walked on together and became friends.

5

At work a curious mental trance would occasionally take possession of me. I came to like monotonous jobs which left my mind free. Sometimes I would gradually lose control over my thoughts. Memories would begin to play before my eyes, and the factory would seem a fantastic vision where I saw workers and machines only through a mist. At such moments my fingers worked with relentless, mechanical speed. Once I turned threads in 270 holes and made altogether more than 6,000 identical arm movements. My mind sank into a complete oblivion of the world, and all night I swam in hallucinations and reveries like a drug addict.

In the fall I was transferred to the Machining Department, a huge white room where countless machines were lined up in impeccably straight rows, and the noise was so hellish that one had to shout into one's neighbor's ear. There I had the thrill of my life starting and stopping the motor, putting my turret lathe into high or low speed, throwing it into reverse, pulling the levers and handles, turning the wheels, and watching the indicators. The docile monster responded sensitively to every touch of my hand and turned out identical finished pieces at equal intervals. It was easy physically, but exhausting mentally. No more dreaming at work. The slightest mistake in the synchronization of movements resulted in a damage to the machine, the product, or my hands. Every day there came a moment when the attention suddenly gave out from overstrain, and an attack of dizziness made things swim before the eyes. I was advised by older workers to stop working for a while at such moments. I have often read that, generally, the two or three first hours of work are the most productive. That is not always true. In the Machining Department we regularly took one or two hours to "warm up." Then, after several hours of efficient work, a short period of mental weakness and distraction would set in. Renewed concentration would follow, and during the last one or two hours we worked at our best and fastest—because subconsciously we strove to get home.

It was fascinating to measure the .001 part of an inch with a micrometer. But it took me some time to learn to read a blue print drawing and set up the turret lathe machine according to it. Suppose you get a blue print calling for 75 screws which have to be made of a 5/8 hexagonal steel bar. The length of the head must be 5/16 of an inch, and the length of the body, 1 inch and 11/16. The thread must fit the gauge and be 1 inch long. Both ends of the screw have to be polished and have their corners cut off at an angle of 30 degrees. And the width of the narrow round body of the screw must be turned down to 1/2 an inch minus .003 of an inch. Well, I did it one night, set up the machine for the job, figured out everything with scales and micrometers, and made the called-for number of screws in the prescribed time, and the foreman checked and approved my work. But often I got hopelessly stuck. Then the assistant would come along, throw all my pieces into the scrap pan because they were .002 of an inch undersized, and reset the machine for me. It was exceedingly difficult for my theoretically trained mind to acquire a machinist's fine sense for exact physical measurements. A simple mechanical problem seemed more complicated to me than an intricate legal case.

There was a symphony of strange noises in the Machining Department. Some machines beat like the tom-toms of the jungle. Some puffed like locomotives. Some whistled, hissed, or howled. Some hummed or purred gently like cats. The steel under the cutter screamed like a human being, and when the huge machine drill pierced a one-foot iron bar the room resounded with the angry roaring of a lion. The men, grimly earnest, worked in tense concentration. Suddenly somebody would shout: "Hey!" A chorus of men would answer him, yelling at the top of their voices. Then they would fall back into silence for hours. Again a laugh would ring out from a corner. For a moment all the men would stop their work, and the entire place would echo with nerve-racking laughter. At first I felt uneasy every time I saw the men lift their heads from the machines. But later I too was carried away and howled with them. It was fun. But underneath it I recognized the need of relaxation from the mental tyranny of the machine.

6

Years ago I had an ambition to become a concert violinist. I am glad I never became one. But I kept up violin playing with that zeal and determination that distinguishes the stubborn amateur, and after some months in Cleveland I began to be asked to play the violin at musical parties in the evenings. I found that many workers in the shop were musical. Some sang, some played instruments, some were members of choirs and bands. One night in the Assembly I whistled the leading tune from the first movement of the Beethoven violin concerto. A handsome young Pole looked up: "Do you sing?" "No," I replied, "I fiddle." "I sing," he explained, "and I knew you must be a musician the way you whistle." We talked music all night while I washed the machines with rags dipped in kerosene and he screwed bolts on them.

When my people overseas heard that I had been compelled to work in an American factory they were worried not so much about the physical hardships I should have to endure as about the social humiliation I should have to suffer. Professional and class standards are so set in Europe that an intellectual who resorts to physical work for a living is considered *déclassé*. Here I saw the sons of rich lawyers and business men spend their college vacations working in a shop. America—we all know—has long ceased to be a pioneer country; but ideas often survive the facts, and certain social standards of the pioneer era still persist here. One of them is respect for physical work. In no European country could I come home all dirty from shop work, lay off my working clothes, take a bath, put on a dinner coat, and play the César Franck or the Brahms D-Minor violin-piano Sonata before an audience in evening clothes at some private house.

One day I was asked by a prominent local organization to give a series of lectures on Central Europe and the Balkans. I spotted a few of my fellow-workers among the audience. The day after my last lecture I put on my overalls again; but my anonymity in the shop had been completely killed by the newspaper publicity, and I was afraid the workers might resent me. As I took the elevator I was greeted with hearty shouts: "Hey, Doc!" or "Here comes the Doc!" They were interested to know whether there was more money in lecturing than in machine running. I told them that, for the time being, I would rather stick to my machine.

After a full year spent in the factory I returned to New York. Looking back upon my year-long experience in this American shop, I am fully aware that it does not give a general picture of the American industrial life. One can arrive at a just evaluation of it only by comparing it with industrial conditions elsewhere, here and abroad. We were paid at an average rate of 84 cents an hour. We worked 40 hours a week, in clean, healthy surroundings. We were given time and a half for overtime. We had time for rest, amusements, and cultural activities. We had a two weeks' vacation with pay. We were treated fairly as men and as workers. The foremen were willing to make exceptions in emergencies and to help out in trouble. Not seldom they would give us time-saving jobs (the so-called "good jobs") when we were behind on our time cards.

But the people whose character left the deepest impression on me were the workers. Humaneness and sympathy were concealed under their brusque ways and manners. On their faces, which sometimes reminded me of those of the peasants in my old country, lines of dishonesty or wickedness were rarely to be found. Many of them came from distant, forlorn corners of the United States, or from far-off, backward countries; they grew into the soil of a new community, excelled at work, and managed to give their children better care than they had enjoyed. When I think how tremendously handicapped they were by lack of means as well as of background and education, I wonder if perhaps they are not more able fellows than I. They were men of simple taste and reasonable, sane attitude toward life. No fanaticism colored their discontent. And their ambitions were undistorted by megalomaniac wishes to make "a career" or do "great things." Their objectives in life were within the limits of the possible. Again and again I feel compelled to reflect upon the question which that young married worker once put to me: "What are you living for?"

Raoul de Roussy de Sales

(1896-   )

RAOUL DE ROUSSY DE SALES is a man who is able to look two ways, for he is the son of a French father and an American mother. At home in both the United States and France, he has been a frequent contributor to *The Atlantic Monthly* and to the *Revue de Paris* and *Europe Nouvelle*. In the United States, he has received the honor of the Strassburger Award (1936) for writings that have strengthened Franco-American friendship; and in France he has been made a Chevalier of the Legion of Honor for the same reason.

Because of its great geographical area and the variety of people who make up its population, the United States as a nationality has always been a problem to Europeans who are accustomed to more national uniformity. What we are and why we are so have always been fascinating problems for the intelligent thinker both here and abroad. Mr. de Sales has attempted to answer these questions, and his statements are thought-provoking. It should be borne in mind, however, that he has not attempted to be either dogmatic or exhaustive in his treatment of the subject.

What Makes an American (1939)

It is strange that the only common denominator accepted by all people today should be the one which most assuredly prevents them from living in peace with one another. That denominator is nationalism, the strongest single motive which inspires the action of modern men.

To define precisely what nationalism means to each individual would fill a volume. A Frenchman once said that nationalism is a certain number of illusions shared by a group of men and women concerning their origin, combined with a common hatred for any other group of men and women sharing another set of illusions. To most people, however, it is something much more noble than that because it represents an extension of the natural love of man for the country where he was born. It implies devotion, duties, and sacrifices under the general assumption that there is some sort of sacred link between each man and a definite spot on the planet.

The question whether nationalism, patriotism, the love of the homeland, is beneficial either to the individual or to the human race as a whole is open to discussion. It might be a much better world if this instinct were eradicated. On the other hand, it might be worse. The fact is that the instinct exists, and that, far from losing its grip on us, on all of us, it is becoming constantly more intense, more exacting, more all-embracing.

I have a definite impression that during my own lifetime the French have shown a tendency to become more French, the Germans more German, the Americans more American. Or, to put it another way, there seems to be an increasing desire on the part of all people to assert more strongly what makes them different

From *The Atlantic Monthly*, March, 1939; reprinted by permission of the author and the Atlantic Monthly Company.

and even antagonistic to one another. And it does not matter at all that—owing to the shortening of distances and the facilities of communications—they are in fact getting closer and more alike in all the visible manifestations of their existence.

It may be that modern nationalism is an instinctive defense against a greater peril—a deadly and overwhelming uniformity. It may also be that in one or two hundred years historians will study this manifestation as one of the most extraordinary examples of mass neuroses that the world has known. Nationalism as we know it may pass, but for the moment it is more powerful than any other idea or even than any religion.

There are, of course, many variations of nationalism, and some think that it is dangerous only in its excessive forms, such as those practiced by the Germans, the Italians, and the Japanese, with their "blood and soil" mysticism, their imperialism, and their racial exclusions. But everywhere we see the same tendency, the same urge to counteract nationalism in one place by more nationalism in another.

2

To a European, no country is more interesting from this point of view than America, and in the seven years I have lived here none has interested me and puzzled me more.

To begin with, it took me some time to formulate to myself an answer to the very simple questions: "What makes an American? How does it *feel* to belong to this nation?"

These questions will naturally sound absurd to an American, and he might retort, "Well, how does it feel to be a Frenchman?" But that is just the point—most Frenchmen can tell you quite clearly what makes them conscious of being French, but I have found it very difficult to obtain from my American friends or from my reading a comprehensive definition of the American nationality.

First of all, it is obvious that the sense of nationality is not less developed in Americans than in any other people. It is quite as real and quite as visible in all its manifestations. But the fact that such expressions as "Americanism," the "American way," the "American outlook," and so forth, have had to be coined seems to indicate that Americans are the first to feel the need of qualifying themselves when they say, "I am an American." More than that, the American consciousness gives an impression of growth. It is not static, and one feels that it still contains tremendous possibilities of expression.

For the moment, however, there is a very important trait in the make-up of the American nationality which does not exist, I believe, in any other. And that is the fact that America is a permanent protest against the rest of the world, and particularly against Europe.

This attitude has both historical and psychological reasons. Most Americans believe today the following facts concerning their nation: (1) that this continent was peopled by men who rebelled against the tyrannies of Europe; (2) that these men dedicated themselves, from the very beginning, to the purposeful establishment of a kind of freedom that should endure forever; (3) that they succeeded, by a "revolution," in breaking away forever from the oppressive domination and the cupidity of European imperialism; (4) that in establishing a democratic government they determined forever the course of political perfection, and that whoever followed another course was on the road to damnation; (5) that although European nations were becoming progressively harmless in relation to the increasing power and resources of the ever-growing America, they remained a potential danger to the integrity of this great nation on account of their deplorable habit of wandering away from the true path of civilization, which is democracy, the pursuit of material comfort and more happiness for everybody on this earth as soon as possible.

An Englishman may have doubts regarding the British Empire, a Frenchman may be discouraged concerning the future of France. There are Germans who are not sure that they represent a superior race. All of them, however, remain thoroughly English, French, or German in spite of everything. The type of American who does not accept America as it is and has misgivings about it —such as Henry James, Edith Wharton, T. S. Eliot, and some others—belongs to a past generation. Today one seldom meets an American skeptic, for the reason that nothing is more assuredly un-American than to entertain any doubt concerning the fact that somehow or other this country will come out all right.

There are many who will find such a statement too sweeping,

and say, for instance, that President Roosevelt is destroying the national ideal, that he is leading the country to ruin, decadence, anarchy, and so forth. But even those objectors are not skeptical about the future of their country. Even they feel that faith in America is what makes them Americans. All their irritation would be assuaged if Mr. Roosevelt were removed, all their confidence restored. This kind of skepticism is skin-deep. It does not affect the soul of Americanism.

This faith, like all faiths, does not engender a passive attitude towards the rest of the world. Americans are tolerant to all creeds and to all convictions, but few people express their distrust and indignation with more vigor whenever some of *their* beliefs are offended. Few people are more conscious that ideas may be more destructive than guns. And rightly so, because if any unorthodox creed really implanted itself in America—if the day came when an American citizen could really feel that his country was not following the right course and that a change was due—the political disunion thus produced would have unforetold consequences. The one serious crisis of this kind that America has known, the Civil War, showed the frightful results of a real political conflict. It nearly made two nations out of one. But this experiment in dissension seems to have served as a lasting lesson. It is difficult to believe that it would be repeated. Unity on the fundamental principles of politics is indispensable to the life of this country. The presence of even a small minority who would question the validity of Americanism would attack at the very core the concept of American nationality itself.

3

The crisis that shook Europe in September 1938 once more brought out the fact that 99 per cent of Americans distrust Europe as a whole, and that they *must* distrust it to retain the feeling that they are Americans.

This is no place to discuss the events leading up to or the consequences of the Munich peace, but the experience was conclusive. American opinion saw in all this affair one main point: democracy had lost out in the struggle, and something hostile to America had won.

Does this mean that many Frenchmen and many Englishmen

do not feel the same way? Certainly not. But even the most ardent opponents of Mr. Chamberlain and M. Daladier, those who feel most bitterly that democracy and freedom are threatened today, do not think that their national integrity—their conception of what is British or French—is involved. Many of them may have become what Mrs. Anne O'Hare McCormick appropriately called "spiritual refugees" within their own country, but—unpleasant as this change may be—it does not go any further.

Not so with the Americans. Most of them today have become isolationists. They despair of Europe and are all the more anxious to protect the Western Hemisphere from the anti-democratic plague that is sweeping the world. And at the bottom of their anxiety to preserve their political institutions, their habits of thought, and their form of civilization, there is more than a prejudice against the revolution brought about by the totalitarian doctrines; there is in the heart of every American the positive fear that his existence, as an American, is endangered.

It may seem presumptuous to say that these two fundamental factors—the permanent protest against Europe, and the faith in one definite outlook on life—are the most important qualifications of an American. One could argue that Americans have a deep attachment to the section of the map which they occupy, and that they would still love it just as much if Hitlerism or Stalinism became the law of the land. This may be so, but it still has to be proved, because for one hundred and fifty years America has known only one form of government, one philosophy of life, and one aim. The elements which make up an Englishman, a Spaniard, or a Dutchman are the same as those that make up an American, but the emphasis is different. For instance, Europeans seem to be more deeply aware of their physical relationship to the place they occupy in the sun than are most Americans.

4

It may be difficult to make this clear to people who profess such a cult of the home, the home town, or the state from which they have come. But, although this love of the motherland is genuine enough, it always appears to a European somewhat abstract, as if it were an acquired taste. Moreover, it is in constant conflict with another impulse, typically American—the urge to

move and detach oneself constantly all through one's life from
any definite surroundings.

This nomadic instinct is too well known to be emphasized. It
has historical causes: the pioneer spirit; the very size of the country; the fact that means of communication, such as railroads, were
available before there really was any place to go to; the urban
civilization attaining a tremendous development without any
marked transition between the village and the big city, and so
forth.

But the relative weakness of the physical love of the Americans
for their country shows itself most strikingly in very trivial manifestations, which, I believe, puzzle every European observer.

For instance, to travel in America is a psychological experience
which cannot be compared with traveling in any other country.
Having visited in the last three years approximately one hundred
cities for the purpose of lecturing, I find today that I have no
memory of more than about ten of them. They are mere names
in my notebook connected with a few incidents, but very seldom
with any characteristic impression of the places themselves. If I
were transported today on a magic carpet to most of these towns,
I should be at a loss to identify them.

The explanation is obvious: there is more monotony in American towns than in those of Europe. There is also the question of
distances. Landscapes and the general surroundings change very
slowly in this huge continent. Someone said that Switzerland
would be the largest country on earth if it were not *folded.*
America is completely *unfolded,* and gives the impression in some
places of being positively stretched out.

The European traveler experiences another strange feeling:
that his ignorance of the geography of the country is usually
shared by most of his traveling companions, who, moreover, seem
to be considerably more indifferent about it than he is himself.
This does not mean that the average American one meets in a
Pullman lounge does not know where he is, or where he is going.
As a matter of fact, he is usually more accurate concerning distances between various points and the time it takes to get from
one to the other, either in a train or in a plane, than a Frenchman
would be in his own country. But his knowledge is abstract. The
railroad timetable and the esoteric map therein seem to give him

all the information he requires. What actually *happens* between two given points, what the physical make-up of the land is, interests only a few.

Here again I suppose the question of size intervenes. Human senses cannot focus on a whole continent the way the painters of the Italian Renaissance could depict on one piece of canvas, and with all its details, the whole familiar area around them which was, in fact, their country. The American must be content with a simplified and purely convenient kind of blue print of the forty-eight states and the broad outlines of endless plains, tremendous mountains, and gigantic rivers.

However, when one is in an American train, the impression of traveling on nothing more substantial than a network of railroad tracks under which there may or may not be America is very disturbing to the European—as disturbing as the obvious fact that the American male reaches the maximum of happiness when, after a night in a Pullman, he goes into the smoking room to wash and shave in his undershirt, splashing and singing like a morning bird for no other apparent reason than that he is nowhere in particular (except far from home), detached from this earth along which he is being carried very fast with the minimum of awareness of its reality.

5

Nostalgia is not an American feeling. True enough, it has been the luck of Americans never to know all through their history the ordeal of exile from America. At one time or another, practically all nations of Europe have expelled some of their citizens for political or religious reasons, and these unfortunate minorities have known this curious human capacity for longing to "go back" where they came from. In recent years this form of suffering has been imposed on larger and larger sections of human beings. Americans, luckily for them, have been spared this experience. Nevertheless, some of them have had to live abroad for more or less lengthy periods. During the 1920's, for instance, several thousands were established in Paris, but, although they occasionally yearned for "home," this yearning was momentary and generally explainable by some local cause of irritation, such as the difficulty of getting accustomed to French coffee, or the amount of rain which falls in France. The imperfections of Parisian steam heat and the difficulty of obtaining orange juice or cereal at breakfast at the Hôtel de la Poste et du Nègre (although it is marked with three stars in the Michelin guidebook) may indeed give a pang to an American heart and bring sweet memories of the faithful radiator thumping away back home and of the corner drug store; but this is a far cry from the horrors of Biblical exodus.

I never saw the American exiles sit, like the Russians, around the equivalent of a samovar—namely, a pot of real American coffee—and indulge in an orgy of misery, with appropriate songs, over the fact that they were so far away from Buffalo or Omaha.

Speaking of songs, it is strange that most of those which express nostalgia come from the Negroes. "Carry Me Back to Old Virginny" is a good equivalent of the Breton "J'aime mieux Paimpol et sa falaise," but it does not express a really American sentiment. As a matter of fact, the number of Americans who want to be "carried back" to Old Virginia or to any other particular place is remarkably small. When it comes to retiring from active life and dying somewhere, they would rather move to a nice climate, if they can, like California or Florida, than to the place where they were born.

I fear that many readers will object to this statement. They will point out that nowhere in the world is there such a love of the family and of the home as in America. They will show me innumerable proofs that all representative and popular expressions of the American soul—such as the movies and advertising, for instance—play up constantly the theme of the American's love for the old homestead, for the state from which he hails, for his Alma Mater, and so forth. This is true, but I will confess that this concerted effort to boost sentiments which are taken for granted everywhere else gives one an impression of artificiality. The fact that the word "home," for instance, can be used and abused to the point of having become meaningless makes one suspect that the millions of people who use it not only do not know what the word really means, but are actually not very much interested in the thing itself.

There are good reasons for this. One is that few Americans live in or near the house where they were born—that is, in their home in the proper sense of the term—because few habitations in

America last as long as a man's life. Not infrequently in small towns one sees a single stone building, standing in the midst of less permanent constructions, preserved as a specimen of the home and dedicated to the town as a museum.

Another reason why the home is more a dream than a reality is the survival of early nomadism which in many parts of the country has blended itself with the sense of instability produced by industrialism and purely urban life. All modern countries are following the same trend; everywhere in the world men are returning slowly to the stage of the Bedouin—with complications. Home, for an ever-increasing number of men and women, is simply the place where they find work, and this place changes for most of them with growing rapidity. But in the Old World this trend towards chronic instability is checked by the toughness of the roots which still attach the individual to his province or village.

In France it is rare to find an industrial worker, an employee, or for that matter any *displaced* Frenchman, who has not kept some contact with his relatives who still live in the village or the small town where he himself was born. And it is usually his ambition to go back there when he is old.

Such roots exist in America also, but, with the exception of the oldest states, they are not very deep or very important in a man's life. There is also the tremendous fact that there are no peasants in America—a fact which alone would explain the curious impression that there is some sort of missing link in the structure of American society. "Peasant" (from the French *paysan*, meaning the man of a *pays*—that is, a very small area which may not encompass more than a village and its surrounding fields) may be a word which sounds badly to American ears, but it nevertheless represents a type of human being whose unchangeability through centuries, and whose total identification with the place where he was born and where he will die, probably constitute the soundest guarantee that some of the strongest virtues and some of the most useful vices of mankind will survive.

There are no American peasants, and this may be the real reason why to so many Americans the love of the land is little more than a poetic expression. It may be the reason why things pertaining to the soil retain a peculiar symbolic quality which is in marked contrast with the poignant connotation that these things have in other countries.

The nearest equivalent to the European peasant is, of course, the farmer, but it is obvious that his outlook on life is more akin to that of the business man than to that of the man who tills the earth. He is already urbanized, and in any event his numbers are rapidly decreasing. Not so very long ago farmers constituted 90 per cent of the population. Now, according to the *Encyclopædia of the Social Sciences,* they make up only 22 per cent.

6

In most countries of the Old World, language creates a bond which is often invoked as a proof of national unity. The national language assumes sometimes a character of sacredness. All through the history of Europe, nations have gone to war for the right to speak and write their own language. It would seem a natural human feeling that, when a man loses the privilege of express-ing himself in his mother tongue, something fundamental in him has been destroyed. He feels that he can no longer defend himself against an alien culture and an alien domination. And, in fact, history proves that this is very often the case.

French happens to be an extremely difficult language to speak or write correctly, even for a Frenchman, but the French have for their language a veneration which has probably no equivalent anywhere else except perhaps in China, among the mandarins. A man who speaks or writes well enjoys an impressive prestige. No politician can get anywhere in France (even if he represents the most uneducated parts of the country) if his style is not approx-imately correct.

Colonel de La Rocque, leader of the once picturesque Croix de Feu movement, failed to achieve real power, not so much because he lacked political ability, but because nearly every day it was possible to pick up a howler in his speeches or in his articles. On the other hand, Léon Blum can address a very tough crowd in the most polished and even precious French and never be criti-cized for being too perfect.

Many Americans cannot understand why European nations do not stop quarreling and form the United States of Europe; but among the chief obstacles is certainly this matter of the language to which each nation, even the smallest, is passionately attached because it has become part and parcel of the people's sense of nationality.

In America, however, no such importance is attributed to the way a man expresses himself. Nobody requires an orator to speak perfect English. Some do and some don't. But this does not affect their prestige or their power in the least. Indeed, the average American audience has a tendency to resent a speaker whose eloquence is a little too punctilious.

The first reason for this attitude towards the national language is that the American language is still in a vigorous state of creation. It offers vast possibilities of development, and it has already (in my way of thinking) made the kind of English which is spoken and written in England seem as dull and ineffectual as weak tea. Contemporary American writing and the forceful rhythm of good American speech are fast superseding British English. But the whole system of communication used by the Americans between themselves is still as unstable and experimental as was French in the time of Rabelais. And so the American purist has not much chance for another century or two.

Secondly, the language which is supposed to be officially that of the United States cannot be considered with great reverence as long as the millions of non-assimilated or partly assimilated foreign-born or children of foreign-born continue to speak their native tongue. According to statistics, out of 123 million American citizens counted in 1930 there were 53 million divided among the foreign-born and their children. Of course, most of these have learned to speak English, and in doing so have enriched their new language with many words and expressions of their own and even, I believe, with certain intonations and a rhythm which are making the American language what it is. But those who spoke Swedish, Italian, or Polish yesterday cannot be expected to feel that the King's English or General Hugh Johnson's has become part of their blood and that it is an important element in their national consciousness.

7

A final factor which makes the concept of American nationality so difficult for the foreigner to grasp is the impossibility of giving a unified picture of a nation which does not really occupy a country, but is spread out all over a continent. The Europeans are used to countries which, however diversified they may be, are built more or less on the same pattern. They are historical conglomerations of various smaller peoples which gradually united under the centralizing domination of a more powerful or more influential conqueror. They are made up of provinces which have retained their original characteristics, but which have in most cases become static. In practically all of them the largest city is the political as well as the cultural capital.

There is, however, no such thing in America, and the more one lives and studies this continent, the greater one's sense of confusion.

An Englishman who has lived here many years said to me: "My job keeps me in Washington, but Washington, of course, does not represent America. When I am in New York, I know also that New York is not America. In San Francisco, my American friends warn me that the Coast is not America. New England is not America; neither is the South. For a while I comforted myself in the belief that America was best represented by the Middle West. But now that I know the Middle West fairly well I have no particular reason to believe that it is more typical of what is really American than any other part of the country. After living ten years in America I still ask myself: Where is America? And my answer is that I don't know, and that I shall probably never find out."

To look at a map of the United States is not helpful; the rectangular boundaries of the states are very disturbing to a European mind. We know that sectional patriotism is strong in the forty-eight states, even stronger in many ways than the regional idiosyncrasies of France, Germany, or England. But how can the inhabitants of these arbitrary rectangles actually feel a coincidence between one of the most primitive instincts of man—his attachment to his native land—and these geometric boundaries? Again one feels the same sense of abstraction which is so characteristic of America as a whole.

8

The truth is that the growth of the American sense of nationality has followed a course inverse to that of older countries. The

European first becomes conscious of himself because he lives in a definite place where his forefathers lived before him, because he speaks a language which has always been spoken there, and because he feels a general sense of physical fixity in his surroundings. The *political* consequences of being a Frenchman, an Englishman, or an Italian are, in a sense, secondary manifestations of his nationality. They are superimposed.

But the Americans began to be *politically* conscious of being a nation before they felt that the land under their feet was really their homeland. It was only after they had broken off their allegiance to the British that they started—very slowly—to realize that America was the particular section of the planet to which they belonged, where their children and grandchildren and great-grandchildren would be born and would die. They began to grow roots after they were already in full bloom as an organized nation.

This—among others—is one of the important reasons why the Declaration of Independence is a certificate of birth not only for the whole American nation but for each American, even today; and why also the Constitution has always had a sacred character, for which there is no counterpart in any other country. It may be a wise political document, but it is even more important as the most genuine and most truly mystical source from which every American derives the consciousness of being himself. If the improbable choice were given to Americans by some great jokester, "Would you prefer to go on living in your country and be deprived of your Constitution and everything that it stands for, or would you prefer to take it with you to some new wilderness?" I am not quite sure what the results of the referendum would be.

Most of the native Americans with three or four generations behind them forget that those who have come after them undergo a process of adaptation. It does not matter whether those who have crossed the seas are conscious of what takes place within themselves when they decide to be naturalized. It does not matter, either, whether they become Americans merely because they are tempted by better opportunities or because they were thrown out of their native land by persecution of one kind or another. The important fact is this: all those who are coming today and those who will come tomorrow are required first of all to accept a certain outlook on life and certain moral and political principles which will make them Americans. These things must take place in their minds and in their souls. Whether they adapt themselves to the landscape, to the architecture of the towns, to the food and drinks of their new country, is secondary. Whether they can speak its language is also not very important. The main thing is that they should be won over to Americanism, which is a set of moral and political doctrines.

Curiously enough, in a country where material changes are extraordinarily rapid, this moral and political frame has the stability of a dogma. For instance, America is the only country in the world which pretends to listen to the teaching of its founders as if they were still alive. Political battles of today are fought with arguments based on the speeches or writings of men dead over a century ago. Most Americans behave, in fact, as if men like Washington, Hamilton, Jefferson, and many others could be called up on the phone for advice. Their wisdom is considered as eternal as that of the Biblical prophets. To show how distinctively American this conception is, one has only to imagine what would happen if Mr. Chamberlain justified his present policy by quoting William Pitt, or if M. Daladier evoked the authority of Danton as a guide.

In fact, to become an American is a process which resembles a conversion. It is not so much a new country that one adopts as a new creed. And in all Americans can be discerned some of the traits of those who have, at one time or another, abandoned an ancient faith for a new one.

This explains, perhaps, the importance of the factor mentioned at the beginning of this article: that, in the make-up of an American, his defiance of the rest of the world, and particularly Europe, is fundamental and unavoidable.

The majority of the people who compose the American nation came from Europe. To uproot themselves and cross the ocean was in most cases a painful operation, but one that was undertaken with hopefulness and courage, because Americanism, as a faith, has a tremendous appeal. But once a man has broken his roots from his native land, the reaction which takes place within himself is not a simple one. It is complex, like the state of mind of a child who has left his home; he may enjoy a sense of liberation while at the same time longing for home, but he also hates that home—because he has left it. America is a nation of prodigal sons who won't go back home—and this accounts for the undercurrent of irritation and bitterness against Europe.

This current is more manifest today than it has been for a long time, and it has now so many obvious justifications that one is tempted to overlook the fact that it is not incidental. Even the Europeans who come here now on a visit breathe a sigh of relief and enjoy the sense of security which they find on this continent. But the national slogan of America, "Thank God for the Atlantic Ocean," is not due to passing circumstances. It is a prayer which has always been heard, and will be heard again even if the Americans have to cross that ocean once more to go to fight "someone else's war."

Of course an increasing number of Americans are wondering today whether God made the Atlantic Ocean wide enough, and President Roosevelt, with general approval, is giving a helping hand to the Creator by building many battleships and many planes which will reënforce this natural obstacle. But it seems to me that the desire to increase the physical defenses of the United States is inspired not so much by the actual fear of a foreign invasion as by the subconscious panic caused by the challenge launched abroad against what is loosely termed democracy—and the more one thinks of that vague word the more it appears to be synonymous with something specifically American.

The American battleships which are being built now may never fire a shot. They are there to defend American ideals more than to protect American soil.

9

If the interpretation I have tried to give of what makes an American is not wholly wrong, it explains why the American is in a peculiar position in relation to the rest of the world. His conception of nationality makes him, in a way, better equipped to resist the degrading forces which are now at work in the world than the citizen of any other country. On the other hand, if these forces (which I call degrading because such is my belief) triumph, they will cease to be considered evil. Quite the contrary. They will be glorified as representing the true course of civilization for the twentieth century, and the American will find himself in the curious position of being isolated, not because he wants to be, but because he will be the last representative of a backward type of humanity that will appear completely out of step with this adventurous Europe that may be emerging under our eyes now. America, which we see clinging so passionately to the political and moral concepts of the nineteenth and even of the eighteenth century, will find itself in an even stronger opposition to Europe than it is now.

What will the American do then? Will he carry on the fight single-handed? Or will he try to cultivate within his own soul a sense of nationality less abstract and less doctrinary, as a compensation for the defeat of his ideals?

For the moment the general tendency is to rely on the possibility of maintaining an unchanged course. In fact, there is no question about that, but it is interesting to note that the "Thank God for the Atlantic Ocean" attitude is not as self-assured as it used to be. Doubt is creeping in very fast, and, as always happens when faith is shaken, the natural instinct is to shout even louder that the reasons to doubt are nonexistent. The affirmation that America has been set apart from the rest of the world, that it can and will fulfill its mission, and that it has been *chosen,* is proclaimed with such eloquence and energy that one has sometimes the impression that it was not God who made the Atlantic Ocean, but the genius of the American people.

In the Progressive Party's platform published last April, for instance, one finds the following statement:

"We believe that this hemisphere—all of it—was set aside by our Creator for the ultimate destiny of man. Here a vast continent was kept virgin for centuries. Here it was ordained that man should work out the final act in the greatest drama of life. From the Arctic to Cape Horn, let no foreign power trespass. Our hemisphere was divinely destined to evolve peace, security, and plenty. It shall remain inviolate for that sacred purpose."

This is a lofty conception, and the immigrant, the pioneer, the refugee, or the oppressed, whether he arrived here a century ago or last week, cannot help being heartened by such words. The question is, however, how much longer can the American maintain the posture of a man who stands on tiptoe on the ground because he feels it is his destiny to keep his head above the clouds?

Walter Lippmann
(1889-   )

ONE OF the most widely read and highly regarded daily columnists in the United States is Walter Lippmann. He was educated at Harvard and since taking his B.A. there in 1909 he has been actively engaged in newspaper writing excepting during the period of his service in the First World War. In 1917 he was Assistant to the Secretary of War, and he also served with the American Expeditionary Force as Captain in the United States Military Intelligence. He has been associate editor of *The New Republic,* editor of the *New York World,* and is at present special writer for the *New York Herald Tribune* and other newspapers. He is a member of the National Institute of Arts and Letters and of the American Academy of Arts and Letters, and is an Officer of the French Legion of Honor. Among his many books, some of which have been widely influential, are: *A Preface to Politics* (1913); *The Status of Diplomacy* (1915); *Liberty and the News* (1920); *Public Opinion* (1922); *A Preface to Morals* (1929); *The Method of Freedom* (1934); *The New Imperative* (1935); *The Good Society* (1937); and *Some Notes on War and Peace* (1940).

Mr. Lippmann's devotion to the democratic organization of society is very sincere. His emphasis on the importance to such an organization of freedom of speech and debate is of great importance to all people who wish to preserve the society in which we live. In the following essay he has pointed out the value of an active and intelligent opposition in the conduct of a democracy.

The Indispensable Opposition (1939)

Were they pressed hard enough, most men would probably confess that political freedom—that is to say, the right to speak freely and to act in opposition—is a noble ideal rather than a practical necessity. As the case for freedom is generally put today, the argument lends itself to this feeling. It is made to appear that, whereas each man claims his freedom as a matter of right, the freedom he accords to other men is a matter of toleration. Thus, the defense of freedom of opinion tends to rest not on its substantial, beneficial, and indispensable consequences, but on a somewhat eccentric, a rather vaguely benevolent, attachment to an abstraction.

It is all very well to say with Voltaire, "I wholly disapprove of what you say, but will defend to the death your right to say it," but as a matter of fact most men will not defend to the death the rights of other men: if they disapprove sufficiently what other men say, they will somehow suppress those men if they can.

So, if this is the best that can be said for liberty of opinion, that a man must tolerate his opponents because every one has a "right" to say what he pleases, then we shall find that liberty of opinion is a luxury, safe only in pleasant times when men can be tolerant because they are not deeply and vitally concerned.

Yet actually, as a matter of historic fact, there is a much stronger foundation for the great constitutional right of freedom of speech, and as a matter of practical human experience there is a much more compelling reason for cultivating the habits of free men. We take, it seems to me, a naïvely self-righteous view when we argue as if the right of our opponents to speak were something that we protect because we are magnanimous, noble, and un-

From *The Atlantic Monthly*, August 1939; reprinted by permission of the author and The Atlantic Monthly Company.

selfish. The compelling reason why, if liberty of opinion did not exist, we should have to invent it, why it will eventually have to be restored in all civilized countries where it is now suppressed, is that we must protect the right of our opponents to speak because we must hear what they have to say.

We miss the whole point when we imagine that we tolerate the freedom of our political opponents as we tolerate a howling baby next door, as we put up with the blasts from our neighbor's radio because we are too peaceable to heave a brick through the window. If this were all there is to freedom of opinion, that we are too good-natured or too timid to do anything about our opponents and our critics except to let them talk, it would be difficult to say whether we are tolerant because we are magnanimous or because we are lazy, because we have strong principles or because we lack serious convictions, whether we have the hospitality of an inquiring mind or the indifference of an empty mind. And so, if we truly wish to understand why freedom is necessary in a civilized society, we must begin by realizing that, because freedom of discussion improves our own opinions, the liberties of other men are our own vital necessity.

We are much closer to the essence of the matter, not when we quote Voltaire, but when we go to the doctor and pay him to ask us the most embarrassing questions and to prescribe the most disagreeable diet. When we pay the doctor to exercise complete freedom of speech about the cause and cure of our stomach-ache, we do not look upon ourselves as tolerant and magnanimous, and worthy to be admired by ourselves. We have enough common sense to know that if we threaten to put the doctor in jail because we do not like the diagnosis and the prescription it will be unpleasant for the doctor, to be sure, but equally unpleasant for our own stomachache. That is why even the most ferocious dictator would rather be treated by a doctor who was free to think and speak the truth than by his own Minister of Propaganda. For there is a point, the point at which things really matter, where the freedom of others is no longer a question of their right but of our own need.

The point at which we recognize this need is much higher in some men than in others. The totalitarian rulers think they do not need the freedom of an opposition: they exile, imprison, or shoot their opponents. We have concluded on the basis of practical experience, which goes back to Magna Carta and beyond, that we need the opposition. We pay the opposition salaries out of the public treasury.

In so far as the usual apology for freedom of speech ignores this experience, it becomes abstract and eccentric rather than concrete and human. The emphasis is generally put on the right to speak, as if all that mattered were that the doctor should be free to go out into the park and explain to the vacant air why I have a stomachache. Surely that is a miserable caricature of the great civic right which men have bled and died for. What really matters is that the doctor should tell *me* what ails me, that I should listen to him; that if I do not like what he says I should be free to call in another doctor; and that then the first doctor should have to listen to the second doctor; and that out of all the speaking and listening, the give-and-take of opinions, the truth should be arrived at.

This is the creative principle of freedom of speech, not that it is a system for the tolerating of error, but that it is a system for finding the truth. It may not produce the truth, or the whole truth all the time, or often, or in some cases ever. But if the truth can be found, there is no other system which will normally and habitually find so much truth. Until we have thoroughly understood this principle, we shall not know why we must value our liberty, or how we can protect and develop it.

2

Let us apply this principle to the system of public speech in a totalitarian state. We may, without any serious falsification, picture a condition of affairs in which the mass of the people are being addressed through one broadcasting system by one man and his chosen subordinates. The orators speak. The audience listens but cannot and dare not speak back. It is a system of one-way communication; the opinions of the rulers are broadcast outwardly to the mass of the people. But nothing comes back to the rulers from the people except the cheers; nothing returns in the way of knowledge of forgotten facts, hidden feelings, neglected truths, and practical suggestions.

But even a dictator cannot govern by his own one-way inspiration alone. In practice, therefore, the totalitarian rulers get back the reports of the secret police and of their party henchmen down among the crowd. If these reports are competent, the rulers may manage to remain in touch with public sentiment. Yet that is not enough to know what the audience feels. The rulers have also to make great decisions that have enormous consequences, and here their system provides virtually no help from the give-and-take of opinion in the nation. So they must either rely on their own intuition, which cannot be permanently and continually inspired, or, if they are intelligent despots, encourage their trusted advisers and their technicians to speak and debate freely in their presence.

On the walls of the houses of Italian peasants one may see inscribed in large letters the legend, "Mussolini is always right." But if that legend is taken seriously by Italian ambassadors, by the Italian General Staff, and by the Ministry of Finance, then all one can say is heaven help Mussolini, heaven help Italy, and the new Emperor of Ethiopia.

For at some point, even in a totalitarian state, it is indispensable that there should exist the freedom of opinion which causes opposing opinions to be debated. As time goes on, that is less and less easy under a despotism; critical discussion disappears as the internal opposition is liquidated in favor of men who think and feel alike. That is why the early successes of despots, of Napoleon I and of Napoleon III, have usually been followed by an irreparable mistake. For in listening only to his yes men—the others being in exile or in concentration camps, or terrified—the despot shuts himself off from the truth that no man can dispense with.

We know all this well enough when we contemplate the dictatorships. But when we try to picture our own system, by way of contrast, what picture do we have in our minds? It is, is it not, that anyone may stand up on his own soapbox and say anything he pleases, like the individuals in Kipling's poem who sit each in his separate star and draw the Thing as they see it for the God of Things as they are. Kipling, perhaps, could do this, since he was a poet. But the ordinary mortal isolated on his separate star will have an hallucination, and a citizenry declaiming from separate soapboxes will poison the air with hot and nonsensical confusion.

If the democratic alternative to the totalitarian one-way broadcasts is a row of separate soapboxes, then I submit that the alternative is unworkable, is unreasonable, and is humanly unattractive. It is above all a false alternative. It is not true that liberty has developed among civilized men when anyone is free to set up a soapbox, is free to hire a hall where he may expound his opinions to those who are willing to listen. On the contrary, freedom of speech is established to achieve its essential purpose only when different opinions are expounded in the same hall to the same audience.

For, while the right to talk may be the beginning of freedom, the necessity of listening is what makes the right important. Even in Russia and Germany a man may still stand in an open field and speak his mind. What matters is not the utterance of opinions. What matters is the confrontation of opinions in debate. No man can care profoundly that every fool should say what he likes. Nothing has been accomplished if the wisest man proclaims his wisdom in the middle of the Sahara Desert. This is the shadow. We have the substance of liberty when the fool is compelled to listen to the wise man and learn; when the wise man is compelled to take account of the fool, and to instruct him; when the wise man can increase his wisdom by hearing the judgment of his peers.

That is why civilized men must cherish liberty—as a means of promoting the discovery of truth. So we must not fix our whole attention on the right of anyone to hire his own hall, to rent his own broadcasting station, to distribute his own pamphlets. These rights are incidental; and though they must be preserved, they can be preserved only by regarding them as incidental, as auxiliary to the substance of liberty that must be cherished and cultivated.

Freedom of speech is best conceived, therefore, by having in mind the picture of a place like the American Congress, an assembly where opposing views are represented, where ideas are not merely uttered but debated, or the British Parliament, where men who are free to speak are also compelled to answer. We may picture the true condition of freedom as existing in a place like a court of law, where witnesses testify and are cross-examined, where the lawyer argues against the opposing lawyer before the same judge and in the presence of one jury. We may picture freedom as existing in a forum where the speaker must respond to questions; in a gathering of scientists where the data, the hypothesis, and the conclusion are submitted to men competent to judge them; in a reputable newspaper which not only will publish the opinions of those who disagree but will re-examine its own opinion in the light of what they say.

Thus the essence of freedom of opinion is not in mere toleration as such, but in the debate which toleration provides: it is not in the venting of opinion, but in the confrontation of opinion. That this is the practical substance can readily be understood when we remember how differently we feel and act about the censorship and regulation of opinion purveyed by different media of communication. We find then that, in so far as the medium makes difficult the confrontation of opinion in debate, we are driven towards censorship and regulation.

There is, for example, the whispering campaign, the circulation of anonymous rumors by men who cannot be compelled to prove what they say. They put the utmost strain on our tolerance, and there are few who do not rejoice when the anonymous slanderer is caught, exposed, and punished. At a higher level there is the moving picture, a most powerful medium for conveying ideas, but a medium which does not permit debate. A moving picture cannot be answered effectively by another moving picture; in all free countries there is some censorship of the movies, and there would be more if the producers did not recognize their limitations by avoiding political controversy. There is then the radio. Here debate is difficult: it is not easy to make sure that the speaker is being answered in the presence of the same audience. Inevitably, there is some regulation of the radio.

When we reach the newspaper press, the opportunity for debate is so considerable that discontent cannot grow to the point where under normal conditions there is any disposition to regulate the press. But when newspapers abuse their power by injuring people who have no means of replying, a disposition to regulate the press appears. When we arrive at Congress we find that, because the membership of the House is so large, full debate is impracticable. So there are restrictive rules. On the other hand, in the Senate, where the conditions of full debate exist, there is almost absolute freedom of speech.

This shows us that the preservation and development of freedom of opinion are not only a matter of adhering to abstract legal rights, but also, and very urgently, a matter of organizing and arranging sufficient debate. Once we have a firm hold on the central principle, there are many practical conclusions to be drawn. We then realize that the defense of freedom of opinion consists primarily in perfecting the opportunity for an adequate give-and-take of opinion; it consists also in regulating the freedom of those revolutionists who cannot or will not permit or maintain debate when it does not suit their purposes.

We must insist that free oratory is only the beginning of free speech; it is not the end, but a means to an end. The end is to find the truth. The practical justification of civil liberty is not that self-expression is one of the rights of man. It is that the examination of opinion is one of the necessities of man. For experience tells us that it is only when freedom of opinion becomes the compulsion to debate that the seed which our fathers planted has produced its fruit. When that is understood, freedom will be cherished not because it is a vent for our opinions but because it is the surest method of correcting them.

The unexamined life, said Socrates, is unfit to be lived by man. This is the virtue of liberty, and the ground on which we may best justify our belief in it, that it tolerates error in order to serve the truth. When men are brought face to face with their opponents, forced to listen and learn and mend their ideas, they cease to be children and savages and begin to live like civilized men. Then only is freedom a reality, when men may voice their opinions because they must examine their opinions.

3

The only reason for dwelling on all this is that if we are to preserve democracy we must understand its principles. And the principle which distinguishes it from all other forms of government is that in a democracy the opposition not only is tolerated as constitutional but must be maintained because it is in fact indispensable.

The democratic system cannot be operated without effective opposition. For, in making the great experiment of governing people by consent rather than by coercion, it is not sufficient that the party in power should have a majority. It is just as necessary that the party in power should never outrage the minority. That means that it must listen to the minority and be moved by the criticisms of the minority. That means that its measures must take account of the minority's objections, and that in administering measures it must remember that the minority may become the majority.

The opposition is indispensable. A good statesman, like any other sensible human being, always learns more from his opponents than from his fervent supporters. For his supporters will push him to disaster unless his opponents show him where the dangers are. So if he is wise he will often pray to be delivered from his friends, because they will ruin him. But, though it hurts, he ought also to pray never to be left without opponents; for they keep him on the path of reason and good sense.

The national unity of a free people depends upon a sufficiently even balance of political power to make it impracticable for the administration to be arbitrary and for the opposition to be revolutionary and irreconcilable. Where that balance no longer exists, democracy perishes. For unless all the citizens of a state are forced by circumstances to compromise, unless they feel that they can affect policy but that no one can wholly dominate it, unless by habit and necessity they have to give and take, freedom cannot be maintained.

Henry Steele Commager
(1902-   )

AFTER an education at the University of Chicago and special study at the University of Copenhagen, Henry Steele Commager became Instructor in History at New York University in 1926 and continued to teach there until his resignation in 1939 to accept a professorship in history at Columbia University, where he is now teaching. He has been for many years an active book-reviewer and writer and is the author of several books, notably, with the collaboration of Professor S. E. Morison, of *The Growth of the American Public* (1931) and, with Allan Nevins, of *The Heritage of America,* an anthology (1939).

Keystones of Our National Unity, reprinted here from *The New York Times Magazine* for November 10, 1940, was published immediately after the election of 1940; it is an exposition of the democratic process in operation and a challenge for its functioning in time of stress. It represents the application of scholarly knowledge to current problems.

Keystones of Our National Unity (1940)

Now that the people have chosen their next President, the solemn warnings, the alarming prophecies, the bitter criticisms, the charges and countercharges that attended the campaign have passed into history.

For months, now, we have heard cries that the Republic was in danger, that democracy was in peril, that we were headed for socialism or fascism, that we were losing, or had lost, our very souls. To an outsider, unfamiliar with American politics, all this might seem very ominous indeed, a prelude to disintegration, a portent of civil war. Actually it is all part of the ceremony of our Presidential campaigns, the normal trappings of party rivalries, and students know that these auspices have attended most of our more important Presidential contests since 1800.

It will be admitted that sometimes this heat becomes excessive and leaves lasting wounds, but it is not entirely unhealthy. For campaigns are the safety valves of American politics. This is how Americans blow off steam, and though the process may be undignified, it is a not unsatisfactory substitute for intrigue or revolution. And the shadow of the war, falling athwart the campaign, emphasized as never before the necessity, the significance, and the value of national unity. It dramatized for us the fact that the American people is a nation.

But what do we mean by this? What is national unity, and in what does it consist? It is easier to ask this question than to answer it, for our response to the term is emotional rather than intellectual. Yet the very fact that our nationalism is so largely an emotion is itself reassuring. We do not have, in the United States, a code of nationalism, a formal philosophy ("happy is that na-

From *The New York Times Magazine*, November 10, 1940; reprinted by permission of the author and the New York Times Company.

tion," wrote Leslie Stephen, "that has no political philosophy").
Nationalism is to be found not in the teachings of the schools
but in the hearts and habits of the American people. Yet this, too,
requires some analysis.

What are the elements of our national unity, and what reason
is there to suppose that these elements will persist and this unity
will survive the present crisis? A nation, said the Comte de St.
Aulaire, is a mission, and the observation is a suggestive one.
Certainly, when we attempt to determine those qualities which
give historical distinction to peoples or nations, it is usually upon
this characteristic that we hit.

The suggestion applies with peculiar force to the United States;
for the United States has had, from the beginning, a mission.
That mission has been to afford an opportunity, on a grand scale,
for an experiment in social and political democracy. This was
what the United States was designed to be—designed by nature
and by man—a laboratory which should test the ability of men to
govern themselves, and which should afford to all men, of all nations and creeds, an equal chance at the good life.

This was what the French statesman, Turgot, meant when he
wrote that "this people is the hope of the human race." It was
what Jefferson meant when he spoke of America as the "world's
best hope," and what Lincoln meant when he referred to it as
"the last best hope of earth," and what Wilson meant when he
called upon his countrymen to lead the way in a world crusade
for democracy.

From the beginning this sense of being embarked together
upon a great experiment in democracy has been an instrument
for national unity. It has been a great common denominator to
Americans north and south, east and west, to first families and
foreign-born, to farmer and laborer, to Hudson River squire and
Hoosier schoolmaster. It has given to Americans, rightly or
wrongly, a sense of being different, and of superiority, and has
inspired, at times, an imperialism designed to confer upon less
fortunate peoples the benefits of the American system. It has inspired loyalty to a society and a nation rather than to a particular class or locality. And it has, more than anything else, drawn

people from the Old World to the New—drawn them to participate in the common venture and to enjoy the common heritage.

Yet democracy, even if removed from the realm of experiment
to that of fact (and it has not yet been entirely so removed) would
not in itself be sufficient foundation for national unity. There
are, of course, other and substantial elements, material and cultural. What are some of these? The first and most obvious is that
of physical expansion—westward across the Alleghenies to the
Pacific.

At first glance this process might seem to be disintegrating, and
indeed many thoughtful observers in the late eighteenth and
early nineteenth centuries feared that the United States was becoming too large for a single nation and that it would inevitably
break up into its natural geographical elements. In any event,
expansion is not in itself nationalizing. What was important
about the process in the United States was that expansion was
westward into unsettled land, and into land which—excepting
Texas—was national domain.

Here, in these successive Wests, local and State loyalties were
submerged, particularism gave way to nationalism. Here were
the melting pots of American society—Yankees and Yorkers and
Carolinians and Kentuckians and Hoosiers, Irish and German
and Norwegian, all fused into Americans. It was no accident of
history, not even of economics, that the West was always the most
American part of America and the most nationalistic.

A second historical factor making for national unity was large-
scale immigration. Here, again, was a process which might have
had very different consequences, which might have aggravated
particularism and disunity. Certainly the German and Italian
colonies in South American countries do not contribute greatly
to the national unity of those states. Yet in the United States
immigration was nationalizing. For from the very beginning
those who came to the New World came because they were discontented with their lot in the Old, because they hoped to find
here a better life for themselves and for their children, to find
religious liberty, social equality, economic opportunity, and justice.

That moving invitation, inscribed on the base of the Statue of Liberty, was implicit in the American attitude throughout the eighteenth and nineteenth centuries:

> Give me your tired, your poor,
>   Your huddled masses yearning to breathe free,
> The wretched refuse of your teeming shore;
>   Send these, the homeless, tempest-tost to me:
> I lift my lamp beside the golden door.

On the whole the immigrants were not disappointed. If they did not find Utopia, they found, for the most part, a better life than that which they had known. And they were, in return, intensely loyal. They were loyal not to a State or a section or a class, but to the United States. Their contribution to national unity was an invaluable one.

These things—the democratic mission, the West, and immigration—have been peculiar to the United States. Other influences making for nationalism are more common to the history of nationalism elsewhere: language, literature, folklore, history, law, education, heroes and symbols.

We inherited our language from England, but we have made it an American language—muscular, racy and idiomatic, wonderfully enriched by contributions from many social groups. We inherited a literature, but we have developed a genuine American literature, whether that of the Authors whose benign countenances graced the cards of that game or the later, more self-consciously American writers who found inspiration in Whitman and Mark Twain.

Folklore and legend, folk song and ballad, are native and reveal an indigenous culture. We have become historically self-conscious—the process began early with Sparks and Bancroft—and the historical memory—the memory of John Smith and Pocahontas, of Plymouth Rock and the Quaker Commonwealth, of border warfare and Indian captivities, of the War for Independence and the naval War of 1812, of Boonsboro and Fort Dearborn and the Alamo, the trek of the Forty-niners, the Lincoln-Douglas debates and the brothers' war—all this has played an incalculably important role in the creation of national unity. We have folk heroes and heroic symbols—Washington and Lincoln and Lee, and for symbol the Constitution which has taken on an aura of sanctity.

This last achievement is worth emphasizing—the creation of folk heroes and of symbols—for it is part of the process of nationalism everywhere. It is not a little remarkable that the youngest of great nations should so rapidly and so effectively have supplied these historical needs.

We have not, to be sure, any mythical founders of the American Republic—no Romulus or Remus, no Horsa or Hengist, no one even of the venerable antiquity of a Charlemagne or a Barbarossa. But Washington's apotheosis has been speedy and impressive, and it may be doubted whether any other folk hero, except Joan of Arc, has so filled the imagination of a people as has Father Abraham. The sanctification of the Constitution, too, has been an illuminating process. It is still, to be sure, a secular document, yet it has become more fully a symbol than any other document except Magna Carta, and a symbol more effective and vital than Magna Carta.

American nationalism, the creation of these and other forces of geography and society and history, has not always had clear sailing. From the beginning the auguries seemed unfavorable, and for many decades storms threatened the success of the venture.

At the time of the formation of the Union many observers were sure that no nation federal in character and democratic in procedure could long endure. The new nation was threatened by dissension within and danger without, by the unsolved problem of distance, by conflicting inherited loyalties, by lack of national traditions or sentiments or habits. It triumphantly survived these perils, only to meet new ones.

The most serious of these—sectionalism—finally brought on disunion and war, and for a time it seemed all up with the American experiment. Yet even here we must not be misled. The American Civil War dramatized profound economic and social cleavages, but it did not indicate that any large part of the American people had repudiated their political institutions. North and South, men asserted that they were the true representatives of the American tradition and the American way of life, that they were fighting to preserve constitutionalism.

The story of the re-creation of the Union and of nationalism after the war is an arresting one. This difficult task was facilitated by the fact that there were no deep-seated differences in political philosophy to be overcome, no ineradicable antipathies to constitution, to democratic processes or to established social institutions. All the forces making for national unity which had existed before the attack on Sumter continued to operate—the democratic ideal, immigration and internal migration; a common language, literature, law, Constitution—and new forces of economic nationalism and of cultural standardization were applied. Within a generation the war had lost most of its bitterness and become a legend; within two generations it was, curiously, a shared heritage and a bond of union.

At no time since Appomattox has national unity been seriously threatened, unless by growing sectional and class exploitation in the economic field. These, to be sure, have seriously disturbed the equilibrium of society and economy, and in perspective we can see that those disturbances were necessary to our national well-being.

Year after year timid men, unfamiliar with our history and without faith in our people, shuddered at what seemed revolutionary threats to stability—at the time of the Granger crusade, during the Greenback campaigns, when labor organized for an eight-hour day and rioted at Haymarket, when liberal legislatures forced railroads and trusts to obey the law, when Populists attacked the citadels of privilege, when Altgeld defended the victims of the Pullman strike, when Bryan called for a new democracy, when imperialism seemed a departure from the teachings of the fathers, when the first Roosevelt thundered from the White House and again when he called for a reform of the judiciary; when Wilson enacted the platform of the new freedom and when the second Roosevelt pushed through a New Deal.

All these things inspired fears and alarms, all of them the Republic has weathered and for most of them it has been the stronger. When we recall how national unity has survived the real crisis of the Civil War and Reconstruction, and how unaffected it was by these sham crises of the past, we should realize that it is not to be destroyed by momentary differences over methods of administration or spoils of office.

Yet all this does not mean that there are not, in the present situation, elements of danger. France, too, had traditions, mission, language and literature and culture, centuries of history; yet France revealed herself, in the present crisis, hopelessly divided. Here, too, there are potential dangers. National unity can be sacrificed, can be frittered away, can be willfully destroyed. It cannot rest permanently on merely spiritual considerations or on tradition and habit. Patriotism itself must have solid bases, must recommend itself to experience and reason.

What are the elements of danger? We need only mention them, for they require neither explanation nor elaboration. If national unity is to be preserved the nation must be kept sound and well. The natural resources of the nation must be conserved, not frittered away; the human resources must be preserved and strengthened, not exploited and weakened. Some solution must be found to unemployment and the nation must restore to its citizens a sense of pride in their contribution to society.

There must be equality not only in politics and law but in social relationships and in economy. We must recall Woodrow Wilson's admonition in his first inaugural address: "There can be no equality of opportunity, the first essential of justice in the body politic, if men and women and children be not shielded in their lives, their very vitality, from the consequences of great industrial and social processes which they cannot alter, control or singly cope with. Society must see to it that it does not crush or weaken or damage its own constituent parts."

Both the material and the spiritual ingredients are essential to national unity. Americans must be aware—not through any artificial process of indoctrination—of their historical heritage. That heritage is rich in material resources—in fertility of soil, and water power, and mineral wealth, and in the incomparable beauty and variety of the land; it is rich in human resources, in the inheritance from the past and the contributions from all quarters of the globe. It is wonderfully rich, too, in history and tradition, in moral and spiritual forces. It is a heritage which, once recognized, will be cherished, and cherished will be preserved.

Part Three

Chapters from American Life

Biography and Autobiography

Part Three

Chapters from American Life

Biography and Autobiography

Venerable men! you have come down to us from a former generation.
DANIEL WEBSTER: Address, at Laying the Corner-stone of the Bunker-Hill Monument, *June 17, 1825.*

All history resolves itself very easily into the biography of a few stout and earnest persons. EMERSON: Essays, First Series: Self-Reliance.

There is no life of a man, faithfully recorded, but is a heroic poem of its sort, rhymed or unrhymed. CARLYLE: Essays: Memoirs on the Life of Scott.

Samuel Eliot Morison
(1887-   )

AWARDED his Bachelor of Arts degree by Harvard College in 1908, Samuel Eliot Morison has spent his life in the study of American history and is at present Professor of History at Harvard. During the summer of 1940 he was frequently in the newsprints as his countrymen followed his cruise in a small sailing boat along the first route taken by Columbus to America. His greatest distinction came, however, in 1922, when he was invited to lecture at Oxford as the Harold Vyvyan Harmsworth Professor of American History. This post Professor Morison held for three years. He is the author of *The Maritime History of Massachusetts* (1921), *The Oxford History of the United States* (1927), *Builders of Bay Colony* (1930), and *Tercentennial History of Harvard University* (1931–36).

About a great leader, a mass of stories and legends always arise, many of which are cherished by later generations. For this reason, the careful historian has a difficult path to tread; without breaking down the true greatness of his subject's character, he must treat his subject with honesty and candor. In this essay, which was delivered in the Sanders Theatre, at Harvard University, on February 22, 1932, the bicentennial of Washington's birth, Professor Morison has clearly set forth those traits of character in the young man which ennobled the mature soldier and leader.

The Young Man Washington

Washington is the last person you would ever suspect of having been a young man, with all the bright hopes and black despairs to which young men are subject. In American folklore he is known only as a child or a general or an old, old man: priggish hero of the cherry-tree episode, commander-in-chief, or the Father of his Country, writing a farewell address. By some freak of fate, Stuart's "Athenæum" portrait of an ideal and imposing, but solemn and weary, Washington at the age of sixty-four has become the most popular. This year it has been reproduced as the "official" portrait, and placed in every school in the country; so we may expect that new generations of American school-children will be brought up with the idea that Washington was a solemn old bore. If only Charles Willson Peale's portrait of him as a handsome and gallant soldier could have been used instead! Or one of the charming miniatures that shows him as a young man exulting in his strength! His older biographers, too, have conspired to create the legend; and the recent efforts to "popularize" Washington have taken the unfortunate line of trying to make him out something that he was not: a churchman, politician, engineer, business man, realtor, or even "traveling man." These attempts to degrade a hero to a "go-getter," an aristocrat to a vulgarian, remind one of the epitaph that Aristotle wished to have carved on the tomb of Plato: *Hic jacet homo, quem non licet, non decet, impiis vel ignorantibus laudare* ("Here lies a man whom it is neither permissible nor proper for the irreverent or the ignorant to *praise*").

Perhaps it is not the fault of the painters and biographers that we think of Washington as an old man, but because his outstanding qualities—wisdom, poise, and serenity—are not the qualities

Reprinted by permission of the President and Fellows of Harvard College.

usually associated with youth. He seemed to have absorbed, wrote Emerson, "all the serenity of America, and left none for his restless, rickety, hysterical countrymen." The Comte de Chastellux, one of the French officers in the war, said that Washington's most characteristic feature was balance: "the perfect harmony existing between the physical and moral attributes of which he is made up." Yet Gilbert Stuart, after painting his first portrait of Washington, said that "all his features were indicative of the most ungovernable passions, and had he been born in the forests, it was his opinion that he would have been the fiercest man among the savage tribes." Both men were right. Washington's qualities were so balanced that his talents, which were great but nothing extraordinary, were more effective in the long run than those of greater generals like Napoleon, or of bolder and more original statesmen like Hamilton and Jefferson. Yet as a young man Washington was impatient and passionate, eager for glory in war, wealth in land, and success in love. Even in maturity his fierce temper would sometimes get the better of him. In Cambridge, at his headquarters in the Craigie House, he once became so exasperated at the squabbling of drunken soldiers in the front yard that, forgetting the dignity of a general, he rushed forth and "laid out" a few of the brawlers with his own fists; and then, much relieved, returned to his study. Under great provocation he would break out with a torrent of Olympian oaths that terrified the younger men on his staff. Tobias Lear, the smooth young Harvard graduate who became Washington's private secretary, admitted that the most dreadful experience in his life was hearing the General swear!

It was only through the severest self-discipline that Washington attained his characteristic poise and serenity. Discipline is not a popular word nowadays, for we associate it with schoolmasters, drill-sergeants, and dictators; and it was certainly not discipline of that sort that made the passionate young Washington into an effective man. His discipline came in a very small part from parents, masters, or superiors; and in no respect from institutions. It came from environment, from a philosophy of life that he imbibed at an impressionable age; but most of all from his own will. He apprehended the great truth that man can only be free through mastery of himself. Instead of allowing his passions to spend themselves, he restrained them. Instead of indulging himself in a life of pleasure,—for which he had ample means at the age of twenty,—he placed duty first. In fact he followed exactly that course of conduct which, according to the second-hand popularizers of Freud, makes a person "thwarted," "inhibited," and "repressed." Yet Washington became a liberated, successful, and serene man. The process can hardly fail to interest young men who are struggling with the same difficulties as Washington— although, I am bound to say, under the far more difficult conditions of depression and mechanization.

Whence came this impulse to self-discipline? We can find nothing to account for it in the little we know of Washington's heredity. His family was gentle but undistinguished. George knew little of his forbears and cared less, although he used the family coat of arms. Lawrence Washington, sometime Fellow of Brasenose College, Oxford, was ejected from his living by the Roundheads as a "malignant Royalist." His son John came to Virginia by way of Barbados as mate of a tobacco-ship, settled there, and became an Indian fighter, so undisciplined as to embarrass the Governor of Virginia as much as the Indians. His son Lawrence, father of Augustine, George's father, earned a competence in the merchant marine and settled down to planting. Love of the land was a trait which all Washingtons had in common: they might seek wealth at sea or glory in war, but happiness they found only in the work and sport that came from owning and cultivating land.

Usually the Washingtons married their social betters, but the second marriage of George's father was an exception. Mary Ball, the mother of Washington, has been the object of much sentimental writing; but the cold record of her own and her sons' letters shows her to have been grasping, querulous, and vulgar. She was a selfish and exacting mother, whom most of her children avoided as soon and as early as they could; to whom they did their duty, but rendered little love. It was this sainted mother of Washington who opposed almost everything that he did for the public good, who wished his sense of duty to end with his duty to her, who pestered him in his campaigns by complaining letters, and who at a dark moment of the Revolutionary War increased his anxieties by strident complaints of neglect and starvation. Yet for one thing Americans may well be grateful to Mary Ball: her selfishness lost George an opportunity to become midshipman in the Royal Navy, a school whence few Americans emerged other than as loyal subjects of the King.

There is only one other subject connected with Washington upon which there has been more false sentiment, misrepresentation, and mendacity than on that of his mother, and that is his religion. Washington's religion was that of an eighteenth-century gentleman. Baptized in the Church of England, he attended service occasionally as a young man, and more regularly in middle age, as one of the duties of his station. He believed in God: the eighteenth-century Supreme Being, a Divine Philosopher who ruled all things for the best. He was certain of a Providence in the affairs of men. By the same token, he was completely tolerant of other people's beliefs, more so than the American democracy of today; for in a letter to the Swedenborgian church of Baltimore he wrote, "In this enlightened age and in the land of equal liberty it is our boast that a man's religious tenets will not forfeit the protection of the law, nor deprive him of the right of attaining and holding the highest offices that are known in the United States." But Washington never became an active member of any Christian church. Even after his marriage to a devout churchwoman, and when as President of the United States the eyes of all men were upon him, he never joined Martha in the beautiful and comfortable sacrament of the body and blood of Christ. The story of the "prayer at Valley Forge" is pure fable, and "George Washington's Prayer" is a pious fabrication. Christianity had little or no part in that discipline which made Washington more humble and gentle than any of the great captains, less proud and ambitious than most of the statesmen who have proclaimed themselves disciples of the Nazarene. His inspiration, as we shall see, came from an entirely different source.

Washington gained little discipline from book-learning; but like all young Virginians of the day he led an active outdoor life which gave him a magnificent physique. When fully grown he stood a little over six feet, and weighed from 175 to 200 pounds. Broad-shouldered and straight-backed, he carried his head erect and his chin up, and showed a good leg on horseback. There is no reason to doubt the tradition of his prowess at running, leaping, wrestling, and horsemanship. The handling of horses, in which Washington was skilled at an early age, is one of the best means of discipline that a youngster can have: for he who cannot control himself can never handle a spirited horse; and for the same reason fox-hunting on horseback, which was Washington's favorite sport, is the making or the breaking of a courageous and considerate gentleman. George may not have actually thrown a dollar across the Rappahannock (though as one elderly punster remarked, "a dollar went farther in those days!"); but his amazing physical vitality is proved by an incident of his reconnaissance to the Ohio. At the close of December, 1753, he and the scout Christopher Gist attempted to cross the river just above the site of Pittsburgh, on a raft of their own making. The river was full of floating ice, and George, while trying to shove the raft away from an ice-floe with his setting-pole, fell overboard, but managed to climb aboard again. They were forced to land on an island and spend the night there without fire or dry clothing. Gist, the professional woodsman, who had not been in the water, froze all his fingers and some of his toes; but Washington suffered no ill effects from the exposure. For that, his healthy Virginia boyhood may be thanked.

His formal education was scanty. The colonial colleges provided a classical discipline more severe and selective than that of their successors,—for higher education had to become painless in America before it could be popular,—but George had none of these "advantages." There were no means to prepare him for William and Mary, the college of the Virginia gentry; his father died when he was eleven years old; and his only schoolmasters were chosen haphazardly, as was natural for a younger son in a land-poor family. Endowed with the blood and the instincts of a gentleman, he was not given a gentleman's education, as he became painfully aware when at adolescence he went to live with his half-brother at Mount Vernon.

In modern phrase, George was "parked" on the estate which would one day be his. Evidently there had been some sort of family consultation about what to do with him; and Lawrence good-naturedly offered to take him in hand, if only to get him away from the exigent mother. Lawrence Washington, his father's principal heir and hope, had been sent to England for his schooling, had served under Admiral Vernon in the War of Jenkins's Ear, and had inherited the bulk of his father's property, to the exclusion of George and the four younger brothers and sisters. The proximity of Mount Vernon to the vast estates of the Fairfax family in the Northern Neck of Virginia gave Lawrence his opportunity. He married a Fairfax, and was admitted to the gay charmed circle of the First Families of Virginia. He was already a well-established gentleman of thirty when his hobble-de-hoy half-brother came to stay.

George was then a tall, gangling lad of sixteen years, with enormous hands and feet that were continually getting in his way. Young girls giggled when he entered a room, and burst out laughing at his awkward attempts to court them. He was conscious that he did not "belong," and made every effort to improve his manners. About three years before, a schoolmaster had made him copy out 110 "Rules of Civility" from a famous handbook by one Hawkins—a popular guide to good manners already a century and a half old; and George was probably glad to have this manuscript manual of social etiquette ready to consult. One of the most touching and human pictures of Washington is that of the overgrown schoolboy solemnly conning old Hawkins's warnings against scratching oneself at table, picking one's teeth with a fork, or cracking fleas in company, lest he commit serious "breaks" in the houses of the great.

These problems of social behavior no doubt occupied considerable space in Washington's adolescent thoughts. But he was also preparing to be a man of action. At school he had cared only for mathematics. He procured books, progressed farther than his schoolmaster could take him, and so qualified to be surveyor to Lord Fairfax. This great gentleman and landowner had much surveying to be done in the Shenandoah Valley, and it was difficult to find men with enough mathematics to qualify as surveyors, or with sufficient sobriety to run a line straight and see a job through. So George at sixteen earned as Lord Fairfax's surveyor the high salary of a doubloon (about $7.50) a day, most of which he saved up and invested in land. For he had early decided that in the fresh lands of the Virginian Valley and the West lay the road to position, competence, and happiness. His personality as well as his excellent surveying earned him the friendship of the

Fairfaxes, liberal and intelligent gentlemen; and this, as we shall
see, was of first importance in Washington's moral and intellectual development.

   That friendship, not the doubloon a day, was the first and most
fortunate gain from his surveying job; the second was the contact
which it gave young Washington with frontiersmen, with Indians,
and with that great teacher of self-reliance, the wilderness. He had
the advantage of a discipline that few of us can get today. We
are born in crowded cities, and attend crowded schools and colleges; we take our pleasure along crowded highways and in
crowded places of amusement; we are tempted to assert ourselves
by voice rather than deed, to advertise, to watch the clock, escape
responsibility, and leave decisions to others. But a hungry woodsman could not afford to lose patience with a deer he was trying
to shoot, or with a trout he was trying to catch; and it did not
help him much to "bawl out" an Indian. If you cannot discipline
yourself to quiet and caution in the wilderness, you won't get far;
and if you make the wrong decision in woods infested with
savages, you will probably have no opportunity to make another.
What our New England forbears learned from the sea—that tough
old nurse who plays no favorites and suffers no weaklings—Washington learned from the wilderness.

   His life from sixteen to twenty was not all spent on forest trails.
This was the golden age of the Old Dominion, the fifteen years
from 1740 to the French and Indian War. The old roughness and
crudeness were passing away. Peace reigned over the land, high
prices ruled for tobacco, immigrants were pouring into the back
country; the traditional Virginia of Thackeray and Vachel Lind-
say—"Land of the gauntlet and the glove"—came into being. Living
in Virginia at that time was like riding on the sparkling crest of
a great wave just before it breaks and spreads into dull, shallow
pools. At Mount Vernon, on the verge of the wilderness, you felt
the zest of sharp contrasts, and received the discipline that comes
from life. On the one side were mansion houses where young
Washington could learn manners and philosophy from gentlefolk. He took part in all the sports and pastimes of his social
equals: dancing and card-playing and flirting with the girls.
When visiting a town like Williamsburg he never missed a show;
and later as President he was a patron of the new American

drama. He loved gunning, fox-hunting, horse-racing, and all the gentleman's field sports of the day; he bet small sums at cards, and larger sums on the ponies—and was a good loser. He liked to make an impression by fine new clothes, and by riding unruly steeds when girls were looking on; for though a graceful figure on horseback he was ungainly afoot. He belonged to clubs of men who dined at taverns and drank like gentlemen; that is to say, they drank as much wine as they could hold without getting drunk—the opposite of modern drinking, the object of which appears to be to get "as drunk as a lord" on as little liquor as possible. Tobacco, curiously enough, made George's head swim; but he learned to smoke the peace-pipe with Indians when necessary without disgracing himself.

On the other side of Mount Vernon were log cabins, and all the crude elements of American life: Scotch and "Pennsylvania Dutch," and other poor whites who as insubordinate soldiers would prove the severest test of Washington's indefatigable patience, and proof of his power over men. The incidents of roughing it, such as the "one thread bear blanket with double its weight of vermin, such as lice, fleas, etc.," which he records in the journal of his first surveying trip, were not very pleasant at first, but he took it all with good humor and good sportsmanship. A little town called Alexandria sprang up about a tobacco warehouse and wharf, and young Washington made the first survey of it. A Masonic Lodge was formed at Fredericksburg, and George, who was a good "joiner," became brother to all the rising journalists and lawyers of the northern colonies. The deep Potomac flowed past Mount Vernon, bearing ships of heavy burthen to the Chesapeake and overseas; you sent your orders to England every year with your tobacco, and ships returned with the latest modes and manners, books and gazettes, and letters full of coffee-house gossip. London did not seem very far away, and young George confessed in a letter that he hoped to visit that "gay Matrapolis" before long.

It was probably just as well that he did not visit London, for he had the best and purest English tradition in Virginia. When Washington was in his later teens, just when a young man is fumbling for a philosophy of life, he came into intimate contact with several members of the Fairfax family. They were of that eighteenth-century Whig gentry which conformed outwardly to

Christianity, but derived their real inspiration from Marcus Aurelius, Plutarch, and the Stoic philosophers. Thomas, sixth Lord Fairfax, was a nobleman devoted to "Revolution Principles" —the "Glorious Revolution" of 1688, in which his father had taken an active part. Of the same line was that General Lord Fairfax, commander-in-chief of the New Model Army, who of all great soldiers in English history most resembles Washington. The ideal of this family was a noble simplicity of living, and a calm acceptance of life: duty to the Commonwealth, generosity to fellow-men, unfaltering courage and enduring virtue; in a word, the Stoic philosophy which overlaps Christian ethics more than any other discipline of the ancients. A Stoic never evaded life: he faced it. A Stoic never avoided responsibility: he accepted it. A Stoic not only believed in liberty: he practiced it.

It is not necessary to suppose that young Washington read much Stoic philosophy, for he was no great reader at any time; but he must have absorbed it from constant social intercourse with the Fairfaxes of Belvoir, neighbors whom he saw constantly. At Belvoir lived George William Fairfax, eight years Washington's senior, and his companion in surveying expeditions. Anne, the widow of Lawrence Washington, was Fairfax's sister, and Sally, the lady with whom George Washington was so happy—and so miserable—as to fall in love, was his wife. Books were there, if he wanted them. North's Plutarch was in every gentleman's library, and it was Plutarch who wrote the popular life of Cato, Washington's favorite character in history—not crabbed Cato the Censor, but Cato of pent-up Utica. At the age of seventeen, Washington himself owned an outline, in English, of the principal Dialogues of Seneca the younger, "sharpest of all the Stoicks." The mere chapter headings are the moral axioms that Washington followed through life:

> A Sensual Life is a Miserable Life
> Hope and Fear are the Bane of Human Life
> An Honest Man can never be outdone in Courtesy
> A Good man can never be Miserable, nor a Wicked man Happy
> The Contempt of Death makes all the Miseries of Life Easy to us

And of the many passages that young Washington evidently took to heart, one may select this:

No man is born wise: but Wisdom and Virtue require a Tutor; though we can easily learn to be Vicious without a Master. It is Philosophy that gives us a Veneration for God; a Charity for our Neighbor; that teaches us our Duty to Heaven, and Exhorts us to an Agreement one with another. It unmasks things that are terrible to us, asswages our Lusts, refutes our Errors, restrains our Luxury, Reproves our avarice, and works strangely on tender Natures.

Washington read Addison's tragedy *Cato* in company with his beloved; and if they did not act it together in private theatricals, George expressed the wish that they might. At Valley Forge, when the morale of the army needed a stimulus, Washington caused *Cato* to be performed, and attended the performance. It was his favorite play, written, as Pope's prologue says,

> To make mankind in conscious virtue bold,
> Live o'er each scene, and be what they behold.

Portius, Cato's son, whose "steddy temper"

> Can look on guilt, rebellion, fraud, and Caesar
> In the calm lights of mild Philosophy

declares (1, ii, 40-45):

> I'll animate the soldiers' drooping courage
> With love of freedom, and contempt of Life:
> I'll thunder in their ears their country's cause
> And try to rouse up all that's Roman in 'em.
> 'Tis not in Mortals to Command Success
> But we'll do more, Sempronius, we'll Deserve it.

These last two lines sound the note that runs through all Washington's correspondence in the dark hours of the Revolutionary struggle; and these same lines are almost the only literary quotations found in the vast body of Washington's writings. Many years after, when perplexed and wearied by the political squabbles of his presidency and longing to retire to Mount Vernon, Washington quoted the last lines of Cato's advice to Portius (IV, iv, 146-154):

Let me advise thee to retreat betimes
To thy paternal seat, the Sabine field,
Where the great Censor toil'd with his own hands,
And all our frugal Ancestors were blest
In humble virtues, and a rural life.
There live retired, pray for the peace of Rome:
Content thy self to be obscurely good.
When vice prevails, and impious men bear sway,
The post of honour is a private station.

From his camp with General Forbes's army in the wilderness Washington wrote to Sally Fairfax, September 25, 1758:

I should think our time more agreeably spent, believe me, in playing a part in Cato with the Company you mention, and myself doubly happy in being the Juba to such a Marcia as you must make.

Marcia was the worthy daughter of Cato, and Juba her lover, the young Numidian prince to whom Syphax says

You have not read mankind, your youth admires
The throws and swellings of a Roman soul
Cato's bold flights, th' extravagance of Virtue

To which Juba replies (II, iv, 49-58):

Turn up thy eyes to Cato!
There may's thou see to what a godlike height
The Roman virtues lift up mortal man,
While good, and just, and anxious for his friends,
He's still severely bent against himself;
Renouncing sleep, and rest, and food, and ease,
He strives with thirst and hunger, toil and heat;
And when his fortune sets before him all
The pomps and pleasures that his soul can wish,
His rigid virtue will accept of none.

Given this combination—a young man of innate noble qualities, seeking a philosophy of life, thrown in contact during his most impressionable years with a great gentleman whom he admired, a young gentleman who was his best friend, and a young lady whom he loved, all three steeped in the Stoical tradition —and what would you expect? Can it be a mere coincidence that this characterization of the Emperor Antoninus Pius by his adopted son Marcus Aurelius, the imperial Stoic, so perfectly fits the character of Washington?

Take heed lest thou become a Caesar indeed; lest the purple stain thy soul. For such things have been. Then keep thyself simple, good, pure, and serious; a friend to justice and the fear of God; kindly, affectionate, and strong to do the right. Reverence Heaven and succour man. Life is short; and earthly existence yields but one harvest, holiness of character and altruism of action. Be in everything a true disciple of Antoninus. Emulate his constancy in all rational activity, his unvarying equability, his purity, his cheerfulness of countenance, his sweetness, his contempt for notoriety, and his eagerness to come at the root of the matter.

Remember how he would never dismiss any subject until he had gained a clear insight into it and grasped it thoroughly; how he bore with the injustice of his detractors and never retorted in kind; how he did nothing in haste, turned a deaf ear to the professional tale-bearers, and showed himself an acute judge of characters and actions, devoid of all reproachfulness, timidity, suspiciousness, and sophistry; how easily he was satisfied,—for instance, with lodging, bed, clothing, food, and servants,—how fond of work and how patient; capable, thanks to his frugal diet, of remaining at his post from morning till night, having apparently subjected even the operations of nature to his will; firm and constant in friendship, tolerant of the most outspoken criticism of his opinions, delighted if any one could make a better suggestion than himself, and, finally, deeply religious without any trace of superstition.

When Washington was twenty years old, his brother Lawrence died. George, next heir by their father's will, stepped into his place as proprietor of Mount Vernon. At this stage of his life, George did not greatly enjoy the exacting task of running a great plantation; he thirsted for glory in war. But he soon began to enlarge and improve his holdings, and in the end came to love the land as nothing else. Late in life, when the First Citizen of the World, he wrote, "How much more delightful is the task of making improvements on the earth than all the vain-glory which can be acquired from ravaging it by the most uninterrupted career of conquests." And again, "To see plants rise from the earth

and flourish by the superior skill and bounty of the laborer fills
a contemplative mind with ideas which are more easy to be conceived than expressed." That was the way with all Washington's
ideas: they were more easily conceived and executed than expressed on paper. Ideas did not interest him, nor was he interested in himself. Hence the disappointing matter-of-fact objec-
tiveness of his letters and diaries.

Nevertheless, it is clear from Washington's diaries that farming
was a great factor in his discipline. For the lot of a Virginia
planter was not as romance has colored it. Slaves had to be driven,
or they ate out your substance; overseers watched, or they slacked
and stole; accounts rigidly balanced, or you became poorer every
year. There were droughts, and insect pests, and strange maladies
among the cattle. Washington's life at Mount Vernon was one of
constant experiment, unremitting labor, unwearying patience. It
was a continual war against human error, insect enemies, and
tradition. He might provide improved flails and a clean threshing
floor in his new barn; when his back was turned the overseer
would have the wheat out in the yard, to be trod into the muck
by the cattle. His books prove that he was an eager and bold
experimenter in that "new husbandry" of which Coke of Norfolk
was the great exponent. There were slave blacksmiths, carpenters,
and bricklayers; a cider press and a still-house, where excellent
corn and rye whisky was made, and sold in barrels made by the
slaves from plantation oak. Herring and shad fisheries in the
Potomac provided food for the slaves; a grist-mill turned Washington's improved strain of wheat into flour, which was taken to
market in his own schooner, which he could handle like a down-
east skipper. Indeed, it is in his husbandry that we can earliest
discern those qualities that made Washington the first soldier and
statesman of America. As landed proprietor no less than as commander-in-chief, he showed executive ability, the power of planning for a distant end, and a capacity for taking infinite pains.
Neither drought nor defeat could turn him from a course that he
discerned to be proper and right; but in farming as in war he
learned from failure, and grew in stature from loss and adversity.

Not long after inheriting Mount Vernon, Washington had opportunity to test what his brother had taught him of military
tactics and the practice of arms. Drilling and tactics, like survey-

ing, were a projection of Washington's mathematical mind; like every born strategist he could see moving troops in his mind's eye, march and deploy them and calculate the time to a minute. He devoured accounts of Frederick's campaigns, and doubtless dreamt of directing a great battle on a grassy plain—a terrain he was destined never to find in this shaggy country. As one of the first landowners in the county, at twenty he was commissioned major of militia. He then asked for and obtained the post of adjutant of militia for the county. The settlement of his brother's affairs brought him into contact with Governor Dinwiddie, a shrewd Scot who knew a dependable young man when he saw one; and from this came his first great opportunity.

At twenty-one he was sent on a highly confidential and difficult thousand-mile reconnaissance through the back country from western Virginia to the Ohio, and almost to the shores of Lake Erie. This young man just past his majority showed a caution in wilderness work, a diplomatic skill in dealing with Indians, and a courteous firmness in dealing with French commanders that would have done credit to a man twice his age. But on his next mission, one notes with a feeling of relief, youthful impetuosity prevailed. Unmindful that one must always let the enemy make the first aggression, our young lieutenant-colonel fired the shot that began the Seven Years' War.

A phrase of the young soldier's blithe letter to his younger brother: "I heard the bullets whistle, and believe me, there is something charming in the sound," got into the papers, and gave sophisticated London a good laugh. Even George the Second heard it and remarked, "He would not say so, if he had been used to hear many." That time would come soon enough. Washington's shot in the silent wilderness brought the French and Indians buzzing about his ears. He retired to Fort Necessity, which he had caused to be built in a large meadow, hoping to tempt the enemy to a pitched battle. But the enemy was so inconsiderate! He swarmed about the fort in such numbers that Washington was lucky to be allowed to capitulate and go home; for this was one of those wars that was not yet a war—it was not declared till two years after the fighting began. The enemy was so superior in numbers that nobody blamed Washington; and when General Braddock arrived with an army of regulars, he invited the young frontier leader to accompany his expedition into the wilderness.

There is no need here to repeat the tale of Braddock's defeat, except to say that the general's stupidity and the colonel's part in saving what could be saved have both been exaggerated. Parkman wrote in his classic *Montcalm and Wolfe,* "Braddock has been charged with marching blindly into an ambuscade; but it was not so. There was no ambuscade; and had there been one, he would have found it." That is the truth of the matter; and whilst Washington's behavior was creditable in every respect, he did not save Braddock's army; the French and Indians were simply too busy despoiling the dead and wounded, to pursue.

Shortly after Washington reached Alexandria, the annual electoral campaign began for members of the Virginia Assembly. In a political dispute the Colonel said something insulting to a quick-tempered little fellow named Payne, who promptly knocked him down with a hickory stick. Soldiers rushed up to avenge Washington, who recovered just in time to tell them he was not hurt, and could take care of himself, thank you! The next day he wrote to Payne requesting an interview at a tavern. The little man arrived, expecting a demand for an apology, or a challenge. Instead, Washington apologized for his insult which had provoked the blow, hoped that Payne was satisfied, and offered his hand. Some of Washington's biographers cannot imagine or understand such conduct. One of them brackets this episode with the cherry-tree yarn as "stories so silly and so foolishly impossible that they do not deserve an instant's consideration." Another explains Washington's conduct as a result of his defeat at Fort Necessity: "Washington was crushed into such meekness at this time that . . . instead of retaliating or challenging the fellow to a duel, he apologized." But the incident, which has been well substantiated, occurred after Braddock's defeat, not Washington's; and it was due to Stoical magnanimity, not Christian meekness. "It is the Part of a Great Mind to despise Injuries," says Seneca the younger, in the L'Estrange translation that Washington owned. The Payne affair was merely an early instance of what Washington was doing all his life: admitting he was wrong when he was convinced he was in the wrong, and doing the handsome thing in a gentlemanly manner. A man who took that attitude became impregnable to attack by politicians or any one else. For a young man of twenty-three to take it, meant that he had firm hold of a great philosophy.

During the next two years, Washington had charge of the frontier defenses of Virginia, and a chain of thirty garrisoned stockades which followed the Shenandoah Valley and its outer bulwarks from Winchester to the North Carolina line. In the execution of this command he showed a prodigious physical activity, often riding thirty miles a day for several days over wilderness trails. His letters show a youthful touchiness about rank and recognition; he sorely tried the patience of Governor Dinwiddie, who, to Washington's evident surprise, accepted a proffered resignation; but he was soon reappointed and took a leading part in General Forbes's expedition against Fort Duquesne. It was merely to settle a question of precedence that Washington undertook a long journey to interview Governor Shirley, the commander-in-chief at Boston. One aide and two servants, clad in new London liveries of the Washington colors and mounted on horses with the Washington arms embroidered on their housings, accompanied their Colonel; for Washington had a young man's natural love of showing off. He stopped with great folk on the way and gave generous tips to their servants; he enjoyed seeing Bostonians gape at the servants in scarlet and white livery—somewhat soiled by travel to be sure, although they had stopped in New York long enough to have everything cleaned, and the Colonel had two new uniforms made in Boston. But Washington never made the mistake of wearing splendid clothes on the wrong occasion. In the French and Indian war he wore a plain neutral-colored uniform instead of British scarlet, and dressed his men as frontiersmen, in buckskin and moccasins, so that they carried no superfluous weight and offered no mark to the Indians.

As a young officer he often became impatient with the frontier folk—their short-sighted selfishness in refusing to unite under his command, their lack of discipline and liability to panic, and the American militiaman's propensity to offer unwanted advice and sulk if it were not taken. But he found something to like in them as he did in all men, and learned to work with and through them. Militia deserted Washington as they deserted other officers, despite the flogging of sundry and the hanging of a few to encourage the rest. Here is plenty of material for a disparaging biographer to describe Washington as a military martinet who had not even the merit of a notable victory; and some of the "debunkers," who have never known what it is to command troops, have said just that. A sufficient reply to them, as well as striking proof of the amazing confidence, even veneration, which Washington inspired at an early age, is the "Humble Address" of the twenty-seven officers of his regiment, beseeching him to withdraw his resignation:

Sir,

We, your most obedient and affectionate Officers, beg leave to express our great Concern, at the disagreeable News we have received of your Determination to resign the Command of that Corps, in which we have under you long served . . .

In our earliest Infancy you took us under your Tuition, train'd us up in the Practice of that Discipline, which alone can constitute good Troops, from the punctual Observance of which you never suffer'd the least Deviation.

Your steady adherence to impartial Justice, your quick Discernment and invariable Regard to Merit, . . . first heighten'd our natural Emulation, and our Desire to excel . . .

Judge then, how sensibly we must be Affected with the loss of such an excellent Commander, such a sincere Friend, and so affable a Companion . . .

It gives us an additional Sorrow, when we reflect, to find, our unhappy Country will receive a loss, no less irreparable, than ourselves. Where will it meet a Man so experienc'd in military affairs? One so renown'd for Patriotism, Courage and Conduct? Who has so great knowledge of the Enemy we have to deal with? Who so well acquainted with their Situation and Strength? Who so much respected by the Soldiery? Who in short so able to support the military Character of Virginia? . . .

We with the greatest Deference, presume to entreat you to suspend those Thoughts [of resigning] for another Year . . . In you we place the most implicit Confidence. Your Presence only will cause a steady Firmness and Vigor to actuate in every Breast, despising the greatest Dangers, and thinking light of Toils and Hardships, while led on by the Man we know and Love . . .

Fully persuaded of this, we beg Leave to assure you, that as you have hitherto been the actuating Soul of the whole Corps, we shall at all times pay the most invariable Regard to your Will and Pleasure, and will always be happy to demonstrate by our Actions, with how much Respect and Esteem we are,

Sir,

Fort Loudoun
Decr 31st 1758

Your most affectionate
and most obedient humble Servants
[Twenty-seven signatures]

There stands the young man Washington, reflected in the hearts of his fellows. As one reads this youthfully sincere composition of the officers' mess at Fort Loudoun, one imagines it addressed to a grizzled veteran of many wars, a white-whiskered colonel of fifty. Colonel Washington was just twenty-six.

A farewell to arms, Washington was determined it must be. Fort Duquesne was won, and his presence at the front was no longer needed. Virginia, the colony which had received the first shock of the war, could justly count on British regulars and the northern colonies to carry it to a glorious conclusion on the Plains of Abraham.

In four years Washington had learned much from war. He found it necessary to discipline himself before he could handle men. He had learned that the interminable boredom of drill, arguing about supplies, and begging for transportation was ill rewarded by the music of whistling bullets; that war was simply hard, beastly work. The sufferings of the border people, the bloody shambles on the Monongahela, the frozen evidence of torture on the road to Fort Duquesne, cured his youthful appetite for glory, completely. When Washington again drew his sword, in 1775, it was with great reluctance, and only because he believed, like Cato (II, v, 85):

> The hand of fate is over us, and Heaven
> Exacts severity from all our thoughts.
> It is not now a time to talk of aught
> But chains, or conquest; liberty, or death.

Nor was Washington one to be rushed off his feet by every gust of war propaganda. Twice, as President of the United States, he courageously resisted popular clamor for war, and cheerfully sacrificed his popularity to preserve peace with England.

From one woman he learned perhaps as much as from war.

Sally Cary, his fair tutor in Stoicism and the great love of his life, was eighteen and married to his friend and neighbor George William Fairfax, when at sixteen he first met her. Beautiful, intelligent, and of gentle birth, Mrs. Fairfax took a more than sisterly interest in the callow young surveyor; and as near neighbors they saw much of each other. Cryptic jottings in his diary for 1748 show that he was already far gone in love. His pathetic letter to her from Fort Necessity in 1755, begging for a reply to "make me happy as the day is long," gives a human note in the midst of his business-like military correspondence. No letters from her to him have been preserved, but from the tone of his replies I gather that Sally was somewhat more of a tease than befitted Cato's daughter. Whatever her sentiments may have been toward him, Washington's letters leave no doubt that he was passionately in love with her; yet gentlemanly standards were then such that while her husband lived she could never be his wife, much less his mistress. What anguish he must have suffered, any young man can imagine. It was a situation that schooled the young soldier-lover in manners, moderation, and restraint—a test case of his Stoical philosophy. His solution was notable for its common sense: when on a hurried visit to Williamsburg in the spring of 1758, to procure clothes for his ragged soldiers, he met, wooed, and won a housewifely little widow of twenty-seven named Martha Custis. She wanted a manager for her property and a stepfather for her children; he needed a housekeeper for Mount Vernon. It was a *mariage de convenance* that developed into a marriage of affection. But Martha well knew that she was not George's first or greatest love, nor he hers.

Twenty-five years later, when Mrs. Fairfax was a poor and childless widow in London, crushing the memories of her Virginia springtime in her heart, there came a letter from Washington. The First Citizen of the World writes that the crowded events of the quarter-century since they parted have not eradicated "from my mind the recollection of those happy moments, the happiest of my life, which I enjoyed in your company." Martha Washington enclosed a letter under the same cover, in order to show that she, too, understood.

Let us neither distort nor exaggerate this relation, the most beautiful thing in Washington's life. Washington saw no visions of Sally Fairfax in the battle-smoke. He did not regard himself as her knightly champion, or any such romantic nonsense; Walter Scott had not yet revived the age of chivalry. Women occupied a small part in Washington's thoughts, as in those of most men of action. No more than Cato did he indulge in worry or bitter thoughts about his ill fortune in love. Suppose, however, Washington had turned out a failure or shown some fault of character at a critical moment, instead of superbly meeting every test. Every yapping biographer of the last decade would have blamed the three members of this blameless triangle. Since he turned out otherwise, we can hardly fail to credit both women with an important share in the formation of Washington's character. And who will deny that Washington attained his nearly perfect balance and serenity, not through self-indulgence but through restraint?

What of other women?—a subject which cannot be shirked in any honest account of the young man Washington. Many of you must have heard, in club or smoking-car gossip, the story of that so-called letter of Washington inviting someone to Mount Vernon, and setting forth the charms of a certain slave-girl. No investigator has ever managed to see this letter, or even found a person who has seen it. The nearest we get is to the man who knows a man who has seen it—but that man for some peculiar reason is always sick, dead, or non-existent when you look for him, or else he refers you to another man, who knows the man, who knows the man that has it. Mr. John C. Fitzpatrick, who has spent much time on the trail of the seductive if mythical octoroon of Mount Vernon, believes that all stories of this sort were started by a spurious sentence in a letter from Benjamin Harrison to Washington during the war, which was intercepted by the British and printed in England. Fortunately the original, a plain letter of military information, has been preserved. But when it was given out for publication to the *Gentleman's Magazine* (of all places), the editor interpolated a jocularly bawdy description of "pretty little Kate the washer-woman's daughter," whose charms the commander-in-chief was invited to share. Of similar origin are the stories of Washington's illegitimate children. Of course one cannot prove a negative to every rumor. I can only state my opinion that, in view of the fact that Washington fell deeply in love at sixteen, and remained in love with the same lady until his marriage, and maintained a reputation for faithfulness under pitiless publicity, he led the life of a Christian gentleman.

Plutarch wrote of Cato, "He had not taken to public life, like some others, casually or automatically or for the sake of fame or personal advantage. He chose it because it was the function proper to a good man." That was why Washington got himself elected in 1758 to the Virginia Assembly, an office proper to a gentleman of his station. He had no gift for speaking or for wirepulling; he showed no talent or desire for political leadership. But he learned at first hand the strange behavior of *homo sapiens* in legislative assemblies. Every one marvels at the long-suffering patience shown by Washington in his dealings with Congress during the war; few remember that he had been for many years a burgess of Virginia, and for several months a member of the very Congress to which he was responsible.

So at twenty-seven George Washington was not only a veteran colonel who had won the confidence and affection of his men, but a member of the Virginia Assembly, a great landowner, and a husband. His youth was over, and he had the means for a life of ease and competence; but the high example of antique virtue would not let him ignore another call to duty. When it came, his unruly nature had been disciplined by the land and the wilderness, by philosophy and a noble woman, and by his own indomitable will, to become a fit instrument for a great cause. There were other colonial soldiers in 1775 who from better opportunity had gained more glory in the last war than he; but there was none who inspired so much confidence as this silent, capable man of forty-three. So that when the political needs of the moment required a Virginian, there was no question but that Colonel Washington should be commander-in-chief.

If he had failed, historians would have blamed the Continental Congress for a political appointment of a provincial colonel with an indifferent war record. If he had failed, the American Revolution would have been something worse than futile—a Rebellion of '98 that would have soured the American character, made us another Ireland, with a long and distressful struggle for freedom ahead. If, like so many leaders of revolutions, he had merely achieved a personal triumph, or inoculated his country with ambition for glory, the world would have suffered from his success. His country could and almost did fail Washington; but Washington could not fail his country, or disappoint the expectations of his kind. A simple gentleman of Virginia with no extraordinary talents had so disciplined himself that he could lead an insubordinate and divided people into ordered liberty and enduring union.

Carl Schurz
(1829-1906)

ONE OF the most picturesque figures in American public life at the end of the nineteenth century, Carl Schurz was born at Liblar, near Cologne, Germany, in 1829. While a student for the doctorate at the University of Bonn, he became involved in the revolutionary movement of 1848–49. When that was suppressed, Schurz was thrown into a dungeon, yet managed a breath-taking escape. As did Francis Lieber a quarter of a century earlier (see p. 173), he fled from Germany first to France and then to England. Emigrating to the United States in 1852, he remained for a while in Philadelphia, but eventually settled in Watertown, Wisconsin, where his wife established the first kindergarten in America. As a result of his vigorous campaiging for Lincoln in 1860, the President appointed him minister to Spain. Craving action, he returned to the United States in 1862 and was made a brigadier-general of volunteers; at the close of the war he was a major-general and was chief of staff to Major-General Slocum in Sherman's army. After the war, he was United States Senator from Missouri, a member of the cabinet of President Hayes, and an editorial writer for the New York *Evening Post* and *Harper's Weekly*.

The Reminiscences of Carl Schurz were published immediately after his death. The selection reprinted here gives a vivid picture of the experiences of a young couple in a new country, their difficulties with the customs and the language, and their adjustment to a new environment. What they went through was the experience of the forbears of many Americans today. One notable feature is Schurz' joy in the freedom of the United States, and in it may be found one source of his devotion to his adopted country.

First Years in America

On the 17th of September, 1852, my young wife and I entered the harbor of New York on board the fine packet-ship *City of London* after a voyage of twenty-eight days. There were at that period steamers—although only a few of them—regularly running between England and the United States. But a friend of ours who had visited this country several times had told us that a good, large sailing-ship was safer than a steamer, and more comfortable to persons liable to sea-sickness. Thus persuaded, we chose the packet *City of London,* a fine ship of about two thousand tons, magnificent to look at. And we did not repent of our choice. Our stateroom was large and commodious, the captain, although a thoroughly sea-bred man, polite and attentive, the table not bad, and the traveling company agreeable. There were several hundred emigrants in the steerage, but only about twenty passengers in the cabin, among them a Yale professor and several New York merchants. I was not yet able to converse in English; but as the Yale professor spoke some German, and two or three of the New York merchants some French, there was amusing and instructive entertainment enough.

Having determined to make the United States my permanent home, I was resolved to look at everything from the brightest side, and not to permit myself to be discouraged by any disappointment.

I knew that my buoyant Rhenish blood would help me much. But I was not so sure as to whether my young wife, whose temperament was not so sanguine as mine and who had grown up in easier conditions and in constant contact with sympathetic people, would be able as readily and cheerfully as I to accept the

From *The Reminiscences of Carl Schurz,* by Carl Schurz, copyright, 1908, reprinted by permission of Doubleday, Doran and Company, Inc.

vicissitudes of life in a new country and a strange social atmosphere. But we were young—I twenty-three years old, and my wife eighteen—and much might be hoped from the adaptability of youth. Still, I was anxious that the first impression of the new country should be bright and inspiring to her. And that wish was at once gratified in the highest degree. The day on which we arrived in New York harbor could not have been more glorious. The bay and the islands surrounding it were radiant with sunlit splendor. When we beheld this spectacle, so surprisingly entrancing after a four-weeks' journey over the waste of waters, our hearts fairly leaped with joy. We felt as if we were entering, through this gorgeous portal, a world of peace and happiness.

As we skirted the shore of Staten Island, with its fine country houses and green lawns and massive clumps of shade trees, a delightful picture of comfort and contentment—Staten Island was then still a favorite summering place—I asked one of my fellow-passengers what kind of people lived in those charming dwellings. "Rich New Yorkers," said he. "And how much must a man have to be called a rich New Yorker?" I asked. "Well," he answered, "a man who has something like $150,000 or $200,000 or an assured income of $10,000 or $12,000 would be considered wealthy. Of course, there are men who have more than that—as much as a million or two, or even more." "Are there many such in New York?" "Oh, no, not many; perhaps a dozen. But the number of people who might be called 'well to do' is large." "And are there many poor people in New York?" "Yes, some; mostly new-comers, I think. But what is called poverty here would, in many cases, hardly be called poverty in London or Paris. There are scarcely any hopelessly poor here. It is generally thought here that nobody need be poor."

In the changing course of time I have often remembered this conversation.

It was not easy to find a place of rest for our first night in the New World. We had heard of the Astor House as the best hostelry in New York. But the Astor House was full to overflowing, and so our carriage had laboriously to work its way from hotel to hotel, through the confusion of omnibuses and drays and other vehicles, up the thundering Broadway. But in none of them did we find a vacant room until finally we reached Fourteenth Street, where the Union Square Hotel, which has subsequently been turned into a theater and then into a hotel again, called the Morton House, offered to us a hospitable abode—a very plainly furnished room, but sufficient for our needs.

The recollection of our first dinner at the Union Square Hotel is still vivid in my mind. It was a table d'hôte, if I remember rightly, at five o'clock in the afternoon. Dinner-time was announced by the fierce beating of a gong, an instrument which I heard for the first time on that occasion. The guests then filed into a large, bare dining-room with one long row of tables. Some fifteen or twenty Negroes, clad in white jackets, white aprons, and white cotton gloves, stood ready to conduct the guests to their seats, which they did with broad smiles and curiously elaborate bows and foot scrapings. A portly colored head-waiter in a dress coat and white necktie, whose manners were strikingly grand and patronizing, directed their movements. When the guests were seated, the head-waiter struck a loud bell; then the Negroes rapidly filed out and soon reappeared carrying large soup tureens covered with bright silver covers. They planted themselves along the table at certain intervals, standing for a second motionless. At another clang of their commander's bell they lifted their tureens high up and then deposited them upon the table with a bump that made the chandeliers tremble and came near terrifying the ladies. But this was not the end of the ceremony. The Negroes held fast with their right hands to the handles of the silver covers until another stroke of the bell resounded. Then they jerked off the covers, swung them high over their heads, and thus marched off as if carrying away their booty in triumph. So the dinner went on, with several repetitions of such proceedings, the Negroes getting all the while more and more enthusiastic and bizarre in their performances. I was told that like customs existed at other hotels, but I have never seen them elsewhere executed with the same perfection as at our first dinner in America. It may well be believed that they then astonished us greatly.

I remember well our first walk to see the town—the very noisy bustle on the principal streets; the men, old and young, mostly looking serious and preoccupied, and moving on with energetic rapidity; the women also appearing sober-minded and busy, although many of them were clothed in loud colors, red, green, yellow, or blue of a very pronounced glare; the people, although they must have belonged to very different stations in life, looking surprisingly alike in feature and expression as well as habit; no military sentinels at public buildings; no soldiers on the streets; no liveried coachmen or servants; no uniformed officials except the police. We observed huge banners stretched across the street, upon which were inscribed the names of Pierce and King as the Democratic, and Scott and Graham as the Whig, candidates for the presidency and the vice-presidency—names which at that time had, to me, no meaning, except that they indicated the impend-ing presidential election and the existence of competing political parties. As to the American politics of the day, I had received only some vague impressions through my conversations with vari-ous persons. My friend Kinkel, who had visited the United States in 1851 in the interest of the revolutionary movement in Europe, had been received by President Fillmore and had described him to me as a "freundlicher und wohlwollender Greis" (an amiable and benevolent old gentleman). Of the political parties he could tell me only that they both seemed to be dominated by the slave-holders, or at least to be afraid of the slavery question, and that most of the Germans in the United States were on the side of the Democrats, because they were attracted by the name of democracy and because they believed that the Democratic party could be more surely depended upon to protect the rights of the foreign-born citizens. The news articles about American politics which I had read in European papers had been, as they mostly have remained to the present day, well-nigh valueless to every one not personally acquainted with American affairs, and my conver-sations with my fellow-passengers had given me little light on the then existing situation. It presented itself to me like a dense fog in which I saw shadowy figures indistinctly moving.

We spent two or three days in trying to see what "sights" there were in the city, and we found that there were none in the line of museums, or picture galleries, or remarkable public or private buildings. Barnum's museum of curiosities, on the corner of Broadway and Ann Street, opposite St. Paul's Church, was pointed out to us as a thing really worth seeing. In the shop-windows on Broadway we observed nothing extraordinary. The theaters we could not enjoy because I did not understand English. The busy crowds thronging the streets were always interesting, but strange—not a familiar face among them. A feeling of lonesomeness began to settle upon us.

Then my young wife fell ill. I called in an old American doctor who lived in the hotel. He seemed to be a man of ability; he certainly was very genial and kind. He knew some French, and thus we could converse. As the illness of my wife became known in the hotel, a spirit of helpfulness manifested itself among the guests, which surprised and touched me deeply—that American helpfulness which was then, and, I trust, is now, one of the finest and most distinguishing characteristics of this people. Gentlemen and ladies, one after another, called upon us to ask whether they could be of any service. Some of the ladies, in fact, now and then relieved me from my watch at my wife's bedside to give me an hour's breathing time in the open air. I then walked up and down or sat on a bench in the little park of Union Square, which was surrounded by a high iron railing. Union Square was, at that period, far "up town." There were above Fourteenth Street many blocks or clumps of houses with large gaps between them, but, as far as I can remember, no continuous, solidly built-up streets. Madison Square showed many vacant lots, there being a field partly planted with corn and enclosed by a picket fence where the Fifth Avenue Hotel now stands. Wandering circuses used to pitch their tents on that spot. But although far up town, Union Square had its share of noisy bustle.

There, then, in that little park, I had my breathing spells, usually in the dusk of evening. They were among the most melancholy hours of my life. There I was in the great Republic, the idol of my dreams, feeling myself utterly lonesome and forlorn. The future lay before me wrapped in an impenetrable cloud. What I had seen was not so different from Europe as I had vaguely expected, and yet it was strange and mysterious. Would my experiences here realize the ideal I had conceived, or would they destroy it? I had to struggle hard against these gloomy musings, and finally I roused myself to the thought that in order to get into sympathy with the busy life I saw around me, I must become active in it, become *of it*—and that, the sooner the better.

During my wife's illness, which lasted nearly a fortnight, I had exchanged letters with some of my German friends in Philadel-

phia, especially with my "chum" of former days, Adolph Strodt-
mann, who had established a small German bookshop there and
published a little German weekly paper—*Die Locomotive,*—and
with Dr. Heinrich Tiedemann, a brother of the unfortunate
Colonel Tiedemann, the Governor of Rastatt, on whose staff I
had served as aide-de-camp during the siege of that fortress. Dr.
Tiedemann had settled down in Philadelphia as a physician and
was in good practice. My wife and I longed for the face of a
friend; and as there was nothing to hold us in New York, we
resolved to visit Philadelphia, not with any purpose of permanent
settlement, but thinking that it might be a good place for a
beginning of systematic study. This it proved to be. We soon
found among the recently immigrated Germans, and also among
Americans, a sympathetic social intercourse, and with it that
cheerfulness of mind which encourages interest in one's surroundings.

   My first task was to learn English in the shortest possible time.
I have, of late years, frequently had to answer inquiries addressed
to me by educators and others concerning the methods by which
I acquired such knowledge of the language and such facility in
using it as I possess. That method was very simple. I did not use
an English grammar. I do not think I ever had one in my library.
I resolutely began to read—first my daily newspaper, which happened to be the *Philadelphia Ledger*. Regularly every day I
worked through editorial articles, the news letters and dispatches,
and even as many of the advertisements as my time would allow.
The *Philadelphia Ledger,* which has since become a very excellent, influential, and important organ of public opinion, was at
that time a small and ill-printed sheet, rather colorless in politics,
which entertained its readers largely with serious editorial dis-
sertations on such innocent subjects as "The Joys of Spring,"
"The Beauties of Friendship," "The Blessings of a Virtuous Life,"
and the like—sometimes a little insipid, but usually very respectable in point of style. Then I proceeded to read English novels.
The first one I took up was "The Vicar of Wakefield." Then
followed Walter Scott, Dickens, and Thackeray; then Macaulay's
historical essays, and, as I thought of preparing myself for the
legal profession, Blackstone's "Commentaries," the clear, terse
and vigorous style of which I have always continued to regard as

a very great model. Shakespeare's plays, the enormous vocabulary of which presented more difficulties than all the rest, came last. But I did my reading with the utmost conscientiousness. I never permitted myself to skip a word the meaning of which I did not clearly understand, and I never failed to consult the dictionary in every doubtful case.

At the same time I practiced an exercise which I found exceedingly effective. I had become acquainted with the "Letters of Junius" through a German translation, and was greatly fascinated by the brilliancy of this style of political discussion. As soon as I thought myself sufficiently advanced in the knowledge of the language, I procured an English edition of Junius and translated a considerable number of the letters from the English text into German in writing; then I translated, also in writing, my German translation back into English, and finally compared this retranslation with the English original. This was very laborious work, but, so to speak, I felt in my bones how it helped me. Together with my reading, it gave me what I might call a sense of the logic and also of the music of the language.

When I began to write in English—letters or other more pretentious compositions—it happened to me not infrequently that in reading over what I had written I stopped at certain forms of expression I had used, doubting whether they were grammatically correct. I then sometimes tried to substitute other forms; but almost invariably I found, upon consulting competent authority, that the phrase as I had, following my instinct, originally put it down, was better than the substitute. In less than six months after I had begun this course of study I was sufficiently advanced to carry on a conversation in English about subjects not requiring a wide knowledge of technical terms, with tolerable ease, and to write a decent letter.

Since becoming known as a speaker and writer in English as well as in German, I have often been asked by persons interested in linguistic studies or in psychological problems, whether while speaking or writing I was thinking in English or in German, and whether I was constantly translating from one language into the other. The answer was that, when speaking or writing in English, I was thinking in English; and, when speaking or writing in German, I was thinking in German; and when my mind followed a train of thought which did not require immediate expression in words, I was unconscious of what language I was thinking in.

I have also often been asked in which language I preferred to think and write. I always answered that this depended on the subject, the purpose, and the occasion. On the whole, I preferred the English language for public speaking, partly on account of the simplicity of its syntactic construction, and partly because the pronunciation of the consonants is mechanically easier and less fatiguing to the speaker. I have preferred it also for the discussion of political subjects and of business affairs because of its full and precise terminology. But for the discussion of philosophical matters, for poetry, and for familiar, intimate conversation I have preferred the German. And beyond this, I have found that about certain subjects, or with certain persons who understood both English and German equally well, I would rather speak in English or in German, as the case might be, without clearly knowing the reason why. It was a matter of feeling which cannot be exactly defined.

Occasionally I have had to translate into German things that I had spoken or written in English, and *vice versa*. And my experience has been that I found translations from my English into my German much easier than translations from my German into my English—in other words, my German vocabulary offered to me more readily an equivalent for what I had spoken or written in English than *vice versa*. I was puzzled by more untranslatable words or forms of speech in my German than in my English. It might be thought that, German being my native language, and the one in which I had been brought up, the German vocabulary would naturally be more at my command. But I have heard the same opinion expressed by other, and among them very competent, persons, who had been brought up in the English language, and had then acquired a very thorough knowledge of German. It is a remarkable fact that, although the German language seems to be stiff and obstinate in its syntactic construction, German literature possesses a far greater wealth of translations of the highest merit than any other, while translations from the German, especially translations of German poetry, into any other modern language are, with very few exceptions, exceedingly imperfect. There is hardly any great poet in any literature such as

Homer, Hafis, Horace, Virgil, Dante, Cervantes, Shakespeare, Molière, Victor Hugo, Tolstoy, that has not had a German translation or reproduction worthy of the original, and in most cases of astonishing fidelity and beauty. Nothing that has appeared in any other language can even in a remote degree be compared with the translation of Homer's "Iliad" and "Odyssey," by Johann Heinrich Voss; and many German translations of Shakespeare's plays, which at first sight might seem fairly to defy the translator's art, have long been among the wonders of the world of letters. On the other hand, the translations into other languages of the masterpieces of German poetry have almost always been more or less dismal failures. Foremost among the exceptions I would place Bayard Taylor's translation of Goethe's "Faust," and the translation by Mrs. Frances Hellman of Gottfried Kinkel's little epic, "Tanagra," which is the most perfect reproduction of foreign poetry in English that I have ever seen. But these exceptions become all the more conspicuous by their rarity.

The extraordinary wealth of German literature in excellent translations—for those translations may well be called a part of German literature—makes the study of the German language a matter of special interest to everyone seeking to acquire a truly liberal education. For German literature is not only exceedingly rich in original works in every branch of mental production, which, owing to the imperfection of the translation into other languages, cannot be fully enjoyed except when read in German, but it contains, in its superior translations, an almost complete treasury of all the literature of the world and of all ages, ancient as well as modern.

In Philadelphia I made my first acquaintances. At that period the Quaker, with his broad-brimmed hat, his straight coat, and his standing collar, and the Quakeress, with her gray dress, her white kerchief covering her shoulders, and her poke-bonnet, were still very familiar figures on the streets of that city. Foremost among them in public estimation at the time stood Lucretia Mott, a woman, as I was told, renowned for her high character, her culture, and the zeal and ability with which she advocated various progressive movements. To her I had the good fortune to be introduced by a German friend. I thought her the most beautiful old lady I had ever seen. Her features were of exquisite fineness. Not one of the wrinkles with which age had marked her face, would one have wished away. Her dark eyes beamed with intelligence and benignity. She received me with gentle grace, and in the course of our conversation, she expressed the hope that, as a citizen, I would never be indifferent to the slavery question as, to her great grief, many people at the time seemed to be.

Another acquaintance of interest we made was that of Mr. Jay Cooke and his family. We met them at Cape May, where at the beginning of the summer of 1853 we went with our first baby to escape from the oppressive heat of the city. Mr. Cooke was then not yet the great banker and financier he became during the Civil War, but he was easily recognized as a man of uncommon ability, energy, and public spirit. The attention of the Cookes was mainly attracted by the beauty, grace, and ingenuous conversation of my wife, in her naïve German-English, and as they were evidently good-hearted people of frank and simple manners, we soon became fast friends and remained so for many years. They were the first family of very strict and active church members we learned to know intimately. They had in their house their regular morning and evening prayers in which not only all the members of the family but also the servants took part, and in which the guests of the house were invited, and, I suppose, expected to join. But there was prevalent in the family an atmosphere of kindly toleration and of buoyant cheerfulness which made everybody feel comfortable and at home. When some years later I was, with many others, Mr. Cooke's guest at his country seat "Ogontz," I saw him one morning in the large hall devoutly kneel down with his family and household to lead in prayer, and then, as soon as the prayer was over, jump up, clap his hands with boyish glee, and cry out in his most jovial tones: "Now let's be jolly!" There was a sort of rustic heartiness in his looks and his whole being which appeared quite genuine and endeared him much to his friends. It is generally recognized that, as a financier, he rendered very valuable service to the country during the Civil War, and I do not think anybody grudged him the fortune he gathered at the same time for himself. When, in 1873, he lost that fortune in consequence of his altogether too sanguine ventures in the Northern Pacific enterprise, and many others lost their money with him, he had much sympathy, and there was a wide-spread confidence that he would faithfully pay all his honest debts, which he did.

During our sojourn in Philadelphia our social intercourse was necessarily limited. But I availed myself of every opportunity of talking with people of various classes and of thus informing myself about their ways of thinking, their hopes and apprehensions, their prejudices and their sympathies. At the same time I industriously studied the political history and institutions of the country, and, as to current events and their significance, my newspaper reading soon went beyond the columns of the *Ledger*. The impressions I received were summed up in a letter which at that period I wrote to my friend, Miss Malwida von Meysenburg. I had long forgotten it when years afterwards it turned up in her "Memoirs of an Idealist," an exceedingly interesting book which has so well held its place in literature that but recently, more than a quarter of a century after its first appearance, a new edition has been printed and widely read.

In that letter I described how the European revolutionary idealists, as I knew them in the old world, would at first be startled, if not shocked, by the aspect of a really free people—a democracy in full operation on a large scale—the most contradictory tendencies and antagonistic movements openly at work, side by side, or against one another, enlightenment and stupid bigotry, good citizenship and lawlessness, benevolent and open-handed public spirit and rapacious greed, democracy and slavery, independent spirit and subserviency to party despotism and to predominant public opinion—all this in bewildering confusion. The newly arrived European democrat, having lived in a world of theories and imaginings without having had any practical experience of a democracy at work, beholding it for the first time, asks himself: "Is this really a people living in freedom? Is this the realization of my ideal?" He is puzzled and perplexed, until it dawns upon him that, in a condition of real freedom, man manifests himself, not as he ought to be, but as he is, with all his bad as well as his good qualities, instincts, and impulses: with all his attributes of strength as well as all his weaknesses; that this, therefore, is not an ideal state, but simply a state in which the forces of good have a free field as against the forces of evil, and in which the victories of virtue, of enlightenment, and of progress are not achieved by some power or agency outside of the people, for their benefit, but *by* the people themselves.

Such victories of the forces of good may be slow in being accomplished, but they will be all the more thorough and durable in their effects, because they will be the product of the people's own thought and effort. The people may commit follies or mistakes ever so grievous, but having committed those follies or mistakes themselves and upon their own responsibility, they will be apt to profit by their own experience. If those mistakes were rectified by some superior authority, the people would be apt to run into the same mistakes again. If the people are left to correct the mistakes themselves, they will more surely progress in wisdom as well as in the sense of responsibility. Whatever stands upon the bottom of the popular intelligence, stands upon far firmer ground than that which rests merely upon superior authority.

"Here in America," I wrote to my friend, "you can see daily how little a people needs to be governed. There are governments, but no masters; there are governors, but they are only commissioners, agents. What there is here of great institutions of learning, of churches, of great commercial institutions, lines of communication, etc., almost always owes its existence, not to official authority, but to the spontaneous co-operation of private citizens. Here you witness the productiveness of freedom. You see a magnificent church—a voluntary association of private persons has founded it; an orphan asylum built of marble—a wealthy citizen has erected it; a university—some rich men have left a large bequest for educational purposes, which serves as a capital stock, and the university then lives, so to speak, almost on subscriptions; and so on without end. We learn here how superfluous is the action of governments concerning a multitude of things in which in Europe it is deemed absolutely indispensable, and how the freedom to do something awakens the desire to do it."

Although I am well aware of its crudities of expression, its inaccuracies of statement, and of the incompleteness of its presentation of American conditions, I quote this letter because it portrays fairly well the workings of the mind of a young man who has been suddenly transplanted from the Old World—its ways of thinking, its traditional views of life, its struggles, illusions, and ideals—into a new world where he witnesses the operation of elementary forces in open daylight, and the realities of free government in undisguised exhibition. I endeavored to get at the essence of truly democratic life, and I still believe that, notwithstanding some errors in the detail of my observations, my general conclusions as to the vital element of democratic institutions were correct.

Some excursions into the interior of Pennsylvania, and to Connecticut, where a distant relative of ours conducted a manufacturing establishment, enlarged the range of my observation. On these occasions I made the acquaintance of a few specimens of the old Pennsylvania Germans, and of the Connecticut Yankees—two distinct elements of the population—both native, for several generations of those Pennsylvania Germans had lived in this country, but so different in language, in habits of thought, and in social traditions, customs, and notions, that the mere fact of their having lived, worked, and exercised the same political rights together in the Republic was to me a most instructive and encouraging illustration of the elasticity and the harmonizing power of democratic government.

What an astonishing spectacle these Pennsylvania Germans presented! Honest, pious, hardworking, prosperous people; good, law-abiding, patriotic American citizens; great-great-grandchildren of my own old Fatherland, who had for several generations tilled these acres and lived in these modest but comfortable houses and built these majestic barns, and preserved the German speech of their forefathers, only mixing it with some words and phrases of English origin. They called all English-speaking people "the Irish," and kept alive many of their old German domestic customs and habits, though they had lost almost all memory of old Germany.

Della Thompson Lutes
(1877-   )

A NATIVE of Jackson, Michigan, Della Thompson Lutes received her education in the schools of that city. Before her marriage, she spent several years teaching, first in the district schools, then in the Detroit public school system. Acceptance of her contributions by several women's magazines opened up a new career for her, and she held successively editorial positions on the *American Motherhood Magazine, Table Talk, Today's Housewife,* and *Modern Priscilla.* Her chief publications are *The Country Kitchen* (1936), *Home Grown* (1937), *Millbrook* (1939), and *Gabriel's Search* (1940).

In her books Mrs. Lutes has portrayed vividly the life in the rural home in America, a life which is distinctly American. The sturdy type of character developed by our farm and small town life has long been valuable in our democratic society. And this character is one frequently mellowed by good humor and sentimentality, as is that of the father in Mrs. Lutes' tale.

Little Runt

Thanksgiving was the day of days, after my father's birthday, for intimate family gathering and unstinted feasting. There were times when my mother resented the invasions of my father's numerous relatives, but on this day she welcomed numbers. Only numbers could provide suitable scope for her prowess as a cook. A meager family of three, even though augmented by a hired man, was no excuse for the array of meats, vegetables, cakes, cookies, pies and puddings and bread, and the orgy of preparation which, on this day, were her great delight.

Such preparations were sometimes in progress far ahead of the eventful date, as in one particular instance when Aunts Hanner and Sophrony, Uncle Frank and Aunt Catherine, with Amelia and Saryette, their daughters, and Uncle Matt and Aunt Martha, who were all within reasonable visiting distance, were invited to partake of the Thanksgiving dinner.

That year a young sow mistook, in the exuberance of her youth, the proper season for mating and, in early fall, presented herself with a lively litter of thirteen husky pigs. All but the thirteenth. The thirteenth was one too many for the calculations of nature and he, being shriveled and feeble, was rooted out of place by the others and repudiated by his mother. My father brought him into the house, scrawny, unable to stand on his little spindling legs, blear-eyed and livid, and laid him on my mother's lap.

"Runt," he said succinctly. "Thought maybe you'd like to put him in a box or something."

My mother placed an old apron on a chair and laid Little Runt upon it. Then she warmed some milk, stuck a finger in it, and let the little creature suck it off. This he did repeatedly until, satisfied and warmed, he fell asleep.

From *The Country Kitchen*, by Della T. Lutes. Reprinted by permission of Little, Brown and Company.

In a few days a bottle was substituted for fingers, and in a week Little Runt not only had a chance but was well on the way to normal pig life. He was given a small box near the kitchen door, and all day his contented grunts, and more demanding squeals as mealtime drew near, were heard.

It became my duty to dump the box, give him fresh straw, and see that he had water.

"Fat him up," said my father, eying Little Runt speculatively, "and we'll have him for Thanksgiving dinner. I've always wanted roast pig for Thanksgiving."

My mother reminded him that he had had roast pig once some years before at Uncle Frank's house and that he had not liked it. In fact he had pronounced the whole dinner an utter failure because he had not liked the pig.

"Fed on sour milk," retorted my father tersely. "Flabby and tough. Frank's too tarnation stingy to feed a pig fit for roasting. Feed the critter up," he advised, "on sweet milk and corn-meal mush, get him nice and fat, and we'll ask the ole curmudgeon over here Thanksgiving and show him what a roast pig's like."

So Little Runt was fed on sweet milk, fresh corn meal and vegetables, and he throve to a state of porcine beauty beyond all rightful expectation, considering his early state.

He was tolerated by Shep, who, after eying him for a few weeks with cold disfavor, finally accepted his presence around the yard with mild lenience, and even allowed him to sprawl full belly-wise in the sun.

He tagged at my mother's skirts when she looked for eggs and when she fed the hens, always sniffing at everything in his path, continuously expressing his affection, gratitude, and general satisfaction in life, with cheerful little ungh-ungh-unghs or a high-pitched protesting squeal.

He allowed me to wash and scrub him until his skin was pink and smooth and firm as that of any buxom farmer's child, and made no serious objection to the still pinker ribbon sometimes tied about his neck. With his little round quirking nose, his small bright watchful eyes, and his upcurled wiry tail, Little Runt was a pig to be proud of—and one to warrant the growth of an affection on the part of the family which without doubt he appreciated and returned.

My father watched the process of his growth with evident approval. He was not as large as the other members of his immediate family, but he was well proportioned, and his contours were such as to stimulate the imagination of the gourmet.

"Going to look pretty good spread out on a dripping pan 'long about the twenty-ninth," observed my father early in November, sitting on the back stoop and watching Little Runt nuzzle the cats away from their rightful pan of milk.

Mother made no reply, and as for myself I looked at my father with positive distaste. How could he be so unfeeling, actually smacking his lips at thought of Little Runt spread out in a dripping pan! Poor Little Runt! I ran and grabbed him up and held him, kicking, squealing, protesting, on my lap, glowering at my father as at an ogre of bloodthirsty proclivities.

"Just how," queried my father at another time, as Little Runt grew in stature and rotundity, "do you make the stuffing for roast pig?"

For quite a few moments my mother did not reply. Her face reflected none of the gustatory fervor that lightened my father's, and she even turned her head away from where he was scratching Little Runt's back with a stick. The subject seemed to lack favor with her as it grew in the approval of my father.

Surprised at her silence, he set his penetrating eyes upon her and said, "Huh?"

"Stuffing?" she repeated with apparent reluctance. "Oh, I make it 'bout the same as for turkey. Little more sage, maybe."

"Umm-m!" My father made pleasant reminiscent sounds in his throat. "Sage! You picked the sage yet?"

"Yes," she replied, "long ago. Savory, too, and all the herbs."

"Put any onion in it?" With the pertinacity of the obstinate mind, he seemed intent upon teasing his always latent appetite.

"Yes," said my mother, shortly, "plenty of it."

After an interval of silence in which Little Runt kept up a running commentary on the salubrious effect of back-scratching, he asked solicitously, "You begun to save up dried bread yet?"

My mother lifted her hands impatiently. "Good gracious!" she exclaimed irritably. "What do you think that pig's goin' to be—an elephant?" With which crushing remark she left the room.

And then, all of a sudden, Little Runt took to following my father about, his nose close to the heel of the man whose favor he seemed to think it vital that he should gain. At first he was merely tolerated, with **much berating** and execrations bordering upon the profane.

"Get out of the way, you dod-rotted, blame little ole fool," my father would exclaim, accompanying the admonition with a thrust of the boot designed to caution rather than to harm. But within a short time, as Little Runt, with porcine stupidity, ignored his master's indifference and increased his noisy attentions, the companionship seemed to be encouraged.

"Come along then, you old cuss-fool," he would invite leniently, "you get under foot and you get your tarnation nose knocked off."

But Little Runt, with the assured experience of all the dumb brethren of the farm in the futility of my father's pretentious bluster, trotted close to heel and thrust his pink nose curiously into the pit his master was digging for winter vegetables, or pried into whatever task he was about.

And into my father's voice crept an extra note of bravado when he referred to the succulent dish so soon to be served upon his plate.

"You goin' to have anything besides roast pig?" he asked of my mother in what was intended for a casual tone, but which certainly bordered upon the anxious.

"Potatoes," replied my mother promptly, "and squash, and boiled onions——"

"I mean any—any other—*meat?*" he persisted in a manner strangely hesitating for one of his forthright spirit. "I didn't know as just the—the—pig'd be enough."

"Well," said my mother judicially, "I didn't know as 't would be, myself, seein' how your mouth's waterin' for it. So I thought I'd roast a turkey. Old Tom's good and fat."

My father's face lightened unwarrantably.

"May be 's well," he replied carelessly. "When you want him killed?"

"Anyway, not yet," replied my mother shortly. "You can kill him when you butcher the pig."

My father rose and went outside, where we heard him vociferously greeted by Little Runt, with his own response made in loud and threatening tones. My mother smiled with her eyes, but her lips were tightly shut as she went about her work of clearing away supper. After that he talked loud and often of the Thanksgiving feast so rapidly approaching. He asked my mother if she was going to put a raw apple or a cooked one in Little Runt's mouth. He enlarged the daily rations of meal and milk and even gave him a few small ears of corn. He cut up pumpkins and fed him bit by bit. He stood by the pen (Little Runt now had a shelter all his own, so, as my father said, he "wouldn't run the fat off") and scratched his back and talked to him, always loudly and truculently of his approaching fate when anyone was within hearing.

My mother grew tight-lipped and stern. She listened to his enthusiasm concerning the succulency of young pork flesh in stony silence, and refused to discuss with him the details of the dinner as his apparently sadistic tendency grew. As for me, I mourned for Little Runt and avoided my father. I likened him to the giant of fee-fi-fo-fum fame, and prayed something would happen to save Little Runt. I even opened his pen and let him out, adjuring him to escape before his day of doom, but the little fool would always follow back to the pen, ungh-unghing and wee-weeing in stupid conceit.

With the imminent approach of the festal day, my father haunted the kitchen. He watched the filling of the cookie jars— gray stone for sugar cookies and a brown glazed one for molasses. He sampled each batch of doughnuts as it came from the kettle and said they were not quite up to my mother's usual standard. He took, at my mother's invitation, repeated tastes of the mincemeat under preparation and with the air of a connoisseur suggested the addition of a *lee-tle* more boiled cider, just a *speck* more of allspice, and, finally, with a tentative glance at my mother's face, just a *touch* of brandy. Adding and mixing and stirring and tasting, together they brought the concoction to what both were satisfied was a state of perfection.

One Saturday about two weeks before Thanksgiving my father came into the kitchen where my mother was making mince pies.

"You know this old receipt book," he said genially, holding it up and tapping the cover lightly with his spectacles.

"Yes," said my mother, eying him with suspicion, "it was my mother's. What of it?"

"You use any of these receipts?" he queried in unctuous tones.

"Sometimes. What you want?" she asked bluntly.

"Why, I don't want anything, 'Miry. What makes you ask that?"

"Because," she said witheringly, "when you talk smooth like that you're generally up to something."

"I found a receipt," pursued my father, sitting down in the rocking-chair by the window and adjusting his spectacles, "I thought maybe you'd like—unless you've seen it."

"I guess I've seen pretty near everything in that book several times over," she told him coolly. "Which one is it?"

He cleared his throat and read: "English Way of Roasting Pig."

"Huh!" exclaimed my mother, pinching down the edges of her crust with a competent thumb. "You don't need to read me anything about English ways of roasting pigs. American ways are good enough for me."

"Still," persisted her obstinate spouse, "this is different. You listen."

She listened.

" 'Put some sage, a large piece of saltish bread, salt and pepper in the inside and sew it up. Observe to skewer the legs back [That's a queer way to put it, ain't it—"observe to skewer the legs back"] or the under part will not crisp. Lay it to a brisk fire [Must have been one of these hearth fires they used to have] till thoroughly dry; then have ready some butter in a dry cloth and rub the pig with it in every part. Dredge as much flour over it as will possibly lie, and do not touch it again till ready to serve; then scrape off the flour very carefully with a blunt knife, rub the pig well with the buttered cloth, and take off the head while at the fire; take out the brains and mix them with the gravy that comes from the pig.' Gosh, 'Miry, sounds like some heathen performance!"

"So it is," interrupted my mother sharply, "and nobody but a heathen'd set and gloat over it!" And, hastily wiping her hands on a towel that lay near, she made an excuse to go to the buttery. My father waited with unwonted patience until she returned and then resumed:——

" 'Then take it up and cut it down the back and breast, lay it into the dish and chop the sage and bread quickly as fine as you can [Seems as if they could have done that before], and mix them with a large quantity of fine melted butter that has very little flour. Put the sauce into the dish after the pig has been split down the back and garnished with the ears and the two jaws. Take off the upper part of the head down to the snout [I thought we'd cut off the head once]. In Devonshire it is served whole, if very small, the head only being cut off to garnish with as above.'

"Well!" observed my father, closing the book and rising, "if that's the way they roast a pig in England I'm glad I'm a Yankee."

And all the time Little Runt was innocently wee-weeing as my father approached his pen with the tri-daily rations, and sniffed and sniffed his fat content as he stuffed his little pink hide to his own doom.

Two days before Thanksgiving my father beheaded Old Tom, filled the big brass kettle with boiling water, scalded and plucked him. The wing tips were cut off whole for brushing the hearth and the tail feathers were finally gathered up and tied together in the form of a duster. He was then handed over to my mother with the somewhat ostentatious remark, "There's your turkey. I'll fetch the pig in tonight. Stib Obart's goin' to butcher him for me."

Turning in the door as at an afterthought, my father continued, "*You* don't want his head cut off, do you, 'Miry? The way that book said the English do?"

I never saw my mother roused to a pitch of real anger in all her life. Her sense of humor was keen and her understanding of my father was deep, and as for *throwing* anything, she never so much, I believe, as tossed a ball. And yet for a moment I thought that, certain as the world, she was going to throw the bowl of suet she was crumbling full at his head. So did he, I think, for he made a quick exit through the nearest door.

The bowl came down heavily on the table and my mother

lifted a corner of her apron to wipe her eyes. As for me, I was
openly bawling. No miracle had happened, no ram in the bushes
to save Little Runt. Stib Obart and his hideous knife stood, a
menacing shadow, in the too near future.

As for my father, there was no understanding him. He had
seemed, especially in the last few weeks, to love Little Runt. He
had fondled him, scolded him, even called to him when not in
sight. He had scratched his back, and now he talked callously
about cutting off his head.

After supper that night he set off with Little Runt, squealing,
kicking, protesting, in a box in the back of the pung, it having
snowed enough during the day to warrant the use of that vehicle.

My mother and I sat close together in the sitting room by the
evening lamp, she mending, I playing half-heartedly with paper
dolls. Our ears were strained to catch, in imagination only, since
the Obarts lived a mile or so away, the shrill, harsh cry of fear
and pain, our eyes seeing crimson splotches on the sweet new
snow.

Along about nine o'clock my father returned. He put the horse
in the barn and then came stomping up to the door—the back
kitchen door where a light had been left burning.

"Where you want him?" he called lustily.

"Put him down cellar," my mother replied. "On the table."

She did not rise, she made no inquiries. She took me off to bed
and sat with me until I slept.

My mother always stuffed her meats at least twenty-four hours
before roasting, so for one day Old Tom hung head down in an
outer room to cool, while the little pig lay supinely upon the
mahogany table in the cellar. I crept down once for a peep at
him, but the sight of the now too-white form sticking stiff, inglorious feet in the air was too much for me. I ran whimpering
upstairs to the comfort of my mother's arms.

Early in the morning of the day before the feast a big bowl of
stuffing was prepared—sage, savory, marjoram, and thyme crum-
bled between the fingers into well-moistened bread; onion chopped
and added; salt and pepper, and lastly the generous half cup of
melted butter, with frequent tastings as the rite proceeded.

When it was finally enriched to my mother's satisfaction, the turkey's ample cavities were filled and sewed. The wings were trussed, the neck bent back; and then, dipping her hand in the moist stuffing, my mother rubbed the entire exterior of the bird with the savory dressing. Over this, paper-thin slices of fat salt pork were laid, and the bird, now in the roaster, was again consigned to the cold room to await his final call to glory.

On Thanksgiving morning the family were early astir. There was much to be done. The company would begin to arrive before eleven and my mother wanted to make progress before they came.

"Once your Aunt Catherine gets here, and your Aunt Hanner, there'll be so much talk I shan't be able to think."

The little pink carcass was brought up as soon as breakfast was over, and at sight of it I burst into tears and fled the kitchen, but could not remain long away. And neither could my father.

Immediately after the early breakfast and the completion of his morning's chores he had shaved, scrubbed his bald pate until it shone, and brushed the fringe of silvery hair and short white beard to a state of bristling order. He put on a clean white shirt and over it a fresh blue "wamus," a sort of short coat made of denim which, with him, took the place of a house coat. He was then ready for the festivities and began to watch the clock as well as the progress of affairs in the kitchen.

Particularly he was interested in the preparation of the pig for roasting.

"You *do* rub it with butter, don't you?" he demanded with eager interest.

"Who said I didn't?" countered my mother a shade tartly, as well she might with a small girl following her about, tiptoe with excitement, and a restless, curious man under her feet when she had a thousand things to do.

More irritable than I had ever seen her she seemed as she rubbed the tender flesh with the buttered cloth and sprinkled it with flour, and especially impatient she seemed with my father, who watched her every move with avid eyes.

And when he asked her if she was going to "observe to skewer the legs back" she lost patience with him entirely. "I wish you'd get out of the kitchen, 'Lije Thompson," she told him hotly, "and go and *do* something. Fill up the woodbox and the water pail, and *stay* out."

He went, and so did I, for I could bear neither the sight of Little Runt in his defenseless state of abrogation, nor my mother's face as she bent over him. I shared her unhappiness in this sacrifice of what seemed like one of the family to man's baser needs, and together we held an unspoken but united animosity toward my father's apparently heartless concern for Little Runt.

The elevated oven, as I remember it, was a monstrous affair, but I cannot recall whether both the turkey and the pig were roasted at the same time, or whether first one was baked and then the other, but I do most definitely know that the odors, as my mother opened the door to baste the browning meats, were such as neither the voluptuous nose of my father nor my own ever-susceptible palate could withstand, and soon we were both back sniffing greedily at the redolent air.

Holidays and company-coming were usually the occasion for exuberant spirits on all our parts, for excited anticipation, chatter, and comment, but today my mother's grim face cast a shadow upon the day and there was small pleasure in the prospect of a bountiful table, the *pièce de résistance* of which was to be our so recent companion.

Time, however, is no respecter of emotion, and as the hours wore on the tempo of activity increased. Potatoes were pared and left in a kettle of cold water that they might not discolor. My father brought a huge Hubbard squash up from the sand pit in the cellar, and broke it into small pieces with the ax. He was not a handy man when it came to household procedures, but on this day he seemed unusually eager to make himself useful. Indeed, as I look back upon it now with mature judgment, I recall that his manner was, for a man of his independent and somewhat truculent disposition, singularly propitiatory.

After chopping the squash into parts, he scraped out the seeds and loose pulp, emptied the waste, and stacked the green and golden sections neatly on the kitchen table.

"Anything more I can do, 'Miry?" he inquired solicitously, only to meet with a suspicious glance from my mother.

"Yes," she said shortly, "you can peel the onions." This was more than he had bargained for, but his quick, rather shocked look into her face brought him no quarter.

"They're in the butt'ry," she said tersely, "and you better peel 'em all."

To my certain knowledge, my father had never up to this time peeled an onion or any other vegetable in his whole life. Nor had he ever washed a dish or in any other way shown any inclination toward self-preservation so far as the preparation of food was concerned. My mother often said that if he were left alone he would probably starve to death before he would cook himself a meal. And now there he was standing at a kitchen table peeling onions and surreptitiously wiping his weeping eyes, while my mother stepped briskly from room to room, her hands filled with one delectable dish after another, her lips grimly set, her eyes unsmiling and hard.

The onions peeled and standing in a pan of water, my father scrubbed his hands in the tin basin, wiped them on the roller towel hanging on the back of a door, and then, without a word or a glance in my mother's direction, put on his hat and escaped.

To a little girl accustomed to basking in the warmth, the approval, the impregnable security of a united family life, there was something oppressive and sinister in the atmosphere of this morning. Still, there was assurance in the wealth of delicacies stored against the day.

In the buttery were the pumpkin pies that had been baked earlier in the morning, the ruffled edges of their biscuit-brown crusts encircling smooth plaques of yellow custard coated with a thin, almost transparent veil of dappled russet and bronze.

From these were exhaled a most flavorsome odor reminiscent of autumn days when the lusty vine strewed its golden fruit wantonly amongst the corn, mingled with the spicy fragrance of cinnamon, nutmeg, ginger, and allspice.

Alongside these were the mince pies baked a week earlier, stored in cold and now brought out to be warmed at the last moment on the oven top. Marked with an "M" they were, and through the delicate tracery of the letter one caught tantalizing whiffs of meat preserved in heavenly juices, apple, currant, and raisin all melted into one sweetly tart aroma, itself bathed in the effluvious bouquet of rich old brandy, such aroma as the Olympian gods may have dreamed of but never met.

Here, too, arranged in glass sauce dishes, pickle dishes, preserve dishes that were the possessions of but ordinary women, but which are now elevated to the high estate of the rare, were pickled peaches with the pointed ears of cloves dotting their amber sides; mustard pickles to neutralize the too-rich content of the young pork; bowls of crimson cranberry sauce; globules of currant jelly for those who did not favor the fruit of the bog; long, green sections of cucumber pickle standing upright in the crystal dish swinging censer-like in its silver frame with hanging fork beside.

And then, here was the comp'ny! Uncle Frank and Aunt Catherine with the two third cousins, Saryette and Amelia. Amelia, fat-faced and smug, the known possessor of a cigar box filled with candy hearts (the kind that said, "Will you be my girl?") which, upon the occasion of a return visit, she would let me look at but never touch; and Saryette, who had been known to faint away upon being unduly chided. A talent openly cultivated, my father declared, and one that a good sound spanking in more formative years would certainly have prevented. And not too late yet.

The horses having been attended to, and greetings exchanged, Uncle Frank and my father betook themselves to the front room, where the round chunk stove sent vibrations of heat quivering upon the air. Aunt Catherine unfolded a voluminous apron from her sewing bag, tied it around her ample waist, and laid capable hands to the setting of the table. By the time Aunt Hanner and Aunt 'Phrony had arrived with the remainder of the guests, the table was dressed in its long white linen cloth, the tall silver caster and its five crystal bottles as a centerpiece, and the various relishes, jellies, and preserves clustered about it.

At two o'clock the family was seated around the board, the turkey, his crisp juicy skin bursting here and there in the plenitude of his stuffed insides, before my mother at one end of the table, and the rosy-brown, crackling-coated, well-rounded porcine frame before my father. The little pig's legs, now untied, squatted wantonly beneath his well-padded hams and shoulders, his golden belly crouched upon the plate.

Scorning what the English recipe was pleased to describe as garnishing, my mother had left the head intact, with upstanding ears and truculently extended snout. In his mouth was a beautiful red apple, polished (for I saw him do it) on the sleeve of my father's wamus, and inserted by him, at my mother's request, into the open mouth after the pig was placed on the table. Over his haunches a small crisp tail upcurled with a realism seldom equaled in culinary lore.

A beautiful creature he certainly was, smoking, steaming, reeking of succulent juices, and rich with fragrance of herbs sun-ripened in our own garden.

"How do I carve him?" inquired my father with suspicious alacrity, poising his instruments above the plate before him, and ignoring the expectant silence with which my mother always recognized the religious tendencies accorded to Uncle Frank. Dismissing the too-previous question as unheard, my mother turned in the direction of her guest and politely inquired if he would like to ask a blessing.

Uncle Frank, knowing my father's contempt for an attitude that he considered lacking in sincerity, waved dismissal of the courtesy.

"Best way to thank the Lord," observed my father benignly, slipping the razor-edged knife well under the skin of the succulent pig and watching with round eyes the free rich juices run, "is to fall to and eat. Pass up your plate, Cathy, for some of the best roast pig you ever tasted in your life. 'Miry'll tend to the turkey."

One by one he filled the huge plates—a slice of well-done pinkish-white young pork, a bit of crackling brown skin, a spoonful of mashed potatoes whipped with cream and butter to a very froth of delectable flavor, a spoonful of the stuffing. My mother, brooding eyes intent upon the work before her, was carving the turkey—a thin piece of white meat rimmed with chestnut-brown, a bit of the dark, laying the pieces on the side of the platter and transferring them to the plates as they reached her.

Finally all were taken care of except Mother, and Father, holding his knife above the riddled carcass, said with odd gusto, "Now, 'Miry, I'm goin' to cut *you* a nice juicy slice."

My mother, struggling to control herself, said, "I don't care for any, thank you," and burst into tears.

We all with one accord turned to look at her, the guests in

astonishment, I with streaming eyes and sobbing breath, and my father in consternation and apparent anger.

"Well!" he said with what would seem to be a righteous indignation. "I been wonderin' if you was goin' to show some signs of feelin', 'Miry. Wait a minute."

He threw down his napkin, shoved back his chair, dashed through the kitchen, snatched his hat from a nail as he went— all, it seemed, in one whirlwind of motion, his guests staring after him in rooted amazement.

My mother wiped her eyes, and in a shamed and shaken voice said, "It was Little Runt. I fed him by hand—he t-tagged us around—I didn't see—h-how he *could*—I d-don't know what he's up to——"

But her tearful, broken apology was interrupted by a confusion of the strangest sounds—a mingling of the sharp, staccato squeals of a struggling pig, snuffles and grunts, my father's voice raised in affectionate abuse, the back door opening.

"Hol' your tongue, you tarnation fool-cuss"—and there he was, white hair flying, hat awry, and in his arms, legs kicking, snout wrinkling, small pink body squirming, was—sure as you live— Little Runt!

"There!" said my father, wheezing a bit from exertion. *"Now what you think?"*

Every chair had been pushed back. Food was cooling on the plates. I had flown from my chair to greet Little Runt and pull him into my lap.

"Why!" cried my mother, gasping. "What—where——"

"Well," said my father, flinging off his hat and smoothing hair and beard, and beaming with satisfaction in his own exploit, "when I see you [addressing my mother] was really *bent* on roast pig for dinner [my mother lifted her hands, opened her mouth, and remained silent], I thought I'd have to fix it some way to save Little Runt's hide. You see," he now turned eagerly to the dumfounded guests, "this was a runt we raised by hand and he took to following me round, so when it came time I didn't have the heart to—so I took one of the others over to Stib Obart's instead." Then, with a swift turn from the still silent table, he addressed the contented, adventuring pig.

"Come along now," he said, and, executing a flank movement,

caught Little Runt by his hind leg and hoisted him to his arms, admonishing him sonorously.

"Thanksgiving for *you,* all right, you fool runt, you, but hogs don't celebrate it in the house," and in an uproar of squeals and protesting kicks Little Runt was borne away.

" 'Lije," said Uncle Frank sententiously in his absence, "always was a sentimental old fool."

"Let me," urged my mother politely, ignoring the remark, "give you some of the turkey."

Almost immediately my father was at his place washed and brushed, passing the squash, asking for the cranberries, urging second helpings where the first were hardly touched. He made complimentary and utterly absurd remarks about Aunt Catherine's fine looks, joshed Uncle Frank about a horse trade he had recently made, and otherwise disported himself as the benignant and genial host. To my mother he was especially considerate, but could not at the last deny himself the pleasure of a subtle thrust which would reflect upon his own clever scheming.

"Well, 'Miry," he said handsomely as the guests, replete with food and hospitable content, drove away in the dusk of blue-white snow and creeping night, "ain't you glad *now* that I done something about Little Runt?"

"You better go feed him," said my mother dryly, which he did. And, so far as I can remember, Little Runt may have lived to a fat old age and died in his pen.

Mark Twain
(1835-1910)

MARK TWAIN, whose real name was Samuel Langhorne Clemens, was born in the village of Florida, Missouri. All his early memories, however, are connected with the river town of Hannibal, where he lived from early infancy to 1853. When Mark Twain was twelve years old, the death of his father put an end to his schooling, and his longer education in the world of affairs began with his apprenticeship to a printer. After a few minor attempts, Mark Twain, who was then living in California, published in 1865, in a New York weekly, a story that was reprinted all over the United States, *The Celebrated Jumping Frog of Calaveras County*. From that time forward, his life was devoted to writing and lecturing. The following are a few of his most widely known works: *The Innocents Abroad* (1869); *The Adventures of Tom Sawyer* (1876); *The Adventures of Huckleberry Finn* (1884); and *A Connecticut Yankee in King Arthur's Court* (1889).

Mark Twain's experience on the Mississippi, both as apprentice pilot and as pilot, fell between the years 1857 and 1861; the Civil War brought this activity to a close. In 1875 he contributed a series of articles to *The Atlantic Monthly* under the title *Old Times on the Mississippi*. In 1883 he published *Life on the Mississippi* in which Chapters IV-XVII are the *Atlantic* material. For the West in the days before the Civil War the romance of the Mississippi river, the splendor of its steamboats, and the exploits of its pilots were subjects of continual conversation. Mark Twain, whose pen-name comes from this river experience, vividly recalled to the memory of his generation and recorded for the benefit and interest of those who have lived since, the exciting and colorful days when every voyage on that great, uncharted stream was an adventure.

A Daring Deed

When I returned to the pilot-house St. Louis was gone, and I was lost. Here was a piece of river which was all down in my book, but I could make neither head nor tail of it: you understand, it was turned around. I had seen it when coming upstream, but I had never faced about to see how it looked when it was behind me. My heart broke again, for it was plain that I had got to learn this troublesome river *both ways*.

The pilot-house was full of pilots, going down to "look at the river." What is called the "upper river" (the two hundred miles between St. Louis and Cairo, where the Ohio comes in) was low; and the Mississippi changes its channel so constantly that the pilots used to always find it necessary to run down to Cairo to take a fresh look, when their boats were to lie in port a week; that is, when the water was at a low stage. A deal of this "looking at the river" was done by poor fellows who seldom had a berth, and whose only hope of getting one lay in their being always freshly posted and therefore ready to drop into the shoes of some reputable pilot, for a single trip, on account of such pilot's sudden illness, or some other necessity. And a good many of them constantly ran up and down inspecting the river, not because they ever really hoped to get a berth, but because (they being guests of the boat) it was cheaper to "look at the river" than stay ashore and pay board. In time these fellows grew dainty in their tastes, and only infested boats that had an established reputation for setting good tables. All visiting pilots were useful, for they were always ready and willing, winter or summer, night or day, to go out in the yawl and help buoy the channel or assist the boat's pilots in any way they could. They were likewise welcomed be-

From *Life on the Mississippi*, by Mark Twain; reprinted by permission of Harper & Brothers, publishers.

cause all pilots are tireless talkers, when gathered together, and as they talk only about the river they are always understood and are always interesting. Your true pilot cares nothing about anything on earth but the river, and his pride in his occupation surpasses the pride of kings.

We had a fine company of these river inspectors along this trip. There were eight or ten, and there was abundance of room for them in our great pilot-house. Two or three of them wore polished silk hats, elaborate shirt-fronts, diamond breastpins, kid gloves, and patent-leather boots. They were choice in their English, and bore themselves with a dignity proper to men of solid means and prodigious reputation as pilots. The others were more or less loosely clad, and wore upon their heads tall felt cones that were suggestive of the days of the Commonwealth.

I was a cipher in this august company, and felt subdued, not to say torpid. I was not even of sufficient consequence to assist at the wheel when it was necessary to put the tiller hard down in a hurry; the guest that stood nearest did that when occasion required—and this was pretty much all the time, because of the crookedness of the channel and the scant water. I stood in a corner; and the talk I listened to took the hope all out of me. One visitor said to another:

"Jim, how did you run Plum Point, coming up?"

"It was in the night, there, and I ran it the way one of the boys on the *Diana* told me; started out about fifty yards above the wood-pile on the false point, and held on the cabin under Plum Point till I raised the reef—quarter less twain—then straightened up for the middle bar till I got well abreast the old one-limbed cottonwood in the bend, then got my stern on the cottonwood, and head on the low place above the point, and came through a-booming—nine and a half."

"Pretty square crossing, ain't it?"

"Yes, but the upper bar's working down fast."

Another pilot spoke up and said:

"I had better water than that, and ran it lower down; started out from the false point—mark twain—raised the second reef abreast the big snag in the bend, and had quarter less twain."

One of the gorgeous ones remarked:

"I don't want to find fault with your leadsmen, but that's a good deal of water for Plum Point, it seems to me."

There was an approving nod all around as this quiet snub dropped on the boaster and "settled" him. And so they went on talk-talk-talking. Meantime, the thing that was running in my mind was, "Now, if my ears hear aright, I have not only to get the names of all the towns and islands and bends, and so on, by heart, but I must even get up a warm personal acquaintanceship with every old snag and one-limbed cottonwood and obscure wood-pile that ornaments the banks of this river for twelve hundred miles; and more than that, I must actually know where these things are in the dark, unless these guests are gifted with eyes that can pierce through two miles of solid blackness. I wish the piloting business was in Jericho and I had never thought of it."

At dusk Mr. Bixby tapped the big bell three times (the signal to land), and the captain emerged from his drawing-room in the forward end of the "texas," and looked up inquiringly. Mr. Bixby said:

"We will lay up here all night, captain."

"Very well, sir."

That was all. The boat came to shore and was tied up for the night. It seemed to me a fine thing that the pilot could do as he pleased, without asking so grand a captain's permission. I took my supper and went immediately to bed, discouraged by my day's observations and experiences. My late voyage's note-booking was but a confusion of meaningless names. It had tangled me all up in a knot every time I had looked at it in the daytime. I now hoped for respite in sleep; but no, it reveled all through my head till sunrise again, a frantic and tireless nightmare.

Next morning I felt pretty rusty and low-spirited. We went booming along, taking a good many chances, for we were anxious to "get out of the river" (as getting out to Cairo was called) before night should overtake us. But Mr. Bixby's partner, the other pilot, presently grounded the boat, and we lost so much time getting her off that it was plain the darkness would overtake us a good long way above the mouth. This was a great misfortune, especially to certain of our visiting pilots, whose boats would have to wait for their return, no matter how long that might be. It sobered the pilot-house talk a good deal. Coming up-stream, pilots did not mind low water or any kind of darkness; nothing stopped them but fog. But down-stream work was different; a boat was too nearly helpless, with a stiff current pushing behind her; so it was not customary to run down-stream at night in low water.

There seemed to be one small hope, however: if we could get through the intricate and dangerous Hat Island crossing before night, we could venture the rest, for we would have plainer sailing and better water. But it would be insanity to attempt Hat Island at night. So there was a deal of looking at watches all the rest of the day, and a constant ciphering upon the speed we were making; Hat Island was the eternal subject; sometimes hope was high and sometimes we were delayed in a bad crossing, and down it went again. For hours all hands lay under the burden of this suppressed excitement; it was even communicated to me, and I got to feeling so solicitous about Hat Island, and under such an awful pressure of responsibility, that I wished I might have five minutes on shore to draw a good, full, relieving breath, and start over again. We were standing no regular watches. Each of our pilots ran such portions of the river as he had run when coming up-stream, because of his greater familiarity with it; but both remained in the pilot-house constantly.

An hour before sunset Mr. Bixby took the wheel, and Mr. W. stepped aside. For the next thirty minutes every man held his watch in his hand and was restless, silent, and uneasy. At last somebody said, with a doomful sigh:

"Well, yonder's Hat Island—and we can't make it."

All the watches closed with a snap, everybody sighed and muttered something about its being "too bad, too bad—ah, if we could *only* have got here half an hour sooner!" and the place was thick with the atmosphere of disappointment. Some started to go out, but loitered, hearing no bell-tap to land. The sun dipped behind the horizon, the boat went on. Inquiring looks passed from one guest to another; and one who had his hand on the door-knob and had turned it, waited, then presently took away his hand and let the knob turn back again. We bore steadily down the bend. More looks were exchanged, and nods of surprised admiration—but no words. Insensibly the men drew together behind Mr. Bixby, as the sky darkened and one or two dim stars came out. The dead silence and sense of waiting became oppressive. Mr. Bixby pulled the cord, and two deep, mellow notes from the big bell floated off on the night. Then a pause, and one more note was struck. The watchman's voice followed, from the hurricane-deck:

"Labboard lead, there! Stabboard lead!"

The cries of the leadsmen began to rise out of the distance, and were gruffly repeated by the word-passers on the hurricane-deck.

"M-a-r-k three! M-a-r-k three! Quarter-less-three! Half twain! Quarter twain! M-a-r-k twain! Quarter-less——"

Mr. Bixby pulled two bell-ropes, and was answered by faint jinglings far below in the engine-room, and our speed slackened. The steam began to whistle through the gauge-cocks. The cries of the leadsmen went on—and it is a weird sound, always, in the night. Every pilot in the lot was watching now, with fixed eyes, and talking under his breath. Nobody was calm and easy but Mr. Bixby. He would put his wheel down and stand on a spoke, and as the steamer swung into her (to me) utterly invisible marks —for we seemed to be in the midst of a wide and gloomy sea—he would meet and fasten her there. Out of the murmur of half-audible talk, one caught a coherent sentence now and then— such as:

"There; she's over the first reef all right!"

After a pause, another subdued voice:

"Her stern's coming down just *exactly* right, by *George!*"

"Now she's in the marks; over she goes!"

Somebody else muttered:

"Oh, it was done beautiful—*beautiful!*"

Now the engines were stopped altogether, and we drifted with the current. Not that I could see the boat drift, for I could not, the stars being all gone by this time. This drifting was the dismalest work; it held one's heart still. Presently I discovered a blacker gloom than that which surrounded us. It was the head of the island. We were closing right down upon it. We entered its deeper shadow, and so imminent seemed the peril that I was likely to suffocate; and I had the strongest impulse to do *some-*

thing, anything, to save the vessel. But still Mr. Bixby stood by his wheel, silent, intent as a cat, and all the pilots stood shoulder to shoulder at his back.

"She'll not make it!" somebody whispered.

The water grew shoaler and shoaler, by the leadsman's cries, till it was down to:

"Eight-and-a-half! E-i-g-h-t feet! E-i-g-h-t feet! Seven-and——"

Mr. Bixby said warningly through his speaking-tube to the engineer:

"Stand by, now!"

"Ay, ay, sir!"

"Seven-and-a-half! Seven feet! *Six*-and——"

We touched bottom! Instantly Mr. Bixby set a lot of bells ringing, shouted through the tube, *"Now,* let her have it—every ounce you've got!" then to his partner, "Put her hard down! snatch her! snatch her!" The boat rasped and ground her way through the sand, hung upon the apex of disaster a single tremendous instant, and then over she went! And such a shout as went up at Mr. Bixby's back never loosened the roof of a pilot-house before!

There was no more trouble after that. Mr. Bixby was a hero that night; and it was some little time, too, before his exploit ceased to be talked about by river-men.

Fully to realize the marvelous precision required in laying the great steamer in her marks in that murky waste of water, one should know that not only must she pick her intricate way through snags and blind reefs, and then shave the head of the island so closely as to brush the overhanging foliage with her stern, but at one place she must pass almost within arm's reach of a sunken and invisible wreck that would snatch the hull timbers from under her if she should strike it, and destroy a quarter of a million dollars' worth of steamboat and cargo in five minutes, and maybe a hundred and fifty human lives into the bargain.

The last remark I heard that night was a compliment to Mr. Bixby, uttered in soliloquy and with unction by one of our guests. He said:

"By the Shadow of Death, but he's a lightning pilot!"

Elizabeth Shepley Sergeant
(1881-   )

LONG a distinguished contributor to the leading periodicals, Elizabeth Shepley Sergeant won wide acclaim for her critical acumen and style, in 1927, when she published *Fire Under the Andes,* a series of biographical studies of recently living and contemporary Americans. Miss Sergeant is a native of Winchester, Massachusetts. She was graduated from Bryn Mawr College in 1903, and in 1912–13 she studied at the Sorbonne and the Collège de France.

The Supreme Court of the United States has long been considered by the people of this country as one of the great bulwarks of their liberties. On its bench have sat many of the great jurists of the nation, and their interpretations of the Constitution have had a general usefulness in adapting it to the changing needs of the people, despite the resentment they have occasionally aroused. Among the Justices none has had a higher reputation than Oliver Wendell Holmes (1841–1935) who served from 1902 until his voluntary retirement in 1932. In her essay Miss Sergeant has given us the real flavor of the man.

Oliver Wendell Holmes

JUSTICE TOUCHED WITH FIRE

Here is a Yankee, strayed from Olympus. Olympians are reputed at ease in the universe; they know truth in flashes of fire, and reveal its immortal essence in cryptic phrase. How disturbing to the solemnities of average mortals, average lawyers, average judges even, is the swift, searching, epigrammatic thought of Mr. Justice Holmes. Even the wise-cracks he loves to fling out are keyed to profundity and wit. He has lived through the most restless periods of American history since the American Revolution itself, yet his early divinations of the law, outlined nearly half a century ago, and his Supreme Court opinions, which have together recast American legal thinking, seem to have been formulated in the elegant leisure that we associate with the classics.

Oliver Wendell Holmes's tall and erect figure, which a ripe and white old age has scarcely stooped; his grand manner, at once noble and dazzling—those have never asked quarter of time. Watch his snowy head for a moment among his younger peers on the bench. Note the set of the shoulders in the gown, the oval contour of the face with its fine, angular New England features, the flow of the level white brows into the thin distinction of the nose, the martial mustachios, with their heavy guardsman's droop and their curved ends of punctilio. The eyes, the most striking feature, give off sparkles of scintillating gray-blue, and have more skepticism and gentle malice than mercy in their depths. Though at bottom Holmes is and looks a simple American gentleman of aristocratic rectitude, he has a spice of the Mephistophelean quality which he himself has recommended to the naïveté of judges.

Reprinted from *Fire Under the Andes* by Elizabeth Shepley Sergeant, by permission of and special arrangement with Alfred A. Knopf, Inc., authorized publishers.

The Justice is listening to a complex argument—listening till his mind, hovering and intent, like the wasp that paralyzes the caterpillar, has driven straight to its heart. Then, while the other judges still patiently listen, he reads over the briefs, calls the pages to bring reports containing opinions relied on by counsel, and is ready, by the time counsel is rising to his peroration, to draft an opinion that will not fail to "strike the jugular."

The jurist who, at fourscore years and five, can command this penetration of essentials, this intense focusing of mental powers, has some rare elixir in his veins. Is it not the true elixir of youth? The youth offered by a young Bostonian to his country in the most heroic of her wars, and thrice wounded, at Ball's Bluff, Antietam, and Fredericksburg? Judge Holmes's clearest genius— the sharp and supple functioning of his mind—in some nameless fashion draws its strength from his curiosity and awe in the face of the mystery of existence. It seems that the near presence of death in those three stern and shadowed years fused his intellect and his emotion in a single shaft of will. It made skeptical philosophy a necessity, but gave to fundamental doubt a practical idealism. It affirmed man's destiny on earth as battle, his chances those of war. But it discovered to him that the root of joy as of duty and the worth of life itself is to put out all one's powers to the full, though the end be dim and the plan of campaign little understood. "Men carry their signatures upon their persons," he has written, "although they may not always be visible at the first glance." The friends of the Justice all know the signature that the Civil War inscribed. It is that of a youthful fighter who somehow inspired the fate of the lonely thinker with the faith of the soldier.

The son of Dr. Oliver Wendell Holmes was a fortunate youth. Born in the flower of New England's cultural dominance, and at the dawn of the Darwinian age into a family at once brahminical, literary, and scientific, brought up at that "autocratic" breakfast-table where a bright saying gave a child a double help of marmalade, he must early have acquired the rich flavor of belles-lettres which in him has ever mellowed the scientific habit. Celebrated men were familiars at his father's house, and from the greatest among them—Emerson—he drew a priceless intellectual ferment. Yet, with his glancing wit and his worldly charm, he might have been tempted away from the isolated path of the original thinker but for the war of secession. It was, in his own view, his greatest good fortune to graduate from Harvard in the class of '61, at the age of twenty, just as this war was beginning, and to learn one day, as he was walking down Beacon Hill, with Hobbes's *Leviathan* in his hand, that he had a commission in the Twentieth Massachusetts Volunteers; a regiment commemorated at last in the Boston Public Library by one of the lions of St. Gaudens that guard the entrance stairway. So the young officer, whom we may see in his uniform at Langdell Hall, at the Harvard Law School, with his visored cap on his knee, in one of those touching little faded photographs which were a sop to parental love—a mere lad, trusting and vulnerable, like all lads who have fought all the great wars—went forth to a baptism that he has never forgotten.

It came at Ball's Bluff: an engagement where the Twentieth Massachusetts got its first crucial trial. There were tactical errors which cost dear. The blues, defeated but "too proud to surrender," as the grays declared, were driven down the cliff on the Virginia shore into the Potomac, where, dying, swimming, drowning in numbers, they yet struggled to transport the survivors and the wounded in the few sinking boats to the island in mid-stream, and then to the Maryland shore, while the river was whipped into a foam of bullets, and darkness fell. Lieutenant Holmes, apparently mortally wounded in the breast, was laid in a boat with dying men and ferried through the night. As he recovered consciousness, he heard the man next him groan and—thinking he probably had his own dose—said to himself:

"I suppose Sir Philip Sidney would say: 'Put that man ashore first.' I think I will let events take their course."

A story written down by the elder Holmes in *The Atlantic Monthly* (not altogether to the pleasure of the younger?) is indicative of another side of the Justice's character. This relates how, after the battle of Antietam, Dr. Holmes started out to search for a wounded son. But the doctor could not find his young hero, though he followed this clue and that. At last, in despair, he was taking a train for the north at Hagerstown, Mary-

land, when, "in the first car, on the fourth seat to the right, I
saw my captain."

"Hullo, my boy!"

"Boy, nothing!" (The original tale does not run quite this
way.) The "boy" had been spending a week much to his taste.
"As he walked languidly along [in Hagerstown], some ladies saw
him across the street and, seeing, were moved with pity and, pity-
ing, spoke such soft words that he was tempted to accept their
invitation to rest awhile beneath their hospitable roof. The mansion was old, as the dwellings of gentlefolk should be; the ladies
were some of them young, and all were full of kindness; there
were gentle cares and unasked luxuries and pleasant talk, and
music sprinklings for the piano, with a sweet voice to keep them
company."

The words call up, along with other images of an America
gone forever, a quaint photograph found in a portfolio in the
memorial Alcove at the Boston Library: a bevy of devout young
ladies in bustles and tight waists and long, flowing skirts, sewing
together on a flag. Such a flag was presented, after Ball's Bluff,
to Company E "by the sisters of Lieutenants Lowell and Put-
nam" with a polished letter from Charles Eliot Norton about
the honor of the Bay State. The Colonel of the Twentieth, by
the way, on first reaching headquarters, and asked by the commanding officer if he had arms, uniforms, and accouterments,
replied proudly: "My regiment, sir, came from Massachusetts."

Back to Massachusetts, then, came young Holmes, to the soil
for whose outcropping rocks and barberry bushes and sand dunes
and old towns built of brick and shingle he has confessed a
rooted affection. He had no path to blaze unless he chose: the
natural Puritan aristocracy from which he sprang awaited him
with its pleasant securities. But there burned in this young man,
as there burns in the Holmes of today, a sense of the valuable
brevity of existence. Life was a rich but a responsible adventure,
and he had a simple democratic conviction, denied to some who
are born under the shadow of Beacon Hill, that "the deepest
cause we have to love our country" is "that instinct, that spark,
that makes the American unable to meet his fellow man otherwise than simply as a man, eye to eye, hand to hand, and foot to

foot, wrestling naked on the sand." Holmes was recognizing fiery energies which later claimed mountain climbing as an outlet. A stern intellectual ambition, worthy substitute for the primitive and heroic, was taking shape. A sentence of his own conjures him up for me, standing apart even in his tested group: "In our youth our hearts were touched with fire. It was given to us to learn at the outset that life is a profound and passionate thing."

It is hinted that among those young ladies of the best families who—Boston being truly a village in the sixties—"knew every carriage in town," the return of a handsome wounded soldier (also the class poet of the decimated '61) made a stir. "That lanky talker of a Wendell Holmes" was an old maid-servant's dictum. Holmes has always loved talking by a fire with a clever and gracious woman, and these ghostly maidens, if they yet lived, could probably tell us why a young man of varied and brilliant parts chose from several possible destinies to enter the Harvard Law School.

For there was also literature, there was above all philosophy. Holmes was not the man to follow in his father's footsteps, or even in Emerson's, though he had in fact qualities as a literary stylist far superior to the doctor's, and gifts as a philosopher which gave a universal impress to his legal thinking. The winds and waves of eternity beat through his writings. "Nerve and dagger," said Emerson, are lacking in the American genius. Holmes the writer has nerve and dagger, as he has in moral and intellectual issues a blade-like courage. But he did not dream, in those tormented days, of being named among great American writers and philosophers. In his twenties this profession of the law which he had elected seemed barren enough. Did he choose it, by a quirk common to New Englanders, for that very reason? Because it was hard, male, undesired? The law enforced more than thought: an activity in the world of men, a reality which the soldier felt bound to espouse, if only that it was so alien to his intuitive bent for inward brooding thought. "It cost me some years of doubt and unhappiness," the Justice has avowed, "before I could say to myself: 'The law is part of the universe—if the universe can be thought about, one part must reveal it as much as another to one who can see that part. It is only a question if you have the eyes.'"

The study of philosophy helped Holmes to find his legal eyes. He likes to tell how he began to read Plato, as an undergraduate at Harvard, and was admonished by Emerson: "Hold him at arm's length. You must say to yourself: 'Plato, you have pleased the world for two thousand years: let us see if you can please me.' " The sequel is pertinent. Young Holmes not only read, but turned off a critical essay which he showed expectantly to his mentor. "I have read your piece. When you strike at a king, you must *kill* him." That shaft went straight to the bull's eye. When Holmes graduated from the Law School he approached his profession in the spirit of scientific and philosophic inquiry. Not as do the practitioners "to whom the law is a rag-bag from which they pick out the piece and the color that they want." Holmes had no consuming interest in practice, considered as winning cases and making money. But he had the hope, as yet scarce conscious, of shooting with true aim at some great intellectual marks. "I suppose the law is worthy of the interest of an intelligent man," he once hazarded, in his anguish of doubt whether it was, to Charles Francis Adams, the Minister to England.

That a philosopher could be, must be, a man of intelligence Holmes was morally certain. Was he not "twisting the tail of the cosmos" with his friend Bill James? One gets from the early letters of William James a fine series of images of two golden and impetuous youths, whetting thought on thought, doubt on doubt, in an upper chamber. In the year 1866 when "Bill" was twenty-four and studying medicine, and "Wendell" twenty-five and studying law, they exchanged acute argument on materialism. A year later, when James had gone to Germany to pursue philosophy, and Holmes had been admitted to the bar, discussions of "our dilapidated old friend the Kosmos" continued by letter— interspersed by affectionate reminiscence from James, of "your whitely lit-up room, drinking in your profound wisdom, your golden jibes, your costly imagery, listening to your shuddering laughter." "Why don't you join the Society for Psychical Research?" James is said to have inquired. To which Holmes: "Why don't you investigate Mohammedanism? There are millions of men who think you will be damned without it. Life is like an artichoke, you pull out a leaf, only a tip is edible. You pull out a day, only an hour or two is available for spiritual thoughts."

Holmes was looking, though he may not have realized it, for a personal philosophy that he could use as a raft from which to take the long, deep plunge into his legal-scholarly pursuits. It is typical—for his power of choice and exclusion, his economy of time and means are facets of his greatness—that he did not continue to flounder about in the philosophic waters, trying this system and that, cursing Jehovah and calling on his angels to save, but grasped the planks that he found near at hand and skillfully fitted them together into the aforementioned raft. *Raft* is too perishable a word. Holmes's philosophy was a tidy boat, formed, for all its pointed nails of skepticism, of sturdy Puritan oak, a shipshape bark, in which he could cruise safely about the cosmos among the other worlds and the stars.

Every speech, every personal letter, every opinion of Oliver Wendell Holmes rests on this hardy and lucid doctrine. Divergent though it was from the philosophy of James—who continued his search for a solution that would fit the fate of Man in general, and for himself tended toward those supernatural revelations and consolations which Holmes's skepticism impatiently repudiated,—the affectionate relation continued through life. And every distant interchange made the old philosophic quarrel flare up. The following statement of Holmes's "platform,"—happily preserved in the James files—though written from the Supreme Court in 1901, "after reading your two pieces about Pragmatism (pedantic name)" might as well have been written in 1875, or, if William James had lived, in 1926.

"It is as absurd (the Justice remarks, with familiar humility, before an expert) "for me to be spearing my old commonplaces at you as it would be for an outsider to instruct me in the theory of legal responsibility—but you see, *mon vieux*, although it is years since we have had any real talk together, I am rather obstinate in my adherence to ancient sympathies and enjoy letting out a little slack to you.

"I have been in the habit of saying that all I mean by truth is what I can't help thinking. The assumption of the validity of the thinking process seems to mean no more than that. But I have learned to surmise that my *can't helps* are not necessarily cosmic . . . philosophy seems to me generally speaking to sin through arrogance . . . I can't help preferring champagne to ditch water, but I doubt if the universe does . . . The great act of faith is when a man decides that he is not God . . . If

I did come out of it [the universe] or rather if I am in it, I see no wonder that I can't swallow it. If it fixed my bounds, as it gives me my powers, I have nothing to say about its possibilities or characteristics, except
that it is the kind of a thing (using this phraseology skeptically and
under protest) that has me in its belly and so is bigger than I. It seems
to me that my only promising activity is to make my universe coherent
and livable, not to babble about the universe."

These passages define a consistent character. Judge Holmes has,
at eighty-five, an intellectual youth that most men of forty cannot
boast. He lives greatly in the brilliant young legal minds of today; believes that there are more men of promise in the present
than in his own youth; receives their ideas with the courtesy, admiration, and speculative curiosity accorded to honored guests.
One of his favorite aphorisms is that the average life of an idea
is fifteen years; another, that the literature of the past is a bore.
Yet it is to be noted (since the laity persist in labeling him a
radical) that, though he admires Proust and finds *Nize Baby*
richly droll, he is more often to be seen, in that dignified Washington study of his, with a volume of eighteenth-century memoirs
in his hand than with a daily newspaper. His own universe, material, spiritual, or intellectual, is not subject to perpetual revi-
sion. His economics, like his philosophy and his literary tastes,
were pretty well settled in the twenties. The foundations of his
legal thinking were laid in the thirties. His domestic happiness,
which continues unbroken to this day, was established at the age
of thirty-one—fifty-four years ago.

Meanwhile he was taking his plunge into the deep waters of
the law. In 1869 James comments that "Wendell" is working too
hard, taking no vacation. In 1870 he assumes the editorship of the
American Law Review. In 1873 appears his important edition of
Kent's *Commentaries,* and in the same year he becomes a member of the firm of Shattuck, Holmes and Munroe. But he cannot
have given much time to practice, for the years from thirty to
forty were a period of intensive research: a time of lonely and
original productivity, often hinted at in his speeches, when he
learned "to lay his course by a star which he has never seen";
and, feeling around him "a black gulf of solitude more isolating
than that which surrounds the dying man," learned also to trust
his "own unshaken will." During these years he offered his life to

the law as completely as he had offered it to his country; and, losing it, found it again in his classic *Common Law,* which dates an epoch in American legal history.

The chapters were written first, as a Boston classic should be, in the form of "Lowell Lectures," and delivered in 1880. Published as a learned volume in 1881, the book was hailed by those competent to judge, both in America and in England, as a great and even a prophetic work. "The law embodies the story of a nation's development through the centuries," we read at the outset, "and it cannot be dealt with as if it contained only the axioms and corollaries of a book of mathematics." "The life of the law has not been logic; it has been experience." Together with the legal essays published before and after in the journals of the period, the book established, as Dean Pound has pointed out, that "functional" and relative view of the law now generally accepted as replacing the anatomical and morphological. Jurisprudence has been considered a self-sufficient science, with traditions all but God-given. Holmes discovered, by following a "right" or some other legal symbol to its early source, that the tradition was based often on some unreasoned survival that had lost all meaning. "The common law"—the phrase, from a later opinion, is famous—"is not a brooding omnipresence in the sky." Holmes emphasized the need of "thinking things rather than words." Pound says that he anticipated the teachers of today by thirty years or more. "The Epigoni could easily forget whose armor they were wearing and whose weapons they were wielding."

Justice Holmes's career as a jurist covers eras of rapid and organic social change and his eminence owes much to the insight—an insight very different from the piling of fact on fact—with which he has held the balance between history, experience, and timely necessity. He scrutinized the historical texts not for antiquarian reasons, not to discover an absolute—for in law, as in philosophy, he knew that he was not God—but for a concrete revelation of "man's destiny upon this earth." And looking back, he began to see the law at last as his constant and all-inclusive mistress: "A princess mightier than she who once wrought at Bayeux, eternally weaving into her web dim figures out of the ever lengthening past . . . disclosing every painful step and every world-shaking contest by which mankind has worked and fought its way from savage isolation to organic social life."

The fame that resulted from *The Common Law* led to a professorship at the Harvard Law School, and before the same year, 1882, was out, to an appointment to the Massachusetts Supreme Bench—"a stroke of lightning which changed all the course of my life." On this bench Holmes spent twenty fertile years, Associate Justice till 1899, Chief Justice till 1902. He managed his court with a practiced hand. But through these Boston years, as now, he wore an air of detachment which marked him, in his native town, with a kind of uncommonness, and so, in certain quarters, with a kind of suspicion. The "village" never queries its failures: Tom Blank is a queer duck, but he is the son of John Blank, the banker. Now Oliver Wendell Holmes, Jr., was never the son of the doctor. He was a peacock with shining plumage; he flew afield and consorted with famous English jurists, like Bryce and Sir Frederick Pollock. He climbed Alps with Leslie Stephen. He enjoyed free spirits, whether Back Bay brahmins, or Jews, or Roman Catholic priests. He invited a labor leader to his home. (Said the man: "You have changed my feeling. I used to see an enemy in every house.") With women he had the ease and gaiety of a Parisian or a Viennese, and sought their company. He was impatient with dullness and long-windedness, suggesting, when Chief Justice, that the lawyers of the state would greatly oblige him by taking a course in risqué French novels and so learn to speak in innuendo rather than at length. Yet, all the while, he was more absorbed by the discoveries of his own mind than by the privileges or limitations of the world about him. The mind accompanied his tall and elegant figure in Boston as elsewhere, a pervasive and skeptical presence at every feast.

At a dinner given by the Boston Bar Association two years before the nomination of Oliver Wendell Holmes by Roosevelt to the Supreme Bench of the United States, the Chief Justice, in his responsive speech, asked himself what he had to show for this half lifetime that had passed—"I look into my book, in which I keep a docket of the decisions . . . which fall to me to write, and find about a thousand cases, many of them upon trifling or transitory matters . . . a thousand cases, when one would have liked to study to the bottom and to say his say on every question which the law ever presented. . . . We are lucky enough if we can give a sample of our best and if in our hearts we can feel it has been nobly done."

This reads like a peroration: it was a prelude to the richest maturity of Holmes's life. Twenty-five more years on the Supreme Bench, a thousand more cases, and the Justice still on the firing line. Nearly half a century altogether that Holmes has been "living through," as judge, the wisdom whose foundations were laid before forty. The phrase is his partner, Shattuck's, spoken in a moment when it seemed to Holmes, after many honors, that he had tasted the full feast of the law: "Now you must live it through." One may relate the words to a comment of Dean Wigmore that Justice Holmes is the only one of the long list of judges of the American Supreme Courts who framed for himself a system of legal truths and general truths of life, and composed his opinions in harmony with the system.

The system was flexible because at bottom it was an attitude of tolerance based on insight into the complexity of human affairs. It has done more than any system of orthodoxies to make the Supreme Court a tribunal, as Professor Felix Frankfurter has said, where inevitable frictions between the individual and society, between the expanding powers of the states and nation could be fought out, instead of a deistic chamber operating by scholastic formulae. Holmes's wish has been ever to harmonize conflicting interests; to see where man's social desires come from, and where they are tending. (He maintains that the "little decisions" frequently reveal more of interstitial change in the tissue of the law than famous disputes about a telephone company.) Though he proceeds from the general to the particular, he repudiates finalities. Behind his generalizations are intuitions of reality.

Minority decisions have probably made Mr. Justice Holmes's reputation with the rank and file. Yet his famous dissents as well as his majority decisions have frequently run counter to his personal prejudice. "The decision of a gentleman," says a Boston friend. The decision of a poet would be equally true. For to Holmes a fire smolders at the core of things which makes them forever plastic and mobile. *Plus ça change, plus c'est la même chose,* says the French skeptic. Holmes feels that the universe may be "too great a swell to condescend to have a meaning," but he is bound to accept the temporary pattern. "The best test of truth is the power of the thought to get itself accepted in the competition of the market. . . . Every year, if not every day, we have to wager our salvation upon some prophecy based upon imperfect knowledge." The Justice never refuses such a wager, but, taking it up, he uses his mind as guide rather than as dictator. His conservative critics cannot point to a single self-interested opinion. His best friends cannot boast that he has ever decided things their way. Indeed, President Roosevelt, who appointed him because he imagined Holmes had "the right ideas"—i.e., T. R.'s—soon was taught a lesson in true judicial-mindedness by Holmes's dissent in Roosevelt's pet case against the Northern Securities merger.

Roosevelt used to urge young men to fight for *their* ideas. So did President Eliot, whose prejudices were the defect of his passion. Holmes the skeptic thinks one idea very like another, but Holmes the New Englander knows well the difference between one aim and another. So his counsel to young lawyers is: Do the handsome thing, young feller! Don't be content to be a lawyer, be a lawyer in the grand manner. If you are sailing an intellectual bark, prepare for rigors, and head for the Pole. Forget subjectivities, be a willing instrument. Wreak yourself upon life. "If you want to hit a bird on the wing, you must have all your will in a focus. . . . Every achievement is a bird on the wing." Key sentences which reveal a freedom from passion that has made the ideal judicial temper.

A judge of the Federal bench tells of driving with Justice Holmes to the Capitol one morning some years ago, in that neat brougham drawn by a fat cob, with a highly respectable colored coachman on the box, in which Holmes used to be recognized on the Washington streets. The Justice had got out of the carriage and was striding off, vigorous and loose-limbed, toward the dome when the younger man called out humorously: "Do justice, sir!" Holmes wheeled: "Come here, young feller!" and then, "I am not here to do justice. I am here to play the game according to the rules. When I was at the bar and Lowell used to beat, I'd say to him: 'Judge, your result may be good, but it's another game I undertook to play. I gave you a thrust in tierce and you countered with a bag of potatoes over my head.'"

When in some summer hour of ease in his home at Beverly Farms on the Massachusetts shore—an unpretentious Victorian house, with a gravel drive and formal flower-beds set with cannas and geraniums—he turns to Pepys' *Diary*—"this and Walpole's *Letters* are the two books if you don't want ideas, and don't want to waste your time"—he looks misty at the duel of two friends who fought for love. When he finds himself in the dentist's chair he recalls that fear of pain and rattling musketry which only the brave admit preceded the attack. His intimate talk still breaks into Civil War slang—"Shut your trap!"—his speeches and letters are full of war metaphors and allusions to this past which he says he "cannot bear to read about," perhaps because his remembered picture is too final to bear the intervention of historians, who describe how Sherman kept Lincoln waiting, and why great battles failed. Writing to Henry James, he is "firing away at high pressure with breech-loading speed." In a speech: "When once the dead fifers of thirty years since begin to play in my head, the laws are silent." In another: "Life is a roar of bargain and battle, but in the very heart of it there rises a mystical spiritual tone. . . . It transmutes the dull details into romance. It reminds us that our only but wholly adequate significance is as parts of the unimaginable whole."

This seasoned judge, this gallant gentleman of the old New England, is the most romantic of contemporary Americans. He starts off for the court every morning at 11:30 as if on an errand for the gods—whereas he is to listen to argument from 12:00 to 2:00; lunch from 2:00 to 2:30; sit again from 2:30 to 4:30. Judge Cardozo has used, of his sentences, the word *phosphorescence*. Always Holmes gives out light. When he returns from the court to the sober dignity of his old house on I Street—formerly it was on foot; now the Chief Justice is likely to drive him a part of the distance; but who can be sure that, disdaining his elevator, he will not still take his stairs two steps at a time?—he will be able, with the young secretary who guards the book-lined antechamber of his library, with the visitor, to search thought and make it glow. The secretary—a new jewel of the Harvard Law School every year—wears an exalted air. He must promise not to get engaged during the period. "But I reserve the right," says the Justice with a twinkle, "to die or resign." With this young mind the Justice twists the tail of the still recalcitrant cosmos, engaged in legal disputation, reads his opinions for criticism as modestly as if he were a novice. Sometimes, but rarely, there is a point of law to look up. For Holmes carries the law in his head, as a prophet the words of the Lord. And the Justice, in his own fine and ornamental script, answers every personal letter scrupulously, almost within the hour. "My messenger is waiting." Off it goes. The eye that falls upon the delicate missive in the cheap plethora of the morning mail has found treasure. Every page has some metaphysical touchstone, some literary epigram or casual heresy. "I must read *Twelfth Night* once more—a little girl tells me Shakespeare is long in getting to the point. I think we take ourselves too seriously."

Mr. Justice Holmes, who has permanently enriched our law, our literature, our philosophy—of whom another distinguished judge has said: "There is Holmes—and there are all the other judges"—takes himself far less seriously than any good Rotarian. The blithe nonchalance, that true humbleness in the face of acknowledged human vanities, seems to his friends a part of his unerring taste. But it provokes distrust in those who need the support of the rolling platitudes of the Fathers. Holmes bears his critics no grudge. His courtesy to his fellows, like his generosity, is basic, and he has an innocent heart. When one sees his gracious figure outlined against his bookshelves full of classics, with their spaces for the books the Lord will omit mentioning, and their gaps for the books of the future, one is struck by its unquenchable youth. The face has a fine fresh color, the voice, with its humorous vain echo of hesitation—mmm—that seems to set off the sparks in the eyes, has clarity and fervor. Maliciously it expunges the name of a popular New England poet from the slate of time, honestly it admits that gentlemen prefer blondes. But it will never allow our modern American idol, publicity, a niche in this hospitable library. If glory is here, she is hidden, diffused into a clear serenity, a scent of tender memory, a vital intellectual replenishment.

Yet do not think of Oliver Wendell Holmes as meagerly recompensed. He has found it well, he says, to have philosophy "the main wind of his life blowing from the side, instead of from behind." He has had his reward in the inspired performance of a daily task, in the constant siege of the eternal verities. Holmes was an infantry officer, at Ball's Bluff, but in the field of ideas he belongs to an arm more mobile. I see him as a light horseman, a fabulous skirmisher, a cavalier for all his "cold Puritan passion," who carries a pennon as well as a lance, and with it "that little flutter which means ideals."

Part Four

Democracy in Action

O America because you build for mankind I build for you.
        WALT WHITMAN: By Blue Ontario's Shore.

Driven from every other corner of the earth, freedom of thought and the right of private judgment in matters of conscience direct their course to this happy country as their last asylum. SAMUEL ADAMS, Speech, *Philadelphia, August 1, 1776.*

Asylum of the oppressed of every nation.
        Democratic Platform, 1856.

She of the open soul and open door,
With room about her hearth for all mankind!
        JAMES RUSSELL LOWELL: Commemoration Ode,
            delivered at Harvard, 1865.

We Americans are children of the crucible.
        THEODORE ROOSEVELT: Speech, *September 9, 1917.*

Nathaniel Hawthorne
(1804-1864)

THE STRANGE gray figure that appeared mysteriously as the champion of the oppressed in this story of Hawthorne must have been not unlike the author's old Puritan ancestor, Major William Hathorne described in *The Scarlet Letter* as the "grave, bearded, sable-coated and steeple-crowned progenitor." Hawthorne had, indeed, the quiet morality of the New England Puritan. He was born in Salem, Massachusetts, and spent much of a recluse life there, poking among the yellowed records of the Customs House where he was employed after 1846 and communing with the spirits of the old Puritans who haunted the place. He had had his college training at Bowdoin, where he knew Longfellow, and had early begun to commit to paper his visions of New England's past. After his marriage to Sophia Peabody in 1841 he lived for a time in Concord and had an intimate contact there with Emerson, Alcott, Thoreau, and other transcendentalists. His record of these years appears in *Mosses from an Old Manse* (1845) and also in *The Blithedale Romance* (1852), a satire on the Brook Farm experiment, with which he had little sympathy. He was Consul in Liverpool from 1853 to 1857, and his extended travels in Italy produced *The Marble Faun* in 1860. To the remarkable novels already mentioned should be added his popular *The House of Seven Gables* (1851). The first series of his *Twice-told Tales*—so-called because told first in magazines and then in book-form—was published in 1837, the second, in 1852.

The Gray Champion was first printed in the *New England Magazine* for January, 1835, and was included two years later in *Twice-told Tales*. In historical background, in vague, indefinite atmosphere, and in moral flavor it is characteristic of Hawthorne's stories. The episode retold is an echo in New England of the rebellion of the people against the "Second Stuart Tyranny" (see p. 60).

The Gray Champion

There was once a time when New England groaned under the actual pressure of heavier wrongs than those threatened ones which brought on the Revolution. James II, the bigoted successor of Charles the Voluptuous, had annulled the charters of all the colonies, and sent a harsh and unprincipled soldier to take away our liberties and endanger our religion. The administration of Sir Edmund Andros lacked scarcely a single characteristic of tyranny: a governor and council, holding office from the king, and wholly independent of the country; laws made and taxes levied without concurrence of the people, immediate or by their representatives; the rights of private citizens violated, and the titles of all landed property declared void; the voice of complaint stifled by restrictions on the press; and, finally, disaffection over-awed by the first band of mercenary troops that ever marched on our free soil. For two years our ancestors were kept in sullen submission by that filial love which had invariably secured their allegiance to the mother country, whether its head chanced to be a parliament, protector, or popish monarch. Till these evil times, however, such allegiance had been merely nominal, and the colonists had ruled themselves, enjoying far more freedom than is even yet the privilege ot the native subjects of Great Britain.

At length a rumor reached our shores that the Prince of Orange had ventured on an enterprise, the success of which would be the triumph of civil and religious rights, and the salvation of New England. It was but a doubtful whisper; it might be false, or the attempt might fail; and, in either case, the man that stirred against King James would lose his head. Still the intelligence produced a marked effect. The people smiled mysteriously in the streets, and threw bold glances at their oppressors; while, far and wide, there was a subdued and silent agitation, as if the slightest signal would rouse the whole land from its sluggish despondency.

Aware of their danger, the rulers resolved to avert it by an imposing display of strength, and perhaps to confirm their despotism by yet harsher measures. One afternoon in April 1689, Sir Edmund Andros and his favorite councilors, being warm with wine, assembled the red-coats of the governor's guard and made their appearance in the streets of Boston. The sun was near setting when the march commenced.

The roll of the drum, at that unquiet crisis, seemed to go through the streets less as the martial music of the soldiers than as a muster-call to the inhabitants themselves. A multitude, by various avenues, assembled in King Street, which was destined to be the scene, nearly a century afterwards, of another encounter between the troops of Britain and a people struggling against her tyranny. Though more than sixty years had elapsed since the Pilgrims came, this crowd of their descendants still showed the strong and somber features of their character, perhaps more strikingly in such a stern emergency than on happier occasions. There was the sober garb, the general severity of mien, the gloomy but undismayed expression, the scriptural forms of speech, and the confidence in Heaven's blessing on a righteous cause, which would have marked a band of the original Puritans when threatened by some peril of the wilderness. Indeed, it was not yet time for the old spirit to be extinct; since there were men in the street, that day, who had worshiped there beneath the trees before a house was reared to the God for whom they had become exiles. Old soldiers of the parliament were here too, smiling grimly at the thought that their aged arms might strike another blow against the house of Stuart. Here, also, were the veterans of King Philip's war, who had burned villages and slaughtered young and old with pious fierceness, while the godly souls throughout the land were helping them with prayer. Several ministers were scattered among the crowd, which, unlike all other mobs, regarded them with such reverence as if there were sanctity in their very garments. These holy men exerted their influence to quiet the people, but not to disperse them. Meantime, the purpose of the governor, in disturbing the peace of the town at a period when the slightest commotion might throw the country into a ferment, was almost the universal subject of inquiry, and variously explained.

"Satan will strike his master-stroke presently," cried some, "because he knoweth that his time is short. All our godly pastors are to be dragged to prison! We shall see them at a Smithfield fire in King Street!"

Hereupon the people of each parish gathered closer round their minister, who looked calmly upwards and assumed a more apostolic dignity, as well befitted a candidate for the highest honor of his profession, the crown of martyrdom. It was actually fancied, at that period, that New England might have a John Rogers of her own, to take the place of that worthy in the primer.

"The pope of Rome has given orders for a new St. Bartholomew!" cried others. "We are to be massacred, man and male child!"

Neither was this rumor wholly discredited, although the wiser class believed the governor's object somewhat less atrocious. His predecessor under the old charter, Bradstreet, a venerable companion of the first settlers, was known to be in town. There were grounds for conjecturing that Sir Edmund Andros intended, at once, to strike terror by a parade of military force, and to confound the opposite faction, by possessing himself of their chief.

"Stand firm for the old charter, governor!" shouted the crowd, seizing upon the idea. "The good old Governor Bradstreet!"

While this cry was at the loudest, the people were surprised by the well-known figure of Governor Bradstreet himself, a patriarch of nearly ninety, who appeared on the elevated steps of a door, and with characteristic mildness besought them to submit to the constituted authorities.

"My children," concluded this venerable person, "do nothing rashly. Cry not aloud, but pray for the welfare of New England, and expect patiently what the Lord will do in this matter."

The event was soon to be decided. All this time the roll of the drum had been approaching through Cornhill, louder and deeper, till with reverberations from house to house, and the regular tramp of martial footsteps, it burst into the street. A double rank of soldiers made their appearance, occupying the whole breadth of the passage, with shouldered matchlocks, and matches burning, so as to present a row of fires in the dusk. Their steady march was like the progress of a machine that would roll irresistibly over everything in its way. Next, moving slowly, with a confused clatter of hoofs on the pavement, rode a party of mounted gentlemen, the central figure being Sir Edmund Andros, elderly, but erect and soldier-like. Those around him were his favorite councilors, and the bitterest foes of New England. At his right hand rode Edward Randolph, our arch-enemy, that "blasted wretch," as Cotton Mather calls him, who achieved the downfall of our ancient government, and was followed with a sensible curse through life and to his grave. On the other side was Bullivant, scattering jests and mockery as he rode along. Dudley came behind, with a downcast look, dreading, as well he might, to meet the indignant gaze of the people, who beheld him, their only countryman by birth, among the oppressors of his native land. The captain of a frigate in the harbor, and two or three civil officers under the crown, were also there. But the figure which most attracted the public eye, and stirred up the deepest feeling, was the Episcopal clergyman of King's Chapel, riding haughtily among the magistrates in his priestly vestments, the fitting representative of prelacy and persecution, the union of Church and State, and all those abominations which had driven the Puritans to the wilderness. Another guard of soldiers, in double rank, brought up the rear.

The whole scene was a picture of the condition of New England, and its moral, the deformity of any government that does not grow out of the nature of things and the character of the people. On one side, the religious multitude, with their sad visages and dark attire, and on the other, the group of despotic rulers, with the high churchman in the midst, and here and there a crucifix at their bosoms, all magnificently clad, flushed with wine, proud of unjust authority, and scoffing at the universal groan. And the mercenary soldiers, waiting but the word to deluge the street with blood, showed the only means by which obedience could be secured.

"Oh! Lord of Hosts," cried a voice among the crowd, "provide a champion for thy people!"

This ejaculation was loudly uttered, and served as a herald's cry to introduce a remarkable personage. The crowd had rolled back, and were now huddled together nearly at the extremity of the street, while the soldiers had advanced no more than a third of its length. The intervening space was empty—a paved solitude between lofty edifices, which threw almost a twilight shadow over it. Suddenly there was seen the figure of an ancient man, who seemed to have emerged from among the people, and was walking by himself along the center of the street, to confront the armed band. He wore the old Puritan dress, a dark cloak and a steeple-crowned hat, in the fashion of at least fifty years before, with a heavy sword upon his thigh, but a staff in his hand, to assist the tremulous gait of age.

When at some distance from the multitude, the old man turned slowly round, displaying a face of antique majesty, rendered doubly venerable by the hoary beard that descended on his breast. He made a gesture at once of encouragement and warning, then turned again and resumed his way.

"Who is this gray patriarch?" asked the young men of their sires.

"Who is this venerable brother?" asked the old men among themselves.

But none could reply. The fathers of the people, those of four-score years and upwards, were disturbed, deeming it strange that they should forget one of such evident authority, whom they must have known in their early days, the associate of Winthrop, and all the old councilors, giving laws, and making prayers, and leading them against the savage. The elderly men ought to have remembered him, too, with locks as gray in their youth as their own were now. And the young! How could he have passed so utterly from their memories—that hoary sire, the relic of long departed times, whose awful benediction had surely been bestowed on their uncovered heads in childhood?

"Whence did he come? What is his purpose? Who can this old man be?" whispered the wondering crowd.

Meanwhile, the venerable stranger, staff in hand, was pursuing his solitary walk along the center of the street. As he drew near the advancing soldiers, and as the roll of their drum came full upon his ear, the old man raised himself to a loftier mien, while the decrepitude of age seemed to fall from his shoulders, leaving him in gray but unbroken dignity. Now, he marched onward with a warrior's step, keeping time to the military music. Thus the aged form advanced on one side, and the whole parade of soldiers and magistrates on the other, till, when scarcely twenty yards remained between, the old man grasped his staff by the middle, and held it before him like a leader's truncheon.

"Stand!" cried he.

The eye, the face, and attitude of command; the solemn yet warlike peal of that voice, fit either to rule a host in the battle-field or be raised to God in prayer, were irresistible. At the old man's word and outstretched arm the roll of the drum was hushed at once, and the advancing line stood still. A tremulous enthusiasm seized upon the multitude. That stately form, combining the leader and the saint, so gray, so dimly seen, in such an ancient garb, could only belong to some old champion of the righteous cause, whom the oppressor's drum had summoned from his grave. They raised a shout of awe and exultation, and looked for the deliverance of New England.

The governor, and the gentlemen of his party, perceiving themselves brought to an unexpected stand, rode hastily forward, as if they would have pressed their snorting and affrighted horses right against the hoary apparition. He, however, blenched not a step, but glancing his severe eye round the group, which half encompassed him, at last bent it sternly on Sir Edmund Andros. One would have thought that the dark old man was chief ruler there, and that the governor and council, with soldiers at their back, representing the whole power and authority of the crown, had no alternative but obedience.

"What does this old fellow here?" cried Edward Randolph, fiercely. "On, Sir Edmund! Bid the soldiers forward, and give the dotard the same choice that you give all his countrymen—to stand aside or be trampled on!"

"Nay, nay, let us show respect to the good grandsire," said Bullivant, laughing. "See you not he is some old round-headed dignitary who hath lain asleep these thirty years, and knows nothing of the change of times? Doubtless he thinks to put us down with a proclamation in Old Noll's name!"

"Are you mad, old man?" demanded Sir Edmund Andros, in loud and harsh tones. "How dare you stay the march of King James's governor?"

"I have stayed the march of a king himself ere now," replied the gray figure, with stern composure. "I am here, sir governor, because the cry of an oppressed people hath disturbed me in my secret place; and beseeching this favor earnestly of the Lord, it was vouchsafed me to appear once again on earth in the good old cause of his saints. And what speak ye of James? There is no longer a popish tyrant on the throne of England, and by tomorrow noon his name shall be a byword in this very street, where ye would make it a word of terror. Back, thou that wast a governor, back! With this night thy power is ended—tomorrow the prison!— back, lest I foretell the scaffold!"

The people had been drawing nearer and nearer, and drinking in the words of their champion, who spoke in accents long disused, like one unaccustomed to converse, except with the dead of many years ago. But his voice stirred their souls. They confronted the soldiers, not wholly without arms, and ready to convert the very stones of the street into deadly weapons. Sir Edmund Andros looked at the old man; then he cast his hard and cruel eye over the multitude, and beheld them burning with that lurid wrath so difficult to kindle or to quench; and again he fixed his gaze on the aged form, which stood obscurely in an open space, where neither friend nor foe had thrust himself. What were his thoughts he uttered no word which might discover. But whether the oppressor were overawed by the Gray Champion's look, or perceived his peril in the threatening attitude of the people, it is certain that he gave back, and ordered his soldiers to commence a slow and guarded retreat. Before another sunset, the governor, and all that rode so proudly with him, were prisoners, and long ere it was known that James had abdicated, King William was proclaimed throughout New England.

But where was the Gray Champion? Some reported that when the troops had gone from King Street, and the people were thronging tumultuously in their rear, Bradstreet, the aged governor, was seen to embrace a form more aged than his own. Others soberly affirmed, that while they marveled at the venerable grandeur of his aspect, the old man had faded from their eyes, melting slowly into the hues of twilight, till where he stood there was an empty space. But all agreed that the hoary shape was gone. The men of that generation watched for his reappearance, in sunshine and in twilight, but never saw him more, nor knew when his funeral passed, nor where his gravestone was.

And who was the Gray Champion? Perhaps his name might

be found in the records of that stern Court of Justice which passed a sentence, too mighty for the age, but glorious in all after-times, for its humbling lesson to the monarch and its high example to the subject. I have heard that, whenever the descendants of the Puritans are to show the spirit of their sires, the old man appears again. When eighty years had passed, he walked once more in King Street. Five years later, in the twilight of an April morning, he stood on the green, beside the meeting-house, at Lexington, where now the obelisk of granite, with a slab of slate inlaid, commemorates the first fallen of the Revolution. And when our fathers were toiling at the breastwork on Bunker's Hill, all through that night the old warrior walked his rounds. Long, long may it be ere he comes again! His hour is one of darkness, and adversity, and peril. But should domestic tyranny oppress us, or the invader's step pollute our soil, still may the Gray Champion come, for he is the type of New England's hereditary spirit; and his shadowy march, on the eve of danger, must ever be the pledge that New England's sons will vindicate their ancestry.

Edward Everett Hale
(1822-1909)

ONE OF THE MOST distinguished of the remarkable group of Unitarian clergymen which New England produced in the nineteenth century was Edward Everett Hale. He was born in Boston and educated at Harvard College, from which he was graduated in 1839. From 1842 to 1856 he was a pastor in Worcester, Massachusetts, and from 1856 to 1903, pastor in Boston; from this last date until his death he was chaplain for the United States Senate. During his nearly seventy years of preaching he yet found time for distinguished literary work. His best known books are *James Russell Lowell and His Friends* (1889), *Memories of a Hundred Years* (1902), and his *Autobiography* (1893; 1900). He wrote two very remarkable and popular stories, *My Double and How He Undid Me,* which appeared in *The Atlantic Monthly* for September, 1859, and *The Man Without a Country,* reprinted here.

The Man Without a Country appeared anonymously in *The Atlantic Monthly* for December, 1863, and became one of the great stories of America. In an article entitled *The Story of a Story* published in *The Writer* for June, 1897, the author tells how he came to write it. "At that time [i.e. 1863]," he wrote, "a western politician of some notoriety (Clement L. Vallandigham) had said that he did not wish to belong to the United States. General Burnside, who was in command of the district where he lived, arrested him and sent him over the border. . . . I had determined to show it is a very bad thing to have no country. I had to show this for a whole lifetime. So I invented a man who expressed this wish when a young man, and who died as an old man after he had tried his experiment." *The Man Without a Country* was written in the dark days of the Civil War, shortly after Lincoln's Gettysburg Address (see p. 182).

The Man Without a Country

I suppose that very few casual readers of the "New York Herald" of August 13, 1863, observed, in an obscure corner, among the "Deaths," the announcement:

"NOLAN. Died, on board U. S. Corvette 'Levant,' Lat. 2° 11′ S., Long. 131° W., on the 11th of May. PHILIP NOLAN."

I happened to observe it, because I was stranded at the old Mission House in Mackinaw, waiting for a Lake Superior steamer which did not choose to come, and I was devouring to the very stubble all the current literature I could get hold of, even down to the deaths and marriages in the "Herald." My memory for names and people is good, and the reader will see, as he goes on, that I had reason enough to remember Philip Nolan. There are hundreds of readers who would have paused at that announcement, if the officer of the "Levant" who reported it had chosen to make it thus: "Died, May 11, THE MAN WITHOUT A COUNTRY." For it was as "The Man Without a Country" that poor Philip Nolan had generally been known by the officers who had him in charge during some fifty years, as, indeed, by all the men who sailed under them. I dare say there is many a man who has taken wine with him once a fortnight, in a three years' cruise, who never knew that his name was "Nolan," or whether the poor wretch had any name at all.

There can now be no possible harm in telling this poor creature's story. Reason enough there has been till now, ever since Madison's administration went out in 1817, for very strict secrecy, the secrecy of honor itself, among the gentlemen of the navy who have had Nolan in successive charge. And certainly it speaks well for the *esprit de corps* of the profession, and the personal honor of its members, that to the press this man's story has been wholly unknown—and, I think, to the country at large also. I have reason to think, from some investigations I made in the Naval Archives when I was attached to the Bureau of Construction, that every official report relating to him was burned when Ross burned the public buildings at Washington. One of the Tuckers, or possibly one of the Watsons, had Nolan in charge at the end of the war; and when, on returning from his cruise, he reported at Washington to one of the Crowninshields—who was in the Navy Department when he came home—he found that the Department ignored the whole business. Whether they really knew nothing about it, or whether it was a "Non mi ricordo," determined on as a piece of policy, I do not know. But this I do know, that since 1817, and possibly before, no naval officer has mentioned Nolan in his report of a cruise.

But, as I say, there is no need for secrecy any longer. And now the poor creature is dead, it seems to me worth while to tell a little of his story, by way of showing young Americans of today what it is to be A MAN WITHOUT A COUNTRY.

·   ·   ·   ·   ·

Philip Nolan was as fine a young officer as there was in the "Legion of the West," as the Western division of our army was then called. When Aaron Burr made his first dashing expedition down to New Orleans in 1805, at Fort Massac, or somewhere above on the river, he met, as the Devil would have it, this gay, dashing, bright young fellow; at some dinner-party, I think. Burr marked him, talked to him, walked with him, took him a day or two's voyage in his flatboat, and, in short, fascinated him. For the next year, barrack-life was very tame to poor Nolan. He occasionally availed himself of the permission the great man had given him to write to him. Long, high-worded, stilted letters the poor boy wrote and rewrote and copied. But never a line did he have in reply from the gay deceiver. The other boys in the garrison sneered at him, because he sacrificed in this unrequited affection for a politician the time which they devoted to Monongahela, hazard, and high-low-jack. Bourbon, euchre, and poker were still unknown. But one day Nolan had his revenge. This time Burr came down the river not as an attorney seeking a place for his office, but as a disguised conqueror. He had defeated I know not how many district attorneys; he had dined at I know not how many public dinners; he had been heralded in I know not how many "Weekly Arguses," and it was rumored that he had an army behind him and an empire before him. It was a great day—his arrival—to poor Nolan. Burr had not been at the fort an hour before he sent for him. That evening he asked Nolan to take him out in his skiff, to show him a canebrake or a cottonwood tree, as he said—really to seduce him; and by the time the sail was over, Nolan was enlisted body and soul. From that time, though he did not yet know it, he lived as A MAN WITH-OUT A COUNTRY.

What Burr meant to do I know no more than you, dear reader. It is none of our business just now. Only, when the grand catastrophe came, and Jefferson and the House of Virginia of that day undertook to break on the wheel all the possible Clarences of the then House of York, by the great treason trial at Richmond, some of the lesser fry in that distant Mississippi Valley, which was further from us than Puget's Sound is today, introduced the like novelty on their provincial stage; and, to while away the monotony of the summer at Fort Adams, got up, for *spectacles*, a string of court-martials on the officers there. One and another of the colonels and majors were tried, and, to fill out the list, little Nolan, against whom, Heaven knows, there was evidence enough—that he was sick of the service, had been willing to be false to it, and would have obeyed any order to march anywhither with any one who would follow him had the order been signed "By command of His Exc. A. Burr." The courts dragged on. The big flies escaped—rightly, for all I know. Nolan was proved guilty enough, as I say. Yet you and I would never have heard of him, reader, but that, when the president of the court asked him at the close whether he wished to say anything to show that he had always been faithful to the United States, he cried out in a fit of frenzy:

"Damn the United States! I wish I may never hear of the United States again!"

I suppose he did not know how the words shocked old Colonel

Morgan, who was holding the court. Half the officers who sat in it had served through the Revolution, and their lives, not to say their necks, had been risked for the very idea which he so cavalierly cursed in his madness. He, on his part, had grown up in the West of those days, in the midst of "Spanish plot," "Orleans plot," and all the rest. He had been educated on a plantation where the finest company was a Spanish officer or a French merchant from Orleans. His education, such as it was, had been perfected in commercial expeditions to Vera Cruz, and I think he told me his father once hired an Englishman to be a private tutor for a winter on the plantation. He had spent half his youth with an older brother, hunting horses in Texas, and, in a word, to him "United States" was scarcely a reality. Yet he had been fed by "United States" for all the years since he had been in the army. He had sworn on his faith as a Christian to be true to "United States." It was "United States" which gave him the uniform he wore, and the sword by his side. Nay, my poor Nolan, it was only because "United States" had picked you out first as one of her own confidential men of honor that "A. Burr" cared for you a straw more than for the flat-boat men who sailed his ark for him. I do not excuse Nolan; I only explain to the reader why he damned his country, and wished he might never hear her name again.

He heard her name but once again. From that moment, September 23, 1807, till the day he died, May 11, 1863, he never heard her name again. For that half-century and more he was a man without a country.

Old Morgan, as I said, was terribly shocked. If Nolan had compared George Washington to Benedict Arnold, or had cried "God save King George," Morgan would not have felt worse. He called the court into his private room, and returned in fifteen minutes, with a face like a sheet, to say:

"Prisoner, hear the sentence of the Court! The Court decides, subject to the approval of the President that you never hear the name of the United States again."

Nolan laughed. But nobody else laughed. Old Morgan was too solemn, and the whole room was hushed dead as night for a minute. Even Nolan lost his swagger in a moment. Then Morgan added:

"Mr. Marshal, take the prisoner to Orleans in an armed boat, and deliver him to the naval commander there."

The marshal gave his orders and the prisoner was taken out of court.

"Mr. Marshal," continued old Morgan, "see that no one mentions the United States to the prisoner. Mr. Marshal, make my respects to Lieutenant Mitchell at Orleans, and request him to order that no one shall mention the United States to the prisoner while he is on board ship. You will receive your written orders from the officer on duty here this evening. The court is adjourned without day."

I have always supposed that Colonel Morgan himself took the proceedings of the court to Washington city and explained them to Mr. Jefferson. Certain it is that the President approved them—certain, that is, if I may believe the men who say they have seen his signature. Before the "Nautilus" got round from New Orleans to the northern Atlantic coast with the prisoner on board, the sentence had been approved, and he was a man without a country.

The plan then adopted was substantially the same which was necessarily followed ever after. Perhaps it was suggested by the necessity of sending him by water from Fort Adams and Orleans. The Secretary of the Navy—it must have been the first Crowninshield, though he is a man I do not remember—was requested to put Nolan on board a government vessel bound on a long cruise, and to direct that he should be only so far confined there as to make it certain that he never saw or heard of the country. We had few long cruises then, and the navy was very much out of favor; and as almost all of this story is traditional, as I have explained, I do not know certainly what his first cruise was. But the commander to whom he was intrusted—perhaps it was Tingey or Shaw, though I think it was one of the younger men (we are all old enough now)—regulated the etiquette and the precautions of the affair, and according to his scheme they were carried out, I suppose, till Nolan died.

When I was second officer of the "Intrepid," some thirty years after, I saw the original paper of instructions. I have been sorry ever since that I did not copy the whole of it. It ran, however, much in this way:

"WASHINGTON (with a date which
must have been late in 1807).

"*Sir*—You will receive from Lieutenant Neale the person of Philip
Nolan, late a lieutenant in the United States Army.

"This person on his trial by court-martial expressed, with an oath, the
wish that he might 'never hear of the United States again.'

"The Court sentenced him to have his wish fulfilled.

"For the present, the execution of the order is intrusted by the President to this Department.

"You will take the prisoner on board your ship, and keep him there
with such precautions as shall prevent his escape.

"You will provide him with such quarters, rations, and clothing as
would be proper for an officer of his late rank if he were a passenger
on your vessel on the business of his Government.

"The gentlemen on board will make any arrangements agreeable to
themselves regarding his society. He is to be exposed to no indignity of
any kind, nor is he ever unnecessarily to be reminded that he is a
prisoner.

"But under no circumstances is he ever to hear of his country or to
see any information regarding it; and you will especially caution all the
officers under your command to take care that, in the various indulgences which may be granted, this rule, in which his punishment is involved, shall not be broken.

"It is the intention of the Government that he shall never again see
the country which he has disowned. Before the end of your cruise you
will receive orders which will give effect to this intention.

"Respectfully yours,

"W. SOUTHARD, for the
"Secretar" of the Navy."

If I had only preserved the whole of this paper, there would be
no break in the beginning of my sketch of this story. For Captain
Shaw, if it were he, handed it to his successor in the charge, and
he to his, and I suppose the commander of the "Levant" has it
today as his authority for keeping this man in this mild custody.

The rule adopted on board the ships on which I have met
"the man without a country" was, I think, transmitted from the
beginning. No mess liked to have him permanently, because his
presence cut off all talk of home or of the prospect of return, of
politics or letters, of peace or of war—cut off more than half the
talk men like to have at sea. But it was always thought too hard

that he should never meet the rest of us, except to touch hats, and we finally sank into one system. He was not permitted to talk with the men unless an officer was by. With officers he had unrestrained intercourse, as far as they and he chose. But he grew shy, though he had favorites: I was one. Then the captain always asked him to dinner on Monday. Every mess in succession took up the invitation in its turn. According to the size of the ship, you had him at your mess more or less often at dinner. His breakfast he ate in his own stateroom—which was where a sentinel or somebody on the watch could see the door. And whatever else he ate or drank, he ate or drank alone. Sometimes, when the marines or sailors had any special jollification, they were permitted to invite "Plain-Buttons," as they called him. Then Nolan was sent with some officer, and the men were forbidden to speak of home while he was there. I believe the theory was that the sight of his punishment did them good. They called him "Plain-Buttons" because, while he always chose to wear a regulation army uniform, he was not permitted to wear the army button, for the reason that it bore either the initials or the insignia of the country he had disowned.

I remember, soon after I joined the navy, I was on shore with some of the older officers from our ship and from the "Brandywine," which we had met at Alexandria. We had leave to make a party and go up to Cairo and the Pyramids. As we jogged along (you went on donkeys then), some of the gentlemen (we boys called them "Dons," but the phrase was long since changed) fell to talking about Nolan, and some one told the system which was adopted from the first about his books and other reading. As he was almost never permitted to go on shore, even though the vessel lay in port for months, his time at the best hung heavy; and everybody was permitted to lend him books if they were not published in America and made no allusion to it. These were common enough in the old days, when people in the other hemisphere talked of the United States as little as we do of Paraguay. He had almost all the foreign papers that came into the ship, sooner or later; only somebody must go over them first, and cut out any advertisement or stray paragraph that alluded to America. This was a little cruel sometimes, when the back of what was cut out might be as innocent as Hesiod. Right in the midst of one of Napoleon's battles, or one of Canning's speeches, poor Nolan would find a great hole, because on the back of the page of that paper there had been an advertisement of a packet for New York, or a scrap from the President's message. I say this was the first time I ever heard of this plan, which afterward I had enough and more than enough to do with. I remember it, because poor Phillips, who was of the party, as soon as the allusion to reading was made, told a story of something which happened at the Cape of Good Hope on Nolan's first voyage; and it is the only thing I ever knew of that voyage. They had touched at the Cape, and had done the civil thing with the English Admiral and the fleet, and then, leaving for a long cruise up the Indian Ocean, Phillips had borrowed a lot of English books from an officer, which, in those days, as indeed in these, was quite a windfall. Among them, as the Devil would order, was the "Lay of the Last Minstrel," which they had all of them heard of, but which most of them had never seen. I think it could not have been published long. Well, nobody thought there could be any risk of anything national in that, though Phillips swore old Shaw had cut out the "Tempest" from Shakespeare before he let Nolan have it, because he said "the Bermudas ought to be ours, and, by Jove, should be one day." So Nolan was permitted to join the circle one afternoon when a lot of them sat on deck smoking and reading aloud. People do not do such things so often now, but when I was young we got rid of a great deal of time so. Well, so it happened that in his turn Nolan took the book and read to the others, and he read very well, as I know. Nobody in the circle knew a line of the poem, only it was all magic and Border chivalry, and was a thousand years ago. Poor Nolan read steadily through the fifth canto, stopped a minute and drank something, and then began, without a thought of what was coming.

> "Breathes there the man, with soul so dead,
> Who never to himself hath said"—

It seems impossible to us that anybody ever heard this for the first time; but all these fellows did then, and poor Nolan himself went on, still unconsciously or mechanically:

> "This is my own, my native land!"

Then they all saw something was to pay; but he expected to get through, I suppose, turned a little pale, but plunged on:

> "Whose heart hath ne'er within him burned,
>   As home his footsteps he hath turned
>   From wandering on a foreign strand?—
>   If such there breathe, go, mark him well"—

By this time the men were all beside themselves, wishing there was any way to make him turn over two pages. But he had not quite presence of mind for that; he gagged a little, colored crimson, and staggered on:

> "For him no minstrel raptures swell;
>   High though his titles, proud his name,
>   Boundless his wealth as wish can claim,
>   Despite these titles, power, and pelf,
>   The wretch, concentred all in self"—

and here the poor fellow choked, could not go on, but started up, swung the book into the sea, vanished into his stateroom, "And, by Jove," said Phillips, "we did not see him for two months again. And I had to make up some beggarly story to that English surgeon why I did not return his Walter Scott to him."

The story shows about the time when Nolan's braggadocio must have broken down. At first, they said, he took a very high tone, considered his imprisonment a mere farce, affected to enjoy the voyage, and all that; but Phillips said that after he came out of his stateroom he never was the same man again. He never read aloud again, unless it was the Bible or Shakespeare, or something else he was sure of. But it was not that merely. He never entered in with the other young men exactly as a companion again. He was always shy afterward, when I knew him, very seldom spoke, unless he was spoken to, except to a very few friends. He lighted up occasionally—I remember late in his life hearing him fairly eloquent on something which had been suggested to him by one of Fléchier's sermons—but generally he had the nervous, tired look of a heart-wounded man.

When Captain Shaw was coming home—if, as I say, it was Shaw—rather to the surprise of everybody they made one of the

Windward Islands, and lay off and on for nearly a week. The boys said the officers were sick of salt junk, and meant to have turtle soup before they came home. But after several days the "Warren" came to the same rendezvous; they exchanged signals, she sent to Phillips and these homeward-bound men letters and papers, and told them she was outward-bound, perhaps to the Mediterranean, and took poor Nolan and his traps on the boat back to try his second cruise. He looked very blank when he was told to get ready to join her. He had known enough of the signs of the sky to know that till that moment he was going "home." But this was a distinct evidence of something he had not thought of, perhaps—that there was no going home for him, even to a prison. And this was the first of some twenty such transfers, which brought him sooner or later into half our best vessels, but which kept him all his life at least some hundred miles from the country he had hoped he might never hear of again.

It may have been on that second cruise—it was once when he was up the Mediterranean—that Mrs. Graff, the celebrated Southern beauty of those days, danced with him. They had been lying a long time in the Bay of Naples, and the officers were very intimate in the English fleet, and there had been great festivities, and our men thought they must give a great ball on board the ship. How they ever did it on board the "Warren" I am sure I do not know. Perhaps it was not the "Warren," or perhaps ladies did not take up so much room as they do now. They wanted to use Nolan's stateroom for something, and they hated to do it without asking him to the ball; so the captain said they might ask him if they would be responsible that he did not talk with the wrong people, "who would give him intelligence." So the dance went on, the finest party that had ever been known, I dare say; for I never heard of a man-of-war ball that was not. For ladies they had the family of the American consul, one or two travelers who had adventured so far, and a nice bevy of English girls and matrons, perhaps Lady Hamilton herself.

Well, different officers relieved each other in standing and talking with Nolan in a friendly way, so as to be sure that nobody else spoke to him. The dancing went on with spirit, and after a while even the fellows who took this honorary guard of Nolan ceased to fear any *contretemps*. Only when some English lady—

Lady Hamilton, as I said, perhaps—called for a set of "American dances," an odd thing happened. Everybody then danced contradances. The black band, nothing loath, conferred as to what "American dances" were and started off with "Virginia Reel," which they followed with "Money-Musk," which, in its turn in those days, should have been followed by "The Old Thirteen." But just as Dick, the leader, tapped for his fiddles to begin, and bent forward, about to say, in true Negro state, " 'The Old Thirteen,' gentlemen and ladies!" as he had said " 'Virginny Reel,' if you please!" and " 'Money-Musk,' if you please!" the captain's boy tapped him on the shoulder, whispered to him, and he did not announce the name of the dance. He merely bowed, began on the air, and they all fell to—the officers teaching the English girls the figure, but not telling them why it had no name.

But that is not the story I started to tell. As the dancing went on, Nolan and our fellows all got at ease, as I said—so much so, that it seemed quite natural for him to bow to that splendid Mrs. Graff, and say:

"I hope you have not forgotten me, Miss Rutledge. Shall I have the honor of dancing?"

He did it so quickly that Fellows, who was with him, could not hinder him. She laughed and said: "I am not Miss Rutledge any longer, Mr. Nolan, but I will dance all the same," just nodded to Fellows, as if to say he must leave Mr. Nolan to her, and led him off to the place where the dance was forming.

Nolan thought he had got his chance. He had known her at Philadelphia, and at other places had met her, and this was a godsend. You could not talk in contra-dances, as you do in cotillons, or even in the pauses of waltzing, but there were chances for tongues and sounds, as well as for eyes and blushes. He began with her travels, and Europe, and Vesuvius, and the French, and then, when they had worked down, and had that long talking time at the bottom of the set, he said boldly, a little pale, she said, as she told me the story years after:

"And what do you hear from home, Mrs. Graff?"

And that splendid creature looked through him. Jove! how she must have looked through him!

"Home!! Mr. Nolan!!! I thought you were the man who never wanted to hear of home again!" And she walked directly up the deck to her husband, and left poor Nolan alone, as he always was. He did not dance again. I cannot give any history of him in order; nobody can now, and, indeed, I am not trying to.

These are the traditions, which I sort out, as I believe them, from the myths which have been told about this man for forty years. The lies that have been told about him are legion. The fellows used to say he was the "Iron Mask," and poor George Pons went to his grave in the belief that this was the author of "Junius," who was being punished for his celebrated libel on Thomas Jefferson. Pons was not very strong in the historical line.

A happier story than either of these I have told is of the war. That came along soon after. I have heard this affair told in three or four ways, and, indeed, it may have happened more than once. But which ship it was on I cannot tell. However, in one, at least, of the great frigate duels with the English, in which the navy was really baptized, it happened that a round shot from the enemy entered one of our ports square, and took right down the officer of the gun himself, and almost every man of the gun's crew. Now you may say what you choose about courage, but that is not a nice thing to see. But, as the men who were not killed picked themselves up, and as they and the surgeon's people were carrying off the bodies, there appeared Nolan, in his shirt-sleeves, with the rammer in his hand, and, just as if he had been the officer, told them off with authority—who should go to the cockpit with the wounded men, who should stay with him—perfectly cheery, and with that way which makes men feel sure all is right and is going to be right. And he finished loading the gun with his own hands, aimed it, and bade the men fire. And there he stayed, captain of that gun, keeping those fellows in spirits, till the enemy struck, sitting on the carriage while the gun was cooling, though he was exposed all the time, showing them easier ways to handle heavy shot, making the raw hands laugh at their own blunders, and when the gun cooled again, getting it loaded and fired twice as often as any other gun on the ship. The captain walked forward by way of encouraging the men, and Nolan touched his hat and said:

"I am showing them how we do this in the artillery, sir."

And this is the part of the story where all the legends agree. The commodore said:

"I see you do, and I thank you, sir; and I shall never forget this day, sir, and you never shall, sir."

And after the whole thing was over, and he had the English-man's sword, in the midst of the state and ceremony of the quarterdeck, he said:

"Where is Mr. Nolan? Ask Mr. Nolan to come here."

And when Nolan came, he said:

"Mr. Nolan, we are all very grateful to you today; you are one of us today; you will be named in the dispatches."

And then the old man took off his own sword of ceremony, and gave it to Nolan, and made him put it on. The man told me this who saw it. Nolan cried like a baby, and well he might. He had not worn a sword since that infernal day at Fort Adams. But always afterward, on occasions of ceremony, he wore that quaint old French sword of the commodore's.

The captain did mention him in the dispatches. It was always said he asked that he might be pardoned. He wrote a special letter to the Secretary of War. But nothing ever came of it. As I said, that was about the time when they began to ignore the whole transaction at Washington, and when Nolan's imprison-ment began to carry itself on because there was nobody to stop it without any new orders from home.

I have heard it said that he was with Porter when he took possession of the Nukahiva Islands. Not this Porter, you know, but old Porter, his father, Essex Porter—that is the old Essex Porter, not this Essex. As an artillery officer, who had seen service in the West, Nolan knew more about fortifications, embrasures, ravelins, stockades, and all that, than any of them did; and he worked with a right good will in fixing that battery all right. I have always thought it was a pity Porter did not leave him in command there with Gamble. That would have settled all the question about his punishment. We should have kept the islands, and at this moment we should have one station in the Pacific Ocean. Our French friends, too, when they wanted this little watering-place, would have found it was preoccupied. But Madi-son and the Virginians, of course, flung all that away.

All that was near fifty years ago. If Nolan was thirty then, he must have been near eighty when he died. He looked sixty when he was forty. But he never seemed to me to change a hair afterward. As I imagine his life, from what I have seen and heard of it, he must have been in every sea, and yet almost never on land. He must have known, in a formal way, more officers in our service than any man living knows. He told me once, with a grave smile, that no man in the world lived so methodical a life as he. "You know the boys say I am the Iron Mask, and you know how busy he was." He said it did not do for any one to try to read all the time, more than to do anything else all the time, but that he read just five hours a day. "Then," he said, "I keep up my notebooks, writing in them at such and such hours from what I have been reading, and I include in these my scrap-books." These were very curious indeed. He had six or eight, of different subjects. There was one of History, one of Natural Science, one which he called "Odds and Ends." But they were not merely books of extracts from newspapers. They had bits of plants and ribbons, shells tied on, and carved scraps of bone and wood, which he had taught the men to cut for him, and they were beautifully illustrated. He drew admirably. He had some of the funniest drawings there, and some of the most pathetic that I have ever seen in my life. I wonder who will have Nolan's scrap-books.

Well, he said his reading and his notes were his profession, and that they took five hours and two hours respectively of each day. "Then," said he, "every man should have a diversion as well as a profession. My Natural History is my diversion." That took two hours a day more. The men used to bring him birds and fish, but on a long cruise he had to satisfy himself with centipedes and cockroaches and such small game. He was the only naturalist I ever met who knew anything about the habits of the housefly and the mosquito. All those people can tell you whether they are *Lepidoptera* or *Steptopotera;* but as for telling you how you can get rid of them, or how they get away from you when you strike at them—why, Linnæus knew as little of that as John Foy, the idiot, did.

These nine hours made Nolan's regular daily "occupation." The rest of the time he talked or walked. Till he grew very old, he went aloft a great deal. He always kept up his exercise, and I never heard that he was ill. If any other man was ill, he was the kindest nurse in the world; and he knew more than half the surgeons do. Then, if anybody was sick or died, or if the captain wanted him to, on any other occasion, he was always ready to read prayers. I have said that he read beautifully.

My own acquaintance with Philip Nolan began six or eight years after the English war, on my first voyage after I was appointed a midshipman. It was in the first days after our Slave-Trade treaty, while the Reigning House, which was still the House of Virginia, had still a sort of sentimentalism about the suppression of the horrors of the Middle Passage, and something was sometimes done that way. We were in the South Atlantic on that business. From the time I joined, I believe I thought Nolan was a sort of lay chaplain—a chaplain with a blue coat. I never asked about him. Everything in the ship was strange to me. I knew it was green to ask questions, and I suppose I thought there was a "Plain-Buttons" on every ship. We had him to dine in our mess once a week, and the caution was given that on that day nothing was to be said about home. But if they had told us not to say anything about the planet Mars or the Book of Deuteronomy, I should not have asked why; there were a great many things which seemed to me to have as little reason.

I first came to understand anything about "the man without a country" one day when we overhauled a dirty little schooner which had slaves on board. An officer was sent to take charge of her, and, after a few minutes, he sent back his boat to ask that someone might be sent him who could speak Portuguese. We were all looking over the rail when the message came, and we all wished we could interpret, when the captain asked who spoke Portuguese. But none of the officers did, and just as the captain was sending forward to ask if any of the people could, Nolan stepped out and said he should be glad to interpret, if the captain wished, as he understood the language. The captain thanked him, fitted out another boat with him, and in this boat it was my luck to go. When we got there it was such a scene as you seldom see, and never want to. Nastiness beyond account, and chaos run loose in the midst of the nastiness. There were not a great many of the Negroes; but by way of making what there were understand that they were free, Vaughan had had their handcuffs and anklecuffs knocked off, and, for convenience' sake, was putting them upon the rascals of the schooner's crew.

The Negroes were, most of them, out of the hold, and swarming all round the dirty deck, with a central throng surrounding Vaughan and addressing him in every dialect and *patois* of a dialect, from the Zulu click up to the Parisian of Beledeljereed.

As we came on deck, Vaughan looked down from a hogshead, on which he had mounted in desperation, and said:

"For God's love, is there anybody who can make these wretches understand something? The men gave them rum, and that did not quiet them. I knocked that big fellow down twice, and that did not soothe him. And then I talked Choctaw to all of them together, and I'll be hanged if they understood that as well as they understood the English."

Nolan said he could speak Portuguese, and one or two fine-looking Kroomen were dragged out, who, as it had been found already, had worked for the Portuguese on the coast at Fernando Po.

"Tell them they are free," said Vaughan. "And tell them that these rascals are to be hanged as soon as we can get rope enough."

Nolan "put that into Spanish"—that is, he explained it in such Portuguese as the Kroomen could understand, and they in turn to such of the Negroes as could understand them. Then there was such a yell of delight, clinching of fists, leaping and dancing, kissing of Nolan's feet, and a general rush made to the hogshead by way of spontaneous worship of Vaughan, as the *deus ex machina* of the occasion.

"Tell them," said Vaughan, well pleased, "that I will take them all to Cape Palmas."

This did not answer so well. Cape Palmas was practically as far from the homes of most of them as New Orleans or Rio Janeiro was—that is, they would be eternally separated from home there. And their interpreters, as we could understand, instantly said, *"Ah, non Palmas,"* and began to propose infinite other expedients in most voluble language. Vaughan was rather disappointed at this result of his liberality, and asked Nolan eagerly what they said. The drops stood on poor Nolan's white forehead, as he hushed the men down, and said:

"He says, 'Not Palmas.' He says, 'Take us home, take us to our own country, take us to our own house, take us to our own pickaninnies and our own women.' He says he has an old father and mother who will die if they do not see him. And this one says he left his people all sick, and paddled down to Fernando to beg the white doctor to come and help them, and that these devils caught him in the bay just in sight of home, and that he has never seen anybody from home since then. And this one says," choked out Nolan, "that he has not heard a word from his home in six months, while he has been locked up in that infernal barracoon."

Vaughan always said he grew gray himself while Nolan struggled through this interpretation. I, who did not understand anything of the passion involved in it, saw that the very elements were melting with fervent heat, and that something was to pay somewhere. Even the Negroes themselves stopped howling, as they saw Nolan's agony and Vaughan's almost equal agony of sympathy. As quick as he could get words, he said:

"Tell them yes, yes, yes; tell them they shall go to the Mountains of the Moon if they will. If I sail the schooner through the Great White Desert, they shall go home!"

And after some fashion Nolan said so. And then they all fell to kissing him again, and wanted to rub his nose with theirs.

But he could not stand it long, and, getting Vaughan to say he might go back, he beckoned me down into our boat. As we lay back in the stern-sheets and the men gave way, he said to me: "Youngster, let that show you what it is to be without a family, without a home, and without a country. And if you are ever tempted to say a word or to do a thing that shall put a bar between you and your family, your home, and your country, pray God in His mercy to take you that instant home to His own heaven. Stick by your family, boy; forget you have a self, while you do everything for them. Think of your home, boy; write and send and talk about it. Let it be nearer and nearer to your thought the further you have to travel from it; and rush back to it when you are free, as that poor black slave is doing now. And for your country, boy," and the words rattled in his throat, "and for that flag," and he pointed to the ship, "never dream a dream but of serving her as she bids you, though the service carry you through a thousand hells. No matter what happens to you, no matter who flatters you or who abuses you,

never look at another flag, never let a night pass but you pray
God to bless that flag. Remember, boy, that behind all these men
you have to do with, behind officers, and government, and people even, there is the Country Herself, your Country, and that
you belong to Her as you belong to your own mother. Stand
by Her, boy, as you would stand by your mother, if those devils
there had got hold of her today!"

I was frightened to death by his calm, hard passion, but I
blundered out that I would, by all that was holy, and that I had
never thought of doing anything else. He hardly seemed to hear
me, but he did, almost in a whisper, say: "Oh, if anybody had
said so to me when I was of your age!"

I think it was this half-confidence of his, which I never abused,
for I never told this story till now, which afterward made us
great friends. He was very kind to me. Often he sat up, or even
got up, at night, to walk the deck with me, when it was my
watch. He explained to me a great deal of my mathematics, and
I owe to him my taste for mathematics. He lent me books, and
helped me about my reading. He never alluded so directly to
his story again, but from one and another officer I have learned,
in thirty years, what I am telling. When we parted from him in
St. Thomas harbor at the end of our cruise I was more sorry
than I can tell. I was very glad to meet him again in 1830; and
later in life, when I thought I had some influence in Washington, I moved heaven and earth to have him discharged. But it
was like getting a ghost out of prison. They pretended there was
no such man, and never was such a man. They will say so at the
Department now! Perhaps they do not know. It will not be the
first thing in the service of which the Department appears to
know nothing!

There is a story that Nolan met Burr once on one of our
vessels, when a party of Americans came on board in the Mediterranean. But this I believe to be a lie; or, rather, it is a myth,
ben trovato, involving a tremendous blowing-up with which he
sunk Burr, asking him how he liked to be "without a country."
But it is clear from Burr's life that nothing of the sort could
have happened, and I mention this only as an illustration of the
stories which get a-going where there is the least mystery at
bottom.

So poor Philip Nolan had his wish fulfilled. I know but one fate more dreadful: it is the fate reserved for those men who shall have one day to exile themselves from their country because they have attempted her ruin, and shall have at the same time to see the prosperity and honor to which she rises when she has rid herself of them and their iniquities. The wish of poor Nolan, as we all learned to call him, not because his punishment was too great, but because his repentance was so clear, was precisely the wish of every Bragg and Beauregard who broke a soldier's oath two years ago, and of every Maury and Barron who broke a sailor's. I do not know how often they have repented. I do know that they have done all that in them lay that they might have no country, that all the honors, associations, memories, and hopes which belong to "country" might be broken up into little shreds and distributed to the winds. I know, too, that their punishment, as they vegetate through what is left of life to them in wretched Boulognes and Leicester Squares, where they are destined to upbraid each other till they die, will have all the agony of Nolan's, with the added pang that every one who sees them will see them to despise and to execrate them. They will have their wish, like him.

For him, poor fellow, he repented of his folly, and then, like a man, submitted to the fate he had asked for. He never intentionally added to the difficulty or delicacy of the charge of those who had him in hold. Accidents would happen, but they never happened from his fault. Lieutenant Truxton told me that, when Texas was annexed, there was a careful discussion among the officers, whether they should get hold of Nolan's handsome set of maps and cut Texas out of it—from the map of the world and the map of Mexico. The United States had been cut out when the atlas was bought for him. But it was voted, rightly enough, that to do this would be virtually to reveal to him what had happened, or, as Harry Cole said, to make him think old Burr had succeeded. So it was from no fault of Nolan's that a great botch happened at my own table, when, for a short time, I was in command of the "George Washington" corvette, on the South American station. We were lying in the La Plata, and some of the officers, who had been on shore and had just joined again, were entertaining us with accounts of their mis-

adventures in riding the half-wild horses of Buenos Ayres. Nolan
was at table, and was in an unusually bright and talkative mood.
Some story of a tumble reminded him of an adventure of his
own when he was catching wild horses in Texas with his adventurous cousin, at a time when he must have been quite a
boy. He told the story with a good deal of spirit—so much so
that the silence which often follows a good story hung over the
table for an instant, to be broken by Nolan himself. For he asked
perfectly unconsciously:

"Pray, what has become of Texas? After the Mexicans got their
independence, I thought that province of Texas would come
forward very fast. It is really one of the finest regions on earth;
it is the Italy of this continent. But I have not seen or heard a
word of Texas for near twenty years."

There were two Texan officers at the table. The reason he had
never heard of Texas was that Texas and her affairs had been
painfully cut out of his newspapers since Austin began his
settlements, so that, while he read of Honduras and Tamaulipas,
and, till quite lately, of California, this virgin province, in which
his brother had traveled so far, and, I believe, had died, had
ceased to be to him. Waters and Williams, the two Texas men,
looked grimly at each other and tried not to laugh. Edward
Morris had his attention attracted by the third link in the chain
of the captain's chandelier. Watrous was seized with a convulsion
of sneezing. Nolan himself saw that something was to pay, he
did not know what. And I, as master of the feast, had to say:

"Texas is out of the map, Mr. Nolan. Have you seen Captain
Back's curious account of Sir Thomas Roe's Welcome?"

After that cruise I never saw Nolan again. I wrote to him at
least twice a year, for in that voyage we became even confidentially intimate; but he never wrote to me. The other men tell
me that in those fifteen years he *aged* very fast, as well he might,
indeed, but that he was still the same gentle, uncomplaining,
silent sufferer that he ever was, bearing as best he could his self-
appointed punishment—rather less social, perhaps, with new men
whom he did not know, but more anxious, apparently, than
ever to serve and befriend and teach the boys, some of whom
fairly seemed to worship him. And now it seems the dear old

fellow is dead. He has found a home at last, and a country.

Since writing this, and while considering whether or no I would print it, as a warning to the young Nolans and Vallandighams and Tatnalls of today, I have received from Danforth, who is on board the "Levant," a letter which gives an account of Nolan's last hours. It removes all my doubts about telling this story.

To understand the first words of the letter, the non-professional reader should remember that after 1817 the position of every officer who had Nolan in charge was one of the greatest delicacy. The government had failed to renew the order of 1807 regarding him. What was a man to do? Should he let him go? What, then, if he were called to account by the Department for violating the order of 1807? Should he keep him? What, then, if Nolan should be liberated some day, and should bring an action for false imprisonment or kidnaping against every man who had had him in charge? I urged and pressed this upon Southard, and I have reason to think that other officers did the same thing. But the Secretary always said, as they so often do at Washington, that there were no special orders to give, and that we must act on our own judgment. That means, "If you succeed, you will be sustained; if you fail, you will be disavowed." Well, as Danforth says, all that is over now, though I do not know but I expose myself to a criminal prosecution on the evidence of the very revelation I am making.

Here is the letter:

"'Levant,' 2° 2′ S. @ 131° W.

"*Dear Fred*—I try to find heart and life to tell you that it is all over with dear old Nolan. I have been with him on this voyage more than I ever was, and I can understand wholly now the way in which you used to speak of the dear old fellow. I could see that he was not strong, but I had no idea the end was so near. The doctor has been watching him very carefully, and yesterday morning came to me and told me that Nolan was not so well, and had not left his stateroom—a thing I never remember before. He had let the doctor come and see him as he lay there—the first time the doctor had been in the stateroom—and he said he should like to see me. Oh, dear! do you remember the mysteries we boys used to invent about his room in the old 'Intrepid' days? Well, I

went in, and there, to be sure, the poor fellow lay in his berth, smiling
pleasantly as he gave me his hand, but looking very frail. I could not
help a glance round, which showed me what a little shrine he had made
of the box he was lying in. The Stars and Stripes were triced up above
and around a picture of Washington, and he had painted a majestic
eagle, with lightnings blazing from his beak and his foot just clasping
the whole globe, which his wings overshadowed. The dear old boy saw
my glance, and said, with a sad smile, 'Here, you see, I have a country!'
And then he pointed to the foot of his bed, where I had not seen before
a great map of the United States, as he had drawn it from memory, and
which he had there to look upon as he lay. Quaint, queer old names
were on it, in large letters: 'Indiana Territory,' 'Mississippi Territory,'
and 'Louisiana Territory,' as I suppose our fathers learned such things.
But the old fellow had patched in Texas, too; he had carried his western
boundary all the way to the Pacific, but on that shore he had defined
nothing.

" 'Oh, Danforth,' he said, 'I know I am dying. I cannot get home.
Surely you will tell me something now? Stop! Stop! Do not speak till I
say what I am sure you know, that there is not in this ship, that there
is not in America—God bless her!—a more loyal man than I. There
cannot be a man who loves the old flag as I do, or prays for it as I do,
or hopes for it as I do. There are thirty-four stars in it now, Danforth. I
thank God for that, though I do not know what their names are. There
has never been one taken away; I thank God for that. I know by that
that there has never been any successful Burr. Oh, Danforth, Danforth,'
he sighed out, 'how like a wretched night's dream a boy's idea of personal fame or of separate sovereignty seems, when one looks back on it
after such a life as mine! But tell me—tell me something—tell me everything, Danforth, before I die!'

"Ingham, I swear to you that I felt like a monster that I had not told
him everything before. Danger or no danger, delicacy or no delicacy,
who was I, that I should have been acting the tyrant all this time over
this dear, sainted old man, who had years ago expiated, in his whole
manhood's life, the madness of a boy's treason? 'Mr. Nolan,' said I, 'I
will tell you everything you ask about. Only, where shall I begin?'

"Oh, the blessed smile that crept over his white face! And he pressed
my hand and said, 'God bless you! Tell me their names,' he said, and
he pointed to the stars on the flag. 'The last I know is Ohio. My father
lived in Kentucky. But I have guessed Michigan and Indiana and Mississippi—that was where Fort Adams is. They make twenty. But where

are your other fourteen? You have not cut up any of the old ones, I hope?'

"Well, that was not a bad text, and I told him the names in as good order as I could, and he bade me take down his beautiful map and draw them in as I best could with my pencil. He was wild with delight about Texas—told me how his cousin died there; he had marked a gold cross near where he supposed his grave was; and he had guessed at Texas. Then he was delighted as he saw California and Oregon. That, he said, he had suspected partly, because he had never been permitted to land on that shore, though the ships were there so much. 'And the men,' said he, laughing, 'brought off a good deal besides furs.' Then he went back—heavens, how far!—to ask about the 'Chesapeake,' and what was done to Barron for surrendering her to the 'Leopard,' and whether Burr ever tried again—and he ground his teeth with the only passion he showed. But in a moment that was over, and he said, 'God forgive me, for I am sure I forgive him.' Then he asked about the old war—told me the true story of his serving the gun the day we took the 'Java'—asked about dear old David Porter, as he called him. Then he settled down more quietly, and very happily, to hear me tell in an hour the history of fifty years.

"How I wished it had been somebody who knew something! But I did as well as I could. I told him of the English war. I told him about Fulton and the steamboat beginning. I told him about old Scott, and Jackson—told him all I could think of about the Mississippi, and New Orleans, and Texas, and his own old Kentucky. And what do you think he asked? 'Who was in command of the Legion of the West!' I told him it was a very gallant officer named Grant, and that, by our last news, he was about to establish his headquarters at Vicksburg. Then, 'Where was Vicksburg?' I worked that out on the map; it was about a hundred miles, more or less, above his old Fort Adams, and I thought Fort Adams must be a ruin now. 'It must be at old Vick's plantation, at Walnut Hills,' said he; 'well, that is a change!'

"I tell you, Ingham, it was a hard thing to condense the history of half a century into that talk with a sick man. And I do not now know what I told him—of emigration, and the means of it—of steamboats, and railroads, and telegraphs—of inventions, and books, and literature —of the colleges, and West Point, and the Naval School—but with the queerest interruptions that ever you heard. You see, it was Robinson Crusoe asking all the accumulated questions of fifty-six years!

"I remember he asked, all of a sudden, who was President now. And when I told him, he asked if Old Abe was General Benjamin Lincoln's son. He said he met old General Lincoln, when he was quite a boy himself, at some Indian treaty. I said no, that Old Abe was a Kentuckian like himself, but I could not tell him of what family; he had worked up from the ranks. 'Good for him!' cried Nolan; 'I am glad of that. As I have brooded and wondered, I have thought our danger was in keeping up those regular successions in the first families.' Then I got talking about my visit to Washington. I told him of meeting the Oregon Congressman, Harding; I told him about the Smithsonian, and the exploring Expedition; I told him about the Capitol, and the statues for the pediment, and Crawford's Liberty, and Greenough's Washington. Ingham, I told him everything I could think of that would show the grandeur of his country and its prosperity; but I could not make up my mouth to tell him a word about this infernal rebellion.

"And he drank it in and enjoyed it as I cannot tell you. He grew more and more silent, yet I never thought he was tired or faint. I gave him a glass of water, but he just wet his lips, and told me not to go away. Then he asked me to bring the Presbyterian 'Book of Public Prayer,' which lay there, and said, with a smile, that it would open at the right place—and so it did. There was his double red mark down the page. And I knelt down and read, and he repeated with me, 'For ourselves and our country, oh, gracious God, we thank Thee that, notwithstanding our manifold transgressions of Thy holy laws, Thou hast continued to us Thy marvelous kindness'—and so to the end of that thanksgiving. Then he turned to the end of the same book, and I read the words more familiar to me: 'Most heartily we beseech Thee with Thy favor to behold and bless Thy servant, the President of the United States, and all others in authority'—and the rest of the Episcopal collect. 'Danforth,' said he, 'I have repeated those prayers night and morning, it is now fifty-five years.' And then he said he would go to sleep.

"He bent me down over him and kissed me, and he said, 'Look in my Bible, Danforth, when I am gone.' And I went away.

"But I had no thought it was the end. I thought he was tired and would sleep. I knew he was happy, and I wanted him to be alone.

"But in an hour, when the doctor went in gently, he found Nolan had breathed his life away with a smile. He had something pressed close to his lips. It was his father's badge of the Order of the Cincinnati.

"We looked in his Bible, and there was a slip of paper at the place where he had marked the text:

" 'They desire a country, even a heavenly: wherefore God is not ashamed to be called their God: for He hath prepared for them a city.'

"On this slip of paper he had written:

" 'Bury me in the sea; it has been my home, and I love it. But will not some one set up a stone for my memory at Fort Adams or at Orleans, that my disgrace may not be more than I ought to bear? Say on it:

" *'In Memory of*

" 'PHILIP NOLAN,

" *'Lieutenant in the Army of the United States.*
" 'HE LOVED HIS COUNTRY AS NO OTHER MAN HAS
LOVED HER; BUT NO MAN DESERVED
LESS AT HER HANDS.' "

Ambrose Bierce
(1842-1914?)

AMBROSE BIERCE, one of the most colorful of American writers, was born in Ohio with a gypsy foot which took him to California, to London, to Mexico, to everywhere, in fact, that his fancy directed and his opportunity provided. At the outbreak of the American Civil War he was just old enough to enlist in the Indiana infantry, and he served throughout the struggle, being twice wounded and gathering in his military experiences material for his *Tales of Soldiers and Civilians*. After the war he drifted to San Francisco, where he turned journalist and fiction writer and contributor to the *Argonaut* and the *News Letter*. From 1872 to 1876 he was on the staff of the London *Fun*, for which he wrote *The Fiend's Delight* (1872), *Nuggets and Dust* (1872) and *Cobwebs from an Empty Skull* (1874), whimsical and often ghastly sketches which brought him into prominence. His *Tales of Soldiers and Civilians* (1891), printed later under the revised title of *In the Midst of Life*, contains his best stories of the supernatural. In 1897 he became Washington correspondent for the *New York American*. In 1913, when he was past seventy, he set out on a quixotic but entirely characteristic expedition into Mexico to fight in the army of the rebel leader Villa. From this excursion he never returned, and it is not known to this day just how the colorful adventurer met his end.

A Horseman in the Sky is the first of the *Soldier* group in *Tales of Soldiers and Civilians*. It is written with Bierce's usual economy of expression and secures its effects of bitter horror with the simplest and most meager of details. The plot has its roots in those too numerous situations of the Civil War in which father and son, each guided by his own conscience and sense of right, found themselves on opposite sides of the tragic struggle.

A Horseman in the Sky

One sunny afternoon in the autumn of the year 1861 a soldier lay in a clump of laurel by the side of a road in western Virginia. He lay at full length upon his stomach, his feet resting upon the toes, his head upon the left forearm. His extended right hand loosely grasped his rifle. But for the somewhat methodical disposition of his limbs and a slight rhythmic movement of the cartridge-box at the back of his belt he might have been thought to be dead. He was asleep at his post of duty. But if detected he would be dead shortly afterward, death being the just and legal penalty of his crime.

The clump of laurel in which the criminal lay was in the angle of a road which after ascending southward a steep acclivity to that point turned sharply to the west, running along the summit for perhaps one hundred yards. There it turned southward again and went zigzagging downward through the forest. At the salient of that second angle was a large flat rock, jutting out northward, overlooking the deep valley from which the road ascended. The rock capped a high cliff; a stone dropped from its outer edge would have fallen sheer downward one thousand feet to the tops of the pines. The angle where the soldier lay was on another spur of the same cliff. Had he been awake he would have commanded a view, not only of the short arm of the road and the jutting rock, but of the entire profile of the cliff below it. It might well have made him giddy to look.

The country was wooded everywhere except at the bottom of the valley to the northward, where there was a small natural meadow, through which flowed a stream scarcely visible from the valley's rim. This open ground looked hardly larger than an ordinary door-yard, but was really several acres in extent.

From *In the Midst of Life,* by Ambrose Bierce, 1891. Reprinted by permission of Albert and Charles Boni, Inc.

Its green was more vivid than that of the inclosing forest. Away beyond it rose a line of giant cliffs similar to those upon which we are supposed to stand in our survey of the savage scene, and through which the road had somehow made its climb to the summit. The configuration of the valley, indeed, was such that from this point of observation it seemed entirely shut in, and one could but have wondered how the road which found a way out of it had found a way into it, and whence came and whither went the waters of the stream that parted the meadow more than a thousand feet below.

No country is so wild and difficult but men will make it a theater of war; concealed in the forest at the bottom of that military rat-trap, in which half a hundred men in possession of the exits might have starved an army to submission, lay five regiments of Federal infantry. They had marched all the previous day and night and were resting. At nightfall they would take to the road again, climb to the place where their unfaithful sentinel now slept, and descending the other slope of the ridge fall upon a camp of the enemy at about midnight. Their hope was to surprise it, for the road led to the rear of it. In case of failure, their position would be perilous in the extreme; and fail they surely would should accident or vigilance apprise the enemy of the movement.

2

The sleeping sentinel in the clump of laurel was a young Virginian named Carter Druse. He was the son of wealthy parents, an only child, and had known such ease and cultivation and high living as wealth and taste were able to command in the mountain country of western Virginia. His home was but a few miles from where he now lay. One morning he had risen from the breakfast-table and said, quietly but gravely: "Father, a Union regiment has arrived at Grafton. I am going to join it."

The father lifted his leonine head, looked at the son a moment in silence, and replied: "Well, go, sir, and whatever may occur do what you conceive to be your duty. Virginia, to which you are a traitor, must get on without you. Should we both live to the end of the war, we will speak further of the matter. Your mother, as the physician has informed you, is in a most critical condition; at the best she cannot be with us longer than a few weeks, but that time is precious. It would be better not to disturb her."

So Carter Druse, bowing reverently to his father, who returned the salute with a stately courtesy that masked a breaking heart, left the home of his childhood to go soldiering. By conscience and courage, by deeds of devotion and daring, he soon commended himself to his fellows and his officers; and it was to these qualities and to some knowledge of the country that he owed his selection for his present perilous duty at the extreme outpost. Nevertheless, fatigue had been stronger than resolution and he had fallen asleep. What good or bad angel came in a dream to rouse him from his state of crime, who shall say? Without a movement, without a sound, in the profound silence and the languor of the late afternoon, some invisible messenger of fate touched with unsealing finger the eyes of his consciousness— whispered into the ear of his spirit the mysterious awakening word which no human lips ever have spoken, no human memory ever has recalled. He quietly raised his forehead from his arm and looked between the masking stems of the laurels, instinctively closing his right hand about the stock of his rifle.

His first feeling was a keen artistic delight. On a colossal pedestal, the cliff,—motionless at the extreme edge of the capping rock and sharply outlined against the sky,—was an equestrian statue of impressive dignity. The figure of the man sat the figure of the horse, straight and soldierly, but with the repose of a Grecian god carved in the marble which limits the suggestion of activity. The gray costume harmonized with its aerial background; the metal of accouterment and caparison was softened and subdued by the shadow; the animal's skin had no points of high light. A carbine strikingly foreshortened lay across the pommel of the saddle, kept in place by the right hand grasping it at the "grip"; the left hand, holding the bridle rein, was invisible. In silhouette against the sky the profile of the horse was cut with the sharpness of a cameo; it looked across the heights of air to the confronting cliffs beyond. The face of the rider, turned slightly away, showed only an outline of temple and beard; he was looking downward to the bottom of the valley. Magnified by its lift against the sky and by the soldier's testifying sense of the formidableness of a near enemy the group appeared of heroic, almost colossal, size.

For an instant Druse had a strange, half-defined feeling that he had slept to the end of the war and was looking upon a noble work of art reared upon that eminence to commemorate the deeds of an heroic past of which he had been an inglorious part. The feeling was dispelled by a slight movement of the group: the horse, without moving its feet, had drawn its body slightly backward from the verge; the man remained immobile as before. Broad awake and keenly alive to the significance of the situation, Druse now brought the butt of his rifle against his cheek by cautiously pushing the barrel forward through the bushes, cocked the piece, and glancing through the sights covered a vital spot of the horseman's breast. A touch upon the trigger and all would have been well with Carter Druse. At that instant the horseman turned his head and looked in the direction of his concealed foeman—seemed to look into his very face, into his eyes, into his brave, compassionate heart.

Is it then so terrible to kill an enemy in war—an enemy who has surprised a secret vital to the safety of oneself and comrades—an enemy more formidable for his knowledge than all his army for its numbers? Carter Druse grew pale; he shook in every limb, turned faint, and saw the statuesque group before him as black figures, rising, falling, moving unsteadily in arcs of circles in a fiery sky. His hand fell away from his weapon, his head slowly dropped until his face rested on the leaves in which he lay. This courageous gentleman and hardy soldier was near swooning from intensity of emotion.

It was not for long; in another moment his face was raised from earth, his hands resumed their places on the rifle, his forefinger sought the trigger; mind, heart, and eyes were clear, conscience and reason sound. He could not hope to capture that enemy; to alarm him would but send him dashing to his camp with his fatal news. The duty of the soldier was plain: the man must be shot dead from ambush—without warning, without a moment's spiritual preparation, with never so much as an unspoken prayer, he must be sent to his account. But no—there is a hope; he may have discovered nothing—perhaps he is but admiring the sublimity of the landscape. If permitted, he may turn and ride carelessly away in the direction whence he came. Surely it will be possible to judge at the instant of his withdrawing whether he knows. It may well be that his fixity of attention— Druse turned his head and looked through the deeps of air downward, as from the surface to the bottom of a translucent sea. He saw creeping across the green meadow a sinuous line of figures of men and horses—some foolish commander was permitting the soldiers of his escort to water their beasts in the open, in plain view from a dozen summits!

Druse withdrew his eyes from the valley and fixed them again upon the group of man and horse in the sky, and again it was through the sights of his rifle. But this time his aim was at the horse. In his memory, as if they were a divine mandate, rang the words of his father at their parting: "Whatever may occur, do what you conceive to be your duty." He was calm now. His teeth were firmly but not rigidly closed; his nerves were as tranquil as a sleeping babe's—not a tremor affected any muscle of his body; his breathing, until suspended in the act of taking aim, was regular and slow. Duty had conquered; the spirit had said to the body: "Peace, be still." He fired.

3

An officer of the Federal force, who in a spirit of adventure or in quest of knowledge had left the hidden *bivouac* in the valley, and with aimless feet had made his way to the lower edge of a small open space near the foot of the cliff, was considering what he had to gain by pushing his exploration further. At a distance of a quarter-mile before him, but apparently at a stone's throw, rose from its fringe of pines the gigantic face of rock, towering to so great a height above him that it made him giddy to look up to where its edge cut a sharp, rugged line against the sky. It presented a clean, vertical profile against a background of blue sky to a point half the way down, and of distant hills, hardly less blue, thence to the tops of the trees at its base. Lifting his eyes to the dizzy altitude of its summit the officer saw an astonishing sight—a man on horseback riding down into the valley through the air!

Straight upright sat the rider, in military fashion, with a firm seat in the saddle, a strong clutch upon the rein to hold his charger from too impetuous a plunge. From his bare head his long hair streamed upward, waving like a plume. His hands were concealed in the cloud of the horse's lifted mane. The animal's body was as level as if every hoof-stroke encountered the resistant earth. Its motions were those of a wild gallop, but even as the officer looked they ceased, with all the legs thrown sharply forward as in the act of alighting from a leap. But this was a flight!

Filled with amazement and terror by this apparition of a horseman in the sky—half believing himself the chosen scribe of some new Apocalypse, the officer was overcome by the intensity of his emotions; his legs failed him and he fell. Almost at the same instant he heard a crashing sound in the trees—a sound that died without an echo—and all was still.

The officer rose to his feet, trembling. The familiar sensation of an abraded shin recalled his dazed faculties. Pulling himself together he ran rapidly obliquely away from the cliff to a point distant from its foot; thereabout he expected to find his man; and thereabout he naturally failed. In the fleeting instant of his vision his imagination had been so wrought upon by the apparent grace and ease and intention of the marvelous performance that it did not occur to him that the line of march of aerial cavalry is directly downward, and that he could find the objects of his search at the very foot of the cliff. A half-hour later he returned to camp.

This officer was a wise man; he knew better than to tell an incredible truth. He said nothing of what he had seen. But when the commander asked him if in his scout he had learned anything of advantage to the expedition he answered:

"Yes, sir; there is no road leading down into this valley from the southward."

The commander, knowing better, smiled.

4

After firing his shot, Private Carter Druse reloaded his rifle and resumed his watch. Ten minutes had hardly passed when a Federal sergeant crept cautiously to him on hands and knees. Druse neither turned his head nor looked at him, but lay without motion or sign of recognition.

"Did you fire?" the sergeant whispered.

"Yes."

"At what?"

"A horse. It was standing on yonder rock—pretty far out. You see it is no longer there. It went over the cliff."

The man's face was white, but he showed no other sign of emotion. Having answered, he turned away his eyes and said no more. The sergeant did not understand.

"See here, Druse," he said, after a moment's silence, "it's no use making a mystery. I order you to report. Was there anybody on the horse?"

"Yes."

"Well?"

"My father."

The sergeant rose to his feet and walked away. "Good God!" he said.

Richard Ely Danielson
(1885-   )

RICHARD ELY DANIELSON was born in Brooklyn, Connecticut, and educated at Yale University. During the first World War he served as captain in the American army. He has been editor of the *Independent* and the *Sportsman.*

Corporal Hardy appeared first in *The Atlantic Monthly* for November, 1938, and was chosen the following year by E. J. O'Brien for his *Fifty Best American Short Stories.* The choice was completely justified, for the story is remarkable for its compression and restraint, for its structural economy, and for the unity with which the point of view of the boy story-teller is maintained. The background of Corporal Hardy's tale is the Battle of Chancellorsville fought May 2–4, 1863. In this bloody engagement the Confederates under Generals Robert E. Lee and "Stonewall" Jackson defeated the Army of the Potomac under General Hooker, although the Confederates were outnumbered two to one. General Jackson was mortally wounded in the battle, but the victory left the way open for the invasion of Pennsylvania that ended at Gettysburg. The Confederate general whose magnanimity protected the courageous Union corporal was General Lee, the most magnificent officer and gentleman in either army.

Corporal Hardy

In those days, during the haying season, it was my duty to keep the men in the fields supplied with sufficient cooling drink to enable them to support the heat and burden of the day. According to our established practice, this cooling drink consisted of cold water from the spring, flavored, for some obscure New England reason, with molasses, and it had to be freshly renewed every hour. We had plenty of ice in the icehouse, but there was a stubborn tradition that ice water was "bad" for men working in hayfields under the hot sun.

So every hour I carried down a brown jug containing the innocent mixture of "molasses 'n' water" to the hands, each one of whom would pause in his work, throw the jug over his upper arm, drink deeply thereof, wipe the sweat off his forehead, say "Thanks, Bub," and go on making hay. I was only ten years old, but it was no hardship to carry the jug, and it was fun to see their Adam's apples working as they drank.

This was routine practice on our Connecticut farm. Mostly the farm hands—"hired men," we called them—came back to the house at noon and ate in the kitchen, after washing up at the pump outside. But in haymaking season each man sought a patch of shade, and his meal was carried to him there, to be eaten in the fields. I suppose the men's overheated bodies cooled off in the wisps of breeze drifting across the scorching "mowings" more effectively and comfortably than would have been possible in a hot summer kitchen. I am sure that my father did everything he could to make their lot as comfortable and healthy as possible. He worked with them, under the same conditions, setting them an example of careful, efficient labor. He differed from his men only in the fact that he was always cleanly shaved, that

Reprinted by permission of *The Atlantic Monthly, The Reader's Digest,* and the author.

he gave orders and directions, and that he wore a silk shirt even in the hayfields. Nobody objected in the least to this token, for he was "the owner," and he had been to college, and everyone admitted that he was fair and square.

On such occasions, when the men were given their "dinners" out of doors, I always carried his victuals to Mr. Hardy, because I liked to sit with him while he ate and listen to his stories. I think he enjoyed talking, in his racy Connecticut vernacular, to such a fascinated audience of one. He was a Civil War veteran, like my father, who, however, had been too young to enlist until the last year of the war and had seen almost no active service. But Mr. Hardy was a soldier. Congress had given him a medal—of honor—and all men regarded him with respect.

As I look back and remember his stories, I think he must have been the most modest man I have ever known. Certainly he never thought of himself as a hero. He would accept no pension. "I'm able-bodied. I can work, can't I?" But, alas, he was not really able-bodied. He had been grievously wounded several times, and in 1895, when I fetched and carried for him and sat at his feet, it was pitiful to see his valiant efforts to fork hay on the wagon or do the other farming tasks which require muscular strength. He was thin and bent, but his face was brown and clean and his blue eyes bright and indomitable.

My father employed Mr. Hardy whenever there was work to give him, and treated him—I did not, at that time, know why—differently from the other hired men. He was poor, he lived alone, he was unsuccessful, and in New England then we rated people by their comparative "success." But he worked stoutly and asked no favors of any one. It was generally conceded that Mr. Hardy, if a failure, was nevertheless a good man.

I remember the last day I served him. I brought him his dinner in a basket—cold meat 'n' potatoes, 'n' bread 'n' butter, 'n' cold coffee, 'n' pie. He was seated in the shade of an oak tree, leaning against a stack of hay. I put the food down beside him and sat down, hugging my knees and rocking back and forth. It was pleasant there, with the smell of the hay and the drone of the bees, and the good, warm feeling of the earth.

Mr. Hardy lay back against the haymow. "Thanks, Jackie," he said. "I don't seem to be hungry today. It's hot and this tree don't give much shade. Why, dammit, it's like that mean little oak tree down to Chancellorsville."

I said, "Oh, Mr. Hardy, you've told me about Antietam and the Wilderness, but you've never told me about Chancellorsville. What was it like?"

He said slowly, "I ain't never told nobody about Chancellorsville, and I don't aim to tell nobody—grown-up, that is. But I'd kind of like to tell somebody that don't know nothing—like you —about it, for the first and last time. You'll forget it, and it would kind of ease my mind."

2

Mr. Hardy hoisted himself a little higher on the haymow and made a pretense of eating some bread and meat.

"Chancellorsville," he said, "was a bad battle, an awful bad battle. We didn't fight good and they was too many of them and I lost my captain."

"Who was he?" I asked.

"Why," he said, incredulously, "you oughta know that! He was Captain William Armstrong, commandin' Company B, 39th Connecticut. 'N' his twin brother, Ezra, was lootenant. He was younger by an hour or so, and they was identical twins. They never was two men as much alike—in looks, that is, for they was quite unlike inside. The lootenant was always stompin' around an' shoutin' an' wavin' his arms, an' the captain, he was always quiet an' soft-spoken an' brave an' gentle. He was a good man— he was an awful good man. I guess he was the best man I ever knowed."

He paused and took a sip of his cold coffee. Then he said, "Why, when we come to leave town to go in the cars to Hartford and then to Washington, their father—he was old Judge Armstrong, who lived in that big place up on Armstrong Hill—the Judge come up to me and says, 'Nathan, you look after my boys,' he said. 'They're younger than you be. You kind of keep an eye on them, for my sake,' he says. 'They is good boys,' he says. 'I will, Judge,' I says. 'I'll do my best.' An' he says to me, 'I know you will, Nathan Hardy.' "

"But tell me, Mr. Hardy," I broke in, for I was not interested in the Armstrong twins, "what happened at Chancellorsville?"

"It was a bad battle, as I said. Them Rebs come charging out of the woods, hollerin' and yellin' and helligolarrupin', and they was too many of them. The lootenant, he kept stomping up and down, shouting, 'Never give ground, boys! Stay where you are! Take careful aim! Never retreat!' Those was his words. I will never forget them, because he meant them. But my cap-tain—I was next to him—says, 'They're too many; we can't stop 'em. Tell the men to retreat slowly, firing as often as they can re-load.' Just then it hit him right in the chest. *Thunk!* was the noise it made; just like thet—*thunk!* I caught him as he fell, and the blood began to come out of his mouth. He tried to speak, but he was vomiting blood dreadful, so all he could do was to make faces, and his lips said, 'Tell Elizabeth . . .' and then he died. I put him down and noticed we was under a mean little oak tree on the edge of our trenches.

"Then they was around us, hairy men with bayonets, stabbin' and shootin' and yellin', and we soldiers had kind of drifted together in groups and the lootenant was shouting, 'Don't re-treat, men!' and he got hit right in the knee and fell down; and so I picked him up and put him across my shoulder and started for the rear. He kep' hittin' me in the face and swearing, 'You damn coward! You left my brother there and you're making me retreat!' I says to him, 'Ezra, be reasonable; I'm takin' you to an ambulance. You ain't fit to fight, and as soon as I can I'm goin' back to bury William. They ain't goin' to shovel him into no trench,' I said. So he stopped hitting at me.

"I was strong then, and I must a carried him a mile or a mile and a few rods when we come to some stretcher men near a house, and I said, 'You take this officer to the nearest surgeon. They got to saw his leg off.' And they said, 'We ain't carryin' no wounded. We're a burial detail.' I said, pulling my pistol out, 'You will be if you don't carry this man. I'm kind of tuckered, but I ain't too tuckered to shoot.' So two of them carried him, and I went along with my pistol till we come to a place where surgeons was carving men up and I handed over the lootenant. He come to as I did so, and said, 'You scoundrel, you made me retreat. I'll never forgive you!' I said, 'Ezra, they're going to saw your leg off and you'll never fight again, but I'll bury William if it's the last thing I do.' He says, 'Is that a promise?' And I says,

'That's a promise. But it ain't a promise to you—it's one I made to your pa.'

"So I stayed with him and helped hold him while they sawed his leg off. They havin' run out of chloroform, it took four of us to hold him. And when it was over he was unconscious, and they put him in a cart with some others and took him away. So I went back to the house where the burial men were loafing. It was pretty ruined, but I found a shingle that was almos' clean and I wrote on it, in the light of a fire, 'cause it was dark then:—

CAPT. WILLIAM ARMSTRONG
COMMANDING CO. B, 39 CONNECTICUT
He was an awful good man

"Then I borrowed a spade from this burial party. We had an argument about it, but I persuaded them with my pistol and I started off toward the Rebel lines. I hadn't gone very far when I come to a place which was thick with men moanin' and screamin' and lots that wasn't sayin' nothing at all. I didn't want to walk on them an' I couldn't help them, having nothing on me but a shingle and a spade and a pistol, an' I decided I couldn't find the captain in the dark anyhow, so I set down and tried to sleep, for I was tuckered. I threw away my pistol. I set there the rest of the night waitin' for the dawn. It was a long time comin'.

3

"When it come gray, I started out with my shingle and my spade and I went along till I was challenged by the Rebel pickets and sentries. I answered, 'Union burial detail. I'm comin' for to bury my captain.' They begun shootin' at me and I don't know as I blame them. I was comin' out of the mist and they couldn't see that I was alone an' wasn't armed. So they shot real hard, and one bullet struck me in the left thigh and I fell down. Fortunately I had a belt, and I sat up and took it off and strapped it real tight over my wound, and my britches was tight at the waist so they didn't come down, and I got up and went on.

"They stopped shootin' and a man with a bayonet got up and said, 'Yank, you're my pris'ner.' And I said, 'I know I be, but I

ain't your pris'ner till I bury my captain.' And I held up my
shingle and spade. He said, 'Where's he lie?' And I said, 'About
quarter mile from here and maybe a few rods, under a mean
little oak tree; and,' I says, 'you take me there and I'll bury him
and then I'm your pris'ner. They ain't goin' to stuff my captain
into no ditch,' I says. He says, 'You may be crazy, Yank, or you
may be a spy. You come with me an' I'll turn you over to the
captain.'

" 'Your captain alive?' I asks.

" 'I reckon so,' he says.

" 'Mine's dead,' I says, 'and I aim for to bury him.'

"So he tuk me away with his bayonet in my back and the
blood was squilchin' in my boot, but I got along to where his
captain was and the captain asked questions, and the Rebel soldier, he tol' all he knew, an' the captain says, 'Where's he lie?'
An' I says, 'By a mean little oak, where our lines was yesterday
mornin'.'

"An' the captain says, 'That ain't far away. I'll send a detail
to bury him.' I says, 'Ain't nobody goin' to bury the captain but
me,' I says. 'After that, I'll be your pris'ner.'

"They was a young man dressed up all pretty with gold braid
on his uniform, and he laughed kind of loud and he says, 'Saves
us the trouble of buryin' him!' an' the captain turns on him, real
stern, and says, 'Lootenant, this is a brave soldier,' he says, 'who
come back under fire and was wounded to bury his company
commander and give himself up as pris'ner. I will not have him
insulted or laughed at,' he says. Then he turns to me an' says,
'What is your name an' rank?'

" 'Corporal Nathan Hardy, Co. B, 39th Connecticut,' I says.

"An' he says, 'Corporal, you and I an' these men,' turnin'
around to the five or six Rebs who was listenin', 'will go together
to find your captain.'

"So we went and I found him, underneath that mean little
oak tree, and he looked dreadful. His eyes was open and they
was an awful lot of blood on his shirt where his coat was open,
and he was lyin' all sprangled out an' undignified. An' the first
thing I done was to straighten him out. I spit on my sleeve and
wiped the blood off his mouth the best I could. An' I closed his
eyes an' buttoned his coat an' crossed his arms. They was kind of

stiff, but I done it, an' I brushed him off and laid him out regular.

"Then I started diggin', an' it would have been easy if it hadn't been for my leg and all the blood in my boot. Six foot four or thereabouts it was, and three foot deep—not as deep as I wanted, but I couldn't dig no deeper, I was so tuckered. But it was an honest grave, for I was real handy with a spade in them days. Then I stood up and said, 'Will two o' you Rebs hand the captain to me?' Which they done, and I laid him in the grave. An' as I stood lookin' down at him lyin' there, I says to myself, 'Ain't nobody goin' to shovel no dirt on the captain's face—nobody, nobody, nobody at all, not even me!' So I took my coat off and laid it over him, coverin' up his face best I could. I didn't want to go to no Rebel prison in my shirt, but I wouldn't have no one shovel dirt on the captain.

"Then the two Rebs pulled me out of the grave, real gentle and considerate. An' then I noticed they was a Rebel general there settin' on a blood horse. How long he bin there I don't know. He looked at me and see I was wounded and peaked, and he says, stern an' hard, 'Captain, what's the meanin' of this? This man's wounded and weak,' he says. 'Do you force wounded men to bury the dead?'

"The captain went over to him and began talkin' to him low and earnest, seemed like, all the time I was fillin' in the grave. An' when I had patted the mound even, so it looked good, and had stuck the shingle in the new earth at the head of the grave, I come over to where the general was, limpin' and leanin' on my spade, an' I saluted,—couldn't help it; I kind of forgot he was a Rebel,—an' I says, 'General, I'm your pris'ner. I buried my captain. I ain't a great hand at askin' favors, an' your captain and these Rebs has been real good to me. But I wanta ask one more. I was raised Episcopal, which was unusual in our town, and so was the captain. I'd kind of like to say a prayer before I surrender . . .' "

4

Here Mr. Hardy seemed to doze for a little. "Where was I?" he asked, rousing after a few minutes.

"You had just gone up to the general and asked if you could say a prayer before you surrendered."

"Yes, yes, so it was. The general said, 'Corporal Hardy, I am an Episcopalian too, and you shall say your prayer.'

"So he dismounted and took off his hat, and he and I kneeled down by the grave, and it was awful hard for me to kneel. And when we was there kneelin' I looked up for a minute and all them Rebs was standin' with their caps off and their heads bowed, nice and decent, just like Northern people. An' then I had a dreadful time, for to save my life I couldn't remember a prayer, not a line, not a word. I had heard the burial service often enough and too often, what with Pa and Ma an' all kinds of relatives, but my brains was all watery an' thin, seemed like, an' I couldn't remember nothin' at all. I don' know how long 'twas till somethin' come driftin' into my mind. It wa'n't from the burial service; 'twas somethin' we used to chant in Evenin' Prayer. So I says it, loud as I could, for I was gettin' awful feeble.

" 'Lord,' I says, 'now lettest Thou Thy servant depart in peace, according to Thy Word . . .' An' I couldn't remember or say any more. The general, he helped me to my feet, spade an' all, an' I looked him in the face and, by creepers, they was tears in his beard. Soon as I could speak I says, 'General, you've been real good to me and I thank you. An' now I'm your pris'ner, wherever you want to send me.'

"An' he says, 'Corporal Hardy, you will never be a pris'ner of our people as long as I live and command this corps.'

"An' I broke in, awful scared he had misunderstood, and I says, 'General, you don't think I was prayin' for *me* to go in peace! I'm your pris'ner; I'm not askin' for no favors. I was thinkin' of the captain—and me too, perhaps, but not that way. I can go anywhere now. I——'

"He cut me short. 'Corporal Hardy,' he says, 'I know to Whom you was prayin' and why, an' I haven't misunderstood you at all. Captain,' he says, 'I want a detail of six men an' a stretcher and a flag of truce to take this brave soldier an'—an' Christian gentleman back to the Union lines; an' I want this message, which I have dictated and signed, delivered to the commanding officer to be forwarded through channels to the Secretary of War or the President. Those people can hardly decline this courtesy, under the circumstances. . . . Wait, Carter, I wish to add a few lines.' So he put the paper against his saddle and he wrote for some time.

"Then, kind of in a dream, I heard the Rebel captain say, 'Sir, if the General permits, I would like to lead this detail to the Union lines and ask to be blindfolded and deliver your message to the Division Commander.'

"An' the General says, 'Captain, I am very glad you made that request, and I commend your behavior. It is only fittin' that the officer escortin' Corporal Hardy with my message should be of field rank, and I shall put in my order for your promotion. You are a pretty good soldier, yourself,' he says—only he didn't say it that way.

"All this time I was kind of waverin' around, but I heard most all they said; and because I was feeble from losing blood an' the battle an' buryin' the captain an' a kind of feverish feelin', things begun to spin around, and I started walkin' this way and that way with my spade, tryin' to stand up, knowin' I couldn't much longer. I heard someone yell, 'Catch him!' An' the next thing I knowed I was in a bed of straw and they was probin' for the bullet in my leg. Then I don't remember nothin' till I woke up in a bed, a clean bed, with a nice lookin' woman leanin' over me, wipin' my head with a cold, wet towel. I says, 'Where am I?'

"An' she says, 'You're in the hospital of the Sanitary Commission in Washington. An' oh, Corporal Hardy,' she says, 'I'm so glad you're conscious, for today the President is comin' to give you the Medal of Honor.' An' I says, 'Listen, sister, I gotta get out of here. I don't care for no President or no medal—I gotta bury the captain. He's lyin' down there under a mean little oak. Gimme my clothes,' I says; 'I want a spade and a shingle,' An' she says, 'Corporal, you buried your captain an' buried him fine. That's why the President is comin' to see you. Now you just drink this and go to sleep for a while, and I'll wake you when the President comes.'

"So I drank it and kind of slept, and when I woke up there was Old Abe, the ugliest man I ever see, leanin' over and pinnin' something to my nightshirt, an' he says, 'Corporal Hardy, even the enemy call you a brave soldier and a good man. Congress has voted you this medal. God bless you,' he says."

5

Mr. Hardy yawned and closed his eyes, and leaned against the haymow. He had told the tale he had to tell—once, to one person.

"But, Mr. Hardy," I said, "what happened to the lieutenant, and who was Elizabeth?" I wanted the story all tied up in ribbons.

"Who?" he said. "The lootenant? Oh, Ezra come back and married Elizabeth and they went to live in Massachusetts. Seems he went aroun' sayin' he couldn't live in no town where people pointed at him and thought he had run away leavin' his dead brother. Naturally no one done so or thought so. But, for all his stompin' and shoutin', he was sensitive, an' he bore me a grudge for takin' him away. I don't see as how I could a done different. I'd promised the old Judge I'd look after his boys an' I've allus aimed to keep my promises."

Just then my father came up to us. It was unlike Mr. Hardy to sit in the shade while other men had started to work again, and Father looked worried. "How are you feeling, Nathan?" he asked.

"Why, John, I'm plumb tuckered out, and that's a fact. I don' know as I can do much more work today. Seems like I never did fare good under these mean little oak trees," and he glanced sharply at me with an expression that was almost a wink. We shared a secret.

Father looked startled, as if he thought Mr. Hardy's wits were wandering.

"I tell you what, Nathan," he said, "You've had all the sun you need. I'll send the wagon and they'll take you up to the house, where you can be cool and rest for a while." And, for once in his life, Mr. Hardy made no protest over having "favors" done for him. Father took me aside. "Jackie," he said, "you run up to the house and tell your mother to make the bed in the spare room ready, and then you go to the village and tell Dr. Fordyce he's wanted. I don't like Nathan's looks."

Before I started running I glanced at Mr. Hardy, and I saw what Father meant. He was pale and flushed in the wrong places, though I hadn't noticed it at all when he was telling me about Chancellorsville.

So Mr. Hardy was put to bed in the spare room, and given

such care and aid as we knew how to give. For several days he lay quietly enough, and, as I look back on it after all these years, I think that the weight and burden of his long, valiant struggle must suddenly have proved too great. He couldn't go on forever. Mr. Hardy was tuckered out.

Then for some time he alternated between unconsciousness and a mild delirium. He kept mumbling phrases: "Take that quid out o' your mouth. 'T ain't soldierly!" . . . "Ain't nobody goin' to bury the captain but me." I knew what lots of his bewildered sayings meant, but there were many which were obscure. I sat with him every day for an hour or so when the rest of the household were busy, and I had instructions to call my elders if Mr. Hardy needed help or became conscious.

One day he opened his eyes and said, "Here I am and I'm real easy in my mind—but I can't just remember what I said." I went out and called my parents, who told me to stay outside. But I listened and I heard Mr. Hardy say, "Call the boy in. He knows what I want said and I can't remember. He's young and 't won't hurt him and he'll forget." So Mother beckoned me to come in and I said, "What can I do, Mr. Hardy?"

"You can say what I said for the captain when I knelt down with the general."

So I knelt down, and, having the parrotlike memory of childhood, I said, "You knelt down and so did the general, and then you couldn't remember any of the words of the burial service, but you did remember something that was sung in the evening, and you said, 'Lord, now lettest Thou Thy servant depart in peace, according to Thy Word . . .'" And I began to cry.

"That's right," he said very faintly, "that's right; that's it. Yes, Captain . . ."

My mother gathered me up and took me out and held me very close, rocking back and forth with me while I wept out how I loved Mr. Hardy and what a good man he was.

And that was why I was sent to my aunt and cousins at New London, where I could swim and fish and forget about battles and wounds and Mr. Hardy. But I didn't forget.

Hamlin Garland
(1860-1940)

THE LAST of the three Civil War stories in the present series was written by Hamlin Garland, a son of the "Middle Border." He was born in West Salem, Wisconsin, the child of a Civil War veteran, but the family moved to an Iowa farm when he was only eight years old. Here he learned the bitterness of farm drudgery that seasons so many of his Middle Western stories. After teaching school for a time in Illinois, he went to a claim in Dakota but soon threw it up and in 1884 went to Boston to write stories. Many of his tales appeared in the *Arena* and *Harper's Weekly*. Among his successful novels and story collections are *Main Travelled Roads* (1891), *Jason Edwards* (1891), *A Little Norsk* (1891), *Prairie Folks* (1892), *Rose of Dutcher's Coolly* (1895), and *Boy Life on the Prairie* (1907). He moved to Chicago in 1893, but after the great success of his autobiographical *Son of the Middle Border* (1917), he made his home in New York City. His *A Daughter of the Middle Border* (1921) is also a distinguished interpretation of life in the Middle West.

The Return of a Private is one of the stories in *Main Travelled Roads*. In it the road which the discharged soldier in faded blue follows home from the war is, like most of Hamlin Garland's main-travelled roads, "long and wearyful" with nought but a life of toil at the end. W. D. Howells' comment on the story is critically sound. The story is, he wrote, "a satire of the keenest edge, as well as a tender and mournful idyl of the unknown soldier who comes back after the war with no blare of welcoming trumpets or flash of streaming flags, but footsore, heartsore, with no stake in the country he has helped to make safe and rich but the poor man's chance to snatch an uncertain subsistence from the furrows he left for the battlefield."

The Return of a Private

The nearer the train drew toward La Crosse, the soberer the little group of "vets" became. On the long way from New Orleans they had beguiled tedium with jokes and friendly chaff; or with planning with elaborate detail what they were going to do now, after the war. A long journey, slowly, irregularly, yet persistently pushing northward. When they entered on Wisconsin territory they gave a cheer, and another when they reached Madison, but after that they sank into a dumb expectancy. Comrades dropped off at one or two points beyond, until there were only four or five left who were bound for La Crosse County.

Three of them were gaunt and brown, the fourth was gaunt and pale, with signs of fever and ague upon him. One had a great scar down his temple, one limped, and they all had unnaturally large, bright eyes, showing emaciation. There were no bands greeting them at the station, no banks of gayly dressed ladies waving handkerchiefs and shouting "Bravo!" as they came in on the caboose of a freight train into the towns that had cheered and blared at them on their way to war. As they looked out or stepped upon the platform for a moment, while the train stood at the station, the loafers looked at them indifferently. Their blue coats, dusty and grimy, were too familiar now to excite notice, much less a friendly word. They were the last of the army to return, and the loafers were surfeited with such sights.

The train jogged forward so slowly that it seemed likely to be midnight before they should reach La Crosse. The little squad grumbled and swore, but it was no use; the train would not hurry, and, as a matter of fact, it was nearly two o'clock when the engine whistled "down brakes."

Published by permission of Mrs. Hamlin Garland from *Main Travelled Roads*, by Hamlin Garland, Harper and Brothers, 1891.

All of the group were farmers, living in districts several miles out of the town, and all were poor.

"Now, boys," said Private Smith, he of the fever and ague, "we are landed in La Crosse in the night. We've got to stay somewhere till mornin'. Now I ain't got no two dollars to waste on a hotel. I've got a wife and children, so I'm goin' to roost on a bench and take the cost of a bed out of my hide."

"Same here," put in one of the other men. "Hide'll grow on again, dollars'll come hard. It's goin' to be mighty hot skirmishin' to find a dollar these days."

"Don't think they'll be a deputation of citizens waitin' to 'scort us to a hotel, eh?" said another. His sarcasm was too obvious to require an answer.

Smith went on, "Then at daybreak we'll start for home—at least, I will."

"Well, I'll be dummed if I'll take two dollars out o' *my* hide," one of the younger men said. "I'm goin' to a hotel, ef I don't never lay up a cent."

"That'll do f'r you," said Smith; "but if you had a wife an' three young uns dependin' on yeh——"

"Which I ain't, thank the Lord! and don't intend havin' while the court knows itself."

The station was deserted, chill, and dark, as they came into it at exactly a quarter to two in the morning. Lit by the oil lamps that flared a dull red light over the dingy benches, the waiting room was not an inviting place. The younger man went off to look up a hotel, while the rest remained and prepared to camp down on the floor and benches. Smith was attended to tenderly by the other men, who spread their blankets on the bench for him, and, by robbing themselves, made quite a comfortable bed, though the narrowness of the bench made his sleeping precarious.

It was chill, though August, and the two men, sitting with bowed heads, grew stiff with cold and weariness, and were forced to rise now and again and walk about to warm their stiffened limbs. It did not occur to them, probably, to contrast their coming home with their going forth, or with the coming home of the generals, colonels, or even captains—but to Private Smith, at any rate, there came a sickness at heart almost deadly as he lay there on his hard bed and went over his situation.

In the deep of the night, lying on a board in the town where he had enlisted three years ago, all elation and enthusiasm gone out of him, he faced the fact that with the joy of homecoming was already mingled the bitter juice of care. He saw himself sick, worn out, taking up the work on his half-cleared farm, the inevitable mortgage standing ready with open jaw to swallow half his earnings. He had given three years of his life for a mere pittance of pay, and now!——

Morning dawned at last, slowly, with a pale yellow dome of light rising silently above the bluffs, which stand like some huge storm-devastated castle, just east of the city. Out to the left the great river swept on its massive yet silent way to the south. Bluejays called across the water from hillside to hillside through the clear, beautiful air, and hawks began to skim the tops of the hills. The older men were astir early, but Private Smith had fallen at last into a sleep, and they went out without waking him. He lay on his knapsack, his gaunt face turned toward the ceiling, his hands clasped on his breast, with a curious pathetic effect of weakness and appeal.

An engine switching near woke him at last, and he slowly sat up and stared about. He looked out of the window and saw that the sun was lightening the hills across the river. He rose and brushed his hair as well as he could, folded his blankets up, and went out to find his companions. They stood gazing silently at the river and at the hills.

"Looks natcher'l, don't it?" they said, as he came out.

"That's what it does," he replied. "An' it looks good. D' yeh see that peak?" He pointed at a beautiful symmetrical peak, rising like a slightly truncated cone, so high that it seemed the very highest of them all. It was touched by the morning sun and it glowed like a beacon, and a light scarf of gray morning fog was rolling up its shadowed side.

"My farm's just beyond that. Now, if I can only ketch a ride, we'll be home by dinner-time."

"I'm talkin' about breakfast," said one of the others.

"I guess it's one more meal o' hardtack f'r me," said Smith.

They foraged around, and finally found a restaurant with a sleepy old German behind the counter, and procured some coffee, which they drank to wash down their hardtack.

"Time'll come," said Smith, holding up a piece by the corner, "when this'll be a curiosity."

"I hope to God it will! I bet I've chawed hardtack enough to shingle every house in the coolly. I've chawed it when my lampers was down, and when they wasn't. I've took it dry, soaked, and mashed. I've had it wormy, musty, sour, and blue-moldy. I've had it in little bits and big bits; 'fore coffee an' after coffee. I'm ready f'r a change. I'd like t' git holt jest about now o' some of the hot biscuits my wife c'n make when she lays herself out f'r company."

"Well, if you set there gabblin', you'll never *see* yer wife."

"Come on," said Private Smith. "Wait a moment, boys; less take suthin'. It's on me." He led them to the rusty tin dipper which hung on a nail beside the wooden water-pail, and they grinned and drank. Then shouldering their blankets and muskets, which they were "takin' home to the boys," they struck out on their last march.

"They called that coffee, Jayvy," grumbled one of them, but it never went by the road where government Jayvy resides. I reckon I know coffee from peas."

They kept together on the road along the turnpike, and up the winding road by the river, which they followed for some miles. The river was very lovely, curving down along its sandy beds, pausing now and then under broad basswood trees, or running in dark, swift, silent currents under tangles of wild grapevines, and drooping alders, and haw trees. At one of these lovely spots the three vets sat down on the thick green sward to rest, "on Smith's account." The leaves of the trees were as fresh and green as in June, the jays called cheery greetings to them, and kingfishers darted to and fro with swooping, noiseless flight.

"I tell yeh, boys, this knocks the swamps of Loueesiana into kingdom come."

"You bet. All they c'n raise down there is snakes, niggers, and p'rticler hell."

"An' fightin' men," put in the older man.

"An' fightin' men. If I had a good hook an' line I'd sneak a pick'rel out o' that pond. Say, remember that time I shot that alligator——"

"I guess we'd better be crawlin' along," interrupted Smith, rising and shouldering his knapsack, with considerable effort, which he tried to hide.

"Say, Smith, lemme give you a lift on that."

"I guess I c'n manage," said Smith, grimly.

"Course. But, yo' see, I may not have a chance right off to pay yeh back for the times you've carried my gun and hull caboodle. Say, now, gimme that gun, anyway."

"All right, if yeh feel like it, Jim," Smith replied, and they trudged along doggedly in the sun, which was getting higher and hotter each half-mile.

"Ain't it queer there ain't no teams comin' along," said Smith, after a long silence.

"Well, no, seein's it's Sunday."

"By jinks, that's a fact. It *is* Sunday. I'll git home in time f'r dinner, sure!" he exulted. "She don't hev dinner usially till about *one* on Sundays." And he fell into a muse, in which he smiled.

"Well, I'll git home jest about six o'clock, jest about when the boys are milkin' the cows," said old Jim Cranby. "I'll step into the barn, an' then I'll say: 'He*ah*! why ain't this milkin' done before this time o' day?' An' then won't they yell!" he added, slapping his thigh in great glee.

Smith went on. "I'll jest go up the path. Old Rover'll come down the road to meet me. He won't bark; he'll know me, an' he'll come down wagging' his tail an' showin' his teeth. That's his way of laughin'. An' so I'll walk up to the kitchen door, an' I'll say, '*Dinner* f'r a hungry man!' An' then she'll jump up, an'——"

He couldn't go on. His voice choked at the thought of it. Saunders, the third man, hardly uttered a word, but walked silently behind the others. He had lost his wife the first year he was in the army. She died of pneumonia, caught in the autumn rains while working in the fields in his place.

They plodded along till at last they came to a parting of the ways. To the right the road continued up the main valley; to the left it went over the big ridge.

"Well, boys," began Smith, as they grounded their muskets and looked away up the valley, "here's where we shake hands. We've marched together a good many miles, an' now I s'pose we're done."

"Yes, I don't think we'll do any more of it f'r a while. I don't want to, I know."

"I hope I'll see yeh once in a while, boys, to talk over old times."

"Of course," said Saunders, whose voice trembled a little, too. "It ain't *exactly* like dyin'." They all found it hard to look at each other.

"But we'd ought'r go home with you," said Cranby. "You'll never climb that ridge with all them things on yer back."

"Oh, I'm all right! Don't worry about me. Every step takes me nearer home, yeh see. Well, good-by, boys."

They shook hands. "Good-by. Good luck!"

"Same to you. Lemme know how you find things at home."

"Good-by."

"Good-by."

He turned once before they passed out of sight, and waved his cap, and they did the same, and all yelled. Then all marched away with their long, steady, loping, veteran step. The solitary climber in blue walked on for a time, with his mind filled with the kindness of his comrades, and musing upon the many wonderful days they had had together in camp and field.

He thought of his chum, Billy Tripp. Poor Billy! A "minie" ball fell into his breast one day, fell wailing like a cat, and tore a great ragged hole in his heart. He looked forward to a sad scene with Billy's mother and sweetheart. They would want to know all about it. He tried to recall all that Billy had said, and the particulars of it, but there was little to remember, just that wild wailing sound high in the air, a dull slap, a short, quick, expulsive groan, and the boy lay with his face in the dirt in the plowed field they were marching across.

That was all. But all the scenes he had since been through had not dimmed the horror, the terror of that moment, when his boy comrade fell, with only a breath between a laugh and a death-groan. Poor handsome Billy! Worth millions of dollars was his young life.

These somber recollections gave way at length to more cheerful feelings as he began to approach his home coolly. The fields and houses grew familiar, and in one or two he was greeted by people seated in the doorways. But he was in no mood to talk, and pushed on steadily, though he stopped and accepted a drink of milk once at the well-side of a neighbor.

The sun was burning hot on that slope, and his step grew slower, in spite of his iron resolution. He sat down several times to rest. Slowly he crawled up the rough, reddish-brown road, which wound along the hillside, under great trees, through dense groves of jack oaks, with tree-tops far below him on his left hand, and the hills far above him on his right. He crawled along like some minute, wingless variety of fly.

He ate some hardtack, sauced with wild berries, when he reached the summit of the ridge, and sat there for some time, looking down into his home coolly.

Somber, pathetic figure! His wide, round, gray eyes gazing down into the beautiful valley, seeing and not seeing, the splendid cloud-shadows sweeping over the western hills and across the green and yellow wheat far below. His head drooped forward on his palm, his shoulders took on a tired stoop, his cheek-bones showed painfully. An observer might have said, "He is looking down upon his own grave."

2

Sunday comes in a Western wheat harvest with such sweet and sudden relaxation to man and beast that it would be holy for that reason, if for no other, and Sundays are usually fair in harvest-time. As one goes out into the field in the hot morning sunshine, with no sound abroad save the crickets and the indescribably pleasant silken rustling of the ripened grain, the reaper and the very sheaves in the stubble seem to be resting, dreaming.

Around the house, in the shade of the trees, the men sit, smoking, dozing, or reading the papers, while the women, never resting, move about at the housework. The men eat on Sundays about the same as on other days, and breakfast is no sooner over and out of the way than dinner begins.

But at the Smith farm there were no men dozing or reading. Mrs. Smith was alone with her three children, Mary, nine, Tommy, six, and little Ted, just past four. Her farm, rented to a neighbor, lay at the head of a coolly or narrow gully, made at some far-off post-glacial period by the vast and angry floods of

water which gullied these tremendous furrows in the level prairie
—furrows so deep that undisturbed portions of the original level
rose like hills on either side, rose to quite considerable mountains.

The chickens wakened her as usual that Sabbath morning
from dreams of her absent husband, from whom she had not
heard for weeks. The shadows drifted over the hills, down the
slopes, across the wheat, and up the opposite wall in leisurely
way, as if, being Sunday, they could take it easy also. The fowls
clustered about the housewife as she went out into the yard.
Fuzzy little chickens swarmed out from the coops, where their
clucking and perpetually disgruntled mothers tramped about,
petulantly thrusting their heads through the spaces between the
slats.

A cow called in a deep, musical bass, and a calf answered from
a little pen near by, and a pig scurried guiltily out of the cabbages. Seeing all this, seeing the pig in the cabbages, the tangle
of grass in the garden, the broken fence which she had mended
again and again—the little woman, hardly more than a girl, sat
down and cried. The bright Sabbath morning was only a mockery without him!

A few years ago they had bought this farm, paying part, mortgaging the rest in the usual way. Edward Smith was a man of
terrible energy. He worked "nights and Sundays," as the saying
goes, to clear the farm of its brush and of its insatiate mortgage!
In the midst of his Herculean struggle came the call for volunteers, and with the grim and unselfish devotion to his country
which made the Eagle Brigade able to "whip its weight in wild-
cats," he threw down his scythe and grub-ax, turned his cattle
loose, and became a blue-coated cog in a vast machine for killing
men, and not thistles. While the millionaire sent his money to
England for safe-keeping, this man, with his girl-wife and three
babies, left them on a mortgaged farm, and went away to fight
for an idea. It was foolish, but it was sublime for all that.

That was three years before, and the young wife, sitting on the
well-curb on this bright Sabbath harvest morning, was righteously
rebellious. It seemed to her that she had borne her share of the
country's sorrow. Two brothers had been killed, the renter in
whose hands her husband had left the farm had proved a vil-

lain; one year the farm had been without crops, and now the overripe grain was waiting the tardy hand of the neighbor who had rented it, and who was cutting his own grain first.

About six weeks before, she had received a letter saying, "We'll be discharged in a little while." But no other word had come from him. She had seen by the papers that his army was being discharged, and from day to day other soldiers slowly percolated in blue streams back into the State and county, but still *her* hero did not return.

Each week she had told the children that he was coming, and she had watched the road so long that it had become unconscious; and as she stood at the well, or by the kitchen door, her eyes were fixed unthinkingly on the road that wound down the coolly.

Nothing wears on the human soul like waiting. If the stranded mariner, searching the sun-bright seas, could once give up hope of a ship, that horrible grinding on his brain would cease. It was this waiting, hoping, on the edge of despair, that gave Emma Smith no rest.

Neighbors said, with kind intentions: "He's sick, maybe, an' can't start north just yet. He'll come along one o' these days."

"Why don't he write?" was her question, which silenced them all. This Sunday morning it seemed to her as if she could not stand it longer. The house seemed intolerably lonely. So she dressed the little ones in their best calico dresses and home-made jackets, and, closing up the house, set off down the coolly to old Mother Gray's.

"Old Widder Gray" lived at the "mouth of the coolly." She was a widow woman with a large family of stalwart boys and laughing girls. She was the visible incarnation of hospitality and optimistic poverty. With Western open-heartedness she fed every mouth that asked food of her, and worked herself to death as cheerfully as her girls danced in the neighborhood harvest dances.

She waddled down the path to meet Mrs. Smith with a broad smile on her face.

"Oh, you little dears! Come right to your granny. Gimme a kiss! Come right in, Mis' Smith. How are yeh, anyway? Nice mornin', ain't it? Come in an' set down. Everything's in a clutter, but that won't scare you any."

She led the way into the best room, a sunny, square room, carpeted with a faded and patched rag carpet, and papered with white-and-green-striped wall-paper, where a few faded effigies of dead members of the family hung in variously sized oval walnut frames. The house resounded with singing, laughter, whistling, tramping of heavy boots, and riotous scufflings. Half-grown boys came to the door and crooked their fingers at the children, who ran out, and were soon heard in the midst of the fun.

"Don't s'pose you've heard from Ed?" Mrs. Smith shook her head. "He'll turn up some day, when you ain't lookin' for 'm." The good old soul had said that so many times that poor Mrs. Smith derived no comfort from it any longer.

"Liz heard from Al the other day. He's comin' some day this week. Anyhow, they expect him."

"Did he say anything of——"

"No, he didn't," Mrs. Gray admitted. "But then it was only a short letter, anyhow. Al ain't much for writin', anyhow.—But come out and see my new cheese. I tell yeh, I don't believe I ever had better luck in my life. If Ed should come, I want you should take him up a piece of this cheese."

It was beyond human nature to resist the influence of that noisy, hearty, loving household, and in the midst of the singing and laughing the wife forgot her anxiety, for the time at least, and laughed and sang with the rest.

About eleven o'clock a wagon-load more drove up to the door, and Bill Gray, the widow's oldest son, and his whole family, from Sand Lake Coolly, piled out amid a good-natured uproar. Every one talked at once, except Bill, who sat in the wagon with his wrists on his knees, a straw in his mouth, and an amused twinkle in his blue eyes.

"Ain't heard nothin' o' Ed, I s'pose?" he asked in a kind of bellow. Mrs. Smith shook her head. Bill, with a delicacy very striking in such a great giant, rolled his quid in his mouth, and said:

"Didn't know but you had. I hear two or three of the Sand Lake boys are comin'. Left New Orleenes some time this week. Didn't write nothin' about Ed, but no news is good news in such cases, mother always says."

"Well, go put out yer team," said Mrs. Gray, "an' go'n bring me in some taters, an', Sim, you go see if you c'n find some corn. Sadie, you put on the water to bile. Come now, hustle yer boots, all o' yeh. If I feed this yer crowd, we've got to have some raw materials. If y' think I'm goin' to feed yeh on pie—you're jest mightily mistaken."

The children went off into the fields, the girls put dinner on to boil, and then went to change their dresses and fix their hair. "Somebody might come," they said.

"Land sakes, *I hope* not! I don't know where in time I'd set 'em, 'less they'd eat at the second table," Mrs. Gray laughed, in pretended dismay.

The two older boys, who had served their time in the army, lay out on the grass before the house, and whittled and talked desultorily about the war and the crops, and planned buying a threshing-machine. The older girls and Mrs. Smith helped enlarge the table and put on the dishes, talking all the time in that cheery, incoherent, and meaningful way a group of such women have,—a conversation to be taken for its spirit rather than for its letter, though Mrs. Gray at last got the ear of them all and dissertated at length on girls.

"Girls in love ain't no use in the whole blessed week," she said. "Sundays they're a-lookin' down the road, expectin' he'll *come*. Sunday afternoons they can't think o' nothin' else, 'cause he's *here*. Monday mornin's they're sleepy and kind o' dreamy and slimpsy, and good f'r nothin' on Tuesday and Wednesday. Thursday they git absent-minded, an' begin to look off toward Sunday agin, an' mope aroun' and let the dishwater git cold, right under their noses. Friday they break dishes, an' go off in the best room an' snivel, an' look out o' the winder. Saturdays they have queer spurts o' workin' like all p'ssessed, an' spurts o' frizzin' their hair. An' Sunday they begin it all over agin."

The girls giggled and blushed, all through this tirade from their mother, their broad faces and powerful frames anything but suggestive of lackadaisical sentiment. But Mrs. Smith said:

"Now, Mrs. Gray, I hadn't ought to stay to dinner. You've got——"

"Now you set right down! If any of them girls' beaus comes, they'll have to take what's left, that's all. They ain't s'posed to have much appetite, nohow. No, you're goin' to stay if they starve, an' they ain't no danger o' that."

At one o'clock the long table was piled with boiled potatoes, cords of boiled corn on the cob, squash and pumpkin pies, hot biscuit, sweet pickles, bread and butter, and honey. Then one of the girls took down a conch shell from a nail, and, going to the door, blew a long, fine, free blast, that showed there was no weakness of lungs in her ample chest.

Then the children came out of the forest of corn, out of the creek, out of the loft of the barn, and out of the garden.

"They come to their feed f'r all the world jest like the pigs when y' holler 'poo-ee!' See 'em scoot!" laughed Mrs. Gray, every wrinkle on her face shining with delight.

The men shut up their jack-knives, and surrounded the horse-trough to souse their faces in the cold, hard water, and in a few moments the table was filled with a merry crowd, and a row of wistful-eyed youngsters circled the kitchen wall, where they stood first on one leg and then on the other, in impatient hunger.

"Now pitch in, Mrs. Smith," said Mrs. Gray, presiding over the table. "You know these men critters. They'll eat every grain of it, if yeh give 'em a chance. I swan, they're made o' India-rubber, their stomachs is, I know it."

"Haf to eat to work," said Bill, gnawing a cob with a swift, circular motion that rivaled a corn-sheller in results.

"More like workin' to eat," put in one of the girls, with a gig-gle. "More eat 'n work with you."

"*You* needn't say anything, Net. Any one that'll eat seven ears——"

"I didn't, no such thing. You piled your cobs on my plate."

"That'll do to tell Ed Varney. It won't go down here where we know yeh."

"Good land! Eat all yeh want! They's plenty more in the fiel's, but I can't afford to give you young uns tea. The tea is for us women-folks, and 'specially f'r Mis' Smith an' Bill's wife. We're a-goin' to tell fortunes by it."

One by one the men filled up and shoved back, and one by one the children slipped into their places, and by two o'clock the women alone remained around the debris-covered table, sipping their tea and telling fortunes.

As they got well down to the grounds in the cup, they shook them with a circular motion in the hand, and then turned them bottom-side up quickly in the saucer, then twirled them three or four times one way, and three or four times the other, during a breathless pause. Then Mrs. Gray lifted the cup, and, gazing into it with profound gravity, pronounced the impending fate.

It must be admitted that, to a critical observer, she had abundant preparation for hitting close to the mark, as when she told the girls that "somebody was comin'." "It's a man," she went on gravely. "He is crosseyed——"

"Oh, you hush!" cried Nettie.

"He has red hair, and is death on b'iled corn and hot biscuit." The others shrieked with delight.

"But he's goin' to get the mitten, that red-headed feller is, for I see another feller comin' up behind him."

"Oh, lemme see, lemme see!" cried Nettie.

"Keep off," said the priestess, with a lofty gesture. "His hair is black. He don't eat so much, and he works more."

The girls exploded in a shriek of laughter, and pounded their sister on the back.

At last came Mrs. Smith's turn, and she was trembling with excitement as Mrs. Gray again composed her jolly face to what she considered a proper solemnity of expression.

"Somebody is comin' to *you*," she said, after a long pause. "He's got a musket on his back. He's a soldier. He's almost here. See?"

She pointed at two little tea-stems, which really formed a faint suggestion of a man with a musket on his back. He had climbed nearly to the edge of the cup. Mrs. Smith grew pale with excitement. She trembled so she could hardly hold the cup in her hand as she gazed into it.

"It's Ed," cried the old woman. "He's on the way home. Heavens an' earth! There he is now!" She turned and waved her hand out toward the road. They rushed to the door to look where she pointed.

A man in a blue coat, with a musket on his back, was toiling slowly up the hill on the sun-bright, dusty road, toiling slowly, with bent head half hidden by a heavy knapsack. So tired it seemed that walking was indeed a process of falling. So eager to get home he would not stop, would not look aside, but plodded on, amid the cries of the locusts, the welcome of the crickets, and the rustle of the yellow wheat. Getting back to God's country, and his wife and babies!

Laughing, crying, trying to call him and the children at the same time, the little wife, almost hysterical, snatched her hat and ran out into the yard. But the soldier had disappeared over the hill into the hollow beyond, and, by the time she had found the children, he was too far away for her voice to reach him. And, besides, she was not sure it was her husband, for he had not turned his head at their shouts. This seemed so strange. Why didn't he stop to rest at his old neighbor's house? Tortured by hope and doubt, she hurried up the coolly as fast as she could push the baby wagon, the blue-coated figure just ahead pushing steadily, silently forward up the coolly.

When the excited, panting little group came in sight of the gate they saw the blue-coated figure standing, leaning upon the rough rail fence, his chin on his palms, gazing at the empty house. His knapsack, canteen, blankets, and musket lay upon the dusty grass at his feet.

He was like a man lost in a dream. His wide, hungry eyes devoured the scene. The rough lawn, the little unpainted house, the field of clear yellow wheat behind it, down across which streamed the sun, now almost ready to touch the high hill to the west, the crickets crying merrily, a cat on the fence near by, dreaming, unmindful of the stranger in blue——

How peaceful it all was! O God! How far removed from all camps, hospitals, battle lines. A little cabin in a Wisconsin coolly, but it was majestic in its peace. How did he ever leave it for those years of tramping, thirsting, killing?

Trembling, weak with emotion, her eyes on the silent figure, Mrs. Smith hurried up to the fence. Her feet made no noise in the dust and grass, and they were close upon him before he knew of them. The oldest boy ran a little ahead. He will never forget that figure, that face. It will always remain as something epic, that return of the private. He fixed his eyes on the pale face covered with a ragged beard.

"Who *are* you, sir?" asked the wife, or, rather, started to ask, for he turned, stood a moment, and then cried:

"Emma!"

"Edward!"

The children stood in a curious row to see their mother kiss this bearded, strange man, the elder girl sobbing sympathetically with her mother. Illness had left the soldier partly deaf, and this added to the strangeness of his manner.

But the youngest child stood away, even after the girl had recognized her father and kissed him. The man turned then to the baby, and said in a curiously unpaternal tone:

"Come here, my little man; don't you know me?" But the baby backed away under the fence and stood peering at him critically.

"My little man!" What meaning in those words! This baby seemed like some other woman's child, and not the infant he had left in his wife's arms. The war had come between him and his baby—he was only a strange man to him, with big eyes; a soldier, with mother hanging to his arm, and talking in a loud voice.

"And this is Tom," the private said, drawing the oldest boy to him. *"He'll* come and see me. *He* knows his poor old pap when he comes home from the war."

The mother heard the pain and reproach in his voice and hastened to apologize.

"You've changed so, Ed. He can't know yeh. This is papa, Teddy; come and kiss him—Tom and Mary do. Come, won't you?" But Teddy still peered through the fence with solemn eyes, well out of reach. He resembled a half-wild kitten that hesitates, studying the tones of one's voice.

"I'll fix him," said the soldier, and sat down to undo his knapsack, out of which he drew three enormous and very red apples. After giving one to each of the older children, he said:

"Now I guess he'll come. Eh, my little man? Now come see your pap."

Teddy crept slowly under the fence, assisted by the overzealous Tommy, and a moment later was kicking and squalling in his father's arms. Then they entered the house, into the sitting room, poor, bare, art-forsaken little room, too, with its rag carpet, its square clock, and its two or three chromos and pictures from *Harper's Weekly* pinned about.

"Emma, I'm all tired out," said Private Smith, as he flung himself down on the carpet as he used to do, while his wife brought a pillow to put under his head, and the children stood about munching their apples.

"Tommy, you run and get me a pan of chips, and Mary, you get the tea-kettle on, and I'll go and make some biscuit."

And the soldier talked. Question after question he poured forth about the crops, the cattle, the renter, the neighbors. He slipped his heavy government brogan shoes off his poor, tired, blistered feet, and lay out with utter, sweet relaxation. He was a free man again, no longer a soldier under command. At supper he stopped once, listened and smiled. "That's old Spot. I know her voice. I s'pose that's her calf out there in the pen. I can't milk her tonight, though. I'm too tired. But I tell you, I'd like a drink o' her milk. What's become of old Rove?"

"He died last winter. Poisoned, I guess." There was a moment of sadness for them all. It was some time before the husband spoke again, in a voice that trembled a little.

"Poor old feller! He'd 'a' known me half a mile away. I expected him to come down the hill to meet me. It 'ud 'a' been more like comin' home if I could 'a' seen him comin' down the road an' waggin' his tail, an' laughin' that way he has. I tell yeh, it kind o' took hold o' me to see the blinds down an' the house shut up."

"But, yeh see, we—we expected you'd write again 'fore you started. And then we thought we'd see you if you *did* come," she hastened to explain.

"Well, I ain't worth a cent on writin'. Besides, it's just as well yeh didn't know when I was comin'. I tell you, it sounds good to hear them chickens out there, an' turkeys, an' the crickets. Do you know they don't have just the same kind o' crickets down South? Who's Sam hired t' help cut yer grain?"

"The Ramsey boys."

"Looks like a good crop; but I'm afraid I won't do much gettin' it cut. This cussed fever an' ague has got me down pretty low. I don't know when I'll get rid of it. I'll bet I've took twenty-five pounds of quinine if I've taken a bit. Gimme another biscuit. I tell yeh, they taste good, Emma. I ain't had anything like it— Say, if you'd 'a' hear'd me braggin' to th' boys about your butter 'n' biscuits I'll bet your ears 'ud 'a' burnt."

The private's wife colored with pleasure. "Oh, you're always a-braggin' about your things. Everybody makes good butter."

"Yes; old lady Snyder, for instance."

"Oh, well, she ain't to be mentioned. She's Dutch."

"Or old Mis' Snively. One more cup o' tea, Mary. That's my girl! I'm feeling better already. I just b'lieve the matter with me is, I'm *starved*."

This was a delicious hour, one long to be remembered. They were like lovers again. But their tenderness, like that of a typical American family, found utterance in tones, rather than in words. He was praising her when praising her biscuit, and she knew it. They grew soberer when he showed where he had been struck, one ball burning the back of his hand, one cutting away a lock of hair from his temple, and one passing through the calf of his leg. The wife shuddered to think how near she had come to being a soldier's widow. Her waiting no longer seemed hard. This sweet, glorious hour effaced it all.

Then they rose, and all went out into the garden and down to the barn. He stood beside her while she milked old Spot. They began to plan fields and crops for next year.

His farm was weedy and encumbered, a rascally renter had run away with his machinery (departing between two days), his children needed clothing, the years were coming upon him, he was sick and emaciated, but his heroic soul did not quail. With the same courage with which he had faced his Southern march he entered upon a still more hazardous future.

Oh, that mystic hour! The pale man with big eyes standing there by the well, with his young wife by his side. The vast moon swinging above the eastern peaks, the cattle winding down the pasture slopes with jangling bells, the crickets singing, the stars blooming out sweet and far and serene; the katydids rhythmically calling, the little turkeys crying querulously, as they settled to roost in the poplar tree near the open gate. The voices at the well drop lower, the little ones nestle in their father's arms at last, and Teddy falls asleep there.

The common soldier of the American volunteer army had returned. His war with the South was over, and his fight, his daily running fight with nature and against the injustice of his fellow-men, was begun again.

Octave Thanet
(1850-1934)

OCTAVE THANET was the pen-name of Alice French who was born in Andover, Massachusetts, but spent her girlhood in Iowa and Arkansas, where her father was a banker and railroad president. Her novels and short stories deal, therefore, mainly with life in the Middle West in the eighties and nineties, and her subjects are largely social. Her interest in the lives and characters of those whom fortune had not treated too well appears in the following titles: *Knitters in the Sun* (1887), *Expiation* (1890), *We All* (1891), *Otto the Knight* (1891), *Stories of a Western Town* (1892), *The Missionary Sheriff* (1897), *The Man of the Hour* (1905), and *Stories That End Well* (1911).

The Old Partisan appeared first in *Chap Book Stories* (1896). Its general theme is that blind loyalty to a magnetic leader which is a frequent phenomenon in a democracy. The object of the old partisan's devotion is James G. Blaine (1830–1893). Blaine was a congressman from 1863 to 1876 and leader of the "Half-breed" Republicans who were opposed by the "Stalwarts." He failed to secure the Republican nomination in 1876, mainly because of a charge of corruption brought against him, but in 1884, although nominated, he was beaten by the Democratic candidate, Cleveland. The Republican convention which forms the background of the story is that of 1895 which nominated William McKinley of Ohio (1843–1901); he beat William Jennings Bryan in a vigorous campaign on the issue of the gold standard. At the time of McKinley's nomination Blaine had been dead for more than two years, but his memory was still fresh with many who had been drawn to him by his personal magnetism.

The Old Partisan

I sat so far back in the gallery that my opinion of my delegate friend dwindled with every session. Nevertheless my unimportant seat had its advantages. I could see the vast assembly and watch the throbbing of the Republican pulse if I could not hear its heartbeats. Therefore, perhaps, I studied my neighbors more than I might study them under different circumstances. The great wooden hall had its transient and unsubstantial character stamped on every bare wooden joist and unclinched nail. It was gaudy with flags and bunting and cheap portraits. There were tin bannerets crookedly marshaled on the floor to indicate the homes of the different States. A few delegates, doubtless new to the business and overzealous, were already on the floor, but none of the principals were visible. They were perspiring and arguing in those committee rooms, those hotel lobbies and crowded hotel rooms, where the real business of the convention was already done and neatly prepared for presentation to the nation. I had nothing to keep me from studying my neighbors. In front of me sat two people who had occupied the same seats at every session that I was present at, a young girl and an old man. The girl wore the omnipresent shirtwaist (of pretty blue and white tints, with snowy cuffs and collar), and her green straw hat was decked with blue corn-flowers, from which I inferred that she had an eye on the fashions. Her black hair was thick and glossy under the green straw. I thought that she had a graceful neck. It was very white— whiter than her face, which had a touch of sunburn, as if she were often out in the open air. Somehow I concluded that she was a shop-girl and rode a wheel. If I were wrong it is not likely that I shall ever know.

The old man, I fancied, was not so old as he looked; his deli-

From *Stories That End Well*, by Octave Thanet, copyright 1911, 1938. Used by special permission of the publishers, the Bobbs-Merrill Company.

cate, haggard profile may have owed its sunken lines and the dim eye to sickness rather than to years. He wore the heavy black broadcloth of the rural politician, and his coat sagged over his narrow chest as if he had left his waistcoat at home. On his coat lapel were four old-fashioned Blaine badges. Incessantly he fanned himself.

"It can't be they ain't going to nominate him today?" he asked rather than asserted, his voice breaking on the higher notes, the mere wreck of a voice.

"Oh, maybe later," the girl assured him.

"Well, I wanted to attend a Republican convention once more before I died. Your ma would have it I wasn't strong enough; but I knew better; you and I knew better, didn't we, Jennie?"

She made no answer except to pat his thin, ribbed, brown hand with her soft, white, slim one; but there was a world of sympathy in the gesture and her silent smile.

"I wonder what your ma said when she came downstairs and found the letter and us gone," he cackled with the garrulous glee of a child recounting successful mischief; "made me think of the times when you was little and I stole you away for the circus. Once your pa thought you was lost—'member? And once you had on your school dress and you'd tore it—she did scold you that time. But we had fun when they used to let me have money, didn't we, Jennie?"

"Well, now I earn money, we have good times, too, grandpa," said Jennie, smiling the same tender, comprehending smile.

"We do that; I don't know what I would do 'cept for you, lambie, and this is—this is a grand time, Jennie, you look and listen; it's a great thing to see a nation making its principles and its president—and such a president!"

He half turned his head as he spoke, with a mounting enthusiasm, thus bringing his flushing face and eager eyes—no longer dim—into the focus of his next neighbor's bright gray eyes. The neighbor was a young man, not very young, but hardly to be called elderly, of an alert bearing and kindly smile.

"I think him a pretty fair man myself," said the other with a jocose understatement; "I come from his town."

What was there in such a simple statement to bring a distinctly anxious look into the young girl's soft eyes? There it was; one could not mistake it.

"Well!" said the old man—there was a flattering deference in his voice. "Well, well. And—and maybe you've seen him lately?" The quavering tones sharpened with a keener feeling; it was almost as if the man were inquiring for some one on whom he had a great stake of affection. "How did he look? Was he better, stronger?"

"Oh, he looked elegant," said the Ohio man, easily, but with a disconcerted side glance at the girl, whose eyes were imploring him.

"I've been a Blaine man ever since he was run, the time Bob Ingersoll nominated him," said the old man, who sighed as if relieved. "I was at that convention and heard the speech——"

"Ah, that was a speech to hear," said a man behind, and two or three men edged their heads nearer.

The old Republican straightened his bent shoulders, his winter-stung features softened and warmed at the manifestation of interest, his voice sank to the confidential undertone of the narrator.

"You're right, sir, right; it was a magnificent speech. I can see him jest as he stood there, a stoutish, good-looking, smooth-faced man, his eyes straight ahead, and an alternate that sat next me— I was an alternate; I've been an alternate four times; I could have been a delegate, but I says, 'No, abler men than me are wanting it; I'm willing to fight in the ranks.' But I wished I had a vote, a free vote that day, I tell you. The alternate near me, he says, 'You'll hear something fine now; I've heard him speak.'"

"You did, too, I guess."

"We could hear from the first minute. That kinder fixed our attention. He had a mellow, rich kind of voice that melted into our ears. We found ourselves listening and liking him from the first sentence. At first he was as quiet as a summer breeze, but presently he began to warm up, and the words flowed like a stream of jewels. It was electrifying: it was thrilling, sir; it took us off our feet before we knew it, and when he came to the climax, those of us that weren't yelling in the aisles were jumping up and down on our chairs! I know I found myself prancing up

and down on my own hat on a chair, swinging somebody else's
hat and screaming at the top of my voice, with the tears running
down my cheeks. God! sir, there were men there on their feet
cheering their throats out that had to vote against him afterward
—had to because they were instructed—no more free will than a
checked trunk!" The light died out of his face. "Yes, sir, a great
speech; never a greater ever made at a convention anywhere,
never so great a speech, whoever made it: but it did no good, he
wasn't nominated, and when we did nominate him we were
cheated out of our victory. Well, we'll do better this day."

"We will that," said the other man, heartily; "McKinley——"

"You'll excuse me—" the old man struck in with a deprecating
air, yet under the apology was something fiercely eager and anxious that glued the hearer's eyes to his quivering old face—"you'll
excuse me. I—I am considerable of an invalid, and I don't keep
the run of things as I used to. You see, I live with my daughter,
and you know how womenfolks are, fretting lest things could
make you sick, and my girl she worries so, me reading the papers.
Fact is I got a shock once, an awful shock"—he shivered involuntarily and his dim eyes clouded—"and it worried her seeing me
read. Hadn't ought to; it don't worry Jennie here, who often gets
me a paper, quiet like; but you know how it is with women—it's
easier giving them their head a little—and so I don't see many
papers, and I kinder dropped off. It seems queer, but I don't
exactly sense it about this McKinley. Is he running against Blaine
or jest for vice?"

The girl, under some feminine pretext of dropping and reaching for her handkerchief, threw upward a glance of appeal at the
interlocutor. Hurriedly she stepped into the conversation. "My
grandfather read a false report about—about Mr. Blaine's sickness, and he was not well at the time and it brought on a bad
attack."

"I understand," said the listener, with a grave nod of his head
and movement of his eyes in the girl's direction.

"But about McKinley!" the old man persisted.

"He's for Vice-President," the girl announced, her eyes fixed
on the hesitating man from Canton. I have often admired the
intrepid fashion in which a woman will put her conscience at a
moral hedge, while a man of no finer spiritual fiber will be strain-

ing his eyes to find a hole through which he can crawl. "Mc-Kinley is not opposed to Blaine, is he?" she asked the man.

"The Republican party has no name that is more loved than that of James G. Blaine," said the man, gravely.

"That's so, that's so!" the old partisan assented eagerly; "to my mind he's a logical candidate."

The Canton man nodded, and asked if he had ever seen Blaine.

"Once, only once. I was on a delegation sent to wait on him and ask him to our town to speak—he was in Cincinnati. I held out my hand when my turn came, and the chairman nearly knocked the breath out of me by saying, 'Here's the man who gave more to our campaign fund and worked harder than any man in the county, and we all worked hard for you, too.' Well, Mr. Blaine looked at me. You know the intent way he looks. He has the most wonderful eyes; look right at you and seem to bore into you like a gimlet. I felt as if he was looking right down into my soul, and I tell you I was glad, for I choked up so I couldn't find a word, not a word, and I was ready and fluent enough in those days, too, I can tell you; but I stood there filling up, and squeezed his hand and gulped and got red, like a fool. But he understood. 'I have heard of your loyalty to Republican principles, Mr. Painter,' says he, in that beautiful voice of his, that was like a violin; and I burst in—I couldn't help it—'It ain't loyalty to Republican principles, it's to you.' I said that right out. And he smiled, and said he, 'Well, that's wrong, but it isn't for me to quarrel with you there, Mr. Painter,' and then they pushed me along: but twice while the talk was going on I saw him look my way and caught his eye, and he smiled, and when we were all shaking hands for good-by, he shook hands with a good, firm grip, and said he, 'Good-by, Mr. Painter; I hope we shall meet again.'"

The old man drew a long sigh. "Those few moments paid for everything," he said. "I've never seen him since. I've been sick and lost money. I ain't the man I was. I never shall be put on any delegation again, or be sent to any convention; but I thought if I could only go once more to a Republican convention, and hear them holler for Blaine, and holler once more myself, I'd be willinger to die. And I told Tom Hale that, and he and Jennie raised the money. Yes, Jennie, I'm going to tell—he and Jennie put off being married a bit so's I could go, and go on plenty of money. Jennie, she worked a month longer to have plenty, and Tom, he slipped ten dollars into my hand unbeknown to her jest as we were going, so I'd always have a dime to give the waiter or the porter. I was never one of these hayseed farmers too stingy to give a colored boy a dime when he done his best. I didn't need no money for badges; I got my old badges—see!"

He pushed out the lapel of his coat, covered with those old-fashioned trade bits of tinsel and ribbon, smiling confidently. The girl had flushed crimson to the rim of her white collar; but there was not a trace of petulance in her air; and, all at once looking at him, her eyes filled with tears.

"Tom's an awful good fellow," he said, "an awful good fellow."

"I'm sure of that," said the Canton man, with the frank American friendliness, making a little bow in Miss Jennie's direction; "but see here, Mr. Painter, do you come from Izard? Are you the man that saved the county for the Republicans, by mortgaging the farm and then going on a house-to-house canvass?"

"That's me," the old man acquiesced, blushing with pleasure; "I didn't think, though, that it was known outside——"

"Things go further than you guess. I'm a newspaper man, and I can tell you that I shall speak of it again in my paper. Well, I guess they've got through with their mail and the platform's coming in."

Thus he brushed aside the old man's agitated thanks.

"One moment," said the old man, "who—who's going to nominate him?"

For the space of an eyeblink the kindly Canton man looked embarrassed, then he said, briskly: "Foraker, Foraker of Ohio—he's the principal one. That's he now, chairman of the Committee on Resolutions. He's there, the tall man with the mustache——"

"Isn't that elderly man with the stooped shoulders and the chin beard and caved-in face Teller?" It was a man near me, on the seat behind, who spoke, tapping the Canton man with his fan, to attract his attention; already the pitiful concerns of the old man, who was "a little off" (as I had heard some one on the seat whisper), were sucked out of notice in the whirlpool of the approaching political storm.

"Yes, that's Teller," answered the Canton man, his mouth straightening and growing thin.

"Is it to be a bolt?"

The Canton man nodded, at which the other whistled and communicated the information to his neighbors, one of whom remarked, "Let 'em bolt and be d——d!" A subtle excitement seemed to communicate its vibrations to all the gallery. Perhaps I should except the old partisan; he questioned the girl in a whisper, and then, seeming to be satisfied, watched the strange scene that ensued with an expression of patient weariness. The girl explained parts of the platform to him and he assented; it was good Republican doctrine, he said, but what do they mean with all this talk against the money; were they having trouble with the mining States again? The Canton man stopped to explain—he certainly was good-humored.

During the next twenty minutes, filled as they were with savage emotion, while the galleries, like the floor, were on their chairs yelling, cheering, brandishing flags and fists and fans and pampas plumes of red, white, and blue at the little band of silver men who marched through the ranks of their former comrades, he stood, he waved his fan in his feeble old hand, but he did not shout. "You must excuse me," said he, "I'm all right on the money question, but I'm saving my voice to shout for him!"

"That's right," said the Canton man; but he took occasion to cast a backward glance which I met, and it said as plainly as a glance can speak, "I wish I were out of this!"

Meanwhile, with an absent but happy smile, the old Blaine man was keeping time to the vast waves of sound that rose and swelled above the band, above the cheering, above the cries of anger and scorn, the tremendous chorus that had stiffened men's hearts as they marched to death and rang through streets filled with armies and thrilled the waiting hearts at home:

> "Three cheers for the red, white, and blue!
> Three cheers for the red, white, and blue!
> The army and navy forever, three cheers for the
> red, white, and blue!"

But when the chairman had stilled the tumult and made his grim comment, "There appear to be enough delegates left to

transact business," the old partisan cast his eyes down to the
floor with a chuckle. "I can't see the hole they made; it's so small.
Say, ain't he a magnificent chairman; you can hear every word
he says!"

"Bully chairman," said a cheerful "rooter" in the rear, who
had enjoyed the episode more than words can say, and had
cheered the passing of Silver with such choice quotations from
popular songs as "Good-by, my lover, good-by," and "Just tell
them that you saw me," and plainly felt that he, too, had
adorned the moment. "I nearly missed coming this morning, and
I wouldn't have missed it for a tenner; they're going to nominate now."

The old man caught his breath; then he smiled. "I'll help you
shout pretty soon," said he, while he sat down very carefully.

The "rooter," a good-looking young fellow with a Reed button
and three or four gaudy badges decking his crash coat, nodded
and tapped his temple furtively, still retaining his expression of
radiant good-nature. The Canton man nodded and frowned.

I felt that the Canton man need not be afraid. Somehow we
were all tacitly taking care that this poor, bewildered soul should
not have its little dream of loyal, unselfish satisfaction dispelled.

"Ah, my countrymen," I thought, "you do a hundred crazy
things, you crush *les convenances* under foot, you can be fooled
by frantic visionaries—but how I love you!"

It was Baldwin of Iowa that made the first speech. He was one
of the very few men—I had almost said of the two men—that we
in the galleries had the pleasure of hearing; and we could hear
every word.

He began with a glowing tribute to Blaine. At the first sentence, our old man flung his gray head in the air with the gesture of the war-horse when he catches the first, far-off scream of
the trumpet. He leaned forward, his features twitching, his eyes
burning; the fan dropped out of his limp hand; his fingers, rap-
ping his palm, clinched and loosened themselves unconsciously
in an overpowering agitation. His face was white as marble, with
ominous blue shadows; but every muscle was strained; his chest
expanded; his shoulders drew back; his mouth was as strong and
firm as a young man's. For a second we could see what he had
been at his prime.

Then the orator's climax came, and the name—the magic name that was its own campaign cry in itself.

The old partisan leaped to his feet; he waved his hands above his head; wild, strange, in his white flame of excitement. He shouted; and we all shouted with him, the McKinley man and the Reed man vying with each other (I here offer my testimony to the scope and quality of that young Reed man's voice), and the air rang about us: "Blaine! Blaine! James G. Blaine!" He shrieked the name again and again, goading into life the waning applause. Then in an instant his will snapped under the strain; his gray head tilted in the air; his gray head went back on his neck.

The Canton man and I caught him in time to ease the fall. We were helped to pull him into the aisle. There were four of us by this time—his granddaughter and the Reed "rooter," besides the Canton man and myself.

We carried him into the wide passageway that led to the seats. The Reed young man ran for water, and, finding none, quickly returned with a glass of lemonade (he was a young fellow ready in shifts), and with it we bathed the old man's face.

Presently he came back, by degrees, to the world; he was not conscious, but we could see that he was not going to die.

"He'll be all right in no time," declared the Reed man. "You had better go back and get your seats, and keep mine!"

I assured both men that I could not return for more than a short time, having an engagement for luncheon.

"That's all right," said the Reed man, turning to the Canton man. "I ain't shouting when Foraker comes; you are. You go back and keep my seat; I'll come in later on Hobart."

So the kindly Canton man returned to the convention for which he was longing, and we remained in our little corner by the window, the young girl fanning the old man, and the young man on the watch for a boy with water. He darted after one; and then the girl turned to me.

No one disturbed us. Below, the traffic of a great city roared up to us and a brass band clanged merrily. The crowd hurried past, drawn by the tidings that "the fight was on"; it choked the outlets and suffocated the galleries.

"He's been that way ever since he read, suddenly, that Blaine

was dead," she said, lowering her voice to keep it safe from his
failing ears; "he had a kind of a stroke, and ever since he's had
the notion that Blaine was alive and was going to be nominated,
and his heart was set on going here. Mother was afraid; but when
—when he cried to go, I could not help taking him—I didn't
know but maybe it might help him; he was such a smart man
and such a good man; and he has had trouble about mortgaging
the farm; and he worked so hard to get the money back, so
mother would feel all right. All through the hot weather he
worked, and I guess that's how it happened. You don't think it's
hurt him? The doctor said he might go. He told T——, a gentleman friend of mine, who asked him."

"Oh, dear, no," said I; "it has been good for him."

I asked for her address, which fortunately was near, and I
offered her the cab that was waiting for me. I had some ado to
persuade her to accept it; but when I pointed to her grandfather's pale face she did accept it, thanking me in a simple but
touching way, and, of course, begging me to visit her at Izard,
Ohio.

All this while we had been sedulously fanning the old man,
who would occasionally open his eyes for a second, but gave no
other sign of returning consciousness.

The young Reed man came back with the water. He was bath-
ing the old man's forehead in a skillful and careful way, using
my handkerchief, when an uproar of cheering shook the very
floor under us, and the rafters overhead.

"Who is it?" the old man inquired feebly.

"Foraker! Foraker!" bellowed the crowd.

"He's nominated him!" muttered the old man; but this time
he did not attempt to rise. With a smile of great content he
leaned against his granddaughter's strong young frame and listened, while the cheers swelled into a deafening din, and im-
measurable tumult of sound, out of which a few strong voices
shaped the chorus of the "Battle Cry of Freedom," to be caught
up by fifteen thousand throats and pealed through the walls far
down the city streets to the vast crowd without.

The young Reed "boomer," carried away by the moment,
flung his free hand above his head and yelled defiantly: "Three
cheers for the man from Maine!" Instantly he caught at his wits,

his color turned, and he lifted an abashed face to the young girl.

"But, really, you know, that ain't giving nothing away," he apologized, plucking up heart. "May I do it again?"

The old partisan's eye lighted. "Now they're shouting! That's like old times! Yes, go it again, boy! Blaine! Blaine! James G. Blaine!"

He let us lead him to the carriage, the rapturous smile still on his lips. The "rooter" and I wormed our way through the crowd back to the seat which the kind Canton man had kept for us.

We were quite like old acquaintances now; and he turned to me at once, "Was there ever a politician or a statesman, since Henry Clay, loved so well as James G. Blaine?"

John William De Forest

(1826-1906)

J. W. DE FOREST was one of the first American realists of definite literary standing. He was born in Humphreysville (now Seymour), Connecticut, and left school early because of the death of his father. After two years in Europe and the Near East he returned to America, married, and divided his time between New Haven, Connecticut, and Charleston, South Carolina. The outbreak of the Civil War, however, found him with his sympathies on the side of the North; he recruited a company in his native state, served as captain, and ended the war as major. After a period in charge of the Freedman's Bureau at Greenville, South Carolina, he retired to New Haven and spent his remaining years in writing novels. Of these the best known is *Miss Ravenel's Confession,* serialized by Harper's in 1866 and reissued by the same house in 1939; it is the story of a Confederate girl in the North during the Civil War days.

An Inspired Lobbyist was first printed in *The Atlantic Monthly* in 1872. It is a burlesque picture of the scheming lobbyist at work, a rogue so clever that the reader is disposed to forgive him in that easy American way which led Ambassador Bryce to say that when Boss Tweed was ruling and robbing New York City, the citizens were so amused that they forgot to be angry.

An Inspired Lobbyist

A certain fallen angel (politeness toward his numerous and influential friends forbids me to mention his name abruptly) lately
entered into the body of Mr. Ananias Pullwool, of Washington,
D. C.

As the said body was a capacious one, having been greatly
enlarged circumferentially since it acquired its full longitude,
there was accommodation in it for both the soul of Pullwool
himself (it was a very little one) and for his distinguished visi-
tant. Indeed, there was so much room in it that they never
crowded each other, and that Pullwool hardly knew, if he even
so much as mistrusted, that there was a chap in with him. But
other people must have been aware of this double tenantry, or
at least must have been shrewdly suspicious of it, for it soon
became quite common to hear fellows say, "Pullwool has got the
Devil in him."

There was, indeed, a remarkable change—a change not so much
moral as physical and mental—in this gentleman's ways of de-
porting and behaving himself. From being logy in movement
and slow if not absolutely dull in mind, he became wonderfully
agile and energetic. He had been a lobbyist, and he remained a
lobbyist still, but such a different one, so much more vigorous,
eager, clever, and impudent, that his best friends (if he could be
said to have any friends) scarcely knew him for the same Pullwool. His fat fingers were in the buttonholes of Congressmen
from the time when they put those buttonholes on in the morning to the time when they took them off at night. He seemed to
be at one and the same moment treating some honorable member in the barroom of the Arlington and running another hon-

From *The Atlantic Monthly*, December, 1872; reprinted by permission of
The Atlantic Monthly Company.

orable member to cover in the committee-rooms of the Capitol.
He log-rolled bills which nobody else believed could be log-
rolled, and he pocketed fees which absolutely and point-blank
refused to go into other people's pockets. During this short period of his life he was the most successful and famous lobbyist
in Washington, and the most sought after by the most rascally
and desperate claimants of unlawful millions.

But, like many another man who has the Devil in him, Mr.
Pullwool ran his luck until he ran himself into trouble. An in-
vestigating committee pounced upon him; he was put in confinement for refusing to answer questions; his filchings were held
up to the execration of the envious both by virtuous members
and a virtuous press; and when he at last got out of durance he
found it good to quit the District of Columbia for a season. Thus
it happened that Mr. Pullwool and his eminent lodger took the
cars and went to and fro upon the earth seeking what they might
devour.

In the course of their travels they arrived in a little State,
which may have been Rhode Island, or may have been Connecticut, or may have been one of the Pleiades, but which at all
events had two capitals. Without regard to Morse's Gazetteer, or
to whatever other Gazetteer may now be in currency, we shall
affirm that one of these capitals was called Slowburg and the
other Fastburg. For some hundreds of years (let us say five hundred, in order to be sure and get it high enough) Slowburg and
Fastburg had shared between them, turn and turn about, year
on and year off, all the gubernatorial and legislative pomps and
emoluments that the said State had to bestow. On the first of
April of every odd year the governor, preceded by citizen soldiers, straddling or curvetting through the mud—the governor,
followed by twenty barouches full of eminent citizens, who were
not known to be eminent at any other time, but who made a
rush for a ride on this occasion as certain old ladies do at fu-
nerals—the governor, taking off his hat to pavements full of
citizens of all ages, sizes, and colors, who did not pretend to be
eminent—the governor, catching a fresh cold at every corner, and
wishing the whole thing were passing at the equator,—the governor triumphantly entered Slowburg,—observe, Slowburg,—read
his always enormously long message there, and convened the

legislature there. On the first of April of every even year the same governor, or a better one who had succeeded him, went through the same ceremonies in Fastburg. Each of these capitals boasted, or rather blushed over, a shabby old barn of a State-House, and each of them maintained a company of foot-guards and ditto of horse-guards, the latter very loose in their saddles. In each the hotels and boarding-houses had a full year and a lean year, according as the legislature sat in the one or in the other. In each there was a loud call for fresh shad and stewed oysters, or a comparatively feeble call for fresh shad and stewed oysters, under the same biennial conditions.

Such was the oscillation of grandeur and power between the two cities. It was an old-time arrangement, and like many other old-fashioned things, as for instance wood fires in open fireplaces, it had not only its substantial merits but its superficial inconveniences. Every year certain ancient officials were obliged to pack up hundreds of public documents and expedite them from Fastburg to Slowburg, or from Slowburg back to Fastburg. Every year there was an expense of a few dollars on this account, which the State treasurer figured up with agonies of terror, and which the opposition roared at as if the administration could have helped it. The State-Houses were two mere deformities of patched plaster and leprous whitewash; they were such shapeless, graceless, dilapidated wigwams, that no sensitive patriot could look at them without wanting to fly to the uttermost parts of the earth; and yet it was not possible to build new ones, and hardly possible to obtain appropriations enough to shingle out the weather; for Fastburg would vote no money to adorn Slowburg, and Slowburg was equally niggardly toward Fastburg. The same jealousy produced the same frugality in the management of other public institutions, so that the patients of the lunatic asylum were not much better lodged and fed than the average sane citizen, and the gallows-birds in the State's prison were brought down to a temperance which caused admirers of that species of fowl to tremble with indignation. In short, the two capitals were as much at odds as the two poles of a magnet, and the results of this repulsion were not all of them worthy of hysterical admiration.

But advantages seesawed with disadvantages. In this double-ender of a State political jobbery was at fault, because it had no headquarters. It could not get together a ring; it could not raise a corps of lobbyists. Such few ax-grinders as there were had to dodge back and forth between the Fastburg grindstone and the Slowburg grindstone, without ever fairly getting their tools sharpened. Legislature here and legislature there; it was like guessing at a pea between two thimbles; you could hardly ever put your finger on the right one. Then what one capital favored the other disfavored; and between them appropriations were kicked and hustled under the table; the grandest of railroad schemes shrunk into waste-paper baskets; in short, the public treasury was next door to the unapproachable. Such, indeed, was the desperate condition of lobbyists in this State, that, had it contained a single philanthropist of the advanced radical stripe, he would surely have brought in a bill for their relief and encouragement.

Into the midst of this happily divided community dropped Mr. Ananias Pullwool with the Devil in him. It remains to be seen whether this pair could figure up anything worth pocketing out of the problem of two capitals.

It was one of the even years, and the legislature met in Fastburg, and the little city was brimful. Mr. Pullwool with difficulty found a place for himself without causing the population to slop over. Of course he went to a hotel, for he needed to make as many acquaintances as possible, and he knew that a bar was a perfect hot-house for ripening such friendships as he cared for. He took the best room he could get; and as soon as chance favored he took a better one, with parlor attached; and on the sideboard in the parlor he always had cigars and decanters. The result was that in a week or so he was on jovial terms with several senators, numerous members of the lower house, and all the members of the "third house." But lobbying did not work in Fastburg as Mr. Pullwool had found it to work in other capitals. He exhibited the most dazzling double-edged axes, but nobody would grind them; he pointed out the most attractive and convenient of logs for rolling, but nobody would put a lever to them.

"What the doose does this mean?" he at last inquired of Mr. Thomas Dicker, a member who had smoked dozens of his cigars and drunk quarts out of his decanters. "I don't understand this little old legislature at all, Mr. Dicker. Nobody wants to make any money; at least, nobody has the spirit to try to make any. And yet the State is full; never been bled a drop; full as a tick. What does it mean?"

Mr. Dicker looked disconsolate. Perhaps it may be worth a moment's time to explain that he could not well look otherwise. Broken in fortune and broken in health, he was a failure and knew it. His large forehead showed power, and he was in fact a lawyer of some ability; and still he could not support his family, could not keep a mold of mortgages from creeping all over his house-lot, and had so many creditors that he could not walk the streets comfortably. The trouble lay in hard drinking, with its resultant waste of time, infidelity to trust, and impatience of application. Thin, haggard, duskily pallid, deeply wrinkled at forty, his black eyes watery and set in baggy circles of a dull brown, his lean dark hands shaky and dirty, his linen wrinkled and buttonless, his clothing frayed and unbrushed, he was an impersonation of failure. He had gone into the legislature with a desperate hope of somehow finding money in it, and as yet he had discovered nothing more than his beggarly three dollars a day, and he felt himself more than ever a failure. No wonder that he wore an air of profound depression, approaching to absolute wretchedness and threatening suicide.

He looked the more cast down by contrast with the successful Mr. Pullwool, gaudily alight with satin and jewelry, and shining with conceit. Pullwool, by the way, although a dandy (that is, such a dandy as one sees in gambling-saloons and behind liquor-bars), was far from being a thing of beauty. He was so obnoxiously gross and shapeless, that it seemed as if he did it on purpose and to be irritating. His fat head was big enough to make a dwarf of, hunchback and all. His mottled cheeks were vast and pendulous to that degree that they inspired the imaginative beholder with terror, as reminding him of avalanches and landslides which might slip their hold at the slightest shock and plunge downward in a path of destruction. One puffy eyelid drooped in a sinister way; obviously that was the eye that the Devil had selected for his own; he kept it well curtained for purposes of concealment. Looking out of this peep-hole, the Satanic badger could see a short, thick nose, and by leaning forward a little he could get a glimpse of a broad chin of several stories. Another unpleasing feature was a full set of false teeth, which grinned in a ravenous fashion that was truly disquieting, as if they were capable of devouring the whole internal revenue. Finally, this continent of physiognomy was diversified by a gigantic hairy wart, which sprouted defiantly from the temple nearest the game eye, as though Lucifer had accidentally poked one of his horns through. Mr. Dicker, who was a sensitive, squeamish man (as drunkards sometimes are, through bad digestion and shaky nerves), could hardly endure the sight of this wart, and always wanted to ask Pullwool why he didn't cut it off.

"What's the meaning of it all?" persisted the Washington wire-puller, surveying the Fastburg wire-puller with bland superiority, much as the city mouse may have surveyed the country mouse.

"Two capitals," responded Dicker, withdrawing his nervous glance from the wart, and locking his hands over one knee to quiet their trembling.

Mr. Pullwool, having the Old Harry in him, and being consequently full of all malice and subtlety, perceived at once the full scope and force of the explanation.

"I see," he said, dropping gently back into his arm-chair, with the plethoric, soft movement of a subsiding pillow. The puckers of his cumbrous eyelids drew a little closer together; his bilious eyes peered out cautiously between them, like sallow assassins watching through curtained windows; for a minute or so he kept up what might without hyperbole be called a devil of a thinking.

"I've got it," he broke out at last. "Dicker, I want you to bring in a bill to make Fastburg the only capital."

"What is the use?" asked the legislator, looking more disconsolate, more hopeless than ever. "Slowburg will oppose it and beat it."

"Never you mind," persisted Mr. Pullwool. "You bring in your little bill and stand up for it like a man. There's money in it. You don't see it? Well, I do; I'm used to seeing money in things; and in this case I see it plain. As sure as whisky is whisky, there's money in it."

Mr. Pullwool's usually dull and, so to speak, extinct countenance was fairly alight and aflame with exultation. It was almost a wonder that his tallowy person did not gutter beneath the blaze, like an over-fat candle under the flaring of a wick too large for it.

"Well, I'll bring in the bill," agreed Mr. Dicker, catching the enthusiasm of his counselor and shaking off his lethargy. He perceived a dim promise of fees, and at the sight his load of despondency dropped away from him, as Christian's burden loosened in presence of the cross. He looked a little like the confident, resolute Tom Dicker, who twenty years before had graduated from college the brightest, bravest, most eloquent fellow in his class, and the one who seemed to have before him the finest future.

"Snacks!" said Mr. Pullwool.

At this brazen word Mr. Dicker's countenance fell again; he was ashamed to talk so frankly about plundering his fellow-citizens; "a little grain of conscience turned him sour."

"I will take pay for whatever I can do as a lawyer," he stammered.

"Get out!" laughed the Satanic one. "You just take all there is a-going! You need it bad enough. I know when a man's hard up. I know the signs. I've been as bad off as you; had to look all ways for five dollars; had to play second fiddle and say thanky. But what I offer you ain't a second fiddle. It's as good a chance as my own. Even divides. One half to you and one half to me. You know the people and I know the ropes. It's a fair bargain. What do you say?"

Mr. Dicker thought of his decayed practice and his unpaid bills; and flipping overboard his little grain of conscience, he said, "Snacks."

"All right," grinned Pullwool, his teeth gleaming alarmingly. "Word of a gentleman," he added, extending his pulpy hand, loaded with ostentatious rings, and grasping Dicker's recoiling fingers. "Harness up your little bill as quick as you can, and drive it like Jehu. Fastburg to be the only capital. Slowburg no claims at all, historical, geographical, or economic. The old arrangement a humbug; as inconvenient as a fifth wheel of a coach; costs the State thousands of greenbacks every year. Figure it all up statistically and dab it over with your shiniest rhetoric and make a big thing of it every way. That's what you've got to do;

that's your little biz. I'll tend to the rest."

"I don't quite see where the money is to come from," observed Mr. Dicker.

"Leave that to me," said the veteran of the lobbies; "my name is Pullwool, and I know how to pull the wool over men's eyes, and then I know how to get at their britches-pockets. You bring in your bill and make your speech. Will you do it?"

"Yes," answered Dicker, bolting all scruples in another half tumbler of brandy.

He kept his word. As promptly as parliamentary forms and mysteries would allow, there was a bill under the astonished noses of honorable lawgivers, removing the seat of legislation from Slowburg and centering it in Fastburg. This bill Mr. Thomas Dicker supported with that fluency and fiery enthusiasm of oratory which had for a time enabled him to show as the foremost man of his State. Great was the excitement, great the rejoicing and anger. The press of Fastburg sent forth shrieks of exultation, and the press of Slowburg responded with growlings of disgust. The two capitals and the two geographical sections which they represented were ready to fire Parrott guns at each other, without regard to life and property in the adjoining regions of the earth. If there was a citizen of the little Common-wealth who did not hear of this bill and did not talk of it, it was because that citizen was as deaf as a post and as dumb as an oyster. Ordinary political distinctions were forgotten, and the old party-whips could not manage their very wheel-horses, who went snorting and kicking over the traces in all directions. In short, both in the legislature and out of it, nothing was thought of but the question of the removal of the capital.

Among the loudest of the agitators was Mr. Pullwool; not that he cared one straw whether the capital went to Fastburg, or to Slowburg, or to Ballyhack; but for the money which he thought he saw in the agitation he did care mightily, and to get that money he labored with a zeal which was not of this world alone. At the table of his hotel, and in the barroom of the same institution, and in the lobbies of the legislative hall, and in editorial sanctums and barbers' shops, and all other nooks of gossip, he trumpeted the claims of Fastburg as if that little city were the New Jerusalem and deserved to be the metropolis of the sidereal universe. All sort of trickeries, too; he sent spurious telegrams and got fictitious items into the newspapers; he lied through every medium known to the highest civilization. Great surely was his success, for the row which he raised was tremendous. But a row alone was not enough; it was the mere breeze upon the surface of the waters; the treasure-ship below was still to be drawn up and gutted.

"It will cost money," he whispered confidentially to capitalists and land-owners. "We must have the sinews of war, or we can't carry it on. There's your city lots goin' to double in value if this bill goes through. What per cent will you pay on the advance? That's the question. Put your hands in your pockets and pull 'em out full, and put back ten times as much. It's a sure investment; warranted to yield a hundred per cent; the safest and biggest thing agoing."

Capitalists and land-owners and merchants hearkened and believed and subscribed. The slyest old hunks in Fastburg put a faltering forefinger into his long pocket-book, touched a greenback which had been laid away there as neatly as a corpse in its coffin, and resurrected it for the use of Mr. Pullwool. By tens, by twenties, by fifties, and by hundreds the dollars of the ambitious citizens of the little metropolis were charmed into the portemonnaie of this rattlesnake of a lobbyist.

"I never saw a greener set," chuckled Pullwool. "By jiminy, I believe they'd shell out for a bill to make their town a seaport, if it was a hundred miles from a drop of water."

But he was not content with individual subscriptions, and conscientiously scorned himself until he had got at the city treasury.

"The corporation must pony up," he insisted, with the mayor. "This bill is just shaking in the wind for lack of money. Fastburg must come down with the dust. You ought to see to it. What are you chief magistrate for? Ain't it to tend to the welfare of the city? Look here, now; you call the common council together; secret session, you understand. You call 'em together and let me talk to 'em. I want to make the loons comprehend that it's their duty to vote something handsome for this measure."

The mayor hummed and hawed one way, and then he hawed and hummed the other way, and the result was that he granted the request. There was a secret session in the council-room, with his honor at the top of the long green table, with a row of more or less respectable functionaries on either side of it, and with Mr. Pullwool and the Devil at the bottom. Of course it is not to be supposed that this last-named personage was visible to the others, or that they had more than a vague suspicion of his presence. Had he fully revealed himself, had he plainly exhibited his horns and hoofs, or even so much as uncorked his perfume-bottle of brimstone, it is more than probable that the city authorities would have been exceedingly scandalized, and they might have adjourned the session. As it was, seeing nothing more disagreeable than the obese form of the lobbyist, they listened calmly while he unfolded his project.

Mr. Pullwool spoke at length, and to Fastburg ears eloquently. Fastburg must be the sole capital; it had every claim, historical, geographical, and commercial, to that distinction; it ought, could, would, and should be the sole capital; that was about the substance of his exordium.

"But, gentlemen, it will cost," he went on. "There is an unscrupulous and furious opposition to the measure. The other side—those fellows from Slowburg and vicinity—are putting their hands into their britches-pockets. You must put your hands into yours. The thing will be worth millions to Fastburg. But it will cost thousands. Are you ready to fork over? *Are* you ready?"

"What's the figure?" asked one of the councilmen. "What do you estimate?"

"Gentlemen, I shall astonish *some* of you," answered Mr. Pullwool, cunningly. It was well put; it was as much as to say, "I shall astonish the green ones; of course the really strong heads among you won't be in the least bothered." "I estimate," he continued, "that the city treasury will have to put up a good round sum, say a hundred thousand dollars, be it more or less."

A murmur of surprise, of chagrin, and of something like indignation ran along the line of official mustaches. "Nonsense," "The dickens," "Can't be done," "We can't think of it," broke out several councilmen, in a distinctly unparliamentary manner.

"Gentlemen, one moment," pleaded Pullwool, passing his greasy smile around the company, as though it were some kind of refreshment. "Look at the whole job; it's a big job. We must have lawyers; we must have newspapers in all parts of the State;

we must have writers to work up the historical claims of the city; we must have fellows to buttonhole honorable members; we must have fees for honorable members themselves. How can you do it for less?"

Then he showed a schedule; so much to this wire-puller and that and the other; so much apiece to so many able editors; so much for eminent legal counsel; finally, a trifle for himself. And one hundred thousand dollars or thereabouts was what the schedule footed up, turn it whichever way you would.

Of course this common council of Fastburg did not dare to vote such a sum for such a purpose. Mr. Pullwool had not expected that it would; all that he had hoped for was the half of it; but that half he got.

"Did they do it?" breathlessly inquired Tom Dicker of him, when he returned to the hotel.

"They done it," calmly, yet triumphantly, responded Mr. Pullwool.

"Thunder!" exclaimed the amazed Dicker. "You are the most extraordinary man! You must have the very Devil in you!"

Instead of being startled by this alarming supposition, Mr. Pullwool looked gratified. People thus possessed generally do look gratified when the possession is alluded to.

But the inspired lobbyist did not pass his time in wearing an aspect of satisfaction. When there was money to get and to spend he could run his fat off almost as fast as if he were pouring it into candle-molds. The ring—the famous capital ring of Fastburg—must be seen to, its fingers greased, and its energy quickened. Before he rolled his apple-dumpling of a figure into bed that night he had interviewed Smith and Brown the editors, Jones and Robinson the lawyers, Smooth and Slow the literary characters, various lobbyists, and various lawgivers.

"Work, gentlemen, and capitalize Fastburg and get your dividends," was his inspiring message to one and all. He promised Smith and Brown ten dollars for every editorial, and five dollars for every humbugging telegram, and two dollars for every telling item. Jones and Robinson were to have five hundred dollars apiece for concurrent legal statements of the claim of the city; Smooth and Slow, as being merely authors and so not accustomed to obtain much for their labor, got a hundred dollars

between them for working up the case historically. To the lobbyists and members Pullwool was munificent; it seemed as if those
gentlemen could not be paid enough for their "influence"; as if
they alone had that kind of time which is money. Only, while
dealing liberally with them, the inspired one did not forget himself. A thousand for Mr. Sly; yes, Mr. Sly was to receipt for a
thousand; but he must let half of it stick to the Pullwool fingers.
The same arrangement was made with Mr. Green and Mr. Sharp
and Mr. Bummer and Mr. Pickpurse and Mr. Buncombe. It was
a game of snacks, half to you and half to me; and sometimes it
was more than snacks,—a thousand for you two and a thousand
for me too.

With such a greasing of the wheels, you may imagine that the
machinery of the ring worked to a charm. In the city and in the
legislature and throughout the State there was the liveliest buzzing and humming and clicking of political wheels and cranks
and cogs that had ever been known in those hitherto pastoral
localities. The case of Fastburg against Slowburg was put in a
hundred ways, and proved as sure as it was put. It really seemed
to the eager burghers as if they already heard the clink of ham-
mers on a new State-House and beheld a perpetual legislature
sitting on their fences and curbstones until the edifice should be
finished. The great wire-puller and his gang of stipendiaries were
the objects of popular gratitude and adoration. The landlord
of the hotel which Mr. Pullwool patronized actually would not
take pay for that gentleman's board.

"No, sir!" declared this simple Boniface, turning crimson with
enthusiasm. "You are going to put thousands of dollars into my
purse, and I'll take nothing out of yours. And any little thing in
the way of cigars and whisky that you want, sir, why, call for it.
It's my treat, sir."

"Thank you, sir," kindly smiled the great man. "That's what
I call the square thing. Mr. Boniface, you are a gentleman and a
scholar; and I'll mention your admirable house to my friends.
By the way, I shall have to leave you for a few days."

"Going to leave us!" exclaimed Mr. Boniface, aghast. "I hope
not till this job is put through."

"I must run about a bit," muttered Pullwool, confidentially.
"A little turn through the State, you understand, to stir up the

country districts. Some of the members ain't as hot as they should be, and I want to set their constituents after them. Nothing like getting on a few deputations."

"Oh, exactly!" chuckled Mr. Boniface, ramming his hands into his pockets and cheerfully jingling a bunch of keys and a pen-knife for lack of silver. It was strange indeed that he should actually see the Devil in Mr. Pullwool's eye and should not have a suspicion that he was in danger of being humbugged by him. "And your rooms?" he suggested. "How about them?"

"I keep them," replied the lobbyist, grandly, as if blaspheming the expense—to Boniface. "Our friends must have a little hole to meet in. And while you are about it, Mr. Boniface, see that they get something to drink and smoke; and we'll settle it be-tween us."

"Pre—cisely!" laughed the landlord, as much as to say, "My treat!"

And so Mr. Pullwool, that Pericles and Lorenzo de' Medici rolled in one, departed for a season from the city which he ruled and blessed. Did he run about the State and preach and crusade in behalf of Fastburg, and stir up the bucolic populations to stir up their representatives in its favor? Not a bit of it; the place that he went to and the only place that he went to was Slow-burg; yes, covering up his tracks in his usual careful style; he made direct for the rival of Fastburg. What did he propose to do there? Oh, how can we reveal the whole duplicity and turpi-tude of Ananias Pullwool? The subject is too vast for a merely human pen; it requires the literary ability of a recording angel. Well, we must get our feeble lever under this boulder of wicked-ness as we can, and do our faint best to expose all the reptiles and slimy things beneath it.

The first person whom this apostle of lobbyism called upon in Slowburg was the mayor of that tottering capital.

"My name is Pullwool," he said to the official, and he said it with an almost enviable ease of impudence, for he was used to introducing himself to people who despised and detested him. "I want to see you confidentially about this capital ring which is making so much trouble."

"I thought you were in it," replied the mayor, turning very red in the face, for he had heard of Mr. Pullwool as the leader

of said ring; and being an iracund man, he was ready to knock
his head off.

"In it!" exclaimed the possessed one. "I wish I was. It's a fat
thing. More than fifty thousand dollars paid out already!"

"Good gracious!" exclaimed the mayor in despair.

"By the way, this is between ourselves," added Pullwool. "You
take it so, I hope. Word of honor, eh?"

"Why, if you have anything to communicate that will help us,
why, of course, I promise secrecy," stammered the mayor. "Yes,
certainly; word of honor."

"Well, I've been looking about among those fellows a little,"
continued Ananias. "I've kept my eyes and ears open. It's a way
I have. And I've learned a thing or two that it will be to your
advantage to know. Yes, sir! fifty thousand dollars!—the city has
voted it and paid it, and the ring has got it. That's why they are
all working so. And depend upon it, they'll carry the legislature
and turn Slowburg out to grass, unless you wake up and do
something."

"By heavens!" exclaimed the iracund mayor, turning red again.
"It's a piece of confounded rascality. It ought to be exposed."

"No, don't expose it," put in Mr. Pullwool, somewhat alarmed.
"That game never works. Of course they'd deny it and swear
you down, for bribing witnesses is as easy as bribing members.
I'll tell you what to do. Beat them at their own weapons. Raise
a purse that will swamp theirs. That's the way the world goes.
It's an auction. The highest bidder gets the article."

Well, the result of it all was that the city magnates of Slowburg did just what had been done by the city magnates of Fastburg, only, instead of voting fifty thousand dollars into the
pockets of the ring, they voted sixty thousand. With a portion of
this money about him, and with authority to draw for the rest
on proper vouchers, Mr. Pullwool, his tongue in his cheek, bade
farewell to his new allies. As a further proof of the ready wit
and solid impudence of this sublime politician and model of
American statesmen, let me here introduce a brief anecdote.
Leaving Slowburg by the cars, he encountered a gentleman from
Fastburg, who saluted him with tokens of amazement, and said,
"What are you doing here, Mr. Pullwool?"

"Oh, just breaking up these fellows a little," whispered the man with the Devil in him. "They were making too strong a fight. I had to *see* some of them," putting one hand behind his back and rubbing his fingers together, to signify that there had been a taking of bribes. "But be shady about it. For the sake of the good cause, keep quiet. Mum's the word."

The reader can imagine how briskly the fight between the two capitals reopened when Mr. Pullwool re-entered the lobby. Slowburg now had its adherents, and they struggled like men who saw money in their warfare, and they struggled not in vain. To cut a very long story very short, to sum the whole of an exciting drama in one sentence, the legislature kicked overboard the bill to make Fastburg the sole seat of government. Nothing had come of the whole row, except that a pair of simple little cities had spent over one hundred thousand dollars, and that the capital ring, fighting on both sides and drawing pay from both sides, had lined its pockets, while the great creator of the ring had crammed his to bursting.

"What does this mean, Mr. Pullwool?" demanded the partially honest and entirely puzzled Tom Dicker, when he had discovered by an unofficial count of noses how things were going. "Fastburg has spent all its money for nothing. It won't be sole capital, after all."

"I never expected it would be," replied Pullwool, so tickled by the Devil that was in him that he could not help laughing. "I never wanted it to be. Why, it would spoil the little game. This is a trick that can be played every year."

"Oh!" exclaimed Mr. Dicker, and was dumb with astonishment for a minute.

"Didn't you see through it before?" grinned the grand master of all guile and subtlety.

"I did not," confessed Mr. Dicker, with a mixture of shame and abhorrence. "Well," he presently added, recovering himself, "shall we settle?"

"Oh, certainly, if you are ready," smiled Pullwool, with the air of a man who has something coming to him.

"And what, exactly, will be my share?" asked Dicker, humbly.

"What do you mean?" stared Pullwool, apparently in the extremity of amazement.

"You said *snacks,* didn't you?" urged Dicker, trembling violently.

"Well, *snacks* it is," replied Pullwool. "Haven't you had a thousand?"

"Yes," admitted Dicker.

"Then you owe me five hundred?"

Mr. Dicker did not faint, though he came very near it, but he staggered out of the room as white as a sheet, for he was utterly crushed by this diabolical impudence.

That very day Mr. Pullwool left for Washington, and the Devil left for *his* place, each of them sure to find the other when he wanted him, if indeed their roads lay apart.

Booth Tarkington
(1869-   )

BOOTH TARKINGTON was born in Indianapolis, the son of a Civil War veteran. He was educated at Phillips Exeter Academy, at Purdue, and at Princeton, where he took a degree in 1893. In Princeton he was interested in music and writing; he seems also to have gained some reputation as a political liberal. He served one year (1902–1903) in the Indiana state legislature. In spite of very serious trouble with his eyes, Tarkington has written persistently and vigorously. The first novel which drew attention to him was *The Gentleman from Indiana* (1899). In 1905 a collection of political short stories, *In the Arena*, reflected something of the mild radicalism of his earlier life. In 1906 appeared what was probably his best play, *The Man from Home*, and ten years later he wrote another popular drama, *Mister Antonio*. A novel, *The Magnificent Ambersons* (1918) won the Pulitzer Prize for literature as did also *Alice Adams* (1922). Tarkington owes his chief fame to his creation of a genuine character, an adolescent youth who is in constant mischief but who is somehow very likable in spite of his callow clumsiness. This famous youngster appears in *Penrod* (1914), *Penrod and Sam* (1916), and *Seventeen* (1916), and has lately made his bow on the screen. Tarkington's *The World Does Move* (1928) is autobiographical.

The Need of Money is reprinted from the author's early political series of stories *In the Arena* and is a half-serious, half-humorous tale of a state senator "honest as the day is long" who ultimately falls from political grace.

The Need of Money

Far back in his corner on the Democratic side of the House,
Uncle Billy Rollinson sat through the dragging routine of the
legislative session, wondering what most of it meant. When anybody spoke to him, in passing, he would answer, in his gentle,
timid voice, "Howdy-do, sir." Then his cheeks would grow a
little red and he would stroke his long, white beard elaborately,
to cover his embarrassment. When a vote was taken, his name
was called toward the last of the roll, so that he had ample time,
after the leader of his side of the House, young Hurlbut, had
voted, to clear his throat several times and say "Aye" or "No" in
quite a firm voice. But the instant the word had left his lips he
found himself terribly frightened, and stroked his beard a great
many times, the while he stared seriously up at the ceiling, partly
to avoid meeting anybody's eye, and partly in the belief that it
concealed his agitation and gave him the air of knowing what
he was about. Usually he did not know, any more than he knew
how he had happened to be sent to the legislature by his county.
But he liked it. He liked the feeling of being a person to be
considered; he liked to think that he was making the laws of his
State. He liked the handsome desk and the easy leather chair; he
liked the row of fat, expensive volumes, the unlimited stationery,
and the free penknives which were furnished him. He enjoyed
the attentions of the colored men in the cloak-room, who
brushed him ostentatiously and always called him (and the other
Representatives) "Senator," to make up to themselves for the
airs which the janitors of the "Upper House" assumed. Most of
these things surprised him; he had not expected to be treated
with such liberality by the State and never realized that he and
his colleagues were treating themselves to all these things at the

From *In the Arena,* copyright 1905, 1933, by Booth Tarkington. Reprinted
by permission.

expense of the people, and so, although he bore off as much
note-paper as he could carry, now and then, to send to his son,
Henry, he was horrified and dumfounded when the bill was
proposed appropriating $135,000 for the expenses of the seventy
days' session of the legislature.

He was surprised to find that among his "perquisites" were
passes (good during the session) on all the railroads that entered
the State, and others for use on many inter-urban trolley lines.
These, he thought, might be gratifying to Henry, who was fond
of travel, and had often been unhappy when his father failed to
scrape up enough money to send him to a circus in the next
county. It was "very accommodating of the railroads," Uncle
Billy thought, to maintain this pleasant custom, because the
members' traveling expenses were paid by the State just the
same; hence the economical could "draw their mileage" at the
Treasurer's office, and add it to their salaries. He heard—only
vaguely understanding—many joking references to other ways of
adding to salaries.

Most of the members of his party had taken rooms at one of
the hotels, whither those who had sought cheaper apartments
repaired in the evening, when the place became a noisy and
crowded club, admission to which was not by card. Most of the
rougher man-to-man lobbying was done here; and at times it
was Babel.

Through the crowds Uncle Billy wandered shyly, stroking his
beard and saying, "Howdy-do, sir," in his gentle voice, getting
out of the way of people who hurried, and in great trouble of
mind if any one asked him how he intended to vote upon a bill.
When this happened he looked at the interrogator in the plaintive way which was his habit, and answered slowly: "I reckon
I'll have to think it over." He was not in Hurlbut's councils.

There was much bustle all about him, but he was not part of
it. The newspaper reporters remarked the quiet, inoffensive old
figure pottering about aimlessly on the outskirts of the crowd,
and thought Uncle Billy as lonely as a man might well be, for
he seemed less a part of the political arrangement than any member they had ever seen. He would have looked less lonely and
more in place trudging alone through the furrows of his home
fields in a wintry twilight.

And yet, everybody liked the old man, Hurlbut in particular, if Uncle Billy had known it; for Hurlbut watched the votes very closely and was often struck by the soundness of Representative Rollinson's intelligence in voting.

In return, Uncle Billy liked Hurlbut better than any other man he had ever known—except Henry, of course. On the first day of the session, when the young leader had been pointed out to him, Uncle Billy's humble soul was prostrate with admiration, and when Hurlbut led the first attack on the monopolistic tendencies of the Republican party, Representative Rollinson, chuckling in his beard at the handsome youth's audacity, himself dared so greatly as to clap his hands aloud. Hurlbut, on the floor, was always a storm center: tall, dramatic, bold, the members put down their newspapers whenever his strong voice was heard demanding recognition, and his "Mr. Speaker!" was like the first rumble of thunder. The tempest nearly always followed, and there were times when it threatened to become more than vocal; when, all order lost, nine-tenths of the men on the other side of the House were on their feet shouting jeers and denunciations, and the orator faced them, out-thundering them all, with his own cohorts, flushed and cheering, gathered round him. Then, indeed, Uncle Billy would have thought him a god, if he had known what a god was.

Sometimes Uncle Billy saw him in the hotel lobby, but he seemed always to be making for the elevator in a hurry, with half-a-dozen people trying to detain him, or descending momentarily from the stairway for a quick, sharp talk with one or two members, their heads close together, after which Hurlbut would dart upward again.

Sometimes the old man sat down at one of the writing tables, in a corner of the lobby, and, annexing a sheet of the hotel notepaper, "wrote home" to Henry. He sat with his head bent far over, the broad brim of his felt hat now and then touching the hand with which he kept the paper from sliding; and he pressed diligently upon his pen, usually breaking it before the letter was finished. He looked so like a man bent upon concealment that the reporters were wont to say: "There's Uncle Billy humped up over his guilty secret again."

The secret usually took this form:

"Dear Son Henry:

"I would be glad if you was here. There is big doings. Hurlbut give it to them today. He don't give the Republicans no rest. he lights into them like sixty you would like to see him. They are plenty nice fellows in the Republicans too but they lay mighty low when Hurlbut gets after them. He was just in the office but went out. He always has a segar in his mouth but not lit. I expect hes quit. I send you enclosed last week's salary all but $11.80 which I had to use as living is pretty high in our capital city of the state. If you would like some of this hotel writing paper better than the kind I sent you of the General Assembly I can send you some the boys say it is free. I think it is all right you sold the calf but Wilkes didn't give you good price. Hurlbut come in while I was writing then. You bet he can always count on Wm. Rollinson's vote.

"Well I must draw to a close, Yours truly

"Your father."

"Wm. Rollinson" did not know that he was known to his colleagues and the lobby and the Press as "Uncle Billy" until informed thereof by a public print. He stood, one night, on the edge of a laughing group, when a reporter turned to him and said:

"The *Constellation* would like to know Representative Rollinson's opinion of the scandalous story that has just been told."

The old man, who had not in the least understood the story, summoned all his faculties, and, after long deliberation, bent his plaintive eyes upon the youth and replied:

"Well, sir, it's a-stonishing, a-stonishing!"

"Think it's pretty bad, do you?"

Some of the crowd turned to listen, and the old fellow, hopelessly puzzled, stroked his beard with a trembling hand, and then, muttering, "Well, young man, I expect you better excuse me," hurried away and left the place. The next morning he found the following item tacked to the tail of the "Legislative Gossip" column of the *Constellation:*

"UNCLE BILLY ROLLINSON HORRIFIED

"Yesterday a curious and amusing story was current among the solons at the Nagmore Hotel. It seems that the wife of a country member of the last legislature had been spending the day at the hotel and the wife of a present member from the country complained to her of the greatly increased expenditure appertaining to the cost of living in the Capital City. 'Indeed,' replied the wife of the former member, 'that is curious. But I suppose my husband is much more economical than yours, for he brought home $1,500, that he'd saved out of his salary.' As the salary is only $456, and the gentleman in question did not play poker, much hilarity was indulged in, and there were conjectures that the economy referred to concerned his vote upon a certain bill before the last session, anent which the lobby pushing it were far from economical. Uncle Billy Rollinson, the Gentleman from Wixinockee, heard the story, as it passed from mouth to mouth, but he had no laughter to greet it. Uncle Billy, as every one who comes in contact with him knows, is as honest as the day is long, and the story grieved and shocked him. He expressed the utmost horror and consternation, and requested to be excused from speaking further upon a subject so repugnant to his feelings. If there were more men of this stamp in politics, who find corruption revolting instead of amusing, our legislatures would enjoy a better fame."

Uncle Billy had always been agitated by the sight of his name in print. Even in the Wixinockee County *Clarion,* it dumfounded him and gave him a strange feeling that it must mean somebody else, but this sudden blaze of metropolitan fame made him almost giddy. He folded the paper quickly and placed it under his coat, feeling vaguely that it would not do to be seen reading it. He murmured feeble answers during the day, when some of his colleagues referred to it; but when he reached his own little room that evening, he spread it out under his oil-smelling lamp and read it again. Perhaps he read it twenty times over before the supper bell rang. Perhaps the fact that he was still intent upon it accounted for his not hearing the bell, so that his landlady had to call him.

What he liked was the phrase: "Honest as the day is long." He did not go to the hotel that night. He went back to his room and read the *Constellation.* He liked the *Constellation.* Newspapers were very kind, he thought. Now and then, he would pick up his pile of legislative bills and try to spell through the ponderous sentences, but he always gave it up and went back to the *Constellation.* He wondered if Hurlbut had read it. Hurlbut had. The leader had even told the author of the item that he was glad somebody could appreciate the kind of a man Uncle Billy was, and his value to the body politic.

"Honest as the day is long," Uncle Billy repeated to himself, in the little room, nodding his head gravely. Then he thought for a long while about the member who had, according to the story, gone home with $1,500. He sat up, that evening, until almost ten o'clock. Even after he had gone to bed, he lay awake with his eyes wide open in the darkness, thinking of the colossal sum. If anybody should come to *him* and offer him all that money to vote a certain way upon a bill, he believed he would not take it, for that would be bribery; though Henry would be glad to have the money. Henry always needed money; sometimes the need was imperative—once, indeed, so imperative that the small, unfertile farm had been mortgaged beyond its value, otherwise very serious things must have happened to Henry. Uncle Billy wondered how offers of money to members were refused without hurting the intending donor's feelings. And what a great deal could be done with $1,500, if a member could get it and still be as honest as the day is long!

About the second month of the session the floor of the House began steadily to grow more and more tumultuous. To an unpolitical onlooker, leaning over the gallery rail, it was often an incomprehensible Bedlam, or perhaps one might have been reminded of an ant-heap by the hurry and scurry and life and death haste in a hundred directions at once, quite without any distinguishable purpose. Twenty men might be rampaging up and down the aisles, all shouting, some of them furiously, others with a determination that was deadly, all with arms waving at the Speaker, some of the hands clenched, some of them fluttering documents, while pages ran everywhere in mad haste, stumbling and falling in the aisles. In the midst of this, other members, seated, wrote studiously; others mildly read newspapers; others lounged, half-standing against their desks, unlighted cigars in their mouths, laughing; all the while the patient Speaker tapped with his gavel on a small square of marble. Suddenly perfect calm would come and the voice of the reading clerk drone for half an hour or more, like a single bee in a country garden on Sunday morning.

Of all this Uncle Billy was as much a layman spectator as any tramp who crept into the gallery for a few hours out of the cold. The hurry and seethe of the racing sea touched him not at all, except to bewilderment, while he was carried with it, unknowing, toward the breakers. The shout of those breakers was already in the ears of many, for the crisis of the session was coming. This was the fight that was to be made on Hurlbut's "Railroad Bill," which was, indeed, but in another sense, known as the "Breaker."

Uncle Billy had heard of the "Breaker." He couldn't have helped that. He had heard a dozen say: "Then's when it's going to be warm times, when that 'Breaker' comes up!" or, "Look out for that 'Breaker.' We're going to have big trouble." He knew, too, that Hurlbut was interested in the "Breaker," but upon which side he was for a long time ignorant.

Hurlbut always nodded to the old man, now, as he came down the aisle to his own desk. He had begun that, the day after the *Constellation* item. Uncle Billy never failed to be in his seat early in the morning, waiting for the nod. He answered it with his usual "Howdy-do, sir," then stroked his beard and gazed profoundly at the row of fat volumes in front of him, swallowing painfully once or twice.

This was all that really happened for Uncle Billy during the turmoil and scramble that went on about him all the day long. He had not been forced to discover a way to meet an offer of $1,500, without hurting the putative donor's feelings. No lobbyist had the faintest idea of "approaching" the old man in that way. The members and the hordes of camp-followers and all the lobby had settled into a belief that Representative Rollinson was a sea-green Incorruptible, that of all honest members he was the most honest. He had become typical of honesty: sayings were current— "You might as well try to bribe Uncle Billy Rollinson!" "As honest as old Uncle Billy Rollinson." Hurlbut often used such phrases in private.

The "Breaker" was Hurlbut's own bill; he had planned it and written it, though it came over to the House from the Senate under a Senator's name. It was one of those "anti-monopolistic" measures which Democrats put their whole hearts into, sometimes, and believe in and fight for magnificently; an idea conceived in honesty and for a beneficent purpose, in the belief that a legislature by the wave of a hand can conjure the millennium to appear; and born out of an utter misconception of man and railroads. The bill needs no farther description than this: if it passed and became an enforced law, the dividends of every railroad entering the State would be reduced by two-fifths. There is one thing that will fight harder than a Democrat—that is a railroad.

The "Breaker" had been kept very dark until Hurlbut felt that he was ready; then it was swept through the Senate before the railroad lobby, previously lulled into unsuspicion, could collect itself and block it. This was as Hurlbut had planned: that the fight should be in his own House. It was the bill of his heart and he set his reputation upon it. He needed fifty-one votes to pass it, and he had them, and one to spare; for he took his followers, who formed the majority, into caucus upon it. It was in the caucus Uncle Billy learned that Hurlbut was "for" the bill. He watched the leader with humble, wavering eyes, thinking how strong and clear his voice was, and wondering if he never lit the cigar he always carried in his hand, or if he ever got into trouble, like Henry, being a young man. If he did, Uncle Billy would have liked the chance to help him out.

He had plenty of such chances with Henry; indeed, the opportunity may be said to have been unintermittent, and Uncle Billy was never free from a dim fear of the day when his son would get in so deeply that he could not get him out. Verily, the day seemed near at hand: Henry's letters were growing desperate and the old man walked the floor of his little room at night, more and more hopeless. Once or twice, even as he sat at his desk in the House, his eyes became so watery that he forced himself into long spells of coughing, to account for it, in case any one might be noticing him.

The caucus was uneventful and quiet, for it had all been talked over, and was no more than a matter of form.

The Republicans did not caucus upon the bill (they had reasons), but they were solidly against it. Naturally it follows that the assault of the railroad lobby had to be made upon the virtue of the Democrats *as* Democrats. That is, whether a member upon the majority side cared about the bill for its own sake or not, right or wrong, he felt it his duty as a Democrat to vote for it.

If he had a conscience higher than a political conscience, and believed the bill was bad, his duty was to "bolt the caucus"; but all of the Democratic side believed in the righteousness of the bill, except two. One had already been bought and the other was Uncle Billy, who knew nothing about it, except that Hurlbut was "for" it and it seemed to be making a "big stir."

The man who had been bought sat not far from Uncle Billy. He was a furtive, untidy slouch of a man, formerly a Republican; he had a great capacity for "handling the colored vote" and his name was Pixley. Hurlbut mistrusted him; the young man had that instinct, which good leaders need, for feeling the weak places in his following; and he had the leader's way, too, of ever bracing up the weakness and fortifying it; so he stopped, four or five times a day, at Pixley's desk, urging the necessity of standing fast for the "Breaker," and expressing convictions as to the political future of a Democrat who should fail to vote for it; to which Pixley assented in his husky, tough-ward voice.

All day long now, Hurlbut and his lieutenants, disregarding the routine of bills, went up and down the lines, fending off the lobbyists and such Republicans as were working openly for the bill. They encouraged and threatened and never let themselves be too confident of their seeming strength. Some of those who were known, or guessed, to be of the "weaker brethren" were not left to themselves for half an hour at a time, from their breakfasts until they went to bed. There was always at elbow the *"Hold fast!"* whisper of Hurlbut and his lieutenants. None of them ever thought of speaking to Uncle Billy.

Hurlbut's "work was cut out for him," as they said. What work it is to keep every one of fifty men honest under great temptation for three weeks (which time it took for the hampered and filibustered bill to come up for its passage or defeat), is known to those who have tried to do it. The railroads were outraged and incensed by the measure; they sincerely believed it to be monstrous and thievish. "Let the legislature try to confiscate two-fifths of the lawyers', or the bakers', or the ironmolders', just earnings," said they, "and see what will happen!"

When such a bill as this comes to the floor for the third time the fight is already over, oratory is futile; and Cicero could not budge a vote. The railroads were forced to fight as best they could; this was the old way that they have learned is most effective in such a case. Votes could not be had to "oblige a friend" on the "Breaker" bill; nor could they be procured by arguments to prove the bill unjust. In brief: the railroad lobby had no need to buy Republican votes (with the exception of the one or two who charged out of habit whenever legislation concerned corporations), for the Republicans were against the bill, but they did mortally need to buy two Democratic votes, and were willing to pay handsomely for them. Nevertheless, Mr. Pixley's price was not exorbitant, considering the situation; nor need he have congratulated himself so heartily as he did (in moments of retirement from public life) upon his prospective $2,000 (when the goods should be delivered) since his vote was assisting the railroads to save many million dollars a year.

Of course the lobby attacked the bill noisily; there were big guns going all day long; but those in charge knew perfectly well that the noise accomplished nothing in itself. It was used to cover the whispering. Still, Hurlbut held his line firm and the bill passed its second reading with fifty-two votes, Mr. Pixley being directed by his owners to vote for it on that occasion.

As time went on the lobby began to grow desperate; even Pixley had been consulted upon his opinion by Barrett, the young lawyer through whom negotiations in his case had been conducted. Pixley suggested the name of Rollinson and Barrett dismissed this counsel with as much disgust for Pixley's stupidity as he had for the man's person. (One likes a *dog* when he buys him.)

"But why not?" Pixley had whined as he reached the door. "Uncle Billy ain't so much! You listen to me. He wouldn't take it out-an'-out—I don't say as he would. But you needn't work that way. Everybody thinks it's no use to tackle him—but nobody never *tried*! What's he *done* to make you scared of him? *Nothing!* Jest set there and *looked!*"

After he had gone the fellow's words came back to Barrett: "Nobody never tried!" And then, to satisfy his conscience that he was leaving no stone unturned, yet laughing at the uselessness of it, he wrote a letter to a confidant of his, formerly a colleague in the lobby, who lived in the county-seat near which Uncle

Billy's mortgaged acres lay. The answer came the night after the
second vote on the "Breaker."

"Dear Barrett:

"I agree with your grafter. I don't believe Rollinson would be hard
to approach if it were done with tact—of course you don't want to
tackle him the way you would a swine like Pixley. A good many people
around here always thought the old man simple-minded. He was given
the nomination almost in joke—nobody else wanted it, because they
all thought the Republicans had a sure thing of it; but Rollinson slid
in on the general Democratic landslide in this district. He's got one son,
a worthless pup, Henry, a sort of yokel Don Juan, always half drunk
when his father has any money to give him, and just smart enough to
keep the old man mesmerized. Lately Henry's been in a mighty serious
peck of trouble. Last fall he got married to a girl here in town. Three
weeks ago a family named Johnson, the most shiftless in the county, the
real low-down white trash sort, living on a truck patch out Rollinson's
way, heard that Henry was on a toot in town, spending money freely,
and they went after him. A client of mine rents their ground to them
and told me all about it. It seems they claim that one of the daughters
in the Johnson family was Henry's common-law wife before he married
the other girl, and it's more than likely they can prove it. They are hol-
lering for $600, and if Henry doesn't raise it mighty quick they swear
they'll get him sent over the road for bigamy. I think the old man
would sell his soul to keep his boy out of the penitentiary and he's at
his wits' ends; he hasn't anything to raise the money on and he's up
against it. He'll do anything on earth for Henry. Hope this'll be of
some service to you, and if there's anything more I can do about it you
better call me up on the long distance.

"Yours faithfully,
"J. P. WATSON

"P.S.—You might mention to our old boss that I don't want anything if services are needed; but a pass for self and family to New York
and return would come in handy."

Barrett telegraphed an answer at once: "If it goes you can have
annual for yourself and family. Will call you up at two sharp tomorrow."

It was late the following night when the lobbyist concluded
his interview with Representative Rollinson, in the latter's little
room, half lighted by the oil-smelling lamp.

"I knew you would understand, Mr. Rollinson," said Barrett as he rose to go. His eyes danced and his jaws set with the thought that had been jubilant within him for the last half-hour: "We've got 'em! We've got 'em! We've got 'em!" The railroads had defended their own again.

"Of course," he went on, "we wouldn't have dreamed of coming to you and asking you to vote against this outrageous bill if we thought for a minute that you had any real belief in it or considered it a good bill. But you say, yourself, your only feeling about it was to oblige Mr. Hurlbut, and you admit, too, that you've voted his way on every other bill of the session. Surely, as I've already said so many times, you don't think he'd be so unreasonable as to be angry with you for differing with him on the merits of only one! No, no, Hurlbut's a very sensible fellow about such matters. You don't need to worry about *that!* After all I've said, surely you won't give it another thought, will you?"

Uncle Billy sat in the shadow, bent far over, slowly twisting his thin, corded hands, the fingers tightly interlocked. It was a long time before he spoke, and his interlocutor had to urge him again before he answered, in his gentle, quavering voice.

"No, I reckon not, if you say so."

"Certainly not," said Barrett briskly. "Why of course, we'd never have thought of making you a money offer to vote either for or against your principles. Not much! We don't do business that way! We simply want to do something for you. We've wanted to, all during the session, but the opportunity hadn't offered until I happened to hear your son was in trouble."

Out of the shadow came a long, tremulous sigh. There was a moment's pause; then Uncle Billy's head sank slowly lower and rested on his hands.

"You see," the other continued cheerfully, "we make no conditions, none in the world. We feel friendly to you and want to oblige you, but of course we do think you ought to show a little good-will towards *us.* I believe it's all understood: tomorrow night Mr. Watson will drive out in his buggy to this Johnson place, and he's empowered by us to settle the whole business and obtain a written statement from the family that they have no claim on your son. How he will settle it is neither your affair nor mine; nor whether it costs money or not. But he *will* settle it.

We do that out of good-will to you, as long as we feel as friendly
to you as we do now, and all we ask is that you show your good-
will to us."

It was plain, even to Uncle Billy, that if he voted against Mr.
Barrett's friends in the afternoon those friends might not feel so
much good-will toward him in the evening as they did now; and
Mr. Watson might not go to the trouble of hitching up his buggy
to drive out to the Johnsons'.

"You see, it's all out of friendship," said Barrett, his hand on
the door knob. "And we can count on yours tomorrow, can't we
—absolutely?"

The gray head sank a little lower, and then after a moment the
quavering voice answered:

"Yes, sir—I'll be friendly."

Before morning, Hurlbut lost another vote. One of his best
men left on a night train for the bedside of his dying wife. This
meant that the "Breaker" needed every one of the fifty-one remaining Democratic votes in order to pass. Hurlbut more than
distrusted Pixley, yet he felt sure of the other fifty, and if, upon
the reading of the bill, Pixley proved false, the bill would not be
lost, since there would be a majority of votes in its favor, though
not the constitutional majority of fifty-one required for its passage, and it could be brought up again and carried when the absent man returned. Thus, on the chance that Pixley had withstood tampering, Hurlbut made no effort to prevent the bill from
coming to the floor in its regular order in the afternoon, feeling
that it could not possibly be killed by a majority against it, for
he trusted his fifty, now, as strongly as he distrusted Pixley.

And so the roll-call on the "Breaker" began, rather quietly,
though there was no man's face in the hall that was not set to
show the tensity of high-strung nerves. The great crowd that had
gathered and choked the galleries and the floor beyond the bar,
and the Senators who had left their own chamber to watch the
bill in the House, all began to feel disappointed; for nothing happened until Pixley's name was called.

Pixley voted "No!"

Uncle Billy, sitting far down in his leather chair on the small
of his back, heard the outburst of shouting that followed; but he
could not see Pixley, for the traitor was instantly surrounded by

a ring of men, and all that was visible from where he sat was their backs and upraised, gesticulating hands. Uncle Billy began to tremble violently; he had not calculated on this; but surely such things would not happen to *him!*

The Speaker's gavel clicked through the uproar and the roll-call proceeded.

The clerk reached the name of Rollinson. Uncle Billy swallowed, threw a pale look about him and wrapped his damp hands in the skirts of his shiny old coat, as if to warm them. For a moment he could not answer. People turned to look at him.

"Rollinson!" shouted the clerk again.

"No," said Uncle Billy.

Immediately he saw above him and all about him a blur of men's faces and figures risen to their feet, he heard a hundred voices say breathlessly: *"What!"* and one that said: "My God, that kills the bill!"

Then a horrible and incredible storm burst upon him, and he who had sat all the session shrinking unnoticed in his quiet, back seat, unnerved when a colleague asked the simplest question, found himself the center and point of attack in the wildest mêlée that legislature ever saw. A dozen men, red, frantic, with upraised arms, came at him, Hurlbut the first of them. But the lobby was there, too; for it was not part of its calculations that the old man should be frightened into changing his vote.

There need have been no fear of that. Uncle Billy was beyond the power of speech. The lobby's agents swarmed on the floor, and, with half-a-dozen hysterically laughing Republicans, met the onset of Hurlbut and his men. It became a riot immediately. Sane men were swept up in it to be as mad as the rest, while the galleries screamed and shouted. All round the old man the fury was greatest; his head sank over his desk and rested on his hands as it had the night before; for he dared not lift it to see the avalanche he had loosed upon himself. He would have liked to stop his ears to shut out the egregious clamor of cursing and yelling that beset him, as his bent head kept the glazed eyes from seeing the impossible vision of the attack that strove to reach him. He remembered awful dreams that were like this; and now, as then, he shuddered in a cold sweat, being as one who would draw the covers over his head to shelter him from horrors in great dark-

ness. As Uncle Billy felt, so might a naked soul feel at the judgment day, tossed alone into the pit with all the myriads of eyes
in the universe fastened on its sins.

He was pressed and jostled by his defenders; once a man's
shoulders were bent back down over his own and he was crushed
against the desk until his ribs ached; voices thundered and wailed
at him, threatening, imploring, cursing, cajoling, raving.

Smaller groups were struggling and shouting in every part of
the room, the distracted sergeants-at-arms roaring and wrestling
with the rest. On the high dais the Speaker, white but imper-
turbable, having broken his gavel, beat steadily with the handle
of an umbrella upon the square of marble on his desk. Fifteen or
twenty members, raging dementedly, were beneath him, about
the clerk's desk and on the steps leading up to his chair, each
howling hoarsely:

"A point of *order!* A point of *or-der!*"

When the semblance of order came at last, the roll was finished, "reconsidered," the "Breaker" was beaten, 50 to 49, was
dead; and Uncle Billy Rollinson was creeping down the outer
steps of the Statehouse in the cold February slush and rain.

He was glad to be out of the nightmare, though it seemed still
upon him, the horrible clamors, all gonging and blaring at *him;*
the red, maddened faces, the clenched fists, the open mouths, all
raging at *him*—all the ruck and uproar swam about the dazed
old man as he made his slow, unseeing way through the wet
streets.

He was too late for dinner at his dingy boarding house, having
wandered far, and he found himself in his room without knowing very well how he had come there, indeed, scarcely more than
half-conscious that he *was* there. He sat, for a long time, in the
dark. After a while he mechanically lit the lamp, sat again to
stare at it, then, finding his eyes watering, he turned from it with
an incoherent whimper, as if it had been a person from whom
he would conceal the fact that he was weeping. He leaned his
arm against the window sill and dried his eyes on the shiny
sleeve.

An hour later, there came a hard, imperative knock on the
door. Uncle Billy raised his head and said gently:

"Come in."

He rose to his feet uncertain, aghast, when he saw who his visitor was. It was Hurlbut.

The young man confronted him darkly, for a moment, in silence. He was dripping with rain; his hat, unremoved, shaded lank black locks over a white face; his nostrils were wide with wrath; the "dry cigar" wagged between gritting teeth.

"Will ye take a chair?" faltered Uncle Billy.

The room rang to the loud answer of the other: "I'd see you in Hell before I'd sit in a chair of yours!"

He raised an arm, straight as a rod, to point at the old man. "Rollinson," he said, "I've come here to tell you what I think of you! I've never done that in my life before, because I never thought any man worth it. I do it because I need the luxury of it —because I'm sick of myself not to have had gumption enough to see what you were all the time and have you watched!"

Uncle Billy was stung to a moment's life. "Look here," he quavered, "you hadn't ought to talk that way to me. There ain't a cent of money passed my fingers——"

Hurlbut's bitter laugh cut him short. "*No?* Don't you suppose *I know* how it was done? Do you suppose there's a man in the whole Assembly doesn't know how you were sold? I had it by the long distance an hour ago, from your own home. Do you suppose *we* have no friends there, or that it was hard to find out about the whole dirty business? Your son's not going to stand trial for bigamy; that was the price you charged for killing the bill. You and Pixley are the only men whom they could buy with all their millions! Oh, I know a dozen men who could be bought on other issues, but not on *this!* You and Pixley stand alone. Well, you've broken the caucus and you've betrayed the Democratic party. I've come to tell you that the party doesn't want you any more. You are out of it, do you hear? We don't want even to use you!"

The old man had sunk back into his chair, stricken white, his hands fluttering helplessly. "I didn't go to hurt your feelings, Mr. Hurlbut," he said. "I never knowed how it would be, but I don't think you ought to say I done anything dishonest. I just felt kind of friendly to the railroads——"

The leader's laugh cut him off again. "Friendly! Yes, that's what you were! Well, you can go back to your friends; you'll

need them!—Mother in Heaven! How you fooled us! We thought
you were the straightest man and the stanchest Democrat——"

"I b'en a Democrat all my life, Mr. Hurlbut. I voted fer——"

"Well, you're a Democrat no longer. You're done for, do you
understand? And we're done with you!"

"You mean," the old man's voice shook almost beyond control; "you mean you're tryin' to read me out of the party?"

"Trying to!" Hurlbut turned to the door. "You're out! It's
done. You can thank God that your 'friends' did their work so
well that we can't prove what we know. On my soul, you dog, if
we could I believe some of the boys would send you over the
road."

An hour after he had gone, Uncle Billy roused himself from
his stupor, and the astonished landlady heard his shuffling step
on the stair. She followed him softly and curiously to the front
door, and watched him. He was bare-headed but had not far to
go. The night-flare of the cheap, all-night saloon across the sod-
den street silhouetted the stooping figure for a moment and then
the swinging doors shut the old man from her view. She returned
to her parlor and sat waiting for his return until she fell asleep
in her chair. She awoke at two o'clock, went to his room, and
was aghast to find it still vacant.

"The Lord have mercy on us all!" she cried aloud. "To think
that old rascal'd go out on a spree! He'd better of stayed in the
country where he belonged."

It was the next morning that the House received a shock
which loosed another riot, but one of a kind different from that
which greeted Representative Rollinson's vote on the "Breaker."
The reading clerk had sung his way through an inconsequent
bill; most of the members were buried in newspapers, gossiping,
idling, or smoking in the lobbies, when a loud, cracked voice was
heard shrilly demanding recognition.

"Mr. Speaker!" Every one turned with a start. There was Uncle
Billy, on his feet, violently waving his hands at the Speaker. "Mr.
Speaker, Mr. Speaker, Mr. Speaker!" His dress was disordered
and muddy; his eyes shone with a fierce, absurd, liquorish light;
and with each syllable that he uttered his beard wagged to an
unspeakable effect of comedy. He offered the most grotesque
spectacle ever seen in that hall—a notable distinction.

For a moment the House sat in paralytic astonishment. Then came an awed whisper from a Republican: "Has the old fool really found his voice?"

"No, he's drunk," said a neighbor. "I guess he can afford it, after his vote yesterday!"

"Mister Speaker! *Mister* Speaker!"

The cracked voice startled the lobbies. The hangers-on, the typewriters, the janitors, the smoking members came pouring into the chamber and stood, transfixed and open-mouthed.

"Mister Speaker!"

Then the place rocked with the gust of laughter and ironical cheering that swept over the Assembly. Members climbed upon their chairs and on desks, waving handkerchiefs, sheets of foolscap, and waste-baskets. "Hear 'im! *He-ear* 'im!" rang the derisive cry.

The Speaker yielded in the same spirit and said:

"The Gentleman from Wixinockee."

A semi-quiet followed and the cracked voice rose defiantly:

"That's who I am! I'm the Gentleman from Wixinockee an' I stan' here to defen' the principles of the Democratic party!"

The Democrats responded with violent hootings, supplemented by cheers of approval from the Republicans. The high voice out-shrieked them all: "Once a Democrat, always a Democrat! I voted Dem'cratic tick't forty year, born a Democrat an' die a Democrat. Fellow sizzens, I want to say to you right here an' now that principles of Dem'cratic party saved this country a hun'erd times from Republican mal-'diminstration an' degerdation! Lemme tell you this: you kin take my life away but you can't say I don' stan' by Dem'cratic party, mos' glorious party of Douglas an' Tilden, Hen'ricks, Henry Clay, an' George Washin'ton. I say to you they *hain't* no other party an' I'm member of it till death an' Hell an' f'rever after, so help me *God!*"

He smote the desk beside him with the back of his hand, using all his strength, skinning his knuckles so that the blood dripped from them, unnoticed. He waved both arms continually, bending his body almost double and straightening up again, in crucial efforts for emphasis. All the old jingo platitudes that he had learned from campaign speakers throughout his life, the nonsense and brag and blat, the cheap phrases, all the empty balderdash of the platform, rushed to his incoherent lips.

The lord of misrule reigned at the end of each sentence, as the members sprang again upon the chairs and desks, roaring, waving, purple with laughter. The Speaker leaned back exhausted in his chair and let the gavel rest. Spectators, pages, galleries whooped and howled with the members. Finally the climax came.

"I want to say to you just this *here*," shrilled the cracked voice, "an' you can tell the Republican party that I said so, tell 'em straight from *me,* an' I hain't goin' back on it; I reckon they know who I am, too; I'm a man that's honest—I'm as honest as the day is long, I am—as honest as the day is long——"

He was interrupted by a loud voice. *"Yes,"* it cried, *"when that day is the twenty-first of December!"*

That let pandemonium loose again, wilder, madder than before. A member threw a pamphlet at Uncle Billy. In a moment the air was thick with a Brobdingnagian snow-storm: pamphlets, huge wads of foolscap, bills, books, newspapers, waste-baskets went flying at the grotesque target from every quarter of the room. Members "rushed" the old man, hooting, cheering; he was tossed about, half thrown down, bruised, but, clamorous over all other clamors, jumping up and down to shriek over the heads of those who hustled him, his hands waving frantically in the air, his long beard wagging absurdly, still desperately vociferating his Democracy and his honesty.

That was only the beginning. He had, indeed, "found his voice"; for he seldom went now to the boarding-house for his meals, but patronized the free-lunch counter and other allurements of the establishment across the way. Every day he rose in the House to speak, never failing to reach the assertion that he was "as honest as the day is long," which was always greeted in the same way.

For a time he was one of the jokes that lightened the tedious business of law-making, and the members looked forward to his *"Mis-ter Speaker"* as schoolboys look forward to recess. But, after a week, the novelty was gone.

The old man became a bore. The Speaker refused to recognize him, and grew weary of the persistent shrilling. The day came when Uncle Billy was forcibly put into his seat by a disgusted sergeant-at-arms. He was half drunk (as he had come to be most of the time), but this humiliation seemed to pierce the alcoholic vapors that surrounded his always feeble intelligence. He put his hands up to his face and cried like a whimpering child. Then he shuffled out and went back to the saloon. He soon acquired the habit of leaving his seat in the House vacant; he was no longer allowed to make speeches there; he made them in the saloon, to the amusement of the loafers and roughs who infested it. They badgered him, but they let him harangue them, and applauded his rhodomontades.

Hurlbut, passing the place one night at the end of the session, heard the quavering, drunken voice, and paused in the darkness to listen.

"I tell you, fellow-countrymen, I've voted Dem'cratic tick't forty year, live a Dem'crat, die a Dem'crat! An' I'm's honest as day is long!"

It was five years after that session, when Hurlbut, now in the national Congress, was called to the district in which Wixinockee lies, to assist his hard-pressed brethren in a campaign. He was driving, one afternoon, to a political meeting in the country, when a recollection came to him and he turned to the committee chairman, who accompanied him, and said:

"Didn't Uncle Billy Rollinson live somewhere near here?"

"Why, yes. You knew him in the legislature, didn't you?"

"A little. Where is he now?"

"Just up ahead here. I'll show you."

They reached the gate of a small, unkempt, weedy graveyard and stopped.

"The inscription on the head-board is more or less amusing," said the chairman, as he got out of the buggy, "considering that he was thought to be pretty crooked, and I seem to remember that he was 'read out of the party,' too. But he wrote the inscription himself, on his death-bed, and his son put it there."

There was a sparse crop of brown grass growing on the grave to which he led his companion. A cracked wooden head-board, already tilting rakishly, marked Henry's devotion. It had been white-washed and the inscription done in black letters, now partly washed away by the rain, but still legible:

HERE LIES

THE MORTAL REMAINS

OF

WILLIAM ROLLINSON

A LIFE-LONG

DEMOCRAT

AND

A

MAN

AS HONEST AS THE DAY IS LONG

The chairman laughed. "Don't that beat thunder? You knew his record in the legislature didn't you?"

"Yes."

"He *was* as crooked as they say he was, wasn't he?"

Hurlbut had grown much older in five years, and he was in Congress. He was climbing the ladder, and, to hold the position he had gained, and to insure his continued climbing, he had made some sacrifices within himself by obliging his friends—sacrifices which he did not name.

"I could hardly say," he answered gently, his down-bent eyes fastened on the sparse, brown grass. "It's not for us to judge too much. I believe, maybe, that if he could hear me now, I'd ask his pardon for some things I said to him once."

Anzia Yezierska
(1885-   )

THE BEST interpreters of our new citizens are the immigrant writers themselves. Anzia Yezierska was born in Poland and came to America with her family as a girl of sixteen in 1901. She worked in sweatshops and factories and in domestic service until, in 1918, she felt moved to record her impressions and experiences and those of her people, and the result was a series of fascinating tales and longer stories. *Hungry Hearts* (1920) is a collection of these stories as is also *Children of Loneliness* (1923). *Salome of the Tenements,* a novel, was published in 1922; it was followed by *Bread Givers* (1925) and *Arrogant Beggar* (1927).

"*The Fat of the Land,*" which contrasts the easy capacity of the younger people in the new world to change their social patterns and the inflexibility of the older immigrants whose habits have been set, first appeared in *The Century Magazine* for August, 1919, and was included in *Hungry Hearts* the next year. It was characterized by E. J. O'Brien as the best short-story of 1919.

"The Fat of the Land"

In an air-shaft so narrow that you could touch the next wall with your bare hands, Hanneh Breineh leaned out and knocked on her neighbor's window.

"Can you loan me your wash-boiler for the clothes?" she called.

Mrs. Pelz threw up the sash.

"The boiler? What's the matter with yours again? Didn't you tell me you had it fixed already last week?"

"A black year on him, the robber, the way he fixed it! If you have no luck in this world, then it's better not to live. There I spent out fifteen cents to stop up one hole, and it runs out another. How I ate out my gall bargaining with him he should let it down to fifteen cents! He wanted yet a quarter, the swindler. *Gottuniu!* My bitter heart on him for every penny he took from me for nothing."

"You got to watch all those swindlers, or they'll steal the whites out of your eyes," admonished Mrs. Pelz. "You should have tried out your boiler before you paid him. Wait a minute till I empty out my dirty clothes in a pillowcase; then I'll hand it to you."

Mrs. Pelz returned with the boiler and tried to hand it across to Hanneh Breineh, but the soap-box refrigerator on the window-sill was in the way.

"You got to come in for the boiler yourself," said Mrs. Pelz.

"Wait only till I tie my Sammy on to the high-chair he shouldn't fall on me again. He's so wild that ropes won't hold him."

Hanneh Breineh tied the child in the chair, stuck a pacifier in his mouth, and went in to her neighbor. As she took the boiler Mrs. Pelz said:

From *Hungry Hearts*, by Anzia Yezierska, published 1920; reprinted by permission of and special arrangement with the Houghton Mifflin Company.

"Do you know Mrs. Melker ordered fifty pounds of chicken for her daughter's wedding? And such grand chickens! Shining like gold! My heart melted in me just looking at the flowing fatness of those chickens."

Hanneh Breineh smacked her thin, dry lips, a hungry gleam in her sunken eyes.

"Fifty pounds!" she gasped. "It ain't possible. How do you know?"

"I heard her with my own ears. I saw them with my own eyes. And she said she will chop up the chicken livers with onions and eggs for an appetizer, and then she will buy twenty-five pounds of fish, and cook it sweet and sour with raisins, and she said she will bake all her shtrudels on pure chicken fat."

"Some people work themselves up in the world," sighed Hanneh Breineh. "For them is America flowing with milk and honey. In Savel Mrs. Melker used to get shriveled up from hunger. She and her children used to live on potato peelings and crusts of dry bread picked out from the barrels; and in America she lives to eat chicken, and apple shtrudels soaking in fat."

"The world is a wheel always turning," philosophized Mrs. Pelz. "Those who were high go down low, and those who've been low go up higher. Who will believe me here in America that in Poland I was a cook in a banker's house? I handled ducks and geese every day. I used to bake coffee-cake with cream so thick you could cut it with a knife."

"And do you think I was a nobody in Poland?" broke in Hanneh Breineh, tears welling in her eyes as the memories of her past rushed over her. "But what's the use of talking? In America money is everything. Who cares who my father or grandfather was in Poland? Without money I'm a living dead one. My head dries out worrying how to get for the children the eating a penny cheaper."

Mrs. Pelz wagged her head, a gnawing envy contracting her features.

"Mrs. Melker had it good from the day she came," she said begrudgingly. "Right away she sent all her children to the factory, and she began to cook meat for dinner every day. She and her children have eggs and buttered rolls for breakfast each morning like millionaires."

A sudden fall and a baby's scream, and the boiler dropped from Hanneh Breineh's hands as she rushed into her kitchen, Mrs. Pelz after her. They found the high-chair turned on top of the baby.

"*Gevalt!* Save me! Run for a doctor!" cried Hanneh Breineh as she dragged the child from under the high-chair. "He's killed! He's killed! My only child! My precious lamb!" She shrieked as she ran back and forth with the screaming infant.

Mrs. Pelz snatched little Sammy from the mother's hands.

"*Meshugneh!* What are you running around like a crazy, frightening the child? Let me see. Let me tend to him. He ain't killed yet." She hastened to the sink to wash the child's face, and discovered a swelling lump on his forehead. "Have you a quarter in your house?" she asked.

"Yes, I got one," replied Hanneh Breineh, climbing on a chair. "I got to keep it on a high shelf where the children can't get it."

Mrs. Pelz seized the quarter Hanneh Breineh handed down to her.

"Now pull your left eyelid three times while I'm pressing the quarter, and you will see the swelling go down."

Hanneh Breineh took the child again in her arms, shaking and cooing over it and caressing it.

"Ah-ah-ah, Sammy! Ah-ah-ah-ah, little lamb! Ah-ah-ah, little bird! Ah-ah-ah-ah, precious heart! Oh, you saved my life; I thought he was killed," gasped Hanneh Breineh, turning to Mrs. Pelz. "*Oi-i!*" she sighed, "a mother's heart! Always in fear over her children. The minute anything happens to them all life goes out of me. I lose my head and I don't know where I am any more."

"No wonder the child fell," admonished Mrs. Pelz. "You should have a red ribbon or red beads on his neck to keep away the evil eye. Wait. I got something in my machine-drawer."

Mrs. Pelz returned, bringing the boiler and a red string, which she tied about the child's neck while the mother proceeded to fill the boiler.

A little later Hanneh Breineh again came into Mrs. Pelz's kitchen, holding Sammy in one arm and in the other an apron full of potatoes. Putting the child down on the floor, she seated herself on the unmade kitchen-bed and began to peel the potatoes in her apron.

"Woe to me!" sobbed Hanneh Breineh. "To my bitter luck there ain't no end. With all my other troubles, the stove got broke. I lighted the fire to boil the clothes, and it's to get choked with smoke. I paid rent only a week ago, and the agent don't want to fix it. A thunder should strike him! He only comes for the rent, and if anything has to be fixed, then he don't want to hear nothing.

"Why comes it to me so hard?" went on Hanneh Breineh, the tears streaming down her cheeks. "I can't stand it no more. I came into you for a minute to run away from my troubles. It's only when I sit myself down to peel potatoes or nurse the baby that I take time to draw a breath, and beg only for death."

Mrs. Pelz, accustomed to Hanneh Breineh's bitter outbursts, continued her scrubbing.

"*Ut!*" exclaimed Hanneh Breineh, irritated at her neighbor's silence, "what are you tearing up the world with your cleaning? What's the use to clean up when everything only gets dirty again?"

"I got to shine up my house for the holidays."

"You've got it so good nothing lays on your mind but to clean your house. Look on this little blood-sucker," said Hanneh Breineh, pointing to the wizened child, made prematurely solemn from starvation and neglect. "Could anybody keep that brat clean? I wash him one minute, and he's dirty the minute after." Little Sammy grew frightened and began to cry. "Shut up!" ordered the mother, picking up the child to nurse it again. "Can't you see me take a rest for a minute?"

The hungry child began to cry at the top of its weakened lungs.

"*Na, na,* you glutton." Hanneh Breineh took out a dirty pacifier from her pocket and stuffed it into the baby's mouth. The grave, pasty-faced infant shrank into a panic of fear, and chewed the nipple nervously, clinging to it with both his thin little hands.

"For what did I need yet the sixth one?" groaned Hanneh Breineh, turning to Mrs. Pelz. "Wasn't it enough five mouths to feed? If I didn't have this child on my neck, I could turn myself around and earn a few cents." She wrung her hands in a passion of despair. *"Gottuniu!* The earth should only take it before it grows up!"

"Pshaw! Pshaw!" reproved Mrs. Pelz. "Pity yourself on the child. Let it grow up already so long as it is here. See how frightened it looks on you." Mrs. Pelz took the child in her arms and petted it. "The poor little lamb! What did it done you should hate it so?"

Hanneh Breineh pushed Mrs. Pelz away from her.

"To whom can I open the wounds of my heart?" she moaned. "Nobody has pity on me. You don't believe me, nobody believes me until I'll fall down like a horse in the middle of the street. *Oi weh!* mine life is so black for my eyes. Some mothers got luck. A child gets run over by a car, some fall from a window, some burn themselves up with a match, some get choked with diphtheria; but no death takes mine away."

"God from the world! stop cursing!" admonished Mrs. Pelz. "What do you want from the poor children? Is it their fault that their father makes small wages? Why do you let it all out on them?" Mrs. Pelz sat down beside Hanneh Breineh. "Wait only till your children get old enough to go to the shop and earn money," she consoled. "Push only through those few years while they are yet small; your sun will begin to shine; you will live on the fat of the land, when they begin to bring you in the wages each week."

Hanneh Breineh refused to be comforted.

"Till they are old enough to go to the shop and earn money they'll eat the head off my bones," she wailed. "If you only knew the fights I got by each meal. Maybe I gave Abe a bigger piece of bread than Fanny. Maybe Fanny got a little more soup in her plate than Jake. Eating is dearer than diamonds. Potatoes went up a cent on a pound, and milk is only for millionaires. And once a week, when I buy a little meat for the Sabbath, the butcher weighs it for me like gold, with all the bones in it. When I come to lay the meat out on a plate and divide it up, there ain't nothing to it but bones. Before, he used to throw me in a piece of fat extra or a piece of lung, but now you got to pay for everything, even for a bone to the soup."

"Never mind; you'll yet come out from all your troubles. Just as soon as your children get old enough to get their working papers the more children you got, the more money you'll have."

"Why should I fool myself with the false shine of hope? Don't I know it's already my black luck not to have it good in this world? Do you think American children will right away give everything they earn to their mother?"

"I know what is with you the matter," said Mrs. Pelz. "You didn't eat yet today. When it is empty in the stomach, the whole world looks black. Come, only let me give you something good to taste in the mouth; that will freshen you up." Mrs. Pelz went to the cupboard and brought out the saucepan of *gefüllte* fish that she had cooked for dinner and placed it on the table in front of Hanneh Breineh. "Give a taste my fish," she said, taking one slice on a spoon, and handing it to Hanneh Breineh with a piece of bread. "I wouldn't give it to you on a plate because I just cleaned up my house, and I don't want to dirty up my dishes."

"What, am I a stranger you should have to serve me on a plate yet!" cried Hanneh Breineh, snatching the fish in her trembling fingers.

"Oi weh! How it melts through all the bones!" she exclaimed, brightening as she ate. "May it be for good luck to us all!" she exulted, waving aloft the last precious bite.

Mrs. Pelz was so flattered that she even ladled up a spoonful of gravy. "There is a bit of onion and carrot in it," she said, as she handed it to her neighbor.

Hanneh Breineh sipped the gravy drop by drop, like a connoisseur sipping wine.

"Ah-h-h! A taste of that gravy lifts me up to heaven!" As she disposed leisurely of the slice of onion and carrot she relaxed and expanded and even grew jovial. "Let us wish all our troubles on the Russian Czar! Let him bust with our worries for rent! Let him get shriveled with our hunger for bread! Let his eyes dry out of his head looking for work!

"Pshaw! I'm forgetting from everything," she exclaimed, jumping up. "It must be eleven or soon twelve, and my children will be right away out of school and fall on me like a pack of wild wolves. I better quick run to the market and see what cheaper I can get for a quarter."

Because of the lateness of her coming, the stale bread at the nearest bakeshop was sold out, and Hanneh Breineh had to trudge from shop to shop in search of the usual bargain, and spent nearly an hour to save two cents.

In the meantime the children returned from school, and, finding the door locked, climbed through the fire-escape, and entered the house through the window. Seeing nothing on the table, they rushed to the stove. Abe pulled a steaming potato out of the boiling pot, and so scalded his fingers that the potato fell to the floor; whereupon the three others pounced on it.

"It was my potato," cried Abe, blowing his burned fingers, while with the other hand and his foot he cuffed and kicked the three who were struggling on the floor. A wild fight ensued, and the potato was smashed under Abe's foot amid shouts and screams. Hanneh Breineh, on the stairs, heard the noise of her famished brood, and topped their cries with curses and invectives.

"They are here already, the savages! They are here already to shorten my life! They heard you all over the hall, in all the houses around!"

The children, disregarding her words, pounced on her market-basket, shouting ravenously: "Mama, I'm hungry! What more do you got to eat?"

They tore the bread and herring out of Hanneh Breineh's basket and devoured it in starved savagery, clamoring for more.

"Murderers!" screamed Hanneh Breineh, goaded beyond endurance. "What are you tearing from me my flesh? From where should I steal to give you more? Here I had already a pot of potatoes and a whole loaf of bread and two herrings, and you swallowed it down in the wink of an eye. I have to have Rockefeller's millions to fill your stomachs."

All at once Hanneh Breineh became aware that Benny was missing. *"Oi weh!"* she burst out, wringing her hands in a new wave of woe, "where is Benny? Didn't he come home yet from school?"

She ran out into the hall, opened the grime-coated window,

and looked up and down the street; but Benny was nowhere in sight.

"Abe, Jake, Fanny, quick, find Benny!" entreated Hanneh Breineh as she rushed back into the kitchen. But the children, anxious to snatch a few minutes' play before the school-call, dodged past her and hurried out.

With the baby on her arm, Hanneh Breineh hastened to the kindergarten.

"Why are you keeping Benny here so long?" she shouted at the teacher as she flung open the door. "If you had my bitter heart, you would send him home long ago and not wait till I got to come for him."

The teacher turned calmly and consulted her record-cards.

"Benny Safron? He wasn't present this morning."

"Not here?" shrieked Hanneh Breineh. "I pushed him out my-self he should go. The children didn't want to take him, and I had no time. Woe is me! Where is my child?" She began pulling her hair and beating her breast as she ran into the street.

Mrs. Pelz was busy at a pushcart, picking over some spotted apples, when she heard the clamor of an approaching crowd. A block off she recognized Hanneh Breineh, her hair disheveled, her clothes awry, running toward her with her yelling baby in her arms, the crowd following.

"Friend mine," cried Hanneh Breineh, falling on Mrs. Pelz's neck, "I lost my Benny, the best child of all my children." Tears streamed down her red, swollen eyes as she sobbed. "Benny! mine heart, mine life! *Oi-i-i!*"

Mrs. Pelz took the frightened baby out of the mother's arms.

"Still yourself a little! See how you're frightening your child."

"Woe to me! Where is my Benny? Maybe he's killed already by a car. Maybe he fainted away from hunger. He didn't eat noth-ing all day long. *Gottuniu!* Pity yourself on me!"

She lifted her hands full of tragic entreaty.

"People, my child! Get me my child! I'll go crazy out of my head! Get me my child, or I'll take poison before your eyes!"

"Still yourself a little!" pleaded Mrs. Pelz.

"Talk not to me!" cried Hanneh Breineh, wringing her hands. "You're having all your children. I lost mine. Every good luck comes to other people. But I didn't live yet to see a good day in my life. Mine only joy, mine Benny, is lost away from me."

The crowd followed Hanneh Breineh as she wailed through the streets, leaning on Mrs. Pelz. By the time she returned to her house the children were back from school; but seeing that Benny was not there, she chased them out in the street, crying: "Out of here, you robbers, gluttons! Go find Benny!"

Hanneh Breineh crumpled into a chair in utter prostration. *"Oi weh!* he's lost! Mine life; my little bird; mine only joy! How many nights I spent nursing him when he had the measles! And all that I suffered for weeks and months when he had the whooping cough! How the eyes went out of my head till I learned him how to walk, till I learned him how to talk! And such a smart child! If I lost all the others, it wouldn't tear me so by the heart."

She worked herself up into such a hysteria, crying, and tearing her hair, and hitting her head with her knuckles, that at last she fell into a faint. It took some time before Mrs. Pelz, with the aid of neighbors, revived her.

"Benny, mine angel!" she moaned as she opened her eyes.

Just then a policeman came in with the lost Benny.

"Na, na, here you got him already!" said Mrs. Pelz. "Why did you carry on so for nothing? Why did you tear up the world like a crazy?"

The child's face was streaked with tears as he cowered, frightened and forlorn. Hanneh Breineh sprang toward him, slapping his cheeks, boxing his ears, before the neighbors could rescue him from her.

"Woe on your head!" cried the mother. "Where did you lost yourself? Ain't I got enough worries on my head than to go around looking for you? I didn't have yet a minute's peace from that child since he was born."

"See a crazy mother!" remonstrated Mrs. Pelz, rescuing Benny from another beating. "Such a mouth! With one breath she blesses him when he is lost, and with the other breath she curses him when he is found."

Hanneh Breineh took from the window-sill a piece of herring covered with swarming flies, and putting it on a slice of dry bread, she filled a cup of tea that had been stewing all day, and dragged Benny over to the table to eat. But the child, choking with tears, was unable to touch the food.

"Go eat!" commanded Hanneh Breineh. "Eat and choke your-self eating!"

"Maybe she won't remember me no more. Maybe the servant won't let me in," thought Mrs. Pelz as she walked by the brown-stone house on Eighty-fourth Street where she had been told Hanneh Breineh now lived. At last she summoned up enough courage to climb the steps. She was all out of breath as she rang the bell with trembling fingers. *"Oi weh!* even the outside smells riches and plenty! Such curtains! And shades on all windows like by millionaires! Twenty years ago she used to eat from the pot to the hand, and now she lives in such a palace."

A whiff of steam-heated warmth swept over Mrs. Pelz as the door opened, and she saw her old friend of the tenements dressed in silk and diamonds like a being from another world.

"Mrs. Pelz, is it you!" cried Hanneh Breineh, overjoyed at the sight of her former neighbor. "Come right in. Since when are you back in New York?"

"We came last week," mumbled Mrs. Pelz as she was led into a richly carpeted reception-room.

"Make yourself comfortable. Take off your shawl," urged Han-neh Breineh.

But Mrs. Pelz only drew her shawl more tightly around her, a keen sense of her poverty gripping her as she gazed, abashed by the luxurious wealth that shone from every corner. "This shawl covers up my rags," she said, trying to hide her shabby sweater.

"I'll tell you what; come right into the kitchen," suggested Hanneh Breineh. "The servant is away for this afternoon, and we can feel more comfortable there. I can breathe like a free per-son in my kitchen when the girl has her day out."

Mrs. Pelz glanced about her in an excited daze. Never in her life had she seen anything so wonderful as a white tiled kitchen, with its glistening porcelain sink and the aluminum pots and pans that shone like silver.

"Where are you staying now?" asked Hanneh Breineh as she pinned her apron over her silk dress.

"I moved back to Delancey Street, where we used to live," replied Mrs. Pelz as she seated herself cautiously in a white enameled chair.

"*Oi weh!* What grand times we had in that old house when we were neighbors!" sighed Hanneh Breineh, looking at her old friend with misty eyes.

"You still think on Delancey Street? Haven't you more high-class neighbors uptown here?"

"A good neighbor is not to be found every day," deplored Hanneh Breineh. "Uptown here, where each lives in his own house, nobody cares if the person next door is dying or going crazy from loneliness. It ain't anything like we used to have it in Delancey Street, when we could walk into one another's rooms without knocking, and borrow a pinch of salt or a pot to cook in."

Hanneh Breineh went over to the pantry-shelf.

"We are going to have a bite right here on the kitchen table like on Delancey Street. So long there's no servant to watch us we can eat what we please."

"*Oi!* How it waters my mouth with appetite, the smell of the herring and onion!" chuckled Mrs. Pelz, sniffing the welcome odors with greedy pleasure.

Hanneh Breineh pulled a dish-towel from the rack and threw one end of it to Mrs. Pelz.

"So long there's no servant around, we can use it together for a napkin. It's dirty, anyhow. How it freshens up my heart to see you!" she rejoiced as she poured out her tea into a saucer. "If you would only know how I used to beg my daughter to write for me a letter to you; but these American children, what is to them a mother's feelings?"

"What are you talking!" cried Mrs. Pelz. "The whole world rings with you and your children. Everybody is envying you. Tell me how began your luck?"

"You heard how my husband died with consumption," replied Hanneh Breineh. "The five hundred dollars lodge money gave me the first lift in life, and I opened a little grocery store. Then my son Abe married himself to a girl with a thousand dollars. That started him in business, and now he has the biggest shirt-waist factory on West Twenty-ninth Street."

"Yes, I heard your son had a factory." Mrs. Pelz hesitated and stammered: "I'll tell you the truth. What I came to ask you—I thought maybe you would beg your son Abe if he would give my husband a job."

"Why not?" said Hanneh Breineh. "He keeps more than five hundred hands. I'll ask him he should take in Mr. Pelz."

"Long years on you, Hanneh Breineh! You'll save my life if you could only help my husband get work."

"Of course my son will help him. All my children like to do good. My daughter Fanny is a milliner on Fifth Avenue, and she takes in the poorest girls in her shop and even pays them sometimes while they learn the trade." Hanneh Breineh's face lit up, and her chest filled with pride as she enumerated the successes of her children.

"And my son Benny he wrote a play on Broadway and he gave away more than a hundred free tickets for the first night."

"Benny? The one who used to get lost from home all the time? You always did love that child more than all the rest. And what is Sammy your baby doing?"

"He ain't a baby no longer. He goes to college and quarterbacks the football team. They can't get along without him."

"And my son Jake, I nearly forgot him. He began collecting rent in Delancey Street, and now he is boss of renting the swellest apartment houses on Riverside Drive."

"What did I tell you? In America children are like money in the bank," purred Mrs. Pelz as she pinched and patted Hanneh Breineh's sleeve. *"Oi weh!* How it shines from you! You ought to kiss the air and dance for joy and happiness. It is such a bitter frost outside; a pail of coal is so dear, and you got it so warm with steam heat. I had to pawn my feather bed to have enough for the rent, and you are rolling in money."

"Yes, I got it good in some ways, but money ain't everything," sighed Hanneh Breineh.

"You ain't yet satisfied?"

"But here I got no friends," complained Hanneh Breineh.

"Friends?" queried Mrs. Pelz. "What greater friend is there on earth than the dollar?"

"Oi! Mrs. Pelz; if you could only look into my heart! I'm so choked up! You know they say a cow has a long tongue, but can't talk." Hanneh Breineh shook her head wistfully, and her eyes

filmed with inward brooding. "My children give me everything
from the best. When I was sick, they got me a nurse by day and
one by night. They bought me the best wine. If I asked for dove's
milk, they would buy it for me; but—but—I can't talk myself out
in their language. They want to make me over for an American
lady, and I'm different." Tears cut their way under her eyelids
with a pricking pain as she went on: "When I was poor, I was
free, and could holler and do what I like in my own house. Here
I got to lie still like a mouse under a broom. Between living up
to my Fifth Avenue daughter and keeping up with the servants,
I am like a sinner in the next world that is thrown from one hell
to another."

The door-bell rang, and Hanneh Breineh jumped up with a
start.

"*Oi weh!* It must be the servant back already!" she exclaimed
as she tore off her apron. "*Oi weh!* Let's quickly put the dishes
together in a dish-pan. If she sees I eat on the kitchen table, she
will look on me like the dirt under her feet."

Mrs. Pelz seized her shawl in haste. "I better run home quick
in my rags before your servant sees me."

"I'll speak to Abe about the job," said Hanneh Breineh as she
pushed a bill into the hand of Mrs. Pelz, who edged out as the
servant entered.

"I'm having fried potato *lotkes* special for you, Benny," said
Hanneh Breineh as the children gathered about the table for the
family dinner given in honor of Benny's success with his new
play. "Do you remember how you used to lick the fingers from
them?"

"Oh, Mother!" reproved Fanny. "Anyone hearing you would
think we were still in the pushcart district."

"Stop your nagging, Sis, and let Ma alone," commanded Benny,
patting his mother's arm affectionately. "I'm home only once a
month. Let her feed me what she pleases. My stomach is bomb-
proof."

"Do I hear that the President is coming to your play?" said
Abe as he stuffed a napkin over his diamond-studded shirt-front.

"Why shouldn't he come?" returned Benny. "The critics say

it's the greatest antidote for the race hatred created by the war.
If you want to know, he is coming tonight; and what's more, our
box is next to the President's."

"Nu, Mammeh," sallied Jake, "did you ever dream in Delancey Street that we should rub sleeves with the President?"

"I always said that Benny had more head than the rest of you,"
replied the mother.

As the laughter died away, Jake went on:

"Honor you are getting plenty; but how much *mezummen*
does this play bring you? Can I invest any of it in real estate for
you?"

"I'm getting ten per cent royalties of the gross receipts," replied the youthful playwright.

"How much is that?"queried Hanneh Breineh.

"Enough to buy up all your fish markets in Delancey Street,"
laughed Abe in good-natured raillery at his mother.

Her son's jest cut like a knife-thrust in her heart. She felt her
heart ache with the pain that she was shut out from their successes. Each added triumph only widened the gulf. And when she
tried to bridge this gulf by asking questions, they only thrust her
back upon herself.

"Your fame has even helped me get my hat trade solid with
the Four Hundred," put in Fanny. "You bet I let Mrs. Van
Suyden know that our box is next to the President's. She said
she would drop in to meet you. Of course she let on to me that
she hadn't seen the play yet, though my designer said she saw
her there on the opening night."

"Oh, gosh! the toadies!" sneered Benny. "Nothing so sickens
you with success as the way people who once shoved you off the
sidewalk come crawling to you on their stomachs begging you to
dine with them."

"Say, that leading man of yours he's some class," cried Fanny.
"That's the man I'm looking for. Will you invite him to supper
after the theater?"

The playwright turned to his mother.

"Say, Ma," he said laughingly, "how would you like a real
actor for a son-in-law?"

"She should worry," mocked Sam. "She'll be discussing with

him the future of the Greek drama. Too bad it doesn't happen to be Warfield, or mother could give him tips on the
'Auctioneer.' "

Jake turned to his mother with a covert grin.

"I guess you'd have no objection if Fanny got next to Benny's
leading man. He makes at least fifteen hundred a week. That
wouldn't be such a bad addition to the family, would it?"

Again the bantering tone stabbed Hanneh Breineh. Everything in her began to tremble and break loose.

"Why do you ask me?" she cried, throwing her napkin into
her plate. "Do I count for a person in this house? If I'll say
something, will you even listen to me? What is to me the grandest man that my daughter could pick out? Another enemy in my
house! Another person to shame himself from me!" She swept
in her children in one glance of despairing anguish as she rose
from the table. "What worth is an old mother to American children? The President is coming tonight to the theater, and none
of you asked me to go." Unable to check the rising tears, she fled
toward the kitchen and banged the door.

They all looked at one another guiltily.

"Say, Sis," Benny called out sharply, "what sort of frame-up is
this? Haven't you told mother that she was to go with us tonight?"

"Yes—I——" Fanny bit her lips as she fumbled evasively for
words. "I asked her if she wouldn't mind my taking her some
other time."

"Now you have made a mess of it!" fumed Benny. "Mother'll
be too hurt to go now."

"Well, I don't care," snapped Fanny. "I can't appear with
mother in a box at the theater. Can I introduce her to Mrs. Van
Suyden? And suppose your leading man should ask to meet me?"

"Take your time, Sis. He hasn't asked yet," scoffed Benny.

"The more reason I shouldn't spoil my chances. You know
mother. She'll spill the beans that we come from Delancey Street
the minute we introduce her anywhere. Must I always have the
black shadow of my past trailing after me?"

"But have you no feelings for mother?" admonished Abe.

"I've tried harder than all of you to do my duty. I've *lived*
with her." She turned angrily upon them. "I've borne the shame

of mother while you bought her off with a present and a treat
here and there. God knows how hard I tried to civilize her so
as not to have to blush with shame when I take her anywhere.
I dressed her in the most stylish Paris models, but Delancey
Street sticks out from every inch of her. Whenever she opens her
mouth, I'm done for. You fellows had your chance to rise in the
world because a man is free to go up as high as he can reach up
to; but I, with all my style and pep, can't get a man my equal
because a girl is always judged by her mother."

They were silenced by her vehemence, and unconsciously
turned to Benny.

"I guess we all tried to do our best by mother," said Benny,
thoughtfully. "But wherever there is growth, there is pain and
heartbreak. The trouble with us is that the Ghetto of the Middle
Ages and the children of the twentieth century have to live under
one roof, and——"

A sound of crashing dishes came from the kitchen, and the
voice of Hanneh Breineh resounded through the dining-room as
she wreaked her pent-up fury on the helpless servant.

"Oh, my nerves! I can't stand it any more! There will be no
girl again for another week," cried Fanny.

"Oh, let up on the old lady," protested Abe. "Since she can't
take it out on any of us any more, what harm is it if she cusses
the servants?"

"If you fellows had to chase around employment agencies, you
wouldn't see anything funny about it. Why can't we move into
a hotel that will do away with the need of servants altogether?"

"I got it better," said Jake, consulting a notebook from his
pocket. "I have on my list an apartment on Riverside Drive
where there's only a small kitchenette; but we can do away with
the cooking, for there is a dining service in the building."

The new Riverside apartment to which Hanneh Breineh was
removed by her socially ambitious children was for the habitually
active mother an empty desert of enforced idleness. Deprived of
her kitchen, Hanneh Breineh felt robbed of the last reason for
her existence. Cooking and marketing and puttering busily with
pots and pans gave her an excuse for living and struggling and
bearing up with her children. The lonely idleness of Riverside

Drive stunned all her senses and arrested all her thoughts. It gave
her that choked sense of being cut off from air, from life, from
everything warm and human. The cold indifference, the each-
for-himself look in the eyes of the people about her were like
stinging slaps in the face. Even the children had nothing real or
human in them. They were starched and stiff miniatures of their
elders.

But the most unendurable part of the stifling life on Riverside
Drive was being forced to eat in the public dining-room. No
matter how hard she tried to learn polite table manners, she always found people staring at her, and her daughter rebuking her
for eating with the wrong fork or guzzling the soup or staining
the cloth.

In a fit of rebellion Hanneh Breineh resolved never to go
down to the public dining-room again, but to make use of the
gas stove in the kitchenette to cook her own meals. That very
day she rode down to Delancey Street and purchased a new
market basket. For some time she walked among the haggling
pushcart venders, relaxing and swimming in the warm waves of
her old familiar past.

A fish-peddler held up a large carp in his black, hairy hand
and waved it dramatically:

"Women! Women! Fourteen cents a pound!"

He ceased his raucous shouting as he saw Hanneh Breineh in
her rich attire approach his cart.

"How much?" she asked pointing to the fattest carp.

"Fifteen cents, lady," said the peddler, smirking as he raised
his price.

"Swindler! Didn't I hear you call fourteen cents?" shrieked
Hanneh Breineh, exultingly, the spirit of the penny surging in
her blood. Diplomatically, Hanneh Breineh turned as if to go,
and the fishman seized her basket in frantic fear.

"I should live: I'm losing money on the fish, lady," whined the
peddler. "I'll let it down to thirteen cents for you only."

"Two pounds for a quarter, and not a penny more," said Hanneh Breineh, thrilling again with the rare sport of bargaining,
which had been her chief joy in the good old days of poverty.

"*Nu,* I want to make the first sale for good luck." The peddler threw the fish on the scale.

'As he wrapped up the fish, Hanneh Breineh saw the driven look of worry in his haggard eyes, and when he counted out for her the change from her dollar, she waved it aside.

"Keep it for your luck," she said, and hurried off to strike a new bargain at a pushcart of onions.

Hanneh Breineh returned triumphantly with her purchases. The basket under her arm gave forth the old, homelike odors of herring and garlic, while the scaly tail of a four-pound carp protruded from its newspaper wrapping. A gilded placard on the door of the apartment house proclaimed that all merchandise must be delivered through the trade entrance in the rear; but Hanneh Breineh with her basket strode proudly through the marble-paneled hall and rang nonchalantly for the elevator.

The uniformed hall-man, erect, expressionless, frigid with dignity, stepped forward:

"Just a minute, madam. I'll call a boy to take up your basket for you."

Hanneh Breineh, glaring at him, jerked the basket savagely from his hands.

"Mind your own business," she retorted. "I'll take it up myself. Do you think you're a Russian policeman to boss me in my own house?"

Angry lines appeared on the countenance of the representative of social decorum.

"It is against the rules, madam," he said stiffly.

"You should sink into the earth with all your rules and brass buttons. Ain't this America? Ain't this a free country? Can't I take up in my own house what I buy with my own money?" cried Hanneh Breineh, reveling in the opportunity to shower forth the volley of invectives that had been suppressed in her for the weeks of deadly dignity of Riverside Drive.

In the midst of this uproar Fanny came in with Mrs. Van Suyden. Hanneh Breineh rushed over to her, crying:

"This bossy policeman won't let me take up my basket in the elevator."

The daughter, unnerved with shame and confusion, took the basket in her white-gloved hand and ordered the hall-boy to take it around to the regular delivery entrance.

Hanneh Breineh was so hurt by her daughter's apparent defense of the hall-man's rules that she utterly ignored Mrs. Van Suyden's greeting and walked up the seven flights of stairs out of sheer spite.

"You see the tragedy of my life?" broke out Fanny, turning to Mrs. Van Suyden.

"You poor child! You go right up to your dear old lady mother, and I'll come some other time."

Instantly Fanny regretted her words. Mrs. Van Suyden's pity only roused her wrath the more against her mother.

Breathless from climbing the stairs Hanneh Breineh entered the apartment just as Fanny tore the faultless millinery creation from her head and threw it on the floor in a rage.

"Mother, you are the ruination of my life! You have driven away Mrs. Van Suyden, as you have driven away all my best friends. What do you think we got this apartment for but to get rid of your fish smells and your brawls with the servants? And here you come with a basket on your arm as if you just landed from the steerage! And this afternoon, of all times, when Benny is bringing his leading man to tea! When will you ever stop disgracing us?"

"When I'm dead," said Hanneh Breineh, grimly. "When the earth will cover me up, then you'll be free to go your American way. I'm not going to make myself over for a lady on Riverside Drive. I hate you and all your swell friends. I'll not let myself be choked up here by you or by the hall-boss-policeman that is higher in your eyes than your own mother."

"So that's your thanks for all we've done for you?" cried the daughter.

"All you've done for me?" shouted Hanneh Breineh. "What have you done for me? You hold me like a dog on a chain. It stands in the Talmud: some children give their mothers dry bread and water and go to heaven for it, and some give their mother roast duck and go to Gehenna because it's not given with love."

"You want me to love you yet?" raged the daughter. "You knocked every bit of love out of me when I was yet a kid. All the memories of childhood I have is your everlasting cursing and yelling that we were gluttons."

The bell rang sharply, and Hanneh Breineh flung open the door.

"Your groceries, ma'am," said the boy.

Hanneh Breineh seized the basket from him, and with a vicious fling sent it rolling across the room, strewing its contents over the Persian rugs and inlaid floor. Then seizing her hat and coat, she stormed out of the apartment and down the stairs.

Mr. and Mrs. Pelz sat crouched and shivering over their meager supper when the door opened, and Hanneh Breineh in fur coat and plumed hat charged into the room.

"I come to cry out to you my bitter heart," she sobbed. "Woe is me! It is so black for my eyes!"

"What is the matter with you, Hanneh Breineh?" cried Mrs. Pelz in bewildered alarm.

"I am turned out of my own house by the brass-buttoned policeman that bosses the elevator. *Oi-i-i-i! Weh-h-h-h!* What have I from my life? The whole world rings with my son's play. Even the President came to see it, and I, his mother, have not seen it yet. My heart is dying in me like in a prison," she went on wailing.

"I am starved out for a piece of real eating. In that swell restaurant is nothing but napkins and forks and lettuce-leaves. There are a dozen plates to every bite of food. And it looks so fancy on the plate, but it's nothing but straw in the mouth. I'm starving, but I can't swallow down their American eating."

"Hanneh Breineh," said Mrs. Pelz, "you are sinning before God. Look on your fur coat; it alone would feed a whole family for a year. I never had yet a piece of fur trimming on a coat, and you are in fur from the neck to the feet. I never had yet a piece of feather on a hat, and your hat is all feathers."

"What are you envying me?" protested Hanneh Breineh. "What have I from all my fine furs and feathers when my children are strangers to me? All the fur coats in the world can't warm up the loneliness inside my heart. All the grandest feathers can't hide the bitter shame in my face that my children shame themselves from me."

Hanneh Breineh suddenly loomed over them like some ancient,

heroic figure of the Bible condemning unrighteousness. "Why should my children shame themselves from me? From where did they get the stuff to work themselves up in the world? Did they get it from the air? How did they get all their smartness to rise over the people around them? Why don't the children of born American mothers write my Benny's plays? It is I, who never had a chance to be a person, who gave him the fire in his head. If I· would have had a chance to go to school and learn the language, what couldn't I have been? It is I and my mother and my mother's mother and my father and my father's father who had such a black life in Poland; it is our choked thoughts and feelings that are flaming up in my children and making them great in America. And yet they shame themselves from me!"

For a moment Mr. and Mrs. Pelz were hypnotized by the sweep of her words. Then Hanneh Breineh sank into a chair in utter exhaustion. She began to weep bitterly, her body shaking with sobs.

"Woe is me! For what did I suffer and hope on my children? A bitter old age—my end. I'm so lonely!"

All the dramatic fire seemed to have left her. The spell was broken. They saw the Hanneh Breineh of old, ever discontented, ever complaining, even in the midst of riches and plenty.

"Hanneh Breineh," said Mrs. Pelz, "the only trouble with you is that you got it too good. People will tear the eyes out of your head because you're complaining yet. If I only had your fur coat! If I only had your diamonds! I have nothing. You have everything. You are living on the fat of the land. You go right back home and thank God that you don't have my bitter lot."

"You got to let me stay here with you," insisted Hanneh Breineh. "I'll not go back to my children except when they bury me. When they will see my dead face, they will understand how they killed me."

Mrs. Pelz glanced nervously at her husband. They barely had enough covering for their one bed; how could they possibly lodge a visitor?

"I don't want to take up your bed," said Hanneh Breineh. "I don't care if I have to sleep on the floor or on the chairs, but I'll stay here for the night."

Seeing that she was bent on staying, Mr. Pelz prepared to sleep by putting a few chairs next to the trunk, and Hanneh Breineh was invited to share the rickety bed with Mrs. Pelz.

The mattress was full of lumps and hollows. Hanneh Breineh lay cramped and miserable, unable to stretch out her limbs. For years she had been accustomed to hair mattresses and ample woolen blankets, so that though she covered herself with her fur coat, she was too cold to sleep. But worse than the cold were the creeping things on the wall. And as the lights were turned low, the mice came through the broken plaster and raced across the floor. The foul odors of the kitchen-sink added to the night horrors.

"Are you going back home?" asked Mrs. Pelz as Hanneh Breineh put her hat and coat on the next morning.

"I don't know where I'm going," she replied as she put a bill into Mrs. Pelz's hand.

For hours Hanneh Breineh walked through the crowded Ghetto streets. She realized that she no longer could endure the sordid ugliness of her past, and yet she could not go home to her children. She only felt that she must go on and on.

In the afternoon a cold, drizzling rain set in. She was worn out from the sleepless night and hours of tramping. With a piercing pain in her heart she at last turned back and boarded the subway for Riverside Drive. She had fled from the marble sepulcher of the Riverside apartment to her old home in the Ghetto; but now she knew that she could not live there again. She had outgrown her past by the habits of years of physical comforts, and these material comforts that she could no longer do without choked and crushed the life within her.

A cold shudder went through Hanneh Breineh as she approached the apartment house. Peering through the plate glass of the door she saw the face of the uniformed hall-man. For a hesitating moment she remained standing in the drizzling rain, unable to enter and yet knowing full well that she would have to enter.

Then suddenly Hanneh Breineh began to laugh. She realized that it was the first time she had laughed since her children had become rich. But it was the hard laugh of bitter sorrow. Tears streamed down her furrowed cheeks and she walked slowly up the granite steps.

"The fat of the land!" muttered Hanneh Breineh, with a choking sob as the hall-man with immobile face deferentially swung open the door—"the fat of the land!"

James Merle Hopper
(1876-   )

AFTER THE Spanish-American War of 1898 the United States
government sent to the Philippine Islands a number of young
teachers whose responsibility it was to carry civilization and
knowledge to the children there. Among these teachers was James
Merle Hopper. He was born in Paris, France, of an American
father and a French mother and came to America with his parents when he was eleven years old. The family settled in California where, in due time, the boy grew up and was graduated
from the state university. He studied law and was admitted to
the California bar in 1900. But he soon gave up his practice
for newspaper work. After a period of teaching French at his own
university he had in 1902–03 the teaching experience in the Phil-
ippines to which allusion has already been made. He was on the
editorial staff of *McClure's* and is the author, with a collaborator,
of *9009,* the story of a convict, and of a volume of short stories
entitled *What Happened in the Night.* The following story appeared first in *McClure's* and was reprinted, with other stories
based on the author's teaching experiences in the Philippine
Islands, in *Caybigan* (1906).

The Struggles and Triumph
of Isidro de los Maestros

I—Face to Face with the Foe

Returning to his own town after a morning spent in "working up" the attendance of one of his far and recalcitrant barrio-schools, the Maestro of Balangilang was swaying with relaxed muscle and half-closed eyes to the allegretto trot of his little native pony, when he pulled up with a start, wide awake and all his senses on the alert. Through his somnolence, at first in a low hum, but fast rising in a fiendish crescendo, there had come a buzzing sound, much like that of one of the saw-mills of his California forests, and now, as he sat in the saddle, erect and tense, the thing ripped the air in ragged tear, shrieked vibrating into his ear, and finished its course along his spine in delicious irritation.

"Oh, where am I?" murmured the Maestro, blinking; but between blinks he caught the flashing green of the palay fields and knew that he was far from the saw-mills of the Golden State. So he raised his nose to heaven and there, afloat above him in the serene blue, was the explanation. It was a kite, a great locust-shaped kite, darting and swooping in the hot monsoon, and from it, dropping plumb, came the abominable clamor.

"Aha!" exclaimed the Maestro, pointing accusingly at the thin line vaguely visible against the sky-line in a diagonal running from the kite above him ahead to a point in the road. "Aha! there's something at the end of that; there's Attendance at the end of that!"

With which significant remark he leaned forward in the saddle, bringing his switch down with a whizz behind him. The pony gave three rabbit leaps and then settled down to his drumming little trot. As they advanced the line overhead dropped gradually. Finally the Maestro had to swerve the horse aside to

Reprinted by permission of the author.

save his helmet. He pulled up to a walk, and a few yards further came to the spot where string met earth in the expected Attendance.

The Attendance was sitting on the ground, his legs spread before him in an angle of forty-five degrees, each foot arched in a secure grip of a bunch of cogon grass. These legs were bare as far up as they went, and, in fact, no trace of clothing was reached until the eye met the lower fringe of an indescribable undershirt modestly veiling the upper half of a rotund little paunch; an indescribable undershirt, truly, for observation could not reach the thing itself, but only the dirt incrusting it so that it hung together, rigid as a knight's iron corslet, in spite of monstrous tears and rents. Between the teeth of the Attendance was a long, thick cheroot, wound about with hemp fiber, at which he pulled with rounded mouth. Hitched around his right wrist was the kite string, and between his legs a stick spindled with an extra hundred yards. At intervals he hauled hand-over-hand upon the taut line, and then the landscape vibrated to the buzz-saw song which had so compellingly recalled the Maestro to his eternal pursuit.

As the shadow of the horse fell upon him, the Attendance brought his eyes down from their heavenly contemplation, and fixed them upon the rider. A tremor of dismay, mastered as soon as born, flitted over him; then, silently, with careful suppression of all signs of haste, he reached for a big stone with his little yellow paw, then for a stick lying farther off. Using the stone as a hammer, he drove the stick into the ground with deliberate stroke, wound the string around it with tender solicitude, and then, everything being secure, just as the Maestro was beginning his usual embarrassing question:

"Why are you not at school, eh?"

He drew up his feet beneath him, straightened up like a jack-in-a-box, took a hop-skip-jump, and with a flourish of golden heels, flopped head-first into the roadside ditch's rank luxuriance.

"The little devil!" exclaimed the disconcerted Maestro. He dismounted and, leading his horse, walked up to the side of the ditch. It was full of the water of the last baguio. From the edge of the cane-field on the other side there cascaded down the bank a mad vegetation; it carpeted the sides, arched itself above in a vault, and inside this recess the water was rotting, green-scummed; and a powerful fermentation filled the nostrils with hot fever-smells. In the center of the ditch the broad, flat head of a caribao emerged slightly above the water; the floating lilies made an incongruous wreath about the great horns and the beatifically-shut eyes, and the thick, humid nose exhaled ecstasy in shuddering ripplets over the calm surface.

Filled with a vague sense of the ridiculous, the Maestro peered into the darkness. "The little devil!" he murmured. "He's somewhere in here; but how am I to get him, I'd like to know. Do you see him, eh, Mathusalem?" he asked of the stolid beast soaking there in bliss.

Whether in answer to this challenge or to some other irritant, the animal slowly opened one eye and ponderously let it fall shut again in what, to the heated imagination of the Maestro, seemed a patronizing wink. Its head slid quietly along the water; puffs of ooze rose from below and spread on the surface. Then, in the silence there rose a significant sound—a soft, repeated snapping of the tongue:

"Cluck, cluck."

"Aha!" shouted the Maestro triumphantly to his invisible audience. "I know where you are, you scamp; right behind the caribao; come out of there, *pronto, dale-dale!*"

But his enthusiasm was of short duration. To the commanding tongue-click the caribao had stopped dead-still, and a silence heavy with defiance met the too-soon exultant cries. An insect in the foliage began a creaking call, and then all the creatures of humidity hidden there among this fermenting vegetation joined in mocking chorus.

The Maestro felt a vague blush welling up from the innermost recesses of his being.

"I'm going to get that kid," he muttered darkly, "if I have to wait till—the coming of Common Sense to the Manila office! By gum, he's the Struggle for Attendance personified!"

He sat down on the bank and waited. This did not prove interesting. The animals of the ditch creaked on; the caribao bubbled up the water with his deep content; above, the abandoned kite went through strange acrobatics and wailed as if in pain. The Maestro dipped his hand into the water; it was lukewarm. "No hope of a freeze-out," he murmured pensively.

Behind, the pony began to pull at the reins.

"Yes, little horse, I'm tired, too. Well," he said apologetically, "I hate to get energetic, but there are circumstances which——"

The end of his sentence was lost, for he had whisked out the big Colt's dissuader of ladrones, that hung on his belt, and was firing. The six shots went off like a bunch of fire-crackers, but far from at random, for a regular circle boiled up around the dozing caribao. The disturbed animal snorted, and again a discreet "cluck-cluck" rose in the sudden, astounded silence.

"This," said the Maestro, as he calmly introduced fresh cartridges into the chambers of his smoking weapon, "is what might be called an application of western solutions to eastern difficulties."

Again he brought his revolver down, but he raised it without shooting and replaced it in its holster. From beneath the caribao's rotund belly, below the surface, an indistinct form shot out; cleaving the water like a polliwog it glided for the bank, and then a black, round head emerged at the feet of the Maestro.

"All right, bub; we'll go to school now," said the latter, nodding to the dripping figure as it rose before him.

He lifted the sullen brownie and straddled him forward of the saddle, then proceeded to mount himself, when the Capture began to display marked agitation. He squirmed and twisted, turned his head back and up, and finally a grunt escaped him.

"El volador."

"The kite, to be sure; we mustn't forget the kite," acquiesced the Maestro graciously. He pulled up the anchoring stick and laboriously, beneath the hostilely critical eye of the Capture, he hauled in the line till the screeching, resisting flying-machine was brought to earth. Then he vaulted into the saddle.

The double weight was a little too much for the pony; so it was at a dignified walk that the Maestro, his naked, dripping, muddy and still defiant prisoner a-straddle in front of him, the captured kite passed over his left arm like a knightly shield, made his triumphant entry into the pueblo.

2—Heroism and Reverses

When Maestro Pablo rode down Rizal-y-Washington Street to the schoolhouse with his oozing, dripping prize between his arms,

the kite, like a knightly escutcheon against his left side, he found
that in spite of his efforts at preserving a modest, self-deprecatory
bearing, his spine would stiffen and his nose point upward in the
unconscious manifestations of an internal feeling that there was
in his attitude something picturesquely heroic. Not since walking
down the California campus one morning after the big game
won three minutes before blowing of the final whistle, by his
fifty-yard run-in of a punt, had he been in that posture—at once
pleasant and difficult—in which one's vital concern is to wear an
humility sufficiently convincing to obtain from friends forgive-
ness for the crime of being great.

A series of incidents immediately following, however, made the
thing quite easy.

Upon bringing the new recruit into the schoolhouse, to the
perfidiously expressed delight of the already incorporated, the
Maestro called his native assistant to obtain the information necessary to a full matriculation. At the first question the inquisition came to a deadlock. The boy did not know his name.

"In Spanish times," the Assistant suggested modestly, "we
called them "de los Reyes" when the father was of the army, and
"de la Cruz" when the father was of the church; but now, we
can never know *what* it is."

The Maestro dashed to a solution. "All right," he said cheerily.
"I caught him; guess I can give him a name. Call him—Isidro de
los Maestros."

And thus it was that the urchin went down on the school
records, and on the records of life afterward.

Now, well pleased with himself, the Maestro, as is the wont
of men in such state, sought for further enjoyment.

"Ask him," he said teasingly, pointing with his chin at the
newly-baptized but still unregenerate little savage, "why he came
out of the ditch."

"He says he was afraid that you would steal the kite," answered
the Assistant, after some linguistic sparring.

"Eh?" ejaculated the surprised Maestro.

And in his mind there framed a picture of himself riding along
the road with a string between his fingers; and, following in the
upper layers of air, a buzzing kite; and, down in the dust of the
highway, an urchin trudging wistfully after the kite, drawn on

irresistibly, in spite of his better judgment, on and on, horrified but fascinated, up to the yawning school-door.

It would have been the better way. "I ought to go and soak my head," murmured the Maestro pensively.

This was check number one, but others came in quick succession.

For the morning after this incident the Maestro did not find Isidro among the weird, wild crowd gathered into the annex (a transformed sugar storehouse) by the last raid of the Municipal Police.

Neither was Isidro there the next day, nor the next. And it was not till a week had passed that the Maestro discovered, with an inward blush of shame, that his much-longed-for pupil was living in the little hut behind his own house. There would have been nothing shameful in the over-looking—there were seventeen other persons sharing the same abode—were it not that the nipa front of this human hive had been blown away by the last baguio, leaving an unobstructed view of the interior, if it might be called such. As it was, the Municipal Police was mobilized at the urgent behest of the Maestro. Its "cabo," flanked by two privates armed with old German needle-guns, besieged the home, and after an interesting game of hide-and-go-seek, Isidro was finally caught by one arm and one ear, and ceremoniously marched to school. And there the Maestro asked him why he had not been attending.

"No hay pantalones"—there are no pants—Isidro answered, dropping his eyes modestly to the ground.

This was check number two, and unmistakably so, for was it not a fact that a civil commission, overzealous in its civilizing ardor, had passed a law commanding that every one should wear, when in public, "at least one garment, preferably trousers?"

Following this, and an unsuccessful plea upon the town tailor who was on a three weeks' vacation on account of the death of a fourth cousin, the Maestro shut himself up a whole day with Isidro in his little nipa house; and behind the closely-shut shutters engaged in some mysterious toil. When they emerged again the next morning, Isidro wended his way to the school at the end of the Maestro's arm, trousered!

The trousers, it must be said, had a certain cachet of distinction. They were made of calico-print, with a design of little black skulls sprinkled over a yellow background. Some parts hung flat and limp as if upon a scarecrow; others pulsed, like a fire-hose in action, with the pressure of flesh compressed beneath, while at other points they bulged pneumatically in little footballs. The right leg dropped to the ankle; the left stopped discouraged, a few inches below the knee. The seams looked like the putty mountain chains of the geography class. As the Maestro strode along he threw rapid glances at his handiwork, and it was plain that the emotions that moved him were somewhat mixed in character. His face showed traces of a puzzled diffidence, as that of a man who has come in sack-coat to a full-dress function; but after all it was satisfaction that predominated, for after this heroic effort he had decided that Victory had at last perched upon his banners.

And it really looked so for a time. Isidro stayed at school at least during that first day of his trousered life. For when the Maestro, later in the forenoon paid a visit to the annex, he found the Assistant in charge standing disconcerted before the urchin who, with eyes indignant and hair perpendicular upon the top of his head, was evidently holding to his side of the argument with his customary energy.

Isidro was trouserless. Sitting rigid upon his bench, holding on with both hands as if in fear of being removed, he dangled naked legs to the sight of who might look.

"Que barbaridad!" murmured the Assistant in limp dejection.

But Isidro threw at him a look of black hatred. This became a tense, silent plea for justice as it moved up for a moment to the Maestro's face, and then it settled back upon its first object in frigid accusation.

"Where are your trousers, Isidro?" asked the Maestro.

Isidro relaxed his convulsive grasp of the bench with one hand, canted himself slightly to one side just long enough to give an instantaneous view of the trousers, neatly folded and spread between what he was sitting with and what he was sitting on, then swung back with the suddenness of a kodak-shutter, seized his seat with new determination, and looked eloquent justification at the Maestro.

"Why will you not wear them?" asked the latter.

"He says he will not get them dirty," said the Assistant, interpreting the answer.

"Tell him when they are dirty he can go down to the river and wash them," said the Maestro.

Isidro pondered over the suggestion for two silent minutes. The prospect of a day spent splashing in the lukewarm waters of the Ilog he finally put down as not at all detestable, and getting up to his feet:

"I will put them on," he said gravely.

Which he did on the moment, with an absence of hesitation as to which was front and which was back, very flattering to the Maestro.

That Isidro persevered during the next week, the Maestro also came to know. For now regularly every evening as he smoked and lounged upon his long, cane chair, trying to persuade his tired body against all laws of physics to give up a little of its heat to a circumambient atmosphere of temperature equally enthusiastic; as he watched among the rafters of the roof the snakes swallowing the rats, the rats devouring the lizards, the lizards snapping up the spiders, the spiders snaring the flies in eloquent representation of the life struggle, his studied passiveness would be broken by strange sounds from the dilapidated hut at the back of his house. A voice, imitative of that of the Third Assistant who taught the annex, hurled forth questions, which were immediately answered by another voice, curiously like that of Isidro.

Fiercely: "Du yu ssee dde hhett?"

Breathlessly: "Yiss I ssee dde hhett."

Ferociously: "Show me dde hhett."

Eagerly: "Here are dde hhett."

Thunderously: "Gif me dde hhett."

Exultantly: "I gif yu dde hhett."

Then the Maestro would step to the window and look into the hut from which came this Socratic dialogue. And on this wall-less platform which looked much like a primitive stage, a singular action was unrolling itself in the smoky glimmer of a two-cent lamp. The Third Assistant was not there at all; but Isidro was the Third Assistant. And the pupil was not Isidro, but the witless old man who was one of the many sharers of the abode. In

the voice of the Third Assistant, Isidro was hurling out the tremendous questions, and, as the old gentleman, who represented
Isidro, opened his mouth only to drool betel-juice, it was Isidro
who, in Isidro's voice, answered the questions. In his role as
Third Assistant he stood with legs akimbo before the pupil, a
bamboo twig in his hand; as Isidro the pupil, he plumped down
quickly upon the bench before responding. The sole function of
the senile old man seemed that of representing the pupil while
the question was being asked, and receiving, in that capacity, a
sharp cut across the nose from Isidro-the-Third-Assistant's switch,
at which he chuckled to himself in silent glee and druled ad
libitum.

For several nights this performance went on with gradual increase of vocabulary in teacher and pupil. But when it had
reached the "Do you see the apple-tree?" stage, it ceased to advance, marked time for a while, and then slowly but steadily began sliding back into primitive beginnings. This engendered in
the Maestro a suspicion which became certainty when Isidro entered the schoolhouse one morning just before recess, between
two policemen at port arms. A rapid scrutiny of the roll-book
showed that he had been absent a whole week.

"I was at the river cleaning my trousers," answered Isidro
when put face to face with this curious fact.

The Maestro suggested that the precious pantaloons which,
by the way, had been mysteriously embellished by a red stripe
down the right leg and a green stripe down the left leg, could be
cleaned in less than a week, and that Saturday and Sunday were
days specially set aside in the Catechismo of the Americanos for
such little family duties.

Isidro understood, and the nightly rehearsals soon reached the
stage of:

"How menny hhetts hev yu?"

"I hev *ten* hhetts."

Then came another arrest of development and another decline, at the end of which Isidro again making his appearance
flanked by two German needle-guns, caused a blush of remorse
to suffuse the Maestro by explaining with frigid gravity that his
mother had given birth to a little pickaninny-brother and that,
of course, he had had to help.

But significant events in the family did not stop there. After birth, death stepped in for its due. Isidro's relatives began to drop off in rapid sequence—each demise demanding three days of meditation in retirement—till at last the Maestro, who had had the excellent idea of keeping upon paper a record of these unfortunate occurrences, was looking with stupor upon a list showing that Isidro had lost, within three weeks, two aunts, three grandfathers, and five grandmothers—which, considering that an actual count proved the house of bereavement still able to boast of seventeen occupants, was plainly an exaggeration.

Following a long sermon from the Maestro in which he sought to explain to Isidro that he must always tell the truth for sundry philosophical reasons—a statement which the First Assistant tactfully smoothed to something within range of credulity by translating it that one must not lie to *Americanos,* because *Americanos* do not like it—there came a period of serenity.

3—The Triumph

There came to the Maestro days of peace and joy. Isidro was coming to school; Isidro was learning English. Isidro was steady, Isidro was docile, Isidro was positively so angelic that there was something uncanny about the situation. And with Isidro, other little savages were being pruned into the school-going stage of civilization. Helped by the police, they were pouring in from barrio and hacienda; the attendance was going up by leaps and bounds, till at last a circulative report showed that Balangilang had passed the odious Cabancalan with its less strenuous schoolman, and left it in the ruck by a full hundred. The Maestro was triumphant; his chest had gained two inches in expansion. When he met Isidro at recess, playing cibay, he murmured softly: "You little devil; you were Attendance personified, and I've got you now." At which Isidro, pausing in the act of throwing a shell with the top of his head at another shell on the ground, looked up beneath long lashes in a smile absolutely seraphic.

In the evening, the Mastro, his heart sweet with content, stood at the window. These were moonlight nights; in the grassy lanes the young girls played graceful Spanish games, winding like garlands to a gentle song; from the shadows of the huts came the tinkle-tinkle of serenading guitars and yearning notes of violins wailing despairing love. And Isidro, seated on the bamboo ladder of his house, went through an independent performance. He sang "Good-night, Ladies," the last song given to the school, sang it in soft falsetto, with languorous drawls, and never-ending organ points, over and over again, till it changed character gradually, dropping into a wailing minor, an endless croon full of obscure melancholy of a race that dies.

"Goo-oo-oo nigh-igh-igh loidies-ies-ies; goo-oo-oo nigh-igh-igh loides-ies-ies; goo-oo-oo-oo nigh-igh-igh loidies-ies-ies-ies," he repeated and repeated, over and over again, till the Maestro's soul tumbled down and down abysses of maudlin tenderness, and Isidro's chin fell upon his chest in a last drawling, sleepy note. At which he shook himself together and began the next exercise, a recitation, all of one piece from first to last syllable, in one high, monotonous note, like a mechanical doll saying "papa-mama."

"Oh-look-et-de-moon-she-ees-shinin-up-theyre-oh-mudder-she-look-like-a-lom-in-de-ayre-lost-night-she-was-smalleyre-on-joss-like-a-bow-boot-now-she-ees-biggerr-on-rrraon-like-an-O."

Then a big gulp of air and again:

"Oh-look-et-de-moon-she-ees-shinin-up-theyre,——" etc.

An hour of this, and he skipped from the lyric to the patriotic, and then it was:

"I-loof-dde-name-off-Wash-ing-ton,
I-loof-my-coontrrree-tow,
I-loof-dde-fleg-dde-dear-owl-fleg,
Off-rridd-on-whit-on-bloo-oo-oo!"

By this time the Maestro was ready to go to bed, and long in the torpor of the tropic night there came to him, above the hum of the mosquitoes fighting at the net, the soft, wailing croon of Isidro, back at his "Goo-oo-oo nigh-igh-igh loidies-ies-ies."

These were days of ease and beauty to the Maestro, and he enjoyed them the more when a new problem came to give action to his resourceful brain.

The thing was this: For three days there had not been one funeral in Balangilang.

In other climes, in other towns, this might have been a source of congratulation, perhaps, but not in Balangilang. There were rumors of cholera in the towns to the north, and the Maestro, as president of the Board of Health, was on the watch for it. Five deaths a day, experience had taught him, was the healthy average for the town; and this sudden cessation of public burials—he could not believe that dying had stopped—was something to make him suspicious.

It was over this puzzling situation that he was pondering at the morning recess, when his attention was taken from it by a singular scene.

The "batas" of the school were flocking and pushing and jolting at the door of the basement which served as stable for the municipal caribao. Elbowing his way to the spot, the Maestro found Isidro at the entrance, gravely taking up an admission of five shells from those who would enter. Business seemed to be brisk; Isidro had already a big bandana handkerchief bulging with the receipts which were now overflowing into a great tao hat, obligingly loaned him by one of his admirers, as one by one, those lucky enough to have the price filed in, feverish curiosity upon their faces.

The Maestro thought that it might be well to go in also, which he did without paying admission. The disappointed gate-keeper followed him. The Maestro found himself before a little pink-and-blue tissue-paper box, frilled with paper rosettes.

"What have you in there?" asked the Maestro.

"My brother," answered Isidro sweetly.

He cast his eyes to the ground and watched his big toe drawing vague figures in the earth, then appealing to the First Assistant who was present by this time, he added in the tone of virtue which *will* be modest:

"Maestro Pablo does not like it when I do not come to school on account of a funeral, so I brought him (pointing to the little box) with me."

"Well, I'll be——" was the only comment the Maestro found adequate at the moment.

"It is my little pickaninny-brother," went on Isidro, becoming alive to the fact that he was a center of interest, "and he died last night of the great sickness."

"The great what?" ejaculated the Maestro who had caught a few words.

"The great sickness," explained the Assistant. "That is the name by which these ignorant people call the cholera."

For the next two hours the Maestro was very busy.

Firstly he gathered the "batas" who had been rich enough to attend Isidro's little show and locked them up—with the impresario himself—in the little town-jail close by. Then, after a vivid exhortation upon the beauties of boiling water and reporting disease, he dismissed the school for an indefinite period. After which, impressing the two town prisoners, now temporarily out of home, he shouldered Isidro's pretty box, tramped to the cemetery and directed the digging of a grave six feet deep. When the earth had been scraped back upon the lonely little object, he returned to town and transferred the awe-stricken playgoers to his own house, where a strenuous performance took place.

Tolio, his boy, built a most tremendous fire outside and set upon it all the pots and pans and caldrons and cans of his kitchen arsenal, filled with water. When these began to gurgle and steam, the Maestro set himself to stripping the horrified bunch in his room; one by one he threw the garments out of the window to Tolio who, catching them, stuffed them into the receptacles, poking down their bulging protest with a big stick. Then the Maestro mixed an awful brew in an old oil-can, and taking the brush which was commonly used to sleek up his little pony, he dipped it generously into the pungent stuff and began an energetic scrubbing of his now absolutely panic-stricken wards. When he had done this to his satisfaction and thoroughly to their discontent, he let them put on their still steaming garments and they slid out of the house, aseptic as hospitals.

Isidro he kept longer. He lingered over him with loving and strenuous care, and after he had him externally clean, proceeded to dose him internally from a little red bottle. Isidro took everything—the terrific scrubbing, the exaggerated dosing, the ruinous treatment of his pantaloons—with wonder-eyed serenity.

When all this was finished the Maestro took the urchin into the dining-room and, seating him on his best bamboo chair, he courteously offered him a fine, dark perfecto.

The next instant he was suffused with the light of a new revelation. For, stretching out his hard little claw to receive the gift, the little man had shot at him a glance so mild, so wistful, so brown-eyed, filled with such mixed admiration, trust, and appeal, that a queer softness had risen in the Maestro from somewhere down in the regions of his heel, up and up, quietly, like the mercury in the thermometer, till it had flowed through his whole body and stood still, its high-water mark a little lump in his throat.

"Why, Lord bless us-ones, Isidro," said the Maestro quietly. "We're only a child after all; mere baby, my man. And don't we like to go to school?"

"Señor Pablo," asked the boy, looking up softly into the Maestro's still perspiring visage, "Señor Pablo, is it true that there will be no school because of the great sickness?"

"Yes, it is true," answered the Maestro. "No school for a long, long time."

Then Isidro's mouth began to twitch queerly, and suddenly throwing himself full-length upon the floor, he hurled out from somewhere within him a long, tremulous wail.

Margaret Prescott Montague
(1878-   )

TO A Virginia woman belongs the credit for having written one
of the most effective stories of the first World War. *England to
America* appeared in *The Atlantic Monthly* in 1919 and won the
O. Henry Memorial award for the best short story for that year.
But Margaret Montague's reputation does not rest on this one
prize story; she is also author of a volume to which this war story
gives the name and of another collection called *Uncle Sam of
Freedom Ridge*. In addition she has recorded in *Up Eel River*
the tall tales of Tony Beaver, legendary hero of the South.

England to America has sentiment without being sentimental.
Against the background of the World War it introduces the elements of youth who give their lives for their country, women
whose anguish is too deep for tears, and blood ties that unite two
countries which can feel and suffer together.

England to America

"Lord, but English people are funny!"

This was the perplexed mental ejaculation that young Lieutenant Skipworth Cary, of Virginia, found his thoughts constantly reiterating during his stay in Devonshire. Had he been, he wondered, a confiding fool, to accept so trustingly Chev Sherwood's suggestion that he spend a part of his leave, at least, at Bishopsthorpe, where Chev's people lived? But why should he have anticipated any difficulty here, in this very corner of England which had bred his own ancestors, when he had always hit it off so splendidly with his English comrades at the Front? Here, however, though they were all awfully kind,—at least, he was sure they meant to be kind,—something was always bringing him up short: something that he could not lay hold of, but which made him feel like a blind man groping in a strange place, or worse, like a bull in a china-shop. He was prepared enough to find differences in the American and English points of view. But this thing that baffled him did not seem to have to do with that; it was something deeper, something very definite, he was sure— and yet, what was it? The worst of it was that he had a curious feeling as if they were all—that is, Lady Sherwood and Gerald; not Sir Charles so much—protecting him from himself—keeping him from making breaks, as he phrased it. That hurt and annoyed him, and piqued his vanity. Was he a social blunderer, and weren't a Virginia gentleman's manners to be trusted in England without leading-strings?

He had been at the Front for several months with the Royal Flying Corps, and when his leave came, his Flight Commander, Captain Cheviot Sherwood, discovering that he meant to spend it in England, where he hardly knew a soul, had said his people down in Devonshire would be jolly glad to have him stop with

From *The Atlantic Monthly*, 1919; reprinted by permission of the author.

them; and Skipworth Cary, knowing that, if the circumstances had been reversed, his people down in Virginia would indeed have been jolly glad to entertain Captain Sherwood, had accepted unhesitatingly. The invitation had been seconded by a letter from Lady Sherwood,—Chev's mother,—and after a few days sight-seeing in London, he had come down to Bishopsthorpe, very eager to know his friend's family, feeling as he did about Chev himself. "He's the finest man that ever went up in the air," he had written home; and to his own family's disgust, his letters had been far more full of Chev Sherwood than they had been of Skipworth Cary.

And now here he was, and he almost wished himself away—wished almost that he was back again at the Front, carrying on under Chev. There, at least, you knew what you were up against. The job might be hard enough, but it wasn't baffling and queer, with hidden undercurrents that you couldn't chart. It seemed to him that this baffling feeling of constraint had rushed to meet him on the very threshold of the drawing-room, when he made his first appearance.

As he entered, he had a sudden sensation that they had been awaiting him in a strained expectancy, and that, as he appeared, they adjusted unseen masks and began to play-act at something. "But English people don't play-act very well," he commented to himself, reviewing the scene afterward.

Lady Sherwood had come forward and greeted him in a manner which would have been pleasant enough, if he had not, with quick sensitiveness, felt it to be forced. But perhaps that was English stiffness.

Then she had turned to her husband, who was standing staring into the fireplace, although, as it was June, there was no fire there to stare at.

"Charles," she said, "here is Lieutenant Cary"; and her voice had a certain note in it which at home Cary and his sister Nancy were in the habit of designating "mother-making-dad-mind-his-manners."

At her words the old man—and Cary was startled to see how old and broken he was—turned round and held out his hand. "How d'you do?" he said jerkily, "how d'you do?" and then turned abruptly back again to the fireplace.

"Hello! What's up! The old boy doesn't like me!" was Cary's quick, startled comment to himself.

He was so surprised by the look the other bent upon him that he involuntarily glanced across to a long mirror to see if there was anything wrong with his uniform. But no, that appeared to be all right. It was himself, then—or his country; perhaps the old sport didn't fall for Americans.

"And here is Gerald," Lady Sherwood went on in her low remote voice, which somehow made the Virginian feel very far away.

It was with genuine pleasure, though with some surprise, that he turned to greet Gerald Sherwood, Chev's younger brother, who had been, tradition in the corps said, as gallant and daring a flyer as Chev himself, until he got his in the face five months ago.

"I'm mighty glad to meet you," he said eagerly, in his pleasant, muffled Southern voice, grasping the hand the other stretched out, and looking with deep respect at the scarred face and sightless eyes.

Gerald laughed a little, but it was a pleasant laugh, and his hand-clasp was friendly.

"That's real American, isn't it?" he said. "I ought to have remembered and said it first. Sorry."

Skipworth laughed too. "Well," he conceded, "we generally are glad to meet people in my country, and we don't care who says it first. But," he added. "I didn't think I'd have the luck to find you here."

He remembered that Chev had regretted that he probably wouldn't see Gerald, as the latter was at St. Dunstan's, where they were re-educating the blinded soldiers.

The other hesitated a moment, and then said rather awkwardly, "Oh, I'm just home for a little while; I only got here this morning, in fact."

Skipworth noted the hesitation. Did the old people get panicky at the thought of entertaining a wild man from Virginia, and send an S O S for Gerald, he wondered.

"We are so glad you could come to us," Lady Sherwood said rather hastily just then. And again he could not fail to note that she was prompting her husband.

The latter reluctantly turned round, and said, "Yes, yes, quite so. Welcome to Bishopsthorpe, my boy," as if his wife had pulled a string, and he responded mechanically, without quite knowing what he said. Then, as his eyes rested a moment on his guest, he looked as if he would like to bolt out of the room. He controlled himself, however, and jerking round again to the fireplace, went on murmuring, "Yes, yes, yes," vaguely—just like the dormouse at the Mad Tea-Party, who went to sleep, saying, "Twinkle, twinkle, twinkle," Cary could not help thinking to himself.

But after all, it wasn't really funny, it was pathetic. Gosh, how doddering the poor old boy was! Skipworth wondered, with a sudden twist at his heart, if the war was playing the deuce with his home people, too. Was his own father going to pieces like this, and had his mother's gay vivacity fallen into that still remoteness of Lady Sherwood's? But of course not! The Carys hadn't suffered as the poor Sherwoods had, with their youngest son, Curtin, killed early in the war, and now Gerald knocked out so tragically. Lord, he thought, how they must all bank on Chev! And of course they would want to hear at once about him. "I left Chev as fit as anything, and he sent all sorts of messages," he reported, thinking it more discreet to deliver Chev's messages thus vaguely than to repeat his actual care-free remark, which had been, "Oh, tell 'em I'm jolly as a tick."

But evidently there was something wrong with the words as they were, for instantly he was aware of that curious sense of withdrawal on their part. Hastily reviewing them, he decided that they had sounded too familiar from a stranger and a younger man like himself. He supposed he ought not to have spoken of Chev by his first name. Gee, what sticklers they were! Wouldn't his family—dad and mother and Nancy—have fairly lapped up any messages from him, even if they had been delivered a bit awkwardly? However, he added, as a concession to their point of view, "But of course, you'll have had later news of Captain Sherwood."

To which, after a pause, Lady Sherwood responded, "Oh, yes," in that remote and colorless voice which might have meant any-thing or nothing.

At this point dinner was announced.

Lady Sherwood drew her husband away from the empty fire-

place, and Gerald slipped his arm through the Virginian's, saying pleasantly, "I'm learning to carry on fairly well at St. Dunstan's, but I confess I still like to have a pilot."

To look at the tall young fellow beside him, whose scarred face
was so reminiscent of Chev's untouched good looks, who had
known all the immense freedom of the air, but who was now
learning to carry on in the dark, moved Skipworth Cary to generous homage.

"You know my saying I'm glad to meet you isn't just American," he said half shyly, but warmly. "It's plain English, and the
straight truth. I've wanted to meet you awfully. The oldsters are
always holding up your glorious exploits to us newcomers. Withers never gets tired telling about that fight of yours with the four
enemy planes. And besides," he rushed on eagerly, "I'm glad to
have a chance to tell Chev's brother—Captain Sherwood's brother,
I mean—what I think of him. Only as a matter of fact, I can't,"
he broke off with a laugh. "I can't put it exactly into words, but
I tell you I'd follow that man straight into hell and out the other
side—or go there alone if he told me to. He is the finest chap that
ever flew."

And then he felt as if a cold douche had been flung in his face,
for after a moment's pause, the other returned, "That's awfully
good of you," in a voice so distant and formal that the Virginian
could have kicked himself. What an ass he was to be so darned
enthusiastic with an Englishman! He supposed it was bad form
to show any pleasure over praise of a member of your family.
Lord, if Chev got the V. C., he reckoned it would be awful to
speak of it. Still, you would have thought Gerald might have
stood for a little praise of him. But then, glancing sideways at
his companion, he surprised on his face a look so strange and
suffering that it came to him almost violently what it must be
never to fly again; to be on the threshold of life, with endless
days of blackness ahead. Good God! How cruel he had been to
flaunt Chev in his face! In remorseful and hasty reparation he
stumbled on, "But the old fellows are always having great discussions as to which was the best—you or your brother. Withers
always maintains you were."

"Withers lies, then!" the other retorted. "I never touched
Chev—never came within a mile of him, and never could have."

They reached the dinner-table with that, and young Cary
found himself bewildered and uncomfortable. If Gerald hadn't
liked praise of Chev, he had liked praise of himself even less, it
seemed.

Dinner was not a success. The Virginian found that, if there
was to be conversation, the burden of carrying it on was upon
him, and gosh! they don't mind silences in this man's island, do
they? he commented desperately to himself, thinking how different it was from America. Why, there they acted as if silence was
an egg that had just been laid, and everyone had to cackle at
once to cover it up. But here the talk constantly fell to the
ground, and nobody but himself seemed concerned to pick it up.
His attempt to praise Chev had not been successful, and he
could understand their not wanting to hear about flying and the
war before Gerald.

So at last, in desperation, he wandered off into descriptions of
America, finding to his relief, that he had struck the right note
at last. They were glad to hear about the States, and Lady Sherwood inquired politely if the Indians still gave them much
trouble; and when he assured her that in Virginia, except for
the Pocahontas tribe, they were all pretty well subdued, she accepted his statement with complete innocency. And he was so
delighted to find at last a subject to which they were evidently
cordial, that he was quite carried away, and wound up by inviting them all to visit his family in Richmond, as soon as the war
was over.

Gerald accepted at once, with enthusiasm; Lady Sherwood
made polite murmurs, smiling at him in quite a warm and almost, indeed, maternal manner. Even Sir Charles, who had been
staring at the food on his plate as if he did not quite know what
to make of it, came to the surface long enough to mumble, "Yes,
yes, very good idea. Countries must carry on together— What?"

But that was the only hit of the whole evening, and when the
Virginian retired to his room, as he made an excuse to do early,
he was so confused and depressed that he fell into an acute attack of homesickness.

Heavens, he thought, as he tumbled into bed, just suppose,
now, this was little old Richmond, Virginia, U.S.A., instead of
being Bishopsthorpe, Avery Cross near Wick, and all the rest of

it! And at that, he grinned to himself. England wasn't such an all-fired big country that you'd think they'd have to ticket themselves with addresses a yard long, for fear they'd get lost—now, would you? Well, anyway, suppose it was Richmond, and his train just pulling into the Byrd Street Station. He stretched out luxuriously, and let his mind picture the whole familiar scene. The wind was blowing right, so there was the mellow homely smell of tobacco in the streets, and plenty of people all along the way to hail him with outstretched hands and shouts of "Hey, Skip Cary, when did you get back?" "Welcome home, my boy!" "Well, will you *look* what the cat dragged in!" And so he came to his own front door-step, and, walking straight in, surprised the whole family at breakfast; and yes—doggone it! if it wasn't Sunday, and they having waffles! And after that his obliging fancy bore him up Franklin Street, through Monroe Park, and so to Miss Sally Berkeley's door. He was sound asleep before he reached it, but in his dreams, light as a little bird, she came flying down the broad stairway to meet him, and——

But when he waked next morning, he did not find himself in Virginia, but in Devonshire, where, to his unbounded embarrassment, a white housemaid was putting up his curtains and whispering something about his bath. And though he pretended profound slumber, he was well aware that people do not turn brick-red in their sleep. And the problem of what was the matter with the Sherwood family was still before him.

2

"They're playing a game," he told himself after a few days. "That is, Lady Sherwood and Gerald are—poor old Sir Charles can't make much of a stab at it. The game is to make me think they are awfully glad to have me, when in reality there's something about me, or something I do, that gets them on the raw."

He almost decided to make some excuse and get away; but after all, that was not easy. In English novels, he remembered, they always had a wire calling them to London; but, darn it all! the Sherwoods knew mighty well there wasn't any one in London who cared a hoot about him.

The thing that got his goat most, he told himself, was that they apparently didn't like his friendship with Chev. Anyway they didn't seem to want him to talk about him; and whenever he tried to express his warm appreciation for all that the older man had done for him, he was instantly aware of a wall of reserve on their part, a holding of themselves aloof from him. That puzzled and hurt him, and put him on his dignity. He concluded that they thought it was cheeky of a youngster like him to think that a man like Chev could be his friend; and if that was the way they felt, he reckoned he'd jolly well better shut up about it.

But whatever it was that they didn't like about him, they most certainly did want him to have a good time. He and his pleasure appeared to be for the time being their chief consideration. And after the first day or so he began indeed to enjoy himself extremely. For one thing, he came to love the atmosphere of the old place and of the surrounding country, which he and Gerald explored together. He liked to think that ancestors of his own had been inheritors of these green lanes, and pleasant mellow stretches. Then, too, after the first few days, he could not help seeing that they really began to like him, which of course was reassuring, and tapped his own warm friendliness, which was always ready enough to be released. And besides, he got by accident what he took to be a hint as to the trouble. He was passing the half-open door of Lady Sherwood's morning-room, when he heard Sir Charles's voice break out, "Good God, Elizabeth, I don't see how you stand it! When I see him so straight and fine-looking, and so untouched, beside our poor lad, and think—and think——"

Skipworth hurried out of earshot, but now he understood that look of aversion in the old man's eyes which had so startled him at first. Of course, the poor old boy might easily hate the sight of him beside Gerald. With Gerald himself he really got along famously. He was a most delightful companion, full of anecdotes and history of the countryside, every foot of which he had apparently explored in the old days with Chev and the younger brother, Curtin. Yet even with Gerald, Cary sometimes felt that aloofness and reserve, and that older protective air that they all showed him. Take, for instance, that afternoon when they were lolling together on the grass in the park. The Virginian, running on in his usual eager manner, had plunged without thinking into an account of a particularly daring bit of flying on Chev's part, when suddenly he realized that Gerald had rolled over on the grass and buried his face in his arms, and interrupted himself awkwardly. "But, of course," he said, "he must have written home about it himself."

"No, or if he did, I didn't hear of it. Go on," Gerald said in a muffled voice.

A great rush of compassion and remorse overwhelmed the Virginian, and he burst out penitently, "What a brute I am! I'm always forgetting and running on about flying, when I know it must hurt like the very devil!"

The other drew a difficult breath. "Yes," he admitted, "what you say does hurt in a way—in a way you can't understand. But all the same I like to hear you. Go on about Chev."

So Skipworth went on and finished his account, winding up, "I don't believe there's another man in the service who could have pulled it off—but I tell you your brother's one in a million."

"Good God, don't I know it!" the other burst out. "We were all three the jolliest pals together," he got out presently in a choked voice, "Chev and the young un and I; and now——"

He did not finish, but Cary guessed his meaning. Now the young un, Curtin, was dead, and Gerald himself knocked out. But, heavens! the Virginian thought, did Gerald think Chev would go back on him now on account of his blindness? Well, you could everlastingly bet he wouldn't!

"Chev thinks the world and all of you!" he cried in eager defense of his friend's loyalty. "Lots of times when we're all awfully jolly together, he makes some excuse and goes off by himself; and Withers told me it was because he was so frightfully cut up about you. Withers said he told him once that he'd a lot rather have got it himself—so you can everlastingly bank on him!"

Gerald gave a terrible little gasp. "I—I knew he'd feel like that," he got out. "We've always cared such a lot for each other." And then he pressed his face harder than ever into the grass, and his long body quivered all over. But not for long. In a moment he took fierce hold on himself, muttering, "Well, one must carry on, whatever happens," and apologized disjointedly. "What a fearful fool you must think me! And—and this isn't very pippy for you, old chap." Presently, after that, he sat up, and said, brushing it all aside, "We're facing the old moat, aren't we? There's an interesting bit of tradition about it that I must tell you."

And there you were, Cary thought: no matter how much Gerald might be suffering from his misfortune, he must carry on just the same, and see that his visitor had a pleasant time. It made the Virginian feel like an outsider and very young, as if he were not old enough for them to show him their real feelings.

Another thing that he noticed was that they did not seem to want him to meet people. They never took him anywhere to call, and if visitors came to the house, they showed an almost panicky desire to get him out of the way. That again hurt his pride. What in heaven's name was the matter with him anyway!

3

However, on the last afternoon of his stay at Bishopsthorpe, he told himself with a rather rueful grin, that his manners must have improved a little, for they took him to tea at the rectory.

He was particularly glad to go there because, from certain jokes of Withers's, who had known the Sherwoods since boyhood, he gathered that Chev and the rector's daughter were engaged. And just as he would have liked Chev to meet Sally Berkeley, so he wanted to meet Miss Sybil Gaylord.

He had little hope of having a tête-à-tête with her, but as it fell out he did. They were all in the rectory garden together, Gerald and the rector a little behind Miss Gaylord and himself, as they strolled down a long walk with high hedges bordering it. On the other side of the hedge Lady Sherwood and her hostess still sat at the tea-table, and then it was that Cary heard Mrs. Gaylord say distinctly, "I'm afraid the strain has been too much for you—you should have let us have him."

To which Lady Sherwood returned quickly, "Oh, no, that would have been impossible with——"

"Come—come this way—I must show you the view from the arbor," Miss Gaylord broke in breathlessly; and laying a hand on his arm, she turned him abruptly into a side path.

Glancing down at her, the Southerner could not but note the panic and distress in her fair face. It was so obvious that the overheard words referred to him, and he was so bewildered by the whole situation, that he burst out impulsively, "I say, what *is* the matter with me? Why do they find me so hard to put up with? Is it something I do—or don't they like Americans? Honestly, I wish you'd tell me."

She stood still at that, looking at him, her blue eyes full of distress and concern.

"Oh, I am so sorry," she cried. "They would be so sorry to have you think anything like that."

"But what is it?" he persisted. "Don't they like Americans?"

"Oh, no, it isn't that— Oh, quite the contrary!" she returned eagerly.

"Then it's something about me they don't like?"

"Oh, no, no! Least of all, that—*don't* think that!" she begged.

"But what am I to think then?"

"Don't think anything just yet," she pleaded. "Wait a little, and you will understand."

She was so evidently distressed that he could not press her further; and fearing she might think him unappreciative, he said, "Well, whatever it is, it hasn't prevented me from having a ripping good time. They've seen to that, and just done everything for my pleasure."

She looked up quickly, and to his relief he saw that for once he had said the right thing.

"You have enjoyed it, then?" she questioned eagerly.

"Most awfully," he assured her warmly. "I shall always remember what a happy leave they gave me."

She gave a little sigh of satisfaction, "I am so glad," she said. "They wanted you to have a good time—that was what we all wanted."

He looked at her gratefully, thinking how sweet she was in her fair English beauty, and how good to care that he should have enjoyed his leave. How different she was too from Sally Berkeley —why she would have made two of his little girl! And how quiet! Sally Berkeley, with her quick glancing vivacity, would have been all around her and off again like a humming-bird before she could have uttered two words. And yet he was sure that they would have been friends, just as he and Chev were. Perhaps they all would be, after the war. And then he began to talk about

Chev, being sure that, had the circumstances been reversed, Sally Berkeley would have wanted news of him. Instantly he was aware of a tense listening stillness on her part. That pleased him. Well, she did care for the old fellow all right, he thought; and though she made no response, averting her face, and plucking nervously at the leaves of the hedge as they passed slowly along, he went on pouring out his eager admiration for his friend.

At last they came to a seat in an arbor, from which one looked out upon a green beneficent landscape. It was an intimate secluded little spot—and oh, if Sally Berkeley were only there to sit beside him! And as he thought of this, it came to him whimsically that in all probability she must be longing for Chev, just as he was for Sally.

Dropping down on the bench beside her, he leaned over, and said with a friendly, almost brotherly, grin of understanding, "I reckon you're wishing Captain Sherwood was sitting here, instead of Lieutenant Cary."

The minute the impulsive words were out of his mouth, he knew he had blundered, been awkward, and inexcusably intimate. She gave a little choked gasp, and her blue eyes stared up at him, wide and startled. Good heavens, what a break he had made! No wonder the Sherwoods couldn't trust him in company! There seemed no apology that he could offer in words, but at least, he thought, he would show her that he would not have intruded on her secret without being willing to share his with her. With awkward haste he put his hand into his breast-pocket, and dragged forth the picture of Sally Berkeley he always carried there.

"This is the little girl I'm thinking about," he said, turning very red, yet boyishly determined to make amends, and also proudly confident of Sally Berkeley's charms. "I'd like mighty well for you two to know one another."

She took the picture in silence, and for a long moment stared down at the soft little face, so fearless, so confident and gay, that smiled appealingly back at her. Then she did something astonishing,—something which seemed to him wholly un-English,—and yet he thought it the sweetest thing he had ever seen. Cupping her strong hands about the picture with a quick protectiveness, she suddenly raised it to her lips, and kissed it lightly. "O little girl!" she cried, "I hope you will be very happy!"

The little involuntary act, so tender, so sisterly and spontaneous, touched the Virginian extremely.

"Thanks, awfully," he said unsteadily. "She'll think a lot of that, just as I do—and I know she'd wish you the same."

She made no reply to that, and as she handed the picture back to him, he saw that her hands were trembling, and he had a sudden conviction that, if she had been Sally Berkeley, her eyes would have been full of tears. As she was Sybil Gaylord, however, there were no tears there, only a look that he never forgot. The look of one much older, protective, maternal almost, and as if she were gazing back at Sally Berkeley and himself from a long way ahead on the road of life. He supposed it was the way most English people felt nowadays. He had surprised it so often on all their faces, that he could not help speaking of it.

"You all think we Americans are awfully young and raw, don't you?" he questioned.

"Oh, no, not that," she deprecated. "Young perhaps for these days, yes—but it is more that you—that your country is so—so unsuffered. And we don't want you to suffer!" she added quickly.

Yes, that was it! He understood now, and, heavens, how fine it was! Old England was wounded deep—deep. What she suffered herself she was too proud to show; but out of it she wrought a great maternal care for the newcomer. Yes, it *was* fine—he hoped his country would understand.

Miss Gaylord rose. "There are Gerald and father looking for you," she said, "and I must go now." She held out her hand. "Thank you for letting me see her picture, and for everything you said about Captain Sherwood—for *everything*, remember— I want you to remember."

With a light pressure of her fingers she was gone, slipping away through the shrubbery, and he did not see her again.

4

So he came to his last morning at Bishopsthorpe; and as he dressed, he wished it could have been different; that he were not still conscious of that baffling wall of reserve between himself and

Chev's people, for whom, despite all, he had come to have a real affection.

In the breakfast-room he found them all assembled, and his last meal there seemed to him as constrained and difficult as any that had preceded it. It was over finally, however, and in a few minutes he would be leaving.

"I can never thank you enough for the splendid time I've had here," he said as he rose. "I'll be seeing Chev tomorrow, and I'll tell him all about everything."

Then he stopped dead. With a smothered exclamation, old Sir Charles had stumbled to his feet, knocking over his chair, and hurried blindly out of the room; and Gerald said, *"Mother!"* in a choked appeal.

As if it were a signal between them, Lady Sherwood pushed her chair back a little from the table, her long delicate fingers dropped together loosely in her lap; she gave a faint sigh as if a restraining mantle slipped from her shoulders, and, looking up at the youth before her, her fine pale face lighted with a kind of glory, she said, "No, dear lad, no. You can never tell Chev, for he is gone."

"Gone!" he cried.

"Yes," she nodded back at him, just above a whisper; and now her face quivered, and the tears began to rush down her cheeks.

"Not *dead!*" he cried. "Not Chev—not that! O my God, Gerald, not *that!*"

"Yes," Gerald said. "They got him two days after you left."

It was so overwhelming, so unexpected and shocking, above all so terrible, that the friend he had so greatly loved and admired was gone out of his life forever, that young Cary stumbled back into his seat, and, crumpling over, buried his face in his hands, making great uncouth gasps as he strove to choke back his grief.

Gerald groped hastily around the table, and flung an arm about his shoulders.

"Steady on, dear fellow, steady," he said, though his own voice broke.

"When did you hear?" Cary got out at last.

"We got the official notice just the day before you came—and Withers has written us particulars since."

"And you *let* me come in spite of it! And stay on, when every word I said about him must have—have fairly *crucified* each one of you! Oh, forgive me! forgive me!" he cried distractedly. He saw it all now; he understood at last. It was not on Gerald's account that they could not talk of flying and of Chev, it was because—because their hearts were broken over Chev himself. "Oh, forgive me!" he gasped again.

"Dear lad, there is nothing to forgive," Lady Sherwood returned. "How could we help loving your generous praise of our poor darling? We loved it, and you for it; we wanted to hear it, but we were afraid. We were afraid we might break down, and that you would find out."

The tears were still running down her cheeks. She did not brush them away now; she seemed glad to have them there at last.

Sinking down on his knees, he caught her hands. "Why did you *let* me do such a horrible thing?" he cried. "Couldn't you have trusted me to understand? Couldn't you *see* I loved him just as you do— No, no!" he broke down humbly. "Of course I couldn't love him as his own people did. But you must have seen how I felt about him—how I admired him, and would have followed him anywhere—and *of course* if I had known, I should have gone away at once."

"Ah, but that was just what we were afraid of," she said quickly. "We were afraid you would go away and have a lonely leave somewhere. And in these days a boy's leave is so precious a thing that nothing must spoil it—*nothing,*" she reiterated; and her tears fell upon his hands like a benediction. "But we didn't do it very well, I'm afraid," she went on presently, with gentle contrition. "You were too quick and understanding; you guessed there was something wrong. We were sorry not to manage better," she apologized.

"Oh, you wonderful, wonderful people!" he gasped. "Doing everything for my happiness, when all the time—all the time——"

His voice went out sharply, as his mind flashed back to scene after scene: to Gerald's long body lying quivering on the grass; to Sybil Gaylord wishing Sally Berkeley happiness out of her own tragedy; and to the high look on Lady Sherwood's face. They seemed to him themselves, and yet more than themselves—

shining bits in the mosaic of a great nation. Disjointedly there passed through his mind familiar words—"these are they who have washed their garments—having come out of great tribulation." No wonder they seemed older.

"We—we couldn't have done it in America," he said humbly.

He had a desperate desire to get away to himself; to hide his face in his arms, and give vent to the tears that were stifling him; to weep for his lost friend, and for this great heartbreaking heroism of theirs.

"But why did you do it?" he persisted. "Was it because I was his friend?"

"Oh, it was much more than that," Gerald said quickly. "It was a matter of the two countries. Of course, we jolly well knew you didn't belong to us, and didn't want to, but for the life of us we couldn't help a sort of feeling that you did. And when America was in at last, and you fellows began to come, you seemed like our very own come back after many years, and," he added, a throb in his voice, "we were most awfully glad to see you—we wanted a chance to show you how England felt."

Skipworth Cary rose to his feet. The tears for his friend were still wet upon his lashes. Stooping, he took Lady Sherwood's hands in his and raised them to his lips. "As long as I live, I shall never forget," he said. "And others of us have seen it too in other ways—be sure America will never forget, either."

She looked up at his untouched youth out of her beautiful sad eyes, the exalted light still shining through her tears. "Yes," she said, "you see it was—I don't know exactly how to put it—but it was England to America."

Martha Ellis Gellhorn
(1908-   )

JOURNALIST, war correspondent, social investigator, and writer, Martha Gellhorn has led an active and varied life. She has served in America as W. P. A. investigator, in Spain during the Civil War and in Finland during the Russian invasion as foreign correspondent for *Collier's*. She has written for *Collier's* and for *Scribner's* and has to her credit a book of short stories, *The Trouble I've Seen* (1936), and a novel, *A Stricken Field* (1940). In 1940 Ernest Hemingway dedicated to her his powerful novel of the Spanish Civil War, *For Whom the Bell Tolls;* and shortly afterwards made her his wife.

Mrs. Maddison Returns to the Land is a New Deal story of social and economic adjustment. Although the story introduces the machinery by which the government relief agencies operate, the essential interest lies in the character of the heroine, a stalwart middle-aged woman who is forced by the indifference and indolence of her children to retreat from her high purpose to re-establish herself and them as independent social units.

Mrs. Maddison Returns to the Land

In the relief office they had read the bulletins coming from Washington via State headquarters, and they had received a good many visitors called field supervisors and field representatives. Under pressure and feeling theirs-not-to-reason-why, they had shipped unemployed families back to the land. It was a Project, which made it vast and important, possible of endless interpretation and confusion, and above all it had to be done quickly. Some of the Relief workers, who had lived long in these parts and knew conditions and what you had to have to farm, and what kind of land they were putting people on, and what the houses meant in ill-health, shook their heads grimly but in wise silence. Rural rehabilitation: in itself a magnificent idea. A chance for men to be again self-supporting; their own masters; captains of their destinies, souls, pocket-books. "It's a fine idea," Mrs. Cahill said, "only nobody seems to have thought much about those Negro shanties we're putting our folks in." Mrs. Lewis, who worked out towards the sawmill district, said it certainly was a fine idea, but she thought there'd be some trouble about medical aid: she also shook her head. "The malaria," Mrs. Lewis said. Miss Ogilvie, who had a sharper tongue than the others, and used to lie awake at night furtively being ashamed of herself for having such a nice bed, said: "It sez, in the bulletins, $105.80 a year is the average cost to the government for rural rehab families; for everything personal. Lissen to me," she said, with the sun shining on her eyeglasses. "That just isn't human. And to think those northerners made all that fuss about slaves. I don't think they got their heads screwed on right up there."

Mrs. Cahill brooded over the present and future of Mrs. Mad-

From *The Trouble I've Seen*, by Martha Gellhorn, copyright 1936 by Martha Gellhorn, by permission of William Morrow & Co., Inc.

dison and her children. She realized that Mrs. Maddison was starving herself, doing some very fine and tricky work with her Relief money in order to coddle Tiny. She liked Mrs. Maddison and thought Tennessee was stupid, sexually awake only, selfish, and that Tiny had so few chances of being a decent or healthy citizen that Mrs. Maddison's sacrifice probably came under the heading of heroic if senseless gestures.

She wanted very much to get Mrs. Maddison away from Tennessee's disaffection, and she also liked Alec, and thought he could do with something to eat for a change. But rural rehabilitation. . . . Something about the name upset Mrs. Cahill, who was fairly simple and usually said what she meant. It was such a vast sound, such a stupendous and splendid idea, and when you got right down to it, it was a chance to live in an abandoned Negro shanty or a badly made, too small, new house; without adequate water, heat or light, with inadequate provision for staple groceries or clothes or medical care: and work until your back broke to raise a crop for which there might or might not be buyers. Obviously it was easier to be in debt to the Government than to private landowners. The Government, being so much bigger, sometimes got a little entangled and forgot to collect on time or just lent you more money to pay back with. But the idea distressed her, still. She talked this problem over with the local administrator and finally she approached Alec, calling on him one day when he was sitting on the river-bank fishing quite hopelessly, but fooling himself into feeling busy.

"Alec," Mrs. Cahill said, "have you ever thought about farming?"

"No'm."

"Would you like to go on a farm?"

Alec thought. He thought about farms as he remembered them and they seemed not unpleasant. Anyhow, a lot better than this overcrowded hut he was living in. And vaguely he had an idea that his mother had baked pies. There would, of course, be a catch in it somewhere.

"I'm not gonna take no Relief," he said rather sulkily.

"It isn't Relief, Alec, it's a loan the Government makes you and you've got some years to pay it back. They give you a certain amount of stuff, farm animals, and tools, and feed, and fertilizer, and seed, and groceries and such; and you make a crop and you pay some money back to the Government."

"Like on shares," Alec said.

"Well." Mrs. Cahill was a little embarrassed. She knew that most enlightened people did not feel the share-cropper system was all that might be hoped. However. "Well. Sort of."

"Who'll go, just me and Sabine or all of us?"

"Well, I thought if we could arrange it, you and your mother and your wife would go—the houses aren't very big and Tiny's so small, it might be better for her to stay here with Tennessee."

"Where'll they live then? Tennessee can't live way off down here with that drunk husband of hers around."

"No, I thought Tennessee could take Mrs. Maddison's house while you're on the farm. That way it'd be all right."

"I'll think about it." Alec was careful not to show pleasure or surprise; he mistrusted the Government and all employers, deeply. It always sounded better than what you got in the end. No sense acting happy; then they'd cut you down even more. But a series of new ideas started in his head: satisfactory images and plans. The first picture he evoked was one of a table groaning with food, home-made preserves and things from the garden and fried chicken from their own backyard and pitchers of milk and corn bread and good pale butter. He tightened his jeans around him and wandered back to find Sabine and tell her warily about the future.

Sabine was sick of their cabin and especially now that Tennessee and the baby were there, and it was so crowded she couldn't properly wash things out, or cook, or ever be quiet. Without saying anything to Alec or comparing notes she too had a vision of wonderful food. And maybe a good dress for coming in to town after the first crop; and some new silk stockings and even a permanent. She said casually that it looked all right to her and better ask Mrs. Maddison.

Mrs. Maddison's reasons were very simple: Tennessee and the baby would have a nice house if she left and then she wouldn't have to go around acting to the neighbors as if she and Tennessee saw each other and behaved as daughter and mother should. When, in fact, Tennessee didn't speak and Mrs. Maddison felt more and more lonely and unwanted every day. And she was getting headaches from the sewing-room; her ten-cent-store glasses didn't seem to be so good after all. And then again, food. And maybe a garden. She saw the house in her mind: a neat little white house with roses all over it and several large magnolia trees and things on shelves in jars, very good to eat, which she had made herself, and curtains at the windows. The Maddisons agreed. Mrs. Cahill wangled. Many papers were made out and signed. Mrs. Maddison had a grand time rushing up to the Relief office, panting and flushed and clamoring for her rights and being stern and saying, I know Mr. Roosevelt wouldn't mean for us not to have oil lamps.

Finally after a month of negotiations they were put into an intimidated Ford truck with whatever baggage they thought necessary or pleasant, and driven to their new start in life. They returned to the land.

.   .   .   .   .   .

"Oh," Mrs. Maddison said. She stood with a rolled patchwork quilt under one arm, and in her other hand, a market basket full of oddments, notably an alarm clock, a potato masher, two bars of laundry soap and some rope for hanging up the wash.

Sabine stared too but she could find nothing to say; and behind her, alarmed but not realizing the extent of the disaster, stood Alec with his mouth open.

"Gimme a hand, bud," the truck-driver said. "I'll help you get the big pieces in but I gotta hurry along; I got some other famblies moving out today."

Alec helped lift down the rusted stove they had brought from his shack, bed-posts, a table, a chest. He went in the house finally, with a chair resting over his head, and stopped in the middle of the floor, looking about him. He didn't know what to do. His instinct and his first desire were to cry out to this man, who was going to leave, "Don't go, don't leave us here." And then quickly, he thought: if only we could go back with him . . . They were so far away; they were so alone and so helpless. What would they do here; how could they live in this place. Suddenly he realized that farming was not a job like salvaging iron: you had to know what to do, and when. And also you had to know what to expect.

Sabine was crying softly behind him. "They shoulda told us," she kept saying. "It ain't right."

Mrs. Maddison was still outside; she had not moved. She didn't notice that the handle of the market basket was eating into her hand and that her arm and shoulder were getting stiff, holding the quilt. These things took time: when you had made a picture, clear and neat in your mind, it took time to erase it. She saw plainly the house she had imagined: white, with roses growing untidily all over it. There should perhaps have been a gray cat asleep on the doorstep in the sun. The curtains would already be up . . . Mrs. Cahill had been very uncertain about moving white families into abandoned Negro shanties: these houses weren't even desirable for Negroes, she had felt, and that—by local tradition—was saying a good deal. It's got a tired look, Mrs. Maddison thought, tired and worn-out and dirty. The kind of place you thought you'd die in, on the days when you were blue. Mrs. Maddison felt that it was too late to start again; what kind of God was it, who was after her? Driving her from one filthy rattle-trap shack to another, driving and driving. She had a right to be tired; she had a right not to try any more.

"Where's Ma?" Alec said.

"Outside."

"C'mon in, Ma," Alec shouted, and there was irritation and despair in his voice; "c'mon in and see the fine house your Relief got us."

She waited a moment longer. It would take a little more courage to go inside, though she could imagine how it was. And she thought: they're young and they're not used to things. I'm the one's got to say something cheerful.

She climbed up the rickety steps. There were two front rooms, both having doors onto the porch. Behind one of them there was a lean-to addition, for a kitchen. It was the simplest form of house. She looked at both rooms and bent a little getting through the low door into the kitchen.

"Well," she said.

They waited. Somehow they felt this was her fault. She was older. She should have known the kind of place they were coming to. They looked at her without kindness.

"Well," Mrs. Maddison said, "I reckon Sabine and me can fix it up so's it'll be all right. It'll be all right in a coupla years."

Alec laughed: "We'll be dead first. We'll freeze in this place in winter. Look," he said. Angrily he ripped more of the torn paper from the walls; light showed through the gaps. "Rain," he said, "we'll be washed outa bed, that's what. And how're we gonna git warm in a place like this." Sabine, catching his anger, kicked her heel hard against the floor and the planking splintered and went through.

"Don't do that," Mrs. Maddison said. "You don't have to show me. But we gotta live here. We don't have no other place to live. So we better get busy about it."

"Your Relief," Alec said in fury. "It's your Relief's doing."

Mrs. Maddison put down her bundles on the floor. She stood up before him, a thin old woman with her hair tightly wobbed on top of her head, sharp-faced and tired, her cheeks fallen in where teeth were missing.

"Lissen to me, Alec Maddison. Don't you talk like that to me. And don't go on saying foolishness. I'd of been dead if it warn't for that Relief. And Miss Lucy's a good woman. And Mr. Roosevelt's a fine man. He's got a good kind face and he's doing what he can for us. Only it takes time. They gotta make mistakes like everybody. But don't you go blaming everything on them. And you jest get busy and set up that bed there, and put the stove where it belongs, and get the pipe fixed up on it, and Sabine, you get busy with a broom and clean out this place and don't look like somebody's stole your last penny. If we gotta live here, we gotta live here. No sense talking."

Resentfully they obeyed her. Mrs. Maddison unpacked what china and pots and pans they had: put clothes and odd bits of linen into the chest. She sang thinly as she worked. She made a lot of noise, too, trying to keep a silence from settling on the house. It's up to me, she thought, they're too young yet. They get discouraged. It's up to me. Suddenly she felt a great pride that their three lives and their happiness and success depended on her: that she was the one who would keep things going, and somehow make a triumph out of this gloomy and decrepit house. It had to be done; it was another job. One more thing to get through before she died. She'd manage it too. The worst thing, Mrs. Maddison decided, would be ever to admit that you didn't have any hope left at all, and that living was too much for you.

.　　.　　.　　.　　.　　.

Alec was a bad farmer, and Sabine an unwilling housewife.
Mrs. Maddison, with love, sought to make excuses for them. It
was true that they had little to work with. The mule named
Thomas was old, embittered and weary. It was no joke plowing
up the field, holding the plow down with blistered hands, behind
that languid and uncertain animal. Thomas had a tendency to
wander off, suddenly bored by the straight line. It was also true
that Alec had to haul water on a crude handmade sled, from a
well about fifteen minutes walking down the road. There was no
well on the place: they rationed water as if they were on a raft,
with the salt ocean swelling ominously about them. And she and
Sabine had to take their clothes to a pond over the hill, a green-
ish pond, where mosquitoes sang their welcome, to wash them.
And there were no screens, and no mosquito-nets for the beds, so
that sleeping was uneasy, a drugged, resentful fight against the
whining pests. And the house; oh yes, Mrs. Maddison told herself, it's bad. But still. She could not keep herself from singing,
a thin monotonous song, as she worked. In the evenings she sat
on the porch alone, beside her pot of evil-burning rags, and
looked over the land. With contentment, and a kind of proud
peacefulness that Alec and Sabine found maddening.

Alec was planting cotton: it was the only pay crop (if there
were buyers) and the Government demanded this. The farm was
twenty acres in all; and he intended to put in eight acres of cotton. By turns, and depending on his anger or where he'd been
plowing, he said: the land's clay . . . it's nothing but sand, no
cotton nor nothing else'll grow . . . rocks, rocks, God I oughta
be plowing with dynamite. . . . The vegetable garden became
Mrs. Maddison's affair: turnips and squash, peas, beans, beets,
carrots, lettuce, potatoes, corn and suddenly, from nowhere, mysteriously, she produced flower seeds: larkspur and asters and a
few brown, frail-looking rose plants, carefully embedded by the
porch pillars. Mrs. Maddison saw everything green and rich already. Later, she thought, when we've made the crop, we'll buy
chickens and a cow. The fullness of life. There might be money
for paint too, and new planks to nail over the rotting floor
boards, and windows later, and yards of bright print for curtains.
It would be a home. She'd live long enough to make it into a
home.

Sabine would get up in the morning, with a fretful look on her mouth, and say " 'Tain't no use doing anything with this house." In silence Alec hitched the plow behind Thomas and set out for the fields. Sabine and Alec worked against their disgust, wearily, and came back at nights to hate this place where they had to live. Mrs. Maddison could find no words to encourage them. Now, before the garden came up, they had to live sparingly on corn bread and sorghum and turnip greens which she bought at the cross roads store five miles away: and the coffee was thin, trying to use as little of it as possible, only colored water: and the milk was oil and yellowish from the can. . . . But in June the garden would be coming on, and there'd be flowers on the cotton. And all summer afterwards they could eat their own things, the fresh green things from their own land; and by September— only five months, only five months—they'd be picking cotton. And then. Maybe Miss Lucy could get them a cow before then. She dreamed as she worked.

There wasn't much to do about the house. The gray, unpainted walls, darkened in places from smoke, always seemed dirty. But, being spring, the broken windows didn't matter so much. She thought about them a good deal and finally wrote a letter with difficulty, to Mrs. Cahill, saying that there were five windows in the house and all broken: now if she could get some cheese-cloth to tack over them, that would anyhow keep out the flies, and maybe when next Alec went to town he could pick up a few boards for shutters in case it rained. And so maybe it would be best if she just knocked out the windows altogether, since they were jagged-like and ugly; and could Mrs. Cahill maybe get her some cheese-cloth. The cheese-cloth arrived, together with a box of tacks, and Mrs. Maddison was as excited as if she'd suddenly been given velvet curtains to hang sumptuously over French windows. . . .

She dug up the garden and planted the seeds. Alec and Sabine together planted the cotton seed in the brown narrow furrows of earth in the fields. Mrs. Maddison was alone in the house all day. There wasn't much cooking to do because finally it always seemed to be pan bread or corn bread and sorghum and whatever else she could find or invent or afford to eke this out. She wanted the garden to be big and the Government had been generous with seeds. She wrote a few letters, almost drawing the words as if each one were a picture, asking for magazines—she would again paper the walls gaily and cleanly. Mrs. Cahill, who could not forget the old woman in that evil, decaying shack, sent her several yards of cheap print in startling colors. Mrs. Maddison made curtains and bedspreads, and hung a length of it over the low door to the kitchen, which at least shut off the sight of that place, if not the smell.

It grew hot. Alec was working without a hat in the fields and he would come back at noon ominously white with the heat. Sabine made a bonnet for herself from newspapers; she worked in bent, broken, high-heeled slippers, the heels catching in the earth, suddenly jerking her ankle sideways. Before they drank the last of the water that they'd hauled in a keg, it was warmish and had a gray flat taste. Mrs. Maddison tended the garden with passion and delicacy, almost luring the seeds to take root and grow. She lay awake at nights thinking of the feathery short green things that would be coming out of the earth. She particularly thought of the flowers. Alec's and Sabine's room had the walls papered now with advertisements: there weren't enough magazines despite Mrs. Cahill's efforts, to do both rooms. In the winter, Mrs. Maddison thought, when there isn't so much work outside, Sabine and I can make rag rugs so it'll be warmer underfoot. In two years, in three years, this place would be a good place: safe and quiet, with things in jars for the winter and every summer plenty in the garden, and a little money coming from the cotton for extras. Safe and quiet: Tennessee and the baby could come too. They'd save money for timber and put up another room. She'd have her family around her. If only they could live it out until the first crop got sold. There were days when her head ached and the garden went black before her eyes: I'm getting old, she thought. And then too she was so sick of the food they ate that it was hard to swallow; it rested uneasily on her stomach. She was thinner.

Alec and Sabine were hoeing now, cutting out the plants that grew too close together, weeding, keeping the grass off, breaking the light dry crust of earth that formed over the plants after rain. They never talked: all three of them lived in an agony of fatigue, hurrying, trying each day to keep ahead of the land which didn't want to be worked over and driven; caring for the seeds which seemed animate, each one with its own fragile and demanding life. At night after supper, Alec and Sabine went to bed. And Mrs. Maddison too weary for sleep, sat on the porch, leaning against one of the thin posts that held it up, trying to ease the aches in her body before she lay down. For a while she would sit quietly thinking of nothing but only identifying the places in her body that meant pain: the shoulders, the center of her back, her knees, her wrists. She waited for the aches to stop being sharp and separate, knowing that they'd merge into a general weariness that was not hard to bear. And then she could look out over the fields, and her garden beside the house. And look at the sky. Things seemed sure to her now: her life and her children's lives were no longer dependent on other people, on the strange fancies of employers, and the rules and regulations of the Government. Yes, they were in debt; but the Government was going to give them time to pay. It wasn't like being on shares or a tenant, when you never knew where you stood. As long as we grow things, Mrs. Maddison thought. She liked the emptiness of the land before her. It's good land Mrs. Maddison said to herself, and we're making something to last. Something for the children. There's nothing wrong with being poor, Mrs. Maddison decided proudly, if you've got your own place, and no one coming to holler about the rent and throw you out; and if you know there's food in your garden, and you don't need to go begging around at every store. It's the begging and not knowing where you're going to be next. "And work," she said suddenly aloud, "Land's sake, no one's ever gonna call my chilrun no-count loafers."

.   .   .   .   .   .

A man came and talked with Alec about the cotton; he said he was the farm supervisor for the rural rehabilitation families around here. A woman came and talked to Mrs. Maddison about groceries and what they needed in the house: she was the home visitor out this way. The callers made Alec mutely angry. He didn't want anybody butting in his business. Even if they acted nice about it. He could get along. Next time they came Mrs. Maddison could just tell them to get the hell out; he'd manage his own farm. Mrs. Maddison, who had an entirely personal con-

ception of Government, was encouraged by these visits. For her,
simply, it meant that Mr. Roosevelt and Mrs. Cahill were not
forgetting her. If they couldn't come themselves they'd send
their people. She was glad of this: she knew Miss Lucy wasn't
forgetting her because there was the cheese-cloth and the print.
But those things were gifts and had nothing to do with the Government. The Government was supposed to be interested and
come around every once in a while and ask how you were getting
on and ask if they could help. Government was like that. She had
been rather boastful with Miss Blythe, who was Mr. Roosevelt's
representative out that way. She'd shown off her not yet producing garden and her house, and extended her arm largely to exhibit their land, the acres which were theirs, which made them
respectable steady rooted people with a future. Miss Blythe had
been flattering about the house and said she'd try to get their
grocery order raised. "Of course," Miss Blythe said, "if you can
manage with it being so small—well that's just that much less
money to pay back later." Mrs. Maddison liked that too; she was
borrowing money, she wasn't begging.

Mrs. Maddison told Alec that Mr. Roosevelt had some right
nice people working for him out this way; but Alec was neither
interested nor pleased.

Sabine and Alec were more than silent; they were sullen now.
They hated everything about the farm, and they had no faith in
it. Alec used to say bitterly he knew his cotton would be bad, or
it'd rain too much later, or there'd be boll weevil; or no buyers.
He didn't believe anything could come of this; he saw the future
as a long half-starved drudgery, slaving for nothing. And the
silent days and the silent nights. Sabine saw herself growing ugly,
her hair straight and unkempt, her hands coarse; no clothes, no
finery, no fun. No girls to gossip with and no dances or any of
the things she wanted. At least, in town, they could get together
with their friends and have a little drink and somebody could
always play a fiddle and they could go uptown and look at the
stores anyhow. But this: working yourself to death and nothing
to show for it. Those hateful ugly selfish little cotton plants.

Mrs. Maddison was going calling. She was in such a good
humor that she had to share it. She walked over the dusty red-
dish roads, with her hat sitting up on top of her head, where it

would shade her, but not press down and give her headache. Her gingham dress was darned till it seemed to be covered with white sores. None of this worried her; she was going graciously to pay a call on Mrs. Lowry and pass the time of day, and talk brightly of the future.

Mrs. Lowry was sitting on her porch fanning herself. She was about Mrs. Maddison's age. Mrs. Maddison said, "Howdy, Mrs. Lowry, fine weather we're having," and they sat down to talk. Mrs. Lowry said it was a treat, she never saw anybody for a month of Sundays and she'd have come to see Mrs. Maddison but they were that busy. "Farming," Mrs. Lowry said; "you just gotta keep at it every second till you die." But she seemed proud of it on the whole. Mrs. Maddison liked her. She thought it would be nice in the winter, when they had more time, and she and Mrs. Lowry could swap recipes and patterns for crocheting. Later, when the vegetables had been canned and the cotton sold.

Mrs. Lowry had been in her house a year. "Lawd knows it's nothin' to look at," she said. "But you ought of seen it when we come. Dirty, I never seen such a place. Now we got our own vegetables put up, and such-like; we're gettin' on all right. It's worst the first year."

Mrs. Maddison agreed.

"The bad thing is the young folks," Mrs. Lowry said. "There's no fun for them. And they don't have no patience, poor things."

"Later," Mrs. Maddison said to Mrs. Lowry, her eyes shining with the thought of it, "when we're all fixed up and everybody's not working so hard, we'll get together and have a barn dance. I see you gotta barn here, and we could sweep it out and fix it up pretty, and everybody bring a little something themselves, and have a real party."

She had said this breathlessly, hurrying before the vision failed her. In her mind, the barn was filled with young men and girls, dressed as she had been dressed when she was young and went to a party. They'd be doing square dances, and the fiddlers thumping with their feet on the floor to keep time. And apple-bobbing. And blind man's buff. All the neighbors there together, being gay and serene, and every man sure of his home, sure of tomorrow, and easy with today.

Mrs. Lowry understood her excitement. "If only the young

folks'll wait," she said. "We'll have a good time yet before we die."

.   .   .   .

Alec lay in his darkened room and Sabine talked to Mrs. Maddison in savage whispers.

"We're going," she said. "Soon's he can move we're going. We're not gonna stay out here to get ourselves killed. Sunstroke," she said, and her whisper was shrill. "He'll be laying in the fields dead next. And me with the malaria. What kinda life is that? They can't make us stay. We hate this place n'we're going quick; n'we're never coming back. So."

Mrs. Maddison twisted her hands in her lap. There were roses now, climbing up the door posts, and even if the posts were unpainted and the house gray and streaked behind them, these were real roses. Next year there would be more and maybe paint, too. The garden was green and just looking at it made you feel rich and safe. She'd been serving her own vegetables now for weeks. Next year, if they had a cow, there'd be butter to put on the new tender carrots and the beets, and the fresh green peas. The cotton was coming out thinly in the fields, but it was only the beginning. She'd gone down and picked a boll, and held the soft white fluff in her hands gently. This was money; of course there'd be a buyer and fine prices. This was more lumber for another room, and shoes, and a buggy, maybe. The worst was over. Things were growing. Larkspur and roses and squash and potatoes and cotton. This was what life meant, if life was good. She'd even gotten her room papered in advertisements now. With money, they could buy boards, make furniture, a solid roof, a whole floor, and paint to make it clean and gay. They had only now to live a little carefully and everything would come to them. They were safe now and what lay ahead was more safety and even ease. In the winter, when they couldn't work after dark and there was nothing much to do anyhow, there were the neighbors. All the things she'd planned and dreamed.

"Sabine," she said softly, "he'll get over it in a day or so. N'you'll get over the malaria. Miss Blythe said she'd send some quinine. We done the work, Sabine. You can't go now. The worst is all over."

"We're going. And don't you try to stop us, neither. You're

old and you don't expect to get any fun outa life. But we're
young. And we're not gonna stay around here and kill ourselves."

"You won't have any fun back in that old shack of yours. You
won't even have stuff to eat. What kinda life is that, then? Sabine, we worked so hard," Mrs. Maddison said. There were tears
in her eyes, but she was not looking at the younger woman. She
was looking out the door, at the roses. For the last month it had
seemed to her that not only Mr. Roosevelt and Mrs. Cahill were
remembering her, but God also. The things she wanted: a home,
and roses, and food, and quiet when the work was over, and a
place to live and be. Tennessee could come in the fall; when
they had a little money, too. She was an old woman and she was
a lucky one: she had everything she could want.

She cried out against this dreadful and wanton thing they
meant to do: leave the land when things were growing; leave the
cotton unpicked and the garden going to weeds and waste. And
the house they'd made into something like a home; let it rot back
again into a worn-out Negro shanty. But she knew they wouldn't
listen to her. Miss Blythe came and argued and so did the farm
foreman: he even threatened Alec, saying "You'll never get a
loan again" and "You're a low quitter, that's what you are."
Alec was ill, and hysterically obstinate; something had happened
to him. He hated the land beyond any explanation. He would
rather starve than stay there; it was a slavery to him and a bleak,
empty, exhausting life, with none of the things that made for
pleasure. Sabine chattered with chills and burned with fever, and
cursed the home visitor and the farm foreman and Mrs. Maddison, and said she'd crawl to town on her hands and knees if she
had to, but she wasn't going to stay out here in this hole and
kill herself, and get ugly, and go crazy with the work, and no fun
ever, ever, ever.

The entire neighborhood got drawn into this, and Mrs. Lowry
stood on the porch with Mrs. Maddison, one day at sunset, looking out over the white beginnings of the cotton, and the green-
ness of the garden and said: "It's a sin and a shame, Flora. They'll
be sorry, too."

Mrs. Cahill drove out in her uncertain Ford and tried to talk
to Alec, who wouldn't listen. Mrs. Maddison could not stay on
alone; the work was too much for her. She couldn't keep the cot-

ton cultivated and do the garden too. "You'd be having sun-stroke next," Mrs. Cahill said and smiled.

"He did have a sunstroke," Mrs. Maddison said abruptly. "It was a real bad sunstroke and he was sick's a baby."

"I know." Mrs. Cahill put her hand on Mrs. Maddison's shoul-der. The old woman would defend those no-count children if they did murder.

"Would you like to take home some roses, Miss Lucy, or some larkspur? It's all gonna be wasted now."

She stood beside her flowers weeping quietly and helplessly. "All wasted," she said. "It all come to nothing."

"Alec deserves a beating," Mrs. Cahill said furiously. "He's selfish, and he's being stupid, too. Sabine's a fool and you couldn't expect anything else of her. But Alec. I'd like to get some big strong man to give him the beating of his life."

"It's only that he's not hisself. He's still weakish from that there sunstroke. But it's gonna be too late when he sees what he done. We'll of lost the place then."

Mrs. Cahill put her arm around Mrs. Maddison's shoulder. "You've done your best, darling. Nobody'll ever blame you. You made a fine place here and somebody'll be lucky to get it, and they'll know what a good worker you are. We'll see you get taken care of all right in town. I'm sorry. I'm sorrier than I can tell you."

"We were all fixed," Mrs. Maddison said. "We could of lived like real people again. Well," she said, "how's things in the sew-ing-room, Miss Lucy?"

Finally Mrs. Cahill drove Alec and Sabine back with her. She thought it would be easier for Mrs. Maddison to have them out of the way. The driver would come with the truck tomorrow or the next day and move Mrs. Maddison and their possessions back into town. The land couldn't be wasted; someone would have to work it and try to profit by it and pay back the debt. Mrs. Cahill drove in angry silence. Once Sabine started to talk to her and she turned and said: "You're a no-count girl, Sabine, and you've got a no-count husband, and I don't want any truck with you. You've broken that poor old woman's heart and you deserve anything that comes to you. I'll drive you to town but I won't act friendly with you."

Mrs. Maddison had something to do. Before it grew dark, before she slept. Now that her son had really done this thing; gone away, not caring for the land or the money he owed. She got out a block of ruled paper and a stubby pencil and began: Dear Mr. Roosevelt. . . .

It was a long letter. She explained Alec's sunstroke and Sabine's malaria, and how hard it had been for over four months, working with so little and the house cheerless and such poor food. She told about everything which excused Alec in his desertion; but loyally, she said too, that the garden was fine now, and the cotton coming up. She hoped he wouldn't be too disappointed in Alec, but Alec was young, and when you were young you were foolish, and did bad things without knowing. She hoped he would excuse Alec. She was grateful for the things Mr. Roosevelt had done, and she would work to pay back the money they owed but she was afraid it would take a long time. Work was so hard to get and money so scarce. She enclosed a short spray of larkspur because she wanted him to know that it was a fine place she was leaving. . . .

She sat alone on the front porch and watched the stars come out. It had all come to nothing. The safety and the ease that was ahead, and the good times, and having a place and being someone. Nothing. The land was fine and beautiful, she thought, and she could smell the roses in the dark.

INDEX OF AUTHORS AND TITLES